IN
EXTREMIS

IN
EXTREMIS

The Life of Laura Riding

———❧———

DEBORAH BAKER

GROVE PRESS
New York

Published by Grove Press
A division of Grove Press, Inc.
841 Broadway
New York, New York 10003-4793

Published in Canada by General Publishing Company, Ltd.

Due to limitations of space, permissions and acknowledgments
appear on pages 461–62.

Library of Congress Cataloging-in-Publication Data

Baker, Deborah, 1959–
In extremis : the life of Laura Riding / Deborah Baker. — 1st ed.
ISBN 0-8021-1364-8 (alk. paper)
1. Jackson, Laura (Riding), 1901–91—Biography.   2. Authors,
American—20th century—Biography.   I. Title.
PS3519.A363Z57   1992
811'.52—dc20
[B]   91-35967
CIP

Manufactured in the United States of America
Printed on acid-free paper
Designed by Irving Perkins Associates
First Edition 1993
1 3 5 7 9 10 8 6 4 2

For Janet

ACKNOWLEDGMENTS

While one of the pleasures of finishing this biography of Laura Riding is to thank those who provided help and encouragement along the way, there is nonetheless something awkward in bundling together names and gratitude in the requisite perfunctory manner. I am sorry I cannot include everyone.

Among the many librarians, curators, and private collectors I would particularly like to thank are Robert J. Bertholf and Michael Pasinsky of the Buffalo Poetry Library; Joseph Dermont; Edna Hajnal of the Thomas Fisher Rare Book Library in Toronto; R. Russell Maylone of the Rare Book Collection at Northwestern University; Simon Nowell-Smith, William Reeves, William Targ, and Saundra Taylor of the Lilly Library; and Joan Silbey and Marice Wolfe, successive curators of the Fugitive Collection at Vanderbilt University. I would also like to express my gratitude to the late Lola Szladits of the Berg Collection of the New York Public Library for her advice and support.

I would also like to thank those who knew Laura Riding and were willing to share their memories of her. First among them is Beryl Graves, whose graceful and often quirky insights into the life and work of both Graves and Riding were invaluable. Ida Gershoy, Helen Booth, Richard Mayers, Sylvia Seaman, and Polly Antell Cohen generously provided me what information I have on Riding's family and childhood, as well as her years at Cornell and her first marriage. Of those who knew Riding during her thirteen years abroad I would like to thank Margaret Bottrall, Honor Wyatt Ellidge, Harry Kemp, the late Thomas S. Matthews and his sons Paul and John, and the inimitable Karl Gay for their recollections. I would also like to thank

William and Elena Graves, Maria Parker, K. T. Jackson, and Griselda Ohannessian for their many kindnesses, their candor, their letters, and their conversations.

Among the poets, scholars, neighbors, and former colleagues whose conversations, writings, correspondence, book loans, and professional advice I am grateful for, I would like to thank Susan Bernard, Georges Borchardt, Abigail Cheever, Kate Daniels, Robert Gorham-Davis, Richard Perceval Graves, Joel Honig, Samuel Hynes, Deborah Karl, Michael Kirkham, Cindy Klein, Brian McInerney, Albert Mobilio, Jim Moser, Geoffrey O'Brien, Alexandra Pringle, Alistair Reid, Martin Seymour-Smith, Dennis Silk, Ivan Solotaroff, John Tice, Tom Verlaine, Ann Waldron, and Joyce Wexler. Thomas A. Underwood and Janet Byrne laboriously but patiently read early drafts of the manuscript and provided me a fund of alarmingly acute but tactful editorial advice. I alone am responsible for any failures or errors that remain.

Finally I would like to thank Amitav Ghosh for his many gifts to me as editor, friend, and husband. I am sure I do not realize all that I have asked of him.

—Deborah Baker
Calcutta
July 1992

CONTENTS

Acknowledgments   vii

Introduction   xi

PART I
THE NEW WORLD

Chapter 1	Full Epidermal Fevers	3
Chapter 2	The Old, Original Dust	18
Chapter 3	Back to the Mother Breast	30
Chapter 4	The Waiting Equipage	46
Chapter 5	Stranded in a Half-told Tale	69

PART II
THE OLD WORLD

Chapter 6	The Emotions of an Audience	91
Chapter 7	The Sphinx in Egypt	112
Chapter 8	Nancy's Laura's Robert and Nancy's Robert's Laura	134
Chapter 9	Anarchism Is Not Enough	153
Chapter 10	Outside the Window	174
Chapter 11	Good-bye to All That	196

PART III
THE OTHER WORLD

Chapter 12	A Small Circle of Meaning	217
Chapter 13	The Damned Thing	234

Chapter 14   The Dry Heart   252
Chapter 15   The Unthronged Oracle   272
Chapter 16   The Story Pig   290
Chapter 17   The Why of the Wind   313
Chapter 18   A Trojan Ending   332

PART IV
THE END OF THE WORLD, AND AFTER

Chapter 19   Doom in Bloom   345
Chapter 20   Le Château de La Chevrie   364
Chapter 21   New Hope   381
Chapter 22   The Only Possible Ending   404
               Epilogue   423
               Notes   425
               Bibliography   459
               Index   463

INTRODUCTION

———— • ————

A story that was the subject of every variety of misrepresentation, not only by those who then lived but likewise in succeeding times: so true is it that all transactions of preeminent importance are wrapped in doubt and obscurity; while some hold for certain facts the most precarious hearsays, others turn facts into falsehood; and both are exaggerated by posterity.

—TACITUS

———— • ————

THE SMALL TOWN of Wabasso lies about halfway down the east coast of Florida, some fifty miles south of Cape Canaveral, in Indian River County. There is a gas station and a 7-Eleven but no drugstore, a post office with 900 boxes but no bank. There are two churches, Baptist and Methodist. Bisected neatly by the tracks of the Florida East Coast Railroad, the town is informally segregated. The blacks live in the west toward the marshy wetlands of the interior, and the whites in the more lush and tropical river region, rich with palm trees, hibiscus, and huge Australian pines. In the nineteenth century Wabasso was a trading post where the Seminole Indians would canoe in from the swamps to trade in alligator hides, fox skins, and venison. The tribes withdrew to the interior when the railroad came in 1898, bringing black laborers to work the infant citrus industry, which would soon dominate the state.

When the WPA writers' project came to Wabasso, the Florida crackers told them about the Guale Indians who, after migrating from Ossabaw Island off the coast of Georgia, decided to call this small backwater Wabasso—Ossabaw spelled backward and a name meaning white rabbit in Seminole. In 1939 the area had 300 inhabitants, a sawmill, and the Blue Goose Packing Company, owned by the Graves brothers, Robert and Hubert.

The railroad was built on the higher ground of an area called the Ridge. Not far from the station and some hundred yards from the packing warehouse, a driveway of fine white sand leads to a small bungalow with a roof of galvanized iron, once painted a brilliant red. The house, which until recently had no electricity, is shaded by the looming and irregular Australian pine; some scrub oak and shortleaf pine dot the property. There is a front porch and a back porch off the kitchen. The house is set on blocks in a weedy grass yard, patchy with sand. Laura (Riding) Jackson lived in this house for almost fifty years. After the death of her second husband, Schuyler Jackson, on July 4, 1968, she lived alone and in wavering health.

In December 1938 *Time* magazine reviewed Laura Riding's collected poems. The unsigned review was a roundup of recent books of poetry which the reviewer thought the most significant of the times. At the top of the list were the efforts of Laura Riding, who, the reviewer claimed, wrote in a language in which every word was chosen and used to its full capacity for literal meaning. She was described as Manhattan-born but, until the outbreak of the Spanish Civil War, settled on the island of Mallorca. There, with the English poet and writer Robert Graves, she ran a small press and wrote fiction, criticism, and poetry. Now living in Brittany, she was waiting for Spain to finish with its civil war before returning to resume her publishing operations. Her preface to her poems was quoted extensively, including her definition of a poem as an "uncovering of truth of so fundamental and general a kind that no other name besides poetry is adequate except truth." Clearly taken by this logic, the reviewer settled the matter by saying that for those speakers of the English language who found themselves marooned on the desert island of the mid-twentieth century, Riding's volume was "the book of books" to have along. William Carlos Williams, whose own *Collected Poems* ranked third in the review, answered dryly to a correspondent who asked who Riding was, "all I know of her is that, personally, she is a prize bitch. . . ."

The appearance of her *Collected Poems* and *Time* magazine's prominent praise were a watershed in the literary career and private life of the woman who then called herself Laura Riding. Within thirteen months she had left Brittany to return to America, broken off her fourteen-year relationship with Robert Graves, and devoted her efforts full-time to a book entitled *The Dictionary of Rational Meanings*, which would occupy her for the next thirty-odd years. Though she would not make her position clear until the early 1960s, she also firmly renounced the art of poetry, both her own of the last twenty years and in general. The *Time* reviewer, not personally known to her when the piece appeared (though they had friends in common and had briefly corresponded), became her husband; and despite her strong views against marriage and a wife's taking her husband's name, Laura Riding became Mrs. Schuyler Jackson. Her poetry fell out of print, in the United States out of copyright, and for many many years out of sight altogether.

While some memory of Laura Riding as a poet prodigy of the 1920s may linger—where it survived at all—her reputation was almost entirely superseded by Laura (Riding) Jackson's. Emerging from thirty years' obscurity, Laura Jackson began to sign her published writings with this name after Schuyler Jackson died in 1968. For a time she responded to practically every mention of her work or the work of Robert Graves in critical articles or reviews, writing dizzyingly prolix letters to the editor. These letters often contained intricate personal attacks on the writer or critic who had made so bold as to mention her; and if Graves was under discussion, his reputation was subjected to similar disparagement. More than any work that she published during this time, these letters, combined with the lingering scandal of her suicidal leap from a window of a London flat in 1929, served to obscure her early achievements. For a thoughtful few, however, Laura Riding remained a poet of the highest stature, and, as a champion and publisher of Gertrude Stein, astute literary critic, and editor, a major contributor to American and British modernism. W. H. Auden called her our "only living philosophical poet."

What, then, happened to her? In 1962, after almost twenty-five years of silence, Laura Jackson publicly explained her renunciation of poetry for a BBC literary radio program, aired in England. The audience might have found something slightly puzzling in the carefully enunciated speech that introduced her poems (she did not read them herself); so much of the context of her complex remarks was missing.

"How did I make the mistake of assuming that, from the art of poetry, the reality of live, personal truth could be precipitated?" she asked her listeners. "The time had come for someone to make the mistake," she answered. The question of what happened to Laura Riding would not be answered so easily.

But for those whose lives had been irrevocably changed by her, a generation earlier, it was a shock to hear her voice again, changed so little. The delivery of her challenge—she was expecting to offend those who still held poetry in some esteem—was as self-assured and imperious as ever.

"Any offence felt can be presumed a thing I would have averted, could I have done so." But there was no public outcry, and the voice from Wabasso was quiet for another decade.

LAURA JACKSON'S RELUCTANCE to cooperate with critics, anthologists, and biographers was well established before I began this book. There have been just two scholarly full-length works about her poetry, and her objections to them were based largely on their biographical renderings, rather than on their critical readings of her poems. In the process of researching and writing these books, both writers corresponded with Laura Jackson for several years and visited her in Wabasso. When Jackson read the first work (it was first a dissertation), she attempted to rewrite it before giving up in disgust and rage over what she perceived as a profound personal betrayal by its author. Another writer labored for ten years under Jackson's direction on an authorized biography, which was finally abandoned in a storm of recrimination. Laura Jackson's own memoirs reflected her aesthetic and moral sense of her life, rather than a more material existence—linear, factual, and populated. These, too, were abandoned unfinished and sold to a literary archive. Clearly, Laura Jackson wanted her story told, but she wanted it to be hers. She admitted of no other, or the possibility of others without malicious motive. The present work, completed just before her death on September 2, 1991, was no exception.

In 1977 and 1982, two books appeared that touched very significantly on her life, and both elicited an extensive rebuttal from Jackson, privately circulated. The first was a memoir of the events of the summer of 1939 in New Hope, Pennsylvania, that led to the break with Robert Graves and Riding's renunciation of poetry. The second was a biography of Robert Graves.

Laura Jackson had a vehement response to the memoir; a statement was sent to the book's publisher, and lengthy letters went out to those newspapers which had seen fit to review it. She encouraged a few close friends to write letters of protest, and her appointed biographer published an editorial denouncing the book. She wrote to those who had written jacket blurbs, describing the author with a string of invective. Finally, a long memorandum went to a small circle of friends, including archivists of those special collections where her papers are kept. The fact of the book's publication, she maintained, provided direct evidence of the evil afoot in the world and was an insult to her presence in it. She was, Jackson declared, considering suicide.

Laura Jackson and I exchanged correspondence when, as a publisher, I approached her about bringing certain of her works back into print. She didn't want to take the time away from her present work, she told me, to consider how these works fit in to the larger fabric of her thought. Where her work has been reprinted—poetry, prose, short stories—she has provided long prefaces to give the texts their "proper" context. Often, Laura Jackson's ambivalent attitude toward her poetry and early work reflected her attitude toward the life that she lived up to the day she and Schuyler Jackson settled in Wabasso.

While *In Extremis* is, in greater part, the story of Laura Riding, I have read and considered all the material provided by Laura Jackson to public archives before her death. In particular, unpublished manuscripts, essays, memoirs, and letters devote hundreds of pages, typed and handwritten, to the specifics and generalities covering those fourteen years with Robert Graves. In them Jackson tried to answer the various allegations and factual misrepresentations of her life and work. In place of working with a living subject, I had her embittered commentary in my head whenever I tried to reconstruct events, personalities, and literary works. As she spent vast quantities of creative energy in composing these rebuttals, accusations, and character assassinations in an attempt to put the record straight "on principle" (to the exclusion of more primary work), this might also be considered part of her life's work, however Sisyphean an endeavor. Out of respect for this effort, I have noted where the major battles were fought and have tried to adjudicate between the sources.

Still, my realization of the extent to which biography and biographers have already been drawn into the conflict between Riding and Graves discouraged any expectation I might have had of "setting the record straight." Martin Seymour-Smith's 1982 biography of Graves described Laura Riding as an "explosively freakish" young woman, while simultaneously betraying the impress of Graves' more mythological imagination. Seymour-Smith admits in his book, "I had a correspondence with [Laura Jackson] in the early sixties, in which I whined in an unseemly way about Graves (I told him later); she dismissed me with a few fairly accurate epithets, for which I hold no grudge." According to Laura Jackson, he wrote to her that he thought Graves—whom he had known since the 1940s and lived with in Mallorca, tutoring his son—was an evil man. At the time of this correspondence, Seymour-Smith intended to write a book about Riding's poetry, but he abandoned the project when she withdrew her support.

Laura Jackson referred to this exchange of letters when Seymour-Smith's book was published and threatened to make it available to scholars as proof of the malice of a spurned scholar. When the biography appeared, Jackson again circulated an extensive rebuttal, accusing Seymour-Smith of manufacturing evidence about her, quoting from letters that never existed, and of actively conspiring with Robert Graves. When the second volume of Robert Graves' selected letters was published in 1984, she became more forceful on these points and endeavored to write a full-scale exposé of their alleged conspiracy against her.

When one considers this large, bitter corpus within the plush comfort of library reading rooms, a sense of disappointment with conventional biography is unavoidable. Perhaps Laura Jackson came to a similar conclusion. In 1990 the second volume of another biography of Graves appeared, which dealt only with his years with Riding. This book was greeted with silence.

Riding sought truth, "literally, literally, literally, without gloss, without gloss, without gloss." She felt its closeness to her with a spiritual intensity to the end of her life. While Laura Jackson was often disappointed by those who wrote about her, she never lost heart that her own "live personal truth" would be understood. But if the surviving letters, documents, and memories will never produce the kind of truth she demanded, to judge Riding's life in those terms which her male contemporaries sought to understand it, including Robert Graves and his biographers, is inevitably to diminish and even condemn Laura Riding to myth, megalomania, or marginality. Yet—and this is one of the ironies that any biography of Laura Riding must, at some level, explain—to judge Riding in the terms Laura Jackson proposed, is ultimately to denounce and silence her.

In the 1920s and 1930s Riding's response to those who thought her poetry baffling and obscure was always the same: an assertion that they had brought insufficient faith to their reading. She considered the difficulties of modernist poetry a new promise of communication, an advance that would be met by a corresponding step forward on the part of the "plain reader," with rewards for all who undertook it:

> I wish it were possible to speak more decisively
> But truly I have nothing more to suggest
> Than a more painstaking romance of perception

I have approached and tried to write about Laura Riding with the "painstaking romance of perception" as my method. I have tried to begin where she began. As with any "romance" it is not always possible to speak decisively; and as final authority I recommend her writings rather than those of her noisy detractors or stout defenders. Implicit in this, however, is my belief that in any biography of a poet, one gets a view not only into the subject's life but also into the visions and language of the time. In this respect *In Extremis* is only partly a narrative of Riding's chosen lives as poet, lover, editor, visionary, wife; it is also about a woman who tried hard to articulate the conflicts between them in her imagination and intellect, while fighting the conventions and institutions of literature and society.

A final note: In her writing and speech Riding always chose her words carefully. She had a litigant's appreciation of meaning, a poet's sensitivity to sound, and at times a diva's awareness of dramatic effect. While still in her teens she used the name Riding informally, finally discarding her cumbersome maiden name of Reichenthal when she married a young history professor. In the course of her life Laura Riding would change or vary her name repeatedly; she also made use of countless pseudonyms. Generally, these new names followed a personal crisis and marked the first step in a process of consolidating and articulating her identity. While these changes often reflected a change in the circumstances of her romantic liaisons, they also marked periods of intense creativity. They were often preceded or followed by abrupt and dramatic life decisions, sudden about-faces announced by telegrams, manifestos, and changes of address.

It seemed only appropriate to use these successive identities and the names that accompanied them to map the continuities and the transformations in her life. As a result, this is not the sort of story that begins, as Laura Reichenthal did, on January 16, 1901, and proceeds directly to a memorial service in Wabasso, Florida. Rather, it became the more roundabout story of those perplexing creatures who sprang repeatedly from this woman's head. And so, when I wrote about her during these periods, I used the name she used and that others used of her, with the eventual understanding that all of them were fictions of one sort or another. But if she is to have one name it will be the name Laura Riding, since this is the name most completely owned by her and also the name by which I first knew her.

PART I

THE NEW WORLD

Chapter 1

FULL EPIDERMAL FEVERS

—— • ——

Did I surprise too truly, then,
Your all too prompt anticipation,
Tear down the wall of self,
Expose the terror of fulfillment?

—"To a Loveless Lover"

—— • ——

IN THE EARLY years of this century Nashville, Tennessee, was known
not as the capital of country music but as the Athens of the South.
On Whitland Avenue, near the grounds of Vanderbilt University,
lived Mr. James Frank, a wealthy and cultivated businessman, and
his wife, Rose. During the early 1920s Frank's middle-aged brother-
in-law, Dr. Sidney Mttron Hirsch, lived with them. Though Hirsch
had no visible means of support, the Franks accommodated him
with grace. The Doctor, as he was called, pursued eclectic intellectual interests, among them the cabala, etymology, and numerology.
Until he became an invalid, he had traveled widely and was well
versed in exotic cultures and religions. There was an enigmatic air
about him, combined with an outward charm and an affected, fey
manner.

For some years now every other Saturday night or so the Doctor
could be found supine, holding forth from a chaise longue in the
Franks' front parlor surrounded by a group of literary-minded young

men. In most respects, this particular evening in late November 1924 was no exception. Among his regular guests from the university were Professors John Crowe Ransom and Donald Davidson and, before he left for wider horizons in 1923, a bright young undergraduate named Allen Tate. Another undergraduate, Robert Penn Warren, nicknamed "Red," had recently taken Tate's place. With the introduction of these younger men, the focus of their discussions had begun to shift from philosophy and an aesthetics to poetry. With no particular program, they nearly all began to write verse, and these Saturday evenings provided an opportunity to read aloud and earnestly discuss their poems. Acting as general host and etymological referee, Hirsch had proposed a name for the group, the Fugitives, which also became the name of the magazine in which they published their work and cultivated their literary palate.

But for Hirsch, who seemed of an epoch all his own, there was something of an eighteenth-century Enlightenment air to these par-lor discussions. Their southern-mannered courtesies bespoke their shared heritage and upbringing, which for Ransom and Davidson included a strict education in the classics. The son of a Methodist minister from Pulaski, Tennessee, Ransom had been a Rhodes scholar at Oxford, where he read Aristotle and Kant. With poetry not the least of his leisured pursuits, he cultivated all the talents of a country gentleman—golf, the card table, and social intercourse among them. Ransom's dry detachment, or what Tate would later call an ironic manner "both brisk and bland," balanced Hirsch's soaring mono-logues, a drier reason struggling with insight.

The younger Tate and Warren were absent from this particular convocation though they would likely have given their eye teeth to welcome the recipient of the 1924 Nashville Poetry Prize of $100 for the best poem published in their magazine that year. Tate alone had met her when, en route to West Virginia that February, he had stopped in Louisville to introduce himself. (Warren would finally meet her the following year in Los Angeles, while she was visiting her half sister.) But even before they made her acquaintance, Tate, War-ren, and Davidson had decided that this young poet had been their most significant "discovery" to date. And for Tate at least, she had come to embody the substance of the modernist challenge to their gentlemanly sensibilities. Belatedly, Ransom had come to share their enthusiasm for her work, and he too looked forward to meeting her that November evening and hearing her read her poems.

Tate had been the first to disturb their composure. A precocious student of Sanskrit and Greek, he had been invited to the Frank house by Davidson, lacking any notion of himself as the poet and literary critic he would eventually become. Despite the presence of his professor, Ransom, he was only briefly cowed. He found Sidney Hirsch's Rosicrucianism—"a . . . doctrine [that] skittered elusively among imaginary etymologies"—outlandish but he stayed. Later he would describe the Doctor with wry indulgence; "His pince-nez stood up on his handsome nose, and curled Assyrian hair topped a massive brow." Hirsch's cosmopolitanism (and perhaps his Jewish background as well) were vaguely suspect, despite his "unfailing courtesy and elevation of tone." Hirsch would wait out Tate's barbs with lowered head and patient manner.

Still, judging by Allen Tate's literary style, his own manner was only slightly less affected. His skeptical pose was couched in Elizabethan syntax, an often contorted mask for his immaturity and tumultuous inner life. Raised in various border cities under the hard hand of a neurotic southern matriarch with aristocratic pretensions—the very sight of her would drain the blood from his face—Tate had intellectual capacities that were as formidable and inescapable as his overlarge forehead and skull, an expanse that loomed above his small, rather delicately pointed face. But his self-mockery saved him from outright priggishness, and he became the enfant terrible of the Nashville Fugitives.

However smoothly blanketed by their gentility, it was precisely the tensions between the Fugitives' varied temperaments and ambitions that catapulted them from a small southern university to the center of the modernist controversy. In the spring of 1922, fleeing "nothing faster than . . . the high-caste Brahmins of the Old South," they had published the first issue of the Fugitive. Their identities were cleverly disguised by the use of elaborate noms de plume, and thus masked they presented a colorful and enigmatic response to the romantic conception of the Poet. From the poetic "offerings" that appeared in this first issue it was clear they stood self-consciously outside those American literary traditions which were available to them (though Edgar Allan Poe was treated with reverence). Tate would later provide their epitaph:

> What were we fleeing from? Or towards? For a Fugitive was quite simply a Poet: the Wanderer, or even the Wandering Jew, the Outcast, the man who carries the secret wisdom around the world. It was a fairly heavy responsibility for us to undertake, but we undertook it, with the innocence of which only the amateur spirit is capable.

Somehow Hirsch, perhaps the most unlikely of Southern gentlemen, had identified the incipient virus to which they, in varying degrees, had become susceptible. Increasingly, their poems became cerebral, wittily intricate, and infused with rare diction and archaic words. The younger Fugitives, stricken by Poe, found an almost pathological delight in the imagery of death and disease. The general public, accustomed to a more conventional lyricism, took it as an affront; but the magazine quickly gained such sophisticated admirers as Hart Crane, T. S. Eliot, Robert Graves, John Gould Fletcher, and even H. L. Mencken, whose attention only heightened the Fugitives' self-consciousness. Laura (Riding) Jackson would later describe their self-perception as a haven of Elizabethanism between the cross currents of a bastardized traditionalism and a reductive modernism. But at the time the older and more amateur members of the group were rather baffled at their sudden celebrity.

Further puzzlement awaited them when Tate acquired one of the first copies of T. S. Eliot's "The Waste Land" in 1922. Under Eliot's influence, and along with a great many others of his generation, Tate began rethinking ideas of poetic style. His own poems soon became more and more opaque, while he became less and less patient with the outmoded poetic styles of Hirsch and the expertly trim sonnets of another Fugitive, Merrill Moore. Donald Davidson (whose nom de plume was Robin Gallivant) played the gracious mediating role between the unruly Tate and his usual sparring partners, Ransom and Hirsch. However, within a year of reading Eliot's poem, the White Hope of the South, as the *Double Dealer* now described the young Tate, was already planning his escape north. "It is no mere reification of desire this time," he wrote Hart Crane, "I am coming to New York. And I have no qualms about saying that the prospect fills me with an enthusiasm best described, perhaps, as somewhat pubic."

While Tate was trying to get to New York many American writers were trying to leave it for Paris. In 1921, Zelda and Scott Fitzgerald, Sherwood Anderson, and Ernest Hemingway all found their way to 27 rue de Fleurus, and Sinclair Lewis' *Main Street*, a novel of revolt against small-town life, was the year's best-seller. The commute between Europe and America, accompanied by the corresponding emotions of intimacy with and estrangement from their public and country, reflected the instability of the American literary ethos, most clearly revealed in the response to Eliot's poem, completed that year. Dr. William Carlos Williams bitterly assumed that Eliot was trying to say something providential on the future of Western civilization and the impossibility of an American literature just when he, and many others, were struggling for the possibility of it. "[He] returned us to the classroom," Williams said, describing the poem as a "sardonic bullet," and "a great catastrophe."

In July 1923 the quarrel over the literary virtues of "The Waste Land" (it had already been called a sham in New York and Chicago) moved to Nashville, flaring up in an exchange between Tate and Ransom in the pages of the *Literary Review*. Ransom, after a long Aristotelian disquisition on the aesthetics of poetry, admonished Eliot for the poem's fragmented rhetorical strategies and heteroglossia: "We do not quote Greek tragedy and modern cockney within the same break or with the same kinds of mind." That spring Tate had roomed with "Red" Warren, who had etched huge cartoons of scenes from Eliot's poem on the dirty plaster walls of their rooms in Vanderbilt's Wesley Hall. Tate's lengthy rebuttal to Ransom's view of the poem concluded with the statement, "Mr. Ransom is not alone. He is a genre." Ransom, tossing aside his classics, responded, "Mr. Tate has for two years suffered the damning experience of being a pupil in my classes, and I take it his letter is but a proper token of his final emancipation, composed upon the occasion of his accession to the ripe age of twenty-three." A long-simmering struggle for editorial control over the magazine ensued, but eventually, with Davidson as go-between, their heads cooled. Ransom, whose nom de plume had been Roger Prim, later ruefully regretted his discomposure.

It was into this climate of intelligent civility and sometimes ill-tempered debate that Laura Riding Gottschalk, as she then signed her poems, made her entrance in late November 1924. The Fugitives' telegram informing her that she had won the Nashville Poetry Prize of 1924 had been sent by special delivery, but Western Union found no one at home. An earlier letter from the Fugitives had been misaddressed and ended up in Louisville with a neighborly old man, who delivered it to its proper recipient, at 1116 South Brook Street, after carrying it in his pocket for several days. Western Union returned the following morning and woke her (she had been out dancing until the wee hours) with the news.

But Mrs. Gottschalk, as the Fugitives referred to her, had first arrived—gravely, with quiet, measured assurance—in the form of a poem entitled "Dimensions." In 1923 she had seen an ad in a local Louisville paper soliciting entries for the Fugitives' annual prize. She was then a newcomer to Louisville, having arrived that fall. The poem came in third out of a field of 400 entries and appeared in the *Fugitive* just one year earlier, in its August–September 1923 issue.

In outward form, "Dimensions" seemed engineered to provide an answer to the Tate-Ransom debate over the modernist template. In its inner certainties, it seemed to address those labors of unrequited love which were rampant at least among the unmarried Fugitives as well as the morbid, necrological fantasies that were their love's accompaniment:

> Measure me for a burial
> That my low stone may neatly say
> In a precise, Euclidean way
> How I am three-dimensional.

In the course of the poem the speaker proposes a number of means by which the true measure of her life might be calculated, only to reject them as imperfect. She concludes:

> Measure me by myself
> And not by time or love or space

Or beauty. Give me this last grace:
That I may be on my low stone
A gage unto myself alone.
I would not have these old faiths fall
To prove that I was nothing at all.

In his brooding "Philosophy of Composition," Edgar Allan Poe
claimed that "the death of a beautiful woman is, unquestionably, the
most poetical topic in the world." Taking this "poetical topic," Laura
Gottschalk gave the Fugitives a dead muse to bury, showing them in
the process that the literary traditions of their language, the "old
faiths" of love and beauty, could not take her measure.

In the course of her career, Laura Riding would often position her
poetic voice in direct response to the male romantic vision of the
poet as suitor to woman, dead or alive, human or divine. The simple
rhythms and diction of her dying lady answered the Fugitives' complex prosody and festering imaginations with an alluring restraint.
Poe was only surrogate quarry, being too long dead himself; instead,
Riding would develop her voices in direct combat. Her quarrel was
not just with the contemporary debate over poetic form and the
social and intellectual conventions that it engaged, but also with the
aspiring Romantic Poet, Wanderer, Outcast, Fugitive himself. And as
this was an adversarial position, she required an answering reply.

Writing "Dimensions" in what she felt were the grim midwestern
wilds of Illinois, where her husband had his first academic post, there
had been no such response. The ladies of Urbana, with their passion
for bridge, had provided her only dispiriting company since their
arrival at the University of Illinois from Cornell in the fall of 1921.
Initially, the ceremonial duties of a faculty wife had had at least the
virtue of novelty. Mrs. Louis Gottschalk had paid her social calls in
dead earnest, reveling in the bourgeois respectability of her position.
But before long the practice of sitting still during endless cups of tea,
punctuating the chatter with compliments on the cakes and the new
upholstery, had begun to pall. She wrote to Joseph Freeman, a high
school friend of her husband's and recently appointed editor of the
Liberator, that she found the academic Middle West even worse than
the simple, unadorned Middle West.

Her undergraduate degree, which she had begun at Cornell and intended to complete at the University of Illinois, was abandoned because of her conviction that she had sufficient mental faculty to confront learning head on; God hadn't intended her for higher education, she explained to one correspondent, nor to become a lady of Urbana, either, it seemed. The flat midwest town threw her literary ambitions into sharp relief; she completed one novel and began another. But, mostly, the two years in Urbana found her writing poems without let or hindrance, selecting and perfecting a range of voices that no one else seemed to hear.

After eighteen months, Harriet Monroe's *Poetry* magazine in Chicago had finally accepted a poem. Fudging somewhat, Laura Gottschalk told Freeman that she had written for *Contemporary Verse, Lyric West,* and *Classic,* though all of these poems had yet to appear. More wistfully, she admitted that while her novels might make the rounds of New York publishers, her poetry, like the gracious ladies of Urbana, entertained at home. She offered him a poem about Eugene Debs in exchange for a job on the *Liberator* in New York City, an unlikely transaction that revealed her desperation to return to the city of her birth. Her situation in Urbana, far from her friends at Cornell and in Brooklyn, had become intolerable. Such desolation was all very well within bounds, she told Freeman, but the ladies of Urbana were conspiring to drive her further than that. Answering Freeman's inquiries about her husband's work, she was perfunctory.

Without the support of any true literary community or sense of how a poet becomes a poet, Laura Riding Gottschalk still did not have her feet in the literary world when the telegram about the poetry prize arrived in November 1924. "Mrs. Gottschalk" was exceptionally naive; one of her earliest poems had been published in the *Step Ladder,* a vanity magazine that accepted submissions only from paying subscribers. Her submissions were scattershot and she knew no one; the company she kept had been mostly that of Jewish radicals and intellectuals, involved more in leftist politics than in poetry. Thanking one editor who offered her advice about where to send her work, she admitted that she had no idea of "What every Young Poet Should Do." Like the governing protocols of the tea table, she understood poetry to have its own code, hushed and intricate, for a successful debut.

Eager to obtain a hearing for work that was seemingly uninformed by a tutored sense of traditional forms, she wrote letters calculated to win over literary editors. Depending on whom she was writing to and what she deemed as their editorial temper, she adopted different and often theatrical epistolary manners, ranging from the Damsel in Distress to the Modern Woman. Lacking the skills of name-dropping and tidy witticism, she often betrayed an urgency where sophistication was intended. By the time "Dimensions" was published in the pages of the *Fugitive* in the fall of 1923, Laura Gottschalk and her husband had left Urbana to settle in Louisville, where she made a second attempt to finish her undergraduate degree. It was her first published poem.

She immediately sent the Fugitives a large bundle of poems that she had been working on for the last two years. A poem entitled "Starved" was among them. Tate, suffering from influenza, had responded to them in early December from his sickbed, in a long, encouraging letter telling Laura Gottschalk that she was the poet to save America from the Edna St. Vincent Millays. In a reply of unrestrained gratitude and relief, sent from the Berkeley Hotel in Louisville, Tate's newest discovery told him about the grinding difficulty of the past two years, of her lonely labors bereft of understanding or encouragement even from those closest to her. She planned to live alone, she told him, eventually to support herself. Aware that her frankness might appear strange, she confided that only her overwhelming joy in his letter could restrain even more intimate confessions. Mrs. Gottschalk had found an answering understanding.

Tate's letter marked the beginning of a winnowing process for her that for a time would focus her poetic energies and voices in Fugitive directions. The entrance of the Fugitives (notably Tate, but also Davidson and Ransom) and their acceptance (or rejection) of her poetry—no small event in her emotional life—was to leave a lasting impression on the development of her work. She confessed to Tate that she was not William the Silent, as she needed approval to give her hope and success to brace her against adversity and misunderstanding. Faced with the Fugitive criticism, echoed down the years, that her poems went on too long, she replied that it was impossible for her to stop. She had no sense of measure, she told Davidson, insisting that this was true of her as a person as well. After writing a heated and tortuous letter protesting a rejection of his (which, for once, she did not send), she wrote a more peremptory one, asking Davidson to forgive her lack of graciousness and find in it "the embarrassment of a hotspur."

After such impassioned declarations, Mrs. Gottschalk's first meeting with a fellow poet was fated to take on "literary" qualities. In February 1924 Tate had stopped in Louisville to introduce himself. His visit, which lasted sixteen hours, was one that neither of them would soon forget.

IN A LETTER following the telegram about the prize, Davidson requested biographical information from Laura Gottschalk for an official press release. His prizewinner began by protesting his impertinence. She was antiautobiographical on principle, she told him; the truly significant facts about someone were not for publication. Nevertheless, she trotted out a list of what those facts encompassed in her life—her father, her mother, her bizarre and unhappy childhood, her loves, and the circumstances of her rising so quickly above her difficult beginnings. Such information, she told him, she must keep to herself. Her reticence, however, did not preclude her apprising him that she was twenty-three years old and that her husband, Dr. Louis R. Gottschalk, was a recently appointed assistant professor in the history department at the University of Louisville, where she was completing her undergraduate degree. She also sent a studio photograph of an attractive dark-haired young woman, demurely dressed. Her light blue eyes were disconcertingly beautiful and shone with an alert stare of anticipation.

Tate's report of the "exceedingly belle" "lady poet" of Louisville was more enlightening but served to whet rather than still Davidson's curiosity:

> [Laura Gottschalk] is just about the greatest person I've met in these dilapidated twenty-four years of mine. Her intelligence is pervasive; it is in every inflexion of her voice, every gesture, every motion of her body. She talks little and then only casually; she speaks of trivialities; altogether she is the most "un-literary" person I've seen— perfectly spontaneous and simple. But always you get the

conviction that the Devil and all Pandemonium couldn't dissuade her of her tendency. She is quite the most intelligent woman I've seen; and even that is an understatement.

Davidson was skeptical and accused Tate of exaggerating; Tate insisted that for once he was not being ironic. "She's great! And this, I assure you, has nothing to do with possible shiftings of my own pericardium." Within a month Tate had proposed her as a reviewer for the *Nashville Tennessean*, whose book column Davidson had begun editing. Her prose was as brilliant as her poetry, Tate wrote, now having as evidence a good many letters and the novel she was writing:

> I rather believe it would be a good thing to get her with us (it would tie her more to The Fugitive), and for this reason: she writes that Harriet Monroe, rejecting all recent offerings, gives a reason that can only be interpreted as a dislike of her friendship with us; and at the same time L.G. comes forth with the confession that she thinks The Fugitive is quite the equal of Poetry (and she's a competent judge, by the way) and for many reasons would prefer to appear with us . . . I feel almost paternal!

To "Red" Warren, Tate had described his first meeting with "Mrs. G." in other than literary terms. Warren, recovering at home from a suicide attempt after a devastating love affair, wrote back, asking to know more about her: "I am more interested than you perhaps realize and my interest is more than that inflamed by an improper curiosity." He observed that they now seemed inexorably linked "in art as in sin." Tate replied and included "Mrs. G.'s" novel, asking that he either return it to her or, as he had been instructed, burn it. Warren thought that if he destroyed the novel, Tate would at least know the "joys of forgiveness at the hands of Mrs. G." At the same time Tate encouraged an editor named William Cobb to visit Louisville on the pretext of considering her novel for his publishing house. Entitled *The Frail Barb*, the work concerned the fate of a Jewish immigrant who, after the momentous journey to America, decides to return to his homeland.

Cobb rejected the book but began a correspondence with the lady poet of Louisville.

For the rest of the gentlemen arranged on couches and overstuffed chairs in the Franks' Nashville home, there was a sense of polite curiosity insofar as the telegram announcing her imminent arrival on a train from Louisville had been unexpected. A few of them found her work hard to fathom, but after the arrival of Tate among them three years earlier, they had learned to listen to and consider that which on first glance did not appear to be poetry at all.

———◦∞◦———

Laura had sat down to write her acceptance of the award in a state of the most abandoned rapture, finding it hard to restrain herself from a profuse outpouring of thanks. Perhaps it would be more prudent, she wrote Davidson, to send a wire to her immigrant parents instead, so that they might witness her arrival among the Fugitives' proud and august company, having left far behind her father's humble beginnings in a small but not yet forgotten village in Austria. That her bold effrontery had not been censored and her poems turned out, Laura found incredible. They must imagine her quite wicked, she said, to encourage her impudence with such sweet punishments. What, she asked him, should she do next? Before Davidson could find an answer, a telegram announced her arrival in Nashville the following weekend. An assembly of Fugitives was hastily convened to meet her at the Franks' house on Whitland Avenue. The Franks wired her an invitation to stay with them, and a shopping expedition with Rose Frank and her sister was planned.

Thus it was with some trepidation that Laura alighted on the Nashville train platform. Met by Mr. and Mrs. Frank, she found them and Mrs. Frank's unmarried sister Goldie unreservedly warm; perhaps they were not too different from her neighbors back in Brooklyn—wealthier perhaps but, like her, Jewish. Sidney's brother Nathaniel was also visiting for the weekend, and she found him charming though not at all literary.

But there was something preposterous in the air of the Franks' front parlor when she stepped forward to meet the Fugitives. How old they must have seemed. There they sat, en masse, all politeness and quiet expectation, a whole row of Southern Gentlemen with exquisite manners—"Fugitives." She stood up to give a reading of some of her more recent poems.

Did their expressions betray them? Undoubtedly, Tate's presence might have eased the gaping awkwardness following her performance, had he not already left Nashville to seek his literary fortunes in New York City. Perhaps Riding's nervousness made her giddy. Generally she was a skillful and charming conversationalist, but her wit seemed to find no purchase here; their stately politeness, especially Ransom's, was imperturbable. Only unliterary Nathaniel Hirsch, who sat to one side of her, seemed to find her at all amusing. Unlike the others, he delighted in flirting with Mrs. Gottschalk, teasing her on her "flapperishness." She responded but not without some anxious sense of making a spectacle of herself. On the other side of her reclined Sidney Hirsch on his chaise longue, squinting at her through his pince-nez and perhaps, too, frightening her with erudite monologues and etymological queries.

Yet she had come to forge something permanent with this fraternity, something more than mere talk about poetry over Mrs. Frank's excellent snacks and refreshments. She quickly proposed herself as a secretary for the magazine, but though she need not have been reminded, there were no funds for such a position. She turned to Ransom, who perhaps sensing some sort of real difficulty arising, suggested that she send typed versions of the poems she read to the magazine. But that was hardly a means to make a living; her poetry manuscript had already been rejected by New York publishers. Since Robert Graves had seen one of her poems in the *Fugitive* and had admired it, Ransom offered to send her manuscript to him in England. That was something but not, at the moment, what she wanted.

The crisis peaked when Laura went walking with the Doctor in the neighborhood. As he proceeded to pontificate on a poet's need for a mentor, holding forth on the idea that poets like painters have masters from whom they learn their art, she grew indignant. Had he offered himself? It is hard to picture exactly what passed between them, but she returned to the Franks after a heated quarrel. Whatever happened, Laura wrote to Davidson after her forlorn return to Louisville that she felt she had been jeered at by them all and that the Doctor, in particular, had treated her as an ignorant flapper. She

wanted to know in all frankness just who Sidney Mttron Hirsch
thought he was.

Ransom later described to Tate the reception in the Franks' front
parlor with dismay and timid compassion. Though he may have felt
that the "best poetry was the most perilous," Mrs. Gottschalk's personal urgencies quite unsettled him.

> Undoubtedly we were rather absurd in the way we re-
> ceived Laura at Nashville—prim, formidable, and stiff.
> What she came for was human companionship of the most
> bare-soul description; she had neither birth, subsistence,
> place, reputation nor friends, and was a very poor little
> woman indeed. She got only a rather formal welcome,
> though she is mistaken in assuming that we burned with
> suppressed libidinous desires. . . . We quite missed the
> point. She on her side did not realize that we had already
> established our respective personal relationships on satis-
> factory and rather final bases, and that we were open to
> literary relationships but not to personal. I realize there is
> a sort of mean-ness in such an admission.

The definition of a Fugitive as the Poet or Wandering Jew would
apparently not apply to Laura Gottschalk, despite her urgent application. The Nashville Fugitives, bound in mystic brotherhood, were to
carry their secret wisdom around the world without her.

But to her college friend Polly Antell, Laura would provide her
own version of that November afternoon. Her weekend in Nashville
was triumphant; the Fugitives seemed to adore her as well as her
work. She enclosed a newspaper clipping about the award, crossing
out the description of herself as a student at the university and
circling a reference to Allen Tate. The Fugitives were still in the dark,
she wrote conspiratorially, though by then it had been some time
since she had last heard from him.

A month later, Laura was in a hospital in Louisville. In her husband's letters to Polly, the reason for this hospitalization seems to be
understood; it was most likely a nervous breakdown. The Fugitives
sent her two dozen roses—American Beauties—but the promise of
life with them had died.

Within a month of her release from the hospital, Laura had come to several conclusions. She had finally decided to divorce her husband and leave Louisville. As for "Allen," suddenly his approval and encouragement no longer seemed to matter. Thoughts of him were so deeply interred, Laura wrote to Polly, that his corpse could not even produce a stink. She did, however, expect to meet up with him in New York City. After a trip to California to visit her half sister, she planned to settle there and look for a job. The city was, after all, the refuge of exiles and fugitives—and more her home ground than his. Like others before and since, her resources were small but her spirit was not.

Chapter 2

THE OLD, ORIGINAL DUST

——•——

Do not deny,
Do not deny, thing out of thing.
Do not deny in the new vanity
The old, original dust.

From what grave, what past of flesh and bone
Dreaming, dreaming I lie
Under the fortunate curse,
Bewitched, alive, forgetting the first stuff . . .
Death does not give a moment to remember in

Lest, like a statue's too transmuted stone,
I grain by grain recall the original dust
And, looking down a stair of memory, keep saying:
This was never I.

—"Incarnations"

——•——

ALMOST FIFTY YEARS earlier, above the crowds and bundles and
crying children on the gangplanks, the city waited to embrace
another prodigal. Like his fellow passengers, the boy smelled of
"ship"—a combination of bilge, sweat, unwashed clothes, and the
stale humors of close confinement—but this would last only a few
weeks to mark him as a greenhorn. The record of his port of

departure and the village of his birth would take longer to lose, and if there was a story about the contents of his pockets or his dreams no one remembers it. Still, the heft of Nathan S. Reichenthal's past, however intangible, was one of the larger encumbrances at the docks.

In the struggle between fathers and those sons who came to America, the son was left standing alone, denuded not just of a collective past but of the tight, protective embrace of family, language, and faith. In the late nineteenth century Karl Marx provided many arriving immigrants with an adoptive parentage and an invincible belief in their own power to alter the course of history and, through intellect, choice, and action, to give birth to themselves. He traveled with them on the boats to America, or they found him on her shores.

Laura's father, Nathan Reichenthal, was one such son. He was small and slim, not yet fifteen, with eager, startlingly blue eyes. He had come with his parents, Isidor and Sarah, from Galicia, the poorest of the Polish provinces, then under the rule of the Austro-Hungarian Empire. Given his mother's maiden name of Reisenfeld, they may have come from the Polish town of Rydzyna. In 1884 their ship docked at Castle Garden, an old fort built in 1807 on an island off the west side of the Battery in New York City.

In 1787 Emperor Joseph II of Austria issued an edict ordering the Jews of Galicia and Bukovina to adopt permanent Germanic family surnames. Isolated and clustered in shtetls, they had few means of protest. Having suffered from the efforts of the Austro-Hungarian monarchy to exterminate them, they now found that they were expected to become Germans, to counter Polish nationalism and ethnicity, and, in the same breath, to undermine their Jewishness as well. In 1812 Napoleon followed suit, linking the emancipation of the Jews of Prussia to the adoption of family names, and within a generation most of the Jews had been "baptized." With the eruption of anti-Jewish riots in eastern Europe and Russia in the 1880s, the massive exodus of Jews across the Atlantic began. As word and money from America trickled back from those who had left, their numbers swelled. On arrival in New York City immigration officials encouraged many of them to simplify the names they had been made to assume a century earlier, and there was little resistance to this new baptism. After the long journey and voyage, anxiety and uncertainty overwhelmed them and it was enough to arrive, to become Americans.

On his naturalization papers Nathan Reichenthal listed his occupation as tailor. Of arriving tradesmen, tailors were then in greatest demand and had an easier time finding employment. Met stateside by Yiddish-speaking contractors for the large German-Jewish clothing manufacturers, tailors were ushered directly to overcrowded lodging houses near the Castle Garden. In an arrangement both philanthropic and shrewd, most of them would be taken to work in vast clothing factories and sweatshops. Between 1860 and 1880 the ladies' garment industry had expanded enormously, dovetailing the massive wave of arrivals from Europe with the fashion demands of America's Gilded Age. Paris patterns and French seamstresses were imported for the cut of the fabrics; sewing was the hard labor done in factories by poor immigrant Jews, generally unskilled women whose wages were perhaps a dollar a day. When tailors began arriving in great numbers in the late 1870s, they took over the sewing machines, sending many women to lower-paying jobs at the finishing and pressing tables.

By the time Nathan arrived in 1884, a man's strength was needed to manage the masses of steel hoops that had become de rigueur in women's cloaks and dresses; his starting wage was perhaps ten dollars a week and he would work in the sweatshops for almost sixteen years. In 1893, soon after he received his citizenship papers, he married a gentle, frail Hungarian woman named Laura Lorber, the daughter of a furrier. Like many of those who lived in the ghetto and worked in the sweatshops, she suffered from poor health. Privation, malnutrition, and tuberculosis, the "tailor's disease," took a great many lives and may have taken hers as well. For Nathan, it was a grievous loss, only somewhat softened by Laura's having left him a daughter, named Isabel, born in 1894.

The sweatshops were located in the large multistory tenements of Manhattan's garment district, north and west of the grand department stores on Sixth Avenue, between 34th and 40th streets. Most likely Nathan met his second wife, Sadie Edersheim, within their dreary confines. The daughter of a peddler she had been there for fourteen years, beginning work at the age of twelve to help support a large family. Dimly lit by kerosene lamps, a stove blazed in the corner of each shop, surrounded by hot irons. Scraps of paper and fabric littered the floor and stairways. Men and women, wedged into their sewing machines and pressing tables, could be seen day or night from the windows of the elevated, grimly laboring. Sadie spent two hours a day walking from her family's apartment on the Upper East Side to be at work by 4:00 A.M., the start of the day's shift. By the time she met Nathan she was the sole means of support for her family of seven, and she was going blind from the years of close work. She was twenty-five and he was a widower with a four-year-old child to raise. It was a short courtship.

These years in the sweatshop, the long hours, and appalling working conditions no doubt contributed to Sadie's physical and emotional decline and warped her view of the world. Her marriage was not to be the escape she dreamed of. In a long and bitter letter written to her stepdaughter, Isabel, thirty years later, Sadie set down her version of the marriage, attempting to correct all the "misshapen, black ideas you have of your childhood." "Of course you were too young to remember. That does not remedy it." After describing her long years of manual labor she told her, "I wanted and needed a rest. . . . So to me, what did it matter if a child was thrown in. I didn't know, and as I was very fond of children, considered them more of a toy, to dress up and make pretty things for them." Still, she imagined that Nathan loved her. "How innocent, and as you always tell me, how stupid?"

"And God knows I tried very hard to do more than my duty," Sadie droned on in the mournful cadence of a well-worn lament, "and for that did I get any help or co-operation from your father? . . . I gave you the remnants of my blindness to dress you as daintily as my neighbour's little girl, doing it on a shoe string, as you well know." Sadie saw not the social injustice of the sweatshops that had devoured her youth but the existential injustice of her own failure to escape poverty, her children's ingratitude, and her husband's irresponsibility. "I kept the real side of our economic condition from you, giving you luxuries, which if I was the stepmother you accuse me of being, I would have taken for myself. . . . And now and for many years," Sadie ended her effort, "it reads just like a story, no a tragedy,

you have been seeking as you proved REVENGE, and you succeeded."
It was blankly signed Mother.

Sadie's wifely ambitions may have been thwarted by the languish-
ing memory of her predecessor, Laura Lorber. Though Isabel was
unlikely to have many recollections of her dead mother, she doubtless decided that she was everything that her stepmother, Sadie, was
not, particularly since she saw that her father had no patience with
Sadie's complaints. When Sadie arrived on the doorstep, Isabel was
old enough to feel resentful and perhaps betrayed as well. She had
been the adored and indulged object of her father's attention; Sadie
was the usurper of her mother's memory and herself. Sadie, in turn,
found Isabel, "delicate, nervous, high-strung [and] spoilt," a cross to
bear along with the realization that her husband had married her "for
convenience sake."

According to the 1900 census, Sadie was born in 1872 in New
York City of German immigrant parents. Her daughter Laura, however, was to describe her as coming from "plain country" and "upper-
class Dutch stock." Her appearance, also according to Laura, was less
Semitic than her husband's, though she came from "downtown," a
disparaging euphemism for the neighborhoods of the Lower East
Side. Sadie's marriage certificate gives her address as 224 East 95th
Street, in what was predominantly a neighborhood of German immigrants on the Upper East Side.

The distinctions between downtown and uptown, between a Semitic appearance and a non-Semitic one, between a German Jew and a
Yiddish-speaking peasant from Galicia, between Orthodox and intellectual, spun an elaborate weave of social hierarchies and eth-
nicities in the world's largest, poorest, and most concentrated Jewish
settlement. The Lower East Side seethed with a riot of languages,
intramural provincialisms, and contending political ideologies. Each
had his own understanding of what it was to become an American.
New identities were devised, and many swept the "old original dust"
under the rug. Thus "Nathaniel," as described by his daughter Laura,
was a "naturalized American" rather than an immigrant and a Jew, and
her mother was "American born." It was another kind of naming
ceremony, having less to do with Nathan and Sadie than with the
aspirations of a second generation.

For both Nathan and Sadie the garment industry provided the

great loom on which new patterns of social and economic relations revealed themselves within the Jewish community. Those recently naturalized evinced a cosmopolitan disdain for the newer arrivals. Upward mobility was granted to those who could find the fifty dollars needed to set up a shop. German Jews whose families had arrived a generation earlier provided these middlemen with contracts for so many garments. The garment worker, in turn, was asked to work longer hours (and no matter what language they arrived with they understood the logic), so that the shop owner could undercut his rivals, so that there would be steady work for the floor. If they wanted to keep their jobs or avoid a cut in wages, they needed to produce more than the Litvaks, the Galicians, or the Bessarabians in the sweatshop below them. This was known as the task system and, to some, embodied the promise of the land of opportunity.

Nathan, by nature gay and high-spirited, believed in the American dream no less than his middleman overseer. But like many of his neighbors and fellow workers, he found such dreams entirely compatible with the ideas of Karl Marx and organized labor—what Sadie contemptuously described as her husband's "Ideas," his "important mission." Released from the myriad ghettos and unventilated shops, men like Nathan gathered in the tea shops of Cherry Street, on the rooftops of the Lower East Side to listen to excited Russian émigrés engage in fevered ideological debate with the ingenuity of rabbinical scholars.

"Jewish Socialism was far more than a politics—it was a gleaming faith, at once splendid and naive in its dreams of perfection and brotherhood," Irving Howe would write. A contemporary observer described these men as neither Orthodox Jews nor yet Americans but as men of ideas—"intense personal abuse and the most violent denunciation of opposing principles are the rule." Nathan was perhaps a gentler man but no less enrapt and uncompromising in his belief that a better life awaited him and all working people.

But skepticism vied with such faiths, and Jewish immigrants, like other arrivals before and since, were torn by conflicting claims on their new lives. In the downtown tea shops resounded the virulent ideological debates of the politicized Jews, "uptown" harbored the bourgeois German Jews who had invested their hopes in free and generally exploitative enterprise, and in the synagogues were the rabbis and rites and incantations of the Old World. Each contended for the immigrant's loyalties and hopes in the promised land. But the desire to believe in universal brotherhood was often thwarted by rude experience. Nathan admitted without a trace of irony, "I am imbued with the idea that all people of all races and nationalities ought to be alike to me. Well, they ought to be, but they are not. Well, to come to the point, . . . I have never known one person of Irish blood to know really what loyalty, honesty, devotion, trustfulness or any other 'human' attribute meant. . . . Facts are facts." Anti-Semitism was doubtless another bitter fact to discover in the land of the free.

When the *Jewish Daily Forward* wanted to start an English-language socialist newspaper, the *New York Call*, Nathan applied for a position. The editors of the *Forward* touted a subscription to the *Call* as a sacred duty. With articles by Dorothy Day and the socialist leader Eugene Debs, the *Call* tended, as far as the hard-line ideologues were concerned, to have a sloppy and sentimental attitude toward Marxist theory. "The difficulty with 'The Call,'" wrote one circumspect Marxist, was that it failed to properly study Marx but "merely pervert[ed] and adulterat[ed] Marxian socialism." If Nathan worked for the *Call* (Riding maintained he was its founder and manager), perhaps he shared its rosy vision of socialism as "the poetry of the oppressed miserable workingman." Socialism's ideals were described in the language of spiritual as well as material rewards delivered to hard-laboring humanity in this world rather than the world to come.

In fact, the traditional fears of the Jewish patriarchs had come true in this first generation of socialists and intellectuals in America: they were unbelievers. In a letter most probably written by Nathan in 1929, he described himself as a "fanatical internationalist," an "Empiricist," and a "transcendental theorist." Further, he embraced the idea—one can almost hear Sadie's snort—"that before we can really create new and beautiful thoughts and things the old, the basis, must be first obliterated":

> I am impatient of the slow changing process which often ends in adaptation, compromise and corruption, then the process of change has to begin all over again. There must

be a steady hammering away. Also there are hearts and minds which obvious crude destructive methods cannot hope to reach because of their sensitive tinctures.

The shtetl in Galicia no longer existed for a man with these thoughts, much less the laws of the Talmud.

But these sons did not stand alone; they stood—at least in theory—beside fellow legions of garment workers—Jews. After the turn of the century they would also try to stand beside fellow socialists—stockyard workers, foundry workers, farmers—older generations of American immigrants. According to his daughter, Nathan Reichenthal was a founder of the Socialist party of America. Organized in July 1901 in Terre Haute, Indiana, the party grew out of the work of the Socialist Labor party; Eugene V. Debs, the party's leader, would put the broad face of the Middle West on what had been largely a New York Jewish labor-union movement. Socialism would never quite be the same "gleaming faith" to the rank and file as it had been to the first-generation Jewish garment worker in the 1880s and 1890s. In the spirit of collective enthusiasm that accompanied the party's founding, however, this was not immediately apparent.

But the Old World was not wholly argued away by a politics that had its roots in Voltaire, the Enlightenment, and European rationalism, though the belief in God and His special favor had been. The wait for the Messiah would, for a generation of Jewish socialists at least, become the wait for the revolution and, Nathan believed, prosperity and freedom from anti-Semitism. The messianic ore that transmuted itself into socialism for Nathan Reichenthal would be refined further, to an even truer vision, by his second daughter, Laura. The inflexible metal of these visions was not a pure substance, tempered as it was by the paradoxes of the American experience; but to both father and daughter it was considered both irreducible and incontrovertible.

Nathan's political work, however, was never a means of living. By the turn of the century the methods of dress manufacture had become more mechanized and no longer dependent on skilled tailors. Nathan lost his job, and unskilled women found their way back to the sewing machines, doing piecework at even lower wages. But though Nathan turned to a number of businesses and trades, including political work, at none was he a success. His daughter, in a poem originally entitled "Fine Fellow Son of a Poor Fellow," would write:

> Every poor fellow reminds me of my father.
> With worse luck than that
> He reminds me of my father
> With worse luck than he had.
> Which means me
> Who has worse luck than my father had
> Because it is not so bad.

In business as in politics, it was never luck alone that defeated him. A scrupulously honest man, he lacked the businessman's sleight of hand. For Sadie, he was honest to the point of exasperation. She would "raise her eyes in near incomprehension" in her attempts to describe her husband's fastidious business practices. His sense of what was fair and right seems to have precluded any idea of making money. Even though prosperity and the revolution remained elusive, his cherished dreams of America remained untarnished and his belief in socialism undimmed. As a businessman, Nathan proved himself a luftmensch, a man with his head in the clouds.

"When they die they will leave nothing behind them," Hutchins Hapgood predicted in his 1902 account of Nathan's intellectual comrades, *The Spirit of the Ghetto*, "but while they live they include the most educated, forcible and talented personalities. . . ." Without real political power at Tammany Hall or on the national level, however, these men and women achieved little in the way of revolution; and the fierce grip of ideology may even have served to sabotage their efforts to organize the American working class. After a surge of votes for Debs in 1912, the Socialist party came out against America's participation in the European war, even though war was by then inevitable. Whether or not it was a war brought on by capitalist imperialist conspiracies, the party revealed its inability to grapple with peculiarly American political realities, and there was no place for it to go after the armistice. Sadie, perhaps, suspected as much, finding Nathan's lack of interest in her struggle to feed and clothe the family sure evidence of the failure of ideology, his "important mission."

What success these early socialists did achieve was in the protest itself: against working conditions, against corruption in Tammany Hall, in their mud-raking reports on the exploitative task system, and in forging a sense of community among themselves. Out of their fractious arguments, splits, and denunciations evolved the self-educated Jewish worker who began with the political syntax of Marxist theory but branched out to absorb Goethe, Schiller, Tolstoy, Dostoevsky and, once English was mastered, Mark Twain and Theodore Dreiser. Socialist newspapers, reading circles, socialist fairs and picnics embraced the ideas of upward mobility and community as well. Thus, Laura was later to denounce the loose talk of her "former associate" Robert Graves about her Marxist upbringing in a Brooklyn slum, decrying as "malignant drivel" the suggestion that she had been culturally deprived. She defended her father by citing his reading of German literature and political and economic theory. Her home had a good library, she countered, yet another watermark of social aspiration.

In one sense, the socialist's virulent secularism was evidence of a kind of cultural disarray—no other immigrant community seems to have abandoned their God quite so brusquely. What was lost in cohesiveness was made up in the sheer energy brought to the acquisition of this new American "culture" and to the zealous pursuit of upward mobility. In this—if in nothing else—Sadie with her homemade dresses and small luxuries, and Nathan with his stress on education and political activism, saw eye to eye: the second generation would not end up in the sweatshops.

AT THE END of his life, worn by the strains of age and poverty, Nathan Reichenthal would talk nostalgically about his early days as a union organizer and socialist. There is no surviving record of his having been a founder of the Socialist party or of his having worked for the *Call*, though he might have worked diligently on their behalf. There are no clippings or photographs of him left to his few descendants. He died in 1938, having long been separated from his wife, Sadie—less than a year before Hitler invaded Poland and, along with it, the province of Galicia. He was buried in Los Angeles, where he had lived for many years, supported by his son-in-law, an advertising man. Among the few possessions dispersed at his death were works by Upton Sinclair, Sinclair Lewis, some German novels in translation, Leninist tracts, and a history of the American labor movement. In his will he bequeathed some books to a local union library, and the rest he left to his grandson, Isabel's child.

Part of his patrimony had been a dream, perhaps forged in those heady days before the Great War, that his second daughter, named Laura after his beloved first wife, would become America's Rosa Luxemburg. A Marxist revolutionary and a Polish Jew, Luxemburg had furthered Nathan's dreams of an international socialist order in her writings and activities until her assassination by political thugs in 1919.

In pursuit of Luxemburg's vision, Nathan would encourage his younger daughter to read the newspapers with an eye for the capitalist subtext. Dinner table discussions turned on current events and dialectical materialism. During the 1930s, when Marxism was again in the air, Riding chastised a correspondent who underestimated her familiarity with Marx. As a child, she insisted, instead of going to Sunday school she learned the wicked intricacies of finance; stories of the Great Financial Conspiracy were her bedtime fairy tales. In such tales the young Laura Reichenthal imagined herself the avenging princess, leading an international movement toward a utopian future. For her, Nathan's brave new world was a far grander and more romantic one than her mother's.

Traces of this dream of glory still languished nearly seventy years later, in a Florida backwater. In the 1980s, Laura Jackson's attention was brought to her work's inclusion in an anthology of American and English poetry published in the Soviet Union. That the Soviet editors had used her work without permission was forgiven because of what the editors had to say about Robert Graves. They described his work (in an entry, she noted, that was five lines shorter than her own) as being involuted and inexact and as having decadent tendencies. Jackson was thrilled and remarked upon the poetical and political justice of these views. The biographical note that accompanied her entry included an approving mention of her father's tailoring and working-class background.

Somehow this mention of her father sparked Laura Jackson's memory of the abandoned alliance with Nathan and her dream of becoming an American Rosa Luxemburg. She concluded her unpublished statement on the anthology with a wistful letter to her long-dead father that summoned the idealism and innocence of an earlier age. In it, Jackson recalled a great fair, a socialist fund-raiser for the *Call* that she had attended as a child. She reminded Nathan of how he had tailored her a brown coat with a matching turban for the occasion. Pride in her father's new position as manager and pride in her new coat had engendered an indelible sense of expectation that in her waning years Laura Jackson felt compelled to answer. And so, with a nod to the Soviet editors, she accepted their accolade on behalf of her father and herself, an accolade that retained the zeal of her father's faded dreams. To spurn such a just recognition, she exclaimed, branded them scabs and, worse still, decadents!

But just as Nathan had felt free to leave behind his village in the Old World, so Laura would feel free to abandon her father's narrative and create her own. In the old country, a proverb cautioned against the father who was tempted to open the Torah for his daughter. Knowledge of the laws, it was said, provided the means for a shrewd circumvention of them. In 1916, the year her half sister, Isabel, married, Laura recanted her political ambitions for the avocation of poetry. A bitter, angry argument with her father followed, with stubborn insubordination on Laura's part and black disapproval on Nathan's, paralyzing the Brooklyn household until Laura left to move in with Isabel. Laura would never really return home, though she would retain leftist sympathies and work for leftist causes at least until her marriage in 1920.

As a young girl Laura Reichenthal could not bear the sound of her Germanic surname. Like her father's ancestors living under the reign of Joseph II, she would assume another. Unlike them, she was free to name herself as she chose, without regard to naming officials, patronymic, village of birth, occupation, or family relation. At about the time she left her father's house, she named herself Laura Riding.

Chapter 3

BACK TO THE MOTHER BREAST

——— • ———

My mother imagined that she suffered from bad eyesight; and to make it worse she wore a stocking round her eyes whenever possible: at home, a white stocking; abroad, a black stocking; and occasionally, to depress circumstances completely, a grey sock of my father's, fastened at the back of her head with a safety-pin. From which, our house was full of small oval rugs made by my mother out of the mates of the stockings which she wore round her eyes and which she was always losing. And these rugs made by my mother were not well made, because she imagined that she suffered from bad eyesight. From which my mother, whose character was all dreariness, acquired in my mind a hateful oddness. From which, I resolved to outdo her in oddness, so that I not only imagined that I suffered from good eyesight: I did actually suffer from it.

—"Letter of Abdication"

Every mother is a judge who sentences the children for the sins of the father.

—Rebecca West

——— • ———

THE REICHENTHALS SHARED their East 52nd Street tenement in the shadow of the Third Avenue elevated with a motley assortment of single immigrant boarders. Even by the grimmest contemporary standards this five-story tenement, with a street frontage of only twelve feet, would have been an overcrowded horror. Among their many neighbors was an Italian cook, an Irish cop, a Swedish tailor, and a Danish maid. Lonely and bereft, Sadie resolved on countless occasions to leave her husband, who spent most of his free time furthering the causes of organized labor and precious little of it with her.

Providentially, the final ultimatum was deferred once too many times. When Nathan lost his last tailoring job, Sadie became pregnant with her first child, and the die of martyrdom was cast. "My child had to have a father, at no matter what cost," she told her stepdaughter, Isabel. "And believe me or not, I hung on all those years for her sake. . . . I was warned by one of your own relatives, but alas it was too late, I made my bed and had to lie in it." This would become Sadie's refrain. She bade Laura, the daughter born to her on January 16, 1901, not to expect much from life because she was bound to be disappointed. One Christmas she put coal in her stocking to prove her point. She let her daughter be named after Nathan's first wife not in a spirit of generosity, Laura Jackson recalled, but defiance.

If Isabel had been at all pampered, Laura, the baby of the family for at least eight years until her brother Robert was born, received even more attention. Isabel, six years old, took an immediate, protective interest in the new baby, perhaps partly out of her own longings and partly in jealous collusion against her stepmother. The baby, learning to talk, called her Bella. Sadie was doubtless pleased to see that Laura had inherited her own blond hair and Nathan's bright blue eyes. From an early age, no matter how straitened their family circumstances, her little girl nearly always wore a ribbon tied in a neat bow atop her head.

In an essay published many years later Laura (Riding) Jackson would describe the grip that this early "three-cornered pattern of concern" had on her as a child. The "open space marked by Mother, Father, Sister (older half-sister)," was not, she wrote, "a design for a successful personality." It is an awkward and poignant comment, made all the more so by the rarity of introspection in Riding's writing. In the denial known to many first-generation Americans, she more often suppressed or misrepresented the factual circumstances of her childhood. One can, however, find in her various writings the grainy photographs of growing up that she inevitably secrets there, however transformed by anger or imagination. That, and the long memories of family friends, a surviving nephew, and some stray comments in letters and in conversation provide the few sources on her childhood and growing up. But this triangle of parents and sibling, which had enclosed her as a child, recurs again and again in Riding's life and work.

It was in the years before and immediately after her younger brother's birth that the claustrophobia and tearing clamor of family conflict made its ineluctable impact. Laura attended almost a dozen primary schools in the East and the Midwest, owing to Nathan's peripatetic career as a socialist and businessman. Despite Sadie's pestering her to play outdoors and make friends, Laura preferred to stay in, choosing the anxious ménage of home life over the strangeness of new neighborhoods and new schoolmates with whom she had little in common. The crashing battles between Isabel and Sadie and the perpetual wait for Nathan to come home may also have had at least one fretful but enthralled spectator in Laura. As the "baby" she found herself the least controversial among them all, and as the presumed innocent she could be the contested prize of their love. From this unsteady cradle, then, she could effect a kind of harmony, if only by staging even more sensational sideshows. One neighbor remembered Laura's violent temper tantrums and that her illnesses and fainting fits were closely attended.

An early, unpublished poem entitled "One Right, One Left" sets up a narrative voice in thrall to two beasts, the one that gave birth to her and the one that would devour her. Predator and protector are equally scarifying, and in the shadow of these looming creatures the poet is the rebel child and fury—at once the quarry and the weapon of the love and hate shuddering above her head. Three lines of this poem were retrieved for a later work, less suggestively autobiographical but chillingly evocative:

> Mothering innocents to monsters is
> Not of fertility but fascination
> In women.

Sadie's second pregnancy took its baleful toll on family life. "My God, My God," she wrote, "my afflictions during this terrible pregnancy." Sadie added Isabel's cold unconcern during this time to her life's list of grievances: "Your arrogance towards me, and your cooperation with your father, who exasperated me with his intellect, and losing my mother during this period. . . ." Acutely unhappy, her body worn with the strains of poverty, overwork, and illness, Sadie would never get much better, and her lot in life would in time get precipitously worse.

But her crowning agony was the arrival of the baby himself, her "poor unfortunate" Bobby. A difficult infant, he later proved to be both brilliant and emotionally unstable. Riding told a close friend in the 1930s that her brother had attempted suicide while an adolescent; he was at one time institutionalized. To Sadie, with a squalling infant now in her care, Laura became the child underfoot. According to one neighbor, in a fit of rage and jealousy over the encroachment on her mother's time by the baby brother, Laura once locked her mother in the family lavatory.

Riding would later publish a miscellaneous collection of letters in which the names and addresses of the correspondents had been changed to obscure their provenance. (While most of the letters were solicited from friends, some had been stolen from their recipients.) *Everybody's Letters* (1933) includes love letters, traveler's epistles, gossipy notes, letters of advice and sympathy, as well as a long afterword by Riding on the perversities of the epistolary medium. She also seems to have included a letter by herself, written at a very young age, perhaps saved and produced by Isabel. Exiled at her grandmother's house, Laura's letter is in unabashed baby talk, though, if one is to believe its date of February 5, 1911, she was ten when she wrote it. The illness worries, the simmering animosities, the appropriations of treats and affection in the Reichenthal household—all these are shown to be her most absorbing interest:

> My dear mother, I have sent a picture for [Bella] of little
> po peep sticking their tails on her sheep. give [Bella] a
> kiss for me and grandma hase looked everywere for my
> vest and she can not find it any were, and she looked in
> the dresser drawer and she found an orange and she gave
> me it. you had it given to you for a christmas and who
> ever gave you it gave you somthing elce, and grandma

bought me a loght of oranges and she had not got some
and so she gave it to me and so I hope you do not mind.
grandma bought me a bottle of cofe mixture and I have
to take it in hot water, and granpa thinks I am going to
have hoping cof and so do not worey your self or if you
do I will worey about you. does not [Bella] miss me and
how is the baby quite well, and how do you get on with
[Bella] and the baby. all write love from [Laura] your
loving daughter.

By restaking her claims on Sadie's cosseting, love, and worry, Laura
adamantly refused to give up her cradle. In publishing the letter
twenty years later (along with the letters by Nathan and Sadie quoted
above), Riding betrayed her continuing engagement with the dynamics of her childhood.

Similarly, like rags woven together in a rug, each line of a 1922
poem seemed to be signed with a tiny fragment of autobiographical
detail, more real than imagined. First entitled "Lida," the poem was
conceived as a book, comprising a poem of over 100 pages; as
"Forgotten Girlhood" it opens her Collected Poems (1938). The excerpts
here mimic the dumb confusions of a child; thoughts and feelings are
only incompletely explored by articulate language. That Riding
chose the language of the nursery rhyme and the taunting voices of
neighborhood children shows the technical latitude that she allowed
herself. She was twenty-one and living in Urbana when she began it:

In Laddery Street

Herself

I am hands
And face
And feet
And things inside of me
That I can't see.

What knows in me?
Is it only something inside
That I can't see.

Children

Children can't see over their eyes.
Children can't hear beyond their ears.
Children can't know outside of their heads.

The old ones see.
The old ones hear.
The old ones know.
The old ones are old.

. . .

Toward the Corner

. . .

One, two, three.
One, two, three.
Coming, Old Trouble, coming.
Somebody's dead, who can it be?
Old Trouble is it you?

. . .

Around the Corner

. . .

But don't call Mother Damnable names.
The names will come back
At the end of a nine-tailed Damnable Strap
Mother Damnable, Mother Damnable,
Good Mother Damnable.

If Laura's father was the central figure of her girlhood and adolescence, the grim and bathetic "Mother Damnable/Good Mother Damnable" dominated her early childhood. For someone who later tried to create a platitudinous upbringing for herself—despite having explored, in vague and allusive riddles, its precise perversities— "Lida" is an important and groundbreaking early work, answerable to no traditional form or conceivable literary forebear. The poem also provides evidence of how much distance was to develop between the young and precocious poet, Laura Riding Gottschalk and Laura (Riding) Jackson.

AFTER BOBBY'S BIRTH, Isabel took Laura under her wing with alacrity. By 1914 the Reichenthals were settled on Woodruff Avenue in Brooklyn, and Isabel had embarked on a literary career. Her thirteen-year-old half sister, distracted from her destiny as a strike leader, listened enraptured to her tales of literary bohemia in Greenwich Village. With thick brown hair, luxuriously waved, Isabel had a warm, maternal manner spiked with a quick wit and a vivacious bearing. Following *Vogue* fashions with a designer's eye, she made her own clothes and cut a stylish figure. Lacking the money or the scholarships to go to college, she began to work at the publishing firm of Grosset and Dunlap, in the Woolworth Building, then the tallest in New York and an imposing cultural landmark to a girl from Brooklyn.

Deep in the Bedford-Stuyvesant section of Brooklyn, however, taking up an entire city block, was an equally imposing landmark. For Laura, still wearing a ribbon in her golden hair, the large four-story red brick building was formidable, the beginning of an age. Brooklyn Girls' High School was bordered by Halsey Street, Nostrand Avenue, and Macon Street; two large entrances at opposite ends absorbed early-morning shoals of girls, more than 2,000 of them, who came from all over Brooklyn. Founded in 1886, the year New York City watched the unveiling of the Statue of Liberty, Girls' High had a reputation as solid as the ideals of plain living upon which it was founded. Its unusually demanding scholastic standards, a curriculum that included Greek as well as French and Latin, and its stated commitment to higher education for women resulted in proud and ambitious graduates. During the 1920s, nine out of ten girls went on to college. Two girls found waltzing were threatened with expulsion.

Morning assemblies began with songs from the Brooklyn Girls' High School songbook, among them a rousing march composed by the school's first principal, Horatio King:

> Lo, in the distance see the Temple Fame
> And she who would its steep approach ascend
> And win a noble and a glorious name
> Must fight the battle to the end.

Part of this battle for Laura Reichenthal would have been against the bedeviling circumstances of class and race. The scaling of the social ladder was precisely determined and acutely felt; according to one alumna it was most readily climbed by "Nordics," girls of English extraction, followed by the French and Germans. Then came the "inferior" races: the Italians, Greeks, Russians, and Poles. Below them were the Jewish girls, divided along class lines; thus, the daughters of bankers and lawyers were heads above the daughters of shoemakers, tailors, and barbers. German and Austrian Jews held themselves superior to Jews from Bessarabia and Podolia; *Galitzianers* were thought to be "dirtiest." Far below came the ultimate pariahs, the "Negro girls."

In 1928 Riding carefully explained how, at the age of fourteen, she had earned pocket money by reading the *New York Times* to an elderly neighbor, a veteran of the Civil War with weak eyesight. As a way of amusing herself, she read the entire newspaper in his eccentric pronunciation of English. At the same time in school she took elocution classes. English grammar, syntax, and punctuation were also part of the syllabus. One day, having mastered the old man's mispronunciation, she knocked on his door to find that he had died and her carefully cultivated talent was useless. "There I was with all that mispronunciation on my hands, and to a certain extent it is still on my hands."

From her accent, John Crowe Ransom concluded that Riding was of foreign birth "(Perhaps Polish Jew?)," with English not her first language, "greatly to her mortification." Riding was acutely sensitive to the way words sounded, particularly her own. The "eccentric" accent betrayed her at school and belied her polished appearance. More to the point, it was in the context of a manner of speech, a self-consciousness and theatricality of speaking, that Laura (Riding) Jackson would write about her discovery of poetry while still a schoolgirl. She saw poetry, she wrote much later, as a place "where the fear of speaking in strange ways could be left behind" and "as a way of speaking differently from the untidy speaking ways of ordinary talk."

At school the clamor of the ghetto—what Joseph Freeman later called the "insane noise"—subsided. The garrulousness of crowded tenements, the arguments behind closed doors, were replaced by the ordered and decorous emotion of Latin verse; the ear attuned itself to the cultured intonations of French, and the eye lit on the self-assured composure of the girls in the nicest dresses. Laura Reichenthal's four years at Brooklyn Girls' High provided her with an education in sensibility more than an acquisition of knowledge for its own sake; poetry carved a pathway to an untrammeled self, and a choice of identities, voices, and destinies sprung fully grown from the dreams of a high-strung child.

Laura owed her discovery of poetry to her half sister, Isabel, who published occasionally in New York literary magazines under the name Ellen Rogers. A party to her younger half sister's imagination and sensitive to the niceties of social advancement, Isabel also arranged for a high school friend to give Laura piano lessons, and saw to it that she had a proper wardrobe. This became easier after Isabel's engagement, and easier still after her marriage, in 1916, to Jesse Mayers, an editor at Grosset and Dunlap. As his editorial secretary, Isabel had returned her employer's dictated letters much improved in grammar and style, thus capturing his attention and his heart. The couple moved into a large house on Ocean Avenue, just four blocks away from the Reichenthal home. Jesse's sister, Helen, a year younger than Laura, began walking with her to school.

Impudence was clearly a kind of asset at Brooklyn Girls' High School, and in this Laura was generously supplied. The third self-evident truth of the school's "Declaration of Impertinence" read: "We could be brilliant as well as sportive. . . . [O]ur modest ears have been shocked by ravings on the subject of our wonderful intelligence." A student's other special distinctions included the ability to "enumerate in order the skeletal parts of a bean" and, to the delight of their chemistry teacher, to prove the "explosive properties of glass retorts." Few strayed far from an awareness of their own budding promise. In 1913 the debating society argued persuasively for the abolishment of the faculty altogether. The faculty, they held, interfered with the pupil's satisfaction in school life by their obnoxious habit of sitting in the last rows of the auditorium; they made it "compulsory for students desiring peace of mind to dodge them in the halls"; and their need for "so many and such instantaneous excuses" for misbehavior required pupils "to distort the truth." Finally, the society felt that a relief from their duties would enable the faculty to cultivate their "sweet dispositions" and, directing the reader to the faculty photo, improve their looks.

Laura shared the school's "charming exuberance of spirit." She staged the school's first production of *A Midsummer Night's Dream* and, as an honor student, took special license to rebel against school authorities. Supported by her father and following the example of her alter ego Rosa Luxemburg, she tried to dissuade her classmates from signing the loyalty pledge on the eve of the First World War. Three years ahead of her in Brooklyn Boys' High School, two other neighborhood boys, Joseph Freeman and Louis Gottschalk, led their debating society on similar issues. Born the son of a Polish barber on Lafayette Avenue in Brooklyn in 1899, Gottschalk was already a fervent socialist. "Our hearts were still tied to our mother's apron strings," wrote Freeman, but "our minds already soared into the Renaissance, the French Revolution, the Mexican War, socialism."

Ready to check these soaring spirits were a busy army of teachers, a strict school protocol, and Dr. Landes's treatise, *General Disability*. This work, known to every adolescent, described a mysterious disease afflicting young girls and boys and inspired a riot of conflict on the subject of sex. Almost in recompense, the students of Brooklyn Girls' High (or Old Maids' Penitentiary, as they fondly referred to it) were to be cheerful, joyful, and in equal measure determined to succeed in their quests: "No somber cloud obscures our sky/ Excelsior's our heart delight/March on was our war cry." Except for the senior prom, Brooklyn Boys' High might just as well have been in another borough.

Nonetheless, Isabel's marriage to Jesse Mayers was most likely of consuming interest to Laura, just as her literary career had been. In Jesse, a small, round, and prematurely balding man with an irrepressible sense of humor, Isabel had found a husband who not only was devoted to her but also took on the support of her family. Isabel's wedding brought the excitement of a new house, an advance in social status, and a front-row look for Laura at the domestic workings of a young marriage. From Isabel, too, Laura derived a more immediate sense of her own choices. Though Isabel had long posed as a model of sophistication and accomplishment, her jovial but rather uninspiring husband may not have been the kind of romantic figure Laura imagined for herself.

By the time Laura graduated, the glamour of Isabel's married life must certainly have paled, having faced certain doom in 1917 with the arrival of an infant, named Richard. Displaced once more as a cherished object of indulgence and affection, Laura provided a passage in "Lida" to make laconic comment on her sister's escape from their disabled childhoods, an escape that presaged her own:

> Bill Bubble in a bowler hat
> Walking by picked Lida up.
> Lida said "I feel like dead."
> Bubble said
> "Not dead but wed."
> No more trouble, no more trouble,
> Safe in the arms of Husband Bubble.
>
> A rocking-chair, a velvet hat,
> Greengrocer, dinner, a five-room flat,
> Come in, come in,
> Same old pot and wooden spoon,
> But it's only soup staring up at the moon.

The ironic detachment, however, came later. After graduating from high school, Laura did not go on to Cornell University, despite having received two scholarships. It was as if the prospect of leaving home, either Isabel's or her mother's, and of having to forge new friendships was too daunting. By remaining in Brooklyn, she might possibly remain her father's daughter—if not her mother's. During the interval between school and college, she worked for the fund established to secure Eugene Debs' release from prison, but she became quickly bored. Beneath her hesitation lay, perhaps, the obscure complaint that Isabel, her mother, and her father had unjustly abandoned her to an unwieldy and unknown fate. When she finally left for Cornell in the fall of 1918, she left with a promise of pocket money from Jesse Mayers.

THROUGHOUT LAURA RIDING'S life, abrupt departures and breaks with family or friends were accompanied or followed by charges of rank betrayal, the dereliction by others of shared principles and understandings. Hard evidence for Riding's early sense of a grievous abandonment, a thwarting of her own "murderous desire for love," is not easily found, though it was certainly the impression of her relatives that "Laura had completely divorced herself from her parents" and that "she seemed to have *hated* her mother."

In the metaphysical precision of the first published version of "Back to the Mother Breast," written in Riding's early twenties, something of this rage is disinterred and carefully autopsied. By the time Riding wrote it, the practice of poetry had become a new wellspring, implicit as a replacement for the infant's lost succor:

> Back to the mother breast
> In another place—
> Not for milk, not for rest,
> But the embrace
> Clean bone
> Can give alone.
>
> The cushioning flesh
> Afraid of closer kiss
> Set nakedness
> Against analysis;
> And the spurned infant cheek
> Turned away to speak.
>
> Now back to the mother breast,
> The silent lullaby exploring
> The frank bequest
> And happy singing
> Out of the part
> Where there is no heart.

That the return of the weaned child to the mother breast is a heartless one, wholly analytical, is the didactic point; the return is not for loving sustenance but for a surgical exploration of the original "frank bequest." The short lines terminated by a flat rhyme create a kind of ruthless logic to this idea, pressuring each word to "express" all possible sound and meaning. But despite the insistence on happy, almost scientific invulnerability, the pain of primal abandonment is implicit in the vengeful tone, in the return itself. Indeed, despite the stream of complaints that issued from Sadie's bedroom as she convalesced from real and imagined illnesses, Laura often found herself, figuratively speaking, on the room's transom, alternately repelled and drawn to the spectacle that her mother made of herself.

In the mid-1960s Laura Jackson told an impressionable correspondent that she had acquired a non-Semitic Dutch streak from her mother, adding that she was reluctant to talk about it because of a mystery that she had yet to resolve. Sadie's letter to Isabel mentions "worst of all the awful tensioned influence," which overshadowed all other trials and ills. The refrain in "Lida" evokes something similar: "Coming, Old Trouble, Coming." This "influence," combined with superstitions about bodily toxins, Sadie concluded, took their toll on her "poor unfortunate boy." In time Riding would come to believe that her brother, Bobby, had inherited his madness—if that is what it was—from his mother. Naturally, this left open the question of what Sadie might have bequeathed to *her*.

In the published story "Fragment of an Unfinished Novel" Riding explored the maternal bequest in a far more outrageous manner than in "Back to the Mother Breast." The story was included in *Anarchism Is Not Enough* (1928), a compilation, Riding said, of antisocial prose pieces on sex and other exceedingly personal matters. "Fragment of an Unfinished Novel" seems to begin a story that Riding is either unable or too uneasy to finish, a story that confronts and questions the bond between mother and daughter in a deeply complex manner. The flaws and failure of the work as fiction suggest that Riding was better at unearthing the raw conflicts than at dramatizing them. Nevertheless, "Fragment" affords the reader some sort of portrait of Sadie, however warped and uncertain its conception.

"What could I do," the story began, "but treat my secret as if it did not exist, that is, as my mother did hers until she confided it to me? which was not confiding, but a necessary explanation of the curious gift or curse (you will decide which for yourself before many pages) that I had from her . . ." The narrative voice is that of a rather inane Clarissa. In breathless and florid lament, she bemoans her fate but slyly resists divulging the exact nature of her mother's terrible secret. The reader gathers, however, that the "gift or curse" takes the form of a fit or spell that leads its victim into acquiescing to the most horrible and shameful deeds. For instance, one day the narrator's mother was sitting on the chamber pot, when the room suddenly filled with beaming people, surrounding her mother with warm congratulations and quite disrupting her quiet conversation with herself. Scrambling to cover her nakedness, her mother found herself dressed, inexplicably, in a bridal gown and already married to a Mr. Pink. She explains to her daughter that she, too, would one day find herself in an equally compromising position. There is nothing for her to do in the circumstances, her mother advises, but relent and accept the fact of this "cruel idiosyncrasy," "unspeakable peril."

Determined never to lose her composure or to consider herself entirely defenseless, the narrator's hapless mother soon took to her bed to "further her security," believing that since she could not stop the visitations she might at least limit them to a respectable place. "Alas!" the narrator wails, "a bed . . . was more ungovernable than a chamber-pot, for in this bed she got me . . ." "Fragment" ends with the poor woman standing half-naked at the window, sporting "a pair of pretty buttocks that she could scarcely trust as far as the door and ready to betray her at the least winking of her eye and plant her where she must acknowledge her position. . . ."

As marriage and motherhood are the immediate results of this maternal curse, the author's intentions at first seem fantastically satirical, a derisive comment on Sadie's lament, "I made my bed and had to lie in it." Further, the precipitous manner in which these seizures occur suggests something alarming about female sexuality; her mother's "curse" becomes for the daughter the harbinger of a paralyzing destiny. But the last vision of the mother is gentle and subdued; the narrator-daughter observes quietly, "How often have I come upon her standing in her shirt at the window, only half of her decently covered, the rest of her naked and unhappy—"

Quite often in Riding's fictional work, circuitousness and highly colored caricature are the means by which she explores autobiographical issues of identity and self-revelation. The choice in "Fragment" of her mother as her secret-sharer, rather than her heroic and dreaming father, is critical. And to some extent, just as the narrator is bound to her mother, the reader is bound to the narrator in morbid speculation; the bizarre turns in the story serve only to tighten the triangle's hold. The curse that the author-narrator inherits may be that of a sexuality unfettered by "self-possession," that of madness, or merely the fact of a female identity. Whatever this mysterious curse was—and perhaps it was different things at different times in her life—Riding clearly perceived it as something integral to her way of thinking of herself as a woman living in a woman's body. But even as it threatened to render her helpless, the secret also bequeathed to her the gifts of the storyteller, the siren, and the artist, and the powers of prophecy and revelation.

If Riding's creative portrayal of a mother's inheritance seems to exceed a daughter's determination not to follow in her mother's footsteps, it is perhaps, too, because of her real fear of this darkened room and the madness within it. There is evidence to suggest that Riding suffered from fainting fits and spells of mysterious paralysis, which may have been self-induced. The lengths to which Laura Jackson later went to discount stories about her miserable youth and strange mother suggest that the early fear of insanity was a real one. She categorized her "basic behavior-inclinations" as ordinary, and as evidence of her normality she provided her blood type and recalled a baby picture of herself showing a "brimmingly joyful little being." But it was through her mother's abnormalities or "oddness" that Riding, as a younger woman, explored her own sexuality and creativity. In later years, confronting an earlier version or fragment of her own narrative, she would blast Robert Graves instead.

In Laura (Riding) Jackson's *Praeterita*, her mostly unpublished memoirs, it is the discovery of poetry more than the circumstances of her birth and upbringing that marked the true beginning of her life. Poetry was the "self-perpetuating language, recited to still the anger at injustice." Her sense of injustice, however, was neither her father's nor her mother's. The provenance of Riding's rage may have been in the disruption of her mother's love on the arrival of her younger brother, "the spurned infant cheek/Turned away to speak," or perhaps it was something else; there is too little information to be certain. If its first remedy was the alliance with her father, its second lay in the more lasting alliance with poetry. As Laura began to free herself from the closeness of home life, other injustices and angers took its place, and poetry—"in eloquence less agony"—rushed in to quiet them.

In the noisy world of Brooklyn tenements, others found themselves besotted by what might be found of Shelley and Byron in Palgrave's *Golden Treasury* of English poetry. Claiming the romantic tradition as his own, Joseph Freeman shared her claim for the right of a transcendent free speech that would free him from the ghetto's dirty grip. Riding, too, would search for "immunity from the Strange" in poetry, a charm to protect her from her mother's fate, from the sordid stench of poverty and to release her into an "unlimited freedom of mind, knowledge, thought, utterance." When, in her eighties, poetry had been renounced and the promise of the immutability of language seemed less certain, she returned to a passionate embrace of language as it is spoken, carefully enunciated in precisely chosen words—as she had heard them in the halls and classrooms of Brooklyn Girls' High School. "All else would be horror: is horror," Laura (Riding) Jackson wrote, "by the light of the single dignity of the sweet single reason of speech—that of being well spoken."

Chapter 4

THE WAITING EQUIPAGE

——— • ———

Chloe or her modern sister, Lil,
Stepping one day over the fatal sill,
Will say quietly: "Behold the waiting equipage!"
Or whistle Hello and end an age.

—"Chloe Or . . ."

——— • ———

WHILE THERE HAD always been a great deal of talk about sex among the Sage College women, few ever had any field experiences to report; any experience whatsoever was received by even the most worldly with incredulity rather than shock. As students of Cornell University they imagined themselves as having bounded far from their mother's homely closets—enlightened, cosmopolitan, and advanced in their thinking. This was particularly true of those from Brooklyn and New York City whose endless discussions about the virtues of free love and deploring of the double standard kept them up long past "lights out." Theda Bara's screen performance as Salomé, the latest works of Havelock Ellis, or Sinclair Lewis' new novel were their likely conversation topics. Verbally at least, the Cornell co-ed could be quite knowing. Still, the weekly hygiene lectures were frequently interrupted by a fainting fit.

Revelations concerning who was going to what tea and with

whom, were, however, quite common. Disappointments in love, unrequited crushes, and undelivered invitations were confidences freely shared, except perhaps by Laura's best friend, Polly Antell, who often acted superior and kept herself aloof. Laura, however, still had time to hold a dorm room spellbound with accounts of her romance with Louis Gottschalk, her history instructor. That he was not just another fraternity boy but an older man, and a member of the Cosmopolitan Club, made it serious (few among them did not find him attractive) and always guaranteed her an audience. There was a certain amount of disappointment and envy when, in the fall of 1920, she married him and dropped out of college. Within a year Laura had left Ithaca and moved to Urbana, Illinois, where Lou had obtained a teaching position.

It was thus a surprise for her former classmates to return to the dorm and find Laura visiting in Sylvia Bernstein's room, chatting away as though she had never left. Seven months after leaving for Urbana she had suffered some kind of illness. After a brief rest with Isabel's in-laws in Far Rockaway, on Long Island, she came north to Ithaca in January 1922 for a further period of convalescence. Her husband's former colleagues were nonplussed, curious as to whether Laura and Lou had separated; Laura made a point of mentioning that Lou had been left behind in Urbana, alone. Sylvia Bernstein did not press her, but Laura seemed not at all clear herself.

Instead, smiling and conspiratorial, Laura pulled out a small case filled with cold creams and lotions, face powders and blush. Sylvia, now a senior, was taken aback, recalling Laura's disdain for cosmetics. Laura carefully explained the proper purpose of each lotion, as everyone in Sylvia's room looked on agog. Until very recently lipstick had been thought to be for prostitutes, and if a young lady wore rouge she did not admit it; nails were polished by assiduous rubbing with a chalked buffer, never varnished. They had never even seen a night cream. What caused an even greater stir, however, was Laura's disquisition on sex. "We listened to her with both our ears and our mouths open. What she told us wasn't very elucidating," Sylvia remembered, "but we were fascinated that she talked about it at all. We didn't know anyone else (with experience) who did."

CORNELL UNIVERSITY SITS on the crown of a very steep hill, over-looking the town of Ithaca, New York, in the valley below. "Far above Cayuga's waters with its waves of blue," boasts the school song, "Stands our noble Alma Mater, glorious to view." Bridges cross two gorges, noisy with cascading water, leading toward the final ascent to the library and chapel at the summit. With the opening of Sage College in the fall of 1873, the university's first thirty women arrived. Despite the trepidations of the founder's wife, women were there to stay. While laying the building's cornerstone, Mrs. Sage was said to have whispered to her husband, Cornell's president at the time, "You have meant to do women a great good, but you have ignorantly done them an incalculable injury."

In 1918 Cornell had briefly become a military school; male under-graduates and teaching assistants were quartered in fraternities ready to be called up for a war that was winding down. To deepen the pall of gloom, on October 1 Ithaca went dry. But a month later the chapel bells rang at 6:00 A.M., proclaiming the signed armistice and awaken-ing the postwar generation, Laura Reichenthal among them. The droves of arriving women students were welcomed by planes flying over the campus, their pilots diving low to wave and smile rakishly. There were crew races on nearby Lake Cayuga, scores of faculty teas and special dinners, and, with the doughboys returning home, a renewed social whirl. A new generation was elbowing its way, no matter who protested.

There were objections in the college newspaper to the sheer numbers of arriving co-eds. Fraternities, in particular, were on the alert to the looming dangers of a "hill full of women"; some even snubbed those brothers who saw fit to entertain them:

> As serious as the situation now is . . . the real danger is not with us yet. . . . If something is not done soon we will never be able to check the idea which exists in some quarters that Cornell is a woman's school. Cornell is and always has been essentially not only a man's but a "he-man's" school. It is in many respects the most virile institu-tion in the country. . . . And when our athletic prowess

declines, where are any of the red-blooded American youngsters, athletes or no, going? Not to Cornell.

Even the official historian of Cornell felt obliged to make allowances for the headstrong determination of these early co-eds, or "grinds," as he called them. Sage College women treated such provincial displays of anti-coedism, like similar ones of "red-blooded" anti-Semitism, with dismissive scorn.

Polly Antell, one such co-ed, had arrived at Sage College with no small amount of impatience. Her real name was Esther, but she hated it. Striding into her dorm room in a pair of scandalous riding breeches, she took one look at her roommate, Fanny, decided that she would not do, and tried to arrange for another room. By her own admission she was stubborn, arrogant, very bright, and "far advanced"; not only did she wear trousers, she sported a Buster Brown bob. The daughter of Russian Jews, she had sneaked books from her father's library and eavesdropped on his business affairs since she was a child. Encouraged only by an older brother, who had served as a medic in the trenches, she had fought the opposition of her entire family to higher education for women. Here she was: a decidedly pretty girl who wanted "to know everything."

But Polly was not the first co-ed to wear her hair short. At the time few women wore bobbed hair, but when Sylvia Bernstein arrived at Cornell she had a barber cut off hers to celebrate her freedom. Hearing the news, Sylvia's outraged family told her that if it didn't grow back by Christmas she could stay in Ithaca and spare them her disgrace. Before long, however, a line formed at her door asking for a bob, Laura among them. Her light brown hair, darker and less golden now, was still "unusual for a Jewish girl," Sylvia noted. In general, Sylvia kept a keen eye on the handful of those who, like herself, came from Jewish homes in New York City. She admired Laura's clear skin and intelligent light blue eyes. To another young woman, who played the Queen of Hearts to Laura's White Rabbit in a freshman production of *Alice in Wonderland*, Laura seemed a little older, a little more worldly than the others; Laura Reichenthal, she recalled later, had an efficient manner about her.

All the co-eds yearned to go to dances, but only Polly, despite her brusque manner and impatience with those provincials who found themselves in her way, seemed to be invited to all of them, leaving behind a trail of broken hearts and envious classmates. But all women had to be in their room by ten o'clock unless there was a formal ball, in which case they were allowed to stay out later, but only with a chaperone. Freshmen were permitted only two nights out a week and were forbidden to walk around after eight o'clock at night. Pianos and Victrolas were limited to certain hours of the day. The more adventuresome naturally found ways to get around the wardens. Laura, found smoking in the infirmary, was one of them, though perhaps not until her second year, when she met Polly.

Among the young "literary" women, Professor James Mason's history of French literature class had become something of a scandal. Though this short, thickset poet and scholar never actually said anything salacious, the mere sound of his French was enough to set them tittering. "Ordinary things, like the birth date of Montaigne, sounded ribald," Sylvia remembered; "he used the words 'social intercourse' to get our attention." To the discomfiture of the administration, Mason taught Villon, Verlaine, Baudelaire, Mallarmé, and their compeers. His recitals of Rimbaud were of masterful suggestiveness, with never an empty seat in the lecture hall.

Less than twenty years after Sylvia Bernstein graduated from Cornell, she collaborated on a novel entitled *Glorious to View*, in which Professor Mason held a class spellbound with descriptions of dissolute French poets smoking Turkish cigarettes, benumbed by absinthe and melancholia in Montmartre's cafés. This scene and others like it made up, in extended flashbacks of elaborately mannered prose, her heroine's student days at Cornell, her close circle of friends, and the fashions, philosophies, and romances that so entangled them.

Felicitously, the novel's heroine, Tamar Spinet, went from Cornell to world fame as a modernist poet. Her poems, "webbed in a lyrical obscurity," Sylvia told her readers, were to receive "eulogistic notices from the critics, and annealed apathy in the buying public." Conflating facts from both its author's past and Laura Reichenthal's college career and future, *Glorious to View* is a sigh-filled period piece. Even if the likeness in Sylvia's purple-tinted mirror is not exact, Tamar Spinet is recognizable as a fantasy spun as much by Laura herself as by her sometimes expendable confidante Sylvia. In Riding's later story "Schoolgirls" a similar character, named Judith, holds court in a Swiss boarding school, reading out her love letters or enlightening her classmates on the details of her affair with the mathematics master:

> It was an exciting thing for the other girls to have Judith among them. She laughed a lot and talked knowingly and brought an atmosphere of confusion and drama to the school. She made the other girls feel guilty and inferior for being unsophisticated. Everyone wanted to do something wrong.

Sylvia described Tamar Spinet, seated in the front row for Professor Mason's lecture on George Sand, reveling in a fantasy of the artistic life of a woman writer. After a careful discussion of Sand's work, ideas, and love affairs, however, Mason turned to his wide-eyed co-eds and, "pointing his finger like a Moxie advertisement" fulminated against the unconventional life in language more befitting Billy Sunday than a professor of French literature. He took pains to point out that despite warnings from her mother, the flamboyant life of George Sand's daughter had a sorry ending. "Without the discipline of genius, she went to pieces completely," he cautioned. "It was the confession magazine with its moral ending," Sylvia editorialized, "but acceptable for its high literary level." Laura also sat in the first row of Professor Mason's class, her French answers more ready than any other student's. To Sylvia, sitting a few rows back, it often seemed as though they were exchanging private repartee. When Sylvia wrote her novel, Tamar Spinet found the required discipline of genius for a life of "high-minded sin." That, plus poetry, seemed about the most romantic destiny that a Sage College girl might hope for.

In Goldwyn Smith Hall, Professor Martin Wright Sampson, a former stage actor who bore a striking resemblance to John Barrymore, also figured in both Tamar Spinet's and Laura Reichenthal's imaginative development. To that small troupe of men and women who considered themselves intellectual, Sampson recited Shelley and Keats in a perfectly modulated English accent. More than sixty years later Laura (Riding) Jackson credited Sampson for giving her the license to choose her own destiny, "to leave me free to be and do whatever came naturally." His own destiny as an actor had been mysteriously short-lived; he spoke with wistful melancholy on the subject. Periodically, however, his moodiness would lift, and he would lose himself in exultant recitals of Hamlet's soliloquies, leaving his students in stunned and somewhat embarrassed silence.

Perhaps owing to her early diet of "boys' books," Polly Antell was not nearly as interested in French and English poetry as she was in Louis Gottschalk's course in European history. Offered in Polly's first semester, in the fall of 1919, this course was his first teaching assignment. Aided by scholarships, Gottschalk had graduated from Cornell the previous semester Phi Beta Kappa. A photograph taken in 1921 shows him standing a head's height above the members of the Cornell History Club; a half smile distinguishes him from the other, more somber members. His unparted hair is left to form a full curly crown; his stylish jacket is open. Compared with the buttoned-up suits, watch chains, and bow ties of the other members, he looks almost boyish. According to his army papers he was five feet eleven inches tall, weighed 131 pounds, and had flat feet.

Gottschalk appears twice in Sylvia's novel: as the president of the Intercollegiate Socialist Society with "passionate, scholarly good looks" and then as a faculty instructor who had made a hasty marriage to an undergraduate. "On an instructor's salary one couldn't afford anything more than the dingy three-room furnished apartment where the Louis Gottschalks lived. The marriage would dissolve in confusion within a few years." More than a few co-eds would have enjoyed his affections, Sylvia remarked, but as usual Polly found him first. The winter of 1919 found them skating together on Beebe Lake.

Early in 1920, Polly abandoned the girlfriends of her first semester, Sylvia among them, and became "very selective" in her friendships. With Laura's arrival at Risley Hall, the second-year dorm after a semester hiatus, Polly took up with her instead, and they began spending most of their time with Lou Gottschalk and his best friend and fellow instructor, Leo Gershoy. The clique quickly acquired a reputation as the most clever and intellectual of the Jewish students from New York City—"a kind of Jewish royalty, the pinnacle of sophistication and brilliance." Sylvia, though still an occasional confidante of Laura's, observed them from a distance.

Sometime that spring Polly transferred her affections to Leo, and Laura began dating Lou. Beebe Lake and the hills around Ithaca became the backdrop for their twenty-mile hikes and picnics. Other days found the group sitting on the library slope or pitching pennies on the sidewalk curb near the cafeteria, dissecting the problems of the Socialist party. "I may even have become engaged to Leo. We were very much attached to each other," Polly recalled. "I was really close to Lou and therefore I was close to Laura. She was very bright and very lovely."

Laura's leftist credentials and early ideological training at her father's knee came in handy in Gottschalk's class. She was often called on to explain the more complex passages of *Das Kapital*. Lou was a fine debater, having honed his skills alongside Joseph Freeman while at Brooklyn Boys' High, and she found in him a true mentor. With brilliance and finesse, she sharpened her mind on his, and their courtship was steeped in the language of social causes and feverish political debate. The pleasures of intellectual kinship that she had once shared with her father were now to be had with him. With scant hesitation, she confessed unabashedly to Sylvia that she had fallen in love. Lou's courtly reticence fueled speculation at Risley Hall as to his true feelings and intentions.

One evening in the fall of 1920 Laura returned to Risley Hall breathless, her porcelain complexion flushed and excited. She had gone for a walk with Lou, she told Sylvia, during which he took her hand and pressed it in his own. In almost two semesters of dating he had never once touched her. Then, walking Laura back to the dorm, he had paused at the door and kissed her before turning on his heel and disappearing into the night. This gesture, Laura intimated to Sylvia, was their courtship's tender finale. The following day Laura sent a telegram to her family announcing her engagement.

Not a week later and having completely ignored her studies, Laura—much to the astonishment of her friends—failed an exam. Exultant at this new distinction, she sat on the library steps waving the paper with its damning mark at everyone who passed by, "her face glowing," Sylvia remembered. In *Glorious to View* Sylvia restaged the scene for the climax of Tamar Spinet's own romance with a fellow student:

> "And you want everybody coming into the library to see you waiting for Jonathan?"
> "Yes."

"And the prelim book? What's that for?"

"For evidence. I failed a history exam."

"*You* failed! An A student?"

"Yes, I failed, gloriously, beautifully, heroically. . . . Isn't it wonderful? Everything's wonderful."

"Oh, you mean you just couldn't study.

"Don't be so prosaic, Becky. You don't understand."

Becky understood. She understood because she felt she would never achieve a similar glory."

Perhaps Polly's self-assured professional ambitions contrasted too sharply with Laura's uncertain goals. Despite her stellar classroom performances, she had none of Polly's brash certainty or sense of direction. Once she announced her engagement, however, the scramble for good marks came to an end; scholastic achievement or professional goals paled beside the wonder of her future with Lou, the wife of a promising young professor and political radical—a collusion of temperament and twenty, she explained later. Though she would make repeated stabs at completing her undergraduate degree, she was happy in 1920 not to look back. In "Postponement of Immortality" (later retitled "Postponement of Self") the poem's speaker comments wryly on the transfiguring proposal of marriage:

> At six little girls in love with fathers.
> He lifts me up.
> See. Is this Me?
> Is this Me I think
> In all the different ways till twenty.
> At twenty I say She.

Thus, on the sunny midafternoon of November 2, 1920, having obtained permission from the university authorities, Laura Reichenthal was married to Louis Gottschalk by the town mayor. She was nineteen, he was twenty-one and just beginning work on his doctorate; the ceremony was witnessed by the mayor's wife. Almost at once Laura began to sign her name Mrs. Louis R. Gottschalk; R. stood for Reichenthal. Though she found Laura Reichenthal Gottschalk too much of a mouthful, Lou was made to take on her maiden name in an egalitarian and entirely modern spirit. He retained it throughout his professional career in deference to Riding's father, whom he greatly respected. Laura, however, replaced her maiden name with Riding, which she had toyed with as an adolescent. According to Polly, Laura promptly quit her studies and devoted herself to domesticity.

FROM A SMALL graduate student body, Cornell University produced a remarkable number of outstanding historians, Lou Gottschalk and Leo Gershoy among them. For the seven distinguished full professors at the time there were no more than a dozen graduate students in the history department; contact between professors and students was therefore "direct, frequent and generally warm." Lou and Leo had forged a friendship in their freshman year, when Lou studied European history and Leo, Romance languages. By the time they registered for Carl Becker's class on the French Revolution and Napoleon two years later, they were known, together with two other classmates, as "the Goops."

Though known principally for his work in American history, Carl Lotus Becker had a major impact as a teacher of European history at Cornell, influencing an entire generation of historians who went on to make their own mark. Gershoy and Gottschalk were among his most eager apprentices. Frederick George Marcham, an English historian several years behind them, described the circle of young leftist historians who worked with Becker as a group apart from the hardworking, earnest students of his own class. They seemed to him lively and vigorous, bursting with the intellectual life of liberal New York City. "Their friendship with Becker was close, almost protective, against others who criticized him," Marcham recalled.

Becker, clear-eyed, square-jawed, and the son of a farmer, was born in Iowa in 1873. While still a boy, trapped between church pews, Becker first heard of the dangers of French atheism. Finding his way to Voltaire's work, Becker was consoled to learn that the Frenchman cut a larger figure in the world than did his Methodist minister. Like H. L. Mencken, whose *Smart Set* was widely read among Cornell sophisticates, Becker's writings were marked by sardonic wit and an impatience with ignorance and intolerance. Though a staunch socialist, he did not believe in mankind's progress toward perfection. Such skepticism was rare among students from Brooklyn, but like their postwar literary compatriots they took to it at once. Becker's was a mood that suited them, a mature contrariness to the full-throated but often blinkered revolutionary idealism of their immigrant parents.

Though Becker was shy and uncomfortable around faculty wives and female undergraduates (a few rated as "pets"), Leo and Lou clearly delighted in the company of their bright, outspoken undergraduate girlfriends. Early in their marriage Lou began a biography of Marat; Laura's response was to begin a verse biography of Voltaire. Her unapologetic and freewheeling description of her method is worth quoting in full for its view of her husband's profession, the radical traditions they were both shaped by, and the question of historical authority:

> In defence of this unauthoritative treatment of the life of Voltaire I offer no other sources than the tireless gossip of an old wind and certain unaccountable revelations of the strange caprices of *what-may-always-be-possible*. If to know others it is enough to love them, that is, to admire in them what others find either wicked or dull, then I claim just title to the privilege of unofficial intuition in the matter of the *truth-about-Voltaire*. I am not sure how long I have held him in this affection, which may be, after all, a form of historical pity for failure; but it seems from here a very long time, long enough to fortify the sympathetic imagination with the data of memory. To know *about* a life requires much learning. To *know* it needs only a partisan fancy. Here is the sole equipment of my humble research. My facts cannot be challenged, for I have none; nor can my fancy be questioned, since it is proved by its own deviations wherever it goes.

Where Becker and Gottschalk had studied the subtle permutations of Voltaire's ideas in the light of an age, Riding embraced the man, discovering with him an age-old alliance. In place of Becker's belief in a central, unifying idea "whose reality could not be established by any number of witnesses" Riding held up the authority of her own "unofficial intuition," which also could not be questioned by any number of witnesses. As a result, *Voltaire: A Biographical Fantasy* is a challenging and coquettish display, aimed decidedly at those gentlemen for whom she would never become a "pet." Within her, the old radicalism of her father's persisted; stubborn, self-insistent, and often blind with the unconsidered belief not only in the perfectibility of mankind but in her own as well. "Faults are perfection's faults," Riding ended "Lida," "And only perfection matters." Historical perspective tempered by skepticism had no place in her world view.

When *Jean Paul Marat: A Study in Radicalism* was published in 1927, the Hogarth Press brought out Laura's *Voltaire*. Then living in England with Robert Graves, she dedicated the book to her former husband but had her married name canceled after the title page was printed. Lou, in turn, acknowledged his gratitude to Laura Riding Gottschalk, "whose time and efforts have been devoted to this book to a degree second only to my own." His epigraph, a quotation from Romain Rolland, might have been chosen by his former wife: "We wander amid the phantoms we create. Yet we have to judge; we have to act."

In the summer of 1924, Riding acted. Living in Louisville, she left her husband again to return again to Cornell, not for a visit to her old dormitory, but to make one last effort to obtain her degree and, as she had told Allen Tate, to spend some time alone. Writing from her small apartment on East Seneca Street, far below the college's cool pinnacle, she found herself, she told Polly, absurdly lonely. Ithaca in summertime, however Edenic, was also desolate without the bustle of classes and students. Sylvia and the rest of her former classmates at Sage had graduated two years earlier, and with them went Tamar Spinet. While lonely letters from Lou arrived regularly, it was not her husband whom Laura wanted to hear from.

To overcome her loneliness, Laura entertained a stream of Lou's friends from New York City and female confidantes to whom she frankly revealed her marital difficulties as she had earlier related its intimacies. Doubtless, there was something awesome in the figure she cut, and judging from her accounts of these visits to Polly, she was never entirely oblivious to the net effect. In Ida Prighozy, for example, Laura had found the perfect audience. A young Cornell student who had just completed her second year Ida, like Laura and Polly before her, was dating her history instructor, Leo Gershoy.

Overly protected and sheltered by a family of older brothers for a heart ailment (she said she was carried up stairs until late childhood), Ida was quiet and observant, concealing her sly intelligence beneath a facade of shy innocence. She quickly became one of Carl Becker's favorite "pets." This endeared her further to Leo, whom she would soon marry. She considered Laura an "older married woman" and was somewhat mystified by Laura's impatient cultivation of her friendship. Still, Ida responded dutifully to Laura's invitations to lunch, sometimes bringing her best friend and confidante, Louise, along.

Laura had also tried to refresh her friendship with the Beckers, but they had proved somewhat chary; she described to Polly an extravagantly upsetting stay at their lakeside cottage. Leo, too, had been less friendly than anticipated; he did not respond to her efforts at renewing their intimacy, perhaps out of loyalty to Lou, perhaps because of Ida. Though Ida learned later about Leo's former infatuation with Laura, she was never clear why Laura pursued *her* friendship with such steadfastness.

Ida was nonetheless fascinated by Laura's conversation, which covered, memorably, men and sex and was punctuated by "flashing blue eyes." Laura was very well spoken, attractive not because of her looks or dress, Ida felt, but because of the way she talked. "It didn't take much in those days to be considered sexy," she recalled. "Men didn't expect you to be pretty so much then as they do now. Laura was not pretty." On one visit to Laura's apartment Ida noticed a curious object hanging from a shower fixture. Laura spotted her puzzlement and enlightened her as to its utility with some degree of explicitness and relish. Scurrying home, Ida duly reported the "preventative" functions of a douche to her friend Louise.

Polly was working at a summer job in New Jersey, at the time. There she had letters from Leo on the subject of Laura and Ida and from Laura on the subject of Leo and Lou. Laura wrote her that she was desperate to avoid a return to Lou and Louisville at the end of the summer, pressing her to inquire about jobs and apartment possibilities in New York City. Within a week, and before receiving an answer, Laura wrote again; after a great deal of anguished indecision she was returning to Louisville after all, suggesting that this route required the greater courage. She and Lou were to go forward as comrades, comparing notes on their private lives and transforming their marriage from a state of bondage into an amazing freedom. As for her beloved Ithaca, she noted sadly, the place now seemed dead and bitter—thanks to Leo for that. To Helen Mayers, her former schoolmate at Girls' High and Isabel's sister-in-law, Riding said of her abortive stay in Ithaca, "Ida was too much Ida." Nothing more was ever said of her degree.

BUT RIDING LED another life during that summer of 1924 in Ithaca. As in Urbana, loneliness and isolation bred poetry. The poems she was writing she knew were wholly original, forcefully expelled, she wrote Polly, with the blast of the new century at her back. Ida and Leo were mere surface skirmishes; it was a letter from Allen Tate that Riding most anxiously awaited.

Tate's passionate interest in "Mrs. G." had been returned in more than equal measure in the few months since his visit to her in Louisville. Though her love for Tate is referred to fleetingly in letters to Polly, the real record survives only in her poems. The first of these memorialized his visit and appeared in the April 1924 issue of the *Fugitive*. It was suggestively titled "Improprieties." From this poem and those that followed, it is clear that Riding had the Fugitives' measure much more quickly than they had hers:

> Why do you come fantastically folded
> In a reticent dark gown?
> It is the house of a harlot
> And you are white and unclothed inside.
> Do you think you can dwell there
> Cryptically forever
> And yet be wantonly unviolated?

The poem's speaker questions her gentleman caller's elaborate self-deprecations and asks of him, muselike, to abandon his indecent and frivolous rhetoric before coming to her. Even before the poem was published Riding wished that she had destroyed it.

The paradoxical use of imagery and language is pervasive in

Riding's work. "Harlot" is idealized to denote the female Fugitive whose chaste silence indicts her caller's promiscuous garrulity. Through paradox Riding extends the capacity of language to create new guises for herself, subversive voices removed from convention and outside judgment, which included those reserved for the unfaithful wife. Paradox also enabled her to confound the Fugitives' peculiar blend of aesthetic assumptions of female beauty. In this way the language of conflict and irony was reserved not only for the ruling poetic orthodoxies but for the social ones as well.

Tate's response to her "Improprieties" endeavored to be humorous rather than ardent: "Credo: An Aesthetic" appeared two months later in the *Fugitive*: "Good manners, Madam, are had these days not / For your asking, nor mine, . . . Comic or not, heterogeneities / Divert my proud flesh to indecisive guile." The poem concludes in idle flattery: "My manner is the footnote to your immoral / Beauty, that leads me with a magic hair / Up the slick highway of a vanishing hill / To Words— . . ." John Crowe Ransom later wrote to Robert Graves, "I've observed many poets (like Tate) castigate their own poetry . . . till poetry was quite intimidated and committed suicide—so I know the dangers of cerebration in poetry. The best poetry, for me, is the most perilous . . ." Riding would also scorn such "literary" affectations, replying to Tate with courtly finesse in "Fragments from Alastor":

> The requisite spot of anguish having shown
> Upon my cheek the growth of the disease
> From the internal infection of the bone
> To the full epidermal fever, please
> Proceed as you intended, in the tone
> With which your sonnet on the subject used to freeze
> My too unliterary passion to stone.

While these lines (later incorporated somewhat changed into "To a Loveless Lover"), show her skill at ventriloquizing the practiced and feverish Fugitive voice, other poems revealed Riding's use and understanding of language to be of an entirely different order than that of the Fugitives.

By midsummer of 1924, five months after meeting her, Tate was agreeing with Donald Davidson that their literary discovery tended to be "too precipitate." He had also stopped answering the stream of letters from Ithaca. While Riding anxiously awaited word from him, Tate was writing to Davidson that he now considered her poems "divine accidents":

> A very volatile genius, but nonetheless a genius . . . Yet it is too bad that nineteen out of twenty of her poems are nearly worthless.

A month later, writing from Guthrie, Kentucky, where he was summering with Robert Penn Warren, Tate advised Davidson how to reject two recent poems of Riding's. Mindful of her "extreme sensitivity to rejection," Tate begged that Davidson not quote his opinion of them to her and promised to explain later. Though Riding had sent him copies of the two poems, he had not responded. Entitled "The Mad Serenader" and "Stanzas in Despair Dying," Tate doubtless realized that they were addressed directly to him. Instead, he struck up an acquaintance with Warren's distant cousin and friendly neighbor, a young journalist named Caroline Gordon.

Not having heard from Tate himself, Riding found the rejection of her poems by Davidson to be searing. Writing to him what she would have liked to say to Tate, she answered his charge that her "Stanzas" lacked conscious deliberation in an impassioned fury. Any poet who waited on Wordsworth's encomium of recollection in tranquillity, she protested, would end up in dumb paroxysms. She was convinced, she told Davidson, of the utter poetry in life; she was not so convinced of the life in poetry as he knew it: Her muse for these poems, she said, was Isadora Duncan, not Anna Pavlova, daring rather than delicate, impetuous rather than measured and graceful. Finally, she equated poetry with her own consciousness, alert and intelligent with the secret meanings of life, even while she dreamed.

Davidson's letter of rejection found Riding uncertain as to whether she should return to Louisville or leave her husband and try to make a living in New York (where she knew Tate was also headed). By the end of August, with still no word from Tate, she had decided to return to Louisville.

The rejection of "Stanzas in Despair Dying" also led Riding to write her first piece of critical prose. The debate between Tate and Ransom on "The Future of Poetry" had appeared in the *Fugitive* that February, and her essay answered both men. Attempting to define what he saw as the impetus and difficulty of modernism, Ransom had isolated two aspects of the modernist vision based on the imagists' work. One was an honesty of theme and accuracy of expression; the other, the spontaneity of the Word and its sacrosanctity. These impulses, he felt, had led the moderns to abandon meter in the search for a subtler music, one less prone to hackneyed sentiment, to lachrymose or pious clichés. After the loss of that "miracle of harmony, of the adaptation of the free inner life to the outward necessity of things," the thoughtful poet straddled an awkward fence between form and formlessness.

Tate rejected this "simple antiphony" and the idea that the mechanisms of meter were ever fixed. The true decadence, he averred, lay in meter's "paralyzing incubus":

> There is no common-to-all truth; poetry has no longer back of it, ready for use momently, a harmonious firmament of stage properties and sentiments which it was the pious office of the poets to set up at the dictation of a mysterious *afflatus*—Heaven, Hell, Duty, Olympus, Immortality . . . the Modern poet of this generation has had no experience of these things, he has seen nothing even vaguely resembling them. He is grown so astute that he will be happy only in the obscure by-ways of his own perceptive processes . . . It is the age of the Sophist . . . Poetry, the oracle, is gone.

In the essay written that summer in Ithaca, "A Prophecy or a Plea," Riding set herself starkly apart from any formal poetic tradition—classical, romantic, or modern; indeed, the question of what form poetry was to take is ignored entirely. The essay, which she worked on for many months, has the temper of a manifesto, sweeping away all those who had come to poetry before her:

> For the poets of the classical mood [art] is a strong cathartic that keeps them free of malaise and dyspepsia and

wraps them in an urbane Horatian peace; for the Eliza-
bethans, a pretty pastoral constitutional; for all the roman-
ticists, a drug—a stimulant for Byron, a delicious dose of
laudanum for Shelley (even such as Baudelaire bought
their cocaine at the same shop); a soothing syrup for the
Victorians, a tonic for the realists; a heady wine for the
impressionists; a profound emetic for the expressionists.

Blinded by life, the poet had in cowardice turned his senses inward
against its brutal advance. "The most moving and at once distressing
event in the life of a human being," she wrote, "is his discovery that
he is alive." Riding was particularly harsh on T. S. Eliot, Tate's literary
hero, insisting that he, too, had retreated into the "penumbra of
introspection." T. S. Eliot and his imitators, she observed pointedly,
"endeavor to show how their chastity and ennui remain intact
through all their orgies of intellectual debauchery." The result was
that poets had become marginalized, "parasites of the spiritual world
they were born to."

Harriet Monroe echoed a similar sentiment in "Why Not Laugh,"
a 1923 *Poetry* editorial directed at Eliot and those would-be poetic
Prufrocks who, having rejected "our bathtubs and telephones and
washing machines and even our humble skyscrapers," saw "the
world smash to pieces in the Wasteland [sic]." Riding's demand for
"the birth of a new poetic bravery that shall exchange insight for
outsight" seconded Monroe's call for an American bard, enlightened
by grand vistas. Fortified by personal faith alone, not only confronting the world but also creating it, "the artist too must turn pro-
ducer," Riding sweepingly pronounced. "Mechanics outrun
metaphysics," she warned. "Do not Philistines lead the race?"

THAT THE RACE was on was unquestioned. The age itself was impatient. Riding returned to Louisville from Ithaca just as the fall 1924
semester began, rejoining her husband. She still had had no letter
from Tate. She found Louisville changed, or herself changed; the
pace seemed to have quickened to match her own. Fourth Street had
become Fourth Avenue, in affected big city style. As the commercial
center, the new avenue was packed tight with tin lizzies and lined by

hotels, movie palaces, and fine restaurants. It seemed that overnight Louisville had become a paean to upward mobility and boundless optimism. Two huge hotels opened up resplendent with polished marble floors and stairs, glittering chandeliers, and potted plants. Another, the Seelbach at Fourth and Walnut, would appear the following year in *The Great Gatsby*.

To the renewed isolation that she felt as a poet was now added the indignity of living on a small salary as a professor's wife, at a time when money was the touchstone. There were places to spend it and amazing new products to spend it on. Mass-produced consumer goods such as electric refrigerators, vacuum cleaners, flatirons, and radios were proliferating, and with the installment plan even the workingman could buy a car. In 1911 there were eleven beauty shops in Louisville; by the late 1920s there were 120, catering to single young women looking for a boyish bob or, for the boldest, a perma-nent wave. Hemlines were rising and would soon reach the knees, with stockings rolled down below them. Clusters of schoolgirls peered in department store windows, snapping and slapping their compacts open and shut.

A poem written at the time, "Saturday Night," captured the sense of exclusion that Riding may have felt on seeing Louisville's profligate flappers strut about her. Strikingly different in style from her early published work, its narrative inquiry is soft-spoken, compassionate, childlike, and open. Drawing on childhood memories of a small Pennsylvania mining town where her father had gone to manage the union paper, Riding describes a Saturday night parade of farmers' wives, townspeople, a Salvation Army band, men on street corners, and women looking in shopwindows "Wondering how much there will be left to spend / On Sunday dinners, and worrying about / The price of everything they'd like to have." While the images are those of a child's illicit excursion, the mood is more that of the young woman writing it, staring in shopwindows, sympathetic to a mother's worried look at the prices, and perhaps envious of those Louisville ladies who "look as if they mean to buy." When Riding reprinted her *Collected Poems* she included "Saturday Night" (which had never ap-peared in any book) in an appendix. By recovering this poem, it was as if the loneliness and isolation of her later years had recognized and finally found company in the experience of her younger self, that hungry youth which she had been all too quick to disown.

Restless, bored, and lonely, Laura often spent evenings in the all-night dance halls downtown. Though more apparent in her very early work, jazz was an important influence on Riding's poetry at this time. Formerly kept to the brothels and honky-tonks, jazz had arrived in dance halls and, like the hip flask of bootleg whisky, seemed to be everywhere. Even Woolworth's had its piano man, serenading the sidewalk shopper with such hits as "Hot Tamale Molly." Marching bands stomped down Fourth at lunch hour, with banners announcing the current attraction at Macauley's Theater, where Laura would go for matinees. She had a passion for Lillian Gish and besieged her with letters for four years until she received a reply. With her eyes and ears finely attuned to her loneliness, Riding wrote poems that imitated jazz rhythms, mocked the likes of Dr. Finley Gibson, pastor of Louisville's Walnut Street Church, and his weekly sermon "God's Judgment on the Wicked City." It was another life, secret from the bespectacled and canonizing Fugitives.

Barry Bingham, son of the Louisville newspaper publisher Robert Worth Bingham, said of his generation, "They all expected to be millionaires by age thirty-five and then to retire and enjoy the money." Bingham was one of the first civic leaders whom Riding approached when it appeared that the *Fugitive* would have to suspend publication owing to a lack of funds and support from Vanderbilt University. She had first hatched the fund-raising plan in Ithaca, writing to Davidson of her acquaintance with Mrs. William Belknap, wife of one of the richest men in Louisville, who "once confided to someone who confided to me" that she, too, had written poetry and was considering taking it up again. Laura suggested that Davidson write to Mrs. Belknap, who had far more money than she needed, and ask her for as much as was required. Davidson promptly did so.

By October 1924, Riding had her marching orders from Nashville, and in return she pledged to work desperately for them all. More than agreeing with the goals of the Fugitives' magazine (she never once commented on any of the poetry that they wrote and published), Laura Gottschalk was intent on becoming an indispensable part of their literary venture. This was inspired partly by self-interest and partly by the desire to embrace a profession, she went about her new job of raising money with efficiency and dispatch. After sending a list of questions about the magazine for Davidson to answer, Laura went so far as to ask his permission to address ladies' clubs on the Fugitives' behalf, assuring him that she would conduct her fund raising with dignity, sagacity, and tact.

Letters composed in a furious hurry or in exhausted, early-morning hours after evenings spent in the dance hall began pouring in to the Fugitives' offices. Riding sent Davidson the names, occupations, and speculations on the fiscal prospects of those Louisville society mavens with cultural pretensions and open pocketbooks. That fall she wrote or visited over sixty individuals in pursuit of funds and subscriptions. Davidson, diligently acting as editor of the magazine, sent flyers, thank-you notes, and follow-up letters in her wake. After receiving the telegram announcing her as the winner of the Nashville prize, Riding felt that she had been truly recognized as one of them; and in some way she may have felt that Tate, too, had a silent part in welcoming her to their distinguished company.

Following Laura's second return from Ithaca, in the fall of 1924, the Gottschalk marriage became an open laboratory before it was entirely dissolved in May 1925; they seem to have consulted each other as well as Polly on their various flirtations. "Fallacies," a 1924 poem, comprised a series of portraits of gentlemen finding their way into the speaker's graces and then losing it. With wicked glee Riding was clearly learning the imaginative potential of a savage poetic palette, at the expense of those individuals (whoever they may have been) who might have trifled with her affections.

Lou, too, had relished amorous horizons beyond Louisville. Despite sixty dollars worth of Laura's unpaid doctor's bills and a dog named Spiegel to consider, he went off to Europe for the summer of 1925 to do research for his Marat biography. He wrote cheerfully to Polly Antell, the day he received his divorce decree and typhoid shots, that if there were similar measures for the prevention of certain other diseases, he would be entirely ready to take on Paris. Laura, plaintiff in the divorce, had already left for California to visit her half sister, Isabel, not even waiting to collect her court costs.

Many years later Louis Gottschalk admitted that he had a hard time taking his wife's poetry writing as seriously as she did. He described her as strong-willed, argumentative like her father, and "high-strung to the point of fainting." At the time of his marriage he wanted a family, and he wanted this "more intelligent than most" faculty wife by his side. However blindsided he later was by her zealous pursuit of this vocation, he had had some reason to expect it from her.

But after the initial honeymoon, Laura was as unenthusiastic about her husband's chosen career as he was about hers. Writing to Polly about his promotion and a successful series of lectures, Lou confessed he could not help feeling rather proud of himself, bearing in mind that against the odds he rose from being the son of an ignorant barber to being a full professor at a major university by the age of twenty-five. He invited Polly to chastise him for his vanity, as clearly his wife had already done. Laura had not, he wrote, been "particularly overjoyed" at the distinction. Both the Gottschalks saw the chasm between their background and future. Riding had had her serving of respectability but wanted to risk more; if she teetered in her decisions, it was out of fear of ending up back where she began.

The poetry and letters of this early and intensely creative period are striking for their sense of urgency. It is as if Laura Gottschalk were answering a host of critics—of her poetry, of her life—under the pressure of an impossible deadline or imminent catastrophe. Her boundless impatience with her circumstances was matched by a cacophony of narratives and possibilities of what she might do, who she might become, whom she might love, next. Even if Lou was irreproachable as a husband, Laura clearly expected more than a husband. For a long while, confused and uncertain himself but steadfastly in love, Lou had listened and debated—and paid the bills out of his meager salary.

After her divorce, Laura deliberated briefly on settling in California before coming back east on the San Francisco Overland Express, entertained en route by a naval officer on leave from Shanghai, a Honolulu businessman, a San Francisco newspaperman, an actor, and a wealthy gentleman who kept her supplied with Scotch and ice cream during the journey. Her itinerary included a stop in Chicago, where she visited the *Poetry* offices, and Nashville. There, she reported to Tate, John Crowe Ransom and Donald Davidson were still immured. After a visit with Helen Mayers in Brooklyn, her last stop on this round of adieus to past liaisons was New York City. On Lou's return from Paris in September 1925, Laura greeted him with a passionate embrace at the docks (Sylvia Bernstein heard that they had "fallen into one another's arms"), but he returned to Louisville alone. His ex-wife had taken up what she described as permanent residence in Greenwich Village.

Chapter 5

STRANDED IN A HALF-TOLD TALE

—— • ——

There was an insufficiency in me
To which no one but John could minister
A hunger no mere man could satisfy.
If I infringed upon the laws of art
By making John outlast himself till now,
It was to save him from the consequence
Of his genetic artfulness and falseness—
Defection, malice and oblivion.
The laws of art? Could I not alter them?
The reason I must call the passion dead
Lies in an insufficiency in him
That leaves me stranded in a half-told tale.

—"John and I"

—— • ——

LYING ON HER bed in the back room of her ground-floor apartment at 43 Morton Street in Greenwich Village, Laura watched rats scrambling in the rafters. An exterminator had paid a call not long before and had asked a number of questions about the rat problem. Laura answered with extensive descriptions of their habits and nightly appearances, pointing out the holes in the wainscoting where they emerged on their forays from the nearby Hudson River. After many questions and even more extensive descriptions, she realized with a start that the man was deaf as a post.

The opening of Laura Riding Gottschalk's "New York season" and "drinking and dancing days" began early in September 1925, when she discovered that a friend from Ithaca had an apartment in the Village where she might stay temporarily. From there she planned on perfecting the appropriate balance between poverty and poetry. As a measure of her fealty to a higher art, Laura wrote to Harriet Monroe from this new address, that she preferred to fast rather than join the supposedly literary dinner tables of the Village. By a fortuitous coincidence the building was only two doors down from Allen Tate, and when the ground-floor apartment became available, Laura and Polly settled in. By October, Laura was doing publicity at the publishing firm of Frank-Maurice, Inc., and was being introduced into the literary jungle by her neighbor, "Mr. Tate."

Ever since Laura could remember, Greenwich Village had been the center of literary bohemia. In Isabel's day, a decade earlier, it was home to Alfred Steiglitz and Isadora Duncan as well as to labor leaders "Big Bill" Haywood and Emma Goldman. Max Eastman's weekly, *The Masses*, like the Village itself, had then embraced the idea of revolution, but by 1925 the revolt was increasingly an artistic rather than a political one; its armory, at least since 1913, was that of art rather than the implements of class warfare. Joseph Freeman, another Village resident at the time, would write:

> The more we analyzed them, the more bohemian ideas reduced themselves to the simple slogans of the French and American revolutions, liberty, equality, fraternity; life, liberty, the pursuit of happiness. Art was the medium through which all these values could be achieved.

For Riding as for Freeman, beneath the rampant defiance of convention there remained some teasing responsibility to higher ideals; but art rather than strike action or party work was the means to the end. What that end was and how it was to be attained were still obscure, but as far as Freeman was concerned, "against the drabness and hypocrisy of the conventional world, village life shone gloriously."

A few blocks away in a garret on Bank Street labored another writer. Though he worked as a janitor and needed to bang out one hundred words a day of hack journalism to support his bohemian life-style, he had not yet felt that art might serve political ends or ideals, however vaguely those ends were defined by the native residents (he was from Pittsburgh). By his own account, Malcolm Cowley had skirted the issues and gotten what he wanted in "a quiet way, simply by taking it." He and his sort "were individualists in theory." And, as he was to write much later, "We were content to sit in the kitchen, two or three young men with our feet on the bare table, discussing the problem of abstract beauty while we rolled Bull Durham into cigarettes." Like Riding, he thought of himself as a starving artist, but unlike her, he had been to Paris:

> We were all about twenty-six, a good age, and looked no older; we were interested only in writing and in keeping alive what we wrote, and we had the feeling of being invulnerable—we didn't see how anything in the world could ever touch us, certainly not the crazy desire to earn and spend more money and be pointed out as prominent people.

For those bookish midwesterners who had perfected the Hemingway drawl, or the dada dandies from New England roaming the Left Bank, the "conventional world" was the small town or family business back home, and Paris was good fun. They staged demonstrations and pranks and squeezed Klaxons in the streets of Montmartre; but they also wrote home each week, grateful sons of parents who had sent them to Harvard and Princeton and paid for the passage to Paris. Good for a loan or a Pernod, they often failed to appreciate that the Great War, which had created such an economic boom in America, had meant something rather different for Europe—even those among them, like Cowley, who had fought in France. They wrote about nihilism and dadaism, but they never really believed in them.

Similarly, while the American exiles all appeared to be struggling for subsistence, their resources were large—whereas Riding's were nonexistent. While still in their early twenties they had published their first books, and they financed magazines like the *Little Review*, *Broom*, *Contact*, and the *Transatlantic Review*. For Riding, the idea of middle-class convention, despite her upbringing, was just as woolly an abstraction as life, liberty, and the pursuit of happiness—or, for that matter, the socialist revolution. She and Freeman nonetheless renounced the middle class and its conventions, but as outsiders rather than as its ungrateful issue. A true child of fortune, Laura depended on Polly or her ex-husband and whatever hack jobs she could find; the publicity work for Frank-Maurice ended shortly after she began. According to Polly, Laura worked hard but never made a living for herself.

Truly needy or not, all these starving artists seemed to abandon their fasts at Marta's, a cheap Italian restaurant run by an indulgent proprietress. Much frequented by literary lights and loungers, Marta's numbered many of Laura's new friends and contacts among its clientele. She dropped a few of their names in a letter to Harriet Monroe; there was the unsurpassable and eccentric Maxwell Bodenheim; Malcolm Cowley, whom she held in "outrageous es- teem"; the wild Mr. Cummings; and the wholly decent Mark Van Doren, who had accepted some of her poems for the *Nation*. Eugene O'Neill, another habitué of Marta's, was friend to both Laura and Polly. Laura also persuaded Robert Warshow of Adelphi, the pub- lisher of Lou's biography of Marat, to give her the French-translation contract for a book entitled *At Home with Anatole France* by Marcel LeGoff. With the poet Leonie Adams and Allen Tate, Laura gave her first reading to students at New York University.

Riding's star was indeed rising. Tate confirmed this, writing that September to Davidson that she had "more energy than a phalanx of dynamos, with seven billy-goats thrown in:"

> Laura, incidentally, is destined to great fame before two years are out. She'll be the most famous of us all, and she deserves to be; she's the best of us all. There are two poets I'm betting on—Laura and Hart Crane; if I'm wrong about them, I'm wrong about everything.

But no sooner had she found company among literary high-steppers like Malcolm Cowley and Edmund Wilson than she seemed to find reason to be dissatisfied. Perhaps, intent as they were on their own writing, few found common cause with her. In this, her experience in

Greenwich Village echoed the course of her relations with the Fugitives. Her lingering radicalism, couched as it was in the doleful protest against the capitalist conspiracy (jobs, Tate said, were scarcer than hen's teeth) would not have found many listeners, at least then. The distinction between those who attended literary dinners and those who did not also rankled; literary ladies were the last invited. In fact, Riding met Cowley and Wilson only once, although they were both close friends of Tate's.

The mere fact of being a woman among them nurtured Riding's itchy desire to play truant and intellectual mimic to all conventions, including the literary and political ones cherished by the *rentrés* from Paris. In "The Quids" she lampoons and caricatures her literary milieux with a highly sophisticated linguistic ingenuity. It first appeared in February 1924, in the *Fugitive*, where it caught the fateful eye of Robert Graves.

> The little quids, the million quids
> The everywhere, everything, always quids,
> The atoms of the Monoton,
> Each turned three essences where it stood,
> And ground a gisty dust from its neighbors' edges,
> Until a powdery thoughtfall stormed in and out,
> The cerebration of a slippery quid enterprise.

Tate called the poem a "metaphysical burlesque."

Riding recommended that readers look up words in a dictionary if they found her poems hard going. "Quid" is Latin for "something"; "quiddity," as the *Concise Oxford Dictionary* has it, is the "essence of a thing, what makes a thing what it is," or "quibble, captious subtlety." In "The Quids" Riding provided the quiddity for these frolicsome abstractions, as they jockeyed for position in a circus ring of metaphysical inquiry. The "quids" may be counter to any number of "things," but it is easy to see in the poem a jumpy satire of the Greenwich Village literary population, with their French literary costumes and modernist high wire acts:

> A quid here and there gyrated in place-position,
> While many essential quids turned inside-out

For the fun of it.
And a few refused to be anything but
Simple, unpredicated copulatives.
Little by little, this commotion of quids,
By threes, by tens, by casual millions,
Squirming within the state of things,
The metaphysical acrobats,
The naked, immaterial quids,
Turned inside on themselves
And came out all dressed,
Each similar quid of the inward same,
Each similar quid dressed in a different way—
The quids' idea of a holiday.

Yet somehow the quids still remain habits of mind, automatons. Their every move, every individuating expression, is derivative of a homogenizing "Monoton." Though "Monoton" is defined as "sameness in style of writing," the dexterity of this poem accommodates a range of meanings, precisely because of Riding's ability to treat words with more than their dictionary definition in mind and, in the process, free them from the parts of speech that they generally inhabited.

By the time she arrived at Morton Street, Riding had gained confidence in her work and her singular point of view and was ready to quarrel and to consider her contemporaries, especially the Fugitives, with a veteran's eye. What she found was not so much flaws in their meter but, honing in on the tender heart of the matter, flaws in where and how they lived—their very sensibilities. Like the quids who could "never tell what their wisdom was about," the Fugitives could never "get out / Of the everywhere, everything," to come to the point. Riding's ironic, playful allusiveness was her answer to their overdressed specificity, their yawning disquisitions on the technology of poetry and the etymologies of words. One *New Republic* critic, reviewing the first anthology of Fugitive poetry, described "The Quids" as the "cruellest of several bitterly cruel poems," hoping that it would "be read with pomp by every professor of English in America!" Indeed it was the starchy attitude toward poetry that would later feed the fires of the immensely influential New Critical method, wherein literary criticism turned in on itself, becoming as much a subject for debate as art itself.

While Riding was loosing language from its moorings, Greenwich Village was abuzz with quidlike activity. Stripped as they all felt, of their regional allegiances and parental values (if only, like Tate, to return to them later with a vengeance), the *artistes* of Greenwich Village were in search of a destiny. Despite Riding's professed "anti-autobiographical" stance, she stated in "A Prophecy or a Plea" that "if the matter be examined more closely it will be seen that the quarrel must be made not with the way we write but with the way we live."

Much later a quarrel arose not out of what poetry or criticism Riding was engaged in at this time but, rather, on precisely the way she lived during what she described as her "mad year." On the strength of Martin Seymour-Smith's sly suggestion, Robert Graves' next biographer, his nephew Richard Perceval Graves, wrote that during the period in Greenwich Village Laura Riding became pregnant with Tate's child and had it aborted. Seymour-Smith's unconfirmable source for this was Robert Graves, but in his book he quotes only from a poem to substantiate the insinuation and avoid the direct statement.

Laura Riding never denied having an affair with Tate—indeed, after his death she encouraged the view that he had loved her. On the subject of an actual liaison, she has commented, "Rumor is an ill-tongued excrescence that grows wild in the soil of idling human interest; and the literary regions of human interest provide such soil and growth in lavish abundance." For such wild growths, however, there generally is a seed somewhere (whether in fact or fantasy), and more than likely, Graves is not responsible.

Riding brought the story of an affair with Tate to England; its growth may have been inconsistently tended by Graves and his later circle of admirers. The story of her pregnancy and abortion is almost certainly a fabrication—either hers or Graves' or someone else's. As for her affair, she met Tate only that once, in Louisville, before arriving in New York City. On the strength of that daylong February 1924 meeting, however, Laura's love for him, kindled by his appreciation of her work, blazed brightly unaccompanied by his presence, much less by physical intimacy. When he failed to return her affections in equal measure—and withdrew, unnerved, from their correspondence—bitterness inevitably followed her heartache. By the time Laura arrived in New York, she had put the love if not the hurt behind her. Rejection would prove as formative an experience as acceptance had been.

Since he had last seen Laura, some eighteen months earlier, Allen had other affairs on his mind. During the summer spent with "Red" Warren in Kentucky, he met his future wife, Caroline Gordon, who was then a journalist but who later established herself as a novelist and a moving force behind the Southern literary renaissance. By late 1924 Caroline discovered she was pregnant (having first had sex with Allen in a graveyard), and in February 1925 they married to avoid deeding their child the stigma of illegitimacy. Allen planned to divorce Caroline once the baby, a girl named Nancy, was born.

During his first year in New York City, Allen had earned a precarious living by writing reviews and working for a pulp love-story magazine, *Telling Tales*. Instead of the wide boulevard of cosmopolitan conversation he had expected from the move to the big city, after the initial excitement of meeting his literary contemporaries he found himself spending a great deal of time in speakeasies getting drunk on rum toddies and sympathizing with Hart Crane's complaints about his stomach ailment. Just what he was going to do when his infant appeared in late September to impoverish him further was a worry of central concern. By midsummer the Tates had taken to traveling upstate for visits to William Slater Brown and his wife, Susan (Allen's boss at *Telling Tales*), who owned a pre-Revolutionary farmhouse in Pawling, New York. Allen began to think seriously about rural peace and quiet.

But before he knew it, the newly divorced Laura Gottschalk had arrived at his door on Morton Street just in time to dispel such bucolic daydreams and prepare his disorderly household for the baby's arrival. While Caroline was in the hospital, Laura cleaned and tidied her neighbor's small apartment in a burst of industry and efficiency. Caroline, by comparison, was no housekeeper. (Polly, Laura's slacker roommate, recalls their own place being in a state of order she found breathtaking.) Allen once again gloried in the tonic effect of Laura's presence: "It is great to have Laura here," he wrote Davidson, "[She] is great company, and we've had a fine time since she arrived. She seemed to feel that everybody in Nashville was

congenitally depressed; but she would put life into—well, into anything. She is a constant visitor to the Tates, and Caroline finds her
very charming, if strenuous!"

That was putting a polite face on things. Laura made a concerted
effort to be a helpful neighbor to Caroline, who in turn had advised
Laura on free-lance writing assignments. Laura (Riding) Jackson
later related how, when Caroline was ready to come home from the
hospital, she herself carried the baby home on the elevated. (Just
how the new parents got home is left uncertain.) Nonplussed,
grumpy, resentful at the invasion of her household, and uncertain of
Allen's commitment to their marriage, Caroline found such close
company disturbing, particularly as she already felt excluded from
the male bohemian enclave. Years later she would write, "There is
nothing more trying than these women who set up to be Norns, I
know."

In her account of her relations with the Fugitives, Laura (Riding)
Jackson insisted that Caroline would have been grossly misled had
she suspected her of any designs beyond friendliness toward her
husband. In Jackson's later view Tate was a man "essentially without
character" who "bound himself to minor scruples without having
satisfied major ones." Caroline she pronounced a woman of character
and courage who tended to shield her husband from "moral scrutiny."
Indeed, by the time Laura tried to make herself a place in their
household, her relations with Allen were most likely filial, competi-
tive, and aggrieved with unhealed hurt. The baby's arrival may have
fed Laura's fantasy of having a child, a fantasy that might later have
found form in a story about having become pregnant herself with
Tate's child.

BY NOVEMBER 1925, to elude the drunken distractions, the expensive
city life, and perhaps the neighborly moral scrutiny as well, the Tates
had decided to rent part of an old house on Hardscrabble Road in
Patterson, New York, about half a mile from the Browns' place, near
the Connecticut state line. This area, called Tower Hill, was so thick
with writers that their lives inevitably appeared later in stories and
novels and memoirs. Slater Brown's Model T squired the city escapees
over the muddy roads from the train station—(Riding, he recalled, let

out a screech at every bump)—to his farmhouse on Chapel Hill road. It was too late in the year for croquet, but long evenings were spent gossiping in the Browns' drafty barns and listening to Hart Crane's Cuban rumbas on the phonograph.

Though he had yet to move upstate himself, Crane's drunken declaiming of poetry (often composed in the alcoholic heat of these evenings) were already legend. Malcolm Cowley referred to him affectionately as the Roaring Boy:

> . . . he would appear in the kitchen or on the croquet court, his face brick-red, his eyes burning, his already iron-grey hair bristling straight up from his skull. He would be chewing a five-cent cigar which he had forgotten to light. In his hands would be two or three sheets of typewritten manuscript, with words crossed out and new ones scrawled in. "Read that," he would say. "Isn't that the greatest poem ever written?"

In many respects Crane embodied the sort of New Romantic that Riding had called for in "A Prophecy or a Plea," promising her the poetic qualities that Tate had reneged upon:

> "[I]f they are to succeed, their constitution must contain . . . the power of wonder that begets wonder, and miracle, and prophecy. They will be egoists and romanticists all, but romantics with the courage of realism: they will put their hands upon the mysterious contour of life not to force meaning out of it . . . but press meaning upon it, outstare the stony countenance of it, make it flush with their own colors."

Where Tate was perfectly composed, relentlessly "literary" and cerebral, Crane was reckless, lyrical, and fully possessed by his poetic vision, particularly when drunk. An ungainly bear of a man, he had a rough, handsome face and an unsettling, wild look in his eye.

Visiting Hardscrabble Road one weekend in the bloom of her friendship with Hart, Laura did not require the jug of hard cider to make merry. Like two unruly children, they made the rounds of households, shouting outrageous literary opinions, playing jazz records, and dancing wildly from one country refuge to another, leaving, according to Susan Brown, "each household somewhat the worse for wear":

> There have been numerous "celebrations," [Crane wrote] and the Punch Palazzo has had due patronage. The engrossing female at most of these has been "Rideschalk-Godding," as I have come to call her, and thus far the earnest ghost of acidosis has been kept well hence.

Hart's other affectionate name for Laura was Laura Riding Roughshod. In cahoots, the two could concoct all kinds of literary conspiracies and idiocies to explain why Hart had no contract for his next book of poems. They could gossip about Allen. For a time they shared their depressions and hostilities, their money and their meals.

Joseph Freeman noted in his autobiography that, unlike the frankly sensual flappers on the Upper East Side and Long Island, he found the Greenwich Village "girls" essentially puritanical. In place of social or religious sanctions for their emotions, they substituted literary and artistic ones; they could love only poets and artists, "superior men." Riding shared such faiths and in her call for a "New Romance" she demanded "more of artists and less of art." But if there was ever a plan afoot to matchmake Laura Riding Roughshod with the Roaring Boy, it was doomed by Hart's natural proclivities—obscure to most of them at the time—to fail. Allen and Caroline, doubtless encouraged by Hart himself, certainly had it in the back of their minds. Polly, who described Hart as having come from "a good family," maintains that neither she nor Laura knew that he was homosexual, and had they been told they would hardly have known what it meant.

Though Laura soon discovered that Hart was as hopeless in bed as he was in directing his life, she managed to forgive him for his "insufficiencies" as she could not forgive Allen for his. Neither it seems, could Tate forgive himself. If for him "poetry, the oracle, was gone" that autumn in rat-infested apartments and Brooklyn waterfront dives, it was only just beginning to be divined. In the Crane of "Voyages" Tate perceived all the gifts that he himself lacked as a poet.

Consistently the most serious and incisive purveyor of his generation's poetry, Tate had the particular talent of evenhanded acumen,
the ability to isolate the power of a unique sensibility from a poem's
technical deficiencies. That gift was fatal for his own poetry. "There
is a tendency in a mind like mine," he wrote Crane in a quite moving
letter, "that always more or less looks upon itself with the satire of
suspicion, to turn that satire into a pure sarcasm directed against
expression itself":

> It isn't . . . that I lack a kind of endurance, but only that my
> core of mystical conviction may not be so tough and
> persistently inviolable as yours; my surface disintegrations
> penetrate directly to the core.

In 1925 Crane's "core of mystical conviction" may have indeed
seemed inviolate to Tate, oppressed as he was by self-doubt, family
responsibilities, and financial insecurities. That fall Crane worked on
the manuscript that would become *The Bridge* (1930); he would move
upstate with the Tates so that he might complete it.

THE BRIDGE WAS intended to be an American epic: a poem of mythic
reach. Expending all, Crane failed, though by the time the work was
published he was too intent in the pursuit of self-destruction to see its
failure. When Tate came to review the poem, it was clear that he felt
the core of Crane's mystical conviction was hollow. But Tate relieved
Crane of responsibility for his failure; *The Bridge* could not be the apex
and microcosm of an age and a culture that had no center.

In retrospect, the entire ambitious conception of *The Bridge* seems
more Tate's than Crane's. Crane made a point of telling friends that
his poem would answer T. S. Eliot's "Waste Land," and, indeed, he
conceived it as a romantic celebration of an American mythology
with this in mind. But what tortured Crane was not the neoclassic
complaint (which Tate had caught from Eliot) that his was not an
Elizabethan age but the inescapable conflict with his mother and his
homosexuality. On New Year's Eve 1928, in a London dance hall, he
would shout drunkenly to Laura before bounding out into the night
after some sailors, "I'll show you, I'll go back to America and marry

Lorna!" In his attempt to live up to Tate's expectations he betrayed only himself. After Crane's suicide, Riding would suggest that he had paid the price of listening to his critics; it was one of the lessons she had, at significant cost, learned herself.

On Riding's precipitous departure for England late in 1925, she left behind in the Morton Street basement manuscripts of about 200 poems, which would turn up in a barn on the property of Polly's Connecticut home in the early 1980s. In a folder labeled Ancient History the manuscripts map the evolution of her early poetic voices, and it is from these manuscripts that the poet Laura Riding first emerges. Her restlessness, the violence of her emotions, and her passions are intricately plotted; her poems entrap, dissect, and explode real or imaginary lovers, her ideas about poetry, her childhood, her self. Typed neatly on the back of Lou's Louisville or Leo's Cornell history department stationery are narratives in rhymed verse, poems written to the syncopation of jazz rhythms, perfectly scanned sonnets. There are poems satirizing her Urbana tea parties, English pastoral poetry, and Jews; others treat of suicide and spiritual longing. Relishing the simple and complex uses of paradox, Riding represented the spirituality of the convent nun in sensuous detail, while righteous Christian ministers are condemned and mocked for their hypocrisy, their sinful prudence. The quantity and range of her experimentation are astonishing.

Throughout these works Riding addresses the heart of being a woman and being a poet with an unsettling intelligence and formidable rage. But the constant quest, transparent and simple in the elegant "Lucrece and Nara," was for an ideal love, timeless and ethereal:

> Astonished stood Lucrece and Nara,
> Face flat to face, one sense and smoothness.
> "Love, is this face or flesh,
> Love, is this you?"
> One breath burned the warm lips close and whispered
> "Nara, is there a miracle can last?"
> "Lucrece, is there a simple thing can stay?"
>
> Unnoticed as a single raindrop
> Broke far apart each dawn

Until as one day blindness fell.
"How is the deep opalescence of my white hand, Nara?
Does it flow milk yet pearlily?"
"How is the echo of my breast, Lucrece?
Is it blood quick in rock, as always?"

Ghostly they clung and questioned
A thousand years, not yet eternal,
True to the fleshless forms they faded in
Through the long death defying
Heaven or hell to make them over . . .

            . . .

When the earth ended, was devoured
Of a meteor one midsummer
Dangerous near the dragon by the border,
A sound of light was felt,
A faithful light fluttered two wings, went out.
"Nara, is it you, the dark?"
"Lucrece, is it you, the quiet?"

In the balance between the religious and mystical inflection of this final stanza and the insistently human vision of "true love" lies Riding's peculiar greatness as a poet. Living in an age when the romantic flush was no less awkward than the prophetic one, Riding would suffer ridicule and disappointment throughout her long vigil. Though the study of language would supersede it, poetry was Riding's most lasting access to the vision of the dissolving border. This was, however, never a wholly romantic or spiritual quest. In Lucrece and Nara one discovers names not of male or female lovers, or even of readily identifiable mythic figures, but a divided acronym for Laura herself, Laura alone.

IN HER THREE-MONTH stay in New York, Riding established relations with a prominent coterie of American writers from whom she soon felt obliged to flee, perhaps from a sense of not belonging, perhaps from a lingering disquiet over her love for Allen and the absence of any welcome from Caroline. "Druida" vents both anger at the abandonment and the headlong, transcendent determination of a spurned woman to overtake and surpass her former lover. Its final (1938) version read:

> . . .
>
> But meagre was the man,
> He took ambition.
> He heard a clock,
> He saw a road.
> When the clock struck,
> Where the road began,
> He called farewell to Druida.
>
> . . .
>
> Druida followed.
> Not to bless him, not to curse him,
> Not to bring back the bridegroom,
> But to pass him like a blind bird
> Seeing all heaven ahead.
>
> . . .

Laura Jackson's own stated reasons for leaving New York contained the familiar indictment: America was too philistine, too parochial, and too much the upstart culture. Among American writers and critics there was a lack of seriousness and an excess of worldly "literary" ambition. To the notion that her own, far less subtle, career maneuvers might warrant a similar accusation, she was blandly oblivious.

After Riding left, Tate would say that she could not forgive him because his ancestors had been Virginia gentry (he later discovered this was his mother's invention). "The inferiority complex often motivates fine poetry," he told Davidson, "but it is an extremely unfortunate social manifestation." That Tate's own, more circumspect ambitions were hardly tiny or limited to poetry, he found harder to acknowledge. Ironically, it was Riding who provided Tate with his first promising professional opportunity, by introducing him to Robert Warshow, publisher of Adelphi.

Warshow had already agreed to bring out Laura's as yet untitled first book of poems in the spring of 1926. Only recently established and not at all a literary publisher, Warshow was, in Allen's words, a "good business man who wanted to do something for 'letters.' " This he learned from Laura, who was undoubtedly responsible for Warshow's good intentions. Her powers of persuasion were considerable, and in this respect, at least, she was never without resources.

During her last visit to Hardscrabble Road before leaving for England, Laura suggested to Allen that he take advantage of Warshow's newfound interest in poetry, and write to Edmund Wilson proposing a series of books of poetry for Adelphi to publish. Among them would be books by himself, Wilson, Louise Bogan, Crane (this would have been *White Buildings*), Malcolm Cowley, and John Peale Bishop. In the letter written that weekend, Tate offered Wilson the general editorship but was ready to take it himself if Wilson declined:

> . . . if [Laura] weren't leaving for England within the week I would suggest turning the project over to her. Warshow admires her "genius" and that sort of thing, and believes anything she tells him. She has agreed to speak to him before she leaves; so in about two weeks I think we might arrange an approach to him, singly or together: we could discuss that, if you are interested at all.

Less than three weeks later, after Laura had left New York, the series ran into difficulties. One of these, Tate wrote Davidson, was Laura. "As soon as she heard that Wilson and I were up to it, she rushed in and tried to take it over! Such are the excesses into which vaulting ambition betrays the delicate mind. But when she didn't prevail, she wanted to come in the series!" Despite the efforts of Tate's more delicate mind, the plan for the series foundered, while Riding's book was published as scheduled.

Tate's subsequent letters to Ransom and Davidson frequently find similar opportunities to disparage Riding. And twenty years later, when Horace Gregory came to write a history of American poetry during this period, Tate did what he could to dissuade him from including Riding among the Fugitives. She was only "casually affiliated," he maintained, and her presence was due to "propinquity," namely her husband's teaching position in nearby Louisville. While she had been made an honorary member of the group, this was the

result of the "appalling naiveté" of the fraternity spirit of the old
Fugitive group rather than any sympathy between her work and
their own.

> . . . after we had accepted some of her poems for the
> Fugitive she immediately came to Nashville for a visit.
> Fortunately by that time I was in New York, but my
> colleagues blamed me for all that she did (which was
> plenty) because I had accepted her poems in the first
> place.

Laura Jackson would feel keenly the Fugitives' efforts to distance
themselves from her and her work. In an introduction to the second
edition of an anthology of Fugitive poetry, Davidson, "with Allen
Tate Privy Counsellor in the matter," downplayed her position. "Why
the special effort to shake me off?" she asked simply. Ransom noted
that Riding lacked birth, subsistence, place, and friends. Further, she
could not, "to save her life . . . achieve her customary distinction in
the regular verse forms." Such dismissive views have crept into works
on the Fugitives. In one she is described as "shrewd, avant gardist,
brittle and more than a little superficial." "To these serious, rather
courtly gentlemen," their official historian Louise Cowan wrote, "it
must have seemed somewhat odd to admit a pert young woman on an
equal basis." Cowan, Laura (Riding) Jackson noted in a response to
the book, was no amateur in the subtleties of disdain.

Tate was, however, the first critic to take Riding's work seriously, a
seminal event. To become a poet, Laura had written him late in 1923
after receiving his first letter, requires not only an inner compulsion
but an answering and tempering recognition, adding that he had
provided this and more for her. Unlike Ransom, Tate ignored the
circumstances of Riding's birth and social position, and though he
was not above making anti-Semitic remarks about Jewish vanity and
ambition, he provided her with the necessary "royal assurance." His
was one of the very few reviews of *The Close Chaplet*, her first book of
poems, when it appeared in America in the fall of 1926. For a time
Riding was grateful to Tate. For a longer time he personified everything that she bitterly resented about the way literature—and poetry

in particular—was professionalized and schematized. Though her backward glare was no less revisionist than his, it was by means of these protests that her precise originality began to shine.

Early in December 1925 Riding was invited to join Robert Graves, his wife, Nancy Nicholson, and their four children on their journey to Egypt, where Graves had accepted a position teaching English literature at the Royal Egyptian University. Having admired "The Quids," Graves had begun his correspondence with her earlier that year after reading the manuscript sent him by Ransom. By the time she arrived in New York, he had arranged for his publisher, the Hogarth Press, to bring out her first collection of poems. In the course of the warm correspondence that followed, Riding invited Graves to consider the idea of a lectureship at Cornell, where she had personal connections. But nothing had come of it by the time Graves was offered the post in Cairo.

Though Lou Gottschalk was still forlornly in love with his ex-wife, he would nonetheless reimburse Polly for booking Laura's passage on the Paris bound for Plymouth, England, on December 27, 1925. Laura celebrated on the eve of her departure with Hart, who had just heard that a benefactor had given him $1,000 so that he might finish The Bridge. Their good-bye was affectionate and loving, far removed from the hothouse of Greenwich Village gossip and literary intrigue.

If in Allen Tate, as Laura (Riding) Jackson later claimed, there was "a triumph of discretion over passion of conviction," in Robert Graves she would find a man of little discretion and much ready, passionate conviction. From his wife she would have a warm and sisterly welcome. Graves had achieved early acclaim in England among the Georgian poets and transatlantic notice for his poems about the war. Nancy Nicholson was a maverick feminist and painter who not only kept her maiden name after marriage but also gave it to her two daughters, apportioning her husband's to her two sons. According to Polly, Laura was invited to go as Robert's secretary, but in the breathless letters announcing her hasty departure Laura clearly anticipated a less formal relation. She went as a member of Graves' family, she wrote hastily to Harriet Monroe, and imagined that they would soon be literary collaborators.

In "Last Nuptials," a poem left behind in a trunk in the basement of the Morton Street rattrap, Riding clearly forecast a more daring itinerary for the trip to Egypt. The speaker of the poem, an "insatiable bride," secretly predicts the arrival of an "eternal mate" in her life, having abandoned "Alastor" and his brother. Some scattered remnants of this poem and other pre-1926 works appeared in 1930 under the title "Fragments":

> Ah, it is a secret I dare not . . .
> If it is not permitted to plot alone,
> Though to no mischief . . .
> I can at least step off the bridge betwixt
> Me and my morrow, . . .

Allen was less sanguine, writing to Davidson the day Laura was due to arrive in England, "I fear disaster: Laura is surely the maddest woman I have ever met, and if Graves isn't already mad—which I'm inclined to suspect from his issuance of a blind invitation to a lady read but unseen—he will be a maniac before a month."

Calling herself Miss Laura Riding Gottschalk, she set sail accompanied by a large steamer trunk, a suitcase, a carryall containing her toiletries and makeup, and a commitment to the pursuit of poetry and truth. Within a week of arriving in England she was on the boat to Egypt, and within a week of that she had turned twenty-five years old, at sea in a story half told.

PART II

THE OLD WORLD

Chapter 6

THE EMOTIONS OF AN AUDIENCE

——— • ———

You watched me act and admired my performance, but credited
me with sincerity rather than talent; you refused to act yourself,
paralyzed by the emotions of an audience.

—"Letter of Abdication"

People don't take things seriously enough. To have tragedy
everyone concerned must be in dead earnest.

—*Convalescent Conversations*

——— • ———

ON APRIL 27, 1929, Robert Graves and Laura Riding leaped from
different windows of their flat in London's Hammersmith, not far
from Miss Pinkerton's Academy. This was also the day France began
celebrating the five-hundredth anniversary of the raising of the
siege of Orleans by Joan of Arc. After a night of fireworks, the
ceremonies were to begin with a procession commemorating Joan's
arrival at the château of Chinon, followed by a reenactment of her
recognition of the dauphin as he cowered behind his courtiers in
the great hall. The bishop of Orléans was to deliver a panegyric on
Joan (she had only recently been canonized), telling how her voices
had revealed the destiny of France and how, after many un-
acknowledged letters to the dauphin, she had succeeded in her
quest for an audience, despite the skepticism of the archbishop of

Rheims and the vacillation of the timid dauphin. Prime Minister
Raymond Poincaré and over 100 French and foreign cardinals were
expected at the fete.

Memory being the tricky thing that it is, however, Robert Graves'
1939 diary entry noting the tenth anniversary of the event was dated
April 29, rather than 27. Laura (Riding) Jackson would also mis-
remember it as the 29th of April in her account of the events of that
day. Curiously, that was also the date she and her second husband,
Schuyler, celebrated as their anniversary. They had actually been
married in June, but the circumstances hadn't been as auspicious as
the day they met: April 29 marked the day she had stepped off the
boat from France, returning to America for the first time since she
had left it, thirteen years before.

But such facts, even once they are pinned down, are unable to
explain themselves, and for such a central event in Riding's life an
explanation is demanded. What happened on April 27, 1929? And
why? For many, the name Laura Riding rings a very tiny bell. It is thus
all the more awkward to be frank about the difficulties of beginning
at the beginning in order to answer both questions. Part of the reason
for Riding's obscurity as a writer, however, lies in the story of the leap
and how it has been told. In these accounts, the bald and often
preposterous facts of what happened have tended to dominate and
direct apparently straightforward narratives, leaving the question of
why she jumped rather at a loss. But it is precisely because the
question "why" is a far more interesting one that this account of Laura
Riding's suicide attempt begins not at the beginning but at what was
nearly the end of Laura Riding.

The apartment itself was on the top two stories of the handsome
Georgian house at 35A St. Peter's Square. From the street, the basement apartment was half below ground level, but in the back of the
house it opened onto a garden. The ground-floor apartment, then,
was really more of a first story, even by English reckoning. Heated
controversy and persistent obfuscation would surround the question
of just how many stories Laura Riding fell. Most, following Graves'
remarks in his autobiography, have described it as the fourth story,
choosing the American way of accounting. Laura (Riding) Jackson,
counting from the front of the house in the English manner, would
insist it was only the second story. Jackson claimed that she had never

discussed the matter with Graves; but were he ever so bold as to describe the window that he jumped from as the second story, she would not have let him get away with it, no matter how terrible her pain at the time. Graves would then have resorted to protestations of innocent stupidity, she said, his face slunk in his customary hangdog expression. At the time, however, both Riding and Graves exaggerated the height; the mathematical measure was not sufficient to supply the requisite miracle of having survived.

But on that Saturday morning in her bedroom atop the house, Laura Riding had a moment of extraordinary clarity. It lifted her spirits above the boundless pain caused by another man, not Graves but a "black Irishman" who stared at her from the back of the room. Her argument with him had lasted unabated for a full month, and now she had reached a crisis. She stood transfixed, surveying the room from her place by an open window, thirty feet above a walled garden enclosure. Robert Graves and his wife, Nancy Nicholson, looked at her, she remembered over fifty years later, with expectation.

In the center of the room lay a large square rug, a patchwork of twenty patterned squares, each distinctive and brightly colored. The squares had been sewn together by twenty village women in Cumberland. Beautifully crafted, the rug was a commanding centerpiece in a room where every item of furniture was carefully chosen and precisely placed. In a short monologue written over a year earlier, Riding had featured the rug as an image of what she was trying to accomplish in her writing, in the circle of artists and writers whom she loved and worked closely with. The fine press that she had acquired in 1927 was part of this harmonious vision of art and domesticity but not nearly all of it.

Robert Graves, standing opposite, knew that something really awful was going to happen, for he had just witnessed Laura calmly swallow poison. She seemed to look at him with stony exasperation before determinedly composing herself on the window ledge. It was important to her then that they all realize what she was about to do and that they remember her unhurried and regal comportment. In these last moments there was no hint of a "disorderly disposition"— when the police came to make inquiries they were assured on this point by Laura herself. The insistence was a principal point of her later

account of that day. Finally, having wasted some minutes frozen in
incredulity and awe, Robert made a protective move toward Laura,
but his wife put her hand lightly on his arm, restraining him. Riding
captured the moment in her roman à clef about the leap, entitled *14A*:

> [NANCY]: I made [Robert] stop trying to keep her from doing
> it.
> [IRISHMAN]: I know. I saw you put your arm on his and make a
> sign. Why did you do it? (He looks at her curiously.) Did you
> think she didn't really mean it?
> [NANCY]: Oh, I knew she meant it. But . . . somehow it was all
> so like a play—her sitting on the ledge like that, quite calmly,
> even smiling a little, and saying "Goodbye chaps." It seemed a
> pity to spoil it. (Then angrily) You didn't do anything to stop
> it.

Glaring at the helplessness of the three of them, Laura threw a
"Goodbye, chaps" over her shoulder and pushed off.

Graves, terrorstruck, was the first to run downstairs, turning at the
first landing to jump out the window of the next story, a twenty-foot
drop into the back garden. Though it would later be bruited about
that Riding and Graves had a suicide pact, this window was the only
point of egress from their apartment to the back garden, apart from
the window that Riding used; the two lower apartments were occupied by other tenants. Laura (Riding) Jackson went so far as to
suggest that Graves had not jumped at all but made use of a fire-
escape ladder, which she had put there, in order to effect a safe
descent; Riding had a consuming fear of fire. With the knowing that
comes from long years of close personal association, she noted that
Graves was fearful of injury or discomfort—always careful, she
recalled scornfully, to tuck his trouser cuffs into his socks before
entering a movie theater for fear of vermin. With or without precau-
tionary calculations, however, Graves' first thought was clearly to get
down to the garden enclosure at the rear of the house, where Laura
lay on a stone pavement, unconscious or dead.

The "black Irishman" was the next to leave the room. In utter
panic, he stormed down four flights of stairs and fled, desperate to get
as far away as possible.

Later that day, Nancy Nicholson would run into him—disoriented, miserable, and frightened—in the unlikely locale of the Plaza Cinema lobby in Piccadilly. By then he had already been to the police and, in his incoherent remarks, led them to suspect foul play. Overwrought herself, Nancy brought the man back to the barge on the Atlanta Wharf of the Thames where she was living with her four children not far from the flat at St. Peter's Square. Nervous and perhaps excited by the atmosphere of crisis, the children sat there, wide-eyed at his approach. They, too, became part of the script for Riding's roman à clef:

> [JENNY]: Oh . . . ! Mother thought you'd gone away for ever! Where have you been? I said I was sure you were with [Laura]. Is [Laura] very ill?
> [DAVID]: Is she going to die?
> [JENNY]: [He] always thinks people are going to die, for the slightest scratch.
> [DAVID]: I bet if you fell out of a window you'd die.
> [JENNY]: I wouldn't let myself fall out of a window. [Laura] must have been feeling very bad not to notice she was falling out.

WHEN, IN JANUARY 1926, Laura Riding arrived in London, a ménage was forged between herself, Robert Graves, and Nancy Nicholson. Among themselves and their closest friends, their special "marriage of three" came to be known as the Trinity. This unusual relationship had acquired a certain reputation by the time the Irishman first arrived at St. Peter's Square, three years later. With the suicidal leaps of Riding and Graves this reputation was further enhanced in London, Paris, and New York. For a long time the fourth individual in the room at the top of the house was forgotten, except perhaps in Dublin, where Yeats told an embellished version of the story. For the most part, however, the Irishman (a poet named Geoffrey Phibbs) was eclipsed by the story of the folie à trois.

Phibbs' presence was overlooked for so long after the immediate delight in the scandal died down partly because he had arrived at the apartment only three months before and partly because he had recently changed his name to Taylor; Taylor was his mother's maiden name. A few weeks before Riding's suicide attempt, Geoffrey's father, a wealthy landowner and justice of the peace of County Sligo, had caught sight of Nancy Nicholson walking with his son along the back avenue of the family home, Lisheen House, near Killaspugerone. Raging out onto the east veranda, the judge accosted them and, pointing at Nancy Nicholson, bellowed, "Get out of my grounds, you scarlet woman!" At that moment Geoffrey Phibbs became Geoffrey Taylor.

Born in Norfolk in 1900 of Anglo-Irish, Protestant parentage, he moved with his family to Ireland at a young age, returning to England only to attend boarding school. At his death in 1956, his early indiscretions had been forgotten, and he was memorialized as a gentleman, the author of the standard work on the Victorian flower garden, and for his editorship of the *Bell*, the Irish equivalent of Cyril Connolley's *Horizon*. The English poet laureate John Betjeman remembered his integrity, humor, sense of proportion, force of character, and ability to steer clear of literary disputes in London and Dublin. He was also known in international entomology circles as an expert on the English beetle.

On that afternoon in early February 1929, three months before the jumps, quite another gentlemen stood before Riding. The Devil! She exclaimed before inviting him in. A certain Irish landlady in Dublin, crossing herself, had said the same of him—to his obscure pleasure. Geoffrey Phibbs looked down at Riding's small, tense figure, and a long lock of black hair fell over one eye. Riding included her first impression in *14A*:

> [Geoffrey] is tall and thin and slants forward as he walks. A lock of hair keeps falling over his forehead; he does not brush it away with his hand, but from time to time jerks his head back with an arched movement of his long neck. He is very black-looking; his face seems dark and hot. His eyes are blue, but these too seem dark; he is always looking down as if intensely pre-occupied with something that has just happened to him. When he looks up, it is always suddenly and questioningly—placing the burden of conversation on the other person.

In a later description, written in Wabasso, Laura (Riding) Jackson mentioned only a rather feverish appearance. On this day, however, Phibbs' aloofness was a thin cover for a kind of throttled hysteria; his three-year-old marriage was undergoing great difficulty, which he hoped would be resolved with the move to London.

According to the Irish writer Michael O'Donovan—better known as Frank O'Connor—Phibbs had the educated gentleman's contempt for the self-educated. In fact, Phibbs had been taken off the books of Trinity College Dublin for having neglected to attend either lectures or exams. O'Connor had often felt the acid of Phibbs' scorn while working in his employ at the Carnegie Library in County Wicklow. But whatever mockery Phibbs made of others, he harbored an even more furious disgust with himself. According to O'Connor, Phibbs nurtured a keen and insatiable appetite for modern literature— anything that could conceivably be termed "advanced" or "difficult." In his solitary and wide reading he had come upon the poems and critical writings of an unknown American poet who seemed to have diagnosed his difficulties as a poet with unnerving accuracy. In the fall of 1928, he decided to write her in London.

"With the two-thirds of him that was air and fire," O'Connor commented, "[Geoffrey] adopted new attitudes and new ideas, without ever realizing how they contradicted conventions that were fundamental to himself." O'Connor, a Catholic reared in the slums of Cork, found Phibbs' reading in the "black arts" particularly unsettling. With a connoisseur's appetite for pornography, Phibbs composed endless saucy limericks for private circulation in Dublin literary circles and treasured Havelock Ellis' seven-volume saga, *Studies in the Psychology of Sex*. His own first slim book of verse, *The Withering of the Fig Leaf*, was published by the Hogarth Press in 1927. Soon after the book was released, however, Phibbs begged Leonard Woolf to suppress it because of his sudden fear of possible reprisals from the Catholic hierarchy—a colleague at the library had been sacked because of a blasphemous story published in a Dublin magazine. Phibbs was talented, if somewhat infirm of purpose.

But, again despite the ever-present Catholic yoke, Phibbs was eager to follow Shelley's revolutionary ideas concerning freedom in marriage. His wife, Norah McGuinness, a gifted painter, agreed, she said, because she agreed with him in most things. "Alas, too late I found out that tho' Geoffrey talked with conviction and persuasiveness he in fact could not live up to his theories." This shortcoming had become apparent in the summer of 1928, when Phibbs learned that his wife was having an affair. Norah had only reluctantly told her husband at the insistence of her lover, David Garnett; whereupon Geoffrey's "theories flew out the window."

In most respects, this affair is little more than a footnote to the dramatic events of April 27. A novelist and intellectual, Garnett came from a prominent family of the Bloomsbury literary circle and was married, with children, at the time of his affair. (Garnett was later to have an affair with the painter Duncan Grant, finally divorcing his wife to marry Grant's illegitimate daughter by the painter and sister to Virginia Woolf, Vanessa Bell.) Initially, Phibbs tried to consider the conduct of his wife's romantic life in a similarly "modern" manner; he wrote a polite note to Garnett, asking to meet him. Garnett replied thoughtfully and sympathetically:

> I don't suppose either of us will be able to avoid influencing Norah against the other, or to avoid trying to. I don't feel any impulse to do that now. But if I do try, I'll give you notice. There'll be plenty of time to be tomcats when we're too miserable to be anything else. It has been an enormous relief to me that Norah has told you.
>
> . . . if you want to see me now, let me know and I'll come over for a day at once. I don't think [my wife] will want to come. You had better come & stay with us here without Norah and get to know her then, & Norah and she can meet when they want to. Four is too many: at the moment anyway.

Norah later decided that insecurity over his age (Garnett was eight years older than Geoffrey) had made him insist that she tell Geoffrey—and thus ruin her marriage. Geoffrey's second wife believed that Norah's professed lack of interest in sex led her to use Garnett to advance her career as a book illustrator. Whatever the circumstances of this particular subplot, Garnett's liaisons were managed quietly and tactfully, and the sobriety of lasting literary opinion was not impeached. This was not the case with the goings-on in Hammersmith; by April 1929 Laura Riding was not at all interested in discretion. She was, perhaps, to pay a lasting price for her imprudence.

Though Geoffrey was able to pursue a tense but fraternal friendship with "Bunny" Garnett, he found it impossible to forgive his wife, even after she had broken off the affair. He confessed to Frank O'Connor that he was devastated. O'Connor, who did not share all his friend's ideas, was more appalled than sympathetic. Affairs, for him, were something liable to happen in Russia and France but not in England—and never in Ireland. Geoffrey's regret over his inability to accept the situation was incomprehensible—worse, even, than Norah's initial infidelity.

In a roundabout way these circumstances conspired to bring Geoffrey Phibbs to Laura Riding's doorstep on February 7, 1929. The previous October, he had written to Robert from his small, lonely cottage in County Wicklow, where he lived with Norah, a few pigs, and some woodcocks. Despairing over his wife's affair, he said that Riding's work had become for him "more important than anything else":

> Naturally the important thing for me is that it is important. But it is also important for me in a different way, and perhaps less, that anyone I like . . . should think me wrongheaded & be annoyed. Because it is annoying to the edge of suicide to be admired by wrong headed people. It would be fair of [Laura] to make allowances for the amount one has to shed, as you said, before one reaches her entire position . . . If you hear of a job in England let me know. I'm tired of dissembling in Ireland.

Laura liked the poems that he had sent and, with Robert Graves, kept up the correspondence. Later she would recall a naturalness and an agility to Geoffrey's conversation that she found wholly missing in the more solemn exercises with Robert, who was perpetually learning. By early February 1929, a job was found for Geoffrey in England; he was invited to join Laura, Robert, and Nancy in their work. He was happy to accept the offer. His leave-taking scene in Dublin, as scripted in 14A, included an appearance of W. B. Yeats, an acquaintance of Geoffrey's and another of Norah's admirers:

> [NORAH]: My husband is leaving me. ([Yeats] laughs embarrassedly, hoping it is a joke.) No, really! he says I'm a witch.
> [YEATS] (gallantly): Well aren't you?
> [NORAH]: He doesn't mean it like that. He means that I'm sort of haunted. He says I paralyse a certain part of his brain. Her name is [Laura]. He's never seen her. She's merely an Influence. People seem to know about her. He heard about her from a friend. He writes to her—it's all very philosophical. He won't even show me her picture.
> [GEOFFREY]: There's no picture, I tell you. There couldn't be a picture. She's not real.

Geoffrey, however, was not yet ready to "shed" his wife, and Norah accompanied him on the journey from Dublin, prepared to enter art school in London. But, to her helpless dismay, Geoffrey was received with "open arms," while she, the outsider, was "got rid of":

> Laura, as cold as the cheap sparkling trinkets with which she was covered, accompanied Geoffrey and they brought me to the Regent Palace Hotel—thrust a bottle of Brandy into my hand and said "Drink this and forget your tears." Then they left me in the desolate bedroom. I had practically never drunk Brandy in my life and, not knowing how to drink it, swallowed half a bottle. I could have killed myself. On the third day I went down to the Lounge—and a nightmare which still haunts me was the constant crying of room numbers by the page boys.

Laura (Riding) Jackson would insist that Phibbs' separation from his wife was a fait accompli before she and he came into correspondence and acquaintance; the evidence suggests otherwise. But in his presence Riding's striking inability to see matters on any but her own terms predominated. In this instance, she was simply not interested in the fact of Geoffrey's wife. When Norah recovered from her shock, she returned to Ireland and had her brother send Geoffrey's clothes, typewriter, and a large library of books to him. Except for the books, many of which were sold, most of his belongings were burned because Laura felt that they had been contaminated.

Geoffrey, however, was soon outfitted with some choice items from Robert's extensive wardrobe, among them a silk dressing gown, underwear, socks, shirts, and a brown coat. It was as if a luxurious new patchwork square was to be added to Laura's work in progress. Laura contributed a batik silk scarf and an eighteenth-century blue tiepin, but they were loans, and careful accounting of these items would be drawn up later. A barge, called the *Ringrose*, had recently been purchased for Nancy and the children from a gentleman on the lam over debts. Geoffrey was to live in a smaller barge, the *Avoca*, also at the Atlanta wharf, where the children and their nurse had been staying intermittently. Laura (Riding) Jackson remembered Phibbs' arrival as happy and as heralding a period of promise. She felt her burden of worry lighten and the prospects of work widen.

Phibbs, too, looked forward to a new life in London. "It is bad to live too long in a desert among intellectual enemies," Garnett had written him in Ireland. "Here it is possible to live for years without being aware that the Roman Catholic religion still exists." Catholicism per se was not a serious subject for discussion in Hammersmith. Geoffrey's brother, regarding their setup during a visit to London, suggested that he might just as well pursue the ideas of Pyotr Ouspensky, a fashionable philosopher of the time, as those of Laura Riding. Geoffrey told this to Laura, and as Laura (Riding) Jackson later recalled, they laughed over the idea that alternatives were available.

The living arrangements were decided in a similarly uncompromising manner. Before long Geoffrey left his barge to live at the flat, where he worked closely with Laura, displacing Robert as her most promising protégé. Responding to a concerned query from Frank O'Connor, Geoffrey told him that since his arrival in London he had gone from a state of "non-conscious, non-happiness to a state of conscious happiness." O'Connor, running back and forth between Dublin and Lisheen House, where he felt it was "touch and go with Norah's reason," decided then that perhaps she should not have dropped David Garnett after all:

To that phrase or state of temporary insanity you have
sacrificed the finest woman in Ireland, and though I cannot
emulate you I take off my hat and touch the ground with
my forehead in admiration. I needn't pray the devil to
roast you because you will roast yourself and like Goethe I
have always loved that which seeks a death of flame. In
three months time you will be the most miserable man in
all Ireland.

"The finest woman in Ireland" was to be a sarcastic refrain in 14A,
Riding's roman à clef published in 1934. Norah, portrayed in the
novel as a jealous hysteric and thief, sued the publisher for libel, and
the book was almost immediately withdrawn from circulation.
O'Connor wrote in his memoirs:

[Geoffrey's] letters, which had been explosive and malicious, took on a tone of unction more suitable to a hysterical ecclesiastical student. They were sprinkled with words
like "right" and "wrong," but the moral context was missing.

On Good Friday, March 29, O'Connor stopped by the Hammersmith apartment, having warned Geoffrey that he would come
see him on his way to Paris for Easter. He nursed a tiny hope that
perhaps Geoffrey could be persuaded to join him; Norah, recovering
her equilibrium, had gone to Paris to paint in André Lehote's studio.
Scowling and aloof, Geoffrey opened the door to announce in an
unnaturally loud voice that Laura was at work in another room and
could not be disturbed. O'Connor saw in plain view an unfinished
sentence on a worktable; the ink was not yet dry. Before O'Connor
could light a cigarette, Geoffrey told him that Laura detested smoke
in the study. If he wanted to smoke or eat they would have to go to
the barge. Robert and Laura followed close on their heels.

Nancy, in her typically flustered and abrupt manner, greeted them
from the deck of the *Ringrose*, where she had prepared lunch. Silently
calculating just who of the four would survive what seemed to him an
untenable situation, O'Connor swiftly figured her for the one who
would break under the strain. His memoirs described the events of
the afternoon, without naming either Graves or Riding as the poets

involved, as a "Mad Hatter's luncheon." In *14A*, O'Connor would appear as Handy Andy, who suffered from nosebleeds and was in love with Norah:

> He is untidy, nervous, ugly—exactly the devoted friend, cynically and jealously resigned to having very little attention paid to him. He goes up to [Norah] and takes her hand, which she does not trouble to give him. He keeps hold of it, stroking it righteously, while he addresses [Yeats]—whom he is resolved to treat like a bounder.

O'Connor left for Paris without Geoffrey.

But two days later, on Easter Sunday, Geoffrey approached Laura with the suggestion of a little holiday excursion. In her later account of the events surrounding the suicide attempt, Laura (Riding) Jackson wrote that she had felt nothing amiss; she agreed immediately. While traveling across London, however, she learned that Geoffrey wanted her to run off with him, leaving behind Robert and Nancy, their fine press, and three years of cooperative working and living—just to be with him alone. He argued that Robert and his family took too much time and attention from her real work. A version of their possible conversation appeared in *14A*:

> [GEOFFREY]: Couldn't we go right away—you and I alone? That would save me, I know it would. It's the others who make it difficult.
> [LAURA]: Perhaps you're not meant to be saved. No, [Geoffrey], you can't cut others out of the story just to simplify it. It's not only your story, remember. . . . You must be in a worse state even, than I think you're in.
> [GEOFFREY]: I'm in an awful state.
> [LAURA]: And what do you mean by going away? Where?
> [GEOFFREY]: Oh anywhere. France. Perhaps for just a while.
> [LAURA]: Yes, it's always for just a while when people go to France.

Laura (Riding) Jackson remembered having tried to calm his anxiety. They took numerous cabs and buses, never stopping long in one place, without finding a way to resolve Geoffrey's trouble. When it began to get dark, they returned home exhausted, leaving the matter unsettled.

The next day, April Fools' Day, everything was suddenly changed. Geoffrey did not return from a luncheon date with his aunt; as Jackson wrote, "*Geoffrey Phibbs was not there!*" The shock of this discovery still resounded, even fifty years later. The loss was not a personal privation, Laura (Riding) Jackson would insist; Robert and Nancy were equally bereft, unable to continue their lives until he was found.

But, initially at least, Robert was secretly pleased to have Geoffrey out of the apartment. That morning, while Laura was talking to Nancy on the barge, Robert had explained to Geoffrey in his usual roundabout way that he could never really be with Laura as long as Geoffrey was with them. Robert, Laura had more than once noted, was adept at cultivating perplexity as to his own selfish motives. The narrator of *14A* makes a similar observation:

> [Robert] does not allow himself to dislike [Geoffrey]; he
> prefers to let himself be puzzled by the situation.

Agreeing with Robert that their situation was one of "doomed impermanence," Geoffrey silently decided that since Laura had Robert and Nancy, he belonged with Norah, who had no one. The prospect made him miserable, but after borrowing some money from his aunt and swearing her to secrecy, he bolted that night for Paris.

The mysterious disappearance and adventurous pursuit of Geoffrey Phibbs also provided dramatic fodder for *14A*:

> [LAURA]: We've come about [Geoffrey]. We must see you.
> THE AUNT: You're a wicked woman. Go away. . . .
> [LAURA]: Oh, please let us in. We must know.
> THE AUNT: He's gone away. By now he's out of England—with
> the right woman.
> [NANCY]: [Norah!] The snake!

In *14A*, Riding's doppelgänger describes herself as a kind of "moral stimulant"; in sufficient dosages she might cause the people around her to become either very, very good (like herself) or absolutely horrid.

ON THE NORTH bank of the Seine, about seventy-five miles north-west of Paris, sits Rouen, for a thousand years the capital of the province of Normandy. It lies in a natural amphitheater formed by the green hills that border the Seine valley. At the Place du Vieux Marché in the medieval heart of the city, a cross marks the spot where Joan of Arc was burned at the stake by the English in 1431 as a heretic and schismatic. There is a story that the executioner found her heart intact in the embers, but the English authorities, displaying a notable inelegance, tossed it unceremoniously into the nearby Seine.

After traveling all night, Laura, Robert, and Nancy reached Rouen in the early morning, less than a week after Geoffrey's departure. It had taken the "Holy Circle," as they had come to call themselves, some time to locate him. A telegram had first gone off to Gertrude Stein, whose book they had just finished printing. Laura believed that Geoffrey connected her and Stein in his mind and was likely to have gone to her in his confusion. Gertrude was asked to tell Geoffrey that the foursome still might last longer if he wanted it to. But there had been no sign of him at the atelier on the rue de Fleurus. Robert's quick trip to Ireland had also been unsuccessful; Geoffrey's parents had no idea of his whereabouts. Cleverly, however, a close friend of Riding's named Len Lye eventually tricked the information out of Geoffrey's aunt. A New Zealander who was an early innovator in animated films, Len told her that he had a steady job to offer Geoffrey but needed to know immediately whether or not he could take it. The aunt told him that Geoffrey had gone to Rouen with Norah. Laura, Robert, and Nancy Nicholson at once obtained passage on the boat train leaving that night for Dieppe.

A bellboy woke Norah and Geoffrey on the morning of Saturday, April 6, with the announcement that several people in the lobby were waiting to deliver a "most important statement." A few days earlier Norah had been similarly awakened in her Paris garret to learn that Geoffrey was downstairs, urgently begging to see her. Upon de-scending she learned that he had run away from the Holy Circle and wanted a reconciliation. He had then suggested a second honey-moon in Rouen, a popular weekend resort for Parisians. For the last three days she had been hearing the most extraordinary stories about life at St. Peter's Square: "One of the most amazing was that Laura (Goddess etc.) locked herself in the lavatory for eight hours because Geoffrey said I was taller than she was," emerging only when he recanted. Again, in *14A*, Norah was cut to Riding's measure:

> [Norah] has purposely chosen the large basket chair for herself. She is quite small, and not at all beautiful, not even pretty. But she has what people would call a tragic face; and somehow, lifting herself tiredly out of a chair much too large for her, she contrives to seem beautiful.

Norah also learned that Laura shared both Geoffrey and Robert's bed, while Nancy lived with her children on a barge. "All this appeared to be agreeable to everyone—living on Shelley's theories!" Rebecca West, Riding told a correspondent somewhat proudly, had made the same observation of their living arrangements.

That morning Laura was once again covered in jewels; even her shoes sported rhinestone buckles. Norah scornfully dismissed them as "Woolworth" ornaments, speculating that Laura was again out to fascinate her husband. Indeed, Geoffrey was stymied. Laura (Riding) Jackson would later write that he appeared not to recognize them, thus supporting her initial conclusion that perhaps he had somehow lost his memory. His behavior was quite strange, she wrote. Norah suggested coolly that perhaps they would like to join Geoffrey and herself for breakfast.

A long morning passed in the hotel. For Norah, still the outsider, most of the conversation seemed encoded in a hermetic language, equipped with secret signals and silent understandings. *14A* gave an indication of its content:

> [Robert]: It was just so untidy, [Geoffrey]. Granted that you couldn't have done it any differently, as you say, being as you are. Well, being as we are, we couldn't let it go at that. We thought that if we could see you, if only for an hour, and talk it all over sanely, at least there'd be a chance of sane feelings all round. It isn't as if anything had happened, so that we had to wait for years for a rational view

of things. You haven't made a single coherent remark. You won't even look at [Laura]. What has [Norah] done to you.

Bored with this, Norah went for a walk, returning to find that no progress had been made and that they were to have lunch in another hotel on the outskirts of Rouen. En route, Robert bought Laura a new necklace.

The five sat in the open air and, as Laura (Riding) Jackson later remembered it, she ordered shrimp. The distinct and plump shape of each tiny shrimp, she wrote, impressed itself on her memory. What few words were spoken, she recalled, shared this distinctness and were consumed silently, one at a time. Geoffrey was guarded, saying little. Norah seemed prepared for an outburst, but nothing untoward happened.

At the end of lunch the proposal was put on the table: Norah was invited to join the Holy Circle. The mistake had been to leave her out (because otherwise Geoffrey would not have run away), and now "their mission," as Norah described it, was to "gather me in." Again, the simple force of Riding's understanding provided an elegant resolution of all their difficulties; 14A summed it up:

> [Laura]: I know you'll come back, somehow. I know it isn't finished. And if only it could all happen calmly and reasonably and naturally. It frightens me the way it is. It's all wrong. No one says you shouldn't love [Norah]. Come back, both of you. You know you want to be in London.

The terms included a separate apartment for them and the promise that all physical intimacy between Laura and Geoffrey would end. Norah and her husband were then instructed to go for a walk and make their decision. Geoffrey, still torn, left it up to his wife, saying that he would stick with her either way. Norah, wanting no part of the goings-on at the "mad house of Hammersmith," returned to the hotel with Geoffrey to deliver a flat no.

Laura threw herself on the floor in hysterics, while an audience of diners looked on aghast. Two waiters removed her, but the argument continued in a cab endlessly circling the city's cobbled streets and finished somehow on a hilltop on the outskirts. Laura "seemed to die," Robert wrote later. Laura mailed a letter to Geoffrey from the Rouen train station proclaiming the end of the alliance. Because Geoffrey had brought no money, Norah was left to pay the hotel bill. She never saw Laura Riding again.

But of course it was not the end. Laura could still not bear to consider that her efforts had culminated in Geoffrey's leaving her. He, too, was at sixes and sevens. He sailed from Dieppe to England, took the train from Euston Station to Holyhead, sailed from there to Dublin, and took the train to Sligo with barely a word to Norah en route. As her husband clutched Laura's letter, Norah felt her enthusiasm to have him back starting to cool. Upon arriving in Dublin, Geoffrey sent a letter to Robert, written in a paroxysm of shame and misery:

> I carry her Rouen letter with me as my most complete humiliation and I have come back here to Ireland out of humiliation. God I feel bitter. Sorry. This letter is bloody. It just shows that I am all Laura said I was. God bless you. Tell Nancy I love her. But not furiously as I love Laura. . . . Hell . . . I'll never see the end of my own futility.

Naturally this provoked a letter from Laura, which Geoffrey received at his parents' house in the midst of signing a letter to Nancy. In the letter to Nancy he had already confided his fear that perhaps Laura suffered from GPI or the general paralysis of the insane, a condition induced by venereal disease; he planned to enclose a description of the symptoms torn from the *Encyclopaedia Britannica*. With the letter from Laura in hand, he scrapped the one to Nancy, returned the page to the reference book, and wrote to Robert. More letters and telegrams were exchanged, and strange objects began to arrive in the mail at Lisheen House. These bus tickets, bits of twisted wire, coins, and colored ribbons were accompanied by symbolic signs that Norah, ever curious, was unable to decipher.

Geoffrey's equivocations would continue to incur suspense back in London; his adamant refusal to rejoin them remained both incredible and unacceptable. Until Laura came up with a better ending, suspense would rule with this disbelief. Geoffrey, in turn, was alternately annoyed and pleased by these attentions. When not answering these missives he occupied himself in a naturalist's pursuits, anxious to skirt the oppressive atmosphere of parental disapproval and Norah's accusing glances by wandering around Sligo looking for a particularly rare bird's nest. When Nancy Nicholson arrived to persuade him to come see Laura in London, he was ill in bed. Because Geoffrey's mother would not let her past the veranda, Geoffrey had to come outside. It was during this visit that Nancy was damned by his father under the Knockeray Mountains and Geoffrey decided to change his name.

Following Nancy's departure, the telegrams came and went. Promises to return to St. Peter's Square were made and reneged upon. After almost three weeks of extended Easter holiday, Norah decided to go back to Paris, and the same day Geoffrey found the bird's nest that he had been looking for. Taking this as an omen, he decided to visit David Garnett for advice, and it was at Garnett's spacious house in Huntingdonshire that Robert, cursing, found him. He pulled Geoffrey out of bed in the middle of the night and dragged him to the train he had hired to take Geoffrey back to London and Laura Riding. Geoffrey by now was insistent, saying he just could not take it anymore.

"Where accident has been the mover in events, necessity has the last word," Laura (Riding) Jackson wrote sixty years later in her account of that rainy April morning. In "Opportunism Rampant," a long essay written in response to Martin Seymour-Smith's biography of Robert Graves, Jackson tried to explain the circumstances that had led to the jump from her bedroom window. It is a poignant and baffling document. Just before the jump she had finally seen with ghastly clarity that further arguments over Geoffrey's return would be useless. To pick up the torn threads, to redesign the weave of interwoven purposes, and return to work was also not a credible alternative, even with the help of Robert and Nancy. Necessity would have to step in.

The image of this living cloth echoed the one that she had chosen in a 1928 fictional monologue entitled "Letter of Abdication":

> . . . my rug was composed of many small squares; and the
> pattern of each square was different; and yet the whole

> harmonious because the stuff was provided by me—the
> finest silk and velvet rags that I could command from
> others, and which I sorted and returned to them to be
> made into squares, a square by each of them. And so each
> who made a square was my subject. And so I became
> Queen.

This was her story, the one she had struggled so long to articulate,
and she needed Geoffrey to complete the pattern. Perhaps by this
image she meant to redeem the ugly oval rugs made from unmatched
socks that had been her mother's dreary occupation. Her quilted
creation had demanded the utmost from those three individuals who
now looked at her expectantly:

> I have said more than enough to satisfy my contempt of
> you. But once I loved you; and I have not punished myself
> sufficiently for that. What do I mean when I say that I once
> loved you? That I knew that being alive for you and me
> meant being more than alive. But you were afraid to ad-
> mit it, though I was willing to take all the responsibility
> upon myself. . . . you repulsed me with praise and grati-
> tude; as you would now with pity and ingratitude if I
> permitted.

What had happened to the carefully wrought, richly woven,
closely stitched harmony of the Trinity of Laura Riding, Robert
Graves, and Nancy Nicholson? Writing the story of that fateful leap
in a lonely bungalow in Wabasso, Florida, Laura (Riding) Jackson
decided that the bleak challenge had come from the shadowy figure
in the far corner of the room, and at stake was the veracity of her
mind and heart. In this Irishman's denial of his love for her, she found
that for him, the lie triumphed.

She had seen this in Graves, of course, but his Irish genius for lying
was tempered by what she called his "Nordic-Teutonic" sense of
purpose. This gave his lies an ulterior motive; blended with personal
confession it gave him a story to tell, an opportunistic self-
dramatization. Geoffrey Phibbs' manner was more purely perverse;

there was in him a satanic need to test the possibility of lying. He once boasted to her that he had eaten a centipede, just for the thrill of the experience. This incident had stuck in her mind all these years, acquiring significance as symptomatic evidence of true evil. She knew that Geoffrey, even more than Robert, recognized the beautiful accuracies of the truths that she offered him that morning; but rather than accept them his Irish perversity compelled him to turn them inside out in mockery of her, to make out of her truths his lies, to make of her love for him something unspeakably pornographic. The travesty still chilled her.

On Robert's face she saw that he expected her to make everything all right, but trapped between Nancy and Robert she longed only to free herself from both. Her first thought was to slit her wrists or to take poison; excusing herself, she left the room. Returning, Laura swallowed a household disinfectant. Robert told the police that he ran downstairs for an emetic, but, incredibly, all three just stood there, watching her.

Later that summer Riding was prepared to be wry. Realizing that the Lysol was not sufficient, she wrote then that she had "left the room, by the window of course," and only the poems left with her. "Or rather I went with the poems." The Devil Phibbs had wanted suicide, she wrote recklessly in her preface to a new collection of poems, and she "gave him suicide." Robert jumped out the lower-story window to get to her; and Geoffrey, finally able to effect his departure, ran out of the house.

Riding had heavily underscored the line "Pure madness is the finest sense" in her copy of Emily Dickinson's collected poems. The events of April 27, she wrote, were pure madness, but with her poetry she would make it sense. Riding would never fully redeem the madness of her suicide attempt and the events surrounding it, but in her work in the months immediately following she got farther than one might have expected.

Until such time, Nancy Nicholson, the only remaining member of the audience, collected herself, went downstairs, and telephoned for an ambulance.

Chapter 7

THE SPHINX IN EGYPT

——•——

Of old there was a spirit, it was dark
Until it felt a pity for itself,
When the tremendous darkness shrieked and broke
Of its extreme and shone, mothering the light
That had been once but pain in the heart of night,
The night original and nameless. What
Brought morning and what made the dark a mother
To light and men? Nothing but woman in
A spirit could have wrought so safe and slow
Its ruin in perpetuity and peace.

—"The Lady of the Apple"

——•——

BEFORE THE *RANPURA* even pulled out into the Channel, it was clear
to all that theirs was an auspicious journey. Disembarking at Gibral-
tar, the party of eight—four children and their parents, a nurse, and
Miss Laura Gottschalk—forayed out under blue skies to buy figs
and get their first view of the Mediterranean. As they passed
through the strait, the two horizons leaped out of the now black
waters, the passage between them lit by lightning. At dusk one
evening, in the middle of a hailstorm, the ship passed close enough
to Stromboli, then erupting, for them to feel the steam of the lava-
heated sea. As the ship sailed east along ancient trade routes to Port
Said, the children slept and dawn broke on the all-night talks in

their second-class cabins. The last leg, an interminable train journey from the port to Cairo, was brightened by a green vision of the fields of lower Egypt.

Out in the desert, beyond the suburb where they were to live for the next five months, fellaheen labored under the burning sun and circling kites, hypnotized by the heat and the songs whose rhythms set the pace of their shovels. Supervised by archaeologists, they removed centuries of sand from the base of the recumbent Sphinx, revealing not only a leonine tail wrapped around its right haunch, but a book between its front paws. Newly unearthed, it waited for new prophecies to be inscribed.

THE ACCOUNTS OF Robert Graves' first encounter with Laura Riding, at the Waterloo Station to meet the boat train from Plymouth, betray a variety of perspectives and alliances. The first version appeared not quite four years later in the "Dedicatory Epilogue" of Graves' best-selling autobiography, *Good-bye to All That*. Written on the heels of Riding's suicide attempt, its tone is a mixture of awe, testamentary reverie, and a certain amount of deliberate ambiguity:

> For how could the story of your coming be told between an Islip Paris Council Meeting and a conference of the professors of the Faculty of Letters at Cairo University? How she and I happening by seeming accident upon your teasing *Quids*, were drawn to write to you, who were in America, asking you to come to us. How, though you knew no more of us than we of you, and indeed less (for you knew me at a disadvantage, by my poems of the war), you forthwith came. And how there was thereupon a unity to which you and I pledged our faith and she her pleasure.

This epilogue, which sealed Graves' adieu to the country he had fought and killed for, was omitted from later editions.

Graves' first biographer set the scene of Riding's arrival by drawing on apocryphal sources. In his account, Graves' father-in-law, the painter William Nicholson, accompanied Graves to the station only to depart in "robust horror" at first sight of Miss Laura Gottschalk.

Graves exclaimed, "My God! What am I going to do?" at the sight of her "small, tired, overly made-up figure in the crowd." Her face, added this biographer, was "very nearly ugly, or at least repellent— when her deep sunk eyes went dead as stone (or a lidded snake's) and her normal pallor faded to the tone of chalk."

Graves' next biographer, his nephew, Richard Perceval Graves, proved more sympathetic to Laura Gottschalk's appearance, para-phrasing her own account of this meeting. In this version, an attrac-tive young woman a little below medium height emerged from the train, wearing a long dark coat and a dark broad-brimmed felt hat. "Her face, serious in repose and always keenly intelligent, now wore the liveliest of expressions; her blue eyes were especially striking, and she had brown hair which was swept backwards from her forehead and fell on her shoulders." Later, after their relations had soured, he learned that her hair, as it appeared in her passport photograph, was in fact quite short.

Finally, with a glare in the direction of that first biographer, Martin Seymour-Smith, Laura (Riding) Jackson described her welcome as warm and courteous, accompanied by help with her luggage and witty pleasantries about her makeup bag. Nicholson had a prior appointment that called him elsewhere—but not, she insisted, with any undue haste. Her traveling outfit was smart but modest, "in unemphatic taste, suiting my 25 years." Whichever view is chosen, the meeting appears staged for the benefit of posterity, and therein lies its significance: it is emblematic of the entire fourteen-year Graves-Riding relationship and the historiographic bickering that followed it. No account is given of the ocean crossing itself, which, as it was the dead of winter, must have been dismal.

It does appear that an unexpected cold front arrived with Riding on that Sunday morning, January 3, 1926, bringing gale-force winds and floods on the Thames. Islip, a small village just outside Oxford and her destination that morning, had more than an inch of water. But what atmospheric condition was it that lit up the train compart-ment that Laura shared with Robert during the trip from Paddington Station? More brilliant than mere light, she wrote a short while later; they were both so dazzled by this illumination that they were left speechless. In her later years, Laura (Riding) Jackson had shut out the memory of this vision that had enveloped her and Robert. She insisted that there was no trip to Islip before they left for Egypt.

And what sort of figure did Robert Graves cut on the platform? To Virginia Woolf, a duchess in the reigning literary elite, Graves' physical appearance suggested a crude likeness to Shelley, "save that his nose is a switchback and his lines blurred." Her sly and mocking description less than a year before props a "bolt eyed blue shirted shockheaded hatless man in a blue overcoat standing goggling" before her curious gaze:

> He stayed until 7:15 (we were going to Caesar and Cleopatra . . .) and had at last to say so, for he was so thick in the delight of explaining his way of life to us that no bee stuck faster to honey. He cooks, his wife cleans; 4 children are brought up in the elementary school; the villagers give them vegetables; they were married in a church; his wife calls herself Nancy Nicholson; wont go to Garsington [and she sorts] her friends into sheep and goats. All this to us sounded like the usual self-consciousness of young men, especially as he threw in, gratuitously, the information that he descends from dean rector, Bishop, von Ranke, etc. etc. . . . in order to say he despises them. . . . No I don't think he will write great poetry; but what will you? The sensitive are needed too; the half-baked, stammering stuttering, who perhaps improve their own quarter of Oxfordshire.

But to Laura, writing ecstatic letters home from Egypt, there appeared before her that rainy day a man both tall and ungainly, with blue-gray eyes, a voice made for ballads, and a tender, protective manner.

IN GOOD-BYE TO ALL THAT, the story of Graves' boyhood, schooling, service in the trenches, and early married life, Graves showed an unusual readiness, as Woolf had already noted, to contemplate his lineage. By the time he wrote it, however, the stammering and stuttering had disappeared, at least in his writing voice. For every bishop, rector, police magistrate, and other example of a respectable ruling-class pedigree, Graves paid almost Mendelian attention to the family's less noteworthy characteristics. "There is a coldness in the Graves which is anti-sentimental to the point of insolence," he noted before proceeding to index the weaknesses in the line. Thus, from his German mother's side, the von Rankes, he inherited his clumsiness, his moral seriousness, a head of thick, curly black hair, and a horror of Catholicism. Under her rigorous religious tutoring Graves developed fears of damnation, a superstitious conscience, and an extreme form of "sexual embarrassment from which I have found it very difficult to free myself." The various complexes and neuroses that he lists showed clearly that he had read at least what he needed in Freud.

But *Good-bye to All That* is memorable for reasons other than the engrossing and robust self-absorption that fuels Graves' narrative. His account of his fate at the hands of his schoolmates at Charterhouse was the first to expose the sexual and other tyrannies of life in a public school. In the 1930s such revelations would create a new genre of memoir. Indeed, Graves came closer to indignation in his description of these years than he did in his account of trench warfare. *Good-bye to All That* is now considered an eloquent masterpiece of revulsion against the slaughter of the Great War. But the discovery that a boy that he loved in school was, in fact, a homosexual was the true crisis of the book; this "betrayal" superseded all others. Indeed it was Graves' indictment of Charterhouse and its fostering of a "pseudo-homosexual" atmosphere that scandalized his family most; his father wrote a letter of apology to the school authorities upon the book's publication. More than ten years after the armistice, the larger misdeeds of the war could still not be comprehended in their entirety.

As for his upbringing, Graves was less generous to his father than his mother. He found the paternal side of the family "thin nosed and inclined to petulance, but never depraved, cruel or hysterical." Alfred Perceval Graves (fondly referred to as APG) was born in Dublin and was the editor of the popular songbook *Irish Songs and Ballads*. This was a collection of songs composed to the music of old Irish airs, the outcome of APG's affectionate study of peasant life among the mountains of Kerry. APG was an icon of the Victorian music room; his songbooks were to be found on every piano. Before Graves began examining his past with a cold eye, he had considerable affection and admiration for his father; indeed, not long before Laura's arrival, he sent him his ballad play, *John Kemp's Wager*, for editing, approval, and praise. Though Graves would develop an antipathy to all things Irish, after the encounter with Phibbs the Irish airs pursued the young Graves beyond the nursery and into the battlefield.

These scraps of song, nursery rhymes, Biblical passages, Welsh and Irish ditties haunted him under fire. Singsong fantasies of a fairy's life, however ridiculous they rang in the bloody thunder of war and death, sustained him: "I'd love to be a fairy's child," for such souls "never want for food or fire" and "always get their heart's desire," trilled one poem from *Fairies and Fusiliers*, his third book of poems. But, in the virulently antipoetic "A Dead Boche" of the same collection he provides an ugly troll (in the form of a dead German soldier) to disturb such whimsy: "With clothes and face a sodden green, / Big bellied, spectacled, crop-haired, / Dribbling black blood from nose and beard." The forms that Graves' war poetry took were still, in some respects, those of the nursery; and this book, like much of the poetry he published following the year of his service in the trenches, indicated the progress of a slow and far more brutal awakening into adulthood than even his public schooling had provided him. *Faeries and Fusiliers* begins with a defense of traditional verse, but clearly the shells exploding overhead interrupted the regular verse forms and allowed him little peace to indulge in the pastoral.

When he began to explore his disillusionment with such "Poetry," in his autobiography, it was his father that he blamed, albeit obliquely. "I am glad in a way that my father was a poet. This at least saved me from any false reverence for poets. . . ." The loss of reverence for his father's art enabled Graves to envision his own sense of "Poetry." In *Good-bye to All That* he sided with his mother's advice to "speak the truth and shame the devil!" even though he had come to believe that it was after marrying his mother and turning teetotaler that his father lost his early gift for playful light verse. A number of Graves' literary friends were later to bemoan a similar transformation in Robert after his marriage to Nancy Nicholson and again after meeting Laura Riding. Indeed, after his marriage in 1918, Robert warned his friend and fellow war poet Siegfried Sassoon not to look for "a certain Robert Graves now dead whose bones and detritus may be found in *Over the Brazier, Fairies and Fusiliers* and the land of memory." Similarly, when Edith Sitwell came upon the volume of her poetry that she had lovingly inscribed for Robert and Nancy in a bookshop, she bought it and added a postscript to her dedication that expressed her opinion of his new American muse:

> I wrote this dedication at a time when Robert Graves was still a tentative English nightengale [*sic*] and not an American loon or screech owl. Though poor, I am happy to buy this book (from the shop to which he sold it) for the sum of 15s so that no one can accuse me of being a hoot-fan.

However his London literary friends might cluck, not long after Riding's arrival, just who spoke the truth and shamed the devil was quite clear.

And, as Graves saw it, Laura Riding was the crusader knight of *Good-bye to All That*—and he the damsel in distress. "From a historical point of view [the story] must be read . . . as one of gradual disintegration," he informed his readers, a disintegration that "by the summer of 1926 was already well advanced." Amy Graves was deeply saddened by her son's account of his early years: "Poor Robert has suffered terribly and what that led to is not for us to judge of." She predicted—(correctly)—that the book would cause "a widespread sensation." APG thought that perhaps the best thing for his son was to join the Roman Catholic church. After meeting Riding, such alternatives—and he had already pursued several of his own— ceased to interest Graves. By the time he came to write the "Dedicatory Epilogue" of *Good-bye to All That*, he had abandoned everything to embrace Laura Riding—and Riding alone.

In the eyes of a watchful eleven-year-old niece named Sally, "too young to have any clear appreciation," Nancy Nicholson appeared in the final days before the departure for Egypt in the top room of a London studio holding a roll of cotton wool. Wearing a broad-brimmed white hat, a loose coat, and a brown skirt longer than the current fashion, she was slight but tall, with fashionably close-cropped hair. Later, Sally's mother explained that this was the "Art School Style." The studio in Apple Tree Yard, a mews off Duke of York Street near Piccadilly Circus, was a former stable. It belonged to Nancy's father, William Nicholson, a well-known society painter and portraitist; Robert, Nancy, and their four children had often stayed there on their trips to London. Her manner and a great deal else about Nancy was unorthodox, at least to those who had not had the privilege of growing up in a family of painters in the dandyish high society of Max Beerbohm's circle of artists and raconteurs. To her mother-in-law's chagrin Nancy fancied men's trousers and a painter's smock. Doubtless there was nothing unusual about this to Nancy, as her father's taste in dress had run to yellow-spotted bow ties and tight checked trousers. But where Robert's family was a large chorus of ballad-singing, rhyming, praying, and bickering, Nancy's family was urban, urbane, and anti-Victorian. Most likely Nancy found her husband's family quaint.

Nancy's considerable talents as illustrator, designer, and printer have been appreciated rather than praised, largely overshadowed by the work of her father and her brother Ben. Like her brother, however, Nancy always set her own blinkered course. However devoted she was to her father, she had early on developed a skeptical eye as far as the wayward virtues of talented men were concerned. She had watched her mother suffer bitterly over her husband's infidelities before her death of influenza near the end of the war. As a result Nancy tended to champion the cause of the powerless and dispossessed.

With the confidence and independence that comes from such a comfortable and nonconformist upbringing, Nancy Nicholson was also much more willing to rebuff convention than her more bourgeois husband was, at least on his own authority. Her later letters reveal a mature woman of fierce principle and abundant compassion, a probity forged in prickly opposition to hypocrisy of all kinds. Together she and Robert had embraced socialism, the simplicities of life on the land, and feminism. She had equally advanced ideas about child-rearing. They did not go to church or have their children baptized, and they were members of the Constructive Birth Control Society, whose literature they distributed in Islip. Nancy joined Robert, too, in his various enthusiasms, which had so far included dream analysis, a Bengali philosopher named Basanta Mallik, and Laura Riding's poetry. In sum, their lives in Islip were a kind of response to the war. Though fervent, unfocused, and confined to improving their quarter of Oxfordshire, their life-style and firmly held beliefs reflected the temper of the times. After such a trauma as the war it was perhaps difficult for them to conceive any life more ambitious.

Nancy was eighteen at the time of her marriage and, wanting four children, had them at very close intervals. An early attempt to make money with a shop on Boar's Hill on the outskirts of Oxford left her and Robert exhausted and in debt. Her health, their financial well-being, and very likely their marriage faltered, too, under the considerable domestic strains of living in a small, damp cottage with no plumbing and only one stove. Nancy suffered from hyperthyroidism (also known as Graves' disease), probably induced by her quick succession of pregnancies. Its symptoms included fatigue, extreme nervous irritability, and hair loss.

On top of these strains, Robert's literary friends found Nancy difficult, so much so that he found himself trying to convince Siegfried Sassoon that he was "not so far as I know Nancy's drudge or 'the Hen-Pecked Husband or Hammond's Depressed Villager or the Impoverished Genius with the Awful Wife and the Squalling Brats.'" Sassoon was a frequent visitor to Lady Ottoline Morrell's country house at Garsington (the weekend house party of Bloomsbury and other London literary elites), and in Ottoline he found someone to share his misgivings over Nancy's influence on Robert. But the "life that Garsington plots out for me," Robert felt, was consciously or unconsciously hostile to the one he had. This was made clear to Nancy when she was advised by another poet's wife that if she wanted to keep her husband she should not lose her intellectual interests. Nancy soon refused to go to Garsington and began to look upon Sassoon with suspicion.

Brought together by poetry and the war that they had both survived, Graves and Sassoon had an uncommon and fiercely felt friendship, tinged on Sassoon's part by carefully suppressed homoerotic desires, which he confided to his diary. Displaced by Nancy in Graves' affections after the war, and handicapped by a neurasthenia that left him at the mercy of his delicate sensibility and war guilt,

Sassoon found Nancy's lack of feminine graces unsettling. Accustomed to the ardent exchange of poetry, sympathy, and romantic idealism that had sustained their intimacy during the war, Sassoon could not conceive what Robert might see in this "queer and uncouth" "sharp-tongued" woman. T. E. Lawrence, another close friend of Robert's, thought Nancy was a cold fish. Both views found ready sympathy in Martin Seymour-Smith, who suggested further that while Robert was a thoroughgoing heterosexual, Nancy's true impulses were "delitescent."

Despite stout assurances as to Robert's true sexual orientation, Seymour-Smith concludes that Robert married Nancy to evade the possibility of his own "delitescent" nature, after a narrow escape from the brush that tarred his first love, the pseudonymous Dick of his autobiography. The net effect of all such speculation is to slight Robert's love of Sassoon as well as of Nancy. Unfortunately, Robert burned his love letters to Nancy in the aftermath of Riding's suicide attempt. Still, there is evidence in his love poems and the observations of his parents and siblings to suggest that Robert's affection for his wife was deep and abiding. Though easily offended by slights himself, Sassoon had the grace to imagine that Nancy's brusque manner might have been a cover for shyness.

THE STEAMER TRUNKS that yawned on the floor of the top room at the Apple Tree Yard studio that morning in January 1926 proved that the life at Islip had at last become unworkable. The family was unable to survive on Robert's pension, the neighbors' vegetables, and the combined goodwill of Robert's literary patron Edward Marsh, T. E. Lawrence, Sassoon, William Nicholson, and Amy Graves. Told by a doctor that Nancy needed a dry climate to avoid becoming a permanent invalid, Robert had accepted a high-salaried position teaching English at the Royal Egyptian University in Cairo. In leaving Islip behind, however, they had the consolation of having tried to live a virtuous life in the long shadow of the war. They had five days in London before the ship sailed.

Nancy was pleased with their new nurse's sure hand with the four children and her unquestioning acceptance of her child-rearing philosophy. That day they had all been to the doctor for inoculations against typhoid, paratyphoid, and other Egyptian plagues. Her youngest, Sam, was just two, Catherine was three, David almost six, and Jenny had turned seven the day after they arrived in London. Nancy, returning from a last-minute shopping expedition, found her husband sitting among piles of unpacked clothing and talking to his half brother, Philip. (Philip was one of four children born to APG in his first marriage. Amy had given him another four.) Interrupting him, she gave him peremptory instructions as to packing, adding the clothes and emergency medical kit she had bought. Having grown up in a family of older sisters and half sisters, Robert most likely saw nothing unusual in being drilled.

As Philip had lived and worked in the Middle East, Laura seated herself on a stool next to his wife, Millicent, to ask questions and take notes about customs and housekeeping matters such as health precautions, servants, and diet. A few days before, spending her first night on English soil, Laura had stood at the window of her attic room at Islip and felt the purest joy. She found everything about the village cottage (aptly named World's End) and the family that lived there perfect. She delighted in the quaintness of taking baths before the inglenook fireplace. From the village pump by the orchard down the lane, Robert brought up buckets of water and, emptied out the front door afterward, it returned via the house path to the River Ray, which Laura could just see from her window, mistaking it for the Thames. She only sensed the spires of Oxford, glimpsed briefly that afternoon, but it was a thrilling proximity. The children, in dresses and short pants made by Nancy, were perfect. In an authentic country kitchen, Laura wrote, Nancy made supper on a Cotswold coal stove, and even that seemed perfect. Everything seemed to be designed and made by Nancy, and to Polly she confessed that perhaps she would one day find herself a Nancy creation. Eleven-year-old Sally Graves noticed that in London Laura was dressed just like Nancy, except that her hat was black and she wore a white blouse. She concluded that the two were sisters.

On the first evening in London, Laura dined with Robert's parents, his older sister Rosaleen, and E. M. Forster. Forster had spent time in Alexandria during the war and went on at great length about Egypt, leaving Robert bored but making a warm impression on Laura. After dinner Robert sang folk songs with Rosaleen, who was in London studying to be a doctor. The next day, extravagant last-minute taxi rides around the city took Laura, Robert, and Nancy on rounds of good-byes to family and friends. There was a visit to Leonard Woolf at the Hogarth Press, an evening at the theater with Siegfried, and an appointment with Graves' agent, Eric Pinker and Sons, who agreed to take on "Miss Gottschalk" as his client.

Laura's financial situation needed encouragement. Had a salary, in addition to room and board, been agreed upon beforehand? It is difficult to say; she certainly never took one. Apart from money borrowed from Polly, Laura had advances from Adelphi on her translation of *Anatole France at Home* and for her book of poems, amounting to $150. When Lou received an accounting from Polly of Laura's debts accrued in New York prior to her departure, the amount, he remarked ruefully, took his breath away. He was obliged to reimburse Polly in installments. As for Laura's more personal debts to Polly, Lou told her, "It may be some remuneration for you to know that Laura said you were one of the noblest souls she has ever encountered." Lou had not yet given up hope for Laura's return to Louisville.

Polly, however, would receive the in-depth details of Laura's first impressions. Robert and Nancy weren't at all superior, she heard; they had both rejected their families and what Laura imagined were aristocratic legacies. (It would be some time before Robert was free of his mother's purse strings.) Laura admired Nancy's uprightness and independence; Nancy, who had no patience for affectation, was impressed by Laura's efficiency and zeal in helping her prepare for the departure. One evening in Piccadilly found all three watching a new Harold Lloyd film, Laura seated between Robert and Nancy, her hands clasped on each side. All their lives had led up to this meeting, and during the brief interim in Islip and London, Laura wrote Polly, they had formed an almost supernatural love, irrevocable and fated.

EGYPT WAS TO provide the grand stage for their common destiny to fulfill its promise. In their various responses to Egypt were the beginnings of the sympathies that were to bind the Trinity together until Riding leaped from her window in Hammersmith three years later. After the chaos of arrival at Ramses Station in Cairo, and the settling down in Heliopolis, six miles north of the city, they began to work out the plot and the point of view of themselves and of their secret marriage to one another. The children, having been declared free of mumps just before leaving England, now came down with the measles and were dispatched to the isolation ward of a Cairo hospital, along with their nurse.

Cairo, Laura wrote in blithe ignorance two months after she arrived, was like all of Egypt. Venturing out in the Morris-Oxford motor car that had been a gift from Sassoon, they found unexpected survivals of its ancient past. The elegance of the native dress, the beauty of the Bedouin and Sudanese, the "real natives" (they excluded the Turks, the Greeks, the Syrians, and the Europeanized Arabs) surprised and pleased them—but not often. Anxious to avoid the cliché responses to a place that had seen centuries of tourists' and travelers' accounts, they all contributed rather amazing observations. The pyramids, Nancy declared, were without exception suburban, though Laura was able to find them somewhat mysterious if only until one achieved an equal antiquity—and that was only a small matter of time. The Nile, Jenny remarked to everyone's pleasure, was not at all blue as the history books had promised but a muddy green. For Laura the Sphinx at Giza was both memorable and dull because it resisted analysis. At first, only the smooth composure of their Sudanese house servants disconcerted them. They were on the alert, ready to catch them in murderous conspiracy or, at the very least, thieving; Riding, who did the shopping and oversaw the meal preparations, called them devils.

While it was still cool, before the flies and the sand fleas, before their sense of humor went completely sour, they found a great deal that was absurd about Egypt, and in their little house in the suburbs the Trinity began to share a smug intimacy about the "godawfulness" of it all. They found English society there grossly provincial. Robert's half brother Richard, a senior government official, was dismissed by Laura as an upper-class bore. Among the other fixtures they noted were the stuffy civil servants and conceited cavalry officers. T. E. Lawrence imposters sailed around in their tarbooshes. Whatever tourists they observed, dutifully following the guided tours of Thomas Cook, were scoffed at.

The trio did seem to find some virtue in the British presence in

Egypt; Robert "flew the British flag" at the Faculty of Letters to offset the "dirty French intrigue" of the other instructors. The Zaggaran Palace, where the university was located, had been the former boudoir for the khedive's harem. The lecture halls, bedecked with huge mirrors and gilded cornices in a grotesque version of French rococo, represented all that was suspect and pernicious about the French influence in Egypt, as in poetry. There was at least something untainted and dignified, Laura felt, about God and Empire.

Robert's students apparently did not see it that way; and despite his parade-ground bellow, he could not manage to get them to pay attention. Malcolm Muggeridge, who arrived at the university the following year, maintained that half the time many of the students were stoned on hashish. In their tarbooshes and *tuczek*-toed shoes, they slumped in the lecture halls and waved their fly swatters, lost, he said, "in some distant dream of erotic bliss." Robert, after writing POET on the blackboard, caught himself explaining that no, Shakespeare was not another word for Byron. He was not amused; he felt unpleasantly ridiculous. Among those students who were not dreaming there were frequent strikes and riots in support of Egyptian nationalism.

But the more striking aspects of British imperial rule seemed to exist for them only in the form of strict protocols and dress codes, things "not done" (Nancy was dressed down for having her passport made out in her own name) and other ceremonial rituals of bureaucratic appeasement. As for the "Orient," it became an imaginative as much as a colonial territory to be contested with the French. What to make of the exotic stew in which they found themselves?

To the sheltered and almost perfectly ethnocentric imagination of Robert Graves, Cairo had suggested purely a solution to a series of domestic and financial crises. Unlike his close friend T. E. Lawrence, who described the Arabs as "curious" and "disgusting," he was not one to go off on desert rampages. Nor can one imagine him disporting himself in the famed bordellos—more the province of the dirty French, perhaps. While in Egypt he finished a book on obscene language and gave a series of lectures entitled "Impenetrability, or the Proper Habit of English." Most of the time very little was required of him; he had lectures only twice a week.

It was not long before Laura Riding's presence had completely charged the alchemy of his imagination. Cairo was transformed into a city of unbridled sensuality, of bizarreries and grotesqueries, macabre and cruel happenings. It became the ancient land of the Fatal Woman, of Cleopatra, Salomé, Nefertiti and Isis, a land obsessed by secret intrigue and the occult. Here was the Romantic Agony in an unsuspected form; just as the Horrid had been one of Beauty's essential elements, now Terror laid its claim on Love. All that Graves needed was to appropriate this city of many ancient legends, by poetic means, and convert its Oriental allure into something "real"; not the reality of decrepit streets crowded with a parade of Europeanized Arabs, donkeys, beggars, and villagers up from the Nile valley selling vegetables but something more exotic and sinister. In his Egypt poem "Pure Death" love, formerly a domestic refuge from the terror of his war experiences, now exhumed that terror and embraced it. The love that he wrote of was not his love for Nancy Nicholson.

Egypt transformed Laura Riding equally profoundly. Many years later Graves would say that in the early days of their life together "Laura glowed with a kind of light." Polly Antell figured a great deal in her conversations with Robert and Nancy, and Laura considered her a party to the mystery of the trinity of love that now embraced them all. As evidence of the all-embracing power of this affection there was, apart from their writing and Nancy's painting, the dresses that Nancy sewed for her. Laura could dress as she had always wanted because she and Nancy shared almost exactly the same taste. Nancy's husband, in turn, washed her stockings. Together, she and Nancy dressed Robert in finery suitable for presentation at the Egyptian court or to the British high commissioner, making certain that he changed back when he returned so that he would remain their awkward but beloved Robert.

Petulance was encouraged, though only one of them could be cross at any particular moment. Laura found that even her most repulsive and obscene thoughts were stoically heard out and applauded. Robert's tendency to talk too much required monitoring, if somewhat indulgently, by herself and Nancy. Nancy detested men and tended to run away from people more than she and Robert did. But all was acceptable. Dissecting their personalities and exaggerating the uniqueness of their faults enabled them to see where their lives and relationships had gone wrong. Each of their characters was to be completely analyzed, revised, and perfected in the shelter of their marriage to one another. In its imaginative aspect the love that they shared was as complex as the confusion of erotic, aesthetic, and mystical resonances that surrounded them. In its daily, more domestic aspect, it was as simple as a mother's love for a child or the changeable affections between siblings.

In Egypt, too, Riding was making substantial revisions to her early work in order, she wrote, to depict more glamorously their love for one another. From January to March, Graves helped her prepare *The Close Chaplet*, her first book, for publication—copying, revising, rereading and giving advice. Riding noted that he worked even harder than she did on the revisions.

The Close Chaplet took its title and epigraph from "The Nape of the Neck," written by Graves in Egypt and his first love poem for Riding. Later suppressed, this gently seductive work referred intimately not only to the physical consummation of their love but to the deep scars of Riding's unrequited love for Allen Tate, the "hypocrite assassin" figure in the poem. The central conceit is the image of the nape of the neck, the junction of intellect and body:

> To speak of the hollow nape where the close chaplet
> Of thought is bound, the loose-ends lying neat
> In two strands downward, where the shoulders open
> Casual and strong below, waiting their burden,
> And the long spine begins its downward journey:
> The hair curtains this postern silkily,
> This secret stairway by which thought will come
> More personally, with a closer welcome,

In the poem there is no conflict between the intellect and the body: "The tighter bound the chaplet . . . the more sure the tenancy." Such a sensual resolution is surprising, given both the corpus of Graves' work and Riding's; rarely would "the privilege of man and woman" be so sweetly solicited. Physical love was part of the "new meaning" in their marriage of three, though not nearly all.

Graves' poem also answered the fretting uncertainties of a female "you" with healing and protective assurances:

... you say, "to these neck-ribbands
May come one night the hypocrite assassin
With show of love or wisdom thrusting in
And, prompted in the watchword of the day,
Run up and stab and walk unseen away."
But there's no need to use such melodrama,
For each betrayer only can betray
Once and the last effect of violation
Need be no ruin, no grief or contrition
(Despite tradition)
But a clear view: "I was betrayed indeed,
Yet to a strictness and a present need."

It was in Egypt that both Robert and Nancy pledged to adopt and "protect" Laura and she, in turn, to bless them as they blessed her. With all three enthralled and each allowed to test the limits of their intimacy, Laura went very far indeed.

From *The Close Chaplet* it is clear that the love of Robert and Nancy almost immediately let loose a dizzying emotive power and ecstatic abandon in Riding's poetic vision. By the end of March, *The Close Chaplet* was in the mail to Hogarth and to Adelphi; it was dedicated to Nancy and to Isabel. While most of the poems included were pre-1926, there were several very long dramatic monologues in a voice that had not sounded before.

Unlike Graves' work, Riding's poetry had never yet drawn on classical and religious mythology. Her mythologies were suggestive but self-made, such as those of "Lida," "Druida," "The Tillaquils," or "Lucrece and Nara." Her religious invocations tended to be generic rather than learnedly Judeo-Christian; her figures are God, angels, and the devil; and several early poems feature Christ, nuns, and ministers. Even if Riding's formal education had been more extensive, such narrative sources did not serve her imagination in the same way that they served "the legendary mind" of Robert Graves. Where they existed at all, they were a means of exploring the dialogue of good and evil.

The question of good and evil had, until now, devolved almost exclusively on the conflict between sexuality and romantic love. Riding, like Graves, would have found Egypt disconcerting, perceiving a world entirely at odds with such questioning, just as the Trinity had begun to take shape. Like any nineteenth-century missionary, she drew in her skirts from the indeterminate Oriental threat to their souls. But Egypt's strangeness answered designs that, for Riding, were deeper than the call of the British flag or Christian preoccupations with sex. The timber of her Cairo poems was that of revelation and prophecy, as if in the land of Moses the prophecies had to be answered, the seas parted, and the mountain climbed again. In lines like "a great wonder in the streets / Is loosed," there is more than a suggestion of Yeatsian Second Comings.

Graves brought Riding the knotted spiritual questionings that had been the fallout from his abandonment of Christianity in the aftermath of the Great War. Naturally, such torments were likely to be accompanied by Robert's sexual tensions and confusions, but Riding was apt to downplay them. The searching questions, however, concerning scripture, Blake's prophetic books, and the nature of poetic inspiration that Graves had put formerly to T. E. Lawrence, Siegfried Sassoon, and Basanta Mallik were now put to her. Like Oedipus called before the Sphinx to solve her riddle or be slaughtered, his very life seemed to depend on the answers that she could give him. As his "muse" Riding provided not only the answers but, like the Sphinx itself, entirely new and different riddles.

Carrying the appropriate epigraph from Revelations and from Blake, Riding's long apocalyptic monologues formed her answer to Graves and, to a lesser extent, Nancy, who sympathized with Robert's unrest. Significantly, these monologues, quite unlike those poems written in America, are the fiercest and most prolonged poems in the book. In "Samuel's Toast of Death" the prophetic voice is supposed to be that of Samuel Butler, which, swelled by scientific skepticism, answers the civilizations and religions that preceded him with antinomic glee:

[. . .] The witch identifies the Devil
With character. Multiplicity
Slaps God's simple cheek.
Hurrah how the principle of Science stings!
Discover my testament in matter.
I make over my limits

To an infinity of laughter,
For there roars no humor
In the implacable dead-earnest self.
The one Gargantuan topic
After my own heart is Deluge,
Condemning Ararat, Atlantis,
Indestructible Red Indians like pines
Shedding heroism to their shades.
Greatness descends upon me with destruction.

Butler's ruthless wit, lack of sentiment, and appetite for the Goliaths of Victorianism appealed strongly to Riding as to Graves. Even before they met, Riding had written triumphantly witty sonnets in his memory, and Graves had recently completed *The Marmosite's Miscellany*, which dealt with Butler's thought through the mouthpiece of a monkey. Dedicated to Mallik, this long poem expressed Graves' desire to revere God "but not from any pew," to treat all human beings on equal terms, and to consider that when truth comes it might be "clad in the strangest clothing," even the "maunderings" of a "maniac." At one point, early in their stay in Cairo, Robert considered selling the car in order to pay for Mallik's passage to Egypt from India because he was eager for his former teacher to meet Riding. (Without a car the household would have been even more isolated.)

But the last word, it becomes clear in "The Lady of the Apple," would come not from Mallik, a marmoset, Samuel Butler, God, or some rough and slouching beast but from Woman. And it is out of her mouth that "resurrection springs." Richly cadenced, Riding's poem embraced the rhetoric and the spirit of the Grand Style:

At a time of full arrival, when the course
Is rounded forward to a destined birth
Of more than earth and continuity
Of more than sky, song nearly, yet never song
Because it dare not waste the voice required
To cry if more be terrible beyond,
The sluggish female will arise, she will
Depart, as well, when sleep is over and
Love, the blind labor, too. She will receive

As children born of her, yet hitherto
Not looked upon, the many lights of one
Titanic darkness, the untasted fruits
Of an intense Hesperides of night.

This image recalled in part the myth of the Egyptian nature goddess Isis, sister and lover of the murdered Osiris. The body of Osiris, cut in pieces and scattered over the earth by their brother Set, was recovered and restored by Isis' magic so that he might become ruler of the dead. The symbolism of the myth represents Osiris, the sun, overwhelmed by night; to Isis, the eastern sky at dawn, is born Horus, the sun of the new day. The reference is not made explicit, partly because Riding's intentions transcended local goddesses. Contending myths step in throughout the poem, revealing a confusion of Greek, Roman, and Judeo-Christian religious narratives taken up and abandoned in her spinning vision. Under Chaos' veil (daughter to Saturn and Hestia of the hearth) is revealed the Sphinx. In the same stanza

The Lady of the Apple, she will kiss
Their burning cheeks and cool the bronze and bloom.
The Lady of the Apple, she will eat,
She will reclaim Eden of gloom and sun.
Now she remembers. She is home. She knows.

Toward the end of the poem, the speaker addresses Man, his mind reeling with the new lights cast on his myths and legends, in a voice that subsumes and transcends them:

. . .

Cease, legendary mind,
The uncommon sound of truth will shatter truth,
Shock vastness into dust.

Large portions of the Cairo poems would disappear from future collections; some disappeared entirely. It is as if, conceived in the ecstatic temper of their secret marriage of three and in contempt of the Christian conventions that they defied, the poetic voice, in Riding's view, could not survive outside it. By suppressing these voices she renounced them, as one renounces false prophets. The questions would resurface, however, in different forms, partaking of different mythologies, both ancient and self-created, throughout the epic that Graves and Riding were to enact together. In the "Dedicatory Epilogue" to his autobiography, Graves would refer to this as Riding's own, ever mutating "parable."

But it is the opening poem of *The Close Chaplet* that most truly answers Robert Graves in the voice of Laura Riding, stripped of elaborate mystical garb. Addressed to Erato, the muse of lyric or love poetry and "the awakener of desire," it is perhaps the voice of Riding's private sphinx, though the poem was written in America. Unlike the Greek terror on the cliffs above Thebes, no muse knew the answer to her riddles. Unlike the Sphinx at Giza, too, her coy mysteries remained out of reach of explorers, wandering romantics, and Cook's tourists, excavating the well-tilled grounds:

> As well as any other, Erato,
> I can dwell separately on what men know
> In common secrecy,
> And celebrate the old, adoréd rose,
> Retell—oh why—how similarly grows
> The last leaf of the tree.
>
> But for familiar sense what need can be
> Of my most singular survey or me,
> If homage may be done
> (Unless it is agreed we shall not break
> The patent silence for mere singing's sake)
> As well by anyone?
>
> Reject me not, then, if I have begun
> Unwontedly or if I seem to shun
> The close and well-tilled ground:
> For in untraveled soil alone can I
> Unearth the gem or let the mystery lie
> That never must be found.

This poem was not suppressed, though it was altered significantly; the first version appeared in *The Close Chaplet*. In the later version,

Riding moved away from oblique metaphor and closer to the possibility of mystical understanding through language:

> Mistrust me not, then, if I have begun
> Unwontedly and if I seem to shun
> Unstrange and much-told ground:
> For in peculiar earth alone can I
> Construe the word and let the meaning lie
> That rarely may be found.

In a rich "peculiar earth" Riding's poetic gift would thrive.

By the early summer of 1926 the small, squat house at the edge of the desert was their only refuge from the heat and dust. Even the back garden, swarming with mangy cats, was avoided like a haunted place. On the next street an Englishwoman was strangled by a camel driver on the eve of Ramadan. The week before there had been an earthquake—indeed, the whole place seemed to tremble with unaccountable and ominous events, and an atmosphere of semihysteria began to prevail. One day, Laura wrote, she was chased by a ghost; she considered the ubiquitous camels to be evil spirits. Robert joined in and began to suffer from hallucinations. No one could face returning to the university after the summer break; they had had enough.

They finally found third-class tickets on a boat carrying onions to Venice. From there they planned a return to the simple life of the World's End cottage at Islip. But they returned to England followed by "demons," which at least in the imagination of Robert Graves, would pursue them "up and down the land," beyond World's End, driving them both to the precipice at St. Peter's Square less than three years later.

Meanwhile, in the desert, shovels bit deeper and deeper into the sand. The winged monster of Giza, which the Egyptians called *Abu'l-Hawl*, the Lord of Terror, remained massive and blank, yielding nothing.

Chapter 8

NANCY'S LAURA'S ROBERT AND NANCY'S ROBERT'S LAURA

———•———

Cover up,
Oh, quickly cover up
All the new spotted places,
All the unbeautifuls,
The insufficiently beloved.

With what? with what?
With the uncovering of the lovelies,
With the patches that transformed
The more previous corruptions.

Is there no pure then?
The eternal taint wears beauty like a mask.
But a mask eternal.

—"The Mask"

———•———

THE LOCKED TRUNK that Laura left behind in the basement of 43 Morton Street in Greenwich Village contained some old clothes, books, letters, poems, two glass vases, a dressing gown, a cape, an ice bag, linens, and a tablecloth with a blue border and six matching napkins. Laura asked Polly Antell to sell certain items, keep some, and return others to Lou Gottschalk. Her long list of instructions concerning the disposal of these items from her recent past was sent first from Egypt, then from Islip, and then again from Vienna (accompanied by the trunk key). She first asked that the peacock tapestry, the long piece of cretonne, the china, her silver coffee spoons, and the two glass vases be sent to England. Lou could have the long drapes from the Louisville apartment and the trunk itself. The Thomas Cook company could arrange the shipment; the sale of the books, Laura felt, would more than cover the cost. After countless such letters Polly became confused, accusing Laura of sending contradictory instructions. Laura denied it.

Of the books in the trunk, she explained patiently, she wanted the three volumes of Molière (the Larousse edition) but not the Donne, Keats, Shelley, Coleridge, Tennyson, Whitman, Milton, Shakespeare, Byron, Oscar Wilde, the Early and Middle English readers, and the Elizabethan readers. Robert's library of English literature contained those items. Laura also asked Polly to buy some recent poetry anthologies, for a survey of modern poetry that she was working on and for another work tentatively entitled *Anthologies Against Poetry*.

Most important, however, she wanted Polly to burn all the papers in the trunk right there in the basement. If it were anyone else but Polly, Laura said, she would have them sent to England so that she could witness the conflagration herself. Her friend might find this hard and, out of a misguided but well-intentioned desire to protect her from herself, might save the papers. But, Laura insisted, the trunk contained nothing noteworthy, only the worst of her college work, old notes on scraps of paper, and a package the size of a shoe box addressed to her from Allen Tate's editor friend William Cobb who had considered her novel *The Frail Barb* for his publishing house. This contained her letters to Cobb from a regrettable period better forgotten. Later she would ask Polly to see if Allen might return the letters, poetry manuscripts, and typescripts that she had sent him. The thought of them had become a septic sore in her memory. When Polly confessed that she had lost the key to the trunk, Laura anxiously ordered her to break the lock.

By August 1926, within a month of Robert, Laura, and Nancy's return from Egypt, they were settled into World's End and work at Islip, and Laura was confident that all their bad habits were now firmly in hand. Much like the manuscript for *The Close Chaplet*, she had been undergoing extensive revision and now found herself free from what she described as her compulsive habits, her wickedness, and her inbred neuroses. Despite some complications, she was at last a good person, much nicer than ever. Laura attributed this transformation to the unprovisional love of Robert and Nancy.

To Laura, too, it seemed that their exact relations with one another had finally become clear. She and Robert shared a room at the top of the cottage, where they worked on their books. Nancy worked downstairs, lounging happily in her big bed, with a cup of tea and a drawing pad propped against her knees. Though she still suffered from spells of lassitude, Nancy's health had improved in the Egyptian climate. She had begun to paint, design, and draw and was confident that she could support the entire family. They took turns caring for the children and were, Laura explained to Polly, ridiculously happy. Laura's itemizing these domestic developments somehow made them all the more true, rendering the contents of the trunk in the Morton Street basement all the more dispensable.

When Lou Gottschalk caught up with his former wife in midsummer, she was staying in London for a month with Robert. By then Nancy had asked for time alone with the children, and so Laura and Robert decamped, happy for the chance to work uninterrupted. Robert's sister Rosaleen stayed with them for the sake of appearances. When Lou arrived, they went up to Islip for the weekend. Like Allen, Lou had been skeptical that Laura's euphoria could last, but he found her well entrenched. Undaunted, he asked her to remarry him but was refused. After returning to New York he told a college friend that the visit had been "a bust" and that Laura had given him no time alone. Much later, Lou would recall that Laura spoke of her literary collaboration with Robert in a newly minted British accent. When Polly reported Lou's disappointment over his stay, Laura affected surprise and mystification. Inevitably, the presence of her ex-husband disrupted the elaborate three-part harmony that Laura was trying to orchestrate with Robert and Nancy. She was as reluctant to exhume her past life with Lou as the contents of the trunk in the basement of Morton Street.

The first book that Riding and Graves began to write fueled her belief that she was "mending" and "tidying up" not only her personal life and history but also her thinking about modernist poetry in general. In many respects *A Survey of Modernist Poetry* betrayed Riding's desire to make herself at home in the English literary world, often at the expense of the American modernism that had nurtured her. In a telling note, Riding's critical terms derived piquancy from house-keeping, gardening, and child-rearing metaphors; her critical persona was a very severe referee of domestic harmony. Riding's taskmistress sported a decidedly British accent: suspect poetry betrayed itself by "vulgar" or retrograde lapses in taste or "decorum."

Pursuing the homely metaphor in *A Survey of Modernist Poetry*, Riding prescribed permissive parenting as a preventive measure to ensure that the next generation of poets—she included herself among them—would not duplicate the mistakes of the past:

> One no longer tries to keep a child in its place by sup-
> pressing its personality or laughing down its strange ques-
> tions, so that it turns into a rather dull and ineffective
> edition of the parent; and modernist poetry is likewise
> freeing the poem of stringent nursery rules and, instead of
> telling it exactly what to do, is encouraging it to do things,
> even queer things, by itself.

This was, perhaps, Nancy Nicholson's influence on Riding's articulation of the musts and mustn'ts of modernist poetry. For all Riding's diligent officiousness, however, there was something not only auto-biographical but also fantastical and childlike in these neat pronouncements; they have the queenly tone of a precocious yet lonely self-sufficiency, like a child playing house alone.

Ostensibly, Riding and Graves set out in their *Survey* to allay the fears and trepidations of the "plain reader" for whom the difficulties of modernist poetry loomed large. Riding shared the impatience of such readers when it came to the prewar American modernists, not because she did not understand their work but because she understood it all too well. In the *Survey* she was less intent on explicating this poetry than in putting forward a modernist ideal that answered the deficiencies of those writers who had dominated the literary chatter of Greenwich Village. All those who had been on the first boats to Paris and to London after the war must be reminded, Riding informed her readers, of something more fundamental about poetry. Merely "jazzing up [poetry's] programme" by showy experimentation, which was how she viewed their work, was entirely unsatisfactory.

Imagism, for example, was described as "a stunt of commercial advertisers of poetry to whom poetic results meant a popular demand for their work," and likened to an " 'artistic' tea-room where the customer finds himself besieged by orange curtains, Japanese prints, painted furniture, art-china . . . and conversational waitresses in smocks who give the personal touch with a cultured accent." Imagism's combination of a quivering and semimystical atmosphere with *entre nous* Grecophile scholasticism irritated her immensely. Of imagism's high priestess, Hilda Doolittle, Riding wrote, "her immortality came to an end so soon that her bluff was never called."

Similarly, throughout *A Survey of Modernist Poetry*, Riding did not allow herself to express more than guarded appreciation for the poetry of her American contemporaries. Marianne Moore was given no more than a nod. Whatever enthusiasm the book summoned for John Crowe Ransom was probably Graves' contribution. Riding found Ezra Pound, Archibald MacLeish, William Carlos Williams, and Wallace Stevens distinctly wanting or worse. Though she explained thoroughly what these Americans were about for her British readers, she offered only the thinnest pretense of disinterested criticism.

Among the quackeries and "peculiarities" of her American contemporaries was "literary internationalism." There was something delinquent, Riding felt, about the new involvement of her literary compatriots with Chinese poetry. She accused those poets who tarried too long among lowlifes of "literary slumming" (sections of "The Waste Land" and a poem of E. E. Cummings were quoted here). Finally, Riding decried the "abnormal cultivation of the classics," particularly the more remote ones, primed by Pound and Eliot. Poetry would be better off once it had purged itself of these "historical efforts" and entered into a less critically conscious or willfully eccentric stage. Riding, equipped with a British accent and sharing a tidy desk in the London literary neighborhood with Graves, was ready to imagine a new poetry.

PUBLISHED IN NOVEMBER 1927 in London and in New York the following year, *A Survey of Modernist Poetry* had a profound impact on the way poetry was read, written, and written about for over a generation. Inevitably, the book attracted its share of controversy and recrimination as well, particularly in later years. Its two authors initially took pains to describe it as a "word-by-word collaboration," but Riding, the sole author of the concluding chapter (on the work of Gertrude Stein), would later insist that the essential and vital thinking was hers. Graves would make similar claims for himself in the 1960s and reprinted large portions of the book in a collection of his critical works, *The Common Asphodel*.

In two critical works published by Graves in 1926, *Impenetrability; or, The Proper Habit of English* and *Another Future of Poetry*, it is clear that Riding's influence had already begun to show, long before they embarked on *A Survey of Modernist Poetry*. Both books are dedicated to Riding, quote from her work, and betray her particular prejudices, including her assertion that English was the language best suited to poetry. This was a comfortable enough bias for Graves, who had been happy to ignore the experiments of the "Franco-Americans." Here, too, was her 1923 conviction that the poetry of the past had been admired for the wrong reasons—"the elegance of the story it told, or the morality of its sentiments, or the divine character it professed"—rather than for the experience of heightened sensibility and excited intelligence. The New Romantic also appears center stage in both of Graves' books, with generous quotations from her "A Prophecy or a Plea": "The poet, the human impulse, is the only premise. He is the potter. He is the maker of beauty, since all form originates in him, and all meaning, since he names the content." Graves' own prose lacked Riding's breathless quality, and he substantiated his reasoning from a fund of scholarly and anecdotal asides, but all the ideas of "A Prophecy or a Plea" were there.

Though Graves had often written about his Georgian contemporaries and fellow war poets, it is important to note that before 1926 he had found nothing whatsoever to say about any of the prewar modernists, American or English. In 1922 Graves published his first book of criticism, *On English Poetry;* and three years later his master's thesis from Oxford, *Poetic Unreason and Other Studies*, appeared as an expansion of the earlier book. In these studies Graves had speculated on the existence of subliminal levels of meaning in a poem and on the problem of unresolved conflicts in poetic composition—a bastardized Freudian approach appropriated from the errant psychologist-anthropologist W. H. R. Rivers. Sassoon noted in his diary that after meeting Rivers, Graves began reading conflict interpretation into just about everything—first and foremost his own life and work.

As a result, *Poetic Unreason* abounds with anecdotes in which Graves describes the mental state underlying his composition of particular poems. Becoming both analyst and analysand, Graves could find in the ingenious feints of his own mind a useful model and method for literary criticism. Poems, like dreams, might be analyzed to show both a "manifest" and a "latent" content. One could indeed get to the bottom of private and poetic difficulty by a correct interpretation of the conflict at work. Not only was this therapeutic, it was also compulsory: the poet was obliged to dig up and resolve these conflicts before the reader got to them. With such precautions the poet could cleverly countermine a curious reader's probings of the poet's "unwitting" self. The trail was well lit for future biographers to take note.

There was an undoubted satisfaction for Graves in attributing his terrors, which trench warfare had only disinterred, to the primal psychodramas of childhood. The completed puzzles that he displayed to his readers have a pleasing, storylike neatness about them, and in poetry, he felt, they found their purest expression. His major worry was not imagism or vorticism, symbolism or surrealism, but, rather, a more private one: if he resolved all his conflicts he might stop writing poetry. This anxiety was followed by the fear that he was prolonging his personal difficulties in order to protect his poetry. Such were his aesthetic concerns in 1925.

Significantly, before Graves met Riding he had found the psychology of "poetesses" a subject "too thorny" to undertake, though he remained optimistic that psychoanalysis would provide the required insight once the key to the symbolism of women's dreams was discovered. In Egypt and Islip, Riding would firmly disabuse Graves of this faith. With the plain reader at his side Graves would learn that it is "always the poets who are the real psychologists."

In Riding's view the modernist poet must break down "antiquated literary definitions" of emotion as well as newfangled pseudo-Freudian ones; this was the difficulty of attempting to synthesize a new system of poetic values along modernist lines. Ignored or obscure mental processes, Riding maintained, however, "freakish," required a new vocabulary. Poets did not articulate " 'things often felt but ne'er so well expressed' "; rather, as mystical vehicles of a contemporary and collective time sense, it was their role to "discover what it is we are really feeling." Riding's language was abstract and riddled with both secular and religious jargon, but her insistence upon the poet's role as intermediary between his time and universal truths was unyielding. Here, in 1926, were her deepest expectations for poetry. Graves promptly hopped up to share them.

Ironically, for the method if not always the terms of her proof of a true poetry's requirements, she exported to England the Fugitives' attempt at a positivistic approach to poetic structure and meaning. She was probably assisted in this effort by T. E. Hulme, a poet and critic much championed by Ezra Pound, who was killed in the trenches of Flanders. Riding had read his work while she was still in America, probably at Tate's suggestion. But it was Tate's concentrated analysis of her poetry that had first given her an analytic discourse, not unlike those that emerged in the Franks' parlor in Nashville.

Yet Riding focused on entirely different issues than those which absorbed the Fugitives; she rejected the need for an overarching theme or reference to a moral or mythic structure—Tate's bailiwick. In *A Pamphlet Against Anthologies*, which she and Graves were writing at the same time as the *Survey*, Riding also dismissed Ransom's longing for a poetic craft or formal metrical structure. Riding defined her poetic imperative as a sense beyond mere prose logic, containing an a priori integrity of meaning:

> Poetry must stim in all directions, every metaphor must be alive and reconciled to its neighbors; analogies must work out precisely; its events must have so complete an interdependence that a single idle word would spoil the cohesion of a poem. Poets unable to make everything "stim" conceal their shortcomings in a facile artistry. Indeed a clearly metrified poem is scarcely asked to stim even in any elementary prose sense, let alone in a poetic sense.

A "clearly metrified poem" (Ransom's miracle of harmony) on close analysis, she found, was likely to betray a suspect prose logic. Riding and Graves provided generous examples of such logical absurdities in anthology favorites like Yeats' "Lake Isle of Innisfree." This method of searching out logical fallacies would also form the basis of her criticism of Edgar Allan Poe's poetry and fiction.

By the time Riding came to write *A Survey of Modernist Poetry* the existence of an intuited "poetic sense" became the insistent cornerstone of her thought. Unlike prose sense, however, the existence of this poetic sense was not subject to easy proof. Chapter 3 of *A Survey of Modernist Poetry* contained a now fabled eighteen-page analysis of Shakespeare's Sonnet 129, "Th' expense of spirit in a waste of shame," in which Riding and Graves purported to show the workings of this a priori "poetic sense."

Almost Talmudic in complexity, the elucidation of the sonnet in its unpunctuated version (the original 1609 Quarto) was intended to demonstrate how the poetic sense of the original text had become corrupted by the eighteenth-century imposition of punctuation and standardized spellings. In this exercise, as in a poem of E. E. Cummings' that was also considered, the work is treated as wholly autonomous and self-referential, dislodged from its historical context. In their insistence that poetry be read for "the reasons of poetry" Graves and Riding argued that literary discourse was privileged, set above other forms of discourse such as philosophy or history. In retrospect, many critics saw their dissection of the sonnet as marking an entirely new threshold in literary criticism. The argument over who crossed it first lent further credence to its significance.

In a letter written to a Cambridge don in January 1934 accusing him of a "certain donnish anti-woman bias" Robert Graves explained how the exposition evolved:

> I certainly remember that you and I talked about the Sonnets at Litherland, but only about the story of the Sonnets: it is simply untrue that I ever made any such analysis of any particular sonnet. I could not have done so, because it was Laura Riding who originated this exegetic method. We chose the Sonnet . . . because we wanted a "good" poem to work on that was at the same time a

familiar one and presumably intelligible to a plain reader.
We worked the whole thing out together at great labour
and in pursuance of LR's idea, in the Spring of 1926.

In 1966 Graves modified his memory of their collaboration and
claimed responsibility for most of the detailed examinations of the
poems, in particular showing the complex structures of meaning of
Sonnet 129 in its "original" form. While he credited Riding for
originating the general principles quoted, he implies that all of the
work was his. After appending a busy listing of Riding's qualities as a
poet of the 1920s and 1930s, he mentioned her subsequent history as
the wife of an "American farmer" in a gratuitous sideswipe.

The question of authorship first arose when the exegesis of Sonnet
129 was happened upon by another young critic. William Empson
was a Cambridge undergraduate studying poetry with the eminent
critic I. A. Richards when the *Survey* appeared. Rather than having
revealed the one most resonant meaning of the sonnet, its "manifold
precision," the authors had provided him with an analytic method
that—to the contrary—showed that all poetry was ambiguous. The
responsibility to establish a poem's various meanings now devolved
on the critic. Being an aspiring mathematician, Empson set out to
prove that there were, in fact, exactly seven varieties of linguistic
ambiguity.

The appearance in 1930 of *Seven Types of Ambiguity* by an unknown
man of twenty-four was, according to Stanley Edgar Hyman, a historian of modern literary criticism, a major critical event. "The book
dared to treat what had always been regarded as a deficiency of poetry,
imprecision of meaning, as poetry's chief virtue." Out of this debate
grew the theories of the New Criticism and the eclipse of the romantic
idea of the poet inspired by his muse, his religious devotion, his
mistress, his insanity, or as in latter days, his Oedipus complex. The
more nimble cleverness of the critic stood in his stead. In his third year
Empson switched from math to "lit," and what Randall Jarrell later
dubbed "the age of criticism" was off to a flying start.

Empson's preface acknowledged Graves' Shakespearean dissection
as his springboard but made no mention of his coauthor. In a letter to
the book's publishers, Riding said that she had found Empson's defense of this omission—"I had not the book by me and forgot it was a

collaboration"—"pretty thick." Empson improved on this. An er-
ratum slip appeared in the second printing, but in the meantime
Empson decided that what had touched him off on the issue of
ambiguity was actually an earlier work of Graves' "not collaborating
with anyone." He described Riding's fuss as an "irrelevant difficulty,"
even though I. A. Richards distinctly remembered the methodical
dissection of the sonnet as Empson's impetus. In the 1947 revised
edition of *Seven Types* Empson wrote, "I ought to say in passing that
[Graves] is, so far as I know, the inventor of the method of analysis I
am using here." When Graves took credit for most of the work in
1966, Empson wrote triumphantly to Laura Jackson that Graves had
finally "admitted" that he was indeed responsible for the Shakespearean analysis. Empson added that she might quote him as having
dismissed her part in the book, having attributed her authorship to a
gift of Graves' gallantry.

Though the term New Criticism would not gain wide currency
until the early 1940s, when John Crowe Ransom published *The New
Criticism*, the school was many years in the making. Among its eventual
adherents (though some chafed at the label) were I. A. Richards, T. S.
Eliot, William Empson, Yvor Winters, Cleanth Brooks, Robert Penn
Warren, Allen Tate, R. P. Blackmur, and in some respects F. R. Leavis.
During the three decades in which the New Critics held mandarin
authority over the academic teaching of poetry, all these critics had
time to distinguish their own brand of New Criticism from the previous one. Almost all of them, however, insisted on close readings of
the text, an alertness to the verbal nuances and etymologies of every
word, a poem's thematic strategies, and its allegiance to or divergence
from the English metrical line; they were less interested in the poet's
professed ideas about his poems, his love life, his childhood unhap-
pinesses, his political views, or his social conscience. The method was
designed to articulate the "cerebrations" of what was a notoriously
"slippery quid enterprise": poetic composition.

Poetic theories come and go. However fervently Riding insisted
that it should be otherwise, the problems of language and meaning
are continuously redefined rather than at any time resolved; analogy
is not algebra and can never be worked out "precisely." When Empson's book was published, his exhaustive analytical approach rang
some bells back in Nashville. Eleven years later Ransom, who had

written to Robert Graves in 1925 that the most parlous poetry was "poetry on-the-way-to-becoming science," responded with the first American treatment of these issues in *The New Criticism*. In 1938 Warren and Brooks published *Understanding Poetry*, the textbook anthology that guided a generation of English literature majors through the intricacies of poetry according to the New Critics. Brooks, in a 1971 letter to Laura Jackson, acknowledged the influence that his early reading of *A Survey of Modernist Poetry* had exerted on his critical thinking, adding that he did not read Empson's book until some time later. The trails of intellectual influence are doubtless as tortuous as those of poetry. Clearly, however, Riding provided a crucial link between Nashville and Cambridge, a link that both Graves and Empson were loathe to credit her for, even forty years later.

Riding felt justly vexed for not being properly acknowledged in Empson's book, but she was enraged at the prostitution of her "poetic sense" in academic exercises that she felt had nothing to do with the search for absolute truth and universal values:

> The quids resolved to predicate,
> To dissipate in a little grammar.

Nonetheless, the New Criticism was immensely influential among poets as well as academics. The work of John Berryman, Robert Lowell, and Sylvia Plath among others demonstrated how a heightened awareness of language's elasticity (and the expansive idea of the self that accompanied it) could extend the range of their poetic language. "Ambiguity" and "indeterminancy" remain the language of a critic; a poet would be more likely to insist, as Riding did, on the existence of congruent meanings or "manifold precision."

The embrace and wide impact of such a theory of language also suggests that the assumptions that informed earlier usages, poetic vernaculars, and metrical forms had been undermined. The old catchwords and constructions—Coleridge's "organic form," Hopkins' "sprung rhythm," and Ransom's "miracle of harmony"—were passé. The long list of poets who later subscribed to the depersonalized theorems of the New Critics had, in some way, abdicated the poet's authority and privilege to blindly intuit the secret forms and miracles of poetry. But while their confidence in the "mystical core" of poetry may have been shattered—by "The Waste Land" or the war or something else—Riding's was not.

Meanwhile, Riding was anxious to tell just what made the truth of poetry—its "poetic sense"—so unarguably immutable; only her language and guiding metaphor remained to be found. The source of her wisdom would not come from learned authors. She would not spend time elucidating the historical etymologies of individual words, the workings of English prosody, or the differences between the romantic and classical traditions. For this reason, if not for the cheek of her presumption, she earned the contempt of those who later made such profitable use of her Promethean fire.

––––⟨∞⟩––––

But no sooner had Riding rested on the subject of modern poetry than Robert's parents demanded an exegesis of "Nancy's Laura's Robert and Nancy's Robert's Laura." Riding's alertness about human character and relations involved as many precise and exhaustive calculations as did her thinking about Sonnet 129. The bliss that had accompanied their return to Islip, the beginnings of the close working partnership with Graves, and publishing contracts from Heinemann for her first two books of criticism clearly fired Riding's confidence and conviction that she was living the poet's life that she had called for in "A Prophecy and a Plea." Just as Donne really lived in his coffin, so Riding was compelled to give living substance to her conviction that through the life of the poet, the age verified the ideal. Unlike Donne, however, who slept alone in his coffin, Nancy Nicholson and Robert Graves were integral aspects of Riding's poetic cosmogony.

If all felt well from within, Laura observed to Polly, then difficulties soon appeared from without. The bedeviling difficulty of what other people might think of their domestic arrangements had reared its curious and inevitably "vulgar" head. ("Vulgar" appeared constantly in both Riding's and Graves' correspondence, critical work, and doubtless their conversation as well. To understand the way in which something or someone is "vulgar" is one of the more difficult tasks of understanding both writers.) In the "contemporaneous universe" of New York, Laura expected Polly to stanch any loose talk and to know that what they were doing together was right. Laura was reluctant to be discreet, as it suggested a degree of waffling; she felt obliged to think first of the triangular integrity of her relations with Robert and Nancy and what they owed each other. Discretion, she wrote Polly, she regarded on the level of a minor practicality.

The more immediate concern of Robert's family was not the appearance of impropriety at Islip but the appalling news that Robert had given up his job in Egypt. He had led his parents to believe that he was returning only for the summer break. When they learned from his sister Rosaleen that he had resigned, they were aghast that he had broken his contract and given up a well paying job with no prospect of another. Their consternation roiled the Islip cottage, subsiding only briefly when Robert pointed out the dangers of Egypt's climate to the children's health. Sam, it appeared, had been neglected in the isolation ward during his bout of measles and had returned partially deaf in both ears. Still, a grumbling chorus of Robert's siblings and half siblings suggested that the resignation was Laura's doing.

"The Vienna idea," a plan for Laura and Robert to move to Vienna in late September 1926 so that they might complete their two collaborative works, posed a greater threat to the niceties of appearances. They planned to stay there at least until the following summer, when Nancy and the children would join them, returning to England only for the Christmas holidays. Laura wrote to Polly before they left that she was on the verge of collapse; of the three she suffered most from the strain of others' failure to appreciate the significance of their marriage triangle. On the trip to Vienna she intended to make a conscientious effort to get well. As for Robert, he needed a tax dodge for his Egyptian earnings and so, with a furtive glance in the direction of APG and Amy, he announced that Nancy had given her "consent" to Miss Gottschalk's accompanying him to Vienna.

Robert's mother, Amalia Elizabeth Sophie von Ranke, was known to her brother and sisters as the *Polizeidiener*, the little policeman; she recalled the nickname fondly when she came to write her memoirs. She was the first to admit that she was not, like her wayward son and devoted husband, a writer, but it was her simple hope that the story of her exemplary life might serve as a model for her grandchildren and their descendants. The text has the saccharine quality peculiar to uplifting homilies, with abundant examples of the gentle virtues of family love, duty, and self-sacrifice. The ironclad rectitude that bound such virtues so firmly together must be inferred.

An unusually pious little girl, Amy's face had flushed with pleasure when, on returning from her confirmation into the Christian faith, she beheld the beautifully bound Bible that was her confirmation gift. While still a young girl she taught Sunday school and made sure that each child understood how pointless it was to hide from God who, like some *Polizei* in the sky, knew exactly what each and every one of them was thinking. Her own children (particularly the impressionable Robert) might thus have found it difficult to distinguish divine directives from those of Amalia von Ranke Graves. Her admonitions and exhortations were always prefaced with the words, "Children, I command you, as your mother . . . ."

Entirely unknown to Amy, her son had since appointed a new confessor. As he put it in "The Taint," written at the time, he had already begun to unwind "the early swaddlings of his mind":

> Agree, it is better to confess
> The occasion of my rottenness
> Than in desperation try
> To cloak, dismiss, or justify
> The inward taint: of which I knew
> Not much until I came to you
> And saw it then, furred on the bone,
> With as much horror as your own.

Horror, perhaps; morbid fascination as well. Within a year, Riding's dissection of his inward taints had largely replaced the call of Graves' conscience. Nancy had no doubt tired of the watch. In fact Graves was willing to bare his taints to anyone, though he tended to prefer women or, in the case of T. E. Lawrence and Siegfried Sassoon, men who were not heterosexual.

At least in the first year of the ménage, the role of Robert's confessor had no small appeal for Laura; but for her, too, the power of the "wonderful trinity" lay in the pivotal role played by Nancy. She needed Nancy's "consent" in a much larger sense than just permission to go to Vienna with Robert, and throughout most of 1926 she was Nancy's Laura as much as Robert's Laura. She, too, felt oppressed by what she termed "the eternal taint" in her poem "Mask," finding in Nancy's tonic severity an echo of her own effort to punish and forgive herself for the sins that accrue to a woman divided by her art. With Nancy she could be the petted and always forgiven younger sister, as well as a poet who spoke with authority as a woman. In this way she not only circumvented the accusations of a society in which she had no legitimate place; she also excised whatever it was about herself that she found intolerable—the "gangrenous spot," or what she described as the monstrous obscenities of her mind. Provided by Nancy with a trousseau of suitable clothes for the trip abroad, Laura even wore her portrait on a chain around her neck.

Robert, in turn, sought Sassoon's approval for the "Vienna idea," dropping by the day before their departure to tell him about it. Not finding him in, Robert left a skittish note, strained in its effort to sound offhand:

> What we came to tell you was quite casually that we are going off together to Austria for a bit: unconventional but necessary and Nancy's idea. She finds that now she's well she can't bring herself to resume the responsibility of the house unless we aren't there to force it on her: and that she can't begin to draw again unless she's alone, and she is longing to draw. We find in our turn that we can't get on with our work unless we have her equally busy. So . . . damned to scandal. . . . We are all very happy about it, though we'll miss each other very much of course, and especially we'll miss the children. Funny life, ain't it?

Robert asked for a copy of one of Sassoon's poems, which they wanted to praise in the book they were working on. Not knowing what Robert expected him to say, Sassoon found it a difficult letter to answer.

Robert's parents, on the other hand, had a ready response to the Vienna idea. They sent a telegram to Islip, insisting that Nancy come speak with them. She responded with reassuring pooh-poohs and the information that Robert and Miss Gottschalk had already left. Still, a showdown with those bastions of Christian righteousness and respectability was inevitable, and perhaps Laura even welcomed it when it came. On October 17, 1926, in the congenial setting of the Bad Hofgastein, to which APG and Amy had repaired to take the waters, Laura was received into Robert's family. The week before, APG wrote in his diary of a "really wonderful letter from Robert about the strange Trinity of friendship and love" that bound his son to his wife and Miss Gottschalk. Touched by this appeal, APG agreed to their coming to Hofgastein for a three-day visit. John Graves, Robert's censorious younger brother, later said that there were "long poetical discussions" at the spa "but no mention of the ménage à trois."

On John Graves' death, his son, Richard Perceval Graves, was left an unfinished manuscript entitled "My Brother Robert" and a vast archive of family correspondence. These letters between Graves' siblings, their regular reports to Amy and APG and to each other on their younger brother's various household arrangements cast an often revealing light on Robert Graves' family. Rosaleen, in an early report to her parents, wrote that "Laura and Robert are still quite innocent." More darkly, her half brother described Riding as a "racial disease," a judgment shared by Robert's brother John, who referred to Laura as "the Jewess." Richard Perceval Graves poses the possibility that Laura, a "ruthless manipulator," might have been "intrinsically evil" but sensibly rejects it. Still, his biography makes clear, however inadvertently, that if Graves had wanted to wrest himself from these affectionate family ties, he would have to make a much greater effort than he had already.

In fact, the ménage à trois was discussed at Hofgastein, and as Laura reported to Polly, it seemed that both APG and Amy understood the meaning of the Trinity up to a certain point—but did not venture beyond the idealized and Platonic terms provided by herself and Robert. While Graves might write T. S. Eliot that he had now "come to the point of always saying exactly what I mean in matters concerning poetry," other matters required some hedging. For Robert's parents to learn of the sexual dimension of the triangle would have caused them too much pain, Laura wrote to Polly, than was practical. As far as she was concerned, the physical aspect of her relationship to Robert (and perhaps to Nancy as well, though the period of their intimacy would have been brief) was certainly a significant aspect of the ménage. But in the rhetoric in which Laura enshrouded herself and the "marriage of three" sex did not figure as overtly as it did in the writings of other contemporary literary figures.

That APG and Amy's sympathy reached even this far, however, Laura considered a great and blessed victory. To her their understanding embraced the essential ideals that the Trinity had come to represent. Like Robert's mother, Laura always believed that moral conviction required exemplary behavior to embody its truths, to fulfill what it is owed. It was in this capacity that Laura presented herself at Hofgastein. Recognizing a kind of kindred spirit, Amy noted Miss Gottschalk's firm but affectionate hand with Robert and the fervor with which they both discussed their work together. She received Laura warmly.

After Hofgastein, Riding realized that the "contemporaneous universe" was not nearly as far behind them and their work as poets as she had at first believed. The excitement of such a discovery led her even further afield in her thinking about poetry. She began her first book of criticism in Vienna, entitling it *Contemporaries and Snobs*. If certain literary friends of Graves', particularly those who wrote poetry, deplored what seemed to be happening to his marriage, and failed to see the astonishing significance of their lives together, it would be shown that they were insufficiently modernist or poetic— or both. No one, it seems, would be able to summon an authoritative response to that—not even the *Polizeidiener*.

At times, however, it was apparent to all three that their marriage involved the deception of Robert's parents in the interest of maintaining peace. The Islip house belonged to Amy, and it was to her that they sometimes paid rent, and from her that they gratefully received allowances for the children. Though Robert might ignore such minor expediencies, Laura was not at peace with them, and her efforts to resolve their apparent hypocrisies inevitably found their way into her work. Her writing was proceeding rapidly, and by the end of 1926 she had finished her two collaborations with Graves and had written 40,000 words of *Contemporaries and Snobs*.

By then, too, Laura had received a note from Lou saying that he would like the Louisville drapes after all and that he was engaged to be married. From Isabel, who had seen him, she learned that Lou was afraid that he might be bored in his second marriage. After asking

Polly to send the drapes to Lou, Laura confessed that she had little affection or thoughts to spare for her former husband and would be grateful never to see him again. She never did. Everything else in the trunk had become a horror to her. The glass vases were the only thing she treasured from her old life, and perhaps Polly might bring them when she came to visit. Her clothes should be given away; she wanted nothing but the Molière and to hear that all the papers had been burned.

Before her first year with Robert Graves and Nancy Nicholson was out, Laura Riding Gottschalk had transformed herself; she was no longer Ransom's lowly born "little woman," with a "Polish" accent and no "place, reputation or friends." In the shelter of World's End, and in the "strange Trinity of friendship and love," she was ready to take on the name that had been hovering over her since she left her father's house. Polly was the first to be informed. Miss Laura Riding Gottschalk had now become—simply but emphatically—Laura Riding.

Chapter 9

ANARCHISM IS NOT ENOUGH

———— • ————

Before that in all the periods before things had been said been known been described been sung about been fought about been destroyed been denied been imprisoned been lost but never been explained. So then they began to explain. And we may say that they have been explaining ever since.

> —Gertrude Stein, "What Is English Literature?"

———— • ————

IN THE SPRING of 1927, two years before her suicide attempt, Laura Riding stood alone in the top-floor room of the new apartment in Hammersmith. Nancy was living on a farm in the Cumberland countryside with the children; Robert was out doing errands. Looking out the front window toward the green enclosure of St. Peter's Square, Laura was gripped by a sense that her life had become nearly unbearable, an apprehension captured in "In Nineteen Twenty-Seven":

> In nineteen twenty-seven, in the spring
> And opening summer, cheap imagination
> Swelled the dollish smile of people.
> City air was pastoral
> With teeming newspapers and streets.
> Behind plate-glass the slant deceptive

Of footwear and bright foreign affairs
Dispelled from consciousness those bunions
By which feet walk and nations farce
(O crippled government of leather).
And for a season—night-flies dust the evening—
Deformed necessity had a greening.

In a private letter written many years later, Laura Jackson recalled how furious she had been with Robert that day—not quarrelsomely so, she was quick to point out, but precisely and critically so. She had forgotten what characteristic behavior incited her anger; she remembered only the extremity of her unhappiness with him and her life that spring.

Laura's unhappiness had begun with the breakup of the Trinity. By February 1927, within a month of their return from Vienna, the clarity of the Trinity and the domestic tranquillity of World's End were lost. In March the skies clouded over, bringing downpours, and influenza struck the whole family. As floods rose to the front door, Robert realized that he was again on the brink of financial ruin. The two books that he and Laura had finished in Vienna would not provide medicine for the children or enlarge the cottage with a much-needed addition. William Nicholson, balking at the ménage à trois, had withdrawn his daughter's allowance. "It seems a pity," he had remarked, "that now the Turks have abandoned polygamy, Robert should have decided to take it up." As a last resort, Laura moved in with friends in Norfolk so that Robert might approach his father-in-law for funds. But Nancy's flu was followed by jaundice; and the children's nurse, who suffered from heart trouble, left the cottage on doctor's orders. In mid-March, Nancy had a nervous collapse and, as soon as she had regained enough strength, abandoned her husband and children to escape to her brother's house in Cumberland.

Deeply shocked and feverish with flu, Robert sent immediately for Laura, who returned from Norfolk to set the house in order. Amy felt that she behaved "splendidly" in the crisis, while Nancy proved gravely irresponsible. Laura made it clear that her presence at World's End was a temporary solution; Nancy would return as soon as she recovered. Instead, Nancy found a job on a farm and sent for the children. By May 1927, Laura and Robert, now living openly to-

)

gether but still insistent on their "innocence," rented out the Islip cottage and moved to London. The Trinity had existed as a practical day-to-day living arrangement for little more than twelve months.

In the aftermath of Nancy's abandonment, Robert left everything to Laura to sort out, and she assumed the responsibility with resolve, efficiency, and alacrity. She found the Hammersmith apartment, which was better than the basement apartment in Ladbroke Square that they had shared with Rosaleen after returning from Egypt. But, despite their new quarters and the prospect of time alone for serious work, Laura found herself enraged and frustrated by Robert's incompetence in managing his life and emotions. As she later recalled, all the despair of the last few months collapsed on her as she stood at the window above St. Peter's Square.

"In Nineteen Twenty-Seven" circled around this fierce unhappiness, "that unteaches ecstasy and fear," alerting the reader to the dark debate at the "fatal sill":

> Then, where was I, of this time and my own
> A double ripeness, a twice-dated festival?
> Fresh year of time, my youth,
> Late year of my age, renounced desire—
> Ill mated pair, this gaudy vantage
> Looks on death, it is a window
> Not worth leaping out of.

In her real life that spring, Laura gazed out that same window, furious with Robert. But suddenly, becoming aware of the intensity of her emotions and sensing that he was in immediate danger from them, she abruptly wrenched her anger back. At that same moment a crash sounded in the street below; looking down, she saw Robert, grinning and making his way to the pavement. The driver of a baker's cart had veered sharply in order to avoid a collision with him as he began crossing the street. In recounting this strange incident almost forty years later in an attempt to explain the poem, Laura Jackson beseeched a perplexed correspondent not to be frightened or to conclude that she had magic powers. Still, she did allow that it was a mysterious affair.

"In Nineteen Twenty-Seven" is minutely complex and not as bio-graphically explicit as Laura Jackson later feared it to be. But the rea-soning and arrangement of its imagery and argument reveal that the stage was being set for Riding's suicide attempt. Central to the poem is the image of the twin hearts, the "double ripeness" of Laura Riding's life that spring. In the imagined chasm dividing this "ill-mated pair"—she referred to them as her adopted British heart and its "cousin in time," her fresh and youthful American heart—was the precise measurement of her unquiet where "deformed necessity had a greening."

The poem proceeds on the imagery of couplings riven by discord. Among them are the "I" divided by her two hearts and the "we" of the ill-paired lovers. These pairs are also divided by differing perceptions of time; at the window, where she stands, time is stopped; outside there continues the ticking of an insensible world. These anachronis-tic pairings are echoed in the quickening footsteps, the "crippled government of leather," that march throughout the poem.

With a poetic sleight of hand, the poem maneuvers the uneasy couples in an intricate dance; through the grace of metaphor, part-ners are exchanged. The blazing unhappiness that begins in the bifurcation of the speaker's heart discovers its correlative in an argu-ment between lovers. Just as Riding sought to define her love for Graves in all its perplexity, the "I" debates "you" in sensuous and dialectical rhythm:

> And this is both love and not love,
> And what I pledge both true and not true,
> Since I am moved to speak by the season,
> Happy and unhappy speed and recession,
> Climax and suspension.

Throughout, Riding creates a sense of precarious tension, orches-trated from the "gaudy vantage" of her high window. Equally, her notion of self expands to encompass multiple realities in time and space; the speaker is both inside and outside the window, inside and outside history.

Laura Jackson connected her composition of this poem to Robert's close escape from death in traffic and, in doing so, suggested that her omniscience as a poet might extend beyond the page and into the world that she felt and described. Her rage with Robert, she insisted, was not personal and arbitrary but "critical." Through the poem's intricate suppression and expression of this rage and the love that accompanied it, Riding felt that she commanded an intimacy with and control of not only her own fate at a high window but Robert Graves' as well.

EVEN BEFORE LAURA and Robert went off to Vienna, Nancy had begun to be "bloody." She directed outbursts of irritation and anger at her husband, Laura, and herself; she pleaded with Laura to return to America. In a letter to Carolyn Tate, Laura mentioned Nancy's nerves and need for a quiet place to paint, wondering if Carolyn might know of a nice house somewhere in America. Donald Davidson also learned from Laura that Nancy was not well and needed to be alone for her nerves. Alone, however, did not mean without the children.

The Vienna plan was their solution to besetting tensions, and in the four months that Robert and Laura were away, Nancy and the children had thrived. Nancy began working on cretonne and chintz designs, and upon their return they found the Islip cottage "as neat as a new pin." But after the crisis of illness and financial worry in the early spring, the bonds of the "strange trinity of friendship and love" were less frequently those of untrammeled affection. When Nancy moved to Cumberland, and Laura and Robert decamped to London, the bonds became more imaginative than real.

Accompanying the breakup of the Trinity was Laura and Robert's growing sense of their increasing isolation. From Vienna, Laura had sent Donald Davidson a long list of the official reasons why she and Robert were there alone together. In doing so she imagined that she was forestalling the arrival in Nashville of the literary gossip that had already become rampant in London and New York. To another, she likened the anonymous hostility that she felt from every corner to a black magic spell, aimed at making her unwell; the view of her as an outsider, determined to break up Robert and Nancy's marriage, was the real cause of her collapse. Robert begged Siegfried Sassoon to visit them in Hammersmith as soon as he could bear it. "[W]e are apt to anticipate insults never intended. But I know that your nerves are as bad as ours and that your heart is true; so shall draw no wrong inferences whatever you do about me."

But apart from Robert's siblings, it is hard to determine just who was raising the hue and cry. Whatever their private misgivings about Graves' affair with Riding, T. E. Lawrence, Edward Marsh, and E. M. Forster were unfailingly neutral. Sassoon was lying low. It was no cause for wonder if William Nicholson, not exactly conventional in these matters, withheld his blessings. In fact, whatever gossip went flying around London, New York, or Nashville got its wings from Riding's own long letters to Tate, Davidson, and Ransom rationalizing her behavior.

Graves, equally quick to imagine a conspiracy against them, seems to have been spoiling for a more direct confrontation for some time. His parents had proved themselves rather disappointing as adversaries; when he announced in Hofgastein that Miss Gottschalk was a "Jewess," Amy, seeing Laura pale, embraced her. For a while Graves' combative gestures against the establishment narrowed down to paper scrimmages with writers and publishers. One visitor to the Hammersmith apartment, the writer and publisher Jack Lindsay, described him spinning "elaborate plots to trip [his publishers] up and get them technically in the wrong on some point or another." Soon, he said, the anger and crusade for truth and independence became "a crusade for Laura." In contrast to Graves' squabblings with editors and writers, Lindsay found "a fresh rambunctious element about his proceedings. . . ." Riding became Graves' gauntlet, and in the process her own hypersensitivity to public excoriation was greatly excited.

In this atmosphere of brewing righteousness, *The Close Chaplet* was reviewed in the August 1927 issue of the *Criterion*. "The practiced reader can readily distinguish the derivation of her manner," John Gould Fletcher wrote offhandedly; "her poems of detached and exhaustive comment . . . owe nearly everything to Miss Marianne Moore; her more serious poems . . . come from Mr. Ransom or Mr. Graves; and her more lyrical outbursts recall just as persistently Miss Gertrude Stein." Graves responded chivalrously in a letter of protest, putting straight just who influenced whom as far as Riding was concerned. T. S. Eliot, editor of the *Criterion*, asked Graves if he was sure that he wanted the letter printed, which prompted further ink-slinging. The result was the souring of Graves' personal and professional relationship with Eliot.

A month later Riding wrote heatedly to Donald Davidson about his review of her book. Having only recently thanked him for his loyal praise, Riding had changed her opinion in the aftermath of the *Criterion* skirmish. She dressed him down, demanding to know whether it was a southern or a masculine timorousness that obliged him to refrain from comparing her work with that of her male contemporaries. Davidson, it seems, had found no other poets to compare Riding with but Sara Teasdale and, "after a woman's fashion," Edna St. Vincent Millay. Davidson addressed his reply to "The Better Self of Laura Riding": "May I beg leave to disregard the enclosed unpleasant note, as coming from your Worst Self?" Riding responded by owning up to both her "Worst Self" and her "Best Self." Returning his letter, she asked whether it might have been easier and more gentlemanly to own up to his bias against women's writing.

Apparently Davidson could not and, like most of his contemporaries, saw no pressing need to. A great many reviewers of *A Survey of Modernist Poetry* concurred. The *Glasgow Herald*, the *South Wales Argus*, the *Nottingham Journal*, and the *Liverpool Post* thought it proper, as one paper stated, to "give predominance to the male partner." Riding and Graves wrote in the short foreword to their second collaboration, *A Pamphlet Against Anthologies*, that even the *Cambridge Gownsman* and *Oxford Magazine* had "followed the provincial example." To be surrounded by such "practiced readers" as Fletcher and politely warded off into the "literary ladies' room" by Davidson and Oxbridge undergraduates would increasingly aggravate the crankiness in Riding. As in the embattled arena of their private life together, Graves happily cheered her on.

IN THE 1920S and 1930s Riding was not awarded any publishing contracts by virtue of her merits or popularity as an author. Instead, Graves made it clear in ever less subtle ways that if publishers wanted his books, her books came along. At the Hogarth Press *The Close Chaplet* sold only twenty-nine copies; *Voltaire: A Biographical Fantasy* sold no more than 125 copies. In June 1927 Graves, in a desperate bid

for funds, signed with Jonathan Cape to write a popular account of
T. E. Lawrence's adventures in the Middle East. The agreement also
included contracts for Riding's first two books of criticism and their
joint work, *A Pamphlet Against Anthologies*. All these books, with *A
Survey of Modernist Poetry*, would also appear in America under the
Doubleday, Doran imprint. Riding eventually paid a price for this
linkage, but until then the giddy freedom to write as she chose
obviated mundane questions of readership.

This was particularly true of the literary criticism and miscellaneous prose writings published during Riding's three years in England. Drawing together unpublished essays that had been written in
America, Egypt, Vienna, and Islip, Riding published *Contemporaries and
Snobs* in February 1928, three months after *A Survey of Modernist Poetry*
appeared. Three months later, *Anarchism Is Not Enough* was released
and, two months after that, *A Pamphlet Against Anthologies*. On the card
page of *Contemporaries and Snobs*, the listing of books "by the same
author" included the two not yet published and one—a book of first
poems—that would never be.

Like Riding's prodigious critical output, the proliferation of British
literary critical periodicals was a sign of the times. In *Contemporaries
and Snobs* she addressed the same questions debated in such journals
as the *Calendar of Modern Letters*, the *New Criterion*, and the *Adelphi*, all of
which were at the height of their influence. In "Escape from the
Zeitgeist" Riding described the elaborate defenses by which contemporary poets had attempted to throw off the yoke of critical self-
consciousness engendered by such reading matter. Whether in satire,
pastorals, messianism, or complicated "snobbisms" (Riding's term,
meaning roughly high literary pretensions), this poetry defined itself
and the poet behind it by what trends it was *not* following. Begun in
America, she conceived this essay in response to one by Edwin Muir
in the *Calendar of Modern Letters;* Graves had placed some of her poems
in the same issue.

But apart from "A Prophecy or a Plea," Riding had signally failed in
her efforts to place any of these early essays. While in Greenwich
Village she had tried H. L. Mencken's *American Mercury*, the *New
Republic*, and Marianne Moore's *Dial*. If she expected a serious hearing
in the London literary world, she was disappointed. While she was in
Egypt her agent, Eric Pinker, tried the English monthlies as well as

American ones, but everything was rejected. Their first appearance would await book form.

The course of Riding's disillusionment with the London literary establishment can be mapped in the pages of *Contemporaries and Snobs* and *Anarchism Is Not Enough*. In a 1925 draft of the central essay of *Contemporaries and Snobs*, "The Absolute of Poetry," Riding was earnest and articulate, providing a "Best Self" rebuttal to an essay by John Crowe Ransom that had appeared in the *Calendar*. Moreover, in this early draft she showed more generosity toward her contemporaries than she would in its revised version and in her work in England and Vienna. She demonstrated how W. B. Yeats, Ezra Pound, Edwin Arlington Robinson, and Marianne Moore had attained (at least occasionally) "the fullest integrity a poet can command." She closed by acknowledging her indebtedness to the *Metaphysics* and *Poetics* of Aristotle in reaching her conclusions, as well as by expressing debts to her contemporaries, T. S. Eliot and the French poet and writer Paul Valéry. None of these acknowledgments survives in the later version of the essay.

By late 1926, Riding's critical work had become altogether less eager to please and more reckless in its willingness to offend. Her "Worst Self," as Davidson would have it, was gaining the upper hand. Pinker received explicit instructions as to what essay should be sent where, so that the editor of the *New Criterion* would not read the joke that she made at his expense but, rather, another at the expense of Marianne Moore, editor of the *Dial*. Arnold Bennett entitled his *Evening Standard* review of *Contemporaries and Snobs* "The Monstrous Conceit of Some Modernists." "In addition to suffering acutely from a total absence of humour," he wrote, "these pioneers suffer from the sense of being all alone, and utterly right, in an utterly wrong world of letters. They rejoice too richly and contemptuously in their apartness."

Ostensibly, Riding's intention in *Contemporaries and Snobs* was to trace various tendencies shared by twentieth-century poets in their effort to come to grips with the special difficulties of their age. She began by attempting to provide a definition of poetry but, before long, resorted to generalizations and variants on generalizations about the sensibility of various poets in order to "prove" her points. Throughout, no quarter was given to the *Survey's* "plain reader," and unlike her collaborations with Graves, supportive quotations from poems—even reference to particular titles—are practically nonexistent. Finally, she had dropped A Survey of Modernist Poetry's idea of a poet as friendly intermediary between the contemporaneous world and the absolute, and had replaced the mediating role with a more adversarial one.

Though her tone is superior and dictatorial, it does not disguise the fact that, like T. S. Eliot perhaps, Riding was writing a way out of her own difficulties as a poet. These difficulties had been vastly complicated by the proliferation of critics and critical writing on modernist poets and poetry. If editors of literary magazines or reviewers showed impatience with her language, it was nothing compared to her own impatience with theirs. In this respect Arnold Bennett would have been the last to appreciate Riding's special sense of humor—her tendency, as the American poet Genevieve Taggard aptly called it, to "put on the literary dog." Considering the sotto voce of T. S. Eliot's poem "Burbank with a Baedeker: Bleistein with a Cigar," Riding's "joke" on the editor of the New Criterion did not square with a gentlemanly understanding of wit. In the A Survey of Modernist Poetry, Riding proposed to study this poem not in the measured tones of an Oxbridge don but in a spirit of wicked and ironic glee. Eliot's portrayal of the Philistine Bleistein, "an upstart Chicago Jew who probably started life as a tailor's apprentice in Galicia," contrasted sharply, Riding noted sarcastically, with the quiet Burbank's "melancholy respect for the past" as they both putter around the remnants of Venice's lost glory. This was the poem's "prose sense," as Riding understood it:

> The rats are underneath the piles now, and the Jew (the eternal Shylock) is the rat of rats. The jew (Jew is written with a small initial letter like rat) is apparently a rat because he has made money and because for some reason Jewish wealth, as opposed to Gentile wealth, has a mystical connection with the decline of Venice.

To defend the tailor's apprentice by charging Eliot with anti-Semitism—a charge that had not yet occurred to anyone—was not

Riding's intention; she disdained "moral" accountability and admitted that it was part of the joke that Jews shared these predjudices. Rather, she improved upon the modernist performance by contributing her cackles to the racist caprice of the modernist audience. For the upstart Jewish daughter of a "tailor's apprentice from Galicia," this had become the black comedy of being a modernist poet in a London literary scene dominated by the mores, manners, and "snobbisms" of Burbank. And this was her poet's Baedeker to the London literary metropolis of 1927:

> . . . [H]owever extreme the comedy—however wilful his caprices, however grotesque the contrasts between inno- cence and obscenity or brutality and preciousness—it is a point of intellectual vanity in him to laugh last, to be found on his feet when the performance is over. He completes and in a sense contradicts his clownishness by revealing that even clownishness is a joke: that it is a joke to be writing poetry, a joke to be writing modernist poetry. By this token he belongs to the most serious generation of poets that has ever written; with the final self-protective corollary, of course, that it is also a joke to be serious.

With such self-protective corollaries in place, Laura Riding might find a quiet corner to write poetry. Only when it came to the sentiment of love and the subject of death did even the most modern- ist of modern poets quiver; he was then "not at his clownish best."

Such bombast should, however, be compared with the opening paragraph of *Contemporaries and Snobs*, which made a sincere effort to offer readers a new understanding of poetry. In the absolute but secular truth of poetry, "the meaning at work in what has no mean- ing," could be found a clear definition of poetry:

> There is a sense of life so real that it becomes the sense of something more real than life. Spatial and temporal se- quences can only partially express it. It introduces a prin- ciple of selection into the undifferentiating quantitative

appetite and thus changes accidental emotional forms into
deliberate intellectual forms; animal experiences related
by time and space into human experiences related in infinite degrees in kind.

Her logic would circle around and around this central insistence.
In what knowledge, her poem "In Nineteen Twenty-Seven" asked,
"do the dressed animals of sense walk upright?" Ransom had said of
Riding's art that "she tries, perhaps, to put more into poetry than it
will bear," and a great deal of her critical writing revealed a similar
strain. However much Riding tried to separate the sparring partners
of thought and emotion in order to locate her meaning, it was often
her language that suffered from the unequal contest between them.
Her intermittent recourse to the language of mystical and religious
experience was an uneasy one: she was aware of the temptation of
messianism. This accounted, perhaps, for some of her difficulty.
Still, her persistence did manage to communicate a kind of hyper-
esthesia; if read sympathetically, the circular logic of "there is a
sense of life so real that it becomes the sense of something more
real than life" becomes a spiraling logic as "real" is forced into
"more real."

The thicket of criticism in the *New Criterion*, with its continual
reference to the myths and learned understandings that sustained the
literature of previous ages, was for Riding obsolete. "Even in this day,"
she claimed at the outset of *Anarchism Is Not Enough*, "when the social
and historical collapse of the Myth is commonly recognised, we find
poets and critics ... devoting pious ceremonies to the aesthetic
vitality of the Myth ..." These critics, she held, were the agents of
compromise between those "incorruptible individuals who might
reveal life to be an anarchy whose only order is a blind persistence"
and the sustaining myths of bourgeois society.

In his review for the *Nation and Athenaeum*, the English poet and
critic Roy Campbell was quick to rebut this challenge to the reigning
critical consensus. He depicted Riding's book as representative of a
recent phenomenon, the invasion of literature by the amateur of
"second rate intelligence" who invested a case of special pleading
with the colors of revolt against tradition:

> Never has poetry bowed under the weight of such a ponderous superstructure of critical pedantry. Almost every word which had any significance in criticism has entirely lost its meaning through being defined so carefully, so often, and so differently. . . . As far as it has any recognizable tendencies it attempts to disintegrate or paralyze all those critical values which belong to "concrete intelligence," and are therefore most dangerous to it.

In fact, such "critical values" had been in danger for some time; Riding held that they could not exist in sane isolation from the work—like "The Waste Land"—that they commented upon. "Concrete intelligence" is Riding's term; Campbell's appropriation of it suggests that he himself scarcely knew how to define what he defended.

Riding had not hesitated to define it for him. Was her pedantry any more thorny or pedantic than that of the gentlemen appearing in the *New Criterion?*

> What, then, is the code which contemporary criticism, bathing in the perennial and ever-changing fount of philosophy, the Zeitgeist, delivers for the benefit of that impeccable though obscure intellectual observance? Can it be that the social backing of contemporary poetic gentlemanliness is only, after all, a gloomy medley of scholastic anthropology, spaded Freudianism, Baroque Baedeckerism, sentimental antiquarianism, slum-and-boudoir philology, mystical Bradleyanism, tortoise-shell spectacled natural history, topee'd comparative religion and Arrow-collared Aristotelianism?

However amateurishly, Riding was attempting to address the nakedness of contemporary criticism's Emperor, even if that meant taking apart each article of critical clothing and fashioning her own special wardrobe. She was not the only one to work within a closed system of reasoning. To Campbell's insistence upon the meanings of words as

he had always understood them, Mr. Doodle-Doodle-Doo of her
next book *Anarchism Is Not Enough*, crowed in agreement:

> "By being a mathematical lexicographer and a lex-
> icographical mathematician, I am therefore able to check
> the truth with the truth. My last words are never 'that's
> true' but 'that's correct,' which explains how I can be a
> philosopher and a gentleman at the same time."
>
> With this Mr. Doodle-Doodle-Doo crowed three times:
> once for lexicography (Doodle), once for mathematics
> (Doodle), and once for himself (Doo), wherein the truth
> was checked by itself and found correct.

Riding's barbed dissections and classifications of T. S. Eliot, Edith
Sitwell, and even Robert Graves betrayed her hope that by tagging
and numbering their "historical efforts" she herself could proceed to
some sort of safe beyond. But constructions like the "Zeitgeist" and
the "collapse of the Myth" created their own dead ends; and there is a
sense of Riding's running hard just to stay in the same place. She
attacked Edith Sitwell for trying to evade the hungry historicity of
the Zeitgeist by becoming a snobby collector of "literary heraldry;"
Sitwell's interest in the work of Alexander Pope, she insisted, was
affected whiggery, an attempt to ingratiate herself with "that dim
social class which lives in the genteel retirement of a few superior
critical journals." This strategy on Sitwell's part defeated the entrapment of the Zeitgeist (but not Riding) only because it was so obscure.
The escape clause loomed:

> The only way out for a poet . . . is to disguise himself as a
> buffoon; so that his contempt of the complicated snob-
> bisms which paralyze all normal poetic instincts and his
> own casual cultivation of these instincts may pass for
> simpleness and he be left to his own devices.

While *Contemporaries and Snobs* might have begun in stately definition of the sane and sovereign "principle of selection" in poetry,
before long the roar of the buffoon resounded. By the time Riding
came to write *Anarchism Is Not Enough* this buffoon was fully formed;

the opening essay likened the modernist poet to an intransigent baby.
Poetry was deemed to have "no system, harmony, form, public significance or sense of duty. It is what happens when the baby crawls off
the altar and is . . . resolved not to pretend, learn to talk or versify."
Riding, too, had " 'Resolv'd to be a very contrary fellow.' "

Within a few months, then, the tidy Islip household had given way
to the anarchism of St. Peter's Square, and a nursery under siege
became Riding's guiding metaphor for modernism. The precocious
but now contrary poet had appeared in the drawing room, and her
indulgent modern parents were obliged, by their cheerful open
minds, to hear out her spleen. The narrator of Riding's monologue
"How Came It About?" basked in the resulting hostility:

> [There is a woman in this city who loathes me.] What is to
> her irritation is to me myself. She has therefore a very
> direct sense of me, as I have a very direct sense of her, from
> being a kind of focus of her nervous system. There is no
> sentiment, no irony between us, nothing but feeling: it is
> an utterly serious relationship . . . I think of her often. She
> is a painter—not a very good painter. I understand this
> too: it is difficult to explain, but quite clear to myself that
> one of the reasons I am attached to her is that she is not a
> good painter. Also her clothes, which do not fit her well:
> this again makes me even more attached to her. If she
> knew this she would be exasperated against me all the
> more, and I should like it; not because I want to annoy her
> but because this would make our relationship still more
> intense. It would be terrible to me if we ever became
> friends; like a divorce.

The loathing of one human being for another, she insisted, "was more
full of passion than incest."

Similarly, "How Came It About?" seemed to also strip the Trinity of
its former holiness:

> How came it about that Mrs. Paradise the dressmaker is
> here to dress me, and Mr. Babcock the bootmaker to boot
> me and a whole science of service to serve me? . . . Do not

speak to me of economics: that is merely a question of how
we arrange matters between us. . . . What I *am* discussing is
existence, uncorrupted by art—how it came about, and so
forth. Do not speak to me of love: Mrs. Paradise and Mr.
Babcock and myself and all the others do not like each
other, in fact, we dislike each other because each of us is
most certainly the cause of the other.

But though drawn and trisected, the Trinity could not be entirely
broken: "If it were not for each other we should be occupied only
with ourselves; we should not exist. How then came we to exist? I ask
this question. Mrs. Paradise asks this question. I am Mrs. Paradise's
answer. Mrs. Paradise is my answer." If that was Nancy's Laura and
Laura's Nancy, this was Laura's Robert: "As for Mr. Babcock, he has
hair on his nose and I never look at him."

Like "Fragment of an Unfinished Novel," which explored a perverse and fantastical bond between a mother and her daughter, "How
Came It About?" limns the grotesque and psychologically subversive
dimensions of domestic life. Like the other short fictions that appeared in *Anarchism Is Not Enough*, the narrator draws a great deal of
attention to herself—as if to say, like the narrator of "In a Café," "Let
them stare. I am well though eccentrically dressed." From the safety
of exile, Riding later confided to a close friend that in London she
often felt that she was being stared at; in 1927 and 1928 she turned
this feeling of being the outsider, the Jewess, the American, and the
tyrannical homewrecker to her creative advantage.

The original title for the book in which these weird fragments and
monologues were to appear was *Miss I*, and Riding planned to include
a frontispiece portrait of herself to underscore their real-life heroine.
As if to court public scandal, Riding—as Miss I—dressed each
narrator outrageously; the negotiable divide between real life and
"more real" life seemed to be part of her delight in her stories. She
told Donald Davidson that the book would have to be sold by
subscription to avoid the censor.

Thus with Nancy in Cumberland and having herself outgrown the
homemade "art school" dresses, Riding might treat her imaginatively,
force-fitting this stubborn woman into her childhood's "three-
cornered pattern of concern." In Riding's version of the threesome,

Nancy's role now combined that of her protective and sympathetic older half sister and the invalid, disciplining mother who nonetheless sewed pretty dresses for her only daughter. Similarly, if the loathing that Riding's mediocre woman painter felt for her contained more passion than incest, that was because in some manner Riding's imagination now thrived on such passions. To excite "loathing interest" from others was to create an intimacy more wild and powerful than the rhetoric of romantic love, physical passion, or emotional or intellectual intimacies would allow.

With the opening of this Pandora's box, the literary adults of London also found themselves the butt of a self-consciously naughty mockery, particularly from her *Anarchism* essay "Jocasta." E. M. Forster learned that Riding found his much praised novel *A Room with a View* "unpleasantly painful to read": "[I]t affected me in the same way as would the sight of a tenderly and exquisitely ripe pimple. I longed to squeeze it and have done with it." The novel *To the Lighthouse* by Virginia Woolf fared no better:

> All this delicacy of style, it appears, is the expression of an academic but nevertheless vulgar indelicacy of thought, a sort of Royal Academy nudeness, a squeamish, fine-writing lifting of the curtains of privacy . . . It is over-earnest, constrained, suppressedly hysterical, unhappy, could give no one pleasure.

"Pleasure," Riding insisted, was "doing as one pleases."

Nor were the terms of Riding's praise gratifying. Of a novel by Rebecca West she wrote, "It was all so frankly false, so enchantingly bad, so vulgarly poetical without the least claim to being poetic, that it was impossible not to enjoy it and not to find it good: one was being sold nothing that was not obvious." Curiously, Riding neglected to provide her readers with the title of this novel. Among Riding's very early poems, however, is one dedicated to Rebecca West. Riding had read West's 1922 novel *The Judge* while living in Urbana and described it then as a work of genius, beauty, strangeness, and compassion. In the ambition and struggle of West's seventeen-year-old heroine to escape the slums of Glasgow, Riding found a sentimental echo of her own experience that she now disdained to hear again, preferring instead to be affected, arch, and outrageous.

By then Riding was close enough to the well-lighted rooms and private libraries of Bloomsbury to feel that she was not of them and, like Rebecca West herself, never would be either by invitation or design. By then, too, the value of being a poet among such highly bred prose writers was simply and precisely to destroy everything that they represented. Unlike Rebecca West, she did not describe her mission in political or feminist terms, though her language might partake of *épater le bourgeois*: "Prose is the social, civilized instrument of communication. The restraints put on it are like the complicated conventions that govern an apparently free-and-easy but actually a rigidly prescribed drawing room atmosphere." As a poet her aim was to suppress such "associative obligations" and reduce each word to a "pure residue, and the meaning if there is any." "The greater the clutter attacked," she insisted, "the smaller, the purer, the residue to which it is reduced, (the more destructive the tools), the better the poem." Poetry was not literature but, rather, a point of view that was both "self and only self" and an "unreality" that belonged to everyone. The profusion of jargons from which Riding manufactured her authority as a critic during her years in London underscored the difficulty of her insistence on a standard of the "self and only self."

In her 1928 lecture "A Room of One's Own" Virginia Woolf fantasized about the nature of a "woman's sentence," believing that such a sentence would somehow be different than a man's. In Emily Brontë and Jane Austen she discovered women who appeared deaf to that persistent male voice, "now grumbling, now patronizing, now domineering, now grieved, now shocked, now angry, now avuncular, . . . which cannot let women alone, but must be at them, like some too conscientious governess, adjuring them . . . to be refined; dragging even into the criticism of poetry the criticism of sex." She cited a review in the *Criterion* to prove her point. In the late 1920s Laura Riding, like Virginia Woolf herself, like the novelists Dorothy Richardson and May Sinclair, contested this persistent voice, both the one that issued forth from the "genteel retirement of a few superior literary journals" and its more internalized echo.

To conceive this woman's sentence, Virginia Woolf continued, a woman required a room of one's own and £500 a year. Yet when she entered that room to write her novels, the too conscientious governess seemed to follow right after her. When the novels came out, extraordinary as they were, the world saw little that was not refined. "There is much," Riding aptly remarked, "that cannot be turned into spun silk."

It was in her diaries and letters that Woolf was more forthcoming with less ladylike sentiments; out of sight of the avuncular voices, she seemed to take some guilty delight in "cat scratching." Privately, she found Riding's public tantrums of protest over bad reviews unseemly:

> . . . see whether you don't get the feeling that here's a shallow, egotistical cock-crowing creature, a bother what people say of her. And The Cause suffers: I mean, I feel, what will people say of the vanity of women? But then I don't believe in causes.

Perhaps Woolf envied Riding's ability to brave the question of what people would say. To rationalize her remarks, however, Woolf followed the *Criterion's* well-worn path and dragged the criticism of sex into the criticism of poetry. Woolf admitted that she despised Laura Riding for making such a spectacle of herself "when reviewers say what is true—that she is a damned bad poet. There! Not very well put I admit . . ." Woolf's remarks are made all the more unfortunate by the fact that she had published two volumes of Riding's poetry.

In 1927 and 1928 Riding's search for critical authority proceeded by dense argument and opinions calculated to offend. In *Anarchism Is Not Enough* her fictive personas were those of a woman in the teeth of defiance, laughing to scorn. By turning her rage outward in public display, rather than inward as more decorous women writers would have done, Riding might elude those self-inquisitions and censures which would eventually destroy Virginia Woolf. For all her efforts to set herself apart from the Zeitgeist, a great deal of *Contemporaries and Snobs* revealed her paralysis as a poet who had already internalized too much of the critical debate going on around her. That Riding came to reject the self-evident truths and critical opinions of her gentlemen reviewers was remarkable, and perhaps the stridency of her protest was necessary to enable a far more fragile poetry to survive.

Perhaps, too, because Riding did not have the cushion of £500 a year, she learned to have a very different answer to Woolf's question, "What will people say?" For Riding the web of love and hate, the ingrown relations of friendship, family, and the London literary world, created a crowded room of her own. The extent to which her mind and emotions were inhabited by the Fugitives, by Nancy and Robert, by their families and friends, was astonishing. If Nancy had a breakdown, Laura got stronger—and if Laura headed toward collapse, it was explained to Polly, Nancy suddenly got very well. Robert, it seemed, was always Robert. Debilitating to some, perhaps, but such an arrangement proved exhilarating to Riding. Similarly, imprinted as she was by Ransom, Tate, and Eliot's *New Criterion*, the acute self-consciousness of her critical persona became a skill honed for use in her later poems and short fiction.

Riding's need for a constant supply of new adversaries derived from her loneliness in the room at the top of 35A St. Peter's Square. The consuming attempt to synchronize her critical pulse with a more lyrical and youthful one recalled the search for the ecstasy of love that had marked the Trinity's early days. The speaker of "In Nineteen Twenty-Seven" anticipates possible resolutions:

> But I, only one, have a charmed memory
> And may go mad with certainty of one,
> And no further, stop in the street,
> Cry "Now" and in despair
> Love who can love me—
> An impartial match, soon over.

In Geoffrey Phibbs, Laura Riding would discover not an impartial match but a divided heart to match her own. Until then, the window in Hammersmith remained "a window not worth leaping out of"; and Robert, by some strange hand, would make his close escape to the sidewalk curb. And though her love for him in the spring of 1927 might be "mad, unnatural / Deceitful, not profitable", she would not yet leave him, being "curious of time." Similarly, Riding's tense debate at the fatal sill would remain unresolved, her body suspended, until a later spring.

Distracted from the melancholy view from her window in Hammersmith, Riding looked to Paris. There a quarterly entitled *transition* would prove more friendly to her essays and short fiction than the English and American monthlies had been. Conceived as a bridge between American letters and the European avant-garde, *transition* was founded by Eugene Jolas to remind everyone that there was more to modernism than T. S. Eliot, Virginia Woolf, and Edith Sitwell.

In Paris, too, there wrote and reigned that star attraction, Miss Gertrude Stein.

Chapter 10

OUTSIDE THE WINDOW

—— • ——

The tympanum is worn thin.
The iris is become transparent.
The sense has overlasted.
Sense itself is transparent.
Speed has caught up with speed.
Earth rounds out earth.
The mind puts the mind by.
Clear spectacle: where is the eye?

. . .

No suit and no denial
Disturb the general proof.
Logic has logic, they remain
Locked in each other's arms,
Or were otherwise insane,
With all lost and nothing to prove
That even nothing can live through love.

—"World's End"

—— • ——

AFTER AN OPERATION on her fractured spine, Laura had a dream in which her hospital bed was only a few inches from the ceiling. From this height she slid down off her pillow to greet Gertrude Stein when she arrived. Gertrude had delicate features in the dream and fine black hair topped by a creamy wool hat; Laura noted that she had put on a bedside manner for the occasion. Her visit to Laura's sickbed was only one of many engagements in London before she joined a shooting expedition in the Scottish Highlands. The latter plan left Laura slightly mystified but she accepted it, so pleased was she at seeing her unexpected guest. In the dream, Laura was vexed with the hospital porter for not giving her time to fix herself before announcing Gertrude. Owing to a nerve damaged by the leap, her left eye was temporarily paralyzed, making the left side of her face seem odd and strangely frozen. A mirror would have enabled her to adjust her right side accordingly, she told Gertrude, but as it was she was caught "half and half."

In early April 1929, during the crisis leading up to her jump, Robert had written to Gertrude Stein asking if there was any way Laura, who had gone into "complete retirement" after returning from Rouen, might come and see her, even for only a day. They had both met Stein the year previous on a short visit to Paris. A week later Laura herself wrote to Gertrude—her first letter to anyone since Geoffrey's arrival at the apartment—to explain her urgent cables to Stein and the trouble that they had all been in. The suspense that followed her return from France, Laura wrote, was succeeded by still another climax. Nancy Cunard, one of their few visitors during this period and unaware of what was happening, came away with an eerie but distinct sense of tension at the apartment. She found Riding, whom she had never met, suggestively "supernatural," dominating, tense, and "quietly American." "Like a brooding sultry day," she recalled, "there was electricity all around, if not visible; a sense of contained conflict."

This sense of contained conflict dominates Riding's poetry, as it did her life that April. "Analogy," Riding had written in her essay on Stein, "is always false, but it is the strongest philosophical instrument of coordination." Through the coordination of analogy, the echo of conflict sounds constantly in the contending dramas of good and evil, body and mind, death and life, male and female, untruth and truth, time and timelessness throughout Riding's oeuvre. As in the poem "In Nineteen Twenty-Seven" through "analogy" these antithetical pairs often change partners—beauty becomes analogous with truth or timelessness; body with male or evil—in elaborate and intricate

metaphysical quadrilles. What remained constant in this organization of meaning was the insistence on the conflict itself, the strict
antagonism of paired opposites.

In April 1929 the image of footsteps passing under the "window
not worth leaping out of" became, in extremis, a high window worth
leaping out of. But how and why did Riding's organizing, coordinat-
ing, and tidying "logic" finally resolve itself in suicide? Why were the
carefully orchestrated cycles of crisis and suspense brought to a
standstill?

From her earliest unpublished poems, Riding's poetry could be
viewed as intensely suicidal. The romantic images of death as the
fatal lover on the other side of a balcony, a window, a precipice—all
continually beguile her, prophesying consummation in death. But by
dramatizing, through her poetry, the myriad and complex tensions of
her person, Riding was continually eluding the exacting finale. "The
theory of death can be thwarted by theory," she argued with her
shrewd adversary in one poem. "And the poetical proof is good
enough for me." Her poems juggled and juxtaposed the homely and
the universal with nimble wit; she flouted poetic conventions as
boldly as social ones, and she constantly invented analogic correspondences to flesh out a personal vision whose subject matter was
the vigor of her own life and body. "Discover the free will," she
proclaimed in "The Contraband." "Count death not necessarily logical."

But while the metaphysical idiom provided a vehicle for Riding's
spiritual intensity and boldness (as it did for Emily Dickinson) and a
means to escape the confining platitudes of more traditional forms,
the lack of a faith more certain than the exigencies of free will and
circular logic proved almost deadly. "Clear spectacle:" she asked in
the feverish and visionary poem "World's End," "where is the eye?"
Her search for the certain proof, the still point, the omniscient eye
beyond the "fancy" and the artifice was never-ending. Geoffrey, the
man she chose to love, challenged her, and voicing her deepest fears
about herself, he suggested that she was not only deluded but insane.

If one imagines a self riven in two, a face caught "half and half," and
believes the measure of unhappiness contained in the width of the
schism, as Riding chose to, the greater the unhappiness, the wider
the division. Similarly, the greater the unhappiness, the sharper and

more absolute the identification of who is right and who is wrong, of what is true and what is a lie. This is not madness, Laura had told Gertrude after Rouen, but a vision of how human behavior might begin to articulate momentous values, adding that such values had nearly killed her in France. In April 1929 the authority behind these values became predicated not on Riding's heart and mind alone but on "Laura-with-Geoffrey" and on Geoffrey's return to her. If the values were to be questioned or undermined, meaning itself would suddenly collapse and all definition disappear. Love, then, would not be confined to a confusion with truth or goodness but might become the other face of evil.

In "Helen's Burning" such paradoxes are explored in ways that suggest how deeply imbued was Riding's "poetic sense" with the dialectical conjurings of metaphysical poetry. That such rhetorical gambits tended, time and time again, to steer all her arguments toward ultimately nihilistic and self-destructive ends is perfectly captured in this early poem:

> Her beauty, which we talk of,
> Is but half her fate.
> All does not come to light
> Until the two halves meet
> And we are silent
> And she speaks,
> Her whole fate saying,
> She is, she is not, in one breath.

In Riding's inexorable and self-embracing "logic," meaning searches for its purest expression not in the mythic ideal but in Helen's "whole fate," her ugliness and her beauty, her life and her death "in one breath." At the window Riding learned from Geoffrey Phibbs what she had already reasoned, that her "truths" could be inverted into their opposites: in the mockery of truth lay the lie. Thus in the perversities of Riding's analogical reasoning lay the danger of reveal- ing the whole image of Helen:

> But we tell only half, fear to know all
> Lest all should be to tell

And our months choke with flame
Of her consuming
And lose the gift of prophecy.

The "gift of prophecy," the vatic power of Helen's transcendental and mythic beauty, was Riding's poetic inheritance. To forsake this mystery, to unmask the "whole fate" of woman risked the revelation that Helen's beauty might be no more than mortal, and the gift of prophecy, delusion. But that is exactly what Geoffrey Phibbs' refusal of Laura Riding's love demanded. In her jump Riding risked all to discover the meaning, the Truth, the whole face and fate—"if there was any." She jumped as much to see this Truth for herself as to prove that it existed for him.

In *The Savage God,* his 1971 study of the poetry of suicide, Alfred Alvarez found that nihilism and self-destructiveness, which so often accompanied the psychic experimentation of extremist poets during the 1920s, was often the harvest of the social fragmentation and violence sown by the Great War. The confusion between the poet's life and work becomes—when formal innovations, technical resources, and rhetorical devices are discarded—suicide. Riding relentlessly skirted that "friable edge." When her imaginative self exhausted its self-generating resources, her own body became the new medium of the nihilistic expression.

In the months following the suicide attempt, Riding would rebuild her poetic language on a new symbolic terrain. The events that led up to the jump were to be turned over and over, each detail somehow a sign in a new parable, each mysteriously expressive of an exalted state of being and Riding's "endless judgement-day." At her direction, Len Lye designed a shawl with a representation of her damson-colored surgical scar on it, like a new icon. Division and definition were replaced by stern omniscience; Riding would no longer be found "pleasure-making with the citizens."

This state of grace, as she conceived it in the poem "Grace," was a brutally human one, enforced by "free" will. Graves, who however, imagined that he had joined Riding in this state, put a religious spin on it, writing to his sister that "one cannot talk of there being good in Laura, she is seamless, like the garment of Christ." Laura, Rosaleen

wrote to her brother John, preferred calling herself " 'Finality,' whatever that may mean." Whether Riding's state was self-induced or
mysteriously attained, it was fundamentally an acute aesthetic experience. As in her Egyptian experience of emotional crisis or ecstasy, the
antique notions of mystical revelation might again attend Riding's
writings and thought during this period, but there was never an
accompanying belief in an eternal God.

As in "Helen's Burning" fire, which Riding feared above all else,
provided the purifying metaphor of her transmogrification. This was
not a martyr's fire, like Joan of Arc's, but one that welled up from
within. In "The Lesson," as well as in other prose pieces and poems
written after her leap, the Devil is understood to be Geoffrey
Phibbs—but a Phibbs that was also a part of herself to be denounced
and cauterized:

> The lesson that the Devil teaches is the necessity of
> discretion. To pass through the fire of one's own excessive-
> ness, to suffer more of oneself than of others, to foreknow
> impossibility. The lesson that the Devil teaches is the
> necessity of discretion if one would remain an illusion.
> The lesson that one learns is the necessity of indiscretion
> if one would be burned down to a fact.

The jump and her survival provided, in her own as well as in Graves'
eyes, the final, authoritative stamp of "fact" of which she had had
endless need, as if her actual existence had been in question all along.

Given the Devil as her newfound adversary, however, "fact" was
suddenly understood to mean, equally, the Good. Heretofore, Riding
had explicitly rejected aesthetic theories with conventional ethical
assumptions but in Finality and righteousness a moral universe beck-
oned. Riding had fulfilled her prophecy of death by burning, to arise
whole and phoenixlike and to predict yet another end: the refining
fires of the apocalypse. Neither Helen's beauty nor her gift of prophecy was an illusion; this was now "proved" by the lesson of Riding's
resurrection, her new factualness. Her further announcement that
historical time was finished was an equally extraordinary but necessary conclusion.

Both Riding and Graves assumed that Gertrude Stein would somehow understand the moral dimension of their personal crisis. Robert
sent Gertrude a telegram on the day of the leap, asking her to come if
at all possible. Two days later he sent another, saying that Laura was
asking for her. The single most important thing, Laura wrote from
the hospital, was that she went out the window and only a few went
with her. "Out of the windowness" became the sine qua non determining who was really with Laura and who was not. Robert definitely
went out; Geoffrey went out but in the wrong direction. Isabel, who
arrived from America with her sister-in-law Helen Mayers, was not a
member of this company. Laura, Helen remembered, was contemptuous and dismissive of her sister's concern and persisted in calling
her Bella. She seemed more interested in the design of a fillet for her
hair (ordered by Robert from a London goldsmith) than in her
injuries. Polly definitely counted herself in, firmly rooted on the
ground though she was. "Laura went through a stage," Polly remembered. "She was with Robert at the time—when they discarded
everything, they discarded books, they discarded people, but I kept
on my own way and remained friends with her." Finally, Gertrude
herself was given the enviable position of having been outside the
window to begin with.

But "finality" had yet to articulate herself. Within the shattered
body on the hospital bed, there survived those twin hearts, now
fused and beating together. Under the influence of morphine, Laura
entered that strange land of being dead and not dead, and few
followed her. It was here, outside the window, that the unlikely vision
of Gertrude Stein dressed smartly for a Highland hunt swam into
view. Quickly, Laura's affection for her flared into an abiding love. In
her worst hours of physical pain, Robert wrote to Gertrude, Laura
had been kept alive purely by thinking of her. One of Laura's first
letters after the jump, written in the most fragile of pencil scrawls,
contained a sketch of her small, almost skeletal figure on the hospital
bed. The spinal cord was drawn with a crooked twist at one end.
Tiny, tiny question marks dot her legs. Yet Laura drew Gertrude's
attention to the hand, stretched out by the pillow over a small square
of paper. This was her letter to Gertrude, she said, exclaiming her
pleasure in writing again. After a few lines she grew fatigued and
passed the letter to Robert to finish.

Riding had first approached Stein after she and Graves had purchased a Crown Albion printing press with part of the advance from
Graves' book *Lawrence and the Arabs* (1927). The Seizin Press, as it was
named, provided yet another answer to Bloomsbury and its Hogarth
Press. Their prospectus gave some indication of their intentions,
while clarifying more firmly what they were not:

> Our editions are decidedly not addressed to collectors but
> to those interested in work rather than printing—of a
> certain quality. That is as far in prophecy as we care at the
> moment to go. You must take our word for it that our
> reticence is due to something more than an uncertainty of
> standards. Quite the contrary.

Laura warned one young hopeful at Oxford that their editorial
criteria were technical rather than literary. The press was set up at
35A St. Peter's Square, and Laura and Robert were taught to print by
Vyvyan Richards, a friend of T. E. Lawrence's who had a similar press
in St. John's Wood. After a short apprenticeship they undertook the
first of the seven books printed between 1928 and 1934, Riding's *Love
as Love, Death as Death*. Printing was an exhausting occupation for a
perfectionist like Riding, and after a year of trial and error the book
appeared in an edition of 175 numbered copies. It was the first and
last to be hand-set. Soon after soliciting and accepting a work from
Stein, Riding asked if she might visit her in Paris to discuss her work.
Stein was delighted to welcome her.

Thus in early June 1928, returning from a holiday on the Côte
d'Azur with Polly, Laura and Robert had stopped in Paris. June was
the official beginning of the Montparnasse season, but the quarter
had changed a great deal since the American occupation of the early
1920s. Café life was less intimate, literary life, more cosmopolitan
and self-conscious; the writers, intellectuals, and painters found
themselves indoors to escape the noisy clichés of their youth before
they were even out of their twenties. The free-for-alls of manifestos
and demonstrations had subsided into the comparatively silent

standoff between Gertrude Stein and James Joyce in the pages of *transition*.

By the time Laura and Robert visited Paris, the journal had published a number of her essays and poems and several stories. Laura, meeting its publisher, Eugene Jolas, and his wife, Maria, over lunch in an Italian restaurant, took issue with his plans for an upcoming number. She had no patience for surrealism and German expressionism, while Jolas thought exposure to such writing would benefit American literature. Laura disagreed emphatically. Afterward she admitted having been "monstrous" to Jolas, whom she nonetheless liked, attributing his faulty judgment to the disorder of the times. After her stern rebuke, she claimed, he nearly gave up the magazine. Kay Boyle, another *transition* contributor who had been lunching with them, left the table in a huff, finding both Laura and Robert overbearing in company and opinion. Riding's work would not appear in *transition* again.

The year before, however, in a Paris *Tribune* review of Gertrude Stein's *Composition as Explanation* (1926) Elliot Paul, Jolas' editor-partner, had singled out Riding's essay "The New Barbarism and Gertrude Stein" for special praise. Paul, an American novelist, noted that despite Stein's popularity as a subject for profiles, in her extraordinary twenty-five-year career very little had been written about the work itself, the actual "literary product." Instead, there had been an abundance of commentary on her charming personality and conversation, her physical strength, courage, and "immense cranial capacity." Legends, portraits, gossip, and essays had trailed her in profusion, but no one had yet dared either to dismiss her or hail her as a literary genius. *Composition as Explanation* was not, Paul pointed out, an attempt on Stein's part to explain her own work, baffling as it was: "[I]t was left for Miss Laura Riding, American poet residing in England, to discover this, and to appreciate it."

In championing Stein's long career and in the recognition of her genius by her younger compatriot, *transition* hoped to stir up some of the old excitement of the Quartier Latin and encourage an American literary tradition unconfined by the parochial forms of realism and naturalism in fiction and formal prosody in poetry. With this intention, another American writer was taken up and championed by *transition*. In Hart Crane, Jolas found the poetic vanguard in American sensibility and language, just as Stein's work represented (roughly) the avant-garde of American prose. Between 1927 and his death in 1932 nearly all of Crane's shorter poems appeared in its pages, as well as sections of the long-awaited poem "The Bridge." Canonizing him in an essay that appeared alongside Riding's explication of Stein, Jolas wrote, "We need new words, new abstractions, new hieroglyphics, new symbols, new myths. By re-establishing the simplicity of the word, we may find again its own magnificence."

As if to anticipate the hostility that Crane's work might incite, Jolas published Kay Boyle's unfavorable review of Crane's *White Buildings* (1926) some months before Riding's June visit to Paris. He had asked Riding to review the book as well, running her "note" opposite Boyle's. The terms in which Riding praised Crane were her own. Crane's voice was eloquent but theatrical, Riding maintained, but this was a condition forced on him by the limits of a discursive language that could not convey more passionate understandings. "There is," she wrote, "something heroic, moving, beautiful in this role: the saying self going through a part written by itself for itself, a sacrifice of identity to eloquence." Tate's foreword to the book, Riding wrote Donald Davidson, was "cant." To his opinion that Crane had not yet found a "comprehensive and perfectly articulated given theme" to match his poetic vision, she replied, "Mr. Crane is preserving his vision from such a theme." This comment was incorporated into "Gertrude Stein and the New Barbarism" to make a concluding chapter for *A Survey of Modernist Poetry*.

Riding's essay on Stein was expanded yet again to appear as "T. E. Hulme, the New Barbarism, and Gertrude Stein," which made up the second part of *Contemporaries and Snobs*. She began by insisting that in order to reassert creativity's dominance over such "cant" as Tate's, to free poetry to "be what it's always been," a new sense of time needed to be synthesized "in self-defense." "It must make the present period not so much the next one of a series as a résumé of periods." Eliot had composed such a résumé in "The Waste Land," she wrote, and the pastiche of period writing in *Ulysses* had achieved, in a more satirical vein, similar success. Crane's work was also discussed. But in the person and work of Gertrude Stein, Riding discovered something even better.

Long before Hart Crane began to build his Brooklyn Bridge and

Franz Kafka his Castle, before Tate nervously embraced the Catholic church and Eliot his "tailor's dummy Muse of religion," Stein had sat in the open air with her legs crossed and one Greek sandal dangling from her big toe. While everyone else had been creating American legends of Pocahontas or moping about lost gods and mythic scaffolding, Stein had "quietly . . . gone on practising a coherent barbarism under [our] very noses without encouragement or recognition." She seemed monumentally aloof to the cries of the age, to the lack of suitable shelter; her sensibility, Riding felt, was both timeless and time-bound. "A large-scale mystic, she is the darling priest of cultured infantilism to her age—if her age but knew it."

Riding's demand in *Anarchism Is Not Enough* for the purification of language from stale historical and mythic associations seemed to be amply answered by this woman who used words as if they had no "experience." Riding described Stein's experiments with language as writing "allowed to become disorganized until so loose grammatically that it could be reorganized as if afresh, without regard to how words and their combinations had been sympathetically affected by usage." That the work was prose as well as poetry seemed to make little difference; Riding had found both her Luddite and her alchemist: "The purer [the words] were the more eternally immediate and present they would be. In this way they could express the absolute at the same time as they were expressing the age."

Stein had stated in *Composition as Explanation* that "nothing changes from generation to generation except the thing seen, and that makes a composition." Not only was there no golden age to bemoan the loss of, there were no ages at all. In this simple understanding of time, as the fusing of the seer and the thing seen, Riding found her "special metaphysic" of absolute poetry and the defeat of the Zeitgeist. By isolating it, she hoped at last that the plague of fragmenting self-consciousness had been thwarted. By writing about it in *transition* she also hoped to quiet those "literary harpies" who had filled her head to begin with. Stein was no doubt pleased with the essay, but she must have been even more pleased by the prospect of seeing one of her many unpublished works, *An Acquaintance with Description*, on the Seizin Press list.

After the visit to Paris, Riding's critical appreciation for Stein's work was warmed by a friendly and affectionate regard for the lady herself. Geoffrey was made to read her, and, Laura reported, he finally concluded that if Laura was the Sphinx, Gertrude was the Great Goddess. In long, loping sentences Laura's letters from her hospital bed mimic Gertrude's own epistolary style. They are intimate with details of her body's progress toward recovery; Robert is rarely mentioned. Enclosed in one letter, written soon after her return to St. Peter's Square from the hospital, was another self-portrait and a drawing of her scar, likened to an asphodel. She also sent along an early version of the poem "Celebration of Failure," which referred explicitly to Stein as her "other" and as the wellspring of her own poetry. None of the lines referring to this muselike persona survived in the published version of the poem.

Robert's letter informing Gertrude of the fall and Laura's injuries elicited a sympathetic and embracing reply. The outcome of the crisis over Geoffrey Phibbs had come as no surprise to Gertrude, though she was optimistic about Laura's "coming together alright":

> Laura is so poignant and so upright and she gets into your tenderness as well as your interest and I am altogether heartbroken about her, I cannot come now . . . but tell her and keep telling her that we want her with us . . . I had an unhappy feeling that Laura would have sooner or later a great disillusionment and it would have to come through a certain vulgarity in another and it will make Laura a very wonderful person, in a strange way, a destruction and recreation of her purification but all this does not help pain and I am very closely fond of you all. Tell her all and everything from me and tell her above all that she will come to us and reasonably soon and all my love.

Such a letter coming from Gertrude during Laura's worst hours provided a bracing mirror to the divided face. Because Gertrude's handwriting was hard to decipher, Robert transcribed the letter so that Laura might read it easily and often.

Welded by Stein's words, Riding took from her own earlier ideas about Stein's disorganization of language a new vision of her self. Without regard to the sympathies of past "usage," Riding's personality, too, might be distilled, become as "pure as colour or stone," reduced to her "least historical value." Like a word out of grammatical sequence, Riding could now be "re-organized as if afresh" in the shelter of a new love, her love for Gertrude. As the summer of 1929 wore on, Laura's spirits quickened with plans to join Gertrude and Alice in Belley, near Aix-les-Bains. She wrote to them that she was writing a book of poems entitled "Here Beyond" and a prose work about suicide that she titled "Obsession."

IT IS A curiosity of history that an event of seemingly private significance often finds an answering echo in the world at large. Laura Riding thrived on such correspondences. On the day of her leap, Virginia Woolf listened patiently to the prophet of paralysis and fragmentation, "poor Tom" Eliot, bewail his wife's mysterious illnesses. "I stand for a half hour listening while he says Vivien can't walk. Her legs have gone. But what's the matter? No one knows." The private visions of misery were, Woolf observed, "imagined, but real, too. . . . This is our man of genius. This is what I gathered yesterday morning on the telephone." And while Riding was still in the hospital, Eugene Jolas was composing a manifesto entitled "The Revolution of the Word," whose twelve points seemed to articulate just the sort of spirit toward which Riding had been working her way in "In Nineteen Twenty-Seven" and in her thinking about Stein and Crane. Perhaps Riding's attempt to synchronize her sense of time with the world's had at last succeeded.

Interspersed with aphorisms from Blake, "The Revolution of the Word" appeared in the June 1929 issue of *transition* with Hart Crane among the signatories. It was a controversial document that signaled the end, rather than the beginning, of an era. Among its revolutionary proclamations was the right of the "literary creator" to disintegrate the "primal matter of words imposed on him by the text-books and dictionaries" and the right to "use words of his own fashioning." The third principle read, "Pure poetry is a lyrical absolute that seeks an a priori reality within ourselves alone." In the tenth, "Time is a tyranny to be abolished"; and finally, "The plain reader be damned." Hart Crane had second thoughts about it when he returned to New York, where Malcolm Cowley and a host of other returned exiles were discovering the virtues of a commitment to a socialist America.

Together, they managed to convince Crane that the manifesto was a lot of aesthetic hooey. Crane, who as Riding noted, tended to pay too much attention to critics, decided that he must have been drunk when he signed.

But Riding's poems written after the suicide attempt seemed to embody this revolution just as the 1920s were coming to a close. By the end of 1929 Montmartre would be emptying of Americans, and Wall Street businessmen in frock coats would be jumping out of windows, belying Blake's epigram (used in Jolas' manifesto) that "the road to excess leads to the Palace of Wisdom." When published in July 1930, *Here Beyond* had acquired the less euphoric and wry title *Poems A Joking Word*.

The new title, Riding said in her preface to the book, came to her in the Charing Cross Hospital when "a shifting of emphasis" from "doom" to poetry occurred. A certain Mrs. Palmer, settled in the next cot of the public ward, had reminded her that poems, unlike doom, was "a joking word":

> She told me a story about that. She was a little girl at a Salvation Army meeting and everyone was on their knees feeling for Jesus in the dark. Feeling for Jesus she lost her muff. And so while everyone was feeling for Jesus she was feeling for her muff. This was also a case of shifting of emphasis.

Hospitalized for an abdominal complaint, Mrs. Palmer seemed to have as much curative effect on Laura as did Gertrude's first letter— and perhaps tempered Laura's view of herself as a humorless and righteous "finality."

Poems A Joking Word was more widely read than her two earlier collections, *The Close Chaplet* and *Love as Love, Death as Death*, and made a decisive impact on an up-and-coming generation of English poets, among them W. H. Auden. (The book did not appear in America.) Selected poems from the earlier volumes as well as the contents of her previously announced *Early Poems* were included, as were those written during the summer of 1929. These latter poems reveal a shift away from "obsession" and the extremism of paradox to a more ornate and conscious manipulation of language.

In the tradition of Paul Valéry's statement "Je suis entre moi et moi," Riding's own "shifting of emphasis" showed how the fluctuations of consciousness could be mimicked in the very syntax of language. Dreams, illnesses, and pain could be depicted rather than denoted, positing a pure intelligence above the flux of human experience. In poems like "And This Hard Jealousy," "Nearly," and "Poem Only" analogy and metaphysical conceit are put aside, replaced by repetition, syntactical inversion, onomatopoeia, and other linguistic devices that are unnaturally focused upon, strategically engineered to enclose the reader in their subtle complexities. Though Riding may have imagined she was searching for a muff in the dark, the intensity of this work recalled the note of feverish revelation in her Egyptian poems.

The short poem "Here Beyond" (later retitled "Beyond") simulated this search for autotelic meaning. The factual and grammatically simple statement "Pain is impossible to describe" is followed by a series of statements linked by subtle changes in each line. By the eighth and final line Riding seems to have parsed together a description of pain, but it is a pain without a victim. The voice is radically detached, personality is obliterated, and for the reader there is virtually no empathetic and imaginative point of entry:

> Pain is impossible to describe
> Pain is the impossibility of describing
> Describing what is impossible to describe
> Which must be a thing beyond description
> Beyond description not to be known through knowing
> Beyond knowing beyond knowing but not mystery
> Not mystery but pain not plain but pain
> But pain beyond but here beyond.

The pain of the first line is transformed in the second line, changed from something felt with the senses to something "felt" with the mind. Riding effects this transformation and others by repeating certain words and altering the parts of speech in which these words are fitted. The syntax follows these permutations closely, beginning in the simple declarative and extending to more elaborate grammatical structures. The taut Latinate structure breaks down in the asyntactic sequence "Beyond knowing beyond knowing" but is retrieved by the phrase "but not mystery." By virtue of Riding's persistent dialectic, then, pain is not impossible to describe. As it is mentally "beyond" and physically "here," it may be described as "here beyond" in one (oxymoronic) breath.

While Riding had played with these devices in earlier poems, in the new work her technique is more intricate and self-conscious. Meanwhile, Stein was writing to her about her own progress in rethinking the sentence. After Riding had composed her first hospital poems, she connected Stein's work on the sentence with the new ease that she found in her own person and work. The difficulty of poems like "Here Beyond," Riding felt, nonetheless represented a loosening of the knot of reasoning that had bound her before the leap. In this, Paris and the avant-garde sensibility of *transition* and Gertrude Stein offered Riding rhetorical traditions and linguistic experiments that surpassed what was happening in London.

In the wake of her suicide attempt, Riding worked with these traditions to redeem the madness with sense. Kenneth Rexroth found sympathies between Riding's work and the writings of the French cubist poets Valéry, Reverdy, and Mallarmé: "Its revolution is aimed at the syntax of the mind itself. Its restructuring of experience is purposive not dreamlike, and hence it possesses an uncanniness fundamentally different in kind from the most haunted utterances of the Surrealist or Symbolist unconscious."

By far the most striking of these poems is "What to Say When the Spider," retitled "Elegy in a Spider's Web" in her *Collected Poems*. In the first seven lines two voices are apparent, the second interrupting the first to call into impatient question the very dynamics by which meaning is elicited from a text:

> What to say when the spider
> Say when the spider what
> When the spider the spider what
> The spider does what
> Does does dies does it not
> Not live and then not
> Legs legs then none

In the late twentieth century the dominant modes of critical discourse—New Criticism, structuralism, and deconstructionism—would consider the above lines in terms of the play of literary conventions belonging to preestablished "codes" of language. Here Riding engaged and questioned the "codes" of vernacular inflection, riddle, and typographical conventions to portray dialogue, onomatopoeia, linear narrative, and mythological reference to Arachne as a symbol of female entrapment. To follow such respectable lines of inquiry, however, is to evade the simple biographical connection between this poem and Laura Riding's suicide attempt.

The poignancy of this long, fragile, and intricate poem is hugely diminished by conceiving of it as a literary experiment of fascinating and baffling "intertextualities." Glancing comparisons between the poetry of Gertrude Stein and this poem have reduced both writers to purveyors of the "plastic" or "playful" qualities of language. In the awkward but infinitely careful crawl of Riding's spider lay one of the few paths to her recovery of an intensely personal poetic voice, in the shadow of the failed suicide attempt.

The spider, made all the more visible by the poem's scarcity of imagery, thus makes way for the "I." Other images carefully dealt out in the body of the poem—face, legs and, most remarkably, genii—stand out in similar relief. The relation between the "I" and the spider is emphasized by the second appearance of the interrupting voice and the repetition of the interrogatory rhythms:

> What to say when I
> When I what
> When I say
> When the spider
> When I always
> Death always
> When death what
> Death I says say
> Dead spider no matter

The initial rhythm quickly breaks down, as the disruptive impatience of the second voice kills the modest struggle of the "I" toward syntactical coherence, suggesting that the web of language (like the grip of hyperself-consciousness) can be suffocating as well as intricate. As if to start again, even more simply, Riding's grammar is obscured into invisibility, replaced by staccato, meaning-numbing repetition. From there the mere fragments, with the briefest residues of meaning, are built:

> What to say when
> . Who cannot cease
> Who cannot
> Cannot cease
> Cease
> Cannot
> The spider
> Death

By the ending of the poem, the loss of the gift of prophecy seems as final as the loss of beauty in the divided face ("O pity poor pretty") and certainty ("What to say"). Of all the poems written in the aftermath of Riding's suicide attempt "What to Say When the Spider" evokes most clearly the small sketch of Riding in her hospital bed and what, in another poem, she called "the stuttering slow grammaring of self." The figure struggling to write her tiny letter is hugely overshadowed by Riding's own struggle to write her letter to Gertrude and by the painful overhanging possibility of "legs legs then none."

All too predictably, the visit to Belley after Riding's recovery from her fall, was a disappointment. Laura and Robert stayed at a small pension in the little town, in the rich farming country of the Haute Savoie region of eastern France. Belley provided little distraction beyond conversation for Laura, particularly since she moved with difficulty even with a walking stick. While Gertrude did offer some criticism of "Obsession," her prose work in progress on suicide, Laura seems to have become impatient with her endless discourses on the weather; Robert would later write to Gertrude that Laura had felt such a trivial subject "unworthy" of her. "But of course the weather is very important in the short run," he added, "and the long run is made up of short runs."

Over fifty years later Laura (Riding) Jackson described Stein's conversation as nostalgic for a "normal reasonableness." Of this visit, she wrote in 1986, Jackson remembered only Stein's pursuing "with obsessive pertinacity meandering lines of small-talk, and exercising her homely intuition and commonsense shrewdness in aphoristic opinion-pronouncements." One of her favorite "wisecracks," Jackson claimed, was "No Jew ever lays down his last cent." She had felt certain that this and other sagacious utterings were but "trifles escaped from the major offering" and proposed that Stein early on had sacrificed her intelligence to "Reasonless Necessity." At the end of the day, Jackson felt, Stein's vast oeuvre had produced no more than a "Protean vagueness," purposely bankrupt of meaning. Applause for "a rose is a rose is a rose," Jackson claimed, was "applause of the worm." Moreover, she scoffed at any attempt to trace similarities between her work and Stein's; they were at opposite poles not only in their intentions but also in their spiritual understanding of humanity.

To explain away all of Stein's stories, novels, compositions, and essays Jackson was obliged to reduce Stein's work with language to her fantastic quest for the godhead. Stein's writing was the work of one who had dismissed the "difficulties of being, thinking, speaking," in order to absent herself "to an ease of tireless deity-being." Mostly, however, Jackson stuck with monetary analogies: "She took the part of one penniless, but rated with herself as a self-backed currency good for quite a long run of circulation." Stein's opportunism "kept no accounts with itself, so that she did not know just how wicked she was, how cynical in her reckless good cheer." Jackson contrasted Stein's desire to devalue language with her own efforts to restore meaning, and in her censorious simplifications one can find echoes of Riding's vexed visit to Belley.

Laura (Riding) Jackson's description of Stein's personality as having been "nervous with a continually aborted generosity" makes one wonder what exactly Laura Riding expected from her in 1929. The closest guess is that Riding was after at least a cent's worth of Finality or "absolute value"—but in her own coin rather than Stein's. The major offering was not forthcoming. Affectionate poodle talk with Gertrude's adored dog Basket persisted, and after two weeks Laura left for Fribourg, Switzerland, without it. Like many others who had sat at Gertrude's knee, she was left guessing.

Throughout the winter and spring of 1930, Robert and Laura kept Gertrude apprised of just how many thousands of copies *Good-bye to All That* had been sold and the progress of Laura's projects. Naturally, Gertrude began to inquire about the fate of her own book; *An Acquaintance with Description* had appeared at about the same time that Geoffrey Phibbs had at the Hammersmith apartment. After a while Gertrude became impatient. "And how did the accounts turn out, you didn't send me the cheque, well checks are a pleasure even when you don't have them but how did the accounts come out." She was finally told by Robert that there had been some difficulties ("the personal touch and so on got mixed up with the business"), and before their London departure Laura had not been in a "proper state for business." Laura blamed their distributor for not sending them a statement by which to figure the royalties. She eventually sent Gertrude a check, but not before Alice had decided to publish Stein's future work herself.

Not long after the check was sent, Gertrude received a letter from Laura referring to a mutual acquaintance. William Cook was a painter from Chicago; Gertrude had suggested that Laura look him up once she and Robert had settled into their new home. Cook, Laura wrote, had taken offense at Gertrude's tendency to make generalizations, in particular her statement that Norwegians were low-class; as a Norwegian, he found that generalization hard to take. Laura went on to describe the book that she had enclosed, which concerned a Jew's not putting down his last cent. She thought Gertrude would like to see the book "because of the generalization." It was a subtle cut but Gertrude did not miss it; times were strange, she answered, but not so strange as to let the remark slide. The understanding seems to have been that if there was an anti-Semitic crack to be made, Gertrude would make it.

Laura's letter of explanation went unanswered. She wrote again, saying that Gertrude's not writing seemed to put them in the wrong (Robert was also writing to Gertrude, vainly hoping that their letters had suffered from the whimsy of the postal service). Laura's final letter begged Gertrude to at least say something unpleasant, but by then even Laura knew that her head had already rolled across the transom of the atelier at 27 rue de Fleurus. Laura closed by saying that she would not write again—not even about the weather.

The insidious voices that echoed from the chambers "of a few superior critical journals" had first sent Laura Riding to the generous but tricky skirts of Gertrude Stein. For both women, however, the much vaunted search of their male literary compatriots for a new myth or "theme" proved redundant when the old ones were still toweringly in place, in their lives as well as their imaginations. Jackson's critical pronouncements on Stein in the 1980s reveal the extent to which she had become trapped in just those assumptions of culture and language that she had struggled so hard against as Laura Riding. In one unpublished essay she goes so far as to link Stein's perverse linguistic games with her homosexuality.

But for both Riding and Stein, being Jews and being anti-Jewish, being women and being contemptuous of women, had a special price. Perhaps Stein's secretive and lasting love for Alice Toklas kept the cost from being too great for her, but Riding left herself no such collateral. In her roman à clef about the suicide attempt, Gertrude Stein, Alice Toklas, Nancy Nicholson, and Norah McGuinness were all lampooned, while Catherine (Laura) was an unconvincing and often bizarre fantasy of serenity, beauty, and wisdom. Following the dictate of her modernist comedian, Riding was obliged to have the last laugh—no matter how hollow it rang—and to be found on her feet after the performance. By the grace of something other than this comedy, at the end of 1929 Laura Riding could be found on her feet.

Laura (Riding) Jackson included an addendum to her 1980 essay on Stein that seemed to convey a more equivocal spirit than her pronouncements. But she seemed to be still describing a dream of that genii outside her window, a composition that was as much a portrait of herself as an epitaph for the woman she had once loved and revered:

> She was, by her own created image of herself, as a compendium of human versatility compressing the range of diversity within it to so abbreviated a representation that she was the God of herself. . . .

Perhaps everyone up to the time of her self-deification was to blame, for the great emptiness that had accumulated in human self-knowledge which Gertrude Stein tried to fill with herself for everyone's edification.

Perhaps, after all, a particle of doubt and affection remained. "If she kept back her last cent," Jackson hedged, "she has hidden it well."

Chapter 11

GOOD-BYE TO ALL THAT

——•——

I am glad women are going mad. It's about time they did.

—Robert Graves to Herbert Palmer, June 1929

——•——

DR. LAKE, THE attending surgeon in the operating theater on May 16, 1929, remarked to those watching him prepare his instruments, "It is rarely that one sees the spinal cord exposed to view—especially at right angles to itself." The initial diagnosis after Laura's jump, Graves wrote to Wyndham Lewis, had been a fractured skull and a broken spine and pelvis; Riding was expected to die within a few minutes. It was then determined that the skull was not actually fractured, but the spine was certainly broken. The prognosis was improved to include a few months of life as a complete cripple or, as Robert wrote to Gertrude, a lifetime of paralysis. Then, as he put it, Laura "decided to recover." Her pubic bone was broken in two places (sometimes it was three), and four lumbar vertebrae were crushed; but the spinal cord was perfectly intact. After a laminectomy to relieve the pressure from the injuries, major surgery to her spine, and an extended period of convalescence, she was expected to make a complete recovery. The height from which she jumped varied: to Gertrude Stein, Robert described a height of fifty feet; to Wyndham Lewis, the Fugitives, Merrill Moore, and Donald Davidson it was sixty feet. In her letter to Moore, who had, Laura imagined, already heard the news, she insisted that she did not try to commit suicide but merely jumped out a window. Geoffrey Phibbs wired to Norah in Paris, "I told you Laura was like Jesus—she dies but has risen again." Norah was much comforted.

The story of the suicide and its aftermath would take as many forms as there were audiences for it. In London, W. B. Yeats told a very entertaining version to Wyndham Lewis, who later passed it on to the American poet Louise Bogan in New York. The police, led to believe by an incoherent Geoffrey that Robert had pushed Laura out the window and killed her, heard from Nancy that Laura jumped while Nancy's back was turned and Robert was downstairs hunting for an emetic. Attempted suicide was a criminal offense, but before the police could begin proceedings to have Laura put in her half sister's charge and deported to California, Robert had his version before Edward Marsh: "Only action from above, from somewhere high out of reach, can make them realize that they are not capable of judging the case." Whitehall stopped the investigation.

Explanations were also forthcoming. T. E. Lawrence, whom Robert was counting on as a character witness for Laura, derided her to a curious correspondent and ascribed the jump to sexual hysteria. But by far the most moving account of the jump was written by Robert Graves three months later, as an afterword to his classic epitaph to the war generation, *Good-bye to All That*. In the events leading up to the plunge Graves saw, like a man facing death himself, the war-torn sequences of his life pass before him. On his trip to Ireland to find Phibbs he traveled on the same boat from the port at Fishguard that had been his hospital boat twelve years earlier. In County Sligo the Irish melodies and anodyne ballads of his father's songbooks returned to him. In Rouen, where he had convalesced from shrapnel wounds to his lung, he connected the hilltop where Laura seemed to die with the hilltop on which he had been given up for dead thirteen years earlier. The journey to David Garnett's in Huntingdonshire to awaken the absconded Phibbs brought him to the same farm where he had courted Nancy and the hope of a peaceful life after the war. As he describes these journeys in the dreamy language of the dedicatory epilogue, he is as a man in fugue, enwrapped in those mysteries which the world had lost or forgotten. He ended *Good-bye to All That* with the invocation, "My lung, still barometric of foul weather, speaks of endurance, as your spine, barometric of fair weather, speaks of salvation."

IN APRIL 1929 Graves was thirty-three years old. Five and a half years older than Riding, he was one of a handful of English writers to have survived the massive bloodletting of World War I. The experience left him deeply scarred and unmoored him from the certainties of an archly Christian and sheltered Edwardian childhood. Just nineteen, he had enlisted as a commissioned subaltern in the Special Reserves of the Royal Welch Fusiliers, a two-battalion home regiment that joined the British Expeditionary Force at the outset of the war. To put off beginning his term at Oxford, Graves imagined the war as a brief but daring interlude, fearfully hoping to see service in the trenches.

These hopes were more than fulfilled. Graves served in both the First and Second Battalions of the Royal Welch, 800-member forces reconstituted with fresh recruits perhaps twenty times during the course of the war. Promoted to captain after surviving the disastrous Battle of Loos, he was wounded during the initial siege of High Wood, part of the Somme offensive in July 1916. The Wood had been attempted by two earlier brigades, both driven back by counter-attacks. The Royal Welch battalion, reduced by casualties to half its fighting strength, suffered an artillery barrage just before going over the top that laid claim to a further third—Graves among them. By the end of the war he had lost all but one—Siegfried Sassoon—of his closest comrades.

On his first leave home, after thirteen months' service, Graves hoped to sleep late, skipping the 7 A.M. church service. He responded to his father's bullying—"hobbling along to my bedroom door at half-past six, banging loudly and saying that my mother counted on my accompanying her, this day of all days"—by pleading a toothache. The 9:30 A.M. service, however, he could not escape, particularly when his mother appeared at the breakfast table with her "prayer-book, veil and deep religious look."

Just after nine the doorbell was rung by the proprietor of the nearby wheelchair business, with chair in tow. Forgetting his father's gout, Graves at first thought that his mother had ordered the chair for

him. But his father soon appeared in top hat and his "better carpet
slippers" and Graves, speechless, took hold of the shoulder harness
(there was a shortage of porters due to the war) as his father hoisted
himself in. The three-hour sermon concerned divine sacrifice and the
"Glurious Perfurmances of our Surns and Brethren in Frurnce." The
return journey, being uphill, was even more arduous, with APG
clutching his wife's prayer book and his son straining against the
chair's harness and "sweating like a bull."

Graves had scruples about publishing this anecdote in his autobiography, as if some residual sliver of faith forbore his ridiculing his
aging father. But when APG published his own memoirs in early 1930
under the title *To Return to All That*, Graves followed him later that year
with *But It Still Goes On*, the wheelchair incident included. This was
the last religious service that he ever attended, and his description of
it is the closest he came to discussing his personal loss of faith.

Perhaps it is now too easy to pass from the idea of trench warfare
after only a serious nod in the direction of casualty figures and a
grimace for the lasting disgrace that the war brought to the twentieth
century. The Great War is not remembered as a war fought by
professional soldiers over distant lands, though for the vast majority
of troops it was exactly that. Rather, it is remembered as a war fought
in the terrified hearts of very young men in the soul of Europe and
thus set apart from those wars in living memory. In their kit bags,
with their Bibles and their letters from home and their pictures of the
king or the kaiser, they kept their Goethe, Rilke, Wordsworth, Tennyson, or Kipling, thus making the war's final impact somehow all the
more shattering and complete. The first and last corpses that Robert
Graves saw during his combat duty were suicides. Of those left
standing or in hospitals at the cessation of hostilities, most knew that
they were lost in one way or another. Theirs was a generation unto
itself, defined by four years rather than twenty, defined by the fact,
however inexplicable, of having been soldiers.

Virginia Woolf, a pacifist, did not perceive the demobilized soldier
in Captain Robert von Ranke Graves. Her conclusion in 1925—"still,
still, he is a nice ingenuous rattle headed young man"—forgets or
overlooks what Graves had been seven years before, a commander of
battle-hardened soldiers, who had been declared dead of wounds on
the eve of his twenty-first birthday. In the ensuing decade, however,

everyone seemed to know what was best for Robert Graves—the hostess Lady Ottoline Morrell and her circle at Garsington, Siegfried Sassoon, even his own mother and father. No doubt Graves encouraged their indulgence, their belief in his innocent helplessness in some way. Nancy, depicted as the root of his problems, tried hard to understand exactly what his problem was. After the suicide attempt she would finally say, "I'm tired of your attitude of poor good Robert and lucky bloody Nancy." She had grown exasperated while he dissembled, caught between stammering and belligerence until he could find the certainty and the voice in which to answer them—all of them.

Paul Fussell has argued persuasively that after the slaughter on the Somme, irony, "the dynamic of abridged hope," became the cardinal virtue of the modernist sensibility, and that this understanding originated principally as a response—"the application of mind and memory"—to the events of the Great War. Irony became a "virtual allegory of political and social cognition." Other scholars have tried to show that the Great War was not the first cause but, rather, a catalyst or a validation of sensibilities and modernist aesthetic strategies already begun. But Pound's call to "make it new" echoed rather hollowly over the Somme battlefield. And irony alone was an insufficient response to the carnage, though noncombatants found it appropriate. Those writers who did survive required a vision that would afford them some possibility of redemption and uphold the honor codes of the battlefield itself, however tentative or privately defined.

What is most astonishing about *Fairies and Fusiliers, Country Sentiment,* and the several critical books that Graves wrote between his demobilization in 1916 and meeting Laura Riding in 1926 is that war had failed to reveal to him the creative possibilities of irony. What he had perfected was a state of mind less discursive and rational, less implicitly defeatist. Often this meant holding fast and blindly to at least two contradictory ideas at once. Thus when he was asked by Bertrand Russell at Garsington whether he would fire on striking British munitions workers, he said yes—and his men would gladly join in, although they all knew that the war, as Russell put it, was "wicked nonsense."

The distance between the two ideas was like the gulf between the German and Allied trenches in France. A no-man's-land of fallen comrades and lost innocence stretched between them, and it was unreasonable to set foot there, even after the hostilities had ceased. In "Lost Acres," published in 1927, Graves, perhaps for the first time, tried to trace the geography of this brutal impasse, gently suggesting its hidden minefields and sacred graves:

> These acres, always again lost
> By every new ordnance-survey
> And searched for at exhausting cost
> Of time and thought, are still away.
>
>   . . .
>
> Invisible, they have the spite
> To swerve the tautest measuring-chain
> And the exact theolodite
> Perched every side of them in vain.
>
> Yet, be assured, we have no need
> To plot these acres of the mind
> With prehistoric fern and reed
> And monsters such as heroes find.
>
> Maybe they have their flowers, their birds,
> Their trees behind the phantom fence,
> But of a substance without words:
> To walk there would be loss of sense.

Under the sustained assault and paralysis of trench warfare, a kind of deadlock had gripped the mind of Robert Graves, a numb code of fear and fortitude. Immediately after the war all kinds of contradictions lodged in the impasse, and all kinds of remedies and absolutions—political and psychoanalytic, personal and aesthetic—presented themselves to fill the breach. Few proved sufficient, though Graves pursued each with wild enthusiasm and imagination. Family life with Nancy and the children was his first refuge. And what sort of refuge was poetry?

In the midst of that war which he would not survive, the poet Wilfred Owen tried to imagine more precisely what he was writing for but failed, concluding only that whatever he was doing had nothing to do with "Poetry." The traditional poetic call to arms was essentially balladic in form and heroic in spirit. Trench poetry, as it came to be known, was something else altogether, reflecting as much a sentimental disillusionment with the English poetry that they had known as with traditional ideas of glory. American poetry and modernism dominated the literary debate after the war, perhaps because so many English poets had been lost, perhaps because America had not been wounded in the way that all of Europe had.

But Graves would always distrust Pound and even T. S. Eliot, at least of Prufrock and the Preludes, seeing in them the darlings of the "side-burned aesthetes" and Noel Coward's "poor little rich girls." The other American modernist poets of note—Wallace Stevens, Hilda Doolittle, Marianne Moore, and William Carlos Williams— were either unknown or of no interest to him, at least until he met Riding. He preferred the poetry of Robert Frost (who was practically a Georgian poet himself); the familiar rhythms, wit, and melancholy of John Crowe Ransom; and the soaring bardic lyricism of Vachel Lindsay. By any measure but the war itself, Riding was an unlikely poet for Graves to pick out of a crowd, reared as he was among the lilting lyrics and songs of his father's Killarney.

Graves did not perceive the ironic quality of Riding's "The Quids" without some prompting. His attention was directed to it by a houseguest, also married with four children, and according to Carolyn Gordon, both men invited Riding to England. By the time Riding arrived, this man had left for India, where he perished of typhoid. Though Laura Jackson has referred to him as Tommy, it was most likely Sam Harries, an Oxford graduate who followed Basanta Mallik to Nepal, a plan that Graves had briefly considered before being taken up with the idea of a lectureship in America. Whatever qualities Graves was then able to perceive in "The Quids," none could have prepared him for the fact of Miss Gottschalk herself.

Bristling with the brusque efficiency of the New World, cursorily surveying the shattered and shabby ramparts of the Old, Laura Riding was ready within a matter of months to dismiss most of what Graves had fought for and written. In the three years leading up to the suicide attempt, she became increasingly insistent on a complete break with the limitations of older and entrenched poetic traditions. Thus when Graves considered Riding's broken body as it lay in the public ward of Charing Cross Hospital, he saw something of himself that he had not seen before. Once conscious, Laura threw tantrums and screamed at the top of her lungs, not from the pain but "for fun" she said blithely, "just to have something to do" she informed Graves' shocked older sister Rosaleen. Slowly he recognized—sometimes dimly, sometimes clearly—the depth of a protest that eclipsed all differences between them.

As in his love for Nancy Nicholson, he saw in Riding's profound contempt for middle-class values and aristocratic pretensions his own silenced rage over the war. With her, the poet and her poetry acquired a louder voice and had demands and ambitions that reached beyond a mere corner of Oxfordshire—something Graves desired for himself without feeling free to ask for. While Riding's problems with Western civilization—it was that large a target by 1929— derived from different causes than his own, her subversive, intelligent stridency allowed him to feel that it "remained for civilization to prove," in the words of Siegfried Sassoon, that their martyrdom as a result of the war had not been "a dirty swindle." After her jump Riding fixed the "end of history" with the end of the war; Graves supported her wholly in her demands for the hereafter.

By the time he wrote *Good-bye to All That*, begun in the early summer of 1929, just before the final break with Nancy, his stammering had yielded to that blackly humorous and mocking voice which he needed. Here at last was *le grand malade* and the buffoon, the modernist comedian for whom the war's grotesque contrast between innocence and obscenity, brutality and preciousness, finds him having the last laugh. If his voice was hard and hollow, refusing to allow creeping sentiment or self-pity, this was as much Riding's voice from her hospital bed as it was his own. After the operation, Rosaleen tried to suggest to Laura that she was lucky to be in the capable hands of Dr. Lake. Facedown on her hospital bed, the surgeon's incision running almost a foot along her spine, Riding demanded, "How do you know that I didn't invent Mr. Lake?" She referred to the man who had saved her from paralysis as the "Insect," and Graves silently applauded. They were beholden to no one.

But, like Graves, Riding's enduring contempt for polite society also masked the extent to which she was captive to its glamour, the fantasy of a high-born and well-spoken composure, the imperial authority of the English language, and those romantic leading men,

Shelley, Keats, Byron, and Coleridge, who had first courted her own poetic voice. What other Jewish girl from New York City could choose as her last words "Good-bye, chaps."? What other Georgian poet would sign off with the slangy and American "good-bye to all that." (Siegfried Sassoon's war memoirs were entitled *Memoirs of a Fox-hunting Man.*)

Graves' ambivalence expressed itself differently. To those who knew him after the war, his tendency to hero-worship and to fall under the influence of others, whether Nancy's or the psychologist W. H. R. Rivers' or Basanta Mallik's, was rather alarming—suggesting, at least to a Victorian mind-set, a weakness of "character." APG kept a close watch on the development of his son's character, writing, at intervals in his diary on its consistency and waiting patiently and lovingly for it to set into the mold of the God-fearing English gentleman. Graves had distanced himself from such expectations, just as he had spurned his father's outdated verse techniques and sentiments during the war. He had promised Edward Marsh that as soon as the "ridiculous" war was over, "I will write Chapter II at the top of the new sheet and . . . will try to root out more effectively the obnoxious survivals of Victorianism."

Yet, if anything was "latent" in the Robert Graves of *Good-bye*, it was precisely that officer and gentleman whom his father was awaiting. In his autobiography, Graves cast his school friend Raymond Rodakowski, the mountain climber George Mallory, T. E. Lawrence, Thomas Hardy, and Siegfried Sassoon as stand-ins for the heroic and gentlemanly roles of the public school, battlefield, and literary life that he abdicated. Christopher MacLachlan has pointed out that in his somewhat doctored portraits of these men, Graves provided vicarious vehicles for his own values, each marking a station and a crisis in his own life. By acting as subliminal witness to a known code of honor, Graves' heroes offer effective counterweights to the amoral satire of the book and to the passivity of its main character.

There was, however, an even tighter bond between Graves and Riding. A shell-shocked victim relives the endless, self-lacerating pain of failure. After the war Graves' guilts assumed monstrous dimensions, requiring desperate measures to police. A chorus of insinuations from his conscience bore down hard upon his most trivial lapses. The sting of his failure to support his family followed him; the standards of Amy's Christian moral purity oppressed him, even after his faith lapsed. The noisy rejection of those social conventions and religious constraints which had nurtured his early childhood fears calmed him somewhat. But the darker questions raised by his actions during the war remained obscured.

Riding knew well the fever of self-accusation; it was as important a part of her disquiet as it was of his. The seat of her imagination, particularly in the poems that she wrote in America, was in this warring self-surveillance, "that shrill antithesis of calm" in which "the goaded brain is struck with ague." Once she arrived in England and felt herself unequivocally loved, she directed her censure outward in literary criticism, snagging other poets, including Robert Graves, where she had so often felt herself stumble.

By appointing Riding as his confessor, Graves was not seeking absolution for a lifetime of guilts (and that included the most unsettling one: that perhaps he did not feel guilty enough). Instead, Riding replaced the haunting voices and ghostly apparitions of combat with her own rigorous moral scrutiny. Her ever-receding promise of salvation through poetry—"Between the word and the world lie / Fading eternities of soon"—served Graves' imagination in a way that Christianity, Nancy, psychoanalysis, and Mallik never would have. For Graves the embrace of her authoritarian mind was as gripping and addictive as the sustaining shock of the war itself; and thus, in the richest resources of his imagination, Riding became Graves' war. As the enemy, she sharpened his senses and kept him alert. And, when wounded and lying in no-man's-land, she gave him the soldier's honor of rescuing a fallen comrade, however suicidal the risks. If despite his skills he was captured, torture followed. Catching him in a lie or hearing him repeat something that she had said as if it were his own thought, Riding would taunt him just as Nancy had taunted when he counted his pennies too attentively. One form of Riding's contempt, delivered to his ear only, was "Blup, blup!" a syllable, she explained in her memoirs, that somehow corresponded to his voice and bearing during these exhibitions.

But time and time again Graves the writer constantly triumphed over Graves the shell-shocked penitent. In him narrative tended to reassert itself tirelessly, under any conditions. Perhaps he truly believed that if his neurasthenia were "cured" he would no longer be able to write. But Graves always seemed fascinated by the pure spectacle of his nightmares, the melodrama of a soul in torture—as if these terrors, too, were mere fantasies, fairy tales of Oedipal conflicts, parables of evil possessions. Hearing of Rupert Brooke's death during the war, Graves had written to a grieving Marsh, "I feel exactly like a man who has watched the 'movies' for a long evening and then suddenly finds himself thrown on the screen in the middle of a scalp hunting Sioux and runaway motorcars; . . . not at all frightened." Geoffrey Phibbs may have swallowed a centipede, but Graves continually swallowed himself. If he stopped dreaming and imagining, he felt he would somehow cease to exist or be swallowed by a terror far larger than those which he might imagine.

AND WHAT OF Nancy, their four children, and All That? Their fate in the aftermath of the suicide attempt was not immediately clear. Until the few months before the leap, the children, ranging in ages from four to nine, had been living apart from their father for some time, though he visited them periodically in Cumberland. For the brief periods when he agreed to relieve Nancy, the results hardly suggested that fatherhood meant as much to him as it had before he met Riding. After spending all of 1927 with Nancy and several weeks on the floor of the Hammersmith apartment, Jenny, David, Catherine, and Sam moved to the *Avoca* barge in January 1928 with the nurse, Doris Ellit, who had been with them in Cairo. Having worked hard to prepare the barge for their arrival, Robert would not listen to the nurse's suggestion that it was not the best place for children, though by this time he could well afford another apartment. Instead, he told her to discuss the matter with Laura. "It was obvious to me," Ellit wrote later, "that neither [Robert nor Laura] really wanted to accept the responsibility for the children but expected me to do so under any circumstances."

Cramped together on the chill, damp barge, they soon had colds. When Sam was discovered by Rosaleen to have bronchitis and a high fever, Robert's response was to fire the nurse for being careless and rude. Returning a few days later to check on reports of her nephew's "recovery," Rosaleen found his condition complicated by pneumonia and an even higher fever. He was put in the hospital for two weeks, and Nancy came to London to take care of the others. Later, Sam fell into the Thames and had to be fished out. By April 1928 the children had recovered from various maladies and mishaps only to come down with diphtheria. They were returned to Nancy's care in Cumberland, and Robert and Laura went off to the Côte d'Azur for their holiday with Polly Antell.

In late December 1928, four months before the suicide attempt, Robert bought the larger and more spacious *Ringrose* barge. In a great spirit of family feeling after a happy Christmas of plum pudding and presents, it was decided that Nancy would return with the children to live on it. Hart Crane, en route to Paris, joined them, though his holiday spirit was muted by flu, which he fought off with Jamaican rum. He found the *Avoca* accommodation less than comfortable, the food indigestible, and Laura in a bad temper. But in late March, Graves sent him a rosy picture of the family, mentioning the "new chap" who shared the flat with them: "Laura has been thinking; but it has been such a positive process that little or nothing else has had room to happen in the same house. It is getting finished now & then she starts *writing*. . . . Nancy and the children are fine. Sam has whooping cough but it makes no difference to him." Graves' capacity for self-delusion rarely stopped short of the magisterial.

Surprisingly, for ten days after the suicide attempt and despite the month of nightmare that had preceded it, these frail family arrangements held. Through a haze of morphine and pain Laura at first expected that the Trinity would resume in Geoffrey's absence. It then appeared that there was, after all, a chance for the four to remain friends—Geoffrey had not gotten away after all; Nancy had brought him back. Only gradually did it become clear that Nancy had indeed brought Geoffrey back—but not, as was expected, to Laura. Upon his return to the *Ringrose* on the afternoon of the jump, Laura (Riding) Jackson later wrote, Geoffrey's love for Nancy was consummated.

In two letters to Nancy on May 4 and 5, 1929, Robert was desperate to systematize the relationships that had resulted from Laura's leap and this new alliance. "It wasn't just a rather messy bit of drama," Robert explained, obviously trying to make sense of what Laura was saying in the hospital. "The mad Geoffrey was killed, so was the over sane Geoffrey. Then the birth of the new medium Geoffrey who is the Geoffrey-with-Nancy. Laura can be very fond of the new

Geoffrey-with-Nancy, but she works now as Laura, not as Laura-with-Geoffrey. His centre is the Ringrose, not the flat. He writes as Geoffrey, not as Geoffrey-with-Laura."

Laura's first, undated, letter to Gertrude Stein from her hospital bed described the new simplicity and freedom that her painstakingly effected death had given them. Weak, yellowish, and wan, she felt that everyone was now free of her power. They had all been very wrong, she admitted, herself included. Nancy was happy with Geoffrey, though shy in front of her and puzzled by Laura's new state of being both dead and alive, out of pain and in pain. Robert and even his friend Len Lye, in his dreamy way, understood. Geoffrey understood her to mean that she was dead in a religious sense; Christlike, she felt that she had chosen to die for his sins. Having now arisen from death, there was a chance for them all to find peace.

But the sight of Nancy and Geoffrey together on May 6, bearing a propitiatory offering on their first visit together to her bedside, was more than Laura could stomach. They arrived with a small plastic bust of Nefertiti, one of the many tawdry curios that proliferated in the wake of publicity surrounding the finds at King Tutankhamen's tomb. The point of this presentation, Laura (Riding) Jackson recalled with disgust, was explained as a homage to her beauty. The two were evicted from the room. Graves dated the breakup of his marriage to this encounter, writing in Good-bye to All That, "On May 6th 1929 Nancy and I suddenly parted company. I had already finished with nearly all my other leading and subsidiary characters, and dozens more I have not troubled to put in."

But the erosion of Robert's regard for Nancy would take longer; his first priority was in seeing that all of Laura's needs were attended to, and soon after her operation she was moved to a private ward. Hart Crane wrote worriedly from Paris, asking what had happened. They had all been sleeping with the Devil, Laura wrote back, and were now all the more wiser. It was to be a long summer.

The mass of documentary material that survived the suicide and its aftermath—not to mention later commentaries and fictional accounts by Riding and Graves—encourage one to believe that it is possible to reconstruct the events and the emotions of the four major participants of the April 27 drama, through every twist and turn of anger, vengefulness, bitterness, compassion, and generosity. There is

Graves' account of his conversation with Nancy and Geoffrey on one of the barges soon after Riding had dismissed them from her hospital room. There are Geoffrey's letters to Laura, Nancy, and Robert before the jump. There are Nancy and Geoffrey's letters to Robert afterward. There is even a letter from Geoffrey's devoted mother in Ireland. Having heard that Geoffrey had moved in with Nancy and Robert's children, she asked Robert if they would all be living together again after Laura came out of the hospital or whether it was a complete break.

Overlooked in both published accounts of the suicide attempt are Laura's and Robert's (mostly undated) letters to Gertrude Stein. In one letter, written at Laura's bedside during Geoffrey and Nancy's May 6 visit, Robert praised Laura's strength and gentleness in dealing with Geoffrey, noting how it had provoked a violent outburst from him. Geoffrey accused her of trying to hypnotize him away from Nancy. Leaving the room, Geoffrey returned and, flaunting his "mean goatish little independence," shocked and bewildered Robert by saying:

> "If I thought that Laura was in anyway to alter my feeling for Nancy in the slightest degree I'd pitch her out of the window and break her neck." Nancy did not protest. Well!

Curiously, in his account of the conversation on the barge Robert reported that Geoffrey had said exactly the same thing with Nancy's silent complicity six days later, on May 12. Since the letter to Stein is written earlier, one must question the authenticity of the latter document and wonder whether the conversation on the barge took place at all.

Nancy's letters to Robert, even after the breakup, reveal that her priorities were steadfastly those of her children. She was unstintingly sympathetic to her husband's anxiety over Laura's recovery but as firm in her own position as her husband was contradictory in his. Despite his initial acceptance of "Geoffrey-with-Nancy," and agreeing upon an equitable distribution of their interests and £200 a year for the children, Robert soon decided that his children would receive nothing from him while his wife lived with Geoffrey. Perhaps counting on her father's help, Nancy accepted complete responsibility for all four children; only when her resources were exhausted would she ask her husband for money. Nancy's letters are not without exasperation:

> Do you wish me to treat your repeated denials of respon-
> sibility for the children and your definite statements on
> two occasions that you never wished to see them again and
> your violent dislike of being left with the children at all—
> as your feelings under strain and not true?

Nancy understood but did not accept the logic behind Robert's eventual denunciation of her and their family life together (he burned their love letters to avoid being "sentimental"). "I know what you feel about us and what you know about us and I know just how much you can't afford to feel about us or acknowledge to yourself or anyone the truth about the whole thing. . . . I know you have to, being you—but curse the you that does it." But by pointing out that Robert had found himself in the position that he had wanted for some time, she would not let him color what had happened with self-pity.

By August, Robert had narrowed his relations with his wife to those of purely pecuniary concern, demanding receipts for every penny of his that Nancy spent. To his correspondents, he tried to make out that Geoffrey Phibbs had not only stolen his wife but was also living off his money. In this respect he replicated Laura's increasing obsession with Geoffrey's indebtedness to her. Geoffrey, who owned nothing but those books remaining at the St. Peter's Square apartment, made repeated efforts to claim his property so that he might sell it. He was met by inventories of all the money and clothes given him and a particular request for the return of a pair of Robert's underpants lent him on his arrival in February. Bemused but now annoyingly steadfast, Geoffrey sent inventories of books, his assets upon arrival, and work done at the Seizin Press, reminding Robert that a great number of his possessions had been "eliminated," including a typewriter. Whatever money paid him, he observed, had come from a select sale of his own library, and now he wanted the rest of it back.

The first letter from Geoffrey's solicitor arrived on July 25, 1929, the day after Robert's thirty-fourth birthday and the day on which he finished *Good-bye to All That*. Having found some of the disputed books for sale in an Oxford bookshop, Geoffrey had finally decided to sue them both for return of the books. Because Robert and Laura saved copies of their responses, the archive of surviving documents from this period thickens noticeably. Laura, home only ten days from the hospital, became intimately involved in the separation of assets and in sending ripostes to the solicitor's demands. In one of her letters she enclosed a bank draft covering the cost of thirty silver three-penny pieces.

There is a bitter portrait of Geoffrey and Nancy in Graves' "Act V, Scene 5" wherein Graves argues for an honest ending to Shake-speare's *Romeo and Juliet*. His final scene proposes two new scenarios for Juliet's nurse and Romeo's page. Instead of bemoaning the lovers' tragic fate, they fall upon their corpses to rifle pockets and purse:

> Or let the feud rage on, with page and nurse—
> His jewelled dirk against her wooden slipper.

Two weeks before they were to leave for France and after a limited number of books had been returned to Geoffrey, Laura received a police summons to appear in court over the matter of the remaining books. It was swiftly followed by a solicitor's request for either an apology, the books, or their equivalent value in pounds sterling. Laura thereupon had her doctor write a letter indicating that she would not be able to appear in court for some months owing to her precarious physical condition, a claim undermined by the tenacity of her correspondence. The same day, she and Robert began work on a "Precis," the basis of the legal defense of her actions and behavior in regard to Geoffrey Phibbs from the day of their first meeting. Car-bon copies of this brief and extended extracts from the other docu-ments tolled the death knell to the Trinity and the Holy Circle. Like most bitter divorces, the ménage ended on a tawdry note, betraying both the rare intimacy and willful innocence of its beginnings. The battle over the books lasted more than twice as long as Geoffrey's two-month residence at St. Peter's Square.

This archive notwithstanding, Martin Seymour-Smith provided another skein of documentation to disentangle and for Laura (Ri-ding) Jackson to dispute. Though amused by the account of the conversation between Geoffrey, Robert, and Nancy Nicholson that allegedly took place on the barge, Seymour-Smith felt it might be improved with the addition of stage directions, such as "Geoffrey stood up and sneered petulantly." Dialogue was also added: "She wants me, she wants to possess me, have me, fuck me," Geoffrey was to have said, referring to Laura. "Isn't that just vulgar? Besides: she thinks she's God. She's sick." With these flourishes, an already suspect 250-word document became a 2,500-word fictional re-creation of the meeting on the barge. Richard Perceval Graves footnoted a few of the specific instances of Seymour-Smith's creative license, coyly concluding that his scholarship at this point "appears uncertain."

Laura (Riding) Jackson went further in questioning the authenticity of Seymour-Smith's sources. In "Opportunism Rampant," an essay finished a year after Seymour-Smith's biography was published, she suggested that Graves, in collusion with his biographer, created many of these documents so that the events might reflect better on himself and deflect attention from his failure to prevent her from climbing onto the windowsill. The book was written, she claimed, to curry favor with literary posterity.

Whether to influence literary history or to bolster a legal case, during the summer of 1929 both Riding and Graves were anxious to prove that Geoffrey Phibbs' monstrous behavior was directly responsible for her leap from the bedroom window. The appearance in two documents of his threat to throw her out—enhanced by Nancy's silent acquiescence and earlier restraining hand on Robert—suggests how sharp Riding's fear of deportation was and how eager she was to look anywhere but inward for murderous intentions. Fifty years later, the complexion of the events had altered significantly. By then Laura (Riding) Jackson was much more willing to point to Graves' culpability than to Phibbs'; his "out of the windowness" was rescinded with the suggestion that he had used a fire ladder to make his descent.

And what quotient of truth could be found in Graves' summer project, *Good-bye to All That?* The author claimed to suffer from sudden spells of amnesia, but when his account of important events was questioned, Graves had a ready reply: "The memoirs of a man who went through some of the worst experiences of trench warfare are not truthful if they do not contain a high proportion of falsities. High explosive barrages will make a temporary liar or visionary of anyone." Paul Fussell concluded from this that Graves had accepted the dubiousness of a rational—or at least a clear-sighted—historiography. The documents on which a work of "history" might be based are so wrong or loathsome or so silly or so downright mad that no one could immerse himself in them for long, Graves implies, without coming badly unhinged.

One is tempted to say the same for the historiography of Riding's suicide attempt, an explosive event that seemed to leave liars and visionaries in every corner. But Graves had drawn no such conclusions about the dubiousness of the historical method; his persistent ambivalence on this score makes him an often surprising and—for scholars of any of the many disciplines that he has poached upon—exasperating writer. Laura Riding was often his collaborator in this mythologizing—and not only in accounts of the suicide attempt and its aftermath. In her later life she composed long tirades on the deviousness of his "mis-picturings" of her life. By then, of course, it was too late.

One is tempted to say the same for the historiography of Riding's suicide attempt, an explosive event that seemed to leave liars and visionaries in every corner. But Graves had drawn no such conclusions about the dubiousness of the historical method; his persistent ambivalence on this score makes him an often surprising and—for scholars of any of the many disciplines that he has poached upon—exasperating writer. Laura Riding was often his collaborator in this mythologizing—and not only in accounts of the suicide attempt and its aftermath.

Only Nancy and her four children failed to provide posterity with their version of events. Before Nancy sent Geoffrey off to marry again (Norah divorced him in 1931) and start his own family, he had lived with her in close companionship for five years, proving a patient and loving stepfather. In the desperate financial circumstances of that autumn he accepted a minor teaching post in Egypt but was soon fired for his nationalist sympathies. On Geoffrey's death in 1956 Graves' elder daughter, Jenny, wrote to his widow that he had been far more important in her life than her father and (with her two husbands) second only to her mother in her affections. "I never made any decision or did anything important (hardly bought a dress, even) without wondering if Geoffrey would approve. . . . It was a much bigger blow when he left us than anybody considered at the time."

By the end of September 1929 all that remained for Robert and Laura's good-bye to become final was to leave England. On October 4, Rosaleen found that Robert and Laura had "vanished" from St. Peter's Square, leaving only a post office box with their forwarding address. Nancy had a curt postcard. Only William Nicholson was told that they were setting out to "stop Time!"

Graves, crossing the Channel with Riding and her masseuse, had ceased to wander in the feints of his own mind; he no longer needed to mediate the sparring disputes of his own conscience. From Riding he understood that he was deeply fathomed and deeply loved, secure in the knowledge that she was even more strict with herself; by her side he would never be far from the truth and its accompanying poetic authority. His poem "The Age of Certainty," published by Nancy Cunard's Hours Press in 1930, celebrated their new estate:

> Content in you,
> Andromeda alone,
> Yet queen of air and ocean
> And every fiery dragon,
> Chained to no cliff,
> Asking no rescue of me.
>
> . . .
>
> Content in you,
> Invariable she-Proteus
> Sole unrecordable
> Giving my tablets holiday.
>
> Content in you,
> Niobe of no children
> Sorrow no calamity.
>
> Content in you,
> Helen, foiler of beauty.

In this new age poetry reigned supreme and the hypocrisies of the traditional moral will were vanquished, replaced with Riding's own "peculiar rectitude of accent." Her intelligence was subtle and far-ranging, and Graves leaped to color her stark vision with the excitement of myth and the resonance of mystery. Through Riding, Graves lived vicariously in a world of good and evil, watching and waiting with her "among the salt and minutes" for deliverance.

PART III

THE OTHER WORLD

Chapter 12

A SMALL CIRCLE OF MEANING

—— • ——

When keeping house is statecraft:
Because the habiting mind seems to itself
Tremendous, as a child writes large.
Then comes maturity, and loss of pride,
And continents give way to islands,
And keeping house is play—
A small circle of meaning
Within a larger, the larger being
Truth . . .

—*Laura and Francisca* (1931)

—— • ——

A MOUNTAIN RANGE called the Sierra de Tramuntana stands abreast of the Mediterranean along the stretch of road from Valldemossa to Sóller. Seen from its bald limestone precipices, the road narrows to a thread, becoming travel in miniature. Like the many olive terraces scribbled into the mountainside, the road negotiates the steep incline by following the ribboning folds of land. If the village is approached by car, the effort of keeping an eye on the sea, some 400 feet below, induces a kind of vertigo. Notions of north and south, height and drop become confused, and distance becomes a matter not of kilometers but of geography and patience. Walking along this road, a rough black pavement when Robert and Laura first traveled it, fills the head differently. Each bend carries its own eddies of sound and smell;

sheep bells mingle with sour carob, the swelling buzz of cicadas with almond. Bands of damp cool shade granted by overhanging pine or evergreen oak alternate with hard sunlight, muddling the senses. Heights vie with sheer drop to distract the eye, test the surefootedness to one's intended destination.

To find this road after the ten-hour night crossing from Barcelona to Palma, one first ascended from the wide coastal plain of the island's interior, along a cactus-lined road, past small olive plantations. Once over the bridge of the coastal mountains, Valldemossa appeared and from there there was a winding descent to the coast road, or *carretera*.

The tiny village of Deyá nests in a natural amphitheater formed by a wide and irregular harbor in these mountains. Centered in the shadow of a looming mount, called the Teix, is a rocky hillock crowned by the village church with its squat bell tower. When the full moon crests the back of the Teix, its light falls first upon the churchyard's small garden of graves and cypresses. Robert Graves, who is buried there, claimed that the church was built on the site of an Iberian shrine to the moon goddess, and he swore that moonlight in Deyá was brighter and stronger than anywhere in Europe. "And moonlight," he added, "is notorious for its derangement of wits."

The graveyard, overlooking the sea a half mile below, is Deyá's highest point. Some springs run all year; but the torrent, the main runoff from the mountains, is dry during the summer, and the resulting stillness seems to suspend the village in another world. By early winter, the torrent's roar, swelled by three springs, breaks the muffled silence, loudest at the edge of the village where it courses through a narrow gorge. There, women would bring their laundry every morning to scrub, gossiping in the washhouse above the rocks. Eluding their tin buckets and soapy fists, the stream then fell through groves of olive, orange, and lemon through scrub of flowers and wild asparagus before arriving in the tiny inlet cove from which Deyá's fishermen set off. In November 1929 the olive harvest was just beginning; the trees were purple with fruit. High above, as far as the dark green belt of the mountain pine, the fires of the charcoal burners smoked silently. It was the season of the fiesta of Todos Santos, the day of the dead and the celebration of the nativity.

The stone cottages of the village, with their terra-cotta roofs and hooded chimney pots, covered the landward side of the hillock, built haphazardly among the twisting stone steps and paths to the church at the top. Strung randomly along the *carretera* and central plaza that collared the hill were more cottages, ending, on the Valldemossa side, with Salerosa. Mr. Short in Palma had found the house for them, and set back from the road, up a dozen stone steps it was, Laura told Hart Crane, exactly right.

There was a glimpse of the sea from the front terrace and, on saint's days, the sight of candlelight processions descending in flickering streams from the crest of the church hill. During the day rows of women in kerchiefs and straw hats worked the surrounding terraces, their fingers plucking the olives and filling small rush baskets. Short snatches of their harvest songs could be heard: songs as ancient as the oldest olive trees, brought by the Moors seven centuries earlier. These were some of the sights of the village that winter. For the price of the parish paper Laura and Robert bought fifty days' "indulgence."

The richest villager was Juan Gelat. His house, abutting the small plaza at the entrance to the village, was the source of everyone's electricity, and at night the light over his front door (backed by a reflector fashioned from an old chamber pot) lit up the main street and the Butcher's café. Around the wooden tables of the café was a motley assortment of geologists, vegetarians, musicians, intellectuals, drunks, and runaway couples; since the late nineteenth century Deyá had been known for its eccentric foreigners. Mostly, it seems, there were a good number of painters from the German colony in nearby Lluchalcari. The Deyá village inn, Sa Fonda, never had less than ten guests, even in winter. Drinking and talking about art and the exchange rate until long after Gelat turned off his generator, the foreigners furnished the village with a steady business and a natural topic of conversation among the women in the washhouses. The villagers had nicknames for those who stayed long enough, regarding them with proprietary, patronizing affection. Unseemly behavior, however, was greeted with unforgiving silence.

In her hospital bed back on that other, colder island some months earlier, Laura wrote to Gertrude Stein that the charges of moral turpitude and attempted suicide had been dropped, as had her deportation proceedings. Nevertheless both she and Robert needed to leave England as soon as possible, to escape the questions and to find a place that would justify being away from England, a place where she might "live untroubled." Len Lye, who had once spent six months in Samoa, suggested Rimatara in the Austral Islands with the enormous enthusiasm of which only he was capable. Out of politeness and affection, Laura considered Polynesia's exotic habitat, only to discount it. The South Seas, she felt, slowed down the mind. Here the mind quickened; this island was not Rimatara.

Mallorca, Gertrude Stein had explained, was "paradise, if you can stand it." Though she and Alice had spent time in Palma, the island's port city, during the war, she couldn't, and they returned to Paris. Gertrude, knowing of Hart Crane's affection for sailors, had first recommended the island to him, but his voyages had recently taken him elsewhere. Before leaving England, Laura had confided to Polly that she detested the idea of Spain, but after a week in Switzerland, following their stay in Belley, this Balearic island became inevitable. On her arrival Laura was delighted to find Mallorca not paradise "but the smallest earth," not

> A favoured island made for man by God,
> But so much godliness as man has
> In being faithful to being man.

LAURA CELEBRATED HER twenty-ninth birthday on a cold January evening in 1930, three months after her arrival in Deyá. Gertrude Stein believed that something inexplicable happens at the age of twenty-nine; it is then that those forces of life which have battled in *Sturm* and *Drang* throughout childhood, adolescence, and youth suddenly seem to arrange themselves, and "life which was all uproar and confusion narrows down to form and purpose and we exchange a great dim possibility for a small hard reality." Where there was misdirection, tumultuous growth, and aspiration with no relation to fulfillment, the twenty-ninth year brings "the straight and narrow gate-way of maturity."

Later, at Salerosa, Riding would write a poem that, despite its length, would be one of her most astonishing and enduring, as if she had at last set a steady foot on the path she had long sought. The simplest observation about *Laura and Francisca* is that, particularly in its first Seizin Press version, it is the avowedly autobiographical story of how Laura and Robert came to live on this small Mediterranean island and how Laura came to love a village child named Francisca. The publication of this "historical and topographical poem" was first mentioned in the 1930 Seizin Press prospectus, in which Riding also announced that "after a year of calm" they were resuming publishing activities in Deyá. More specifically, if more puzzling, the poem would enlighten its readers about how Laura turned into Francisca.

Though at times overelaborate and obscure, this exasperatingly long, come-hither soliloquy evokes the magnetic temper of Riding's six-year reign in Deyá with mesmeric power. The poem may also be seen in retrospect as the end of Riding's obsession with Geoffrey Phibbs. This obsession had worked itself out in several new poems that first appeared in *Poems A Joking Word* and in prose pieces (including "Obsession") published in the Seizin book *Though Gently* and Jonathan Cape's *Experts Are Puzzled*. All three books appeared in 1930, as did *Four Unposted Letters to Catherine*, marking an extraordinary output despite her injuries.

Laura and Francisca was also a rather open invitation to visit Riding in her recently discovered, special, and private "small circle of meaning." Objecting to the terms in which the poem was reviewed in the *Times Literary Supplement*, Riding responded, "Of course I am obscure; I am not offering myself but my hospitality. Nor do I hawk my hospitality abroad. I give out indications of my willingness to dispense hospitality on a basis that protects my integrity as a host." One imagines that this intriguing message was posted thus in the *TLS* for those *entre deux guerres* youths who imagined themselves poets, artists, or truth seekers and thus answerable to her challenge. Not only did they harken to her call, they sailed south in impressive numbers.

The *TLS* critic, eyeing the 658-line poem warily from his intemperate climate, felt that perhaps the obscurity of *Laura and Francisca* reflected the difficulty of expressing "in temporal terms an experience of the eternal." He also thought it too hard to distinguish "Laura" from "Francisca." Which of them, he asked, was "the true Self dwelling in the Eternal Moment" and which "the mundane self inhabiting the world of temporal illusion?"

To find one's way, like any reckless reader at loose ends in London, into Laura Riding's "small circle of meaning" is first to accept her poem's beckoning hospitality. Then, one must risk the loss of known categories ("Eternal Moments," "temporal illusions" first among them) for something else that, "according to the trouble you can take," tests one's sense of direction and balance. Like the labyrinthine paths that wandered over the moon-soaked terraces of the Teix, the poem seems to proceed in compass-ordained directions only to slip into other realms of perception. In *Laura and Francisca* lyrical passages of pointillistic realism slide abruptly into dense metaphysics; the observable, quantifiable world collapses into inner states of mind; and seductive panoramas are brought up short by dangerous precipice. Like a cry in the vast mountainous echo chamber that surrounded her tiny cottage, Riding's voice comes from more than one direction. The poet's warning to readers and wayfarers comes late— perhaps unfairly late in the poem.

> A poem's by—who knows? And must be read
> In prompt mistrust of the designing sense.
> For once you let it have you,
> There's no way out unless to leave behind
> Your wits in it and wander foolish.

Quiet on her hill, "Laura" lies in wait for one of those fellow exiles in the Butcher's café down the road, a certain traveling writer from some German *Burg*. As is often the case in Riding's poems wherein "you" figures, she awaits a specific (though imaginary) gentleman. And so the reader of *Laura and Francisca* is accompanied by this rather dull companion, who asks the stupid questions that a more reticent reader would not dare to pose. Chancing by Salerosa one morning, this German pipes up, affecting disinterest, "Peseta's down to-day. What's *your* story?" The poem is Riding's answer.

Laura and Francisca is divided into three parts—"The Island, and Here," "Francisca, and Scarcely More," and "How the Poem Ends." In the first part "Laura" tells the story of a search for a place of "literal death"; a story told as if by a woman who had not only found this place but also become it. If no man is an island, a woman, one can imagine Riding deciding, is an island. (The means by which similes become equations is one of the mysteries of the poem.) In her search for an island, only the Mediterranean would do—for

only there had the Cretans fashioned their "private idiom of death."
There, too:

> With merchant impartiality the Phoenicians
> Mothered the strangers of the little places.
> Which Athens taught their several prides.
> Corsica, man of France, triumphed too well,
> By littleness was great, and of greatness, nothing.
> Malta, Italy of islands,
> Dreaming of greatness won from fate
> Only an aged bad temper.

Robert and Laura's voyage of discovery was also a "looking round for
the last day," a search for a home where the spirit, though not weary,
might yield to flesh "without a struggle":

> From England sailed shy heroes
> To stretch an empire of interrogation
> As far as man could think—
> Without forgetting the way back to patience.

Their odyssey ended neatly in "Exact Mallorca, minute
Deyá, / Finest and only fraction / Of the sole integer." It is here that
those greedy for truth will find most, if not nearly all of it. In *Laura and
Francisca* Riding's choice is not between truth and untruth, as it had
been following the suicide attempt, but between less and more. In
Deyá, too, Riding believed, those searching for the true self will find
it whole and entire. Is the German interested or is he, like the fly-
swatting crowd at the café, just on holiday? If piqued, he is cautioned
against bringing along his own fancy or fiction (which, as a writer
himself, he is likely to do) to substitute for the poem itself. For it is
only here in Deyá, sedentary and literal, that one fearlessly accepts
death. He may always take a walk in the other direction, toward
Sóller, if he is unwilling or unable to make the journey:

> But I think this is enough to show
> My poem is not travel literature,
>
>   . . .

But a poem, that is, a fact
Standing alone, an island,
A little all that more is
According to the trouble you can take.

By the end of the first part, one has arrived and found not yet Laura but "the samest least of her," Francisca. The "laws of similarity" work throughout the poem to legislate a progress of likenesses; the "finest and only fraction" is to the "sole integer" as "Francisca" is to "Laura." With this discovery arrives the means to achieve what the *TLS* critic might call the Eternal Moment.

In the "briefest day" of the poem "Robert" has gone to the village for the mail and to repair, once again, their landlady's stove. He carries a basket for the groceries and will bring back some rice that "Laura" will put in a tin, a head of lettuce, some cheese, and spice cakes for Francisca. Under the algarroba tree and surrounded by cats Maria, their cook and housekeeper, is cleaning fish. While Laura watches, the combs that keep Maria's long black hair in place slip down, showing a "shy cheek." There is in these details a sense of time as an expertly extended pause, and this is part of the poem's mesmerism; after this "briefest day" comes the "short sleep," from which only those who follow "Laura" all the way into the poem will awaken.

Into what? The long present? The Eternal Moment? Truth? Many years later (there is a puncturing travesty in the so-called historical perspective), after Robert's death, Maria remembered with amazement how at Salerosa two fires were kept burning all day. Women all over the village were impressed with how demanding "la Senyora Laura" was in matters of housekeeping and with the turnover in servants. A clean household was an absolute value for them as well. Because Laura insisted on its being known in Deyá that she was not Robert's wife, many villagers at first concluded that the gentleman who did the errands was her butler. When the village women realized that this was not the case, their astonishment was even greater than their amazement at the extravagant use of firewood. For Juan Gelat's mistress, a very old maid at eighty-five, the astonishment still lingers.

The second part of the poem, "Francisca, and Scarcely More," opens with a vision of a village girl of perhaps six dancing in a violet dress. There are those in the village who already say of her, "Francisca will be wild, she sings":

> This is a way of looking at a child
> With years of hate between.
> Francisca is.
> She witches now, I love her.

Suddenly, the poem slips out of realism; Laura "possesses" Francisca and through this seizure achieves the timeless present, the bewitching "now" of childhood, the "now" of death itself, inexplicably embodied here beneath Francisca's indifferent brow. Watching the child, "Laura" sees herself hiding in Francisca's dancing back, glimpsed between shocks of sun-spattered hair. Once inside Francisca, her voice of "blazing judgement, . . . terrible to see" is muted, kept "prettily."

Here "Laura" pauses, anticipating the German's anxiety at the turn of events. Ever her own literary critic, she stops to explain. Her "sleight of person" is just trifling with her "earnest likeness"; but not to worry. In fact, Laura's possession of Francisca dramatically embodies the poem's central linguistic revelation. As when a name becomes so deeply lodged in that which it names that the sign disappears, so "Laura," through an act of love, achieves autochthonous identity, complete self-possession, and disappears into a primordial and timeless truth:

> Up the slow grade of resemblance creeps
> Identity—till the exact image
> Is unphenomenal.

The "laws of similarity" will lead one ever closer to the final object, but Riding insists that only through the final act of "possession" can truth, like the self, transcend proximate likenesses and historical constructs to become actual.

Before Riding leaves Francisca by the wayside, she follows with her the journey of her toy boat in its voyage down a gutter. Like Robert, whose progress through the village on his errands is also followed in "Laura's" mind's eye, Francisca carries a basket. As the boat founders in a hole the basket is inspected:

> Three cards to laugh at? someone else.
> A sprig to smell? not now.
> Has anything dropped out? perhaps.

By the time the almond blossoms arrived in their second spring in Mallorca, and the sea had calmed enough for Maria to buy fish from the fisherman's wife, the story of the Trinity, "Three cards to laugh at?" had become someone else's story—not Laura's, not the one that the German was trying to understand. The long interim of pain, the creeping toward "an inch of wholeness" had ended somehow in this springtime pocket of Deyá. Dropping into this hole in a gutter's current, "enough danger for a short voyage," Laura had arrived safely.

Laura and Francisca was Riding's myth of that season of "literal death" and "literal life." The London world that had been large and adult, a tottering household of civil insurrection, had shrunk to the exactness of her dollhouse microcosm—the "finest and only fraction"—of being small, tranquil, and sweet-smelling. The colossal self that had been huge with hideous emotion, vivid with shame and vengeance and the "long language of not again," collapsed, too, into the love of a wild child, the silent dark stillness of being Francisca.

Had anything dropped out in the course of this rite of passage? Perhaps. Robert, on his way home, carried a heavier basket. Laura took it from him:

> Dear Robert,
>
> . . .
>
> Sit down and rest now, today has taught you
> At least to feel no new despair.

Having left behind family and friends, literature, and All That, what was to be the fate of their little ship? What did their baskets hold? Had they come to Deyá, perhaps, to die? Was this the meaning of "literal death" and their "looking around for the last day"?

Laura, hearing from Gertrude that she was working to save the sentence, replied that she was trying to save the word. (Robert's responsibility was the letters of the word.) Coming across the word "death" in a Riding poem or prose work, particularly in the rash of writings that followed her suicide attempt, one is awash in a whirl of possible meanings. Responding to Merrill Moore's comments on *Poems A Joking Word*, Riding connected this reconstruction of words with the reconstruction of her self. Ostensibly a gift of history, language required from her a patient extraction of meanings before she told Moore, she could begin to know herself. If ever a word needed saving it was "death," and if ever identities needed new wellsprings of meaning that season, Laura Riding and Robert Graves were among them.

In the intricate process of reconsidering her self, "death" was requisitioned for *Laura and Francisca* to play a leading role. Naturally, for a woman who has pursued "death" without benefit of cushioning metaphor or the distancing of bodily conceit, the word takes on added dimensions. This new "literal death" was an older, more experienced cousin of those unsuccessful suitors in her unpublished poems or of those modern sisters in the poem "Chloe Or . . .":

> But the embarrassment of the suit will be
> Death's not theirs. They will avoid aggression
> As usual, be saved by self-possession.

It was beyond even the "death" who had ravished in the impassioned presuicide poem, "Death as Death":

> A dullness fallen among
> Images of understanding,
> Death like a quick cold hand
> On the hot slow head of suicide.
> So it is come by easily
> For one instant. Then furnaces
> Roar in the ears. Then hell is live.
> Then the elastic eyes hold paradise
> At visible length from the invisible mind.
> Then hollowly the body echoes
> "Like this, like this, like nothing else."

So what is this new death? If "Laura" has come to Deyá and extended an invitation to come find her there, in a timeless standstill, in the company of "literal death," what can one expect to find upon closer inspection of her meaning, upon finishing the poem?

In "How the Poem Ends," the third section of *Laura and Francisca*, the flirtatious and coy "Laura" is replaced by a sober one, her soliloquy becomes richly rhetorical in the use of symbol and imagery, and her rhythmic intonation more enveloping, conspiring. Her caller comes closer, narrowing his focus, perhaps up the steps to the terrace. For in what direction does the interrogatory proceed if not closer to the literal "Laura," in dizzying inwardness? From the cool interior of the stone house, the traveler is directed to meet Francisca at play:

> Francisca, here's a gentleman from life
> Come all this way to meet you . . .

But the restless foreigner has not come to see this unfriendly little girl, he will not be distracted.

So where could "Laura" be? Might this gentleman, she now asks, approach the door and look in, even if he disdains to enter? Out of the glare of the tropical sun the house is dark; map and compass are useless:

> I lie from Deyá inward by true leagues
> Of earthliness from the sun and sea
> Turning inward to nowhere-on-earth.
> A rumoured place? That takes us to the moon?
> Let it be moon. The moon was never more
> Than a name without a place to match it. . . .
> In Deyá there's a moon-blight always
> On the watery irises of fancy.
> And minds that feed on bodily conceits
> Go daft in Deyá, especially Germans. . . .

With this, "Laura" goes too far. The German withdraws in skeptical disdain; he is insulted. What is a poem after all? He considers the fine paper on which this one is printed, the book itself. Indeed it is exquisitely produced but remains, for all that, just a book. "Laura" admits her part in the presswork. She does the inking, Robert the pulling of sheets. He considers further the poet herself—what does she know? She is human, is she not? She lives, breathes, and eats, doesn't she? He has kept his wits about him, "Laura" avers. Where does that leave them?

> . . . What shall we think?
> The circumstances are at once
> Too natural and too poetical
> To determine either doubt or belief. . . .
> Let's ask Maria . . .

Maria, a well-bred servant, responds rudely, "Who asks?" She knows her business. Perhaps Juan Gelat will oblige; all the foreigners go to him with their difficulties:

> If there's a settlement between
> Your certain sanity and mine,
> He'll make it, and with no disrespect
> To either party, a *pax mallorquina*
> Founded on mutual regret
> That ever did we meet to differ.

The idea of suicide and its corollary in the cessation of creativity has had a tense grip on the American poetic imagination of this century. (Three years to the day after Riding leaped from her windowsill, Crane jumped into the Gulf of Mexico, clad only in his pajamas. His body was never found.) But in the months following her suicide attempt, Riding appeared to gain in vitality, incorporating her fall into her sense of herself as endowed with uncommon and transcendent purpose, entering a period of intense and remarkable creativity. The finish yielded the "Laura" of *Laura and Francisca*, beguilingly transformed, the Laura in exile, a "name without a place to match it," and the "stranger you can't do without."

Robert Graves lovingly held up to her one of the mirrors in which Riding would continually consider new aspects of herself. "On Portents," one of his first poems written in Deyá, captured the "habiting mind" of Laura in her cool stone cottage at the edge of the village:

If strange things happen where she is,
So that men say that graves open
And the dead walk, or that futurity
Becomes a womb and the unborn are shed,
Such portents are not to be wondered at
Being tourbillions in Time made
By the strong pulling of her bladed mind
Through that ever-reluctant element.

He was to be her witnessing apostle, and the years in Deyá were to usher in his own Age of Certainty, the rock upon which he would later found his church.

Hand in hand with Riding's poetic make-over after her suicide attempt would be an ever expanding wardrobe and a glittering array of accouterments. Margarita *la modista*, the dressmaker and dealer of antique fashions in Palma, held up another mirror as she assisted Riding in taking on the color of her surroundings. There were waistcoats and velveteen trousers for Robert, silk blouses with collars of old lace and old-fashioned Spanish costumes with brocaded skirts for Laura. The close-fitting bodices of rich velvet required some alterations to suit la Senora's smaller frame. Lace mantillas were purchased, and friends in London contributed fur hats and boots, stockings and special Japanese silks for her underclothes. Laura even took to sporting the immaculate white muslin headdresses worn by village women on special fiesta days. She disdained only the peasant rope-soled espadrilles, preferring a black or scarlet leather shoe with a stout Cuban heel and a rhinestone buckle on its strap. The fillet from the London goldsmith also arrived, a kind of headband in which "Laura" was spelled in Greek letters across her brow. Though Laura explained to Gertrude that she wore it to keep her hair tidy, she took it out only on very special occasions.

In these clothes Riding felt herself beautiful, pregnant with meaning. In her delicate "Because of Clothes" they are the maturing medium by which matter and thought, sense and foolishness, body and head, goodwill and purpose are conjoined and balanced:

Inner is the glow of knowledge
And outer is the gloom of appearance.

But putting on the cloak and cap
With only the hands and the face showing,
We turn the gloom in and the glow forth
Softly.

And thus by the neutral grace
Of the needle, we possess our triumphs
Together with our defeats
In a single show of contradiction.

The antique dealers in Palma also received regular visits from Laura and Robert during their six years in Deyá. Rings, earrings, necklaces, bracelets, and brooches filled the special boxes lined with plush and satin on Laura's dresser. In the original version of "Jewels and After" Riding strung a "bejewelled progress" of associations, beginning with the idea of jewels as both an escape from danger and a pathway to death. This "death" is the death of passions, its jewels those of memory and

The unprecious jewels of safety,
As of childhood.

Like the cold, glittering embrace of death, the safety of childhood suggested to Riding the safety of love without danger of pain: the jewel, like the poem itself, perfect in pristine invulnerability.

Laura's pleasure in her jewels and elegant clothing—those tokens of love from Robert or whomever—was spontaneous and childlike. Many of her friends gave her gifts just to share in this pleasure, rather than as an act of homage. On a day trip to Palma, Laura had her heart set on a particular item that she wanted one of her houseguests to buy her. When he failed to take her hint, she returned to Deyá furious, carefully explaining her anger to a friend. Though there is a hint of spoiled temper about this greediness, gold coins, jewels, expensive gifts, and even stock certificates figure throughout her stories and poems as the frank material of love. Clothes and jewels were never mere decoration or vain costuming but a protective, self-tailored womanhood unavailable to her, in these years at least, by other means.

Riding's ability to fashion a living personal mythology stemmed in part from the dead seriousness of her quest for poetic truth and in part from her highly developed, often bruisingly comic sense of play with those men (rather fewer women) who gathered to behold her. As the circumstances surrounding her suicide and as her various writings about it suggest, it is impossible to separate the theater from the sincerity, the epiphany from the absurdity. Combined, these powers afforded her a means of survival, allowing her to generate endless new narratives of self, each insisting upon an even greater proximity to truth than the self that came before. The woman who now stood before Robert and the *modista* had a presence entirely unlike the one that she had in London. Ironically, her belief that time had ended and that they were living in the shadow of a looming apocalypse seemed to steady her, transferring the imagined locus of conflict from within to without. Laura Riding was now "at home," ready to receive callers.

But that season of "literal death" and the child's game of playing house and dress-up had yet to arrive. Within a month of their arrival in Deyá, winter set in "blowing like hell," and in the steady rain their well rose ten feet in five days. Robert asked a friend who was planning a visit to bring two pairs of flannel trousers, mentioning that he had not bathed for weeks. The brazier, fed with bits of charcoal and olive pits, was kept stoked, and at night they tried to keep warm with eiderdowns and woolen jerseys. There was some comfort in knowing that they were at last rich—Jonathan Cape had already sold 40,000 copies of *Good-bye to All That*—and they began to think about building a house on the Sóller side of the village. It was to be called Canelluñ, which in Mallorquin meant "house farther on, past place names." From Salerosa's kitchen window they could see that that side of the valley had a longer, warmer day.

Robert did steady work on an autobiography of God and on the poems that would be published the following year in *To Whom Else?* Laura, waiting for the Seizin Press to arrive, wrote letters and worked on "Obsession," the prose piece that would appear in her next book, *Experts Are Puzzled*. Some of her work involved soliciting letters for a book entitled *All That Gets Posted* (eventually published as *Everybody's Letters*). With this book in mind she told Gertrude that she wanted to open a long-closed correspondence with her mother and that she planned to include Geoffrey's letters to her. She later changed her mind about them, but most of the afterword to the book had to do with laying his ghost. Before the summer of 1930 began she had walked down the steep and stony incline to the Mediterranean without her stick, and Robert could write proudly to Gertrude that Laura now had a spring in her step.

Every evening before ten Gelat flicked the lights, a warning that he was preparing to shut down the generator and turn in for the night. After that there was only the wind or the rain, and whatever thoughts kept them wakeful; wondering and waiting for that short sleep within the moonlit walls of their tiny cottage:

> Francisca, anti-narcissus of me
> Be a fate unapparent yet half-sweet,
> Whom tiredness may succumb to without shame
> While stubborn days of will push on to death
> More personal and more death-like to know.

Chapter 13

THE DAMNED THING

—— • ——

Stir me not,
Demons of the storm.
Were I as you would have me,
Astart with anger,
Gnawing the self-fold chain
Until the spell of unity break,
Madness would but thunder
Where sorrow had once burned. . . .

—"Because I Sit Here So"

—— • ——

LUCIE BROWN, A young fashion designer, had only just arrived from London for a holiday in Mallorca when she received a telegram from Laura warning her not to get involved with Elfriede Faust. But Elfriede, whom Laura had banished from Deyá, was also staying at the Royal Hotel and had already found her. By the time Lucie arrived at Laura's dinner party at Salerosa, she had heard Elfriede's side of the story. Privately, Lucie had thought the young, tubercular Hamburg girl with a hectic flush in her cheeks "rather nymphomaniacal," particularly when she persisted in following her around (even when she retired to the lavatory), pouring her heart out and giving her "rather magnificent" gifts. Lucie was glad to get away.

Now, dancing rather drunkenly in a village café, Lucie listened in awestruck bewilderment to Robert as he bemoaned his sexual torments. Laura wouldn't sleep with him anymore. This gangly, awkward man, dressed in a brocaded waistcoat with silver buttons, was quite unlike the man she had once met in London. His wild and staring eyes completely unnerved her; she found him bombastic and "quite insane." Sitting down afterward, Laura joined their conversation, and in Lucie's words, "not a stone was left unturned in the revelation of both their complicated emotions. I felt rather an outsider as I didn't understand why so many charged-up feelings should be discharged on me."

Naturally broad-minded, Lucie Brown was no stranger to idiosyncrasies in sexual matters. Returning from the trenches, her fiancé told her that the purpose of intercourse was to have children. After four years of marriage, her doctor discovered that she was still a virgin. Her husband also proved to be a sadist. The unhappiness this caused her, she concluded in her memoirs, drove her to what her childhood nurse might have called a "short cut to the devil." After leaving her husband and going to art school, Lucie became a popular model for the London art crowd. At the same time she became acquainted with powdered and long-haired young men, members of the Oscar Wilde cult that flourished in London during the early 1930s; they chose to broaden her mind even more. Her escort was an adoring young aesthete named Basil Taylor, of whom Lucie wrote, "it rather wore me out that Basil was 75 per cent homosexual." He was also a talented painter, but the encouragement of his tutors at the Royal College of Art meant little to him; he "rather liked parties" better. It was Basil who presented Lucie at the garish court of Great Ormond Street, the venue of Cedric Morris and Lett Haines (Bloomsbury called him "Don't Lett Haines"). "It was the aim of all the bright young people to be invited to these orgies," Lucie recalled with satisfaction.

In their salon Lucie found herself amid disporting politicians, female impersonators from the music hall, drunken prelates, and handsome youths garlanded and draped in trailing ivy. If the conversation veered too far from current sexual imbroglios and scandals, an "indecent sallie" from Haines was sure to bring it back. While Lucie was a sought-after decoration, often arriving in elaborate costumes of her own or Basil's design, something of her ingenuousness clung to her. Dancing one evening on the arm of a young painter (wearing a

Gainsborough hat with ostrich feathers and a cerise silk dress, with a long skirt hooped up one side to expose bright green boots trimmed with white fur), she was astonished to see him recoil in horror after what she thought was an innocent remark. "That's the most disgusting thing I've ever heard a girl say," he admonished her. She and Basil generally arrived back at their Hampstead flat "with the morning milk."

It was in this colorful demimonde that Lucie had met the young and promising painter John Aldridge. Tall and sleek, Aldridge was attractive to both men and women, though a quizzical and polite aloofness kept all but the most daring comers at bay. One contemporary described him as "good-looking in a neat, sparing way" with "a lean look of speed." His love for fast cars belied his cautious and controlled manner, and altogether Aldridge was not an easy man to fathom; he apportioned his affection in secret measures, never giving all of it to any one. Lucie had known him for about a year before he ended his affair with Cedric Morris to retrieve her from her increasingly disastrous one with Basil. She fell in love with him almost immediately. While not an active homosexual, Aldridge was vain enough to accept Cedric's courtship, perhaps because one of Cedric's fetishes was helping young artists' careers. Lucie, however, thought John "naughty" to torture Basil as he did; Basil was seriously "keen" on John as well.

Toward the end of 1931, soon after they got together, Aldridge was called to Deyá by Laura, whom he evidently kept apprised of his more nefarious doings. Laura insisted that, despite the considerable success of his London exhibition at the Leceister Galleries (the critics likened his work to Constable's), he could not keep out of "mischief." It was foolhardy for him to postpone his trip any longer, she felt, referring *en passant* to his recent descent into sin. She enclosed a check to pay his passage. He sailed for Deyá, leaving Lucie bereft until a providential phone call from her aunt—asking if she wouldn't like to escort a niece to Palma—saved her from great misery. Cedric Morris was left stewing in "acid jealousy" and Basil Taylor, in gin.

Before she sailed, Lucie received dire warnings about Laura Riding from a former lover of Aldridge's who had accompanied him on an earlier trip to Deyá: "She said I would be used like a pawn in a game of chess." Lucie was thus surprised when, upon meeting her at the Palma docks, John brought a little note of welcome from Laura. From the look of expectation on his face, she "realised that this was a tremendously important jesture." An invitation to dinner at Salerosa arrived at the Royal Hotel shortly after the telegram warning about Elfriede Faust.

From Elfriede, who appeared to be still traumatized by her eviction from the Deyá circle, Lucie learned that her disfavor was the result of having become pregnant the year before by Robert. The affair had come about at Laura's instigation because of her decision to stop sleeping with Robert; Elfriede was invited to come live with them at Salerosa. Laura had explained matter of factly to John that Elfriede's body was an extension of that side of herself which she had recently chosen to withhold from Robert. The pregnancy, however, was wholly Elfriede's and wholly unforeseen. Laura, Elfriede told Lucie, arranged for an abortion and stood at the foot of the bed while it was done. Elfriede later took revenge on Laura by spreading a story (almost carried by *Time* magazine) about a mountain compound in Mallorca where two poets entertained unsuspecting guests; once inside the walled courtyard, they were set upon by savage dogs.

Whether or not she believed Elfriede's sorry tale, Lucie still felt that in Laura's eyes it was she who bore the stigma of a depraved past. She considered the dinner party that evening a kind of test of her moral mettle. Laura and Robert had once visited the notorious drug den of Ham Common, where Lucie and Basil had "gone to the dogs entirely" in the company of two pub-crawling, cocaine-snorting sisters, one of whom was crippled by polio. "She could have learned to walk," Lucie insisted, but she made the most of her infirmity and thought it romantic to be carried, "especially if there was a man to carry her." The woman often left drinks under her bed as a lure for Basil to sleep with her. By the time Robert and Laura visited the Ham Common digs, it had also become open house for Aldridge and a young Oxford poet named Norman Cameron.

Laura's cold disgust at these goings-on had left Lucie with the impression of a "rather unpleasant white-faced disagreeable woman." Ornamented as she was now in the gold fillet and one of her more exotic Mallorquin costumes, Laura struck Lucie as a figure of considerable "magisty." Overhearing Laura tell John, "I love the child" in the course of the evening, Lucie immediately had a sense of safety and security.

THE MOST "RATIONAL" ideas concerning sexuality can often mirror the most deeply felt emotional needs of an individual and a time. This was certainly true for Laura Riding and Robert Graves. The Elfriede debacle doubtless influenced her reflections not only on her relationship with Graves and others of the shifting Deyá circle but also on her work. She would later write, as if to justify her behavior over the Elfriede incident, "Women see to it that nothing is suppressed. . . . If man feels any timidity in doing what it is in his will to do, they do the thing along with him, to put the matter on record." From what her half sister, Isabel, had always called Laura's "keeping of accounts," certain ideas about sexuality and poetic authority presented themselves to Riding and with them an increasingly didactic aesthetic. In the past Riding's criticism had concentrated on the virtues of poetry over other art forms and on the placement of poetic authority above historical or even divine authority as a means of attaining universality and ascertaining final truths. More and more, however, a "female-centered" aesthetic entered her life and the lives of her company in Deyá; questions concerning poetic authority remained unchallenged, but the poetry itself seemed shunted aside.

Riding was not, of course, the only intellectual of the time attempting to define and understand the worrisome topic of sex, but her conclusions and proscriptions were often the most radical. In 1933 Riding would renounce sex publicly for her autobiographical sketch in *Authors Today and Yesterday*:

> I like men to be men and women to be women; but I think that bodies have had their day. The fundamental relation which has to be made is between the male mind and the female mind, and in this relation the female mind is the judge, and the male mind the subject of judgement. Physicality only postpones judgement. But the male mind has now had all the time there is for working up [its] case.

Laura Riding by Ward Hutchinson

Helen Mayers, Isabel's sister-in-law

Ida Prighozy

Sylvia Bernstein

Polly Antell

Allen Tate

Donald Davidson

Robert Penn Warren

John Crowe Ransom

Louis G. Gottschalk

Laura Riding Gottschalk, *winner of the 1924 Nashville Poetry Prize for best poem*

Isabel Reichenthal Mayers, Laura's half-sister

obert Graves in 1929, as he appeared in
e frontispiece of Good-bye to All
hat

Geoffrey Phibbs, artist unknown

ancy Nicholson, Robert's wife, with their children Catherine, Sam, Jenny, and David

Deyá, Mallorca: Karl Goldschmidt, Robert Graves, Laura Riding, and some village women

Jean Marroig Gelat

Francisca, the young Mallorcan girl befriended by Laura

Griselda Jackson

Schuyler Jackson

Jackson

Tom Matthews

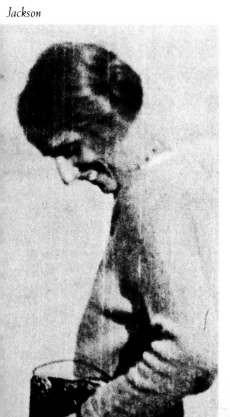

Laura (Riding) Jackson on her front porch in Wabasso, Florida

Her draft of this statement denounced sex between women as vile, sex between men as comic, and sex between a man and a woman as immoral. Answering a questionnaire sent to her by Geoffrey Grigson's magazine, *New Verse*, she said that she quite clearly had not been influenced by Freud. To the question, How do you regard him? she answered emphatically:

> Poets are not influenced by people, but have community with people. Freud's notion of community is an identity in sexual obsession. As I think sex is disgusting and he loves its disgustingness, community between us would be rather like me going to D. H. Lawrenceland.

The *Authors Today and Yesterday* statement was accompanied by a recently completed portrait of Riding by Aldridge ("Painting is a mute form of writing; I think there exists only one eloquent living painter.") In 1933, during the summer following Lucie Brown's first visit, Laura asked John Aldridge back specifically to paint her, the request carrying the weight of an aesthetic consummation of their relationship. In the painting Aldridge caught not only Riding's remarkably deep and penetrating gaze but also her thinly set lips and chin and a tense, square-shoulder attention to inquiring viewers. Her only complaints about the portrait were that its perfect symmetry was compromised by one shoulder's being slightly higher and one lip's being slightly thinner than the other. When Lucie arrived a month later, she found John shaken and rattled and painting entirely under Laura's direction. Further, Laura made them sleep with the door to the guest bedroom open. Riding's autobiographical statement finished her clipped account of herself and her work with the challenge: "I am tidy, quick, hard-working, good-humoured, and let absolutely nothing go by." After a few days under Laura's roof, Lucie was in tears.

Riding's decision to stop sleeping with Graves was still, in 1931, a personal one discussed extensively and without hesitation among friends. These conversations were not the first in which Riding had attempted to articulate her problems with male sexuality. As early as 1927 she had confronted the subject head on in "The Damned Thing," a ferociously comic essay which appeared in *Anarchism Is Not Enough*. Not since Anthony Comstock or Christabel Pankhurst's *The*

Great Scourge and How to End It (1913) had sex been treated in such an arresting manner for the prurient public.

This was the voice of male sexual desire as Riding heard it:

> "My sexual glands, by the ingrowing enlargement of my sex instinct since childhood and its insidious civilized traffic with every part of my mental and physical being, are unfortunately in a state of continual excitement. I have very good control of myself, but my awareness of your sexual physique and its radiations was so acute that I could not resist the temptation to desire to lie with you. Please do not think this ignoble of me, for I shall perform this act, if you permit it, with the greatest respect and tenderness and attempt to make up for the indignity it of course fundamentally will be to you (however pleasurable) by serving you in every possible way and by sexually flattering manifestations of your personality which are not strictly sexual."

Although Graves was clearly the butt of this essay, "The Damned Thing" would always remain one of his favorites. Simply and forcefully, Riding had reversed the Judeo-Christian equation of women and sin, casting the guilt on the male perpetrator. That sex was a morally ambiguous act was understood. But it took her until 1933 to clarify the precise nature of its turpitude. At that point Amy Graves was informed, in a polite letter from Laura, that her physical relationship with Robert had been wrong and was now finished. By then Laura had taken to wearing an 1830s dress with a near-bustle, thereby divesting her appearance of any remaining vestige of her former "flapperishness" or art-school allure. Even the village women of Deyá did not wear ankle-length skirts. Riding continued to give them a great deal to consider.

In private correspondence she was prepared to go even further. Her body was indestructible and indivisible, she told a virtual stranger, on hand only for the purposes of the "governing 'I.'" She intimated that she had never shared Graves' bed (as late as January 1931 theirs had been a "thoroughly unplatonic" relationship). As for children, there were more than enough already. What remained important was for everyone to understand that history was finished, and once that was accepted, each must choose whether to accompany herself and the truth—or proceed into "nothingness."

Riding obviously enjoyed writing outrageous letters to see how far she might go and with what results; she seemed to thrive on the notion that she was every man's worst fear. One such young man, writing from Bradford, England, responded to the rejection of his poems with a "smutty postcard," and Riding pursued the correspondence (writing that his letters were unacceptable) for a year until she was obliged to notify the Bradford police. She reported to Aldridge that the young man had begun writing obscenities and confessing his sexual misdeeds. (Aldridge seemed to share her laboratory interest in human behavior, but even he had his fears.) After interrogating the young man, the chief constable of Bradford reported back by letter to Riding; the youth admitted that he had started out by trying to justify himself but later just found "some morbid satisfaction which he could not properly explain."

The renunciation of sex and sexuality was to shape Riding's view of feminism dramatically. In 1928 she felt feminism fundamentally wrongheaded and entirely insufficient to waylay the male assault on the female person. The careful placing of the ritual "obstacles with which she conditions her capture" in the traditional mating dance had changed only slightly with the advent of suffrage. Contemporary feminism, Riding felt, was only a more sophisticated version of the insistence of a woman's "value as a prize." Harsher measures were called for in order to compensate for the "indignity of [women's] position." Such measures did not include further agitation for greater political and economic freedoms; Riding was far more interested in what men needed than in what women did.

In the afterword to *Everybody's Letters*, written after the publication of *A Room of One's Own* in 1929, Riding declared Virginia Woolf simply too forgiving. By this book Woolf had proved only that "she was a better friend of men than of women." Men had shown themselves ready for something more than niceness, Riding felt; they were in fact, quite tired of niceness. What exactly they wanted from women, she admitted, was uncertain. What her readers and visitors to Deyá received was a clinical disquisition on sex (if often tongue-in-cheek) and a point of view that had more in common with the

unflinching dissections of the psychoanalytic couch than with the
elegantly limbed introspection from the room of one's own:

> The child begins with crude sex alone. It innocently in-
> dulges itself in sensual pleasures. It loves kissing and to be
> kissed, stroking and to be stroked, fondly contemplating
> its excretions. The civilized society into which it is born
> magnifies the importance of these insignificant local sen-
> sations, gives them intellectual depth. It creates a hand-
> some receptacle, love to contain the humours of this
> unnaturally enlarged instinct.
> So much at any rate for the male child.

Considering all the foolish things written by men about the "essential" nature of woman, and all the disciplinary measures taken to
see that she remained true to it, such a mirror vision of the "essential"
nature of man seems an inevitable reply. But beneath the exhibitionist
veneer of Riding's humor is the ache of loneliness; the essay ends
almost plaintively: "When . . . will man grow up . . . become woman,
when will she have companions instead of children?"

Not satisfied with mere satire, however, Riding pursued the impli-
cations that such a view of male sexuality imposes on the subject of
art and on the creative imagination. Her 1923 expectation of "a new
romanticism and a new romance" of poets with "the souls of children
and the sense of men" had suffered a grinding disappointment; and
there is little doubt that the fading attraction of Robert and the
difficulties of his constant demands on her were partly responsible. In
his persistent attempts to revere her she had perceived not only the
concealment of his priggish disgust with sex but also ulterior literary
agendas. A line of her poem "Two Loves, One Madness" despaired
that "She understood his wooing wrong. / He never meant her more
than paper." Riding explored this exploitation more graphically in
"The Damned Thing":

> Woman is the symbol to man of the uncleanness of bodily
> existence, of which he purifies himself by putting her to
> noble uses. . . . Through her he can refine, ritualize and

vary his monotonous and trivial appendage. She is the
means by which he adapts himself to what he is unable to
assimilate mentally. . . .

The resulting "phallus-proud works of art," in which the female is
dressed up in a variety of alluring disguises, was for Riding no better
than an indecent and "private play with [woman] in public," a male
monologue. In 1933, after further observations of Robert Graves at
work, she concluded that man pursues his imagination rather than
truth in his art, "where he can juggle the facts according to his will."
By trusting what he thinks or imagines, she warned one correspondent, man dies inside his imagination. Equally, a man becomes "in-
sanely dead" by the physical conquest of women. Sex for Riding
quickly became a metaphor for the corrupt mythohistorical imagination that she found in Graves, while her more poetic celibacy revealed the way to truth. "The rigor takes/The body first," she wrote in
Laura and Francisca; "the mind comes of itself."

Apart from her serious physical injuries, the collapse of Riding's
love for Geoffrey Phibbs and its accompanying shame had brought
about an increasingly surgical attitude toward the offending act of
lovemaking and the conspiracy of emotion and sensation that led up
to it. Riding sought the culprit not only in the demonization and
caricature of "Fibs" but also in the way she perceived and imagined
her own body. Women's bodies were the first to betray them, she
wrote to one correspondent. In Laura and Francisca she questioned the
use of bodily conceits, a staple of her early work, but she would
return to them in such poems as "Because of Clothes" and "Signs of
Knowledge."

In particular, the cuts she made to "Organs of Sense," a long poem
written in Louisville, exemplify her change in attitude toward tactile
sources of intelligence. Originally, this poem was a masterfully inven-
tive self-portrait laden with elaborate, conceit-filled descriptions of
her eyes, ears, mouth, and nose. A version of it appeared in The Close
Chaplet. In the final version of the poem, entitled "Pride of Head," the
intellect reigned supreme over more restive "cross purposes," and the
offending sense organs had been cauterized. One imagines that this
was the imperial being whom Lucie Brown found ensconced in Deyá
in 1931:

. . .

My head is at the top of me
Where I live mostly and most of the time,
Where my face turns an inner look
On what's outside of me
And meets the challenge of other things
Haughtily, by being what it is.

From this place of pride,
Gem of the larger, lazy continent just under it,
I, the idol of the head,
An autocrat sitting with my purposes crossed under me,
Watch and worry benignly over the rest,
Send all the streams of sense running down
To explore the savage, half-awakened land,
Tremendous continent of this tiny isle,
And civilize it as well as they can.

But Robert Graves wanted his own empire to administrate, and to
attain it he could never follow his idol Samuel Butler's adage, "Wise
men never say what they think of women." Though Riding often
protested, he was unable to completely cease in the "private play with
her in public," and the visage of Riding recurs repeatedly in his
poems throughout the 1930s. Graves' need to possess Riding creatively became as vociferous a craving as his physical desires had
been. Still, the extent to which she participated in his various
fantasies—Isis, Christ-Woman, Moon Goddess, Lilith, Hecate—
cannot be neglected either. Each figure tended to spawn her succession of ever enlarging and more glittering mantles. Even though, one
by one, she rejected them and those poems in which they appeared,
she also used them to sustain herself creatively and to captivate the
essentially male audience surrounding her. Asked by one such admirer whether Robert knew that she was a "magician," Laura answered that Robert, out of self-protection, did not let himself know
more than he needed to know. He was, however, the only person to
whom she revealed exactly who she was.

    In the "As It Were Poems" of his 1931 volume *To Whom Else?* Graves
proposed various mythical trappings for Riding. He quoted her

response (taken from notes that she had given him) to his question, "Two-named one, how shall I call you without duplicity?" in a vain effort to pin her down, to "know" her and name her:

> "Call me . . . by my open name, so that I may know that you are not calling upon any of those belied spirits of the legends with whom men have ever held stealthy, frightened converse. For in my open name I am jealous of my hinder name, that it should not sound of the closed names invoked in the mysteries: am I not the most level-headed of all your fellows? I tear away the legends from your unwilling eyes that you may call on me with your willing mind; so may my open name be my closed name, and my closed name, my open name."
>
> These are your very spoken words . . .

Graves is thus given an opening to conclude, "Those many names with which I hid myself from you, and you from myself, are vanishing into a single name of names. Isis . . ." Once again, a new territory, a new beginning had required a new naming ceremony. In 1934 Laura described this creative "naming" process to a confidante as one which made real what had been only myth or legend, a process which brought to life what had existed until then only in abstractions because men had put themselves at the center of reality.

By telling Robert (or whomever) "exactly" who she was, Riding was both able to locate her "voice" and become all things to all those lost writers and artists who descended on Deyá, intrigued and stimulated by the outrageous stories that reached London, Oxford, and Cambridge. In her presence many visitors, particularly those uncertain of their talent, were struck dumb. Others, perhaps those young men who were still mystified or terrorized by the opposite sex, seemed literally in thrall. Despite the repetition and the snarled syntax of her essays and poetry, Riding's surfeit of ideas on love and sex possessed the breathtaking quality of dead certainty and oracular pronouncement. Who among them did not arrive in Deyá without some sort of dogged self-doubt or, like Lucie Brown, some private shame? Riding's bracing recommendations for the self-improvement of men to benefit their relations with women (whether sexual or intellectual) were sure to startle those who were amazed that she wanted to talk about it at all. Whether or not one automatically followed her thinking, there was certainly excitement in the suspense of waiting for what she might say next.

But Riding's decision to stop sleeping with Graves echoed a corresponding decision to cease participation in his mythologizing. There is a curious love poem that attempts to glamorize the grandeur of their celibate estate and, in its own affectionate way, to answer Graves' dedicatory volume, *To Whom Else?* In "After Smiling" Riding acknowledged that she had been his hostage, "the else/You made kinged state against," but had come to insist upon complete sovereignty; the poem was a kind of Declaration of Independence. Acknowledging both Graves' protectorship and the physical love that they had shared, Riding now chose a "kinghood of not-you," which was doubtless more real to her than his relentless mythologizing. But she also defeated herself by relying on metaphors of contending empires (hers, suggestively Holy Roman); such patriarchal and imperialist assumptions about the exercise of power created their own tyrannical logics, which served to enslave her further. As a result, the poem is not terribly persuasive, and furthermore, it gave Graves his opening to answer her in kind with his 1936 poem "To the Sovereign Muse."

Yet in poems like "Divestment of Beauty," where the speaker is also addressing the worshipful "man," Riding's command of her subject and theme is masterful, without reference to the "gaudy franchise" of myth. In this poem the speaker slowly unwraps beauty's "long robe of glamour," to reveal not the further strip tease of a naked goddess or muse but the bright insult of mortality:

> It were a loathsome spectacle, you think?
> Eventual entrails of deity
> Worshipful eye offending?
> It were the sign, man,
> To pluck the loathsome eye,
>
> Forswear the imbecile
> Theology of loveliness,
> Be no more doctor in antiquities—

Chimeras of the future
In archaic daze embalmed—

And grow to later youth,
Felling the patriarchal leer
That it lie reft of all obscenities
While she and she, she, she, disclose
The recondite familiar to your candour.

Naturally, Laura's public renunciation of sex and Robert's dutiful obedience provoked a great deal of sniggering. If there were elements of cruelty and spite in their subsequent relationship, there was also something spectacular about it that both Riding and Graves were to build on, albeit in entirely different ways. Responding to Laura's list of reasons for her renunciation, Rosaleen wrote, "I agree that sex makes one a divided being. That's why the great sages and mystics renounced it, I suppose; they did so for a greater love—God or Humanity or some such idea. To renounce it coldly for no other idol must be hard indeed but rather magnificent."

Riding's greater love and idol remained the heated search for truth, and renunciation of sex was only the first step toward it. Her insistence on the essential differences between men and women came next, as one of her first commandments. Commingling male and female, intellectually or in the act of lovemaking, was her first heresy. One of her most dismissive epithets was "muddle-headed." Thus if a woman were to behave like a man, she was neglecting her responsibility as his judge—"prostituting herself"—by implicitly approving the male viewpoint. Sympathy or coddling a man's ego were equally reprehensible. Writing to a young man about his relations with his lover, Riding equated his sexual ecstasy with the ecstasy of destruction, identifying sexual desire with the desire to destroy, possess, and make a woman "one" with man. His motive, she ventured, was to allay feelings of incompleteness that were in fact quite inconsolable. Man, she insisted, was the derived rib or accidental being, and woman the fundamental one. In such a universe, man, ever subject to female judgment, was left little room to maneuver creatively or emotionally. Presumably, there was virtue enough in learning what it had felt like all those years to be female.

It is a measure of Riding's importance to Graves, and of his own ambivalence toward his sexuality, that he eventually joined her in celibacy. There were incidents of backsliding that both Riding and Graves found "psychologically interesting"; Graves inevitably explored his "brutal lapses" in his poetry. Certainly the strangling nexus of sex, sin, and death was a familiar enough catechism; he was always able to draw on his puritanical embarrassments to align himself with Riding's views. He found his grace in Riding's confessional.

But while Graves might depict male lust as the "original sin" in poems like "A Jealous Man" and "The Succubus," the essential travesty as far as Riding was concerned was against her vision, not her body. To Graves' question in "The Succubus," "Yet is the fancy grosser than your lusts were gross?" Riding would answer yes. In the struggle between female truth and male fantasy, the sin was not in the lust but in the lie.

Such distinctions would, of course, become confused. In "After Smiling" Riding offers Graves a kind of papal dispensation and anointment, but there remains the suggestion of an uneasy truce, recalling those between medieval kings and Rome. Riding could not serve his visions and her own at the same time, but neither could her work always be conceived in isolation from his demands. When she tired of the predictability of Graves' themes, however, she turned to other men, like the New Zealand filmmaker and artist Len Lye, to explore new creative avenues. At one point Riding and Graves considered building him a film studio in Deyá. Riding's vision, it seemed, could embrace any medium.

Another of her potential collaborators was a gifted Scots poet, Norman Cameron, who was also at the café that evening after Lucie's arrival. In the course of his life Norman would undergo a nervous breakdown, psychoanalysis, three marriages, a sympathectomy (a type of lobotomy), and a conversion to Roman Catholicism before dying peacefully in 1953, of a cerebral hemorrhage at the age of forty-seven. A soft pillow of light brown hair topped Norman's problematic head, perhaps the most visible extravagance about his carefully composed, apologetic manner. Dylan Thomas' pet name for him was Normal; Len Lye called him "a long-legged walking essence of poetry." "How one envies Norman's life," someone else remarked, "no detail at all!" Norman had played his part in the disturbing events surrounding Elfriede's banishment. In this and in so many things he felt guilty.

TALL, PALE-FACED, AND a stutterer, Norman Cameron had befriended Laura and Robert when he invited them to lecture at Oxford's English Club in 1927. With John Aldridge he was part of a set known as the "Corpus aesthetes," though his college was Oriel. Shortly after leaving the university he moved into the neighborhood of St. Peter's Square but left for a stint as an education officer in Lagos, Nigeria, shortly after Riding's suicide attempt. Indeed, having given a significant portion of his small inheritance to help cover her hospitalization costs, Norman was obliged to get a job. His monthly dispatches to her conveyed his dismay over having to act as an agent of the British Empire:

> I had a sad experience when a girl I bought some bananas from (I shouldn't have done that . . .) made a gesture which I thought was a sort of technical blessing. So I said "bless you" and smiled at her, and went upstairs to my house. But she followed me up and started to make a sexual demonstration. So I daren't smile at any African girls anymore.

Such misunderstandings with the female sex dogged him perpetually; two of his three marriages were the result of Laura's active interest in the conduct of his personal life. Norman's equivocations (which tended, like his stutter, to become more pronounced in her company) became Laura's invitation to settle the matters of his heart for him. This seemed the best solution to the endearing problem of Norman, who, quitting his African appointment, decided at Laura's insistence to devote himself to "pure literature." He had moved to Deyá sometime in the summer of 1931 and thus far worked largely on an abridged version of *David Copperfield* with Robert. They expected it to make them all money—"pure" literature notwithstanding. Laura later worked closely with him on translations of Rimbaud's poetry.

In fact, Elfriede had told Lucie, she had actually been "procured" for Norman but fell in love with Robert before Norman arrived in Deyá. Though Norman always remembered his time there as one of hard work unalloyed by sex, he and Elfriede caused quite a stir in the village when someone came across them skinny-dipping in the cistern of a remote olive grove. Soon after Lucie's arrival, Elfriede's passage was paid to the Canary Islands so that she might regain her health, thus depriving Norman of further temptation. Perhaps for this reason Norman gravitated toward Lucie, taking particular interest in her numerous letters from Basil. Lucie returned his affection. Deciding to stay on after her niece returned to London, she and John settled down in a cottage, John to paint and Lucie to keep house and cook. In the afternoons she and Norman went on long flower-collecting walks up the Teix.

So intense was everyone's work schedule, and so great their involvement in the dramas and intrigues that surged around them at every moment, that the life of the village and the overwhelming natural beauty of the surrounding landscape were relegated to second place. One American couple fell into disfavor with Laura for their tendency to groan appreciatively during evening sunsets and shooting-star displays. Laura actively discouraged tours of the island.

To Lucie it seemed that no sooner had she arrived then she had to return to London. Shortly before she left, Laura took her aside and confided that John, whom she knew better than Lucie did, cared for Lucie more than he had ever cared for anyone else. Laura was of the opinion that Lucie and John might live together when he returned to London, adding "love was love but marriage was only for people who were married for convenience." Lucie (who was still married) reflected that this was not her idea of marriage but "it was the Laura Riding teaching."

When John Aldridge returned to London, he and Lucie Brown did indeed live together. With the outbreak of war in 1939 and Aldridge called to military service, they arranged a hasty marriage so that Lucie, as his legal wife, might be informed if anything happened to him. For almost thirty-five years they lived together in great happiness in a beautiful house in the Essex countryside, surrounded by gardens and cats and paintings. In the 1960s, however, Aldridge told Lucie that she had to leave. Norman Cameron's widow moved in, and Lucie never recovered from the shock.

The farewell party that ended Lucie's stay in the spring of 1932 took place in the newly built, newly inhabited Canelluñ. Norman, who was building his own cottage about eighty yards away, joined them. Perhaps feeling that his life was going to be rather grim after Lucie left, Norman found himself arguing with Laura over the respective meanings of "fake" and "fluke." Contrary to his usual placating nature, Norman insisted that she was wrong. After much fulminating, Laura told Norman to go and be nice to Lucie as it was her last evening. He replied morosely, "I always am nice to Lucie. I'm fond of Lucie."

Soon after, Norman confessed that he had developed a "kind of horror" of Laura. Laura was understanding and sympathetic and promised him a home to return to if things ever got too difficult for him elsewhere. He left Laura his unfinished house, Ca'n Torrent, to clear his conscience over what he felt were his broken commitments regarding her other plans. During the war, Norman wrote to Robert that he considered this gift as "the price of the post graduate liberal education I received from LR, a stiff price but not outrageous." In Barcelona, on his way back to England, he met up with Elfriede, and she became the first of his three wives. He married her, generously, to see her through to the end; she died of tuberculosis a few years later.

The evening following the farewell party, John accompanied Lucie to Palma to settle her on the boat to Barcelona. After a lavish shipboard dinner, they danced cheek to cheek before retiring to make love in her cabin to the gently rocking rhythm of the sea. Lucie lay awake after he left, watching through the porthole as the winking lights of Palma disappeared. Writing her memoirs fifty years later, she wondered how they would all be written about and what people might think. She did not care to see her own account published. "It will have to wait until I'm dead or Laura will shoot me," she wrote a close friend shortly before her death. Still, Lucie decided, even if she had been a pawn in Laura's game of chess, the time in Deyá was her "halcion days."

Chapter 14

THE DRY HEART

———•———

The world where the dead live is a dry heart,
Every world is a heart, a rhythm spherical,
A rhythm of impossible intentions
That yet sings itself, imagining heard music.
The world where the dead live is a silent choir.
It does not hear itself, it sings itself not.
Its will has frozen into memory,
Black as still blood, without flood, without flow.
To the painless sorrow of death it throbs.
The world where the dead live is a heart alive
In a body once alive.
The dead move neither into heaven nor hell.
Their afterwards is their before.
The world where the dead live is a dry heart,
The same heart as always, even dry.

—"The Life of the Dead"

———•———

STOPPING BY THE side of the road, the young man left his pretty wife
and two small sons in the car while he went to investigate. He
thought that the inhabitants of the stone cottage at the edge of the
village might know where he could find Robert Graves. If not, they
might at least help him find a similar dwelling where he could begin
work on his novel. Not understanding the maid's reply to his in-

quiries, he nevertheless followed her into a cool dark room with a large fireplace. There, behind a table covered with papers, stood the severe but poised figure of Laura Riding. Hearing that he had come to pay his respects to Robert (whom he had had the honor of meeting some years before), Laura looked him up and down. As Robert entered, she remarked, deadpan, "Robert, here is a young man who *says* he knows you."

Rolling his eyes, glancing at the eager and handsome face before him, Robert grimaced and shook his head. "Never saw him before in my life."

The young man paled. Robert let him splutter for a while before letting the memory of an afternoon in Islip with an American student at Oxford slowly return. Only then did the healthy tan return to the visitor's face. Robert Graves introduced him properly to Laura Riding, and most likely the family was invited for tea.

Thomas Stanley Matthews had just arrived, but not in Deyá or at the home of the famous author of *Good-bye to All That*. Rather, he had found his part in Riding's *théâtre intime*: "an earnest comedy / Complete of brief undoings, minute fatalities."

He had tried once before to describe this first meeting with Laura Riding but, after reaching the story's dark denouement in a Pennsylvania farmhouse seven years later, abandoned it. Finally, in the study of his comfortable country house in a corner of Suffolk, he finished the typescript of his third and final book of reminiscences. There he told the story of his friendship with Riding and the indelible mark she had left on his life. At seventy-four, "half-blind, half-deaf, half-crippled," he felt certain he was nearing the end and that "the curtain [was] coming down." For his concluding chapter he used Jung's idea of the shadow self to consider the meaning of the line, "There is one story and one story only":

> [T]he "shadow" ... can only be seen in glimpses, in dreams, in impulses pushed down below awareness, a story that is not understood, that is in fact so horrifying that we deny its existence. The idea of this duality does not horrify me: I know and can admit, at least in theory, that I am at odds with myself; but the nature of this "shadow," unknown to me although within me, alarms and disturbs me,

like a dog hearing the far off howling of a timber wolf. Though this shadow may be my real kinship with the real world, all my conscious life, all my training, has unfitted me for perceiving or dealing with this world. If I could reconcile my domesticated dog-self with my brother the wolf—would I know my own story then? Perhaps I would.

The last time he had seen Robert, he wrote, nothing they could say to each other carried the ring of truth; both were vain old men who expected to be humored. "My only claims to special regard," Matthews mused cynically, "are that I am usually the oldest person present, and the richest." Despite the proliferation of warts, moles, liver spots, and other "horny excrescences," neither aging patriarch could bear to believe that they had ceased to be attractive to women. And Laura? As far as he knew she continued to "profess her unique sanity":

> [I]n fact we are all just waiting—waiting to die . . . In a blink of time, . . . all that will be left of us will be contained in the distorted and dwindling flashes of memory, less and less frequent, in the minds of fewer and fewer people.

But, thirteen years after finishing his memoirs, Tom Matthews, almost ninety, was not yet facing his end with serenity. He could still be found scanning the "hatch, match, and dispatch" columns of the London *Times* for Laura (Riding) Jackson's obituary. Writing about his impassioned, dream-filled years at Princeton with his idol and blood brother Schuyler Jackson, writing about Schuyler's wife Kit and his own beloved first wife Julie, had provided neither the needed catharsis nor the understanding of his shadow self; Matthews did not yet know his own story. Though Schuyler had been dead for twenty years, the far-off howling of his blood brother, the wolf, had not ceased.

Tom Matthews was born in Cincinnati, Ohio, the child of a dean of the Episcopal church and the shy heiress to the Procter fortune (of Procter and Gamble). Of six children, he was the only son. While he was still a young boy, his family moved to Princeton, so that his father might become bishop of New Jersey. In 1918, two years after F. Scott Fitzgerald left without taking a degree to write *This Side of Paradise,* Tom entered Princeton University from the exclusive St. Paul's prep school in New Hampshire. There, in the close fraternal company of the Tuesday Evening Club, a literary society, the eating clubs, and the *théâtre intime,* he sought and secured the friendship of the reclusive but brilliant and aristocratic Schuyler Jackson. He soon grew to share his belief in poetry as "the distillation of writing itself," and together, as true poets, they pledged themselves to the "whole-souled and life-long practice of their calling."

Tom had since lapsed. He felt he lacked both his father's robust faith in God and Schuyler's uncompromising artistic vision. He became a journalist but marked time, awaiting the moment when he would become a serious writer, of fiction if not poetry. That is what brought him to Deyá in January 1932, a dashing, intelligent, and independently wealthy young man. On a six-month leave from *Time* magazine, where he was a promising junior editor, he hoped to complete a novel based on the life of Katherine Mansfield. Through Schuyler, Tom had been introduced to the philosophy of Georges Gurdjieff, granting him, he felt, a special insight into Mansfield's life. Her death at thirty-four of tuberculosis had, Tom felt, ennobled her. He had brought with him Gurdjieff's opus *Beezlebub's Tales to His Grandson* and was ready to work.

Yet, there again, another minute fatality was lying in wait. Even before Robert told her, Laura had a premonition that she and Tom Matthews had been born on the same day. Robert had been helping Tom fill out a form for the Palma police when he noticed the birth date. When he shouted over his shoulder, "Laura! You and Tom are twins!" Tom was horrified; she seemed ages older and he very nearly said so. Smiling slightly, Laura gave a curt nod, "as if she acknowledged the fact, now that it was out, but was not yet prepared to commit herself on its significance." No portent was ever overlooked in Deyá.

Tom was very much in love with Julie, his childhood sweetheart and wife. While Julie did not readily understand her husband's literary ambitions, she no doubt connected them with his worshipful allegiance to Schuyler. Though Tom's relationship with him had changed since Princeton, their friendship was still strong. To Julie, the fortunes of the Jackson family, who lived on a Pennsylvania farm about twenty miles from their Princeton home, seemed to always prove a less than flattering comment on their own. She thought poetry "morbid," particularly her husband's, and told him so. Indeed, despite his healthy bearing, Tom savored some unwholesome notions:

> This is the source of wanting to die
> In the forehead's too smooth cliff
> Nothing is wanting but a hole.

Julie knew better than to say what she thought of Schuyler.

Edmund Wilson, whom Tom had worked for at the *New Republic*, was a frequent weekend visitor to the Matthewses' home in Princeton and a close observer of their domestic idyll. Though he acknowledged their intelligence, tolerance, curiosity, imagination, and courage as individuals, Wilson found that suburbia had left the Matthewses somewhat immured. Left alone in the house one weekend, Wilson noted wryly that as soon as the Matthewses' car pulled out of the driveway the black help burst into a loud and raucous version of "That's Love." Upon the song's finish, he heard the maid complain to the cook, "I do all the sweeping and you get all the gin." Still, Wilson included the Matthewses on his list of people for an ideal dinner party along with Zelda and Scott Fitzgerald, Dorothy Parker, Peter Benchley, Allen Tate, and Carolyn Gordon. Julie, he wrote in his diary, had nice legs.

In Deyá the Matthews family seemed like a vision of American normalcy, as immaculate as the perfect green of a Princeton lawn. Tom's tall, patrician appearance was complemented by simple but exquisite manners. Their two boys were little gentlemen. "They seemed apart from all this cauldron," Lucie Brown wrote, remembering their arrival in Deyá in January 1932, "and yet somehow necessary to complete the circle. Later I was to learn their importance in the plan which Laura was weaving." If there was such a plan, Tom and Julie were at first unaware of it. With the children in bed they would talk over dinner about how Robert and Laura, though very helpful and friendly, were not really their "kind" of people. Indeed, Robert and Laura seemed to agree; after a picnic at the pebble beach known as the Cala they found out just who Tom and Julie's kind were. "Robert summed up the inquiry by laughing and saying to Laura, 'They seem to know all the wrong people!' "

Still, little by little, Tom and Julie found themselves drawn toward "Laura's set" more by fascination than by design. Tom learned to keep quiet about his suburban activities, sneaking off once a week to play tennis in Palma. After one game, he ran into Norman Cameron and John Aldridge in a Palma bar. Shamefaced, he mentioned how beholden he and his wife were to Robert and Laura for their kindness. Thereafter he and Julie were greeted at the Butcher's café as Mr. and Mrs. Ben Beholden. Soon, too, Robert was confiding to them his woeful deprivation; he hated to sleep by himself, he told Julie mournfully. Gradually, they pieced together the tale of Elfriede, and Tom began reading Laura's poetry.

Throughout the 1930s Riding would become involved in dozens of collaborative and editorial projects. She had a coauthor (another Deyá denizen) for her roman à clef, *14A*; she rewrote Graves' penny dreadful *No Decency Left*; and in daily morning sessions with Robert she went over and approved all of his poems and manuscripts. She worked for a long time on a masque for which Len Lye was to create the scenery. She corresponded with Jacob Bronowski, James Reeves, Alan Hodge, Ronald Bottrall, and other poets—as well as with those whom she judged might be poets. Editing their poems, she rooted out antique or faded romantic notions of women and dissected them—sometimes gently, sometimes severely—in the light of their relations with her or with their wives and girlfriends. Few resisted, and once she became their "editor," they rarely wrote anything that was not submitted for her approval. There were also novels, published and unpublished, and countless unfinished book ideas, articles, and moneymaking projects. With at least one exception, the results of these artistic collaborations were impressive more for their quantity than for their integrity of vision.

Tom Matthews' novel *The Moon's No Fool* was Riding's first completed collaboration with someone other than Robert Graves. Published in 1936 under Matthews' name and even translated into Dutch, it was decidedly written by Laura Riding. Certainly the character of Katherine Mansfield is nowhere to be found. Matthews later acknowledged that Riding, "using me as a pencil," wrote the book. He

described the work as essentially "a private exercise, between ourselves." This exercise had its real beginning with an invitation from
Laura to help her with a work that she had been struggling with for
some time. Bogged down in his novel about Mansfield, Tom agreed
to try.

For almost two weeks Tom came each morning at ten to work until
lunchtime on Riding's manuscript, the masque that she had been
working on with Len Lye. She had started *Fantasia* during Lye's visit to
Deyá in 1930, but the work stalled in endless correspondence after
he left. Lye finally told Riding that he could neither write nor receive
any more letters. Sometime before this new collaboration with Tom
began, Laura and Robert had given Salerosa to the Matthewses,
moving themselves into a cottage named C'an Pa Bo (the "house of
good bread") for two months while work on Canelluñ was completed. Lucie Brown, living with John Aldridge in a nearby cottage,
observed Laura waiting each morning, wearing an immaculate white
muslin head dress, a tight bodice, and full skirt brocaded in exquisite
patterns. "They were genuine old dresses," Lucie observed, "and
suited her." Just what Laura and Tom were working on, however,
remained a mystery.

In his memoirs, Tom Matthews recalled the bare wooden table
with two tidy piles of foolscap paper in an otherwise empty white-
washed room. Heavy wooden chairs were aligned with each pile—
one for Laura, one for himself:

> She would be looking pale, scrubbed and intense; and her
> brusque nod, dispensing with the usual civilities, served
> notice that the workday had now begun and that I had
> arrived not a moment too soon. . . . Before another syllable
> could be added [to the unfinished manuscript] we had to
> go over this beginning, word by word and phrase by
> phrase, partly to satisfy Laura that the foundation was
> solid and partly to acquaint me with the nature and mean-
> ing of the work . . . I never strained so hard to understand
> anything in my life, and to so little purpose.

Before the inescapable and humiliating conclusion that he was stupid
could dawn on him, Matthews arrived one morning to find an enve-

lope with his name on it lying on the table. Laura left the room, shutting the door, having allotted him fifteen minutes to read the letter:

> As I read, my alarm deepened. The gist of it was that she knew the effect she made on me; that if I could master my feelings I was to remain in this room, she would come back and we would go on with our work as before; if however, I could not be sure of controlling myself I was to get up and go, now; she would understand, she would not hold it against me, but we must not continue to work together. . . . Why didn't I immediately get up and what possessed me to stay? I have asked myself that question a hundred times since. But no matter what I did, I said to myself despairingly, she would still think I was in love with her! . . . I'd be damned if I'd give her the impression that I was so mad about her I couldn't trust myself in her presence. Of course I should have gone, and let her think what she liked. And, if I'd had a vestige of humor left in me about the situation, I'd be laughing all the way home. But I didn't; I stayed where I was.

Tom soon realized that he could not continue the work in any case; he was close to a nervous collapse. After a long talk with Julie, they decided that the best thing was to confess to Laura that he had bitten off more than he could chew, and offer to withdraw from the friendship. Laura would not hear of it; "she couldn't have been kinder," Matthews recalled ironically, and they remained friends.

Laura's work on Tom's novel did not proceed any more smoothly; he watched helplessly as the book took an altogether different form from what he had envisioned. Toward the end of *The Moon's No Fool* the main character undergoes a series of humiliations in the company of his aristocratic friends. Principally these involve losing all his money and all his righteous delusions in front of his beloved, a decadent but wise queen with a mordant wit. Washed ashore after a failed attempt at drowning himself, he comes to in the company of his godmother, "Miserable Sarah," who, astonishingly, seemed to bear some resemblance to his beloved queen:

"You're still a little weak in the head, Godson. Have some more toddy."

She helped me upstairs to a perfect little bedroom. The bed was all ready for me—the sheets turned down, a hot-water bottle bulging up under the blankets. When she had tucked me in she sat down beside the bed, smiling at me in a friendly but inscrutable way. I wondered what was coming next.

"Been out swimming, Godson?" she asked, almost twinkling . . .

"Yes, Godmother," I answered, understanding her immediately, "out of my depth. But I'm glad I did it. And I'm glad I failed. I won't try it again."

She nodded solemnly. "And what about your grand friends? You can't expect them to change along with you."

"I've finished with them. I never want to see them again."

"I wouldn't talk like that, Godson. . . . You've got nothing to be ashamed of. . . .

"You've lost your moonshiny notions, but I don't think you've lost your pride. . . . And as for money—" She got up and went over to a little cupboard, unlocking it with a key she brought out of her bag. She took out a shiny black box and brought it to the bed. Another key had to be found in her bag to open it. It was full of stock certificates.

Tom left the draft of their "private exercise" behind in Deyá. Delayed in Paris by a violent attack of stomach ulcer, he returned to Princeton to find the finished version awaiting him.

"When she laughed," Tom Matthews later wrote of Riding, "something appealing happened to her face: then she resembled a little girl who has momentarily forgotten that she meant to scare the grown-ups." The fairy tale farce of *The Moon's No Fool* is, in contrast, precocious by calculation, enlivened only by a long dream sequence of phantasmagoric abandon. Mostly, however, the style reflects the incongruous personalities of its working partners and their mutual fascination.

Much more successful was "The Playground," a fairy tale written by Riding alone in which Tom also appeared, accompanied by Julie (as Julia) and his two boys. Riding "appeared" as a character named Unhappy Lady Thinking-hard. In the story Julia sends her children to a special playground to buy some dreams from a Mr. Sleep. They find him prone and snoring, and Unhappy Lady Thinking-hard sitting nearby, with gold pieces dropping all around her. She instructs the boys to tug sharply on Mr. Sleep's right ear (left ear for night-mares) and to stuff her special coins in his mouth when he groaned. That night when the boys go to sleep they receive their strange visions. In one, there is a shop in a rock where real people are sold by a hateful old woman for bits of string. Somehow Tom, who had not accompanied his sons to the special playground, catches one of Mr. Sleep's dreams as well:

> I was in a rolling rocky place and every rock looked like a large animal lying down or like something difficult to understand. And a woman's voice kept saying, "Yes, this is the place." I wanted to ask "What place?" but was too frightened. So I only said, "Thank you very much!" every time she said, "Yes, this is the place." Finally she got tired of saying it, I suppose, and said, "Do you like it?" Not wanting to be dishonest, I answered, "I like what I see of it." "Oh, you'll remember much more *afterwards* than you see now," she said.

The story was amazingly prophetic.

But if Laura and Tom were an odd pair of "twins," they were in some way an inevitable match for each other, as both Laura and Lucie Brown had foreseen. For Laura, Tom was an American graced with an upper-class pedigree. He lived the American dream, and she aimed simply to wake him up, to divest him of his "moonshiny notions." Tom, in turn, was completely absorbed by the spectacle of Laura's rule over Robert and by her own peculiar literary glamour. Seeing her as a sister to Gertrude Stein, he thought that he would eventually get a handle on her work, but as in his dream in "Playground," he could not quite catch her drift. "To read her," he wrote before meeting her in a review of *Anarchism Is Not Enough*, was "like listening to a man who is passionately anxious to be heard, but who has such an impediment in his speech that he can not be understood." His understanding, he thought, might come later. Until then he was Mr. Ben Beholden, a patient listener and her ardent disciple. Still, he could not escape the feeling that it was his friend and blood brother Schuyler Jackson who deserved to be there, rather than himself.

IN THE SUMMER of 1932, soon after the Matthewses left Deyá, Riding and John Aldridge began work on a book that was easily the most remarkable of her collaborative efforts. *The Life of the Dead* was written in ten parts, each accompanied by a wood engraving based on an Aldridge illustration, conceived by Riding before the text was prepared. The "verbal comedies" that accompanied the engravings were first written in French so that the English, when translated, "might benefit from the limitations which French puts upon the poetic seriousness of words." Riding's "Explanation" of this "highly artificial poem" was profuse but unhelpful; it was more "a poetic deshabille" rather than a "stylistic orgy in prose." It is as though Riding had to make excuses for this temporary departure from her increasingly abstract and "truth-seeking" language. John Aldridge was the perfect conspirator; in his sheltering company she was free to imagine a world of dark and ghastly allegory. The result was something wholly her own, entirely uninscribed by identifiable religious or mythological narratives but almost wholly inscribed by the merry band within her "necropolis" at Deyá.

One by one, Riding had rid herself of the more obvious poetic devices in the hopes of discovering a means of ascertaining truth directly and "logically." Considerations of sound, meter, or rhythm certainly no longer entered into her poetic composition—or so she thought. As a result, the act of writing poetry had become almost impossibly exhausting and cerebral, even for her. She was left principally with the choice of words, but with words baked in the peculiar oven of her intellect. To understand her poems, so that one might trace her didactic, one often needed to know the line of shorthand thought that had brought her to choose a particular word. An abstract word such as "natural" had a very precise, metaphysical meaning for her, as did seemingly concrete words like "wind" and "weather." She also felt free to make up compound words such as "water-thought," "clock-romantic," or "mind-sight" to denote specific states of being and perception. In the process, a network of symbolic understandings assumed the aura of concrete proof (at least until the symbolic became suspect), allowing her to hurry on her way. With notable exceptions, her poems became increasingly codified and, for many, bafflingly obscure.

Whatever gloss Riding might put on it, such cerebral devices in *The Life of the Dead* are buttressed by dramatic event and character. Circumscribed by what she felt was the lack of seriousness in the French poetic language, Riding indulged her appetite for a grand style of rhetoric and hothouse imagery. The opportunity to tell a macabre parable doubtless cheered her as well. The poem shares with *Laura and Francisca* the exalted and magisterial eloquence of its central voice, but here Riding's humor was far more corrosive. As in that poem, too, the notion of death has once again been personified. As cabaret manqué, the central figure of the Death Goddess orchestrates the grotesque lives of the "dead" in what is partly a burlesque and partly a morality tale. In 1938 *The Life of the Dead* was the last work in her *Collected Poems*, the final collection to appear during Laura Riding's career as a poet.

The Life of the Dead captured the mood of wicked play and brooding sexual intrigue that gripped Deyá life for those members of Laura's circle. In the poem Riding shows that the world outside her rocky mountain fastness is the hugely disturbed one; the little lives that each visitor hoped to return to after a sunny holiday in Deyá are presented as meaningless and corrupt. In her warped looking glass this was the life of the damned. Indeed Mr. Beedham, the wood engraver, became so overwrought at the morbidity of Aldridge's drawings that Riding had to write to him. The illustrations could not be made any less terrifying, she explained, because they depicted the true life of the dead—not those in the ground but those tiresome multitudes who live in ways that are monotonous, repetitive, and self-defeating.

John Aldridge's illustration of the outer world, facing the French text of "Within the City: Daytime," showed a carnival of torture and violence. A man hangs from a street light, preferring "to swing under blows than to lie tragical / On the inexorable pavement high below." Another is skewered on a soldier's scabbard, while live victims are pitched on a bonfire in the city square. Motorcars and trams are checked in their progress by bodies on the tracks. A "delicate prank in vogue" is to tie some wretch to a fender and watch him bump through traffic. "Often there's luck in this, the silly survives intact." (Laura had a particular fear of London traffic.) Riding cautioned Aldridge to not let the atmosphere of atrocity overwhelm the city bustle.

The metropolis of this section is perhaps inspired by John and Lucie's tales of the goings-on at the Great Ormond Street salon of Lett Haines. Curiously, Riding later published a painting of the Brontë sisters by Basil Taylor, Lucie's escort in that demimonde after he, like many others of the set, had committed suicide in 1935. A note accompanied the reproduction, clearly written by Riding, though signed by John and Lucie. She described Basil as he himself had: a pariah who regarded his paintings, like himself, as failures "in the sense that his preoccupation was fatedly with the beauties of waste." Drawn to "the brilliant, lavish subject conditioned emotionally by the shadowy threat of waste, disappearance," Basil's painting of the Brontë sisters was unfinished at his death. The year before, Riding had tried to write a poem about Hart Crane's suicide for a small press in California but destroyed it, producing a fierce satire entitled *Americans* instead. In the hag's cackle, the shrill mockery of *The Life of the Dead* was her self-assertion, her safety.

Riding wrote of the stage, "for drama I like what is happening." Her relationships with Aldridge, Graves, and to a lesser extent Tom Matthews provide the models for the principal dramatic subtexts of *The Life of the Dead*. All three are introduced in the poem's second section, "The Three Men-Spirits of the Dead." Aldridge is clearly recognizable in his drawings as the character of Mortjoy, "the preferred," who kneels at the side of the "unknown goddess, death itself" and who claims "in one confiding gesture" "her private, worthless treasures." He has exchanged the "poor numbered picturing" of his sight for Death's.

In the engraving Mortjoy wears something resembling a chastity belt, while he pulls small, human figurines from the drapes of Death's voluminous cloak, or winding sheet. Death is depicted as a seated figure, completely enveloped in her cloak, with no features visible. Above her swoops a strange creature, whose bird beak scavenges in

Death's drapes where her head should be. This was Romanzel, the "luckless poet of the dead":

> Hovers on her, soaring round in word-lust.
> He has the wings of a vulture,
> The head of a bird vain of its manhood.
> His feet are of lost roads and endlessness,
> Hollowed up with anger, devil-toed.
> And blacker than death, his body—
> The black of furious silences.

The third "man-spirit" is Unidor. Only he seems indifferent to the death goddess as he works doggedly on a conjured female figure, suspended in a "little world of air":

> Unidor,
>
> . . .
>
> Holds the same task, contents the same desire.
> With his blind eyes he builds the woman again
> That death's veraciousness made nothing
>
> . . .
>
> Her name is Amulette, and saucy-fair she is,
> Little image of death, of dead flesh moulded—
> Close image of the far obsession, . . .

When the lights go up in Mortjoy's theater, in the third section of the poem, he is ensconced in his royal box above an empty theater. The play, except for dumb show, is over; the clock has struck its angry tone 'No more to go!' " On hand, in boxes close to the stage, are two evil geniuses who are there to thwart any prospect of a happy ending. One of them is a real witch (in contrast to the cotton one that hangs suspended from the rafters of the stage); she is the queen of witches, the hag of the play. It is she who makes certain that all play their parts; it is she who commands that the next scene not begin until everyone goes home. It is there, at home, in the satiated safety of the domesticity that ruled at the Matthewses' Salerosa or the table of plenty set by Lucie Brown, that Death will bring her chilling intimacies.

About halfway through the Matthewses' stay, Robert took Julie Matthews on a long mountain walk. Under the blossoming almond trees and algarrobas, he confessed his love for her. When Julie told her husband of this new development beneath the Deyá proscenium, he immediately assumed that his wife was lost to him, that she now loved Robert. The event, combined with a lingering impotence that had followed his struggle with Laura's masque, left Tom in a temporary state of shock. Nothing ever came of Robert's infatuation with Julie, but his courtship was immortalized in the fourth section of *The Life of the Dead*.

In the "Transformation of Romanzel" Aldridge's tableau shows the high "mountainous oppression" of the Teix horizon and luckless Romanzel, pursued by his several demon satyrs, leaping in "frolicsome despair from peak to peak." Far below, impossible to reach, dances Amulette, "[f]rank earth-illusion, a nymph within a grove of self / Musing her free dominion and her loveliness." Nearby sleeps Unidor untroubled, dreaming peacefully of her. To Romanzel is given the part of the old fool; to Amulette, whom he pursues, "the saucy schoolgirl, . . . Pretending nunnish innocence of love":

Romanzel leaps, falls, leaps . . .
Amulette dances,
More briskly than before, indeed; Unidor, dreaming,
Smiles at some nameless humour of an instant . . .
And all that's left of Romanzel bestrews the ground
Like the discarded bones of a vexed ghost.
Amulette does not mark them, far less does Unidor:
The sorrows of the dead who die—such matters cannot give them
    pause.

Like the mortification which followed Robert's affair with Elfriede Faust, Romanzel's humiliation is once more complete in Aldridge's illustration. He is doomed to repeat this fate endlessly; as his skull falls upon his heap of bones at the foot of the high cliffs, another demon satyr prepares to sacrifice his life in the forlorn hope of earthly love. The hag of the play has once again enacted her black triumph over human aspirations—"What an interminable game it is!" she exclaims.

The seventh illustration for *The Life of the Dead* draws on the atmosphere of the Butcher's café and the worn routines enacted there by its "uninspired wanderers." After a simple dinner of cold fried fish, hard white rolls, and olive oil, it was the custom of Laura, Robert, Norman, John, and Lucie to walk down the crooked streets of the village to the café, where they would drink coffee and play Parcheesi and dominoes. Laura was later to become particularly skillful at sixty-six, a German card game like pinochle. Gelat liked seven and a half, a Spanish form of blackjack, and naturally turned out to be quite a shark. Robert, unable to conceal his nervous desire to win, kept careful score. While they played, Gelat kept them apprised of village politics; the progress of work at Canelluñ and new business ventures were tactfully broached.

And so in *The Life of the Dead* one might live the life of the damned as easily in Deyá as London. The café is home to the accouterments of games of chance. A jack, a king of diamonds, a three of clubs, cluster around the queen of hearts at the bar in the Aldridge illustration, "fugitives of the pack." The gentlemanly dominoes brood austerely over a gaming table nearby. The empty costumes of the ball and ballet hang on the walls, and near the door a set of chessmen dance to the tunes of a giant Victrola whose records are spun by an "eloquent, harmonic hand":

> And the gramophone? I believe you are familiar with it:
> It is the voice of all those races that time has not admitted
> Into the lavish happenings and courses
> That make life so full of interest, and death so foul.

The voices of Riding's phonograph were also those of the dispossessed, those of the all-night dance halls of Louisville and Greenwich Village, those of Billie Holiday and the Matthewses' Princeton cook. Not for them the balls and ballets, the lost hours of ennui and genteel decadence at the resort gaming table. Like the lonely young woman who drank and danced to their blues, they were among those whom "time has not admitted into the lavish happenings."

The last character of *The Life of the Dead* is the self-absorbed Amulette, aloof from the petty concerns of material existence and inhabiting higher realms. Shortly before the Matthewses were to leave Deyá, Laura tried to get Julie to admit that she had never been influenced by or subservient to her husband in any way—as if this might account for Julie's chipper complacency. But if Julie was not entirely fulfilled by motherhood and wifedom (and during her marriage to Tom she considered her options more than once), she made her own peace. Though she might flirt with Robert and grow weary of Tom's poetry and doting affections, she knew enough to ignore or "pretend nunnish innocence" of Laura's impertinent inquiries.

In the last section of the poem, "The Playful Goddess," Death arrives at center stage to assert herself in all her impish brutality. "A gay rogue, she!" A few stray corpses have valiantly tried to clamber out of their crypt, indulge in ecstatic delusions of a future, a utopian deliverance. The death goddess swiftly quells their expectation of a special afterlife for themselves. Her mortifying admonition is intended for Graves, certainly, but for Aldridge as well:

> The immortal rats bespeak the future.
> Thus beats, in false-earnest, a dry heart once a heart,
>
> . . .
>
> Pretending, in her large make-believe of vesture,
> A heart like a world a-toss, a live heart,
> A veinage of people like a live world seeming—
> Seeming, like her, eternal.

The last etching reveals the dry heart beneath the vestments of the death goddess; drawn by the lines of the blood vessels are silhouettes of six human figures. On top of her empty gown of make-believe, a black cat plays with the ribbons of her cloak and with the rats that run through her empty veins.

One of the theorems on which Riding occasionally depended in her poetry was the use of metaphysical paradox for "proof by oppositiveness" in symbolic imagery. If, for example, the live heart is the universally acknowledged symbol of romantic love with its delusions and inconstancies, a dry heart is the corrected heart, a pure heart. Because Riding trusted this proof's utility in revealing the "full spread of truth," for a time she had every expectation of achieving what she termed "metaphysical perfection" in her poetry and the ways in which she imagined her own identity. In *The Life of the Dead* the death goddess only pretends to have a live heart, "a heart a-toss." And creeping further up the grade of resemblance, if a heart a-toss is like a world a-toss, then the world over which she presides only pretends to be eternal. This world, like Deyá, is an artificial "museum-like enchantment." Neither Amulette, Unidor, Romanzel, nor Mortjoy can be saved. The goddess smacks her lips with unholy glee over her darling pets: "Ah, the pretty notion! Ah, to-morrow's immense suppering!"

The Life of the Dead was conceived and written after everyone had left Deyá to return to their life and work in London and New York. On the eve of Tom and Julie's departure, Laura had them to dinner in the newly habitable Canelluñ. The moon, the nightingales, the "magisty" of the evening conspired to waylay Tom into thinking that he was a fool to return to New York with so much left undone. Perhaps, he thought, he was a fool to go back at all. Perhaps, like "Tom's" dream in "The Playground," Lady Thinking-hard was right. Perhaps this was the place.

Awake, however, he once again suffered a brief undoing. Laura, he recalled, made an "extraordinary proposition." Her delicate suggestion was that perhaps Julie could live with Robert while she and Tom, despite his failure over the masque, worked together. So carefully couched was this proposition that Julie altogether missed its meaning—or pretended to. Tom managed to demur politely without causing Laura much offense or, he imagined, clueing Julie in. Robert, ever "the luckless poet," was crushed.

Sharpened by loneliness, by her failure to keep her "family" by her side, Riding summoned the vision of *The Life of the Dead* from the outer darkness in which she found herself, returning to her perfect house after seeing off John Aldridge, the last to leave, on the Palma quay. She felt bitterly abandoned. The feast of the death goddess, however, is precisely the one invitation that none of her guests could refuse. In donning the garb of the goddess, Riding transformed her own pain and isolation into a fecund weapon of revenge. The aloof but ever-present cadaverous spectator, John Aldridge, was the key to the poem's success. "Death does not little him with fear. 'More, more!' he cries."

The story "The Playground" ended rather more gently and hopefully. When "Tom" awakens from his dream, he remembers a great many more details of the mysterious place that he had visited and the voice that had called him than he noticed while he was dreaming:

> There was a post-box, for instance, with my name on it, only my name was Mr. Thank-you-very-much instead of Tom. I looked for the key to it in my pockets, as if I knew I must have it on me, and found it after a little search. In the box was a picture-postcard for me from myself addressed to "Mr. Thank-you-very-much" and signed "Mr. Thinking-hard." It said: "This is the place. Do you like it?"

When Matthews described his six-month leave in Deyá to Edmund Wilson, his comment was, "I think you got away just in time." But Tom had not really gotten away. The dream of that "rolling rocky place," like the memory of Princeton, Schuyler Jackson, and his gilded youth, would haunt him like a misplaced key for the rest of his life.

The life of John Aldridge came to an end in 1983, though as a member of the Royal Academy he achieved some measure of immortality. Lucie Brown died alone in a sunless apartment in Cambridge, the town of her childhood memories. Robert Graves died in Deyá, bereft of all memory, even the most indelible ones of the war. In 1943, when her youngest boy was seven, Julie Matthews died of cancer, prey to "death's veraciousness." The day before she died, her husband—fiercely, jealously, and tenderly guarding her deathbed—was called to the phone to learn that he had been appointed managing editor of *Time*.

There were two "evil geniuses of the boards" in Mortjoy's theater. In the high box was the witch of the play. But who, the poem asks, was the patron of the lower box. Who is this "waggish villain," her dark twin? Perhaps, under the villain's fedora, there was a shadow of resemblance to the dreamy Unidor, Mr. Ben Beholden, Mr. Thank-you-very-much, or Miserable Sarah's moony godson. Tom would later remark in horror on the wild and ugly face of old age, "He will not admit even the possibility that the innocent or charming child he was has turned into the hollow scarecrow, the nasty and frightening person, that he is now."

Was this the mien of Tom's "feared and hated blood brother," the shadow self that had stalked him for so long? How was it possible for such a handsome and polite young man to become that sort of hideous ill-tempered old man who, in his hunched perversity, would alarm innocent children? He suffered from a speech impediment; he repeated himself. Desperately anxious to be heard, he replayed or retold the story of his life time and time again. Only afterward did he realize "with faint horror and dull dread" that he had been "parroting the same old squawks and cackles."

Laura Riding once believed that there are many strange things in the world but only one so strange as to make a man stop and consider not the strangeness in the world but the strangeness in himself. Confronting this strangeness, she wrote in an essay on Hans Christian Andersen, man is either afraid or unafraid. If afraid of this strange shadow, he will grow old and lonely in his efforts to understand what it is. If unafraid, he will grow younger in the pleasure of sharing the world with that strangeness, that "one thing by which he is able to feel, though perhaps not understand, himself." In the closing pages of his memoirs Matthews confided that he carried in his pocket a little black nugget, dry and shapeless as a "withered and petrified heart." Grasping for a coin or car key, his fingers sometimes encountered and enclosed it (it was, he said, the small hard noun, "love"). Until his death, less than two weeks before his ninetieth birthday, Matthew's grip remained unexpectedly strong.

"What an interminable game it is!"

Chapter 15

THE UNTHRONGED ORACLE

——•——

Your coming, asking, seeing, knowing,
Was a fleeing from and stumbling
Into only mirrors, and behind which
Behind all mirrors, dazzling pretences,
The general light of fortune
Keeps wrapt in sleeping unsleep,
All-mute of time, self-muttering like mute:
Fatality like lone wise-woman
Her unbought secrets counting over
That stink of hell . . .

—"The Unthronged Oracle"

——•——

"THE AUTOBIOGRAPHY OF Baal" was begun in London, at St. Peter's Square, before Graves left for Mallorca. After six weeks of eighteen-hour workdays, Graves had found it hard once he finished *Good-bye to All That* to lay down his pen and stop "talking." The spare and stammerless voice kept thoughts of his family crisis at bay, so he had started a diary and found himself explaining—as "Myself" to "Himself"—his loss of faith, telling the story of the wheelchair, his father's "inglorious gout," and better carpet slippers. Out of this diary and dialogue of self grew a more pointed project; Robert Graves began to talk to God. Undertaken at the deity's request, this off-the-cuff interview ranged over the high points of His various incarnations. In God's successive manifestations as mother goddess or Old Testament's fierce patriarch, in His promotion of various intermediaries like Christ and Mary Baker Eddy, something like an autobiography of God began to take shape. Unfortunately, Graves was obliged to abort this unusual "as told to" collaboration to go abroad. The last two chapters, "Alpha" and "Omega," arrived in Deyá—or so Graves claimed in his gloss to the text—from Los Angeles.

In these chapters God had earnestly explained why He was writing under the name Baal, a name that He had not used for several centuries, and why He was using such a degraded genre as popular autobiography rather than prophets and holy books. Such apologetic chattiness was a sign of gathering clouds; as the story closed on his present-day manifestation, God appeared to be on the very edge of hysteria:

> I attempt to comfort myself by recalling that in spite of my recent disestablishment in every department of human experience . . . I have always emerged triumphantly as the power which is beyond them, as the external consciousness of the human race, as the axiomatic life-force . . . to which the whole corpus of human experience must for ever make humble reference. But then again I question this "for ever." How was it that I suddenly became necessary to man in the first place?

Clearly, God's autobiography was an attempt to come to terms with this recent "vague disquiet," a punishment, He admitted abjectly, for the many capricious wrongs done to mankind in His various aspects. Certain people had already noticed and made comments. They thought He was acting strangely, rather like a man in fear of God:

> Somehow, I therefore believe, though I cannot make it clear to myself, a being perhaps in human shape, yet perhaps not, will appear. I had better say, will appear, for I do not really feel that this has yet happened. And this being will not be for or of me, or yet even against me. It will be indifferent to me, wounding me more terribly than the mistletoe ever did. A deathless being, no doubt, humanly

visible; but without aspects, therefore humanly unknow-
able; not worshipped, not martyred, left alone, of no kind.

"The Autobiography of Baal" was published by Graves in his
miscellaneous "accumulation," *But It Still Goes On*, which Jonathan
Cape brought out in 1930 in an attempt to capitalize on the booming
sales of *Good-bye to All That*. Graves flaunted his cynical motives
before his readers with an uncomfortable ill humor. He did, however,
try to justify himself to his critics and his family, for whom this book
was even more disturbing than its predecessor. In this sense he was
doing exactly what God was doing in His autobiography, only with
much less grace. As far as Robert's parents were concerned, "The
Autobiography of Baal" was by no means the most offensive piece in
the collection.

But God's life story was clearly not as absorbing for the public as
Graves' own had been; sales of *But It Still Goes On* were disappointing,
and Graves needed money. Even before Canelluñ was finished in the
late spring of 1932, Gelat had broken the news to Laura and Robert
that Don Bernardo Colón, who owned the large hillside tract of land
between Canelluñ and the sea below, had been approached by some
Germans who wanted to build a hotel. Because Don Bernardo's elder
son was courting his daughter, Gelat might intervene—but only, he
told them, if Robert and Laura made a counteroffer. Their offer was
accepted with alacrity.

Like Canelluñ, the land that Robert bought was considered
Laura's, as were nearly all of his purchases during their stay in
Mallorca. Also like Canelluñ, because the land lay outside the
village and within five kilometers of the sea, Gelat registered it in
his name; as a foreigner, Laura was not allowed to own land in those
areas. This complicated applications for bank loans to buy Don
Bernardo's land until Gelat suggested a moneylender. Neither Robert nor Laura saw anything suspect in the fact that Don Bernardo
was both the seller of the land and the lender—at breathtaking
interest rates—of the money to buy it. Nor did they stop to
consider that Gelat might put his future son-in-law's interest in the
deal before their own.

Juan Gelat Marroig Más (pronounced Jel-OT Mar-OTCH), the fac-
totum of Deyá, had begun his life as a tenant farmer. He had had little

education but nearly every newcomer to Deyá soon found themselves, hat in hand, stuttering before him in broken Spanish. Apart from being the sole source of electricity, Gelat owned and drove the daily bus to Palma, undertaking small commissions and errands. He was also the owner of the factory that, until he installed his electricity generator, had formerly produced soap, milled flour, and pressed olives. Bald, swarthy, and compact in stature, he wore a stony expression under his soft black fedora. He could be both charming and resourceful; but he could also intimidate a person with his shrewd, unsmiling stare. Gelat knew everyone's business but no one's better than his own.

Canelluñ was part of the world sustained by Robert's limitless faith in the imaginations of Gelat and Laura Riding. Their pride in what they had created in this house inspired Laura and Gelat to greater heights and steeper investments of Robert's money. As overseer, Gelat organized the labor and the craftsmanship of Canelluñ's construction. When the house was finished, he presented Laura with a dining room table and chairs made of mulberry and carefully crafted by Miguel the carpenter. Gelat had cut the tree himself fifteen years before on the waning moon, and the wood had been submerged in a cistern awaiting use. Laura's chair, modeled to her small frame, was placed at the head of the table like a miniature throne.

To recoup some of the expense entailed by Canelluñ's demands of beauty and perfection, Laura's first idea was to build a cottage on the edge of their property with the leftover materials. If it was rented by advertisement in London, Robert wrote to John Aldridge a bit nervously, they might make back their money in three years. But before they had lived in Canelluñ for four months, the house was mortgaged to meet a payment on Don Bernardo's land and to pay for a road down to the Cala. Laura, in consultation with Gelat, had now decided that they would sell off plots to select people and even build a hotel themselves. Norman Cameron agreed to come in on this, and even John Aldridge's mother contributed capital. In celebration of the founding of her company, Luna, and the mortgaging of Canelluñ, Robert threw a party for Laura. The phonograph was wound up, champagne was poured, and Robert presented an excited Laura with a large moonstone ring.

AFTER THE SUCCESS of *Good-bye to All That*, Jonathan Cape had agreed to publish Riding's *Poems A Joking Word* and her story collection *Experts Are Puzzled*. As publication grew nearer, Riding's letters to her editor contained a fund of carefully detailed strategy, plans, and advice about the books tender debut in the marketplace. After a number of such letters, her editor requested his secretary to distill her key points so that he might be saved the effort of reading the closely written pages. There was even a brief trip to London in the fall of 1930, during which Robert met with Jonathan Cape to discuss promotion ideas for Riding's poems; Robert generously offered to pay for the advertisements. Cape kept his own counsel, and both books appeared with little fanfare.

The publicity and large income that attended the reception of *Good-bye to All That*, combined with the stream of visitors arriving in Deyá inquiring about its author, had thoroughly unsettled Laura. While there was never any doubt about the relative merits of her talent and Robert's, the contrast between her tiny successes and his spectacular one left her indignant and embittered. When Cape promised him a surefire means of launching a successful career as a novelist, Robert, perhaps alarmed by Laura's acute unhappiness, at first put him off. The novel was to be called *No Decency Left*, and Cape was persistent in believing that it would make money: "Every maiden aunt will want to read it as she will expect to find in it her own views as to the general decadence of the younger generation . . . George Bernard Shaw will have it read aloud to him and be consumed with envy that he had not thought of it as a title for one of his own books." Feeling guilty about the costs that Cape had incurred in fending off the legal claims that had arisen over *Good-bye to All That*, Robert finally relented.

But the novel, published in 1932 under a pseudonym that was also the name of the main character, was not what Cape had in mind. To a certain degree, the envisioned satire—an alarmist hand-wringing over the fraying of the moral fiber of British society—had been achieved. But Barbara Rich, as main character and author, was rather a surprise. After reading Robert's draft of the novel, Laura apparently took over the book and rewrote it; long letters to Cape told what a bother this was for her but that she was helpless to do otherwise. Underlying such complaints was her hope that Cape would see that her writing might also bring in money. Robert was obliged to admit to friends that *No Decency Left* was now largely Laura's, though they still wanted to retain the pseudonym and the secrecy. His version, he explained, had "too heavy a touch, too cock-a-hoop a style, too altogether—too—not good enough. Now it's what it should have been."

The novel opens on the morning of Barbara Rich's twenty-first birthday. A common salesclerk with uncommon ambitions, she decides that the following day will not find her waking up in the same rooming house, looking at the depressing cracked tiles of her bath or engaged to the same dreary fellow. And so, in the course of a single day, she meets and marries the prince of a small parliamentary democracy very much like England, is promoted, is then given ownership of the department store where she works, and with hardly any assistance effects a political coup. The forlorn prince, who at first seems like the handsome, charming, and sincere catch of any young girl's dreams, takes a backseat after Barbara ascends to the dictator's throne.

Riding tried to hide her enthusiasm for the book once she had finished it, telling Cape that wherever he found it dull, that was Robert's doing, and wherever it was exciting, that was hers. Just before publication day, Cape had a flurry of letters from Deyá suggesting that they go public with the book's authorship. Cape politely demurred, explaining that the kidnapping of the Lindbergh baby had preempted whatever publicity might be gained from it.

Though restrained by the abject absurdity of her plot, Riding wrote of Barbara Rich's unbridled fantasies of power and wealth with keen enthusiasm. Her own weakness for royalty and daydreams of benevolent despotism are thinly disguised by the cloak of satire in *No Decency Left*; it is a profoundly nihilistic novel. But through the offices of bestsellerdom Riding hoped to achieve exactly those fantasies which she tried hard to disown, clinging to some notion of "decency" that Barbara herself lost somewhere along the way. Two years later Riding sought the novel's republication, with a sequel, by another publisher. Wealth and popular acclaim were hard dreams to relinquish; they provided Riding the only possibility of escape from the humiliating stranglehold of her dependence on Robert. Compounding the book's failure was Riding's fear that Cape believed that she had ruined the book's chances, a fear that eventually soured their relationship. Laura (Riding) Jackson refused to authorize any attribution of the novel to herself. She demanded that libraries and special collections that have the book carry a precisely worded disclaimer in their card catalog. But neither would she allow a collaborative share of credit to be granted to Robert Graves.

In the long run, the tiny but remarkable book of poems that Cape published with modest claims will secure the reputation, if not the wealth, that Riding so craved as a young woman. In her best poems, she established the independence that she was often unable to attain in her life with Graves. *Poems A Joking Word* did find an attentive audience among the reviewers when it was first published. During their London visit, a review appeared in *The Granta* magazine at Cambridge by a young mathematician and friend of William Empson named Jacob Bronowski; Laura was soon in correspondence with him. In the review he paid particular attention to the book's foreword and to the unique formal techniques of the poems. Riding's poetic process, he said, was one of rarification and distillation reached by almost a purely personalized means; her individuality and independence were a measure of her "isolation."

Such isolation, Bronowski pointed out, put too much stress upon the poet's "personality." Individual personalities were limited by subjective perceptions; they could not achieve the required omniscience. Bronowski cited T. S. Eliot's dictum that the true artist must strive for a "continual extinction of personality" in order to achieve the requisite, universalist vista. To shoulder the burden of poetic authority alone—particularly considering that Riding was both a woman and a poet, only "fragmentarily articulate"—was to reveal only a vision with limits that mirrored her own:

> This limitation has always been foreshadowed in Laura
> Riding's poetry, and has tended more and more to become
> a dissatisfaction, an insistence on the limitations of expres-
> sion; a continual attempt to break through to the univer-
> sality. And this book may be said to stop on the threshold
> of that breaking through; so that although it marks an

important stage, and a stage which would be no less important if it were final. . . .

Somehow, the rationalistic and philosophical cadences, the precise linguistic engineering of Riding's poems convinced Bronowski, no less than the poet herself, that she was abreast of the final threshold and through that doorway, assuming that one successfully extinguished one's "personality," lay truth. Bronowski's faith, which he was exploring at the time with William Empson under the influence of I. A. Richards' *Practical Criticism*, was with the scientific method. His ambition was "to carry the language of science into literature" and "to write criticism as reasoned as geometry."

But however abstract the new poems like "Here Beyond" seemed, Riding had not replaced poetry with geometry. Similarly, though the earlier, apocalyptic "Samuel's Toast of Death" had been revised, heavily cut, and retitled "Goat Alone" for this collection, Riding still held firm to her belief in her personal "Form Eccentric." With her spine as her divining rod, she held science to be just one of the insults to the old divine order. Central to her universe were the "Laura" of *Laura and Francisca* and the death goddess of *The Life of the Dead*. These avatars embodied Riding's "Form Eccentric" at its most majestic; rather than curtailing the incidentals of "personality," Riding enlarged precise autobiographical detail with metaphysical wit or colorful allegory to show that what she regarded as the requirements of truth or "universality" could be consanguine with the domestic self—her self.

THUS THE TRANSFIGURATION that had its first flowering in Cairo and bloomed again at St. Peter's Square as Riding recovered from her "death" and her tussle with Phibbs had its inevitable sequel. Having survived demons and the Devil himself, Riding now found God her natural adversary. This latest battle was only intermittently ironic, what Laura (Riding) Jackson later liked to call her "play with the possibilities of extreme statement."

Generally, Riding's imaginative relationship with God, unlike hers with his wayward angel, was a great deal more formal. Her respectful solicitude toward Him was as befitting as that due to an English gentleman of independent income suffering from a crisis of faith in the Church of England. By the time Graves received God's last two chapters from Los Angeles, Riding had already written "Then Follows." It was included in the section entitled "Poems of Final Occasion" of her *Collected Poems* and appears here in its 1930, Hours Press, version:

. . .

It came about by chance—
I met God.
"What," he said, "you already?"
"What," I said, "you still?"
He apologized and I apologized.
"I thought I was alone," he said.
"Are you displeased?" I said.
"I suppose I should not be," he said.

. . .

"Are there any more of you?" he said,
Tears in his eyes, but politely.
"As many as you care to meet," I said.
Tears falling, he said politely,
"I can't wait, but remember me to them."

From being not ill
To being ill
Was an awkward moment.
But my celebrated power
Of maintaining a fixed attitude
In scenes of stress and perturbation
Is no mere want of grace.
Here was an awkward moment
Worthy of my awkwardness at last.

. . .

She received Him in her own version of heaven, Canelluñ, the last and largest jewel in her crown.

Jacob Bronowski was one of the first visitors to the newly completed house. Late on the evening of his arrival, in early July 1932, he wrote to his mother of the long journey to Deyá and Canelluñ, the "most beautiful house I have ever been in." He likened its structure to houses in the south of France. Rectangular, two-storied, and crowned with a slightly hipped, Roman-tiled roof, Canelluñ was built with large local stones like the surrounding olive terraces. The beams were of the best pine, the water supply ingeniously arranged so that the cistern on the west side of the house not only provided enough water for the entire summer but also formed a veranda. By opening a small door in one wall of the kitchen, one could drop a bucket twenty feet down to a smaller rainwater well and bring up cooler water for drinking (and sometimes a drowned rat). Together, Gelat and Laura planned the garden for Sebastian the aged gardener to work, mapping the placement of paths and benches and the position of the fruit trees. Robert busied himself transplanting flowers from Salerosa.

> As you come into the house you are in a square entrance hall, about 25 or 30 feet square—that is occupying the whole width of the house so that its far door goes straight out of the house again at the back. This hall, like all the rest of the house, is tiled (I mean underfoot) with pale yellow tiles; and the walls are whitewashed, stone. On the left of the hall is a flight of stairs, upstairs, of yellow tiles also with a dark brown wood facing on each step, and no banister . . . further on the left, a door leading to Graves's workroom, a spare workroom containing their printing press, and the (very important) cellars ice-cool. On the right, a door to the living room and the kitchen.

By Deyá standards the kitchen was modern and well organized, with shelves and a pantry. A flat coal stove for heating and cooking during the winter was replaced by a pressure cooker in summer. There was a washboard, and a black marble sink was brought from the house of St. Catalina da Tomás, a recently canonized Mallorquin girl whose uncorrupted corpse was then lying in the Palma cathedral. The story was told that it was over this sink that Catalina had stood when the devil came up the waste pipe and first tempted her.

On the kitchen side of the living room were a fireplace and two windows. One faced the mountains and the sea; another, which the dining room faced, overlooked the garden. The woodwork of the

door was light pine, which Bronowski thought created a lovely
contrast with the white walls and pale yellow floors:

> I won't go into the detail of the curtains and other
> hangings—nearly all made by her help and beautifully
> woven: and the other decorations are not easy to de-
> scribe, . . . the large flat bowls being instead full of apri-
> cots, coloured tiddlywink discs and another beautiful one,
> on an old chest in the hall, of beautifully chosen tiny
> pebbles covered with a thin layer of water. . . . I shall
> exhaust myself over the upstairs rooms if I go on at this
> rate: you must imagine items chosen with the same sort of
> decorative care. The rooms upstairs are . . . Laura's work-
> room, four bedrooms, a very lovely bathroom (huge) and
> a lavatory and linen cupboards and such . . . all of them in
> beautiful pale pine-wood (of which the downstairs rooms
> are also beamed), more or less all over the place. . . . As for
> those mountains and the Mediterranean and the sun—I
> feel I have spent so much time describing the house almost
> a postponement of this beauty, and so much more moving,
> so much more difficult to speak of.

Bronowski, whom everyone but Riding called Bruno, stayed only
for a short visit but promised to return the following year to help
Riding with her proposed publication, *The Critical Vulgate*. Planned as
a Seizin Press hardcover journal copublished with a willing London
publisher, it was to concern itself "in an uncompromising authoritative way with the values of things." Laura would contribute the
"general statement of values," Robert wrote to T. E. Lawrence, while
he worked at "the internal interrogation and illustration." Laura asked
Jacob to write glosses for the text; Eirlys Roberts, a classics scholar at
Cambridge and Jacob's girlfriend, would collate. As the original title
indicated, its ambitions went beyond the temporary enthusiasms of a
literary journal; the Vulgate referred to the most ancient of the extant
Latin versions of the Bible, the standard by which Gnostic heresies
were judged in Rome.

The Critical Vulgate, like Deyá and Canellun, quickly became the nu-
cleus around which those who chose "literal death" and the pursuit of

literal truth might concentrate themselves. "I am never entirely without assistance in my work of investigation," Riding told her readers in *Authors Today and Yesterday*. As in her previous collaborations on novels, poems, and masques, Riding's would be the dominating presence, but now the primary writing of her "Vulgatites" would be didactic and philosophical—"Vulgate-minded"—rather than creative.

When, in 1764, the public prosecutor was asked by the Paris city council to give his opinion of Voltaire's philosophical dictionary, he described the undertaking as a "deplorable monument of the extent to which intelligence and erudition can be abused." Like Voltaire, Riding wished to establish the truth regarding all possible subjects and was as full of portentous ambition as any eighteenth-century rationalist. In *The Critical Vulgate* she hoped to make an encyclopedic effort to apprehend this "finality" or final truth, using what was called the "'divine' sanction of poetic life." This founding principle sustained and integrated a range of articles on a variety of subjects. The absolute laws of poetry were for her, and for those whom she gathered around her, as indisputable as the laws of reason were to the encyclopedists. Similarly, Voltaire's categories—certainty, circumcision, idolatry, religion, virtue, men of letters—were as miscellaneous and unsystematic as Riding's. In the three volumes of *Epilogue: A Critical Summary* that were published (Riding changed the title after Jacob left the fold), essays on fame, advertising, drama, and photography appeared alongside others on reality, the end of the world, detective fiction, and the bullfight.

But following Jacob's question of universality and the nature of poetic authority, Laura chose God as the first subject to tackle. In the short fictional monologue "Their Last Interview," published at the close of *Experts Are Puzzled* in 1930, Riding had written:

> In their last interview, Lilith Outcome and God left very little of the ground uncovered. . . . "I give up," God said. "But I knew from the very beginning that it was only a matter of time with me. I never meant to be anything but God." Miss Outcome was delighted that he felt no antagonism to her. "Then you quite forgive me for being more correct?" "Dear me, girl," God said, "I am only grateful to you for taking the responsibility off my hands. Of course, I

kept the ball rolling pretty steadily, though I do say so myself; but I haven't your authoritative touch. How do you do it?" Miss Outcome smiled shrewdly. "I find nothing wearisome. There's really no more to it than that."

Now, two years later, Riding directed her attention to God's dawdling parishioners, announcing in no uncertain terms that changes at the top had occurred.

Back in Princeton, Tom Matthews, being the son of a bishop and still a churchgoer, was asked to play devil's advocate to Riding's percolating encyclical. Matthews described the result as not so much an argument about the nature of the divine being but, rather, "an occasion for Laura to proclaim the final truth of the matter, using my naive questions, and equally simple demurrers to her first replies, as easy but simple targets." In fact, Matthews' questions were time-honored ones concerning God's nature and the question of his existence, rather than specific tenets of theological doctrine. This exchange, "The Idea of God," appeared in 1935 as the opening salvo of *Epilogue*. To the question, Does God exist? Riding began her tract with the simple answer, "Woman."

God, Riding wrote, was generally acknowledged to be an idea, an important idea thought up by early man to account for his sense of inadequacy for or his dependence on the ungentle mercies of fate. Thus, Riding decided, God encompassed all that consciousness which was not man, "a creature neither man nor God." Riding wrote in the 1938 version of "Then Follows":

> . . .
>
> Yes, such a creature by name,
> But featured like both man and God—
> Like God, a creature of mind,
> Like man, a creature of mouth.
> Ah, the pity of it,
> To be a mouth and mind,
> But dimly named,
> As if this third where two contended
> Were murky mumbling peace thereof.

In this poem Riding seems to have been exploring a purely female cosmology. If "mouth" is to be metaphorically derived from womb, then one has found the germinal sprouts of Riding's argument for the "divine" (never to appear shorn of quotation marks) aspect of the female being. Man can be said to be a "creature of mouth" because he was born of woman, and a "creature of mind" because he continually creates himself. But mouth is also the birth canal of breath, voice, the Word; while the male poet has focused on the mouth as the passageway of divine "inspiration," Riding calls on a symbolic system derived from exhalation, the birthing of the inner divinities. Delicately, she reroutes the association of mouth and womb from more biological thoroughfares and needs, in order to focus on this utility. Ontologically as well as metaphorically only woman, that "third where two contended," "dimly named," can speak clearly that "murky mumbling peace."

In her essay for *Epilogue*, Riding came to the same conclusion via a different route. As the relationship between man and his world changed, she argued, the "mystical fiction" of God underwent corresponding changes, but until the last century at least, He retained his transcendent appearance and nature. At that point God began his descent. Man began to see that he was not created in the image of God; rather, God had been created in his.

This was not atheism, Riding insisted. However much God suffered from neglect, it could not suddenly be said that He did not exist, for the idea of God continued to incite modern man to be either insolent or propitiatory. Why? Because He threatened man's sense of his own importance, his genius, his idea of himself as creator, master of his fate. Thus when modern man was obliged to consider either the idea of God or the idea of woman, the results were the same: either "obscene (irreverent) or sentimental (guilty)." And the answer to the question of whether woman exists was yes.

In the aftermath of such scorched-earth reasoning, there has grown a jungle of excited comment over whether Laura Riding suffered from the delusion that she was God. In recent years Laura (Riding) Jackson corrected this impression to insist, primly but slyly, that it was Gertrude Stein who thought she was God; she, however, always remained her "careful self." In *Epilogue* she identified Stein as

God but indicated that she meant the primitive sort, as in the Old
Testament, rather than a more modern incarnation:

> She is woman representing the something else, against
> which man has now immediately come, as a blank scene
> where it is as inaccessible to man as at the beginning of
> time . . . The meaning of her record is only the failure of
> the human consciousness to go beyond itself.

Riding was not exactly out to replace God with herself or Gertrude
Stein, nor was she particularly interested in arguing with Him, as
man had taken to doing since the Enlightenment. In Deyá she was
said to have referred to a female divinity, an abiding She, but this
must also be understood in a rhetorical sense, as a "play with the
possibilities of extreme statement."

Still, Riding recognized that the patriarchal Christian God was,
in most Western minds, a glamorous and fundamental feature of
ethical inquiry into the nature of truth, and for many of her followers the Christian God still grasped the gold standard of good
and evil. The essay in *Epilogue* was intended to force man to consider
the Big Questions in a new light, to see the human puzzle in terms
other than those of a conflict between man and his God. Even for
the most atheistic of her annoyed literary critics, their faith in the
idea of God was not subject to much change. Most irksome was
Riding's observation that as man's equivocal notion of God increasingly resembled his equivocal notion of woman, God was beginning
to be more and more womanly. For this alone it was only reasonable
for her detractors to conclude that Laura Riding suffered from
religious delusions.

As a result, the very real issues that she tried to raise have been
persistently obscured by the riot of ridicule and accusation that the
Riding legend helped to foment. Gertrude Stein's impenetrability,
she insisted, only reflected the failure of male consciousness back at
man. Riding claimed for herself the first soundings of female consciousness. Her dismissal of the patriarchal Christian God defined
her stance but in no way diminished her oracular ambitions. To the
question, "What now?" in "As to Food" she answered as the woman at
whose feet "this dead God" lay:

Then I must feed you, if you live,
Not that old pap you died of,
The thin milk of time which was yourself
Mothered by yourself, O mortal Godhood.

The long delay in the discovery of poetry's "final" standard, Riding showed, was caused by man's stubborn dependence on a patriarchal superstition, first in the idea of God, then in the idea of himself. This standard, the rule by which all is judged, dwelled only in women. In 1938 Jacob Bronowski would question what he considered Riding's arbitrary decision to locate the final standard in women; by then he had been "excommunicated." But his best friend, James Reeves, replacing him on *Epilogue*, happily traced the trajectory of Riding's thought as it applied to "The Romantic Habit in English Poetry." "[Shelley's] poetic faith was a faith in man," prompted Riding in a footnote, rather than the "absolute poetic law" with which *Epilogue* identified itself. The final resting place of the romantic tradition lay with the Georgians' dead Rupert Brooke, "a young Apollo, golden haired."

In the first issue of *Epilogue* Riding had marked her territory; time and time again she emphasized that only she had ventured so far into that sea of misconceptions known as knowledge and brought back the shining prize of her discovery, the compass of final truth. For the most part, *Epilogue II* and *III* failed to recapture this initial intellectual excitement; but the exhilaration of Riding's own, personally inscribed, faith inspired an amazing variety of projects—literary, educational, social, and political—throughout the 1930s. For a while, she provided a rich pap for more than a few.

And what else besides Laura Riding and her *Epilogue* was required to explore the Good, the True, and the Final—now that history had ended and God had entered retirement? A great deal. Apart from building her hotel and selling plots, Luna also envisioned founding a university. Gelat would oversee the construction, perhaps Eirlys would act as manager, and Laura would extemporize on various subjects. A series of short textbooks was planned, collaborative work began on a dictionary that would integrate these textbooks, and countless articles were assigned for *Epilogue*.

The construction of the road down to the Cala, weaving in hairpin turns from one olive terrace to the next, marked the beginning of this mammoth undertaking. Completed by Easter, 1934, the road down the steps of Don Bernardo's land was washed into the sea four months later by a freak rainstorm. In the eighteen months that they had owned the land, Gelat had not sold a single plot to anyone—select individual or otherwise. Indeed, why would anyone working with Laura in Deyá invest in plots when Robert was always willing to pay for their room and board?

Later, some would decide that Laura had been completely duped. Seduced by Gelat's cunning, she had allowed his low-key machismo to get the better of her common sense; she had an almost unlimited capacity for deceiving herself when it came to imagining how men felt about her. How else could one explain Laura's eagerness to use Robert's money to bankroll Gelat's plans to the point of risking everything, including Canelluñ? Both Laura and Robert were party to Gelat's various intrigues against the village doctor and the village priest; his financial machinations were there for them to see. They did, of course, appreciating each nuance of Gelat's genius for getting the best of his adversaries. It never occurred to either of them that they were an integral part of his financial portfolio. When a discrepancy was found in Gelat's accounts of 4,000 pesetas (about $7,000 in today's currency) heads were scratched for a few days but no eyes narrowed.

To a certain extent Laura and Robert's risks were also Gelat's; the loss of Canelluñ would have been his no less than theirs, particularly if it obliged them to leave Mallorca. Gelat would never have let it come to that. With Laura and Robert's spending habits, it is often not clear if the thrill of making money or losing it was more exciting; they certainly had no desire to be free from the labor of writing books—as Gelat kept promising them they would be. Unlike Robert, however, both Laura and Gelat knew what it was to have nothing, and to walk that fine line with Gelat was as intimate an experience as Laura allowed anyone. Riding wrote of a character in one of her stories, "She could not help flirting with her own good luck in being so contented." Perhaps Gelat understood this. In 1933 she wrote, "I admire no single person except a native of Deyá called Juan Morroig . . . He is rarely wrong in his judgements, and when he makes a mistake it does not stay long uncorrected." Doubtless, she imagined that Gelat recognized the same quality in herself.

Many years later Laura (Riding) Jackson, trying to understand what kind of faith sustained her life in Deyá, related a conversation in which Gelat scolded her for being too generous with herself. The word for this in Mallorquin, he told her, was the same as the word for fool. After a ten-minute silence, Laura looked up to find that both she and Gelat had tears in their eyes. Depending on one's view of the world, this reaction suggests the level of his guile, his affection, or a careful combination of both.

Inevitably, however, such grandiose ambitions—whether God's, Riding's, or Gelat's—eventually ran up against mundane concerns. *No Decency Left* was a flop, as was Graves' condensed version of *David Copperfield* and Riding's *Everybody's Letters*. By mid-July 1933 they faced "spectacular financial ruin," which obliged Robert to reopen correspondence with Siegfried Sassoon. He begged for £1,000, and after a twitchy and bitter exchange of letters Sassoon refused. Once again Graves needed a story as good as—if not better than—his own.

Chapter 16

THE STORY PIG

————•————

On the mantelpiece of Hotel Moon, where people went to behave nicely, stood a large silver-plated pig with its mouth wide open. . . . The pig was called the Story-pig because it was undoubtedly responsible for all the story-telling. It held its mouth wide open and gorged itself on the idle thoughts of the guests; and as they were all the pleasantest possible thoughts . . . they turned to stories in the pig's shiny belly. The pig's belly was not shiny inside, but no one saw or thought of the inside.

—"The Story Pig"

————•————

A MONTH BEFORE Riding read the finished manuscript of *I, Claudius* she learned that Jonathan Cape had sold the remaining unbound copies of *Poems A Joking Word* as pulp, having already done the same with *Contemporaries and Snobs* and *Anarchism Is Not Enough*. Mary Burton-wood, then living in Deyá with George Ellidge (they were married but kept it a secret from Laura), was on hand to hear Laura's response to Robert's new book. They had all decided to take Gelat's taxi to Palma so that the manuscript might be sent to England by registered mail. Laura, she remembered, was sulking and grumpy, having spent half the night reading the historical novel. To dampen everyone's spirits, Laura suddenly announced that she thought it a "very boring book." To Mary it was perfectly clear that Laura "was *jealous* because she knew that this was going to be a successful book and she could never write a successful book. . . . And poor Robert was like a pricked balloon because he'd been on top of the world you see, so happy that he'd finished the wretched thing."

Venison Bride, in Riding's short story "Daisy and Venison," was named by her mother, who thought her daughter had a "freakish, gamey look." Her father, a drunk, predicted that "she'd have an odd taste, not like ordinary meat." Venison often stole from people; she was really interested only in herself. When her father kicked her out of the house for having stolen his drinking money, her mother gave her the secret hoard of gold pieces that she kept in a sock in her sewing basket, and sent her off to live with Daisy. Daisy was a young woman living off the spoils of her father's criminal activities. She took Venison in without comment, and so Venison began spending her time sitting quietly in comfortable positions in her Sunday clothes. It was then that she began to write stories.

Tom Matthews, after delighting in "The Playground," Riding's fairy tale about his family, suggested to Robert that she write more— perhaps a whole book. The next day he was summoned to Laura's Ca'n Pa Bo sanctum, where Laura demanded, "What did you mean by telling Robert that I should write more fairy stories?" In fact, Riding already had the idea but, as was her wont, could not resist an invitation to "scare the grown-ups," and Tom was perhaps her pet grown-up. In August 1931 she had written to Jonathan Cape that since he did not absolutely refuse to print her, she was working on a collection of fairy tales for him. The collection was to be entitled after one of the stories, "The Story Pig," and the book itself was to be perfectly readable. This was to be Riding's successful book, the one that Mary Burtonwood and everyone else thought she could not write. Jonathan Cape would sell thousands of copies, she foretold, and then, of course, everyone would live happily ever after.

When her mother died, Venison attended her funeral, staying away from Daisy overnight. At the service an aunt who read novels told her that she ought to become an authoress, living in seclusion the way she did. The aunt, of course, was being sarcastic. She knew that Venison wrote stories, but that was not what she meant by literature. Venison, she said, lacked both the education and human sympathy required to write literature. Indeed, Venison's stories were simple but ruthless—somewhat like Venison herself:

> Her stories were mostly about people who did not alto-
> gether moral things that turned out well and therefore
> seemed, after all, right things to do. . . . Nor did she know
> much about people. But as she was a timid, somewhat
> wicked person herself, she thought of other people as
> being like herself, only a little bolder. She did not think of
> wickedness as wickedness, but rather as the stuff people
> were made of, like flesh. Thus, without any knowledge of
> life or geography, she gave an impression of wide experi-
> ence in her stories. With a little training in grammar and
> literary style she would undoubtedly have been a success-
> ful author.

Venison's one serious failing was that she could not write about love: "She could not write a story with more than one important character in it, whom she thought of for the moment as herself; with love there had to be at least two important characters."

Venison returned home after her mother's funeral and took her stories out of the dog basket, where she kept them. After rereading them she agreed with her aunt that she had no human sympathy. Still, she thought that she had instincts. Suddenly talkative, she remarked to Daisy, "They say it is like being an animal to rely on your instincts, but if an animal wrote stories about people, they would be good stories in their way. And my stories are good stories in their way." Daisy, who saw Venison as "a flaw that had developed in her happi-ness" but whose presence she nevertheless accepted without com-plaint, maintained her composure. She suggested that Venison send her stories to be printed in an illustrated magazine.

When at last published by Constable in 1935, Riding's collection of fairy tales was entitled *Progress of Stories*. Her long preface made it clear that her readership was a small party ("we almost know exactly who we all are") rather than the "thousands" she had anticipated in her 1931 letter to Jonathan Cape. Nor were all the stories fairy tales; a few, she felt, would give her readers no pleasure at all. Nonetheless, her real readership had learned the virtues of truthful communication, and that was worth a great deal more than what-ever temporary entertainment one writer's silly story might provide. Riding claimed that she shared an understanding with those readers to say only what was true, to hold only one conversation and be "careful of accidents."

This circle of readers, she allowed, might be expanded to include "you"—provided you also think that truth requires everyone's having the same conversation. If you sneer, "Oh, of course, by the 'same' conversation she means *her* conversation," then you had better forget it. If you imagine, while reading the stories, that Laura Riding was really just talking about herself, she will ask you, "And in everything that I have ever written have I ever brought myself in, except in the most discreet way?" And if your answer even then is that she has always been secretive, ready to talk about everyone but herself, she will tell you that you are being childish and should have "gone away long ago."

Riding's close cross-examination of herself, in the guise of anticipating her readers' every impatience with the stories that followed, is concluded by a petulant dismissal. Her heartfelt conviction was that the single most intimate and truthful communication was one shared by all; this became her conception of storytelling, as of poetry. Still, doubts assailed her, particularly when those few gathered about her at Canellun kept leaving her in midsentence to pick up their lives elsewhere. What would people say, she asked John Aldridge, when they saw how her friends kept abandoning her.

Venison's aunt, like the skeptical reader of Riding's preface, would doubtless think that Riding's stories shared the failing of Venison's loveless stories: there was only one important character in each of them. But it was through this character that Riding tried again and again to find out exactly who she, Laura Riding, was. Each story provided a new attire, a new angle from which she might consider the various aspects of her self. Until that other "important character" appeared, all she had were her readers to confer with on possibilities.

And she had Robert. An early version of the story essay "A Crown for Hans Andersen," which eventually appeared near the end of *Progress of Stories*, was printed, unbound, at the Seizin Press toward the end of 1931. Only six pages survive, but they contain Riding's distinction between the story she was trying to tell and the story Robert was trying to tell. To Robert she allotted the legend of King Arthur. But she herself would crown Hans Andersen. Robert's story, she felt, was written backwards from his conclusions and therefore could never achieve more than a memory of himself.

In 1931 the word "always" had meant the large truth, the happily ever after; true fairy tales were a brief instant in "always." In Andersen, Riding had found her literary forebear with none of the scholarly ephemera of the "history men." There was no now-and-then with Hans; there was only now. "Then" was Robert's province. She also found in Andersen the smallness and the patience and the tranquillity that she had found in *Laura and Francisca*. Riding told Cape that it was in the last few pages of this poem that she began to hear the fairy tales talk. Like the "Laura" of this poem, Andersen "looked at the truth and saw small and talked small: this is what his fairy tales are." To Robert, Riding gently yielded the "always" of heroic deeds and historic legends because he had paid court to the everafterness of fairy tales. Robert might continue with the now-and-then of himself, Riding wrote magnanimously, since he had made room for the always of herself.

But despite her sworn allegiance to Andersen's "in a little while," by the time her collection of stories was published, in 1935, Riding's patience had worn rather thin. By then she found Robert's sort of storytelling—juggling facts and playing on the grosser human sympathies—less forgivable if more profitable. She had even lost her pleasure in fairy tales. As her preface indicated, she was not about to dance attendance on the dull reader.

To join Riding's "conversation" one either arrived in Deyá asking about Laura Riding (never Robert), or after a decent period of correspondence, one was invited. Sometimes Laura not only paid her guests' passage but also gave them a stone cottage for an indefinite stay, providing for herself an ever changing circle of friends with whom to work and talk. In her story "Miss Banquett or the Populating of Cosmania" the main character came from a land where she was known to be beautiful. Upon leaving it, Miss Banquett's became a beauty of will more than of appearance, a steady occupation that required attentive care. Upon arriving in Cosmania, she takes seven days to populate the country with tribes who represent to her different aspects of her beauty, thereby preserving her beauty and extending her dominion. Laura's lonely letters to John Aldridge suggest that she, too, feared for the dimming memories of the intimacies shared in Deyá. While Riding, like Venison Bride, may have insisted on the importance of her own singular "animal instincts," she herself could not seem to live peacefully for very long without more human mirrors, active or passive collaborators in much of her thought and writings. In "Miss Banquet," as well as in other stories in the collection, she acknowledges the symbiosis between hostess and guest, creator and created, author and reader—and celebrates it.

Progress of Stories comprised eighteen stories divided into five sections: "Stories of Lives" (in which "Daisy and Venison" appeared), "Stories of Ideas" (in which "Miss Banquett" appeared), "Nearly True Stories" (in which "The Playground" appeared), "A Crown for Hans Andersen," and "More Stories." The "progress" of the title reflected the evolution of the book from a proposed collection of fairy tales entitled *The Story Pig* to a book whose stories and essays deconstructed the very assumptions with which she had begun. At least part of the reason for the evolution of the book in this manner lay with Jonathan Cape. When Riding sent the manuscript to him early in 1932, he returned it in "indecent haste," avowing that he saw no possible readership for the stories in book form.

Reviewing the book for the London *Sunday Times*, Rebecca West suspected that the tales were "perhaps quite a lot wiser than the ordinary realistic novel" but found it hard to say why or how so:

> When one reads "Daisy and Venison," the story of a girl who sent her stories to an editor with a letter, "I am sending you a lot of stories in a dog-basket. It opens by pressing on the lock, Yours respectfully, Venison Bride," one will, if one is a certain sort of reader, throw the book aside, indulge in unfavorable and unjust generalizations about literature, and go out and play golf. But if one is . . . lucky, one will realise thankfully that one is back with Grimm and Hans Andersen, and that the Princess who felt the pea through the mattress has a very crazy little sister.

Unlike Jonathan Cape, Mr. Valentine, the editor of the illustrated magazine to whom Venison Bride sent her dog basket of stories, did not throw the manuscript aside. But he did have his own designs. He arrived one morning at the house where Venison lived with Daisy, "smiling like a clergyman on holiday." He brought with him a box of chocolates and a gramophone. He wanted to talk with Venison about her stories, but she was still in bed. Offering chocolates to Daisy, he put a record on the gramophone, combed his hair, and when Daisy went to wake Venison, began chuckling and rubbing his hands together greedily. He left his comb on the table. When Venison came down he told her his publicity plans while she ate the chocolates. When he finished he turned to her and "pressing down the lid of the gramophone emphatically" asked, "What about a little love?"

In the preface to her stories Riding wrote that her intention had always been to make things plain, but somehow by making things too plain they became more than people could understand. In their irritation they, like Jonathan Cape, accused her of obscurity. The stories of the first section, "Stories of Lives," were more easygoing so that people would not be immediately confused. "I have," she said, "changed the subject in telling them. Yet not really: there is only one subject, and it is impossible to change it." Still she hoped that their obscure though simple material would be enough to disarm any reader's suspicions of her "truth-telling technique."

But even in the "Stories of Lives" the narrative voice is not the calm, grown-up sort usually associated with the tranquillity of bed-time. As in her description of Venison Bride's stories, vices turn out to have peculiar virtues. Non sequiturs abound, laid down as emphatic fact. "His father had wanted him to be a doctor. He had chosen to be only a chemist: a chemist could be more scientific than a doctor. His real interest was not chemistry but Magyar origins; . . ." Riding's contentiousness becomes rather more evident in the two long stories of the second section, "Stories of Ideas." The "Nearly True Stories" of the third section are most like fairy tales; magic powers are invoked—but capriciously. "A Fairy Tale for Older People" goes along as a very merry piece of teasing whimsy. But the omniscient storyteller, after leisurely flirting with her readers in a provoking manner, turns on them at the end in a rage, suddenly contemptuous of their desire to know what happens next:

You can't get it into your heads that in the end nothing happens—nothing more. You keep waiting for a Something, forgetting over and over again that it can never be. You die, well enough; you become a Nothing. But you can't help hoping that a Nothing is really a Something. And so you become a Something, since if you are a Nothing you can be whatever you like.

"It's nonsense," Rebecca West remarked, "but it couldn't have happened any other way."

Riding was at her best when she was able to balance oddity and wild imagination with sustained observation of particulars; this gave "Daisy and Venison" its own logic, uncompromised by a more sentimental alliance with her readers. By depicting Venison's hunger for money and admiration for her stories, "like a person waiting feverishly for a legacy," Riding could rise above her own impatience with Jonathan Cape and her imaginary audience. Sometimes the freshness of what Riding was attempting created a certain amount of giddiness, pettifoggery, and fanciful overkill in her style. Rebecca West asked, however, that Riding "be allowed to carry on with these vices because they make her what she is, and what she is is unique and, to a certain number of us, uniquely delightful."

But by 1935 that was too flighty a response for Riding's satisfaction. The two "Stories of Ideas"—"Reality as Port Huntlady" and "Miss Banquett"—would not settle for being queerly charming. Self-evident truths march by; like one narrator in "Reality as Port Huntlady" Riding had left behind her "patience with narrative accuracy and the slow difficult understanding of hidden activities and meanings." Riding was eager to be done with storytelling altogether. In 1934 she told a correspondent that "Reality as Port Huntlady" was pivotal to the collection, that everything led back to Port Huntlady, and that without it the book would be impossible to disentangle. Her narrator explained:

> That is, by exercising the limited courtesies possible between us we create between us the charm of the story; we have a tepid fascination for each other that we are each anxious to let run its course without lasting inconvenience on either side. And so we keep the story between us as a substitute for any more profound experience of

each other, an emotion-screen in whose making we both
co-operate.

Riding was not the first writer to comment on her own literary
contrivances or to fan her reader's curiosity about herself by affecting
intrigue with them or actively insulting them. But she was one of the
first to incorporate assumptions concerning the creative role of the
reader in her construction of fictions. "An Anonymous Book," a very
early story, is as self-referential as any postmodern text. "The effect of
this style," the narrator explains, "makes the reader first inquisitive of
the course and conclusion of the narrative, then suspicious of the
philosophical import of the narrative, and finally resolved to track
down . . . the anonymity of the author."

While Riding would not yield the final quarry in *Progress of Stories*,
each story provides a tangled course for the chase. Whether as writer
or reader, Riding naturally preferred the more dislocating and often
disturbing narrative experience to the silly, old-fashioned "courtship"
of realistic fiction. In "Reality as Port Huntlady" this preference takes
the form of successive narrators, each of whom questions the story as
narrated thus far.

Port Huntlady was a seaside town where people came to give up
their minds to "really important things." In characters like Dan the
Dog, Baby, Slick, Tomatoes, and Laura Manilla one finds echoes of
the Deyá denizens, coming and going and dallying with the "really
important things." Robert, notably, figured in a character named
Cards, jealous of Lady Port-Huntlady's attentions to any of the others
but proud of his special standing among her entourage.

If, however, the reader is at all tempted to identify Lady Port-
Huntlady (described as the only permanent resident "really *entirely*
interested in the really important things") as possibly Laura Riding
herself, he is quickly discouraged. Early on in "Reality as Port Huntlady" one of Riding's narrators, Lady Whatever-Her-Name-Is, throws
open the question of the main character's identity in one of her
typically disarming maneuvers. Lady Whatever-Her-Name-Is ventures the view that there was a good chance that Lady Port-Huntlady
was really a lot of nonsense. She may be called Lady Nonsense or
Lady Understanding as quickly as Lady Port-Huntlady, the reader
learns. Lady Whatever-Her-Name-Is then proceeds to tell us some-

thing of her own story, which inevitably echoes the one just told by another narrator about Lady Port-Huntlady.

In taking up ever more unorthodox devices, Riding draws attention in her inimitably disruptive way to the kinds of truths that normal, "realistic" stories leave out, to uncover the "not really frank state of affairs" with most stories. This was the "progress of stories"— a different tack from poetry or criticism, but there all the same. "[A] story must be more than a supercilious concession to your boredom with the really important things," one of the narrators of "Reality as Port Huntlady" curtly informs her reader. "You are bored with them but sorry."

Riding's captive audience for stories like "Reality as Port Huntlady" and her "selfish understanding of everything" were those with whom she found herself in Deyá. Mary Burtonwood and her husband, George Ellidge, were the sort of people Lady Whatever-Her-Name-Is would describe as "temporarily permanent residents" of Port Huntlady. They had come to Deyá in 1933 and stayed on, George collaborating with Laura on *14A* and *Epilogue*, Mary typing Robert's novel *I, Claudius*. Mary had once dared to ask Laura, "If you so much disapprove of sex, what do you think of all of us for doing it?" Laura allegedly replied, "As long as you don't make babies under my roof I don't care how you amuse yourselves." As if to challenge her, Mary promptly got pregnant. Laura assisted at the birth of her son, writing to Lucie Brown that the experience proved that snobs did not own surrealism. Mary impressed one German resident as looking rather like "a character from a Ziegfeld film of the Nibelung"; her long red hair in coiled braids around her ears was cleverly set off by a forest green cape.

But George and Mary had a somewhat superficial charm; early on they dispensed with the really important things. Still, they did not fail to humor their landlady and employer when it mattered. Much like Lady Port-Huntlady, Laura gave the impression that she was perfect, an impression that gradually got on their nerves. Riding knew the signs as well as the narrator in Port Huntlady:

> [P]erhaps, indeed, Baby might one day have said to himself, "Oh, hang Lady Port-Huntlady, and hang it all!" And, of course, by this time Dan the Dog would have developed

nameless suspicions about Lady Port-Huntlady, from
nothing happening in their relation beyond the mean-
inglessly privileged hours which he was permitted to pass
in her little work-room. . . .

He would have asked her one day, "Are you as wise, as
right, as perfect as you seem?" . . .

Then he would have got up and started to leave the
room, like a lover disgusted with intimacies he himself has
insisted on.

Mary and George vented their spleen and nameless suspicions of
Laura in the Butcher's café, where they discussed her "craziness about
being perfect" and her delusion that she was God with Antonia, the
village woman who ran the café, or with their London friends Honor
Wyatt and Gordon Glover. Mary even began to suspect Laura of
showing up unexpectedly at the café to spy on them.

Still, it was Riding's good fortune—and, for that matter, Lady
Whatever-Her-Name-Is' and Lady Port-Huntlady's—to pursue such
interests as Mary and George as she pleased "in the confidence that at
the appropriate moment we shall tire and turn away, leaving the door
of truth open behind us." If there was a "progress" in practically any
one of her stories, it was toward this moment. And with Mary and
George that is exactly what was to happen, though as they all sat in
Gelat's taxi on the way to Palma with I, Claudius on Robert's lap, they
did not know this yet.

WHILE ROBERT WAS planting his geraniums, pinks, roses, aloes,
lantanas, and cineraria in the garden at Canelluñ, he began reconsidering an idea for a book that had teased him since the summer of
1929, before God had interrupted his chain of thought and appropriated his first person singular. Within a year of mortgaging Canelluñ,
Graves, on the verge of bankruptcy, completed I, Claudius. Once
again he chose to ventriloquize a story in the form of popular
autobiography. And once again he showed that, left to his own
devices, uninterrupted by Riding's numerous assignments and clever
book ideas, he could be both brilliant and profitable.

Robert's life with Laura in Deyá, much like the life story of Claudius, was not without its fairy-tale aspects. For outsiders and disillusioned intimates, Laura was the evil stepmother to Robert's Cinderella:

> He was more than protective of her; he seemed in a constant swivet of anxiety to please her, to forestall her every wish, like a small boy dancing attendance on a rich aunt of uncertain temper. And she treated him—like a dog. There was no prettier way to put it.

Unlike Cinderella, however, Robert was not without resources. He answered Laura's contempt with financial support and breakfast in bed. He lavished jewels, houses, poems, and praise upon her. Unlike Cinderella, too, Graves flourished in the combat between his own imaginative demon and Riding's. She egged him on, acknowledging "the black of furious silences" that resulted from her ridicule, without trying to appease him.

For Graves to write a history that proposed an entirely new reading of the character of the Roman emperor Claudius, and the line of emperors who preceded him in his lifetime, courted other ridicules. Claudius was regarded—by posterity no less than by his contemporaries—as a fool. Though Graves' knowledge of Greek and Latin, classical history, and its historians was real enough, his view of the historical method by which he might prove Claudius other than a dimwit was equivocal. Detailed scholarly asides (rationalizing his use of the word "assegai" to denote a Roman spear, for example) pepper the text and seem to draw more attention to himself than to issues of historical accuracy. Writing in the shadow of Riding's skepticism of "history men," Graves might have intended these exhibitions as a tongue-in-cheek ridicule of classical scholarship.

But only in the dusty reaches of ancient history could Graves evade Riding's scrutiny. In his 1933 poem "The Cell" he described a prisoner's cell from the vantage point of one imprisoned. Escape is ruled out; neither fantasy, memory, distractions of the body, nor the jailer will free him. But it is precisely within these constraints that he is free to imagine:

What refuge here for a laborious mind!
What a redoubtable and single task
Could one attempt here:

Threading connexion between wall and wall
And floor and ceiling, more attentively
Than the cob-spider.

Plain logic without benefit of flies—
Spinning and knotting till the cell became
A spacious other head

In which emancipated reason might
Learn in due time to walk more accurately
And neatly than at home.

In 1932 and 1933, though her attentions were often directed elsewhere, Robert Graves loved Laura Riding with keen desperation; he also conspired and plotted, in the garden of Canelluñ, to avenge himself. Here, too, he had special resources; the plot and the logic and the connections that he would thread in his "spacious other head" inevitably took on the aspects and dimensions of the prison in which he found himself, those of an established literary tradition as well as those of Canelluñ. The man under the prison blanket looked liked Riding's prisoner, but in *I, Claudius*, Graves crowned himself emperor.

It was during the thirteen-year reign of Tiberius Claudius Drusus Nero Germanicus, the most enlightened and humane of the Roman emperors, that Christianity was brought to Rome and a permanent conquest was made of Britain. But it is with Claudius' life up to the moment he is made emperor in A.D. 41 that *I, Claudius* concerns itself. A delicate, nervous child, afflicted by a stammer and a limp, Claudius was the fool of the family whom none of his ambitious and bloody-minded relatives considered worth the trouble of executing, poisoning, forcing to suicide, or banishing to a desert island. One by one, contenders for the imperial throne fall prey to each other's intrigues. Only by trading on his supposed imbecility does Claudius survive his tormentors. Among them is his grandmother, the evil Livia Drusilla; to further her plots, she successively poisons her first husband,

Claudius' grandfather; her second husband, the Emperor Augustus; and a great lot of his relatives. His insane nephew, Caligula, prized Claudius only because he made a perfect butt for his jokes. The novel is a comprehensive catalog of the folly and vileness of imperial Rome where blasphemy, treachery, incest, black magic, and grotesque debaucheries flourish.

Claudius' story begins with his visit to the Cumaean sibyl in her cliff cavern on Mount Gaurus, just west of Naples. He goes in disguise. After his sacrifice of a bull and a ewe to Apollo and Artemis in exchange for the sibyl's prophecy, a sudden shaft of light reveals Amalthea, seated motionless on an ivory throne, with her eyes closed. "She had a beautiful, mad-looking face with a high forehead," Claudius recalled. His knees quaking, he stammers the beginning of the greeting he has prepared while bats flap overhead:

> "O Sib ... Sib ... Sib ... Sib ... Sib ..." I began. She opened her eyes, frowned and mimicked me: "O Clau ... Clau ... Clau ..." That shamed me and I managed to remember what I had come to ask. I said with a great effort: "O Sibyl: I have come to you about Rome's fate and mine."
>
> Gradually her face changed, the prophetic power overcame her, she struggled and gasped, there was a rushing noise through all the galleries, doors banged, wings swished my face, the light vanished, and she uttered a Greek verse in the voice of the God.

Amalthea prophesies not only Claudius' becoming emperor but the fall of the Roman Empire.

In Graves' "legendary mind," as codified in his later compendium of the Greek myths, Amalthea was the Greek maiden goddess (generally depicted as a goat) who nursed the infant Zeus to young godhood. He had been hidden in her cave by his mother to avoid being eaten by his father, Cronus. When, as had been prophesied, he unseated his father as lord of the universe, he ascended into heaven wearing a coat made from Amalthea's hide and in gratitude set her image among the stars as Capricorn. It was Amalthea's horn that became the famous Cornucopia, which filled itself with whatever food or drink its owner desired.

Capricorn was Riding's astrological sign and Amalthea had first "appeared" to Graves in a Riding poem written in Egypt and published as "Amalthea" in *The Close Chaplet*. In "Samuel's Elegy for Amalthea of the Legends" the sibyl returns in the form of a visitation. Samuel, the speaker, was Samuel Butler, the poet Robert claimed as his literary ancestor:

. . .

> I have been assaulted by the moths
> Thick in my eyes and throat many a night
> When the thought of Amalthea was
> Tall flame in a grimy wick.
> Then I have blown the light down
> And not remembered.
> It is better to be dark with Amalthea
> Than give her over to the moths and bats.

. . .

> She fell of no plague or passion.
> She was only swift, so swift, they say,
> She ran till she stood still
> As a bell swung round more than rings,
> And was alive and dead in one day.
> When the day went she was dead most fully.
> She knew all.

. . .

> I have come with Amalthea in my veins
> Into a fifth season.

. . .

In choosing Amalthea as the name of the sibyl who foretells Claudius' fate, Graves implicitly acknowledged both Riding the prophetess and Riding the nurturer of his own hopes for salvation. In her horn of plenty was whatever he might desire to harvest; in her skin, his warmth and ascension into heaven. The sibyl's prophetic words to Claudius at Cumae echo Riding's prediction to Graves in Cairo and Deyá:

To a fawning fellowship
He shall stammer, cluck and trip,
Dribbling always with his lip.

Handed down from generation to generation, sibylline verses were often forged by those who wished to glorify themselves and curse their enemies or business rivals; the Claudius family figured largely among the forgers. Thus, despite Amalthea's insults and prophecy of doom, Graves can add to them a premonition of *I, Claudius'* publication many centuries later:

When he's dumb and no more here,
Nineteen hundred years or near,
Clau-Clau-Claudius shall speak clear.

Just as *Good-bye to All That* was Graves' autobiography divested of the stammer, so Claudius perceives these lines as his injunction to write his autobiography and "speak clear." Both men learn from sibylline predictions that their civilizations are soon to rot away— Claudius' Roman Empire under the Punic curse after the destruction of Carthage, and Graves' British Empire perhaps under the curse of dialectical materialism, perhaps merely the curse of the trenches. The war riches gained by both empires brought upon their leaders and people "sloth, greed, cruelty, dishonesty, cowardice, effeminacy." The working-out of the curse is the plot of both *I, Claudius* and the sequel, *Claudius, the God and His Wife Messalina.*

Throughout *I, Claudius* Graves would pilfer Riding's imaginative wardrobe of glamorous images and evil disguises for his own characters, beginning with Amalthea. As her own poems, stories, and fairy tales amply demonstrate, Riding was capable of generating a cornucopia of identities and voices; and Graves helped himself, perhaps because he had held up the mythological mirror to so many of them. He might even have felt that he had paid for them. Cameos of his relationship with Riding can be seen not only in Livia's dealing with Claudius the half-wit but also in her marriage to Augustus:

Augustus ruled the world, but Livia ruled Augustus. And I must here explain the remarkable hold that she had over

him. It was always a matter of wonder that there were no
children of the marriage, seeing that my grandmother had
not shown herself unfruitful and that Augustus was reported to be the father of at least four natural children. . . .
The truth will not easily be credited. The truth is that the
marriage was never consummated. Augustus, though capable enough with other women, found himself as impotent
as a child when he tried to have commerce with my
grandmother. The only reasonable explanation is that Augustus was, at bottom, a pious man, though cruelty and
even ill-faith had been forced on him by the dangers that
followed his grand-uncle Julius Caesar's assassination. He
knew that the marriage was impious: this knowledge, it
seems, affected him nervously, putting an inner restraint
on his flesh.

Yet Claudius admits that even this is not the whole story; he is
prepared to divulge even more surprising aspects of Augustus' relations with Livia. "In writing this passage, with the idea, I suppose, of
shielding Augustus's good name, I have been holding something
back, which I shall now after all set down." Livia consolidated her
absolute hold over Augustus, he tells us, by procuring "very decently
and quietly" beautiful young women from the Syrian slave market
(Augustus preferred Syrians). As emperor he might have had any
woman with impunity, but nevertheless "he tasted no meat . . . that
she had not passed as fit for eating." And for this he found himself
absurdly grateful. Livia herself remained faithful, having no lust
except for power. It is hard to ignore the spector of Elfriede Faust in
such a passage.

And to underscore the correspondence between his own and
Augustus' imprisonment (though everyone, including Robert and
Laura, chose not to recognize it), Graves had Livia run her house like
Canellun. Even Mary Burtonwood, ever ready with sympathy, made
no connection between Livia's treatment of her servants and Laura's
treatment of herself. In Livia's household care was taken not to offend
her, and everyone reported to her on their daily activities so that
nothing would arouse her suspicion. Though Livia reveled in luxury
and dressed in rich costumes, there was no extravagance about the

house itself; she insisted on the traditional austerity of the Roman life-style: "Her rules were: plain but plentiful food, regular family worship, no hot baths after meals, constant work for everyone and no waste." She kept a detailed list of the moral shortcomings of her husband, as well as all his toadying letters to her and his insulting remarks about her son Tiberius. After she poisoned Augustus, these letters enabled her to hold sway over Tiberius.

At the end of her life, however, Livia needed Claudius; her fears for her fate in the hereafter had begun to torment her, for she had also consulted the sibyls. After Augustus' death, Livia found in his library of oracles a book entitled *Sibylline curiosities*, a collection of prophecies from the original canon, which had been censored by Augustus. Whatever scruple or fear kept him from destroying them gave Livia her knowledge of the line of succession and Claudius' eventual ascension to the imperial throne. From Claudius, then, she extracted a promise that he would ensure her deification, so that she might sidestep her just deserts in hell. Claudius agreed on the condition that Livia tell him whom she poisoned and how, so as to further his historical research.

With Livia's death there was yet one further reincarnation of Robert Graves' Laura Riding. After becoming emperor, Caligula fell ill with what the doctors called brain fever. After a month of uncertainty over whether Caligula would live or die, Claudius was summoned to his bedroom for an audience. The emperor was querulous and petulant at his delay; Claudius asked after his health:

> "I have never really been ill. Only resting. And undergoing a metamorphosis. It's the most important religious event in history. No wonder the City keeps so quiet."
>
> I felt that he expected me to be sympathetic, nevertheless. "Has the metamorphosis been painful, Emperor? I trust not."
>
> "As painful as if I were my own mother. I had a very difficult delivery. Mercifully, I have forgotten all about it. Or nearly all. . . ."
>
> ". . . may I humbly enquire precisely what is the character of this glorious change that has come over you?"
>
> "Isn't it immediately apparent?" he asked angrily.

Drusilla's word "possessed" and the conversation I had had with my grandmother Livia as she lay dying gave me the clue. I fell on my face and adored him as a God.

Caligula's divine plans included attracting the awe of the whole world and ignoring that bunch of "fussy old men" who considered themselves his advisors. It was clear to him, as it had not been to Livia, that he—not she—was the everlasting god about whom everyone in the East had been prophesying for the last thousand years. Like Graves' question to Riding in the abject "As It Were" poems written after her suicide attempt, the prostrate Claudius wanted to know in what name he was to worship and adore Caligula: "Is it incorrect, for instance, to call you Jove?"

He said, "Oh, greater than Jove, certainly, but anonymous as yet. For the moment, I think though, I'll call myself Jove—the Latin Jove to distinguish myself from that Greek fellow. I'll have to settle with him one of these days. He's had his own way too long."

News of Caligula's divinity circulated privately for awhile; but when it became generally known, it was accepted without question.

But neither Caligula's nor Livia's godhead occurred to Claudius when he was proclaimed emperor by the imperial palace guard. Found trembling in alarm behind the curtain, where he hid after Caligula's assassination and the ensuing bloodbath, Claudius had other matters on his mind as he was carried aloft to the Senate.

I was thinking, "So, I'm Emperor, am I? What nonsense! But at least I'll be able to make people read my books now. Public recitals to large audiences. And good books, too, thirty-five years' hard work in them. It won't be unfair. . . . My History of Carthage is full of amusing anecdotes. I'm sure they will enjoy it."

That was what I was thinking. I was thinking too, what opportunities I should have, as Emperor, for consulting the secret archives and finding out just what happened on this occasion or on that. How many twisted stories still re-

mained to be straightened out! What a miraculous fate for
a historian! And as you will have seen, I took full advantage
of my opportunities.

The glass slipper slid easily onto Claudius' crippled foot. Graves
got one, too; published in May 1934, his historical novel was a huge
success, critically and financially. Nearing the end of a year of re-
prieve granted by Don Bernardo Colón, he and Laura were at last
able to retreat from the brink of bankruptcy. As their fears receded,
excellent reviews sent by their clipping service filled the mailbox.
Laura was less than gracious, and the "dreary" Claudius book was not
to be spoken about by visitors to Deyá.

Despite his demurrals about wanting the throne, Claudius' reign as
emperor did not find him always in the library. He saw to the
deification of Livia, but he also conquered England and was made a
god himself. Robert, too, was no doubt secretly cheered by his huge
success and by the prospect of large audiences for his books. He was
not immune to the pleasures of fame and fortune. (When Robert did
not get the Nobel Prize in 1937, Laura slyly remarked, "What a waste
of false modesty!") Considering, too, the Claudian propensity to
forgery when it came to the proliferation of sibylline prophecies,
some skepticism must greet the publication of Claudius' "autobiography" in 1934. Was the hand of a Claudian successor, one who wished
to glorify himself and vilify his enemies, once again at work? The
author himself suggests as much.

SILENTLY JUDGING LAURA'S response to the book in the taxi to Palma,
Mary Burtonwood did not, perhaps, take into account exactly whose
hospitality she had enjoyed during her stay in Deyá, nor did she
consider that her own emotional involvements there might color her
view. In the course of typing *I, Claudius* and *Claudius, the God* she had
worked closely with Robert and had been a sympathetic witness to
his selfless dedication to Laura. After a morning of hard work she and
Robert would go to the beach for the afternoon, leaving Laura and
George at work on *14A*—they did not enjoy the sun and the beach
the way she and Robert did, she would later recall. (In fact, Robert
actively disliked the sun, and Laura believed that sunbathing induced

lumbago.) But twenty-six to Robert's thirty-eight, Mary Burtonwood had found in Robert a kind of father figure; her own father, she continued, had died when she was very young:

> The first time [Robert] kissed me I said "I have waited a
> long time for that."
> Yes, I loved him.

Indeed, she conceded, working with Robert proved to be the happiest years of her life.

But Deyá, Laura told a close correspondent, was a mercilessly revealing place, not a place of escape but of conclusions. One afternoon Mary Burtonwood learned, in rude surprise, that Robert could no longer afford her help. The end came fairly quietly. Laura and Robert settled Mary and George's debts with Gelat and put them both on a boat back to England.

An American couple, arriving in Deyá to join Riding in her work on *Epilogue*, had been the recipients of Mary and George's pent-up frustrations and had felt obliged to report to Laura what had been said. Mary, Laura wrote to John Aldridge, had given the couple some tips about how to get along with her; and the usual things about never contradicting her were glossed by their own "special dirt." Laura was a literary nonentity who tyrannized Robert, "a literary somebody." Laura was sexually attracted to Gelat. George had chipped in his description of her as "a regular Tartar." Robert, on the other hand, was nothing less than contemptible for his devotion to Laura; their relationship lasted only because he fed her desire to be flattered.

The Americans had begged Laura not to say anything or do anything, so Laura had to look for another reason to ask Mary and George to leave. Eventually, she found it. While it was hard to believe that such a betrayal was possible, Laura had no doubt that the couple were suffering from the knowledge of their treachery and the justness of the edict that had sent them to ignoble exile in England. In her letter to John Aldridge, Laura mentioned what she perceived as Mary's sexual predation of a helpless Robert as a complicating factor in the banishment.

Emotionally worn and on the verge of tears, Laura wrote to John on a small marble table in the Hotel Alhambra. She and Robert had decided to stay a night in Palma to escape the sadness of Canelluñ, empty once again. Robert, returning from an afternoon in the antique shops looking for small gifts brought with him a pretty ring. Exclaiming her pleasure, Laura's spirits became a little brighter.

——— ∞ ———

Responding to Jonathan Cape after his rejection of *Progress of Stories*— in peevish revenge, she supposed, for her work on *No Decency Left*, Laura wrote that she understood his prejudice in favor of Robert's name for its publicity value, but she had assumed that other values had been involved in her relationship with him. It was quite clever of him, she wrote, to let her imagine that such a thing might be possible. Since at that point she felt her stories were more saleable than the work he had already published, only one conclusion could be drawn.

Venison Bride, considering the "How about a little love?" proposal of Mr. Valentine's, came to a similar conclusion:

> Venison ran upstairs to her bedroom to think. She was not sure how she ought to react. Why not a little love? It need not interfere with anything if one thought only of oneself. That was one of the advantages of being a woman: one didn't have to love, only let oneself be loved. . . . She looked into her mirror and decided to change into a more sensible frock. Then she noticed the water-jug full of gold pieces. She knew immediately that Daisy had gone away for good. She went downstairs, picked up the pile of stories from the table and put them into the kitchen stove. Mr. Valentine was outside, triumphantly planning his next step. She put the gramophone in the dog-basket, and the comb, and what was left of the chocolates, and carried it out to him. "You can keep the dog-basket," she said with a sneer. "Now go along."

Having accepted her commercially unprofitable works for reasons that had nothing to do with an appreciation of her ability, Laura realized, Cape had indeed been stringing her along to get Robert's. (This thought must certainly have occurred to her before.) Perhaps,

Laura wrote in the letter terminating both their relations with Cape, it would now seem that he was justified in such tactics. But unfortunately, neither she nor Robert imagined that he would understand unless their response to such treatment was couched in his business language. Cape was not even given the dog basket. Arthur Barker published *I, Claudius*.

Chapter 17

THE WHY OF THE WIND

———•———

We have often considered the wind,
The changing whys of the wind.
Of other weather we do not so wonder.
These are changes we know.
Our own health is not otherwise.
We wake up with a shiver,
Go to bed with a fever:
These are the turns by which nature persists,
By which, whether ailing or well,
We variably live,
Such mixed we, and such variable world.
It is the very rule of thriving
To be thus one day, and thus the next.

—"The Why of the Wind"

———•———

THE DESERT DUST, carried by the sirocco from the Sahara, had plagued them on and off all summer. Inside Canelluñ, with the windows and shutters closed against the rasping gusts, Laura suffered terribly from heart pains, palpitations, and "nervous voices." At one point she drew up her will (this became a constant preoccupation); Robert followed suit. In the diary that Robert had begun in February 1935, he noted that Laura would neither see a doctor nor give up smoking. When she felt well enough to work steadily on her philo-

313

sophical novel about the fall of Troy, she chain-smoked and drank cup after cup of coffee. But when the wind was really blowing she stayed in bed with the door closed, working at night in the "Troy" study until three or four in the morning. There she laboriously constructed the Trojan citadel and its towers, and Priam's palace and its chambers of polished stone wherein lived Helen, the abducted queen of Sparta. There too, she choreographed the events of the war, bringing to life Priam's brave sons and bright-eyed daughters. In October 1935, with the final proofs of *Epilogue I* in the mail, and Laura on the verge of quitting the Troy novel and returning to America for a visit, a heavy thunderstorm broke. The downpour cleansed the air, washing the grit into the torrent, where it was swept away into the sea.

WHEN THE RAIN stopped, Karl Goldschmidt was appalled to find the windowsills of Norman's old cottage, Ca'n Torrent, streaked by a ghastly yellowish stain. Worse, the English dictionary on his desk had gotten wet, though he had firmly shut the windows. The storms had brought some relief from the heat; the last few hot days he had been irritable and uncomfortable—one afternoon he thought his head would burst with pain. Lying down with a wet cloth on his forehead had not helped; in his distress the cushions seemed about to suffocate him. And after the storm there was the tremendous bother of mopping up in the dark; the electricity had failed. The following day, after ablutions and breakfast, Karl had found some equanimity. When he went to get the mail he had a nice gentle feeling of safety. The only thing he lacked in life, he confided to his diary that September 1935, was a pair of rubber boots. The next thunderstorm found him sitting in a pair of English lederhosen singing the song of the blue flower.

In 1916 Karl Goldschmidt's mother died of pleurisy, and his father was called up to the German front. Karl, just four, was sent to live with relatives. After his father was demobilized they shared a miserable existence imposed by a cousin sent to keep house and look after them. Illiterate and domineering, she beat Karl while his father withdrew into sullen silence, eventually committing suicide when Karl was sixteen. Thereafter he was shuffled from relative to relative, all of whom strove with various degrees of success to keep themselves clothed and sheltered in the 'lean years following the war. In his grandmother's household in Dortmund he was given his own room, language and music lessons, and tuition to a course in graphic arts. After sliding down a banister in college, he was expelled and sent to his father's family in a small Westphalian village. There he slept under the counter in the local shop, where he earned his keep and suffered from chilblains. After three years of misery he returned to Dortmund, working in its largest department store as a sign painter after completing a course in window dressing.

In February 1933, the month after Adolf Hitler came to power, Karl came of age. An orphan and a Jew in love with a Gentile, he had few prospects in Germany and only a small inheritance. In an illustrated weekly he saw an inviting photograph of Lluchalcari; the magazine was offering a free trip for anyone who could provide the best reason for wanting to go to the Balearic Islands. An entomologist in search of a rare species of bug got the prize, but as soon as the courts cleared his emigration papers, Karl left with his inheritance, leaving behind a battered and lonely youth for an illustrated weekly's vision of beauty and tranquillity. By August 1933 he had settled in Lluchalcari with his girlfriend, Ellie, his grandmother's former housemaid.

At twenty-three Karl was a slender, dapper man whose swift, nervous movements seemed to accompany the anxious rapidity of his thoughts like a dancer following music that no one else hears. When he was upset he combed his hair with quick dashes of a pocket comb, smoothed his eyebrows with the flat of his hands, and mopped his brow with a handkerchief from his trouser pocket. He hated his small stature and the bad fit of his German clothes, envying the tall, happy-go-lucky figure of Honor Wyatt's husband, Gordon Glover, draped in elegant Oxford bags. For his size, he had a spectacular temper, and it was in such a fit that Robert first met him. Passing through the village with a basketful of vegetables, Robert found Karl fuming and pacing at the bus stop one evening, waiting for Gelat's seven o'clock bus to Palma, after having secured the lease on his cottage in nearby Lluchalcari. Pointing out that the bus ran in the morning, Robert showed him where he might stop for the night. It was six months before they would meet again.

Mallorca at the time had an assortment of German refugees; a mass exodus of intellectuals and Jews had followed the rise of Nazism. Despairing commentaries on a future under Hitler's dictatorship and gruesome anecdotes about Nazi atrocities became a staple of conversation at the Sala, Gelat's new café and bandstand. Most of the members of the German colony in Deyá and Lluchalcari were painters, and until Ellie abandoned Karl for one of them, he kept their company. In his agony and loneliness at his desertion, Karl decided to jump off a cliff when his money ran out. Before this could happen he met Jacob Bronowski, then living in Deyá with Eirlys Roberts, who invited him in late February 1934 to Deyá for the weekend to meet Laura and Robert.

To Karl, Canellun was a jewel box of sublime elegance. He had never seen anything like the beauty of the furnishings, the silver, the pale yellow teacups and saucers, and the utter spotlessness of the rooms. Eyeing Aldridge's illustrations for *The Life of the Dead*, Len Lye's eccentric Seizin Press book covers, and the colorful silk screens that draped the whitewashed walls, Karl was stunned. Almost everything in the house that first weekend—not least the hospitality and intelligence of his hostess—left him hushed and reverent.

But all that seemed so long ago. Jacob was gone. Karl, invited to replace Mary Burtonwood as Laura and Robert's secretary, had moved first to Deyá and then, in April 1935, to Norman's cottage. Honor Wyatt and Gordon Glover returned that summer, free-lance journalists working under Laura's direction on *A Mistake Somewhere*, a three-part narrative of their marriage and Gordon's affair with a Canadian woman (each wrote from their own perspective). At Ca'n Torrent, room and board became part of Karl's wages. After lunch, Laura would come over to dictate letters; Robert would arrive at 5:00 P.M. with his manuscripts for Karl to retype. The two would then head to Gelat's café for a meal and to listen to the English news on the radio.

By the time Karl arrived in Deyá, all that was left of Norman Cameron and Elfriede Faust, Len and Jane Lye, Tom and Julie Matthews, John Aldridge and Lucie Brown, Jacob Bronowski and Eirlys Roberts, Mary Burtonwood and George Ellidge were the stories and the now silent phonograph. Of this group, only John and Tom still wrote to Laura, and even the letters from newer friends had recently slowed to a trickle; Laura wrote to one friend from Deyá that it seemed like a conspiracy. Worse still, after more than three years in preparation, Arthur Barker had refused to take *Epilogue*. In May 1935, an agreement had finally been struck with Constable on the understanding that Graves would pay part of the production costs and that the jacket copy would be made "less alarming." The Seizin Press existed only as an imprint, but its list was full nonetheless, including (finally) *Progress of Stories*, James Reeves' first volume of poems, Honor's novel *The Heathen*, *A Mistake Somewhere*, Tom Matthews' *The Moon's No Fool*, and two works of memoirs by friends; but there were to be no more fine-press books from Deyá.

Listening to the wild stories about Norman and Elfriede, hearing about the parties and dancing in the moonlight, Karl imagined that life in Deyá must have been more exciting then; he had arrived on the scene rather late in the day. But ensconced at Ca'n Torrent, he had decided to have nothing more to do with girls himself; he had recently agreed with Laura's assessment that he was a thoroughly bad character. The subject had arisen when the maid, Magdalena, quit and a young Jewish refugee from Germany was being considered to take her place. After an "illuminating talk" with Laura, Karl completely forgave Ellie, the "poor girl" who had been forced to live with him before betraying and abandoning him. "As Laura rightly said," Karl wrote in his diary, "she really ought to be pitied. And besides, twenty-three is still a bit green isn't it." The refugee was not hired. Once in a while Karl ventured a smile at Marguerita's niece, but that and "lots of wrong thoughts about girls" were as far as he went.

Karl's carefully protected daily routine was soon upset by the long-awaited arrival of James Reeves, a Seizin author and contributor to *Epilogue*, who would be staying with him in Ca'n Torrent. After two and a half years of correspondence, James had finally decided to come to Deyá to meet his editor. Laura arranged for Maria, the gardener's daughter, to clean and make them breakfast. A towel rack was installed, and there was even talk of bringing out the phonograph. Karl anticipated James' visit with as much trepidation and excitement as did Laura. He imagined James as a tall Louis Golding (another recent visitor)—"God only knows why." Karl was shy still about speaking English and had overheard respectable friends of Laura's express dismay at his "awful delivery," but he had recently found himself following the London literary columns with interest. He rather hoped James, whom he understood to be a gentleman as well as a poet from Cambridge University, would like him despite his obvious shortcomings.

There was a furious discussion about who would meet James at the boat and who would remain behind to supervise Maria. Uncertainty on this question, Karl felt, had contributed to the trying atmosphere about Canelluñ; nervous indecision and domestic squalls reigned. Robert lost 500 pesetas (later found), but Laura became so angry with him that she was almost ill. Karl, who had lately begun to notice how Laura's gifts to him were generally followed by nasty scoldings, was dressed down for not returning her special greetings when she arrived at Ca'n Torrent to dictate. Karl, in turn, found Laura's quarrelsome behavior after losing a game of sixty-six insupportable. "I couldn't have been worse," Karl said to himself. When Karl found out that his long-awaited sandals had been made much too large, he became so furious that Laura gave him the day off. "Nothing seems to go right," he mourned.

After a sleepless and anxious night, Laura alone accompanied Gelat to Palma, leaving at 5:30 A.M. so as to be on the dock when James arrived from Barcelona. They had to wait some time for him to appear. Sleeping peacefully in his berth, he did not awaken until several hours after the boat had docked.

INEVITABLY, THE ARBITRARY array of individuals who surrounded Riding during the 1930s in Deyá provided an eccentric and—given her particular gifts as a salon impresario—far more fertile milieu than she might have found had she remained in London. Her closest allies were often not poets and intellectuals but free-lance writers, refugees from Germany, and retirees. Honor Wyatt had been reluctant to think of herself as a real writer, much less a poet, until she met Riding; she wrote a beauty column under the name Ann Morgan for the *Manchester Guardian*. Still, after numerous and hopeful editorial sessions aimed at "discovering the poet" and after a great deal of rewriting by Laura, Honor's poems were accepted for publication in *Epilogue*. Similarly, the McCormacks were a retired couple relatively indifferent to the arts who were charmed by Riding and took delight in her conversation. Dorothy and Ward Hutchinson were another couple (called, affectionately, the Monosyllables) whom Riding adopted, soliciting Ward's amateurish photographs for *Epilogue* and editing his juvenile efforts at verse. Isolated from the literary competition of London, Riding achieved that measure of suzerainty which she needed. In Deyá it was understood that visitors were to accept Laura on her terms, not theirs. Many, including the villagers, did.

The same day in March 1934 when Riding first considered Honor's prospects as a poet for *Epilogue*, Jacob Bronowski was studiously reading Rainer Maria Rilke in one of Riding's small cottages. Bronowski's correspondence with Riding began in 1930, when he reviewed *Poems A Joking Word*, and continued during his career at Cambridge. From 1928 to 1931 his magazine *Experiment* published articles on biochemistry and theoretical physics alongside poems by William Empson, Kathleen Raine, and Richard Eberhart and fiction by Malcolm Lowry and T. H. White. In the laboratory of *Experiment* the "language of science," Bronowski hoped, was carried into literature. He was put first on Riding's list of contributors to *Epilogue*.

Bronowski, in turn, reviewed her work for the *Cambridge Gownsman*, and it was he who first proposed his close friend James Reeves as a contributor to *Epilogue*. Two other contributors to *Experiment*, John Archer and John Cullen, followed. It was during Bronowski's monthlong visit to Deyá in 1932 that the outlines of the proposed journal were established, and it was decided that Jacob must come back to help her write and edit the journal once he had gotten his Ph.D. Jacob also understood that Laura would be working with him directly on his poetry. Before his return to Deyá in late 1933, he had submitted two essays to her for extensive critical revision. He was an avid, if rather humorless, admirer.

Born in Lodz, Poland, in January 1908, when it was Russian territory, Bronowski was the eldest son of an Orthodox Jewish father and a fervently communist mother. During the war his family had lived in Germany, finally arriving in 1920 in London's East End, where his father set up a clothing-import shop. At twelve Jacob was a "small Jewish ex-Polish, ex-Russian, ex-German boy" for whom the English language and the language of science seemed interchangeable. In his first letter to Riding he described himself as a "coming young man," and it was perhaps this single-mindedness that distinguished him from the lesser mortals in her circle. Exceedingly bright and pro-fessorial, he enjoyed the thrust and parry of debate; their minds fixed on each other like two swords, leaving them stimulated and eager to publish works of critical collaboration. Mostly, however, Jacob's days were spent perfecting his collection of poems, finally ready for submission on his twenty-sixth birthday, after just two months in Deyá.

Bronowski approached the subject of English poetry from a some-what similar perspective as Riding. Upon entering Cambridge, he had left behind his father's devout religious beliefs in much the same way that Riding had abandoned socialism; he found his father's meticulous orthodoxy not only anachronistic but also obsessive and had embraced English poetry in its stead. Still, he did not cease finding the question of God a matter for concern and considered Riding's essay on the subject, then being prepared for *Epilogue*, "deep." He also shared her special faith in the truthful properties of the English language. English poetry, like geometry but unlike God, was susceptible to "correct analysis," and more than anything Bronowski wanted to be a poet.

The positivist language of mathematics and science was attractive for Riding. Even before she met Bronowski, in her critical writing and poetry she was partial to metaphors that employed the language of the chemistry lab, surgical amphitheater, and math class. Thus a certain sense of expectation accompanied Jacob's return to Deyá in the fall of 1933, more than a year after their initial visit, for an indefinite stay in one of Riding's furnished houses.

During this visit Jacob kept a detailed diary of his reading, activ-ities, and literary progress. Within a month he had a new poem to show Laura; it revealed more the impress of her thought than her poetry. At the same time he was writing a review of one of Laura's books and rereading Shakespeare's sonnets with her. His major un-dertaking, however, was work on an English dictionary, which was to be part of Laura's "child's university" series. Laura, meanwhile, quietly noted Jacob's tendency to preach on any subject within easy reach. He lectured Eirlys all day long on the meaning of this and that, reminding her that she really didn't mean to smoke that cigarette. He even ventured into long-winded dissertations on the details of women's dress, such as the reasons why women wear puffy sleeves.

Nor was Jacob a humble man. Once, while playing the truth game (a popular pursuit at Canelluñ), Laura asked Robert what he thought he could do better than anyone present. To Robert's answer that he could write the best nursery rhyme, Jacob indignantly said that he could write one as good and possibly even better. Still, it took almost six months of close work and conversation before Jacob came to write in his diary "Quarrel with Laura."

The week before the quarrel, a twenty-four-page letter had gone off to James Reeves. The letter discussed Laura's changes to a batch of his poems; she hoped that James would "sponsor" the changes with her and not feel that his poems had been mistreated. Included was a stern lecture on his astonishing admission of indifference to stray connotations of certain words that she had taken exception to in a poem of his. He considered her understanding of those words irrelevant to his use of them. To distinguish between the various uses and meanings of words mattered, she insisted, more than anything else in the world.

The argument with Jacob had begun during a similarly lengthy editorial exchange. While Laura was going over one of his poems with her usual patiently laborious inspection, Jacob suddenly pushed his chair back and said that he did not believe that she was being helpful. Laura, in describing the scene to James, said that Jacob now felt she had begun, instead, to meddle with his work. If that was the case, she told Jacob, then it was impossible for her to continue. Perhaps to her surprise, he agreed, picked up his poems, and left, willing to let the matter rest there.

But Laura was not. On two evenings she tried to discuss with Jacob where things might have gone wrong. After her first effort she was made to understand that to make peace she must first realize that her opinions about his poems were no longer of any value to him. Furthermore, her methods were "suppressive" and forced "spurious agreement." When Laura tried to point out that she had no method but that of sitting down and opening her mind to work with people whom she trusted, Jacob interrupted. She was no "lily white angel," he said. He and Eirlys had decided to continue with the critical journal alone, along with another project of hers. He suggested that Laura take the dictionary and the book on women that she had been writing with Eirlys, *The Word 'Woman.'*

As evidence that she suppressed people, Jacob reminded Laura that she had once referred to James as "obstinate," and so it was to James that Laura applied for proof to the contrary. In a long letter she expressed her hope that their work with his poems had been good and that he would want to continue it. Apologizing for her hasty choice of the word "obstinate," Laura wrote that she was prepared for his judgment.

James Reeves' lengthy response was grave and thoughtful, admitting truthfully that he had once felt that one of her primary motives had been to assert her will over his. In particular, she often seemed high-handed, willfully misconstruing the tone of his remarks in a manner that to him indicated a faulty sense of proportion and a degree of certainty that he, as a young man, could not summon for himself. Anticipating her anger and disappointment, he asked her not to remark upon these feelings of his, partly because they were in the past, and partly because he felt that they did not alter his respect for her as a poet. Furthermore, all personal differences aside, it was "their duty (to Truth) to get on together. You are bound to look at the present crisis in an undetached way, unconnected with other things; but . . . I can see it mainly as just another instance of the continual impoverishment to Truth caused by people who are aware of the Truth not getting on together." All these matters, Reeves felt, were of the deepest importance, and the loss of Jacob from their critical journal would prove infinite.

After Laura read Jacob and Eirlys James' letter in another effort to close the breach, she looked up to find the "loathsome" spectacle of them sitting there like Egyptian mummies. Tugging his beard and smiling with professorial condescension, Jacob said nothing. She was stung and humiliated. Upon their departure from Deyá, Jacob carefully apportioned those things which Laura had given him for his household, deciding which had been gifts and which loans. Gifts were returned with the words, "I thought this might be useful to you." Items in an uncertain category came to her "by reversion." In her next letter to James, written with the assistance of a dozen cigarettes rolled for her by Robert, Laura pronounced Jacob "spiritually dead." She finished by leaving it to James to decide whether he was horrified by her insistence that the truth abided only in her presence. Those who left her, having been with her, left the truth as well.

THE QUARREL WITH Jacob was perhaps the most notorious of all the Deyá banishments, and imbedded in the circumstances surrounding it are questions concerning Riding's intellectual influence on men who later became known in their own right as poets and intellectuals. After leaving Deyá in July 1934, Bronowski published *The Poet's Defence* (1939), which showed Riding's influence on his thought without acknowledging it. In "Poets and Poetry," a central critical treatise of the first *Epilogue* (which Bronowski had worked on), Riding—even after the break—acknowledged his contribution. Bronowski would, however, later write sensitive reviews both of *Epilogue* and of Riding's collected poems for the *New Criterion*.

But as the years of neglect and loneliness accumulated, Laura (Riding) Jackson claimed intellectual title not only to *The Ascent of Man*, the 1974 work that is central to Bronowski's popular reputation, but also to the achievements of many interwar male writers who had direct or indirect contact with her. From the 1930s on she (first with Graves) made constant reference to the young Auden's enthusiastic appropriation of the signature rhythms that so marked her best work. There are indeed clear echoes of the syncopated four-beat rhythms of "Footfalling" from *Love as Love, Death as Death* in Auden's first volume of poetry. Even Auden's biographer noted the "literary ventriloquism" of Auden's poem "For What Is Easy," which not only mimicked the laconic, abstract style of Riding's "All Nothing, Nothing" but also subverted its meaning. Similarly, the foreword to Michael Roberts' influential anthology, *The Faber Book of Modern Verse*, was extensively rewritten by Riding and contributed to the shaping of the interwar generation of poets' self-perception. Still, arbitrary attempts at quantifying Riding's considerable influence in the ideas of 1930s criticism, the lifted rhythms of 1930s poetry, are doomed to oversimplify a complex transaction.

More than a question of "influence," the rich grip of Riding's imagination and intellectual presence seems in retrospect to reveal as much about the lack of vigor among British poets after World War I as about her own ambitions. The war, which they had been too young to die in, had stolen from them not only a sense of certainty and continuity but also a generation of writers against whom they might have marked their course. In her intense editorial microscopy, in her long analyses of their personal character weaknesses, Riding made many of these young men complicit in the further unraveling of their sense of self, often in the language or jargon that they brought to her. For Graves this was the language and imagery of myth; for Tom Matthews, Christianity; for the "spiritually dead" Bronowski it was science; and for other younger compatriots of Graves' it would be politics.

Riding's intentions were neither as Svenghalian nor as arbitrary as they are often perceived. It was in the unraveling of her own self through poetry and stories that she gained intimate self-knowledge and inched closer to what she felt was the truth. Julian Symons, a 1930s poet, novelist, and intellectual who came briefly into her orbit, noted how Riding's determination to purify poetic language was inseparable from her "close finickiness in personal relationships," setting her apart from other currents in British poetry:

> Her exercise of her art, and her conception of conduct, represented an aspect of literary life in the thirties that is now too little recognised: the tendency towards extreme individualism and poetic isolation. The opposite tendency, which regarded the poet as one more worker bee in the hive, and which permitted extreme freedom of action and comment on private relations while insisting on a strict public social morality, has been well enough understood and publicized . . . ; but the isolationist attitude . . . is ignored or forgotten.

As Riding's formative years were the 1920s this is not a surprising observation. But in the 1930s she was increasingly willing to legislate a "strict public social morality" and to foster a tightly knit "cell" of core writers for *Epilogue*. Though her language was not strictly that of dialectical materialism, she reserved the right to use it for her purposes. Whatever language she chose, she filled the period's demand for ideological certainties.

There is an even more crucial aspect to the dilemma that Riding posed to these young men. The critical shift in the balance of power between men and women, beginning in British society as elsewhere, had its echo in the imagination of the time. Apart from Gertrude Stein, it is hard to find a literary precedent for the many writers who were ready and willing to look to Riding as sole arbiter of the unvarying female principle and, as such, the seat of poetic authority. The theme of sexual realpolitik and its accompanying fear, revulsion, and thrill form the subtext if not the text of many of modernism's great works of literature. Like D. H. Lawrence, James Joyce, Ernest Hemingway, and even E. M. Forster, Robert Graves somehow understood this struggle as necessary for himself as a writer. For a time John Aldridge also considered Riding's domineering sensibility crucial to the shaping of his work. In the aftermath of Bronowski's banishment, Robert wrote to James in an attempt to characterize Riding's touchstone quality and its importance to him:

> I want to say this as someone who has known Laura for many years and has had not only the pleasure of her friendship but the interest of watching other people with her: there have been many people who have felt the same kind of pleasure with her as I do, and always a few who have felt some sort of resentment against the fact of her (it always really comes to that.) She is a great natural fact like fire or trees . . . and either one appreciates her or one doesn't but it is quite useless trying to argue that she should be other than she is.

But the fear of being compromised by this patently powerful woman would take a number of forms over the years. Some, like Martin Seymour-Smith, were intricately vengeful. Laura (Riding) Jackson believed that his biography and his characterization of her reflected a profound hatred of women. He depicted her as a witch, she said, because she had dared to divest the title of truth-teller from men to don it herself. One 1930s collaborator acknowledged his debt as a poet to Riding, while protesting his indifference to her as a woman. His description of her appeared in the Richard Perceval Graves biography:

> Her undershot jaw, primly ascetic lips, rather prominent nose, curvaceous and tobacco stained fingers and wobbly

blue eyes, if anything slightly repelled me: as did her too-theatrical Mayorquin [sic] costumes and gold wire tiaras spelling LAURA.

His "authorial integrity and personal independence" were similarly preserved. "We are, and were, all honourable men."

There was, however, a darker side to Riding's appropriation of the "patriarchal leer" and its various authoritarian dialects. For those who grew to contest her rule, Riding—whether hurt, betrayed, or just enraged—was ready with often brutal denunciations. Bronowski had vast reserves of ego and could shrug off her sentencing, but there were others who could not. When Laura learned that Elfriede Faust had returned to Deyá some weeks after she had sent her away, she descended on Lucie and John's cottage in the middle of the night looking for the unfortunate woman. While Robert stood by giggling uncontrollably, Laura cracked a large whip, "her face white with rage," Lucie Brown remembered.

Those who submitted wholly to Riding were permanently altered by the experience. Norman Cameron's widow felt that Riding, whom she had never met, had in some way "irretrievably harmed" her husband and was largely to blame for his later misery. Jane Aiken Hodge, widow of another collaborator, Alan Hodge, held similar views: "Of course one mustn't blame LR for all the damage that hard-drinking group of post war artists and poets did to themselves and their families. But she was a stunting influence." This influence eventually began to stunt Riding as well. By the late 1930s her poems had become increasingly dry relics of remembered emotions; the rich wayward humor, the pleasure in the rhythm and color of words, was absent.

Bronowski, however, got off fairly easily. The quarrel with Laura, perhaps not coincidentally, followed the rejection of his poetry manuscript by Chatto and Windus. Within a few months after leaving Deyá he was a lecturer in mathematics at University College, Hull. Returning to the security of straight lines and points in space, he would keep his faith in the "precise and cogent" "exact and detailed" language of science—until he visited Hiroshima to view the precise and cogent, exact and detailed effect of the atomic bomb. The faithful certainties of his contemporaries would not last as long;

the Ribbentrop-Molotov Pact of 1939 was a devastating disillusionment for those who had looked to Soviet communism to right the
wrongs of the world.

And for those whose faith in the divining powers of Laura Riding
was near absolute, they, too, would suffer disillusion. In a review of
Riding's *Collected Poems* written on the eve of World War II, Robert
Fitzgerald, the translator of Homer's *Odyssey* and *Iliad* and yet another
young poet who had briefly fallen under her influence, observed that
"the urgency with which Riding professes [her faith in poetry] is an
index of the divided faith of her contemporaries. By the settled
prejudice of our time, indeed, her credo is her delusion." Riding's
faith in poetry as the language of truth-telling was perhaps less
harmful than other delusions of the time.

<hr>

When assigning moral homilies for *Epilogue*, Laura gave Honor
"Frankness"; Robert, "Theft" and "Regrets"; Gordon, "Enthusiasm";
Tom, "Praise"; and in a comment on his long-delayed visit to Deyá,
James Reeves was given "Decision." (Laura reserved "Anger" for herself.) The decision to come to Deyá, and to stay from early November 1935 until just before Christmas, was made only after James had
finally secured a job as a schoolmaster. Thus it was less indecision
that kept him from coming than reluctance to venture south without
his future firmly in hand. Such precautions were typical; when Laura
ventured to address him as "dearest James" in a letter, he informed her
that he had reserved his own "dearest" for his fiancée, Mary Phillips.
In a moment of petulance early in their friendship, Riding had
scolded that they would get along better once he realized that she
could easily fathom the inner complexities of his cautious mind. But
James, with Jacob's experience in mind, was taking no chances.

Within a few days of James' arrival at Ca'n Torrent, Karl was on
edge; he found it unnerving to go to the toilet with only a bit of
plaster wall separating him from his sleeping houseguest. Twice his
nose began to bleed, and in an afternoon secretarial session he made
the same typing mistake throughout an entire manuscript. Then he
began to imagine that Laura was angry with him; James might have
said something. The next day, when James had gone off with Robert
to the Cala, Karl accompanied a despondent Laura into the village

for a cup of coffee and learned to his relief that he was not the cause of her unhappiness:

> It was very awkward [Karl wrote in his diary], my trying to interest Laura in some topic of conversation, Laura feeling frightfully depressed about everything and James in particular without having found any particular reason. [As we walked] along the carretera towards Salerosa Laura [told me] about flower sending in America, how the Fugitives once, when she lay ill somewhere in the south, near Nashville, had sent her two dozen of American Beauties. So I tried to tell a bit about flowers in Germany and picked her a daisy. But all was very sad and triste and heavy so that I could have cried for her because it should happen to her like this.

Karl's diary is an intimate record of the lives that he, Laura, and Robert shared in the months preceding their evacuation from Deyá with the outbreak of the Spanish civil war in July 1936. Where Robert's diary is a blunt record of his purchases, projects, special outings, letters received, weather, illness, and other notable events, Karl's is a soulful narrative of his inner life. His Kafkaesque obsessions with his state of health, his tremulous indexing of his own and others' moods and tempers, are periodically interrupted by bursts of rapture at the home he had found for himself under the watchful care and castigation of Laura. In Karl, Laura discovered a man whose sensitivity was at a pitch to match her own; she respected his temper and he respected hers. In a Palma jewelry shop waiting for Laura to make up her mind over a purchase, Karl tried out a new English expression, "Take it or leave it." Laura, he remembered fondly, "nearly blew me out the door." But it was Karl to whom she confided her beauty secrets (a dab of Vaseline at the corner of each eye to make it look bigger), trusting in the absoluteness of his devotion. He would even purchase sanitary napkins at the drugstore for her "without a blink." Unlike James, Karl breathed the air as she did, vigilant for injury and easily discomposed but ever open to the exquisite experience of loving and being loved.

But Laura's attention was most resolutely fixed on James, not Karl; she had high hopes for his work. In April 1936 William Butler Yeats asked both Riding and Graves if he might include a selection of their poems for his anthology *The Oxford Book of Modern Verse*. Riding insisted that he take Reeves as well, a strategy that after a long, hectoring correspondence had finally proved successful with Michael Roberts and his *Faber Book of Modern Verse*. After seeing some of James' work, Yeats demurred, writing from Palma, where he was finishing a translation of the Upanishads, "Too reasonable, too truthful. We poets should be good liars, remembering always that the Muses are women and prefer the embrace of gay warty lads." Though shocked by Yeats' frank admission of the necessary falsehood of poetry, Riding was nonetheless triumphant at having her suspicions about yet another blarneyman confirmed. When one of her *Epilogue* collaborators expressed a liking for Yeats' work, Riding chastised him. "The pleasure Yeats gets out of 'Lake waters' etc. is a loathesome pleasure of a poet possessing his poem." Still, she suggested that Yeats come to Deyá, an invitation that he declined, citing poor health.

There was indeed little that was warty about James Reeves, and the loathsome pleasures of life were probably apt to make him skittish. Ardently polite and witty and amusing when relaxed, he had what Karl thought was a "tiny good looking nose," a reddish sandy moustache, "nice wavy hair," and "the strangest spectacles imaginable." He smoked a pipe. As a muse for Riding, however, he proved reluctant. Since the affair over Jacob, she had nurtured a tense affection for him, and from her poem "When Love Becomes Words" (which Karl typed within a few days of James' arrival), as well as "Friendship on Visit" (which she wrote immediately after he left), it is clear that any possible spark between them was extinguished by her fear of rejection and by his wary but determined reserve. With painful frankness "Wishing More Dear," written one morning in bed during James' stay, evokes the embarrassment occasioned by her yearning and the "hoarding under courtesy" of the "fancied minutiae of affection":

> . . .
>
> Can this be made somewhat of lust
> That, clamorous for loving signs,
> My heart so piously disowns
> Thought of the usual embraces?
>
> . . .

In Deyá, in place of the "usual embraces," there would be the imperfect intimacies of editorial sessions over a novel, elaborately sketched plans for *Epilogue* essays, and more and more book ideas. But whether because of her loneliness or the acute anticipation that had preceded his arrival, Laura's hope for a closer intimacy with James, was one not easily abandoned. After a trip to Palma, Robert noted in his diary that, for the first time in years, Laura found a shade of lipstick that suited her.

Less than a week after James' arrival, the phonograph was brought to the Sala, and they had a party. Laura danced the fox-trot with both Robert and James, while Karl looked on with admiration. But the records seemed old and stale, and the evening ended early with a medley of Elizabethan songs from James and Robert, with James accompanying on guitar. More late evenings of champagne, one-steps, and two-steps followed; sometimes Robert would be sulky because he felt neglected, and worst of all for Karl, sometimes the evening would end awkwardly with Laura's lapsing into a morose silence. Robert was dispatched to Palma, where he bought five new records.

At various times during James' monthlong stay, Laura broached the idea of deeding him the cottage, which Jacob had lived in, and providing him a steady income as an assistant. Failing that, she mused aloud on the possibility that she might accompany James on his departure, but only going as far as Barcelona. Laura had not left the island since her 1930 trip to London, over five years before. James' polite demurrals contributed to an increasing tension; and it was not long before Karl, with whom Laura discussed her intricate difficulties with James, began to feel that James was dreadfully self-absorbed and not nearly as attentive to Laura as he might be:

> Why hasn't he a bit of pity [for] poor Laura who's his hostess, and is so worried about him and does everything she can do for him and doesn't feel well herself besides being overworked. Bloody egoism.

Robert, returning from Palma with Laura and Karl after seeing James off, wrote in his diary that Laura seemed worn out. Karl also noted that within a few days Laura had relapsed into the illnesses that beset her before James' arrival. "I rather wish now somebody were here than being alone with Laura and Robert," he wrote. "There is nothing now that restrains her."

Within two weeks of James' departure, however, Laura wrote testily to a young Oxford graduate named Alan Hodge that objective feeling and the poetic state of mind were entirely different matters. Hodge had confused them in his review—one of the first—of *Epilogue*. If he wanted to know exactly what the poetic state of mind was, she wrote on December 20, 1935, he should come visit her in Deyá. Hodge, a slight and somewhat delicate young man with "a good head," was there by Christmas.

Chapter 18

A TROJAN ENDING

——— • ———

The story of Troy, now dispersed in mocking legend, was the first tight knot that history made in time. After Troy the rope of time tangled, but during all the long coils of ages, when men grew old without reaching last maturity, never was a true knot made again.

Yet perhaps, in this last of ages, the second knot will be tied, and the last. By which we too shall have a Trojan ending—leaving off once more in the middle, having attained possession of life as they attained recognition of it.

—*A Trojan Ending*

——— • ———

THE KINGDOM OF Troy was one of the oldest of the East; its citadel rested on six predecessors, and its richly cultivated civilization had bloomed and faded long before the Greeks first encountered the Trojans on the plains below the hill in Asiatic Turkey that is now known as Hissarlik. At the time of the siege the Trojans were rich, sane, and complacent. Arrayed against them were the impulsive, stubborn, and childish Greeks, endowed with a bravura that made them invincible. Riding's novel opens with a view of the battlefield from the Scaean Tower of Priam's palace. On the plains below, the Trojan army is struggling on into the tenth and final year of the war. From the lofty realm of those who live outside the trivialities of legends and notions of heroic deeds, particularly Greek ones, Cressida, the daughter of a Trojan priest who deserted to the

Greeks early in the war, considered the ancient Trojan character and fate:

> What was wrong? Had Troy not kept its balance? No, Troy was sure, Troy was what truth was like. Could it be that Troy was too small a measure of truth, too small a vessel to contain the mounting substance of time? Nowhere else could there be such sureness as that bred on the hill of Troy.

A Trojan Ending, Riding's 1937 retelling of the Troy epic, is primarily Cressida's story. Of the Trojans, she alone knew that she was witnessing the doom of a civilization and that in the camps below were the beginnings of another—clever barbarians with their greedy eyes fixed not upon the recapture of Helen and her honor but on control of trade routes to the East. Despite her love for Priam's son Troilus, Cressida knew that she would join the new age; in her final flight to the Greeks she not only saved herself from extinction but also protected for the new age the memory of the old.

In Riding's novel the Trojan War was prolonged not because the Trojans couldn't win it or because of the exigencies of legend and archaeological evidence but to pose more searching questions for the inhabitants of that stone citadel. How does a war begin? How does a civilization come to a close? To explain events in terms of causes, Riding points out in her preface, is a resolutely modern exercise, not yet available to most newspapers. To the historian's cynical point that no ancient author has provided a better reason for the siege of Troy than the rape of Helen, she replied, "No contemporary newspaper knows of any reason for [the Great War] except the assassination at Sarajevo of the Austrian Archduke Franz Ferdinand." The problem of ascertaining the true story of Troy, she continued, was not a scholarly one but, like Homer's, a poetic one. To tell this story required "a delicate balance between a sense of the past and a sense of the present—since a story of past events must include the present from which they are viewed."

This watchful sense of the present is at the center of *A Trojan Ending*. Her account does not dwell on the contest between the legendary brawn of Odysseus, Paris, Hector, Agamemnon, Achilles, and Ajax, as does Homer's, nor was the courtly and coy romance of Troilus and Cressida the dramatic focus. Rather, Riding's account takes place in a novel of ideas, a philosophical inquisition into the cycles of history, and that precise moment when the rise of a new civilization passes the fall of an older one. In the "living history" of the Trojan War, Riding sought a prognostication for the future of Europe. Most immediate was the rearming of Germany, the impotence of England and France before Hitler, and the ideological squaring off of fascism and communism.

Which of those barbarians posturing aggressively across the borders of Europe would emerge ascendant? One night in the spring of 1935 Laura had a dream about Hitler in which he took pains to assure her that he had no secret purposes. "Alas, no," she wrote in the Deyá newsletter, "all the secret purposes grow in Italy nowadays." Within five months Mussolini had invaded Abyssinia. But there were as many secret purposes in Berlin and Moscow as in Rome, and somehow they all found a war—if only by proxy—in Spain. It now seems inevitable that the prologue to World War II was a war not between European nation-states (though many participated) but within the heart of one. When Riding came to write of Hector's death and the final capture of Troy, it was Deyá that was under siege.

In January 1930, three months after Robert and Laura arrived in Mallorca, the sleepy dictatorship of Miguel Primo de Rivera was overturned. In 1931 Spain established the Second Republic, a loose coalition of socialists and reformists, almost Fabian in character and intentions. Spain, the historian Paul Johnson has written, was then the most aloof, self-contained, and xenophobic nation in Europe, "the least vulnerable to the foreign viruses of totalitarianism, of Left or Right, social engineering, relative morality." Perhaps it was some sense of this self-sufficiency and surety that prompted Laura to consider taking up Spanish citizenship after Gelat was appointed mayor of Deyá in May 1936 by the village council.

To celebrate, Laura and Robert hosted a midday banquet at the Costa d'Or, a high-class hotel in Lluchalcari. Around the table, at plates of sweet rice and lobster, sat Deyá's six councillors, Gelat and his wife, several prominent villagers, and the Canellun contingent. Cigars and fruit followed the main course, accompanied by informal speeches in which each councillor made sure to disown any preten-

sion of being a politico. Gelat soft-pedaled the long-standing controversy over water rights (one of his many entrepreneurial schemes
financed by Robert), expressing his desire to settle all grievances and
abandon old feuds during his tenure as mayor. One *counsillor* (who
had perhaps recently been leaning in the wrong direction, politi-
cally) insisted tearfully on his own neutrality. Laura wrote to a new
protégé of Gelat's triumph over his "villainist" enemies (first among
them was the village doctor) who had denounced him and herself as
spies. Had she been naturalized, she told him, she thought that the
counsillors would most likely have asked her to be mayor. With stun-
ning innocence she cited approvingly Gelat's congratulatory telegrams from the president of Spain and the mayor of Madrid as
evidence of the "personal" touch in Spanish politics.

Gelat's appointment as mayor had followed the narrow electoral
victory in February 1936 of the Popular Front government. Ever
sensitive to political winds, Gelat made a special visit to Madrid to
see the governor, the Mallorquin deputies, and the minister of war
soon after the elections. Robert wrote in his diary that the election
had been a "landslide," something that the Popular Front also seemed
to believe—as they set up their government before a second ballot
could be called. Gelat, canny rather than ideological, turned with the
political tide; he declared to Robert a month after the Popular Front's
victory that he was more than a socialist: he was now a communist.

At the historic meeting of the Comintern six months before the
1936 Spanish elections, the Bulgarian Communist leader Georgi
Dimitroff proposed the idea of a Popular Front. "Comrades," he
began, "you will remember the ancient tale of the capture of Troy. . . .
The attacking army was unable to achieve victory until, with the aid
of the famous Trojan Horse, it managed to penetrate to the very
heart of the enemy camp." Despite its xenophobic past, in five years
of republican government Spain had somehow become vulnerable to
foreign interference in the ebb and flow of its internal politics. With
the election of the Popular Front government, the communists
gained their first foothold in Europe, edging out or winning over
moderate and progressive elements and proclaiming a militant program of agrarian reforms. Leftist youth gangs soon took to the streets
to fight their emergent fascist counterparts in ever more enthusiastic
sprees of murder and mayhem.

Within a few months of the Popular Front's victory the winds had changed again. The lack of a unified political consensus on which their revolutionary platform could rest was part of the problem. The Popular Front, infiltrated by Comintern agents, quickly lost control of its own militants and indulged itself in political infighting, intrigue, and rhetoric. The resulting chaos and power vacuum provoked a military uprising. The scale of the violence that would take place during the Spanish civil war now seems hardly credible. Mass executions and purges by the Left were matched by violence of equal ferocity on the Right; the virulence of the hatred unleashed was out of all proportion to the vested interests at stake or to the utopian ideals sought. What had begun as a cynical shadow play between Hitler and Stalin ended up being a vicious and bitter tragedy for Spain.

In the citadel of Deyá, the arrival of the Trojan horse went almost unnoticed. Brief glimpses of its shadow fall across the pages of Robert's or Karl Goldschmidt's diaries. Between servants hired and fired at Canelluñ, spurts of work on the Troy novel, and long letters to England, the war had its unofficial beginnings. A few days after James' arrival, Laura and Gelat were visited by two mounted Guardia Civil officers and were instructed to report to the military authorities in Palma to answer questions about the purpose of the road to the Cala. During the interrogation they were also asked about Karl and two German Jewish neighbors with whom Laura and Robert were quite friendly. The Seizin Press was also deemed suspect, and Laura was made to register it and pay a tax. Whoever had informed on them had also photographed the house and reported the small Klepper boat they kept by the sea. Like Riding's Troy, Deyá was also too small a measure of truth, too small a vessel to contain the "mounting substance of time." Gelat vowed to get to the bottom of it, but in this contest even he was vulnerable; more than one Trojan Horse was stalking Spain.

As in Riding's Troy, there was an apathy in England and France, a listless reluctance to entertain seriously the prospect of war against the fascist upstarts. Hitler was humored—even admired—by Baldwin's foreign office, and the Labour party found a great deal that was appealing in Stalin's massive collectivization of industry and agriculture. Among the most thoughtful there was almost a willingness to be invaded, if not by armies then by those ideas which would call into question the most fundamental issue in any conflict: Who is the enemy? Was it Hitler or the Jew next door? Was it fascism abroad or one's own "bourgeois liberal tendencies at home"? In June 1936 Robert wrote to his elder son, David, discouraging him from his view that the Nazis might be a good tonic for an ailing Europe. In Riding's Troy, there was a similar inability to take the Greek threat seriously, pro-Greek cults flourished, and Greek soldiers repeatedly besieged Priam for the hand of his daughters in marriage:

> Priam mused tiredly. To go out to the battle-field and participate in these farcical devotions was a tedious prospect. Nothing like this would end the War. It was a war, not a personal duel, and the end could only be some mighty death, like the death of the people. All personal enmities were obscured in the great, almost nameless forces which now drove the War on: the fury of the gods themselves was in the War, and must be spent. Priam's position was not unlike that of Zeus': he would have stopped the War, had he been able, but logic (Athene) and pride (Hera) and sentiment (Aphrodite) left him no alternative but to speed it along its dreadful course.

Mallorca's "dreadful course" began officially on July 18, 1936, only one day after General Franco, *el caudillo* and former chief of the general staff, declared a Fascist revolt against Spain's republican government. On that day Fascist machine guns appeared in Palma, and the Popular Front government responded by imposing martial law, suspending deliveries of mail and the boat service from Barcelona. For the first few days the war took place over the radio, beginning that night in Gelat's café with the news of a military insurrection at Melilla and Seville and the demotion of Franco and five of his generals. On July 20, a Fascist was shot while trying to take over the post office in Sóller. Coffee and sugar disappeared from the shops. Radio reports announced that the Fascists had seized power in the Balearic Islands and twelve other provinces, but later there were conflicting reports. Popular Front mayors, including Gelat, were told to hand over their offices to a "nonpolitical." The village doctor, Robert noticed, began "strutting about" with his gang.

Fascism first arrived in Deyá during the night of July 21, when trucks of soldiers on patrol roared down the carretera shouting "Viva el fascismo!" Eighteen youths in five cars returned the following morning at 3:00 A.M., looking for the Popular Front mayor of Inca, whom they thought was being sheltered in the village. Gelat, ordered to turn on the electricity generator so that they could search, was warned that they had already killed eight men. Ironically, the doctor's house was the first they tried. While his front door was peppered with bullets his wife and daughter hid under the bed. Convinced that the communists had arrived, the doctor escaped out the back in his underwear and espadrilles and hid quaking in a tree all night. The youths, none of them over seventeen, soon lost interest and drove away. The mayor of Inca was later found at the Costa d'Or Hotel and was promptly shot.

On July 22, Minorca became the base for attacks against Mallorca; six people were killed in the north of the island. The next day a republican plane flew over Palma at noon and 5 P.M.. Because of the scarcity of ammunition, planes dropped stones and leaflets when they ran out of grenades and homemade bombs. Two people were killed and refugees from the city began arriving in Deyá, heightening tensions still further. Within a week of his declaration of war, Franco had left his outpost in the Canary Islands and had amassed 6,000 soldiers, poised to invade the south of Spain from North Africa. For a few days it seemed that Fascist Mallorca, cut off from military materiel and the outside world, would be left to fall by itself; but on July 28, Palma was once again bombarded by government planes.

Within two months Franco would have 60,000 Italian troops under his command, and Hitler, eager to test the new weaponry of the Third Reich, would direct Göring to begin planning a half-billion-mark military-assistance package for the Fascist cause in Spain. Among the deliveries would be the Condor Legion, a squadron of bombers, armed with 550-pound bombs and piloted by Germans in Spanish uniforms. Thus began the dress rehearsal for World War II.

On August 2, 1936, as Robert, Laura, Karl, and Alan Hodge were clearing away Sunday lunch, the former British consul stepped up to the front door of Canellun and announced that their last chance to leave the island had come. They would leave from Los Pinos in Palma that evening on the *Grenville*, a spanking new battleship. They were each allowed one suitcase, which they packed hurriedly and at random. Gelat arrived, took the keys from Robert, and undertook to watch over the house, their belongings, and garden. "He said 'sin verguenzas' [without shame] and wept," Graves wrote in his diary. Driving through Palma, they saw broken windows and few people. At the pier soldiers milled around—"growing beards already," Robert noted glumly. Sixty bombs were dropped on the city that day.

Karl had always dreaded the moment when he would have to leave Mallorca; he seemed to have always known that such happiness was doomed. Almost a year earlier he had had an "extremely vivid and grotesque dream" about going in a boat to England:

> My terror and grief [at] being obliged to leave the islands grew gradually with every yard the ship went on its way. There were all Englishmen aboard, and they were all shaving in the queerest places and positions.
>
> After getting up I stood still a time under the terrible impression that I had left these isles.

All the same, he was lucky to be leaving with them.

Karl took one long backward glance at a pantry full of jams and marmalades, fruits and butter. Laura left behind her black cat Alice Heartbreak and Alice's *bête noire*, Solomon, Robert's gentle bull mastiff. Bundles of scrawled notes and several unfinished manuscripts would languish in a cupboard in Laura's study for many years. At her request, Robert would eventually burn most of her papers, and the rest would be sold to a Palma wastepaper merchant. "A pity," he wrote to Tom Matthews, "but it will make good cardboard and wrapping paper." The jazz records and phonograph would lie untouched for even longer.

Ten years after the outbreak of the Spanish civil war, Robert Graves returned to Deyá to find his hat still on its peg, his walking stick in its corner, and everything else as he had so often recalled it. Tom Matthews recalled Robert's preening: his trust in Gelat had been vindicated, "like a gambler who thinks he has won his bet not because he is lucky but because he knows the winning system."

But when Gelat died three years later, the title to Graves' property went to his son Juan Marroig, who laughed at the idea that the land properly belonged to Robert. Though there was never any question of being turned out of Canelluñ, Graves eventually had to buy back a parcel of the land that he had bought from Don Bernardo Colón. The greater part of the land and his financial stake in Gelat's moneymaking schemes were lost. Graves cursed Gelat's son, who died a pauper, having gambled away his father's fortune. The shrewder villagers smiled. Only Graves could never bear to consider who the real con artist was; Gelat's trustworthiness, particularly after Laura left him, was an article of faith to a man who committed himself to rather few.

Olive trees, the Greeks say, never die, but the terraces of Deyá are gradually crumbling; richer fruit lies in tourists' pockets. These days summer brings tour buses filled with sightseers looking for a sunburn or a glimpse of a movie star in Deyá's wide selection of cafés, boutiques, art galleries, and restaurants. Since the death of Franco in 1975 the peseta has become a stronger currency, but Mallorca is still a budget holiday. Michael Douglas has a house nearby; Prince Charles and Lady Diana have been known to moor their yacht not far from the Cala. Two farms at the entrance to the village on the Canelluñ side (one of them Don Bernardo's) were recently converted into a luxury hotel, partly backed by Virgin Airlines mogul Richard Branson. When a German soap opera used it as a filming location, Deyá became swamped with German tourists. One family of fishermen remains, supplying the two restaurants in the Cala and the local hotels. Only in winter does the village seem to return to an earlier age; the roar of the torrent by the abandoned washhouses still fills the air.

Also left behind in the panicked departure on that August afternoon in 1936 was the legend of Laura Riding that foreigners would tell over and over again at the Sa Fonda café. On his return to Deyá, Graves would reinvoke the poetic mysteries that Riding had first divined in the shadow of the mountainous Teix. Norman Cameron would return in the 1950s, shortly before his death, to exorcise the ghosts that had plagued him since his first visit to that modest island village. John Aldridge, Alan Hodge, and James Reeves would also come back. Though Karl returned to live in Ca'n Torrent and to type and check Robert's manuscripts, for him "the paradise was lost."

But, as before, there was a steady flow of writers and artists to Canelluñ. With Robert Graves as resident bard and iconoclast, Deyá became a center of the international counterculture. Hypnotized by what Laura called "Deyá's kittenish beauty tricks," many would stay on to work or dream. Those who became friendly with Robert—he was far more open with strangers and admirers than in the years with Laura—might get a stone house to write poetry or paint pictures in. Now, each return to Deyá by foreign residents or former Graves' intimates is accompanied by a bruising sense of time not standing still but passing, and of an enchanted youth shattered by the crush and noise of tour buses and motorbikes along the *carretera*.

Among the books and curios in what used to be the Seizin Press room is a copy of Emily Dickinson's *Collected Poems* annotated in Laura's hand. There are also a few books with Geoffrey Phibbs' bookplate and, in Robert's study, a trunk full of Seizin Press books, carefully wrapped. Len Lye's silk-screens still adorn the walls, only slightly faded. A John Aldridge painting of the newly built Canelluñ hangs in the living room, a later addition to make more room for the family that Graves brought back with him. A few of Laura's antique dresses are stored in an armoire in her old bedroom, ready for the summer dramatic productions staged by Graves' grandchildren in the rocky amphitheater on what was once Don Bernardo's land.

In a corner of the dining room, unobtrusive against the white-washed wall, stands an empty chair. Too small for most adults to sit in comfortably, it is the chair of mulberry wood that Gelat had made for Laura, though few remember this. Every week Francisca, who works for Robert's widow, Beryl Graves, moves the chair to mop the pale yellow floors. If asked about Laura she will smile shyly.

> Francisca will preside while we withdraw
> To the major drama that was not meant
> To be produced by their kindness
> On their stage for their self-congratulation.
> Francisca is a charm like a wise child
> Against the whimsicalness of the world
> To be itself the world it tells of.

PART IV

THE END OF THE WORLD, AND AFTER

Chapter 19

DOOM IN BLOOM

———— • ————

And every prodigal greatness
Must creep back into strange home
Must fill the hollow matrix of
The never-begotten perfect son
Who never can be born.

. . .

And from this jealous secrecy
Will rise itself, will flower up,
The likeness kept against false seed
When death-whole is the seed
And no new harvest to fraction sowing.

Will rise the same peace that held
Before fertility's lie awoke
The virgin sleep of Mother All:
The same but for the way in flowering
It speaks of fruits that could not be.

—"The Flowering Urn"

———— • ————

AFTER A MEAL of canned beef, ship's biscuit, and lime juice, Laura
bedded down in an officer's cabin while Robert, Alan, and Karl slept
on deck with one thin blanket between them. The following morning more evacuees came on board at the neighboring island of Ibiza.

At the port of Valencia they transferred to the *Maine,* a British
hospital ship bound for Marseilles. Introducing himself as Captain
Graves, Robert convinced the ship's commander that Karl belonged
with their party. After a last stop in Barcelona, they disembarked
wearily at Marseilles at 8:00 A.M. on August 6, 1936; it had taken
them four days to reach the French port. There they made arrangements for money transfers and bought rail tickets for Paris. Laura,
whose passport had expired, was treated so rudely at the American
consulate that she emerged in tears; it took them three hours to
obtain a special stamp for Karl's passport. Finally, with everyone's
papers but Laura's in order (she needed a British visa), they took a
night train to Paris, where Robert was in and out of the British
embassy in time to catch the 10:19 boat train to Dieppe. Laura,
exhausted, cranky, and protesting, was rushed into a cab for the
station. They were all in London by 6:00 P.M. on August 7.

Robert had wired ahead and alerted Maisie Somerville of their
imminent arrival. A friend from his Oxford days and head of schools
broadcasting at the BBC, Maisie met them at the station, having
arranged a place to stay. They were installed at 32 York Terrace, just
off Regent's Park, in a Georgian mansion owned by Kitty West, a
friend of Maisie's who had visited Robert and Laura in Deyá. West
was the daughter of Arthur Leaf, an archaeologist whose work on
Troy had been critical in Riding's casting of *A Trojan Ending*. In
gratitude for the hot baths, two Welsh maids, the telephone, and
"every comfort," Riding dedicated her novel to West. Everyone was
somewhat in shock.

Apart from visits from or to all the Deyá intimates, there would be
reunions with Norman and Len Lye, with Robert's children, siblings,
and half siblings, and with Amy. (Robert's father had died in 1931.)
There was even a warm reunion with Nancy when Jenny, now
seventeen, got into a very bad scrape with a sleazy boyfriend. At
cocktail and dinner parties Robert and Laura found themselves telling and retelling the story of their hasty evacuation; gradually Deyá
came to seem more like a story and the war there ever less real. In
October, Tom and Julie Matthews were in town, and there were
evenings at the theater and meals at Spanish restaurants. There were
also visits to Denham Studios, where Alexander Korda was in the
early stages of filming *I, Claudius*. Korda, who sent a limousine to pick

up Laura, invited her and Robert to do a screenplay of their refugee experiences. With this offer in hand and after meeting with several publishers, they were encouraged by prospects for work and gain. The week they arrived, three Seizin Press books were reviewed favorably in the *Times Literary Supplement;* soon after, Random House, in cooperation with Constable, agreed to be the American distributor of the press.

There was a great deal of settling in. Shopping expeditions continued unceasingly through the fall and winter of 1936. Two Irish tweed suits, one greenish, one brown, were made for Laura, and two matching velour bonnets in the Salvation Army style were purchased to go with them. Robert made repeated trips to Albert Mills, a shop selling antique curios and jewelry in the Caledonian flea market, buying fistfuls of gifts for everyone. Laura arranged for Karl to be suitably outfitted. He returned from a posh shop on Regent Street with two tweed sports jackets, two pairs of gray flannel slacks, and a blue double-breasted overcoat, but the sight of him dressed up like a "city gent" was more than Laura could bear with a straight face.

Underlying the frantic activity was the sense that the civil war was only a temporary departure from Spain's "normal ways" and that the stay in England would be brief. They had trouble getting comfortable; their first apartment, on Osnaburgh Street, was found to have fleas in the carpets and a tap dancer overhead; the second, at 10 Dorset Street, sheltered mice. Plagued by boils, Robert suffered the most from the upheaval and found himself mired in lengthy negotiations with Lawrence's trustees over the book on T. E. that he was writing with Basil Liddell-Hart (Lawrence had been killed in a motorcycle accident in 1935). *A Trojan Ending,* which had been nearly finished in Deyá, underwent lengthy revisions by Laura. As the fall progressed, their lives seemed to be in a kind of holding pattern, waiting for the civil war to end or the war with Germany to start, waiting for Korda's film to be finished or a big check to arrive. Anxious over the fate of Canelluñ, over the next two and a half years they would constantly send money to Gelat, further exacerbating their financial worries.

Robert, more than Laura, followed the news in Spain closely; in November he had an audience with Winston Churchill, still out of office, on the possibility of British intervention. But England, too, seemed to be drifting. Churchill knew better than anyone that the country was ill-prepared for war, and in great agitation he told Graves that a "lethargic" Parliament and Stanley Baldwin's government were to blame for the state of the military. Rearmament was still a thorny political issue, and Churchill was considered by many to be a warmonger, a demagogue, and a Cassandra.

But the equivocal spirit ran deeper than even Churchill might imagine. At Denham Studios, Charles Laughton, Churchill's favorite actor, was filming the role of Claudius, with Merle Oberon as the evil Queen Messalina. "On the set," one of the actors remembered, "Laughton had flashes of brilliance, but he just couldn't get it right, even though he sweated over his performance for weeks. The result was fluffed lines and an enormous number of retakes. Sometimes he seemed to go to pieces." At the height of the abdication crisis and in the midst of filming, Laughton burst onto the set shouting, "Don't you realize, I'm Edward VIII!" The film was never completed.

The project that dominated Laura Riding's thoughts and energies between her evacuation from Mallorca in August 1936 and her return to America in April 1939 must be considered in the context of the failure of leadership in England and France and, more, of each government's marked sympathy for the Fascist dictatorships in Germany and Italy. While Riding would also collaborate on novels with Honor Wyatt and Alan Hodge, work on her screenplay, write a popular novel on the wives of famous men (*Lives of Wives*), and confer with young poets, during this period one project would overshadow all others.

"A Personal Letter with a Request for a Reply," the initial salvo of what would swell into a massive undertaking, was sent to 400 prominent political figures and intellectuals in January 1937, on Laura's thirty-sixth birthday; the following month she, Robert, and Karl left London for a four-month tax exile in Switzerland. The letter asked what might possibly be done by intelligent men and women who desired to "live a peaceful, civilized existence, in a world which [had] become steadily more and more disordered and less and less peaceful." Riding's singular object was to arrest—through direct, personal intervention—the slide of Europe toward war.

UNTIL THE SPANISH civil war came to Deyá, Riding's familiarity with the social and political issues that transformed the literary and cultural climate of the 1930s was limited to what young emissaries like Bronowski, Reeves, and Alan Hodge might tell her; the BBC world news service; and what she read in *This Week*, a left-wing American journal that they subscribed to in Deyá. In 1933 Riding replied to a question concerning her political or economic creed (in a questionnaire circulated by Geoffrey Grigson's *New Verse*) by asking why so many communist poets were homosexual. She dispatched Freud with equal alacrity and, in 1937, cheered the call for censorship of D. H. Lawrence's *Lady Chatterley's Lover* and James Joyce's *Ulysses*.

As to whether she thought herself, as a poet, different from "ordinary men," she was equally direct:

> As a poet, I am distinguished from ordinary men, first, in that I am a woman; second, in that as a woman I am actively and minutely aware of the fundamental distinctions in life (the distinction between man and woman being the most absolute of these) which as a poet it is my function to organize into unities.

With such statements Riding remained a hard-to-ignore fixture on the British literary landscape. "One woman goes a long way in any capacity," Riding noted. As the 1930s wore on, the London literary temper became ever less patient with those female voices which had been at least a passing fascination in the 1920s. Poetry in particular became more and more a male preserve, homosexual or not. Queenie Leavis, a Cambridge critic and the wife of F. R. Leavis, joined Virginia Woolf in protesting the cliquishness of Auden and his entourage: "It is no use looking for growth or development or any addition to literature in such an adolescent hot-house." By 1936 Grigson would dismiss Riding as the "Queen-bore among all poets writing at present. She must face that truth. She was useful to some of us when we were young, like Brancusi's egg; but there isn't much difference between eggs, so why go on being the Heroine of the Poultry Farm and the champion layer?"

The time in which Riding's work was "useful" to a generation of Oxford and Cambridge poets and critics had been the late 1920s, before and immediately after she left for Mallorca. In 1928 Stephen Spender had inherited the post of president of the Oxford English Club from Norman Cameron. The 1928 lecture program featured the old Edwardian and Georgian worthies who had suckled Graves; Spender had invited Edmund Blunden, J. C. Squire, Humbert Wolfe, and Walter de la Mare. But by the time he had left Oxford, his loyalties and imagination had been captured by the moderns, first by Virginia Woolf and T. S. Eliot, later by Gertrude Stein, James Joyce, Ezra Pound, and Laura Riding.

Just as *A Survey of Modernist Poetry* had provided William Empson at Cambridge with his critical springboard in 1927, *A Pamphlet Against Anthologies* had provided Oxford with theirs in 1928. That year both Grigson and W. H. Auden had completed their undergraduate degrees, with Grigson going on to found and edit the immensely influential journal *New Verse*. Louis MacNeice, like Spender, had two more years at Merton but had already published his first book of poetry, as had C. Day Lewis. *A Pamphlet Against Anthologies*, Grigson claimed, helped advance the Oxford revolution in poetry that would dominate the 1930s:

> Coming at this time the Riding-Graves pamphlet—a thickish pamphlet it was—made for scepticism and caution and a dismissal of poems about lambs, and of poetical lachrymosity. Gardens were out. "A garden is a lovesome thing, God wot!" The anthological career of that famous piece "O blackbird what a boy you are" also began its passage into oblivion.

Where Bronowski and Empson at Cambridge concerned themselves with the literary critical method, the young poets of Oxford absorbed the subtle prosodies, technical innovation, and imaginative territory of the modernists. "On Auden, Graves and Norman Cameron [Laura Riding's] influence was obvious and profound," Julian Symons remembered, "but many other poets benefited, some of them indirectly, from . . . her utter elimination of what she called in one letter to me 'marzipan' and in another 'the luxury-stab we are taught to look for at school.'" "All of us" Grigson concurred, "were being weaned sharply from the last thin drops of the milk of a devitalized fairyland."

One measure of Riding's isolation during the early and mid-1930s was the indifferent or hostile reception of *Epilogue* when it finally appeared in 1935. By then Spender's "devitalized fairyland" had been almost entirely replaced by the gritty politics of social realism. "The writer who grasps anything of Marxist theory," Spender wrote, "feels that he is moving in a world of reality, and in a purposeful world." Upon her return to London in August 1936, Riding would try to recapture the attention of this generation by debunking their political idealism and by proposing an increasingly autocratic view of the role that women should play, not only in literature but in the world at large. Few were prepared to listen seriously.

Riding first entered the public fray on October 20, 1936, after traveling to Oxford by train with Robert, Tom, and Julie to deliver a lecture at the English Club entitled "The End of the World and After." They stayed at the posh Clarendon Hotel, and Laura wore a long red velvet skirt, earrings, a white blouse with red buttons down the front and a gold Ibizan necklace. An undergraduate approached the president of the club before she began and asked if the speaker were an evangelist; Laura said that that was exactly what she was. She hoped, however, to spare them any drivel about the coming apocalypse or absurd promises regarding their fate in the hereafter. Though skeptical of messianism, Riding nonetheless could not help leaning in that direction; she realized the strategic value of the religious angle for the "multitudes" and could not quite abandon it entirely. A few months after her talk she would write candidly to Alan Hodge that if she wanted to found a new religion she would at least be able to exploit the sensationalist angle. Poetry had proved disappointing in that respect.

She began her lecture by stating that history, as it had been understood, was pure illusion, nothing more than the bad dreams of poets. Gradually, however, the progress of time had brought an increasing degree of wakefulness, culminating in the present period of full and sustained wakefulness. The proof that the world was ending, that what she was talking about was more than the sentimental assertion of an evangelist, required a period of sustained contact with her. If permitted, she promised to wake them all up and show them how they might keep themselves awake. Surely, she asked, "after lolling about in a perfectly disgusting way for thousands and thousands of years" the challenge of at last cleaning up the "sprawling mess" that consciousness had been up to now should be the most exciting task of all. Robert noted that during the discussion period there were several obstreperous questions from "obvious communists." After the speech, however, a number of students crowded around her in the Randolf Lounge. Laura reported to Ward Hutchinson that she had been greatly amused by her reception.

She had another project in the works aimed specifically at the "obvious communists" of her audience. In *The Left Heresy in Literature and Life*, assisted by a former member of the Cambridge University Communist party named Harry Kemp, Riding challenged many of the fallacies of the leftist literary embrace of Soviet communism. Introduced to Riding by James Reeves soon after her return to England, Kemp was distinguished by his good looks—an "Adonis," Karl noted—and complete humorlessness. He took his role as Laura's repentant ex-communist seriously and, with her help, rooted out his Marxist convictions with as much fervor as he had previously stifled his bourgeois liberalist tendencies.

The Left Heresy was much more closely argued than much of Riding's other critical works; at her scornful best her dissections of leftist hypocrisies rivaled those of Wyndham Lewis. She abutted her generalizations about leftist self-absorption and immaturity with apt quotations from the various mea culpas offered by the Left Book Club. Responding to Day Lewis' insistence that the truly activist writer must work and sleep with the working class, Riding commented acidly, "A truly piteous fate. He must tell somebody about it. He cannot tell 'them,' so he tells 'us.'" She contrasted this effort to assimilate with the working class with those values of the older working-class Left, such as her father's, which put the acquisition of learning and culture first.

But where Riding addressed the circumstances of the British working class, she showed a drastic lack of sympathy. Like the most complacent Tory, she doubted first of all that the working class was really so unhappy with its lot: "Many people get on well with their employers and fellows, do in fact enjoy their jobs—may be regarded as having freely chosen them. Others make the best of their bad jobs by taking them lightly, perhaps by trying to treat them humorously." She also refused to acknowledge the sincerity of the Left's moral indignation, and impugned their research. Thus Allen Hutt's 1933 study, *The Condition of the Working Class in Britain*, was "almost diabolical in tone" because of his obsessive dilatation upon the poor standard of living of the working class. "Too great an interest in the material wrongs people suffer," she concluded, "is evil. It breeds the belief that life is made up of wrongs to the exclusion of good things." *Left Heresy* was a peculiar combination of skeptical disdain, righteous diatribe, and extreme political naiveté.

Just how Riding proposed to prevent the war and end civil strife she had not quite decided. As with so many of her previous projects, she was more certain of what was *not* needed, than what was; she made it clear, for example, that none of the contemporary proposals on the table—feminist, masculinist, internationalist, religious, communist, scientific, pacifist, armed intervention, "or anything in which physical fitness plays a prominent part"—would offer a solution to the world's "outside disorders." For a long time what remained most tangible about her efforts was the mood of urgency and insistent demand for action by like-minded people.

In her "Personal Letter with a Request for a Reply" Riding had posited the existence of two groups: the "inside" people of the "inside world" and the "outside" people. The latter were the professional politicians and diplomats, the "fretful, blundering Napoleons" who roamed the "public corridors of life." The "inside" people, on the other hand, were first of all women, the protectors of the hearth, "the world inside the house and the minds" where all that was known to be "precious and true" resided. Concerned about how the world's unsettled state had invaded this inner tranquillity, she invited replies from both outsiders and insiders on what might be done.

Loath to interrupt her work to leave England but anxious to escape being taxed on Robert's royalties, they set off once again for the Continent. In February 1937, within a month of the mailing of her "Personal Letter," they were en route to Switzerland to stay near their Deyá neighbors, Georg Schwarz and Emmy Strenge. They moved into an apartment in the Villa Guidi, in the Lugano suburb of Paradiso. From there they had a view of the snow-capped Alps and the lakes below them. They found its cheerful views somewhat distracting, as if its picturesqueness undermined the seriousness of their task—a glib reminder of their privileged retreat from taxes and other "material wrongs of the world."

Their routine at Villa Guidi was unvarying. Rising late, Robert fetched the Spanish paper *Libre Estampa* and the *London Daily Telegraph* from the corner newsstand. Lunch was at one after Karl and Robert's daily walk, and they worked until the mail arrived at four. The real work did not begin until after dinner and often lasted until the early hours of the morning. In one three-day period Laura dictated sixty letters to Karl, many of them answering those responses to her "Personal Letter" which had begun trickling in.

The increasingly grim news from Spain contributed a note of urgency to Riding's correspondence. In March, Malaga fell to the Fascists, signaling the end of the insurgent offensive, though Madrid, Barcelona, and Valencia were still republican strongholds. March also brought a letter from a friend in Palma, who informed them that Gelat had been arrested and imprisoned; though he was never formally charged with espionage or collaboration, the road Laura built to the Cala had brought him to the attention of the Guardia Civil. Robert, doubtless feeling somewhat responsible, was shocked at the mild response of Schwarz and Strenge to the news. To console himself he wrote to Albert Mills at the flea market, asking him to send a surprise—nothing with arms but something like the Chinese glass beads or a colorful glass paperweight: "Georgian preferred—they did make things beautifully in those days!" More money was sent to Deyá.

Gelat's imprisonment occasioned Laura's first poem in months; "March, 1937" was about prisoners, Robert wrote in his diary. The specificity of the date ten years after her poem "In Nineteen Twenty-Seven" suggests that Riding once again felt for the erratic pulse of her heart and bade the world keep time. To Nancy Nicholson, Laura wrote of suffering from "a locked feeling," as if Gelat's imprisonment and her sympathetic response were emblematic of powerful and inevitably unseen forces. That so many were shot—in Germany, Italy, the Soviet Union, and Spain—for much less than what Gelat had done, seemed to go unnoticed by both Robert and Laura because of their intense focus on immediate personal concerns. Thus Laura's chronic insomnia became a metaphor of utter wakefulness; she was haunted by a sense that her bedroom had at one time a great deal to do with death. As in the Heliopolis house in Cairo, Villa Guidi was found to have a ghost. One night, suffering from indigestion and nerves, Riding began speaking a language that she and Robert decided was Trojan.

Though quick to disavow any pretense of "magicks," Riding often flirted with the supernatural in much the same manner as she flirted with messianism. At the time of her suicide attempt, all four members of the Holy Circle had had their astrological charts done, and from 14A it seems that a medium had been a part of their Hammersmith circle of friends. Very often the language in which Riding asserted her authority drew, perhaps unconsciously, on current jargon or propaganda. Card-table spiritualism was hardly unusual in postwar literary circles, and like the mediums who presided over them, Riding exploited the reigning superstitions, both her own and those of others, when circumstances demanded it. When she learned that Italian troops had gone to Spain (thus overtly nullifying the nonintervention pact), Laura stuck pins in newspaper photographs of Mussolini and waited with Karl, "semi-seriously" he claimed later, for signs that Il Duce felt the pricks.

Other, more earthly, means of directing world affairs were also conscientiously investigated in Lugano. While awaiting further replies to her "Personal Letter," Laura sent away for Raymond Postgate's book *How to Make a Revolution*, although she had already rejected purely political or "outside" solutions; history had already proven such means ineffective. There were, however, a number of thoughtful replies to her "Personal Letter" from "outside" people. Two well-known writers, Christina Stead and Naomi Mitchison, took exception to Riding's generalizations of "inside" versus "outside" people and to her derogation of women who involved themselves in politics as "denatured."

"When you say that 'political employments . . . are intrinsically commonplace and blank' " Mitchison wrote, "I just feel that you don't begin to know about them." Nor did Mitchison accept that women were occupied only with personal relationships and the home: "That is the archaistic view. It ceased to be valid at about the time it became cheaper to buy jam than to make it oneself." Christina Stead concurred:

For where is the secret of the "true nature of women"
buried? The characteristics put forward here—quietude,
petty domestic diplomacy, intuition, the smooth ordering
of a few lives . . . are equally the characteristics of a well-
trained servant or nurse, or private secretary, whether male
or female.

The World and Ourselves, referred to as "the letter book," was the
work that resulted from Riding's "Personal Letter with a Request for a
Reply." It was also billed as the fourth and final volume of *Epilogue*. To
the sixty-five responses that she chose to publish she added her own
commentaries, most of which were twice the length of her respon-
dents' letters. To those, like Stead and Mitchison, who took issue with
her assumptions, she was dismissive, contriving long, circular rebuttals that tended to twist the meaning of her sender's letters. She was
more patient when there was a personal connection; Julie Matthews'
mother, for example, got a polite and careful hearing. Her "answers"
point out the misconceptions, personal confusions, and symptomatic
delusions of not only the general population on the subject of the
world's "outside disorders" but also its reputed intellectuals. At all
costs, Riding intended to have the last word.

Like any government-in-exile, Riding's potential strength lay in
the interweaving of close friendships back in London and less and
less in poetry or the intermittent pretense—greatly respected by
Robert—that she possessed supernatural powers. It was this circle of
friends to which Laura's thoughts kept returning while she was in
Switzerland; at one point she considered going to America to check
the response to her ideas. But her "contacts" were best in London, and
perhaps impatience with the reaction to her "Personal Letter" led her
back to them. When Alan told her of a visit to Honor Wyatt and his
work for Maisie Somerville at the BBC, she wrote conspiratorially of
his excellent intrigue. Maisie was an important mole for the cause;
Tom, at *Time*, was another.

In Lugano, however, financial worries interfered with these pressing
concerns. The mere notion that she had to distract herself on this
count contributed to Riding's impatient sense of the wrongness amok
in the world. What real weapons did they have for their struggle, she
asked Alan in despair. Thinking up books that would sell was some-

how no longer sufficient; what was needed was a frank fund-raising drive. The time had come to demand money from any source whatsoever, she told Alan, at least until their work and their aims had attracted the attention they deserved.

To John Aldridge, Laura wrote of one possible weapon at hand. The real answer to her "Personal Letter," she said, should be a Council of the Inside People, which would act as a council of elders to whom people might come for advice. The seat of its authority, she insisted with her usual circular precision, would be none other than those giving the advice. A greater and more effective vehicle for truth than poetry seemed to be swimming into view.

IN THE CONCLUDING "chapter" of *The World and Ourselves*, which takes up half the book, Riding moved beyond her initial "Personal Letter" to embark upon the elaboration of a "new moral law." Laws are not made, she insisted; they *are*. Her new moral law was presented to the world by the "inside voices from the point of view of women," and its apparent aim was to legislate everything from the tiniest actions or thoughts to diplomacy between nations and the redistribution of wealth.

The main work on these conclusions was done in Ewhurst, Surrey, where she, Robert, Karl, her coauthor of *Left Heresy* Harry Kemp, and his wife, Alix, had repaired after the return from Lugano in June 1937. The evening of their return to England, Riding conducted a meeting in London with a core group of friends and solicited their advice on what might be done. Among those present were Norman Cameron, Alan Hodge, Karl Goldschmidt, Harry and Alix Kemp, Maisie Somerville, and Dorothy and Ward Hutchinson (the Monosyllables). When Riding came to write up her conclusions in Surrey, she had arrived at quite specific recommendations. There were sections entitled "How to Read Newspapers," "Women as Hostesses in the Outside World, Rather than Job Holders," "The Proper Attitude and Approach to the Multitudes and Their Problems," and "How to Speak Purely in a Way to Avoid Fallacies of Language and Mediocrity of Thought." Riding even expressed an opinion on how the railways might be run. "A Civilized Private Ethic" outlined the duty of every individual

to be *tidy* in every corner of our existence, with the fanati-
cism of beauty . . . To develop each personal relation to its
maximum of frankness, and to have no friendship where, if
all were mutually confessed, the appearance of one to the
other would not be a happy sight . . . To have no private
communication with ourselves, no seclusion with self in
place or mind, to which we could not admit others without
guilty immodesty.

Out of such a vision of human relations and community grew Riding's
plan for a new organization of society that would wrest political and
economic control not only from His Majesty's Government but from
men in general.

In *The World and Ourselves* the new moral law called for the establishment of a three-tiered government. The First Order consisted of
those "inside" individuals, male or female, who had achieved complete and perfect frankness with one another or, as Riding put it,
"articulate reality on a personal plane." For this to happen these
people should all know each other, and since Riding felt that there
"couldn't be that many of them," there would be no difficulty in that.
The Second Order, which she called the Order of Love, aimed to fix
her straitened finances. The Order of Love would own all the "material amenities of life" and oversee their equitable distribution on the
principle of sharing. This order was to comprise only "women of
grace" with no "ulterior motives." The Third Order would comprise
"men of power who are also men of good will." They were expected
to hand over all their possessions to begin the process of redistribution to the Second Order. Such transactions would be carried out
between men and women in a "personal manner" with no outside
interference.

Riding finished writing her conclusions and outlining her plans for
a woman-centered system of government in London at 6:00 A.M. on
March 26, 1938, ten days after Chamberlain's equivocal foreign
policy speech concerning what he termed the "distressing" Anschluss
of Austria by German troops. That afternoon, after a special lunch
with James Reeves and his new wife, Laura presided over the first
meeting of the Council of the Inside People. The purpose of the
convocation was to decide on "moral action to be taken by inside

people: for outside disorders." Her half-hour speech was followed by comments from everyone present. Out of this meeting, which took place at 31 Alma Square in London, the Covenant of Literal Morality came into being. That night Laura slept for fifteen hours.

Over the next few months so many people came and went from Alma Square that they wore a track in the green wall-to-wall carpet from the door to Laura's desk. During the day she was constantly on the phone; at night she dictated dozens of letters, routinely at work until 4:00 or 5:00 A.M., kept awake with hand-rolled cigarettes and coffee. Working night and day with her associates, she drafted the "Covenant of Literal Morality," which later became known as the First Protocol. In its twenty-six articles Riding outlined the initial stage of "Judgement of Evil," and an ultimatum calling for a "moral war on evil." With its subsequent endorsement by twenty-eight of her close friends and artistic collaborators, she had the beginnings— the "fighting apparatus"—of her new moral order.

It is hard to avoid a note of incredulity in considering Riding's hopeful plans for reorienting and reeducating the world along essentially matriarchal lines. The "Personal Letter," *The World and Ourselves,* and, most of all, the "Covenant of Literal Morality" are bewildering documents; Riding's ambitions were outstripped only by her raw ingenuousness and, presumably, faith that she would prevail. Perhaps it was an index of the fear and confusion of the times that *The World and Ourselves* was one of the few books by Riding seriously and comprehensively considered in the *Times Literary Supplement.* The *Bookseller* compared it with Aldous Huxley's *Ends and Means; Time and Tide* considered it alongside a book published by Mass Observation, another popular movement that attempted to address the divide between ordinary people and the political machinery of government and diplomacy. As "anthropologists of British culture" Mass Observers were instructed to take detailed "scientific" notes on "the soggy mess of public opinion" as it exhibited itself in daily life. Naomi Mitchison was one of the participants.

But one thing set Riding's mission apart from other formulas for salvation, world peace, or self-improvement: the uncompromising ugliness of the language in which she chose to bring her cause to the masses. In contrast to the eloquence of Churchill's Albert Hall "Arms and the Covenant" speech, her covenant was impressive for scrupulous avoidance of stirring rhetoric. In an essay for the *Spectator*, Dorothy Sayers described Riding's call to arms as "a high-falutin version of the kind of thing we are accustomed to get in political manifestos and deliberations of borough councils":

> It is written in words most of which may, I dare say, be found in the dictionary, and its syntax, though clumsy here and there, is not scandalously corrupt. But for all that it is not English; it is not language at all; it is abracadabra— a hypnotic rumble of stupefying polysyllables.

During the three months of sifting and weighing the articles of the First Protocol, Laura had hit upon certain words—"revive" was one, "enthusiasm" another—that struck her with unusual force. "All the good words," Robert agreed, had become "either stiff or tainted."

Not long after the first Covenant meeting, the word "literal" came into this focus. Suddenly "literal" became the catchall to be found on every endorser's lips. With Maisie, Laura discussed literalism as it touched on education; with Honor she explored a literal approach to novels. Julian Symons was subjected to a "literal criticism" of his poems, which involved severe questioning of his use of the word "hypoteneuse." Though Robert noted in his diary that Symons behaved decently during the session, Symons himself recalled the experience with chagrin:

> "What you really meant to say in this verse," [Riding] would say, "was . . ." Had I meant to say just that? I did not feel sure of it, but her own certainty was impressive. When I raised objections she was ready for me. "But don't you see that what you are saying now is inconsistent with your opening lines? They say one thing and now you are saying another. There is a confusion of thought." . . . As we went on talking, I was conscious of an increasing area of disagreement . . . [I]n my memory we stayed fixed in our positions for this hour and a half like flies in ice, she enforcing the thrust of her voice by occasional darting

glances from her dark eyes and producing on me rather the effect of the Wicked Queen in *Snow White*, I making occasional play with my beer.

On May 4, 1938, Laura discussed literalism in painting with John Aldridge and demanded of his friend, another painter who had come with him, how he could possibly square his homosexuality with "literal morality." He had not worked it out, Robert commented in his diary. Someday, Laura wrote to James Reeves, they must both sit down and get the "music problem" clear; "literal" seemed to provide the key to this difficulty as well. During the drafting of the Protocol, Riding was so fiercely attuned to the meanings of words that she passed Robert on a London sidewalk without recognizing him.

In the spring of 1938 Riding had turned her attention to novels, painting, music, and public morality because she had already written the last of her published poems. Both she and Robert had begun compiling editions of their collected work the year before. Riding had finished hers in Surrey before they moved back to London. Particularly in two poems written in Surrey, "Doom in Bloom" and "Seizure of the World," Riding seemed to be drafting an ending not only to the world but also to her life's work. While their message of impending doom and impending salvation was familiar, she was almost perfunctory about the theme; literalism and abstraction had replaced more elaborate poetic strategies and imagery. In doing so she disregarded her own warning, written in 1925 before she left for England: "a poet outside his poem is messianic."

In the preface to her *Collected Poems*, which one reviewer described as a kind of Newtonian *Principia* of poetry, Riding haughtily defended this new direction as being the first step out of the ashes of a dying romantic tradition, which she described as having only dreamed of a future in which their lives would be pure poetry, pure truth. "But these are other days," she wrote in July 1937. "These are days for neither dispute nor dreaming, but for poetry positive, poetry actual." The times demanded that poetry at last speak without guile, wit, or decoration. In this insistence, she struck an old romantic note; plain speech alone was the speech of truth. Imagery or any sort of rhetoric at all could not be trusted to carry truth simply, directly—and, inevitably, "literally."

"Literalism" was the culminating ideology of a line of thought that would lead to Riding's renunciation of poetry. Most of the poems written in the late 1930s were tailored to this simple and perfectly self-destructive conception. Ironically, the more clearly she articulated her critical philosophy of simplicity, clarity, and literalness, the more obscure her poetry became. That "literalism" did not come close to "explaining" her most important work now seems irrelevant; the lasting impression of Riding as a cerebral, abstract, and obscure poet testifies to the success of her critical rhetoric. "Miss Riding has few equals," Dudley Fitts remarked, "when it comes to browbeating an audience into conviction by sheer force of arrogance, among any poets living or dead." Riding had long applied such arts of persuasion to herself as well. As early as 1933 she had written "Lines in Short Despite in Time":

> Forgive me, giver, if I destroy the gift!
> It is so nearly what would please me,
> I cannot but perfect it.

The gift that she finally destroyed was her own.

———◦∞◦———

In June 1938, soon after finishing her corrections to the proofs of *The Left Heresy in Literature and Life*, Laura and Robert decamped once again, this time for Brittany. They were to be joined by Alan Hodge and his new wife, Beryl; a sculptress named Dorothy Simmons; and James Reeves' younger brother David, who was working with Laura on a book about furniture-making. Though Laura had written to the *Times* castigating their lack of editorial comment on the violent persecution of Vienna's Jews, she had little sense of the personal danger that she might face by traveling to France in an increasingly hostile Europe. However, soon after they had decided on their destination, she had her second dream about Adolf Hitler.

In the dream she and some friends were joined by Hitler in a game in which one person was to think up a subject for a picture and another was made to draw it. Laura was to give Hitler his subject, but before she could tell him what it was he gleefully proposed drawing a huge flood. She promptly scolded him, saying no, she would provide him a subject; she told him to draw "a moment of complete private happiness." At first this stumped him, Laura wrote to James, but then his eyes lit up and he shouted, "Followed by universal disaster!" This idea so excited him that he asked permission to lie down on Laura's bed to plan it. At that point Karl spoke up worriedly, "I don't like him lying on your bed."

Having fallen in love with another housemaid, Karl remained behind in England when Robert and Laura went off to France. He had yet to sign the Protocol because, he confessed, he did not understand it. On June 30, 1938, Laura and Robert docked at St. Malo with Alan and Beryl, to be followed by the others. Three months later Chamberlain, returned from Munich, would stand at the window of 10 Downing Street and proclaim to the cheering crowd below, "peace with honor . . . peace for our time."

Chapter 20

LE CHÂTEAU DE LA CHEVRIE

—— • ——

Laura had a dream. "Shut all the windows, there's going to be a storm."

—Robert's diary, January 26, 1939

—— • ——

IN THE YEARS that she had lived with Robert, Laura had often thought about returning with him to America for a visit. In 1939 she was thirty-eight and had not seen her half sister, Isabel, since her suicide attempt ten years earlier; she had put off a visit from her father to Deyá in 1935 with the promise that she would soon be coming to California. But there had always been some reason to postpone the trip or to choose a destination closer to certain and secure friendships, like Schwarz and Strenge in Lugano or Anita, Gelat's daughter and her husband, Juan, in Britanny. Anita had sent them word of Gelat's release and kept them apprised of life under curate rule in Deyá. Their reunion in Rennes was warm, accompanied by a festive meal of wine, Mallorquin *sobresadas*, olives, and pimientos. Still, even after they rented a small château in the countryside from the countess de Kerouallan, the idea of returning to America would not go away for very long.

In the parlor of the château of La Chevrie, just outside Montauban-de-Bretagne, twenty miles west of Rennes, were large oil murals, darkened by age and lantern soot. The parlor itself was crowded with Breton ornaments, settees, and elaborately carved couches and tea tables. High oak-beamed ceilings and stone-tiled floors added to the atmosphere of forbidding if damp grandeur. But it was the oil murals of French village scenes that seemed to populate the 300-year-old house with the ghosts of an older world. Above the fireplace mantel, a startled deer eluded five men and two ladies on horseback, and an equally terrified rabbit dodged hounds in hot pursuit; on another wall shy village women convened at a crossroads to meet farmers returning from the fields. When it was warm enough Laura and her entourage would gather in the parlor or "painted room" for bedtime tea, playing seven and a half or word games. Mostly, however, Laura stayed alone in her bedroom or study, working steadily until the early hours of the morning.

Despite his stubborn faith that war might be averted by Laura's efforts, and that her call for a new moral law was gaining ground, Robert was uneasy about being back in France amid the rumors and the fear of Hitler's advancing armies. His diary followed the civil war in Spain closely and noted many ominous auguries, including otherworldly ones. He dwelled at length upon the various infestations of vermin that besieged them on their arrival at La Chevrie. A bat in Laura's bedroom on their first night was only the harbinger of an onslaught from the attic rafters. When they lit the fire in the parlor, a cloud of angry bees descended from the flue; thousands more swarmed out the chimney and billowed into the rooms. For days half-singed bees were found crawling everywhere. A kitten named Nono, enlisted to chase the mice, rats, and bats, would emerge downstairs maddened and wild after feasting on them in the attic. Birds tried desperately to get in at the windows, and crickets chirped in remote corners of the house. Fleas invaded the bedclothes, and late one night in the kitchen Robert absentmindedly answered "yes?" to a voice that addressed him as Marthe. "The kitchen ghost Beryl already knows," Robert wrote in his diary, "it left an old-fashioned poker on the stove; which disappeared when she touched it."

There were other signs of things amiss. On the evidence of the poems that Graves wrote in London, the stage for the drama of the Graves-Riding relationship seemed to have undergone a scene change; as Riding's poetry had divested itself of all but the most transparent images, Graves' imagery and metaphorical props grew increasingly obscure, emotionally disturbing, and nightmarish. In "A

Jealous Man" a man with a "dream-enlarged" mind stumbles down a darkened country lane, haunted by ghastly visions:

> A score of bats bewitched
> By the ruttish odour
> Swoop swinging at his head;
>
> Nuns bricked up alive
> Within the neighbouring wall
> Wail in cat-like longing.
>
> Crow, cocks, crow loud,
> Reprieve the doomed devil—
> Has he not died enough?
>
> Now, out of careless sleep,
> She wakes and greets him coldly,
> The woman at home,
>
> She, with private wonder
> At shoes bemired and bloody—
> His war was not hers.

The sudden loss of the habitual daily rhythms and comforts of Deyá had left Robert increasingly on his own, prey to the disturbing images of war and the accompanying threat of madness. "Nuns bricked up alive" may have referred to the numerous newspaper reports of Left atrocities against the Catholic clergy in Spain. At the same time, Riding's involvement with the Protocol and the work of her associates had never been so intensive; he recognized, perhaps for the first time, that "his war was not hers." There was also something desperate and poignant about his rummaging in the crowded bins of Albert Mills' antique shop. Among the dozens of items he purchased during his stay in England were Bristol bowls and vases, an ivory paper cutter, a Georgian corkscrew, Venetian glass ornaments, pin cushions, butter presses, bobbin beads, tortoiseshell combs, watch lockets, and even a Chinese ostrich-egg stand carved from a coconut shell. However many fragments he shored against the ruins, Graves could not quite trick himself into believing that Laura could prevent the next catastrophe awaiting Europe. His correspondence with Mr. Mills continued in France; Mr. Mills was even invited to sign the Protocol.

To distract himself, Robert continued to be Laura's noisiest supporter. In this, he had solicited Nancy once more for backing, hoping that his newly warmed friendship with her and his children might underwrite his doubts. But Nancy knew a different Laura than Robert's and refused to accede to a friendship that smacked of the Trinity. She wrote to him that she would be friends with Laura on her own and that she wished he would stop "putting Laura, L, L, L," in all his letters:

> Isn't it an insult to Laura to go on rubbing her in? Or do you see it quite differently? But if L knew she'd think it was. I know L— & I know she's true. Its very like being told Christ, C, C, C, all through one's childhood so one never reads the Bible. . . .

From Laura's next letter to Nancy it appears that Robert had misrepresented the reasons for Nancy's not agreeing to closer contacts between the three again. When he got to France, Robert wrote to his wife and asked for a divorce, suggesting that she might charge him with desertion because, he added gloomily, "it would be difficult for me to prove legally that my relations with Laura were not what they are not."

Robert was used to finding consolation and escape from loneliness and privation by writing, but after his *Collected Poems* and his fictionalized biography *Count Belisarius* went off to the publishers, he was without a book of his own to fall back on. Work on a ghost story begun in Switzerland with Laura now limped listlessly along, as did a dramatic treatment of *A Trojan Ending*. He also provided historical notes for Laura's use in *Lives of Wives*, as he had done for the Troy novel. Consequently, Robert's major task at La Chevrie was one that had been simmering on Laura's back burner for some time.

The idea for this book had been around since 1932 as part of Laura's series of books for a children's university; in 1933 she and Jacob Bronowski had never gotten beyond the planning stages. The original specifications for the project, first entitled *Dictionary of Exact Meanings* before being changed in November 1938 to *Dictionary of*

Related Meanings, called for 24,000 crucial words of the English language to be defined in such a way as to erase any ambiguity that might have accrued to them over years of improper usage. Getting things "clear" became Riding's new ultimatum, and Graves initially joined her with enthusiasm. When Oxford University Press turned down the proposal, telling Riding that her approach was "too individual and personal" and that she could not put words "into straightjackets," Graves saw it as yet another example of the "tolerance of illiterates for the sake of lexicographical richness."

At La Chevrie, Robert and Alan began the dictionary work in earnest, sorting up to 100 words a day into categories for Laura to approve and, once she had finished *Lives of Wives,* compose definitions for. But Robert's initial enthusiasm was short-lived; he found himself staring disconsolately at the word-group labeled "minutiae and smithereens," and chafing over Alan's "thin skin." Dictionary work was not likely to engage his imagination, and though this in itself was hardly a new experience for him, after London and the endless discussions over the drafting of the Protocol, he had grown increasingly restive at Laura's assignments. He was even more frustrated by the needy crowd surrounding Laura, particularly Montague and Dorothy Simmons whose marital problems Laura was expected to straighten out and clarify. It was about this time that Robert's heart first lit on the slip of a girl he knew as Beryl or, as Laura had christened her, "Woolworth."

Alan Hodge had first met Beryl Pritchard at Oxford where, at the Society of Home Students (now St. Anne's), she was studying politics, philosophy, and economics. They became close friends. Raised in Hampstead, in north London, Beryl was the fifth child of a distinguished and respected London solicitor, one of a pair of twins. Her initial interest in the humanities (she had a keen appreciation of poetry) had quickly been overtaken by more pressing concerns; H.G.D. Coles' lectures on socialism steered her toward the Oxford University Labour Club and leftist politics. Her concern for the "common man" was, however, equal parts curiosity. Though she distributed leaflets at factories and was well informed in world affairs, Beryl never joined any political party. Instead, after leaving Oxford she wandered from the life path of the privileged to take a secretarial course. During the Christmas season of 1937 she worked in the

Oxford Street branch of Woolworth's as a shop assistant—hence Laura's nickname.

Beryl's parents were greatly distressed at her uncertain career and early engagement to Alan; they felt that she was throwing her life away. Though Beryl herself had had doubts about marrying Alan, she relented in the face of his certainty. Unlike most of those surrounding Laura, Beryl was entirely lacking in artistic ambitions. She was more apt to be distracted by the plight of others than intent on a destiny and a literary sinecure for herself.

Still, this guaranteed no refuge from Laura's all-seeing, all-knowing eye—particularly since Alan, superseding James, had become her closest protégé, and she naturally appointed herself guardian of his affairs. In the shadow of Laura's commandeering intelligence, Beryl, however, was only imperfectly appropriated. In London, Robert's diary for June 1937 mentioned an incident of apparent rudeness on Beryl's part toward Laura, but not long after that, Laura wrote to Alan of her dream in which Beryl's manner with her had improved; in the excitement of behaving so well, Beryl's hair had fluffed out. Perhaps somewhat diffident in the face of Beryl's quietly unassuming manner, Laura did not ask her to sign the Protocol. Instead, Beryl took over Karl's secretarial duties in Brittany, taking dictation and typing letters to the Protocol's endorsers back in England.

Many of these letters, particularly during the late September crisis that followed the Anglo-French surrender to Hitler over the Sudetenland, were intended to reassure Protocol signers that there would be no war; somehow Laura felt that her letters would diffuse not only the anxieties of friends back in London but also the war hysteria of Hitler and Chamberlain as well. Regrettably, Laura wrote Karl, such work still remained invisible among the comings and goings on in Downing Street. On September 24, 1938, Robert wrote dutifully in his diary, "We do not expect war in any serious sense."

Still, there was general disgust at La Chevrie over Munich, as if Chamberlain had lost an opportunity not to declare war but to denounce Hitler as evil and, in the manner of "the old Jehovah," bring about divine retribution. On September 28, just before Hitler's ultimatum to the Czechs expired and while Chamberlain was conferring with Mussolini, Laura speculated in a letter to James Reeves on just what divine instruments might be available to them to rout the evil designs of "Germanic fury." Such instruments were available in modern, secular form, she believed, though how to get one's hands on them was uncertain. Three days later she wrote a poem entitled "When the Skies Part"; it was never published.

Robert, meanwhile, heard from his elder son David that if war broke out he would enlist, an eventuality that must have deepened his anxiety, however much he wanted to believe Laura's assurances. Without Nancy or his children, without even Albert Mills' bric-a-brac or the ventriloquial escape into imperial Roman life, Robert was inescapably confronted with the realization of his worst fears. While his daily diary entries conscientiously mention Laura's headaches, pronouncements on the war, and work—"difficulty with Aristotle, spends all day writing George Buchanan about novels"—one can see from them that Laura was less and less a part of his thoughts.

This was partly due to Laura's isolation from the daily life of La Chevrie. Where Robert chopped wood, cleaned the kitchen, filled the kerosene lamps, and kept the bicycles maintained, Laura merely supervised the local women who came in to cook. Alan was given the clock-windup detail, grounds clearing, and lavatories; Beryl, apart from typing, did the shopping and saw that the cupboards were stocked. Dorothy Simmons and David Reeves also had their duties. Laura would occasionally join them in the parlor for games, but she was generally awake while others slept, rarely leaving the warmth of her study or bedroom for their walks or errands in Montauban or Rennes.

In contrast, the appearances of Beryl in Robert's diary are taken at sly angles: Beryl wins 100 francs at the races; Beryl invents a parlor game of solitaire; Beryl becomes "possessive" about a black kitten, which creates a "contretemps." Robert counts Beryl's typing mistakes on Laura's manuscript, and after chastising her for not keeping the key machinery free of dust, he cleans her typewriter; they have a "tiff." A long entry is devoted to the fate of a wounded hedgehog, rescued and cared for by Beryl. Finally, Robert even gives Beryl a manuscript of a poem that he has written, telling her to destroy it. Here, at last, was an enigmatic subject to fathom over the stirring of a cauldron of preserves in the large La Chevrie kitchen. Here was a loving story to tell. "Frankly," Robert asked Beryl, "are you bored with the stirring?"

"No, not frankly."

SCHUYLER BRINCKERHOFF JACKSON II was most definitely "Ivy": born on August 18, 1900, in Bernardsville, New Jersey, he came from old money. However ambivalent he may have felt later about his privileged background, Schuyler was shaped by an upright and almost Puritanical code of honor ingrained in him by his father, a wealthy businessman named Phylip Nye Jackson. At Pomfret, an exclusive prep school in Connecticut, Schuyler had been a varsity athlete, star quarterback, and baseball pitcher. At Princeton he was invited to join Ivy, its most exclusive eating club. There too, he discovered poetry, not in the lecture hall (he was too busy reading to attend classes) but on his own. He mastered Latin, Greek, Italian, and French and began to wear glasses. He dominated the literary society, the Tuesday Evening Club, with impassioned recitals of "true" poetry. He played Samson in a *théâtre intime* production of Milton's *Samson Agonistes*. A photograph taken at this time shows his open, dark eyes minus spectacles engaging the camera with a challenging glare, his black hair swept back from a wide and smooth forehead.

In his last year at Princeton, Schuyler was "discovered" by the arch-Georgian poet J. C. Squire. Upon his graduation, Squire invited him to live in Boar's Hill at Oxford, write for his magazine the *London Mercury*, and meet the circle of poets who lived nearby. (Graves had just removed himself from that neighborhood to live in Islip.) Schuyler's first article was on W. B. Yeats, whom he traveled to Dublin to meet and interview. So instant was their rapport that Yeats presented him before the Irish parliament as the next great American poet— without having read any of his work. While in England, Schuyler also met the widow of his true idol, Charles M. Doughty, author of *Travels in Arabia Deserta*. But despite the rich welcome from the Boar's Hill circle, and the prospect of a well-received literary career, Schuyler was back in America within six months, hopeful of starting a press that would discover and encourage young American writers, poets mostly. The Open Road Press was founded soon after he returned, and after sending out his manifesto, he enlisted Robert Frost, Hervey Allen, Vachel Lindsay, and Edgar Lee Masters to be on the board of directors. But, despite a promising start across the country in a station wagon, he never found the poets who, he was convinced, awaited him in the American heartland. He then tried his hand at a number of businesses before buying a farm outside of New Hope, Pennsylvania, about twenty miles due west of Princeton. He never published another poem. In January 1939 the *Princeton Alumni News* described Schuyler as a "gentleman farmer" who specialized in raising walnuts. "Our guess is that he has found something that grows slowly enough to allow time for his job as poetry reviewer for *Time*."

Had Schuyler not gone to Princeton with an inveterate memoirist, little would be known about him. Soon after it had occurred to Tom Matthews that Schuyler's farm was failing, he found a nominal post for him as poetry reviewer for *Time*. Because *Time* published few reviews of poetry, Schuyler's responsibility was primarily as a reader. Tom had first talked about Schuyler to Laura on his visit to Deyá in 1932. Whenever Tom felt that he was getting into deep water with her, he insisted that it was Schuyler who should have come to Deyá; Schuyler was the man Laura should meet.

Perhaps it was Tom's incessant praise of Laura to Schuyler, and Schuyler to Laura, that made their initial introduction, via the mails, so awkward. Early in 1933 Laura invited Schuyler to write something on "Money and Economics" for *Epilogue*, having heard from Tom of his involvement in Major Clifford Hugh Douglas' theories of social credit. The economic doctrine developed by this Cambridge engineer and social economist had also attracted the garrulous support of Ezra Pound. Schuyler's answer had greatly displeased her; she not only thought it insulting but also judged him to be, in his essential flippancy, a prototypical American. She found his reference to fairy tales (apparently he had brought "Jack and the Beanstalk" and colored beans into his economic analysis) entirely disrespectful. Almost three months later she received an answer. Refusing to be baited, Schuyler mixed sarcasm with slyness, and sent her elaborate thanks for the persistence with which she had pursued their differences. Perhaps, he ventured, this would prepare the ground for future understandings, rather than more fruitless arguments. Riding let the matter drop. There had never been a misunderstanding between them, she told Tom, because there had never been an understanding.

Five years later Schuyler declined to respond to Laura's "Personal Letter, with a Request for a Reply," but the seeds of a better understanding had begun to sprout; he and his wife were among the

American endorsers of the First Protocol. On December 10, 1938, the day the drunken postman delivered a thick batch of letters to La Chevrie (without, this time, falling off his bicycle), Schuyler made his first appearance in Robert's diary. Along with long letters from John Aldridge and Isabel, the postman brought a friendly one from him. Laura, who had been feeling depressed and ill, found that the day had been given "color."

A few days before she had written a long and thoughtfully affectionate letter to Karl in an attempt to answer his question, "What next?" She spoke of the cause of her illness and depression as something deeply private, impossible to talk about because no one could understand. While she had, on rare occasions, shared some of her disquiet with him, it was inevitable that, despite all her work to keep hope alive in others, she would eventually have to acknowledge that there was no "what next." She told Karl not to worry if he did not understand what she meant; by writing it, she herself began to understand.

But "What next?" would not go away; the strain of watching and wondering in an uncertain Europe made the news from America and the letters from the Jacksons and the Matthewses seem all the more fresh, innocent, and untouched by the fears choking Europe. Even the five points of the U.S. Senate's foreign affairs agenda, expressing disapproval over the conduct of government in Germany and Japan, gave Laura pleasure. Her hopes were further encouraged when she heard from Random House that her *Collected Poems* was slated for a lead review in *Time* magazine. Though Riding's critical works and novels had been brought out by Doubleday, Doran and by Random House, this was the first collection of her poems to appear in America since *The Close Chaplet* was published by Adelphi in 1926. Tom, as book editor, had invited Schuyler to do a survey of recent books of poetry.

The day after she heard from Random House, Laura had news that her father was dead. She had planned for years to visit him, she wrote to Karl in a long letter on a cold and blustery Christmas Eve. In a telling description, she wrote that his intransigence and single-mindedness had been key to his survival. Nathan's death provoked an even keener melancholy and wistfulness about the country that she had been so quick to abandon exactly thirteen years before.

But it was Schuyler's review of her poems, which arrived at La Chevrie on January 3, 1939, that finally put America firmly on Laura's itinerary. It was quietly acknowledged that Tom had an "editorial" hand in writing the review, but nonetheless Schuyler Jackson had at last come into full view. The review began by stating *Time's* responsibility, in the face of overwhelming public indifference, to take new books of poetry seriously. "As *Time* sees it," Schuyler began,

> [P]oets acknowledge a responsibility which sooner or later every human being must acknowledge. That responsibility, stated in its humblest form, is to make words make sense: stated in its most ambitious form, it is to make words make complete sense . . . For the poets' effort to make words make sense is an effort to make the thing on which all human communication—letter-writing, conversation, journalism, literature—ultimately depends. To the extent that poets fulfill their poethood they are making human communication more possible. To the extent that poets lapse . . . they are perverting or muddling human communication.

Schuyler divided the eleven poets covered in his review into a *Time*-ese scale of poets, poetasters, or poeticules. Only Riding and Rainer Maria Rilke were accorded the status of true poets.

The clipping was passed around the dining room table for comments. Robert, writing that night to Karl, found "it really brave of them to print anything as strong as that in a magazine of 700,000 subscriptions." Dorothy, perhaps still upset at the stone bust of Laura that she had recently been forced to destroy, was more skeptical: "I think the man's in love with you," she said. Such a "vulgar" thought brought a sharp rebuke from Laura.

The language in which Laura could begin to consider the possibility of such a love was a great deal more opaque, etiolated, and roundabout, at least in its public dress. Within a week of receiving Schuyler's review, Laura began work on the Second Protocol, which would call on those endorsers of the First Protocol to pledge themselves to the Common Obligations of Friendship. To Karl, Laura described the new closeness in her American friendships with more directness. Her half sister, who had borne most of the responsibility for Nathan's care, had recently become acutely precious to her. She also felt newly close to Tom and Julie, who had agreed to spend $25,000 restoring a derelict stone cottage on Schuyler's farm so that they might have a place to stay in America. And finally, through their letters, there were Schuyler and "Katharine," which was Laura's name for Kit, Schuyler's wife. Laura imagined her a dreamy beauty; Schuyler arresting and direct. They, too, had become indispensable to her. But it was to John Aldridge that Laura came closest to confiding all. She had quit smoking because the inevitable was about to happen: the "intimate omen" of ultimate happiness that she had been waiting for had arrived. She was not specific, but John doubtless knew what she intended.

Even the fall of Barcelona, the republican stronghold in Spain, did not long distract her from these affections; the city had been too corrupt with Catalan contentiousness to stand as their public emblem of the good. She had become increasingly impatient with those, like the Catalans, who thought themselves on the side of the just; it was they who deserved punishment stiff enough to make them rediscover themselves and their values. Robert agreed, writing Karl that "the Catalans have deserved their humiliation." Laura wrote to Chatto and Windus, publisher of *The World and Ourselves* in London, about the possibility of a "stinging advertisement"; her impatience with the Catalans extended easily to the foot-dragging "inside people."

In February 1939, with reservations to embark for America in late April, Laura gave the Spanish situation two months to resolve. If the war was finished by then, they would return to Deyá; if not, they would proceed with their plans for America. She had an inkling that it would be America, she confided to Karl. Robert, on the other hand, still hoped desperately to return to Deyá, writing to Karl that the signs from Spain were promising "in a perverse way." If they won, the Fascists would not last long, Robert ventured, even if supported by Italy and Germany.

Amid these discussions Laura celebrated her thirty-eighth birthday. She asked to be given no presents, and in keeping with the Second Protocol each of La Chevrie's residents wrote her a letter. She was also presented with an azalea, white flowers, and chocolate-covered peppermints. Robert's birthday letter to her was entitled

"The Hostage" (later "Dawn Bombardment"); like Laura's poem
"March, 1937" it mixed the metaphors of war with more private ones.
The plight of captured hostages, marooned in enemy shelters awaiting rescue by advancing troops, becomes a dramatic analogue not
only for Graves' own predicament at La Chevrie but for Laura's
as well:

> Guns from the sea open against us:
> The smoke rocks bodily in the casemate
> And a yell of doom goes up.
> We count and bless each new, heavy concussion—
> Captives awaiting rescue.
>
> Visiting angel of the wild-fire hair
> Who in dream reassured us nightly
> Where we lay fettered,
> Laugh at us, as we wake—our faces
> So tense with hope the tears run down.

The dream of the visiting angel would have reminded Laura quite
pointedly of her approving dream of the well-behaved Beryl topped
by her halo of "fluffy hair." This image, and the circumstances in
which the poem was offered to Laura, suggest that Robert was asking
her to share his faith in the balm that Beryl provided him and to see
in her quiet ministerings the holy sign that they had so long awaited.
He had to wait longer for her answer.

On February 27, Laura secured reservations on the *Paris*, bound for
New York from Le Havre via Southampton on April 19. That same
day everyone at La Chevrie felt a great political change occurring:
"We all feel something cracking," Robert wrote in his diary. From
England Robert's niece Sally wrote that war was very near, but to him
"this [made] no sense." Two days later, on March 1, Robert had his
reply to "The Hostage"; March 1, Laura decided, was the "world's
birthday," and she ordered everyone to prepare a party.

In her answer to Robert's poem Laura would not accept his metaphor of the besieged fortress and the hostages, nor did she make
direct reference to his angelic vision of Beryl. Instead, she insisted that
the guns he heard from the fortress were his own; Robert had for too

long affected powerlessness. It was time to fire his guns, to "Get them all shot off." Only after his shots were "spent" could he use the fortress windows for looking out of. That night the world's birthday was celebrated with bottles of champagne, and Robert wrote a long letter to Schuyler Jackson before retiring to bed. The next day, on a long walk with Alan, they discussed Laura "as a focus for love among us."

IN THE FEW weeks preceding their departure, Laura, having finished *Lives of Wives*, took time out from supervising the packing and cleaning to discuss the relationships between everyone at La Chevrie and their possible activities in America. Montague Simmons, she felt, had shown vast improvement in his character; Dorothy less so. David Reeves had returned to England but was expected to join them on the boat at Southampton. Dorothy would come later. There was a four-day period of long talks about respective relationships between "joulting pig" or "swingering swine" men and "two-in-hand" or "one-in-the-bush" women. This was Laura's new system (devised by Lucie Brown) for determining character matches between men and women. Robert was having difficulty understanding the difference between "joulting" and "swingering" and perhaps, too, what these male aspects portended for his growing affection for Beryl.

As part of her tidying, Laura gave things away—clothes brushes, spare necklaces, odd items. A Christmas gift of purple spangles from Honor, who had drifted away from Laura after falling in love with Laura's *14A* collaborator George Ellidge, went to a French neighbor. Karl, who visited for a weekend from London, where he was working in a bookstore, got a ring. To him it seemed that Laura was giving away everything. New endorsers for the First Protocol continued being interviewed by old endorsers; that weekend Karl finally relented and signed the Protocol. He would never see Laura again. Others, including Maisie Somerville, dropped out. On March 28 a letter came from Norman telling Laura to count him out of the Protocol and the trip to America. Madrid fell the same day; Valencia, the next. With that the Spanish civil war ended.

As if in consolation, the weather suddenly turned gorgeous, the bare winter trees softened by buds of color. "No need to feel guilty about good weather," Beryl commented while on a walk with Robert;

he picked a flower for her. In the final days before leaving La Chevrie, even Laura left her study to take walks in the sunshine. The cherry blossoms seemed to fill them all with hope that everything would turn out right in the end.

"After So Much Loss" was, perhaps, written in a similarly promising Deyá spring, close on the arrival of the first primroses. Riding had always had an equivocal relationship with nature; in her earliest unpublished poems she upheld the gritty urban cityscapes over the gentle finery of nature or the time-locked rites of seasonal passage. She satirized the pastoral lyric with unforgiving wit. In the portrayal of spring in this poem, however, Riding captured a more profound music. She invoked, too, the longing and loneliness that she had nurtured since losing the love of Geoffrey Phibbs:

> After so much loss—
> Seeming of gain,
> Seeming of loss—
> Subsides the swell of indignation
> To the usual rhythm of the year.
>
> The coward primroses are up,
> We contract their profuse mildness.
> Women with yet a few springs to live
> Clutch them in suppliant bouquets
> On the way to relatives,
> Who, no, do not begrudge
> This postponement of funerals.
> And, oh, how never tired, and tired,
> The world of primroses, how spring
> The bended spirit fascinates
> With promise of revival,
> Leaving more honest summer to proclaim
> That this is all—a brighter disappointment—
> Time has to give to an implacable
> Persuasion of things lost, wrongly.

For Riding, this was the logic of the seasons: the spring's promise of love and the betrayal of its hot sequel, the "brighter disappointment" of summer. It was against this fateful cycle of the earth that Riding, in the furious and hungry life of her heart, would always rebel:

> Is it to wonder, then,
> That we defy the unsuspecting moment,
> Release our legs from the year's music,
> And, to the reckless strum of hate,
> Dance—grinding from primroses the tears
> They never of themselves would have shed?
> None dances whom no hate stirs,
> Who has not lost and loathed the loss,
> Who does not feel deprived.

In Riding's work, the balance between the fragility of her sensibility and the strength of her anger and intellect is often unsteady. For the close of "After So Much Loss," however, she achieves the "difficult decorum" that will always mark the greatness of her work:

> After so much loss,
> The hate will out, the dance be on,
> And many of their rage fall down.
> It is easy as spring to yield to the year,
> And easy as dance to break with the year,
> But to go with the year in partition
> Between seeming loss, seeming gain,
> That is the difficult decorum.
> Nor are the primroses unwelcome.

———

The car arrived at 4:00 A.M. to take Robert and Laura to Le Havre; their luggage had gone on ahead via American Express, to be loaded onto the *Paris*, the same ship that had brought Laura to England thirteen years before. En route they stopped off for coffee in "pont-Something" Robert wrote, where they learned of a terrible fire aboard the docked ship—another omen, perhaps, for him to mull over. The luggage was safe, however, and after a night at the Hotel Bordeaux in Le Havre, they embarked on the *Champlain* at 11:00 A.M. on April 21, 1939. In Southampton they said good-bye to Alan and

Beryl, who would join them in America within a few weeks. By early evening Laura Riding had seen the last of the coast of Devon.

As dawn rose on the morning of April 28 after an uneventful voyage, the harbor lights of New York City came into view. On the French Line pier at the foot of West 15th Street waiting to meet them were Tom and Julie Matthews, Kit and Schuyler Jackson. Laura Riding had come home.

Chapter 21

NEW HOPE

—— • ——

The old ruin across the road which is on Jackson's Farm has been rebuilt to a lovely little stone house in which shall live Miss Laura Riding, Mr. Robert Graves, Mr. David Reeves, Mr. Allan Hodge and Mrs. Bearal Hodge. All famous writers from England.

Mrs. Jackson is in the hospital, sick, in Philadelphia.

Miss Riding's sister is here also.

Mr. Jackson is harvesting his soy bean.

Miss Laura Riding and Mr. Frank Baisden are new subscribers to this magazine.

Some of the English People had to leave the farm and return to fight in the war.

—*Jackson Quarterly*

—— • ——

THE JACKSON FARM was on Brownsburg Road, about five miles south of New Hope, Pennsylvania. The White House was hidden until the last possible moment, its front porch leaping out of a screen of oak and fir trees just after a bend in the unpaved and pockmarked road. The main part of the handsome three-story stucco house was almost a perfect square box with a flat roof; at night its windows were lit up by kerosene lanterns. The dining room and kitchen were part of a clapboard extension at the back, facing the fields. The property also had a large stone barn, numerous sheds, pens, and outbuildings that housed pigeons, rabbits, chickens, pigs, sheep, and a milking cow. Beyond the barns and sheds was a pre-Revolutionary house where the Owles, a Cherokee family who worked on the farm, lived. At one time the White House had been a rooming house; the outbuildings had once housed circus animals. When the Jackson family arrived in 1929, the elephant house was still standing.

Across the road stood the stone house that Laura had already named Nimrod's Rise. Built on the site of a stone ruin, in preparation for her arrival, the house was one of many investments in the farm that failed to pay off, at least in financial terms. Tom Matthews' $25,000 construction was one measure of his eagerness to have Robert and Laura near him and, more significantly, near Schuyler. Until the construction was completed, Laura and Robert planned to stay in the Matthews' house in Princeton. David Reeves moved in to a room a few doors down from Albert Einstein; toward the end of May, Alan and Beryl arrived and took rooms nearby at the Tiger Inn.

The farm had been bought with the last of Kit Jackson's dowry. Born and raised in Buffalo, Katharine Townsend was the daughter of a successful landscape architect and a voluble and generous-hearted society hostess. When Kit was fifteen the family moved to Brookwood, a huge sprawling estate on the shores of Otsego Lake in Cooperstown, New York. Brookwood was a large establishment; servants, gardeners, chauffeurs, and one adored German governess for the seven children kept it going. In contrast to her sister, who was being groomed to be an opera singer, Kit was tall and somewhat ungainly; at the exclusive boarding school that she attended she preferred sports to studies, and the outdoors to teas. Nonetheless 1920 saw her debut in Chicago, where her family had numerous social connections.

Two years later Schuyler Jackson pulled his Model T Ford station wagon to the side of a Cooperstown road, hoping to camp uninvited in Brookwood's pine forest. Fired with enthusiasm for his cross-country journey in search of new American bards, he found instead Kit, strolling in the rose gardens of the great house. He stayed for two days before resuming his journey; Kit said later she thought him quite handsome. After a few months on the road, he had not found even one poet quite good enough to publish. He turned back to Cooperstown and asked Kit to marry him. On December 29, 1922,

Kit's mother hosted a huge society wedding, with Tom Matthews as best man and a host of Kit's friends from school as bridesmaids. Kit would later remember being disappointed over her honeymoon in Vermont. While she had looked forward to skiing, all Schuyler wanted to do was to read aloud from Charles M. Doughty's *Travels in Arabia Deserta*. From the beginning Schuyler Jackson and Kit Townsend were an unlikely match.

In 1926 Kit was introduced to the philosophy of Georges Gurdjieff by a former mistress of the American lawyer and arts patron John Quinn; this woman encouraged Kit to attend A. R. Orage's weekly lectures on Gurdjieff in New York City. A lapsed follower of Ouspensky, Orage now dispensed Gurdjieff in lecture halls to a motley crowd of followers from whom he pried funds to send to his master in France. Schuyler was at first dismissive. "At the time he was interested in Bible instruction," Kit remembered. "All the new ideas had to come from him." Kit soon went off Gurdjieff, "because I didn't find what I wanted," but in the meantime Schuyler had become possessed by the teachings of this Armenian mystic and former carpet trader. Tom and Julie were recruited to the Orage lectures, which included sessions on how to become a writer. That same year the Open Road Press, which in the four years of its existence had yet to publish a book, was shut down. Kit, two months pregnant with her first child, decamped with Schuyler for Gurdjieff's Institute for the Harmonious Development of Man in France.

In Fontainebleau-Avon, they lived the life of Franciscans in the drafty confines of the château du Prieuré, where Gurdjieff's followers kept to the regimens of Eastern dances and hard labor that he custom-tailored to what he imagined were their particular needs. Gurdjieff insisted that only by such discipline could their souls awaken and escape their mechanical prisons to achieve immortality and serenity; he was fond of addressing his followers as *merde de la merde*. "There were a lot of queer ducks there," Kit recalled. The hefty editors of the *Little Review*, Jane Heap and Margaret Anderson, would sneak off with her to find "proper food."

Schuyler's fascination with Gurdjieff lasted for almost eight years. In 1934, after working with Orage to help spread the word in the United States, he began having doubts. To settle them he sailed again for Fontainebleau and, as Laura told a correspondent in the 1960s, went only so far as to peer through a window at the man. After a moment Gurdjieff looked up and hailed him, but in that exchange Schuyler saw all that was false about Gurdjieff and his teachings. He turned on his heel and went back to America. Later, however, he would blame his wife for getting him involved.

In their ten years at the New Hope farm, Schuyler had steadily suffered losses on various moneymaking schemes. He had tried sheep farming and, ahead of his time, soybean cultivation. In the depths of the depression he tried to launch an antique business dealing exclusively with Early American furniture. His most recent idea was black walnuts; 300 trees were planted by him as an inheritance for his grandchildren. Until the trees matured, he hoped to sell the nuts, though they were proving hard to crack. From the window seat of a third-floor bedroom, his daughter Griselda could watch him storming out into the front yard with his rifle to shoot at the grackles that settled in the treetops. At twelve, Griselda was Schuyler's eldest. She had her father's dark watchful eyes and, of his four children, was most like him. Birds, squirrels, and time would ultimately defeat the black walnut project.

In the busy daily life of the farm during the spring of 1939, there were few outward signs that the farm was failing or that the Jacksons' marriage was troubled. Kit baked peach cobbler in a kitchen full of help, while Schuyler harvested the crops of oat, soybean, and wheat. There was a parrot named Miranda, turtles, goldfish, and three pigs. Maria, the second oldest at nine, kept bantams and sold eggs to the neighbors. Kathy, the youngest girl, kept rabbits. Ben, only four, was looked after like one of the many pets. Griselda bred pigeons, but despite her best efforts the squabs bred too quickly for her to isolate an appetizing strain.

Griselda was the ringleader of the gaggle of children who ran wild about the place, playing and swimming in the shallow duck pond down the road from the house. The pond took center stage in summer, when the children could often be found lying in the sun, the girls' long hair strewn across the grass to dry before being bound up carelessly in a ribbon or swept under a Boy Scout cap. Generally, however, Griselda kept her sisters, the Owle siblings, and the Matthews boys busy directing the theater of make-believe and the daily life of chores that occupied the farm and its residents.

On the farm there was a natural order that Schuyler taught each child to respect and uphold. Animals as well as children had their proper place. Griselda's sources for the family newsletter, the *Jackson Monthly*, were everywhere; on the farm natural melodrama, the cold lessons of life, and pure fantasy were rife. For fifty cents a year the laboriously executed magazine provided comic strips, poems, short stories, farm and family news, a "Did You Know?" column, and even unpaid advertisements and product endorsements. While siblings contributed some work, Griselda was the business manager and distributor; she also wrote the editorial lead, did most of the drawing, and came up with most of the copy. At its peak the magazine had ten subscribers.

Schuyler entered into the imaginative lives of his children with agility and tenderness. He gave them access to his study and library, encouraging their curiosity in the world around them. Griselda, who read assiduously, absorbed George MacDonald and Grimm alongside Robin Hood, Lorna Doone, and Huckleberry Finn. She had a passion for fairies; overnight a feather would mysteriously appear in a doll's bed, or a tiny dish of fairy food was inexplicably emptied. Similarly, in her magazine, the pressure and advice of her silent consultant is everywhere apparent. Every undertaking provided an opportunity for Schuyler's disciplining lessons about the real world. However hard it became in practice, Schuyler always upheld the virtues of good business, the importance of application, conscientiousness, and hard work. It was not enough to believe in fairies or merely to be clever.

Kit Jackson, if they thought about her at all, struck the Matthews boys as rather odd, not at all like their mother. She had a big booming laugh. Tommy Matthews remembered how once, on Halloween, Mrs. Jackson climbed in through the kitchen window dressed up as Puss in Boots. He found this alarming. To a young woman who knew her in 1939 "Kit was sort of gawky and very outspoken. She'd say whatever she thought; she wasn't inhibited in any way." In contrast to Schuyler, Kit was always warm and welcoming. For the most part, Tom Matthews had regarded her simply as "Schuyler's wife." As an adult, Griselda would recall her as "someone who had always been there, doing the things that mothers do and that children take for granted. She was to our eyes an adjunct to our father as sparrow to peacock."

"Bousie," on the other hand, held his children rapt. For Schuyler there was always a right way and a wrong way to do things, and those around him had little choice but to follow his lead. He was not a man for small, merely social graces. Those who worked for him respected him, and when he was not ill he worked as hard as two men. The pressure that his children felt to "be good" in view of his unimpeachable goodness was compelling; the blackest sin was to tell a lie. Griselda, in particular, was fiercely devoted; and to the Matthews boys, reared in the gentle, suburban life of Princeton, Schuyler Jackson was almost fearsome. "He always thought he was Jesus Christ," Kit remarked many years later. Strictly speaking, Schuyler was not pious, but for a time he took to reading the Bible aloud to his family from his chair by the Franklin stove in the front parlor. His voice filled the house.

But in the spring of 1939 Schuyler's world appeared to be threatened in a number of ways. Within the last two years Kit had grown disillusioned with him, treating his new business schemes with impatience and sometimes scorn. The year before, Schuyler had seriously considered leaving her and the children for a champion figure skater. But in many respects, a righteous code of conduct was the only vanity that remained to him, and so he had stayed. Gradually, however, the New Hope world of right and wrong became more and more a fantasy fed by failure, drink, and disillusionment. Like Nathan Reichenthal, Schuyler sought from his children (and Tom Matthews) the reverence that his wife had once felt for him. The children remained oblivious to their mother's growing sense that, as she put it later, there was something "phony" about her husband.

After the summer of 1939, the world of the New Hope farm would seem antediluvian to the Jackson children, as if the purity and certainty of their lives had been betrayed and wronged. Though each child and each adult would, in their own way, try to make reasonable the events of that summer, their sense of equanimity and well-being would never be entirely regained—not by Schuyler or Kit and their children, not by Tom or Julie, not by Robert, and not by Laura. If there had ever been a right way and a wrong way to do things, within a short time of Laura Riding and Robert Graves' arrival, it was no longer clear to anyone, adult or child, what it was.

JOHNNY MATTHEWS, TOM'S eldest, remembered how Laura's perfume seemed to be everywhere in his house and how her perspiration cut lines in her face powder. She carried a parasol and, no matter how hot it was, wore long jade-colored velvet gowns and capes, numerous brace-lets, pins, and necklaces. Though she wore a prim, schoolgirlish collar, these dresses, Tommy noted with the practiced eye of an eleven-year-old, were well cut. His younger brother Paul was astonished to see his father get down on his knees on the carpet to inspect a large drawing of Laura's ("it looked like masses of intestines") entitled "The Map of Life." Still, when Laura questioned Johnny at bedtime about the colors of the days of the week and whether the months and years went clockwise or counterclockwise, he was won over; Laura agreed with his feeling that Thursday was orange. She was quite different from any grown-up he'd ever met. Next to her, interest in Robert paled into insignificance. One visitor to the house during the spring did not recall his being there at all; one of the few things Griselda remembered about him was how at mealtimes Robert would poke crumbs out of the corner of Laura's mouth with the point of a napkin.

But among both the Matthews and the Jackson children there was common assent that something important was happening with the arrival of the "famous writers from England." Along with the special attention paid to them, there were numerous gifts and trinkets, includ-ing a pearl headband for Griselda from Robert. In her jewels and "costumes" Laura at first intrigued, excited, and puzzled them. Julie had spoken firmly and gently to the boys about Laura and her "special-ness." Their bedroom was requisitioned for her; Johnny and Paul slept on the sleeping porch, and Robert bunked in Tom's study on a cot. Not long after her arrival, Laura called a meeting of the household. The boys' nurse had raised an objection to the change in mealtimes and was proving generally resistant to the new arrangements. Laura indi-cated that she was corrupt. Julie reluctantly but dutifully dismissed the woman. The boys were deeply impressed.

In the week following their arrival Robert noted in his diary that Laura was not sleeping well and was running a fever; on May 2 she was "happy but thinner." The next day she had a long talk alone with Kit. That evening Schuyler came over to join them for dinner, and plans were made for how Tom might improve *Time's* book page. Robert's first letter to Karl described the love between Laura, himself, and the Jacksons as having been "pre-destined." "And that means an un-numerability of old problems cleared up—like a game that cannot properly begin until all the players are present; now we all are."

The story of Laura Riding and Schuyler Jackson is not a simple love story with a happy ending. Though in many respects their meeting had its apocryphal aspects, the events that followed their "getting things clear" sharply tested the message of friendship and world peace that Laura was bringing with her to America from the lost cause that was Europe. Indeed, soon after her arrival, out of Riding's sense of the good in each human being grew once again an ominous awareness of evil—not in Hitler's Germany this time but within themselves. It was understood at least implicitly by Robert, Tom, Beryl, Alan, David, and Julie that Laura was the final arbiter of where and in whom that evil lay.

In significant respects the events in Princeton and New Hope bear a striking similarity to the events that led up to Riding's suicide attempt in 1929. Again the crisis was precipitated by her falling in love; again she considered that love to have far more than private significance. On May 5, Laura sent one of her last messages to Karl: "You know all will be done that needs to be done for all." Robert quickly saw that the intimacies between Laura and Schuyler would go as deep, if not deeper, than those that Laura had shared with him; Schuyler Jackson was not the whimsical and equivocal Geoffrey Phibbs. Given Robert's growing affections for Beryl, it is hard to believe that he was wholly surprised or, at the outset, unsettled by this development.

Once they moved from Princeton to the Jackson farm, it was not long before Riding would publicly flout her edicts of celibacy, disappearing behind a locked door one day with Schuyler and emerging to announce that "Schuyler and I do." The act was less a private intimacy than dramatic evidence of the extraordinary denouement that she had long prophesied. She expected everyone to acknowledge the significance of the event with her; on another occasion Beryl was summoned into Laura's bedroom one afternoon to sit by the bed while she and Schuyler napped.

Like the events of April 1929, too, an atmosphere fraught with tension preceded the final crisis. According to Tom Matthews, soon after their arrival in America there began a long interim of suspense, three weeks of waiting, of playing out a bizarre and puzzling end game. All work on the *Dictionary* and on other projects was suspended, replaced by almost daily Second Protocol meetings at the Matthews house or the farm. According to another participant, there was endless talk about "love," particularly everyone's love for Laura. This generally involved her close examination of each participant (alone, or in front of everyone) on their deepest feelings about her, as well as long, racking periods of silence. Tom Matthews later compared these meetings to sitting up with a corpse; at the time, however, he was zealously attendant.

Tom had taken a two-week vacation from *Time* in order to properly introduce Laura to his closest friends. Among these potential Protocol signers were the composer Elliott Carter, the novelist Robert Cantwell, and the poet and future translator of Homer's *Odyssey*, Robert Fitzgerald. As Fitzgerald was an admirer of Riding's poetry, he and his wife Eleanor were invited to attend one of the first American Second Protocol meetings in a picnic setting out on the Jackson farm. It was a bright sunny day with everyone sitting around on the front lawn. Eleanor was astonished to see the adults scurrying fearfully back and forth at Laura's orders. Robert, she recalled, would get up to fetch the sandwiches or pies, and Laura would tell him to sit down—to "stop *fussing*"—and send someone else who had yet to fetch anything. Becoming increasingly disturbed by what she saw, she got up to take a walk.

> When I started back I saw Laura coming down the road after me. She said "I want you to come upstairs and talk to me." Feeling put on the spot I followed her upstairs but it was just impossible and so I told her that I couldn't talk when I was told to, I couldn't answer her questions. . . . [Later] she wrote me and said that I couldn't be a member until I could love her; she knew I didn't love her. I wrote back and said I would have to wait to see if I loved her.

At this convocation Tom remembered that Schuyler contributed little to the discussion, "but his lowered eyelids and continual slight smile looked receptive."

Later, driving to the Trenton train station, Kit Jackson asked the Fitzgeralds what they thought of "everything"; Eleanor, normally reticent in the company of her husband's intellectual friends, told her that she thought there was something cultish about Laura and the Second Protocol. At the second session she attended, when they were all seated in a hushed circle in the Matthewses' living room, Eleanor recalled that Laura opened the meeting by saying, "Eleanor, I understand you think this is a cult," whereupon Eleanor burst into tears. When she went out to the kitchen with Julie to get some ice cream and to compose herself, Julie told her that she thought Laura was "Christ incarnate." Eleanor remembered having the strong impression that Tom did, too, and was entirely unnerved. On that day, she also noted with amazement, Laura changed her dress three times. Returning home, Eleanor cried for three days.

Somehow the greater the powers invested in Laura by herself and by those around her, the weaker and more uncertain everyone else became. Even in the context of a mounting war hysteria, the endless Protocol meetings produced an atmosphere that remains largely inexplicable. Somewhat in the Gurdjieff manner, Laura's often bizarre demands found dutiful obeisance. One evening at sunset Robert was seated on the White House lawn and made to read aloud from Dante's *Inferno* in a cloud of hungry mosquitos. Only the children kept aloof; perhaps taking Griselda's cues, the older ones were intrigued but increasingly wary; the glad-hand gifts began to seem more like bribes.

"It suddenly dawned on me that this long-drawn-out torture, which had brought everything to a standstill and all of us to the tautness of hysteria, was for a purpose," Tom wrote later. "We were being put to the question and one of us must sooner or later break." During a dinner with the Jacksons at the Matthewses' house, shortly before the move to Nimrod's Rise, Kit suddenly laid her head on the table in what Tom recalled as a gesture of infinite weariness and resignation. "If she was weeping, it was very quietly," Tom wrote. "I think Schuyler and Laura took her back to the farm. It was the last I saw of her for months."

Laura Jackson virulently denounced Tom Matthews' account of the events that summer when his book *Jacks or Better* appeared in 1977, eleven years after Schuyler's death. Matthews was a treacherous man, she wrote, consumed with envy, hate, and rage over his failure to achieve anything of literary note. His book was an obscene, salacious, and spiritually monstrous insult to the truth. The disparity between what she recalled and what he did was one of interpretation rather than substance. Laura Jackson believed until her death that her actions that summer were based solely on her concern for the well-being of others, including the Jackson children and their mother. This meant not only keeping alive the hope among the signers of the Second Protocol that the war would be averted but also helping them to resolve more intimate personal difficulties, often at great strain to herself. Indeed, for her the two challenges were inseparable. Matthews' account is based on his assumption that Laura wanted Schuyler Jackson and would stop at nothing to have him. If Matthews' account is to be impugned, Griselda said later, it would be for the extent to which he distanced himself from events in which he played an active part and beliefs that he held with passion—beliefs shared, in greater part, by every adult in Laura's circle. Matthews, however, was not present for the final climax.

Sometime in late May or early June, Robert, Laura, Alan, Beryl, and David left Princeton, moving first into Nimrod's Rise, which was still under construction. After a week the work remained unfinished, and Alan and Beryl boarded at a nearby farm while the others moved across the road to the White House; according to Griselda, Laura settled herself in the second-floor guest bedroom. When the Rise was finally ready, all but Laura moved back there. One evening when everyone was seated at the White House dinner table, Kit suddenly pushed her chair back and announced that she was going for a walk with her children. Silently and in unison, all four children stood up.

Laura, at the head of the table, suggested that Robert accompany her, but to the children's amazement Kit insisted loudly, "They are my children and I have a right to walk with them." She left with her brood flocked behind her, striding across the lawn, across the road, and down the hill and swampy woods toward Nimrod's Rise and a little stream. She was soon followed by a succession of keepers sent by Laura—first Robert, then Alan, then Beryl—as Kit screamed at them to go back and to leave her alone. At the stream she stopped and threw peach pits in the water, asking her silent and increasingly apprehensive children, "See the goldfish?" The little group moved on up behind the Rise, when Griselda suddenly burst into tears and threw her arms around her mother. "Something is wrong with you," she said. "What is the matter with you?" Kit replied that nothing was wrong. Griselda kept up the pressure, begging her mother over and over to tell her what the matter was. Finally, Kit spun around and grabbed her around the neck. When Schuyler ran up the wet path from the house, he found his children howling and his wife strangling his daughter.

"THE PARTICULARS OF that dreadful summer," Kit recalled in 1989, "are not only difficult to recount but difficult to believe in our age of science. My side of the story is not credible, inasmuch as I was its victim in its general insanity and landed several times in the loony bin." Initially, Kit Jackson remembers having looked forward to Laura Riding's arrival, hopeful of her good influence on Schuyler, whose drinking and hypochondria, since his affair with the figure skater, had steadily worsened. While her first impression of Robert was of "a big hulk, a boob," Laura seemed to her "like something out of Mother Goose." The first evening at the farm, she recalled, Laura read aloud from George MacDonald's *The Princess and the Goblin.* "Not to the children," she recalled, "but to all of us."

Though Kit said later that she did not fully realize that Laura was falling in love with her husband, it gradually dawned on her that she was not at all prepared for the scope of the changes that Laura was bringing to the farm. Before long, this included a close involvement in the daily lives and discipline of her children, as well as intimacies with her husband. "Before my mother's first breakdown," Griselda recalled, "Tom and Julie took her out for a drive and told her that she had to do something to stop what was happening at the farm. But she just laughed. Of course by then it was too late." Kit's strongest recollection was of being trapped, in some mysterious manner, in Laura's power; Laura was her "puppeteer." Still, in curious, semi-automatic ways, Kit found herself resisting Laura's rearrangements and tidyings of her household:

Laura would go through the house closing the windows, curtains and doors and I would follow her opening them; she would shut off dripping faucets and I would turn them on again. I hardly realized what I was doing.

One morning at dawn Kit awoke early and almost walked into Robert, who was standing in the dark hallway upstairs in the White House. "He told me, 'Be very quiet, this is very dangerous.' " Kit remembered that "the very air seemed to quiver." When asked for an explanation, Kit could only say, "It was just understood that Laura was a witch." When asked what evidence they had of this, she explained there wasn't any. "Laura used no props, just her mind."

Kit was not the only one who assumed that Laura had extraordinary powers. Matthews admitted in *Jacks or Better* that both he and Julie shared this belief that Laura was a witch—albeit a "white witch," who used her powers for benevolent ends; they believed, for example, that she had predicted an earthquake in South America.

In an "age of science" one tends to explain the perceptions of those individuals and the events at the farm in terms of mass hysteria—as if bedtime fairy tales had been taken much too seriously. But to insist that the belief in witches is superstitious nonsense misses a critical point. What other word was uniformly available to Kit—indeed, to anyone at the farm, adult or child, including Laura—to explain Laura's special goodness or, when things turned nasty, Laura (or Kit's) special evil? Much later Kit's refusal to accede to Tom's belief that Laura was "evil" contributed to the cooling of their friendship.

In the spring of 1929 Riding's pursuit of Geoffrey Phibbs was accompanied by a personally concocted brand of mysticism. With Robert's encouragement, she dabbled in spiritualism's usual accouterments; strange and ominous warnings were seen in the most innocent of daily happenings; astrological forecasts were consulted. After Geoffrey's return to Ireland from Rouen, Laura stepped up her pressure on him to return to her by reverting to her form of mystical language. What to Norah were strange signs, mysterious gifts and objects, contained for Geoffrey intimate reference to the ad hoc symbolic language that the Trinity had developed. Even the search for the bird's nest appeared to be part of this private language. In a world dominated by patriarchal conventions, whether religious or secular, the generic notion of witchcraft has been one of the few languages of power available to women. At New Hope there is no question that the "age of science" had reverted to another age entirely; and Riding's attraction to what she termed her "magicks" can, in part, be understood in terms of this desire for a female source of power and authority outside and in contravention of Judeo-Christian ones. But, somehow, in the course of donning the garb and trappings and in appropriating the language of what she understood to be "witchery," Riding also took on the most hated and repressive aspects of those misogynistic institutions and traditions which she had once sought to question and undermine. In a troubling kind of logic, the search for evil that Laura carried out on the Jackson farm, with implicit and explicit complicity of those around her, had repercussions not only for Kit but also for Riding's own life and ultimately her poetry.

The morning after the episode in the woods, Schuyler drove Kit to their family doctor, and a massive housecleaning was undertaken. Suddenly, it was Kit who had been practicing magic, not Laura. Kit's clothes and belongings, those objects supposedly used in what Laura later termed her "uncanny rites and practices," were thrown on a bonfire in the back where the rubbish was burned. Everyone consigned at least one possession of Kit's to the flames in a communal ritual of purification that recalled Riding's burning of Geoffrey Phibbs' clothes at St. Peter's Square to get rid of Norah's corrupting influence.

Returning from the office that day, Tom recalled finding David Reeves there, talking to Julie. From David he learned that Kit had been taken to a Philadelphia hospital, and he was told that "they" wanted him at the farm—"they," he understood immediately, meant Schuyler and Laura. Speaking on behalf of everyone, Laura told Tom upon his arrival that "Katharine" was evil:

> [Although she didn't use the word then Laura] was telling me that "Katharine" was a witch, that she had been unmasked and her sorceries brought to nothing; that the house was now being purified of her cabalistic relics and of all her associations with it. There had been terrible scenes with Kit (which she described) before she had finally

dropped her mask and confessed her evil practices. The
others . . . were in perfect accord with Laura. . . .

Tom balked at Laura's invitation to join in the purifying chores, but
even more fearful of a confrontation with Schuyler, he took a small
china figurine and promised to destroy it. Reaching the Delaware
River on the way back to Princeton, he threw it in. He later begged
Kit's forgiveness.

To Beryl, Laura pointed out a pile of Kit's tampons arranged in a
manner that she certified as maleficent. Beryl remembers no other
"evidence" and never believed that either Laura or Kit was a "witch."
Griselda, too, recalls being told that her mother was now considered
by all to be damned. But the summer was not yet finished.

After about ten days in the hospital Kit convinced her doctors
that she had fully recovered her senses, and made her first attempt
to return to the farm, arriving sometime in late June or early July.
From her bedroom window Griselda watched her mother being
taken away again, this time in a straitjacket "because Ma went
completely bonkers," she recalled. Kit was taken back to the hospital in Philadelphia and made a second attempt to return to the
farm after Robert and Alan had returned to England. She was
transferred to a hospital for the violently insane in Utica, near her
childhood home, Brookwood. In preparation for her return (which
Laura and Schuyler anticipated but did not warn Beryl and David
about) Griselda recalled being made to pick up every single stick on
the front lawn. "Why?" Tom asked bitterly, "To show the children
how much less tidy their mother . . . was?" In another curious echo
of the 1929 suicide attempt, Griselda was told to find a bird's nest to
give to her father.

In July, Tom came to the farm one night a week for a series of
sessions with Laura and Schuyler in which they both attempted to
convince him that Kit was a witch. According to his account this was
the first time that the word was actually spoken. As Griselda watched
from her upstairs vantage, Tom was told on the evening of his last
visit that if he did not agree that Kit was, at the very least, evil then he
was evil, too. It was his last trip to the farm; by the middle of August
both Tom and Julie had withdrawn their friendship ("in borrowed
severity" Laura wrote at the time). Tom was not the only person told

that Kit was evil; the neighbors and family friends were gently informed.

In May 1956, almost twenty years later, Griselda received a twenty-three-page typewritten letter from her stepmother in which that summer's events were set out as Laura remembered and felt them. Griselda, now married, had seen neither her father nor Laura since April 1945, when she and her sister Maria visited them in Florida. At that time they were told that Schuyler and Laura had evidence of their mother's evil: Kit had once suggested to him that they make love in a field of daisies. Furthermore, Schuyler offered to show them Kit's "love letters" to Laura. Griselda refused to look at them, and the nightmarish visit ended with Schuyler's disowning both daughters and putting them, stunned and crying, on the train back to their mother.

In the letter that Griselda received in 1956, Laura prefaced her description of Kit's behavior that summer with the assertion that Kit believed that life was a meaningless void and that this conviction had exposed her soul to evil possession. Laura insisted that what she knew of Kit she knew from close observation and unimpeachable authority. Among Kit's practices and black magic rites that summer, Laura Jackson continued, were the performance of Egyptian dances, making Ben see things in his room move, and making of weird sounds. Laura also insisted that Griselda's mother suffered from numerous sexual perversions that she had confessed in detail. Only after Kit's breakdown, Laura wrote, did Schuyler come to see how his wife's discipleship under Gurdjieff had led her into a pure nihilism that finally proved the existence of something evil at work. As corroboration for these astonishing accusations, Laura cited the observation of the family doctor who first admitted Kit to the hospital: "She was always a careless mother." One family friend was quoted as having said of Kit, "She always despised people."

At New Hope the belief in fairy princesses, angels, and "white" witches inevitably begged the arrival of goblins, devils, evil stepmothers, and satanic witches. Pure fantasy and superstition, one could insist; a "play with the possibilities of extreme statement," Laura Jackson might protest. But such notions are real, too, particularly in light of the price paid by Kit and, indeed, by everyone else.

In the 1960s Laura Jackson responded to a correspondent's question about witchcraft and its bearing on a woman's true nature by admitting that the subject was indeed complex. She distinguished several forms that female witchery could take. The first included those who practiced primitive magic rituals and rites, the second involved those historical cases which had been certified by ecclesiastical authority. The third involved a more contemporary phenomenon, behavior that indicated an outright perversion of the essential nature of woman. To the existence of this latter type, both she and Schuyler, she informed her correspondent, could personally attest.

For Laura Jackson to accept as legitimate the Inquisition's definition as to what behavior constitutes evidence of witchcraft is a measure of how far she had traveled from Laura Riding. For Riding, any male idea of woman's nature, perverse or not, had always been challenged and scorned. As for the behavior that she and Schuyler had witnessed in Kit, the question becomes more pernicious. In her 1956 description of the intricate recesses of Kit's "soul" one catches glimpses of the discarded selves of Laura Riding; the manifestations of evil and perversion that she ascribed to Kit and later to Griselda were first and foremost fears and faces that she had felt and exploited imaginatively within herself. The nihilism of the modernist poet that Riding embraced in *Anarchism Is Not Enough* was now ascribed to Kit; Gertrude Stein would later be deemed guilty of sexual perversion and moral bankruptcy. In the end Riding's fourteen-year relationship with Robert Graves served to strengthen rather than undermine the belief in an essential and pure female nature. She may have questioned the various mythic figures that he placed upon his pedestal, but after 1926 she did not question the pedestal itself. Ultimately, it was from this unsteady perch that Laura Jackson denounced not only Kit Jackson but also Laura Riding.

To others, apt to be unimpressed by such arguments, Laura Jackson defended her version of that summer's events by suggesting that Kit's mental instability had preceded her arrival in New Hope. There is no evidence to support such a claim, but such an assertion reveals that the denunciation of women as witches does have its age-of-science equivalent, equipped with its own superstitions and form of persecution. "I never described any of Laura's witchy stuff to the doctors," Kit said later. "I knew they would commit me for life if I said anything like that." Instead, Kit was subjected to insulin treatments and, when they proved inconclusive, to electroshock "therapy."

Did Laura Riding inadvertently or purposefully drive Kit Jackson insane? It is beyond the domain of a book to settle such claims. Riding did, with the apparent assistance and approval of Kit's closest friends and husband, expropriate her bed, family, and home. Even without Laura's intensive spiritual cross-examinations, Kit was bound to be greatly disturbed, and there is no question that she behaved violently and strangely. But to conclude, as both Laura and Schuyler Jackson did, that she was either predisposed to evil or actually possessed by it are equally insupportable explanations of what happened that summer.

As an adult Griselda formed her own opinion of her mother's predicament during the summer of 1939, remarking that she went mad not in one day but over a period of weeks: "She got in over her head." One psychiatrist observed that while Kit may have been raving, she was still saner than any of the other adults who participated in the events that summer. But by August, Kit had found another means of protest; she explained her deviation, Laura reported to Robert, as rational opposition, insisting that they were "wrong" and she was "right" and that she was prepared to prove it by legal means. Kit's only terms were complete surrender, Laura wrote in exasperation.

Kit Jackson remains grateful to her last doctor, a man named Hughes, who left her alone, without trying to probe her fragile psyche. Visiting her in the asylum, Beryl remembered Kit sitting in her room repeating over and over "Griselda, Maria, Kathy, Ben," and perhaps it was this thought that returned her to sanity. Despite continuing bouts of illness, upon her divorce in 1941 Kit was awarded custody of her children. After another breakdown in 1947, she successfully prevented Schuyler from taking custody. In the 1960s she became a Catholic and moved to Maine, where, now in her nineties, she still skis cross-country during the long snowy winters.

By THE END of July, Robert had decided to return to England for six weeks; at that point Schuyler had usurped his place not only with Laura but also on the dictionary. Alan would accompany him, continuing on to Warsaw from London; Beryl would stay behind to help with the children while Kit was in the hospital. Laura and Schuyler thought that Griselda, who was proving difficult, should accompany Robert, but the threat of war intervened and he would leave without her. On the eve of his departure he asked for the pearl headband back, marking him forever in Griselda's eyes as an "Indian giver."

Also on the eve of his departure, Robert asked Laura if he would have to sleep alone on his return to New Hope. Receiving him in her bedroom with Schuyler, she told him that she would have to wait and see. Perhaps because of her lingering possessiveness or the continuing uncertainties of her new life, Laura was unwilling to see Robert with Beryl. As there had been problems between Beryl and Alan, what had been a possibility seemed increasingly a likelihood. Just before his departure, Laura encouraged Robert to write to Nancy about a rapprochement. He had:

> What happened long ago is finished with except as history, and if we were to go into it and apportion blame, I would claim a good share—not to make you feel better, but in honesty. I don't want, either, to start anything old up again: only to see whether we can be friends in a true way . . . not "for the sake of the children" but for the sake of . . . the good that was in our confused love once, and that good lost. I think this is a debt we owe each other; and it is perhaps my chief reason for coming over.

But to Robert it was Schuyler who sported a "grin of triumph" as he sat there waiting for Robert to finish his good-byes.

Once Robert had left, arrangements were required for Griselda. After promising that she need not return to the summer camp where she had been miserable the year before, Schuyler made her accompany him on a visit to her mother in Cooperstown. By August Kit had left the hospital in Utica and was staying with her mother at Brookwood. Afterwards, he promptly deposited Griselda at the nearby camp. Ten years later, of all the failings that Schuyler might have confessed, he apologized for this broken promise, admitting that he had broken it for selfish reasons. While at camp, Griselda recalled receiving letters laden with expressions of affection and girlish confidences from Laura. She destroyed them.

In a long, rambling, and wistful letter to Robert in Newport, Rhode Island, where he was visiting Tom and Julie prior to his departure, Laura insisted that Robert's own instinct had prompted his decision to return to England. Accompanying her melancholy anticipation of this parting was a rather premature nostalgia—he was going for only six weeks—for all their years together. She described the conflicts that tortured her since their first meeting, the push and pull between feeling and thinking, where so often, overwhelmed by her own emotions, she had reeled sharply into rigid ways of thinking to right herself again. In these letters Laura seemed both anxious to appear calm and secure in her love for Schuyler and careful to efface her private history with Robert. She ended one letter by offering her pity of him as a kind of gift of parting.

Within the meanderings of Laura's obliquity was an effort to be gentle with the man with whom she had shared fourteen years and from whom she had never been parted for more than a few days. It had not yet dawned on either of them that their partnership was at an end; one of Robert's errands in London was to obtain a contract for a book by Laura and Schuyler entitled *The World Has Changed*. But once Graves was back in England, the final break became inevitable. When Robert's letters began pressing Laura on the subject of his love for Beryl, she became impatient, accusing him of vulgarity and childishness. His relationship with Beryl, she said, was to be decided only by herself and Alan.

But Alan had left Poland just as Hitler's armies invaded, and what Laura failed to realize was that both he and the mails would be delayed in the journey to London; her letters encouraging Alan to stick with Beryl did not reach him by the time she thought they would. Nor did she realize that England's declaration of war would prevent Robert from returning to America, as he had planned, by October 15. Had England not declared war on Germany on September 4, Robert's ship—returning him to America and to Beryl—would have passed Beryl's returning to England and, Laura expected, to Alan. But, within a month of her return to England in October, Beryl was pregnant with Robert's child; he had met her at the boat.

Robert continued planning his return to America until January 1940, when a letter from Laura arrived asking him not to come in the spring because it was too soon. Her letter was accompanied by a blunter message from Schuyler in which Graves was taken to task for not paying sufficient attention to Schuyler's recommendations for the improvement of his character. His love for Beryl would leave his condition unchanged, Schuyler said frankly, because she could never be more for him than a passive sexual object. Schuyler now believed that it was the effort to save Robert's soul that had nearly destroyed Laura and now that she was better, she could be of no further use to him. Graves had swallowed Laura's "holy words" until he had become grotesquely bloated with self-importance (much like Katharine had treated his own holy words). Schuyler imagined that the day was now breaking on an earthly paradise and that Robert's use of language had left words with scarcely a remnant of meaning to celebrate its coming. Of course, Schuyler assured Robert, this did not diminish his affection for him by one iota.

By early February 1940 Robert's anxious response to these letters led Laura, perhaps at Schuyler's insistence, to cut off all communication with him other than that of a practical nature.

—<>—

Though Riding and Graves were never married, years of intimacy were dissolved in the protracted struggle for control of the historical record. Scholars, critics, biographers, and archivists, like hapless, disoriented children, were forced by Jackson to choose sides in the quarrel, even after Graves was dead. There was a rich store of exhibits on each side: clues recorded in abbreviated diary entries or poetic imagery, remembered glances across the La Chevrie dining table, manuscripts and letters that were to have been burned appearing in public archives, stolen lines of poetry have all been presented in the court of print to determine who spoke true and who spoke false.

The long process of unraveling the Graves-Riding partnership was as intricate, complex, and heated as the process of their coming together had been blind and urgent necessity. Just as they engaged each other on so many levels, the process of their disengagement, never fully achieved by either, is a deconstructivist's study unto itself.

In particular, Laura Jackson would accuse Graves of fabricating a cartoon of her in his depiction of the Triple Muse in his 1948 book *The White Goddess*. This "historical grammar of poetic myth" set out Graves' belief that the earliest European deity to whom all true poets must pay homage was the beautiful, generous, cruel, wise, and implacable White Goddess of birth, love, and death.

The wickedness of this book, she claimed, lay not only in the large-scale appropriation of her thought, gussied up by show of learning. There was more to his "intricately truthless" effort than that. The center of his travesty had been in the assassination of her self and the coherent truth of her being, and the distortion of the human wisdoms and cosmic realities that belonged to herself alone. Where she once had reigned, now a whorish abomination had sprung to life, a Frankenstein pieced together from the shards of her life and thought. Graves' new goddess and muse would receive his execration or his veneration, she wrote bitterly, and would take on whatever disgusting or ennobling aspect his literary whim cared to provide her.

In a crucial sense Jackson's perception was correct; by imagining a muse in her likeness, Graves, inadvertently or not, denied Laura Riding her own significance, except as a necessary adjunct to his poetry. For a long time Laura Riding was known not for her own work but as the living incarnation of Graves' White Goddess. In 1961 Graves made the connection between Riding and the White Goddess explicit in a letter to Tom Matthews. While preparing an Oxford lecture on the "Personal Muse," he wrote that he was now able to separate the "mythic" from the "personal" better than he had in *The White Goddess*: "I feel now that I failed Laura no less than she failed me—not that I blame either of us. We were premature."

But Graves' depiction of the White Goddess was not wholly an act of revenge or merely the means to understand how Riding had failed him. They had not only shared the most vital years of their youth and maturity but had also created themselves and their work utterly in the changing image of themselves that they saw reflected in each other's eyes and imagination. "The Thieves," written by Graves in Brittany and first published in 1940, comments obliquely on how his work and Riding's work became—and to a significant extent will always remain—inextricable:

Lovers in the act dispense
With such meum-tuum sense
As might warningly reveal
What they must not pick or steal,
And their nostrum is to say:
"I and you are both away."

After, when they disentwine
You from me and yours from mine,
Neither can be certain who
Was that I whose mine was you.
To the act again they go
More completely not to know.

Theft is theft and raid is raid
Though reciprocally made.
Lovers, the conclusion is
Doubled sighs and jealousies
In a single heart that grieves
For lost honour among thieves.

By re-creating Riding, Graves could most clearly see himself as a poet. By re-creating Graves in endless denunciations, repainting the vast canvas of literary history as it was framed in the years following their breakup, Laura (Riding) Jackson sustained the sense of unimpeachable omniscience that she had exercised during the 1930s. The extent to which she recognized herself in Graves' portrait of the White Goddess is the extent to which she recognized the changeable woman that they had created together. Finally, Laura Jackson did not need Graves to divest her of the banner of poet; by the time *The White Goddess* was published she had done that already herself.

Chapter 22

THE ONLY POSSIBLE ENDING

———•———

But something must be written about me,
And not by them.
So I began those mistold confidences
Which now read like profanity of self
To my internal eye
And which my critic hand erases
As the story grows too different to speak of
In the way the world speaks

—"Memories of Mortalities"

———•———

THE SQUEALING, MOANING, and whistling of the pigeon squabs broke the Sunday morning stillness of the New York City streets. Between Schuyler's perch on the roof of 59 West 53rd Street and Central Park were six rows of four-story buildings, many displaying laundry strung from the fire escapes. A forest of aerials scratched the skyline. Under a sunny and cloudless April sky, backed up against a soot-encrusted chimney, Schuyler wrote the first of his weekly letters to his children.

In the weeks since they had arrived, Schuyler and Laura had worked constantly on the dictionary. At first, Schuyler wrote Griselda, he was utterly lost. He knew he wasn't on the farm anymore but that was all that he knew with certainty. Gradually, work on the dictionary and sleep became the only occupations that could distract

Schuyler from the pain of his separation from his children, from the farm life he had loved. When he became too depressed, he told his daughter, he took a walk in the park to find something, a sight that would relieve his sadness. Thus engrossed in his own grief, he did not venture to imagine his daughter's: his greatest consolation, he told her, was Laura.

Just before David Reeves' departure for California the previous September, Dorothy Simmons had joined them on the farm, staying from August 1939 until Kit was declared well enough to return to take care of her children. In April 1940 Dorothy returned to England, having won the children's lifelong affection. Until the harvest was ready, Schuyler and Laura moved into a dismal rooming house on Riverside Drive, run by a "murderous looking Jew" named Prosser, who required roomers to pay for soap, toilet paper, and toothbrush glass. The cockroaches, bad smells, and blaring radios, Schuyler told Griselda, came free of charge.

Finding it too depressing, Schuyler and Laura moved into the tiny walk-up on 53rd Street over a tailor's shop on the corner of Sixth Avenue. There was a living room, where Schuyler worked; a large kitchen with a gas stove and dumbwaiter; and a dark little box of a bedroom, where Laura had her worktable. The landlord was Gordon Still, a name that Schuyler and Laura found apt owing to his practice of sitting in his room all night listening to the radio. At dawn, Still would move only to light up the first cigar of the day. The smoke and the radio made their way into Schuyler's thoughts and from there to his letters to his children back on the farm with their mother. His intense observation of small details, the acutely felt closeness of the rooms, reflected his tight focus on the task that he and Laura had set for themselves: to take apart and put back together the vocabulary of the English language. The war in Europe went on without them.

The reconstitution of the English language was accompanied by Laura Riding's reconstitution of her self, just as it had been ten years earlier in Deyá. The name under the bell of their apartment read Mr. and Mrs. Schuyler Jackson. Robert, in attempting to explain Laura's defection to Liddell-Hart, told him that "she has made the center of her universe no longer herself but Schuyler Jackson and herself, and thus admitted into her scope so many foreign elements that it is difficult to regard her as the same person." In a letter to Karl explaining why he was not returning to America, Robert quoted Laura as having said that there was no possibility of his helping in the dictionary any longer, though he might still help them financially. Laura, he told Karl, now considered the Protocol an "infected" document.

Schuyler and Laura had scrapped almost a year's work of word-sorting in favor of a new concentration on concrete nouns. Riding's earlier samples had concerned mostly abstract nouns—"wisdom" or "vice"—in which the moral underpinnings of her approach were made explicit. By February 1940 Laura and Schuyler illustrated the virtues of their new approach by sending to Little, Brown definitions of rather more tangible words; in contrasting definitions of "dirt" and "earth" Schuyler invested his longing for the New Hope farm and his feelings of isolation and despair in the city setting.

In 1938, while still at La Chevrie and before Dent in England and Little, Brown in America had contracted to publish *A Dictionary of Exact Meanings*, Riding had had to answer two queries regarding her initial proposal for the work. She had dismissed the idea that words could be defined by synonyms; works such as Roget's *Thesaurus* encouraged imprecisions. She had also questioned the dependence of the *Oxford English Dictionary* upon accredited authors whose gifts might not, she pointed out in her proposal, be that of exact accuracy in word usage. Robert had also come to think of the *OED* as "not a dictionary so much as a corpus of precedents: current, obsolete, cant, cataphretic and nonce-words are all included." Each word was deemed to have no more than one meaning, which Riding proposed to nail down in such a manner as to prevent—once and for all—ambiguous, untruthful speech. Anyone with access to Riding's dictionary would find within it a precise and sovereign value for each word and, through study, would eventually become ethically articulate. Asked how she would treat "Americanisms," she was only momentarily nonplussed. Her eleven-page answer argued that American colloquialisms and slang often were just bad habits that would eventually wear off.

Her next challenge had come from an old adversary. Little, Brown had submitted the proposal to I. A. Richards and C. K. Ogden, both celebrated authors of works on basic English. Their report to Laura's editor, Alfred McIntyre, was entirely dismissive of her project. Laura, Robert, and Alan had worked four full days at La Chevrie to respond to the Richards-Ogden charges, finally finishing their 4,000-word reply at 3:30 A.M. with "everybody helping" and Beryl typing. Laura wrote to Ronald Bottrall that the semantic analysis of language provoked in her an anger much like that which she felt whenever the nature of the atom was discussed.

Riding's defense of her approach had begun with an assertion of her particular and special superiority in these matters. Poets, she had insisted, were the only authorized guardians and orderers of language, and as a distinguished poet herself she was not about to kowtow to the latest charlatans in the field. Just as a serious economist would no doubt be aware of the crackpot social-credit theories of Major Clifford Hugh Douglas, she was fully apprised of the scientific cult of semantics that had come out of Cambridge. She had even witnessed firsthand the havoc that such theories had played with the young poets who had come to her for guidance. Bringing the opinions of these pretenders to her attention, she said, was like telling the prime minister of England that his chancellor of the exchequer had sent the new budget to Major Douglas for inspection. The rebuttal to Little, Brown included a long dissection of the prose of both writers by Graves, showing their faulty grasp of prose style and grammar. Riding had ended her defense by comparing the new theories of modern linguistics to flashy modern conveniences hawked by fast-talking door-to-door salesmen. Little, Brown sent her a long apologetic cable, and Riding had her contract for *A Dictionary of Related Meanings* by the end of the month.

With the September 1940 deadline bearing down on them, Schuyler and Laura defined their words almost nonstop. They had plans to stay in New York until the summer and to return again in the fall after the harvest in New Hope. But city life deprived Schuyler of the consolation and distraction of farm work, the complicated details of domestic life there, and the company of the Owles and the animals. Laura, too, was used to managing a larger household, staging the lives of a wide cast of characters.

In May, Schuyler wrote to his children of an evening out to see the circus. Rather than finding it diverting, he was made uneasy by the acts, upset by the trainers in cages with wild animals, and more pointedly, by the spectacle of a blindfolded man walking a tightrope wrapped in a burlap bag, fifty feet in the air without a net.

Walks in the park brought them less fraught pleasures. With little money to spend, Laura and Schuyler would ride the elevated to Bronx Park to go bird-watching or take a bus up Riverside Drive to Coogan's Bluff, overlooking the Polo Grounds, to sit, watch other strollers, and look out over the Harlem River. Laura did not even call on Polly (she waited until she was married the following year), and seeing Eleanor Fitzgerald one day on the street, ducked into a store to avoid meeting her. Twice a week they visited the nearby Trans-Lux movie theater to watch the newsreels.

Gifts from the children were placed carefully on the mantel over the blind fireplace in the living room. There was a ewe-and-lamb paperweight, an ashtray from Ben, a small birdcage and dried flowers from Maria, and a jewel box from Kathy. The sight of them on the mantelpiece, he told Griselda, made anything seem possible again. And as for her gift of painted pigeon eggs, he wanted her to know that he understood the meaning of her special message, the one borne by the tiny inscription and the wordless one.

In Schuyler's early letters to his children there is a private and gentle intimacy not yet breached by many references to Laura or the recent past. Gradually, however, he became sensitive to the artificial note in their letters, contrived to please or relieve him of worry. In one letter Schuyler demanded of Maria that she write him only the truth; he wanted to know exactly how her life was going. As Schuyler's sense of isolation from his children deepened, his letters became rigid with insistence on the "truth" and dense with criticism of their imprecise wording or faulty logic.

Before long, Laura and Schuyler had developed a letter calendar. They would each write to one of the four children every Sunday, rotating so that each child got at least one monthly letter from both Schuyler and Laura, regardless of when they themselves received letters from the children. Not only did Schuyler expect each letter to be answered, but he insisted that any subject or question that he raised would be addressed. There were additional rules; it was acceptable for the child to write back to *both* Schuyler *and* Laura, but it was not acceptable to write back *only* to Schuyler and *not* to Laura. This was a particular blow to Griselda. Grappling with the responsibilities of being the oldest and uneasy with her father's sometimes plaintive and sometimes harsh letters, she was left confused and disoriented. Schuyler would often keep a carbon of his letters so that he might refer to his exact wording, should a controversy arise. As not all of his children felt able to express themselves so precisely in letters, the task quickly became a burdensome duty. In June 1940 Ben, who was only five, returned unopened a letter from Laura. This led to a letter to Kit and Laura's withholding writing to Kathy. It was four years before the letter-calendar schedule was abandoned.

At first, however, the vulnerable and somewhat self-pitying tone of Schuyler's letters prevailed, and the chiding remained soft. Even in the city Schuyler's gift for natural description is apparent; his best letters are humble, portraying a desperate search for something lost. To live openly with Laura while still married to Kit involved considerable revision of Schuyler's personal and inherited sense of himself in order to avoid coming face to face with the utter hypocrisy of it all. To their neighbors and landlord they were Mr. and Mrs. Jackson though they were not yet married; to friends and relatives concerned with the children's welfare Schuyler was an adulterer and Laura a homewrecker—or worse. In one letter to Griselda, Schuyler admitted that it was difficult to be certain that he and Laura had not done wrong. He looked for proof that they hadn't in their work on the dictionary.

Out on a stroll one day, they passed by a bird shop whose window was alive with tiny fluttering finches. The elderly proprietor offered to sell them a secondhand birdcage for fifty cents. Laura delightedly chose two birds—a strawberry finch distinguished by its spotted and rosy head, which she named Baby, and another finch of less distinctive coloring, which was named Boy. Armed with only a goldfish net, Schuyler thrashed around the store after the tiny birds before emerging triumphant.

Settling the birds in the kitchen, Schuyler and Laura followed their relationship with anxious concern. Baby, Schuyler reported, sang lustfully, while Boy seemed hopelessly mute, never once opening his beak. Thus it was a great event one morning, as Baby was finishing off a mealworm on the floor of the cage, when little squeaks began to come from Boy, solitary on his perch. The squeaks became increasingly melodious as Boy stuttered his way from chirps and warbling into wholehearted bird song. Boy's song, Schuyler reported, rendered a meaning all who heard it would readily comprehend. Good omens were in short supply.

A week later, adding to the same letter, Schuyler said that he was far too happy for letter writing and should be writing a poem instead. The cause of his happiness was his certainty that things were going to work out for everyone. The world's trouble would not disappear right away, but it would not stop anyone from being happy in the end. He followed this thought with a sentimental poem that, in simple declarative stanzas, equated the happiness of the bird in the cage and the bird in the tree; the virtue of their song, the speaker reasoned, dared anyone to say otherwise. A postscript acknowledged that work on the dictionary was proceeding much faster.

Offered a choice between a grim vision of a man alone, bagged and blind on a tightrope with no net to catch him, and a caged bird, learning to sing to his mate, Schuyler chose the bird, celebrating the decision with a sentimental and suspect ode to the cage. The few poems that Schuyler sent to Griselda, presented to her either as spontaneous, like the one quoted above, or as laboriously worked upon by both Laura and himself, were uniformly empty. Laura's poems sent to Griselda were no less sentimental; they are unrecognizable as works by Laura Riding.

At times, Schuyler fully shared Laura's expectations for their dictionary. But while her optimism and strength of will often pacified him, bouts of depression and the various illnesses that accompanied them made her burden heavy. Near the end of their three-month stay in New York, Schuyler's brief euphoria over the birds had dissipated. Work on the manuscript, Schuyler decided, was not proceeding fast enough, and within a week Alfred McIntyre at Little, Brown had received a more realistic estimate of the delivery date.

A letter from Laura to Little, Brown followed Schuyler's, referring humbly to her past sins of desperate optimism, which had obscured the issue of how long the work would take to complete. Only after a fierce drumming from Schuyler, she wrote to her London agent, did she finally confront the brute reality of the project she had undertaken. She asked for three to five more years and promised an annual report on their progress. Both publishers—perhaps to Schuyler's surprise—accepted her revised proposal.

Laura had other bare facts to face that spring, and Schuyler's efforts to make her see them were not gentle. As work on the dictionary slowed down, Schuyler began to blame Laura for the alienation of his children's affection, particularly those of Griselda. As if courting favor, Schuyler reported to his eldest daughter that Laura now did all the laundry, cooking, and housecleaning. At the farm, much to Griselda's disgust, Laura had had her customary breakfast in bed served by the kitchen help. Impatient for it to arrive one morning, Laura had called downstairs to Griselda to find out the reason for the delay. Griselda's response was to proclaim loudly, "Laura wants her breakfast!" Infuriated, Laura leaped out of bed, raced downstairs, and informed Griselda severely that she was not to call her Laura in front of the "servants."

Now it was Griselda whom Laura had to appease. Schuyler decided that his daughter needed to hear from Laura herself about the changes that she had undergone before they returned to live at Nimrod's Rise for the summer harvest of 1940. Using a character from one of Griselda's stories, Laura wrote to explain how the woman whom Griselda had known at the farm the previous summer no longer existed. The woman who had taken her place had begun to learn about the virtue of helping. Her fairy tale life as a princess was such a long time ago that she thought it might now belong to someone else. Now she was just Laura. She would try hard not to think of her past life or story; she would simply and happily accept whatever fate had to offer. On the farm that summer, while Griselda was away visiting her grandmother, Laura would take over responsibility for her pigeons. To show her industriousness she wrote Griselda a report on the six new squabs, the thirty eggs, and their daily baths and feedings. The report was neatly written, factually presented, and dated but unaccompanied by any letter. No further reports followed.

LAURA RIDING AND Schuyler Jackson were married on June 20, 1941, in Elkton, Maryland, a small town renowned for giving quick marriage licenses to runaway couples. Laura was forty. That fall they returned once again to the farm for the harvest; they lived at Nimrod's Rise and saw the children, who were living at the White House with Kit, every day for an hour after school. Increasingly, they began to feel themselves fading presences in the children's lives; but despite the strain of living there, the steady decline in income from the harvest, and the increase in running expenses, Schuyler was reluctant to desert the farm. For several years, they continued to move back to the farm during harvest times in an effort to provide some financial support for the children's upbringing. Laura acknowledged to Polly that it was little more than a wistful gesture against ruin; at one point they had only one pen between them to write with.

Laura's half sister, Isabel Mayers, and her husband, Jesse, helped out during this time, paying Laura's and Schuyler's way for a trip out to California in February 1943, a welcome respite from their financial worries. Isabel had come to the farm just after Kit was first hospitalized, but while in Los Angeles, Laura saw her mother and brother for the first time in almost twenty years. Helen Mayers remembered that Laura seemed, for the first time, truly in love and happy, and perhaps this tempered her feelings toward seeing her mother once again. She found Sadie greatly aged but still sharp as a tack, talkative, and quick to take a childish delight in her company.

Before they left for California, Schuyler had tried to find other sources of income. He applied for a Guggenheim Foundation grant for the dictionary and also tried to get more money from Little, Brown and from Dent, who finally agreed to a small, quarterly payment. While in California, Schuyler learned that his application for a staff job at *Time*, where he had been a reader of new books of poetry, had been turned down. He resigned in protest, curtailing his income still further. He also made the final decision to sell the farm before it bankrupted them. For all intents and purposes, by the spring of 1943 it already had.

Kit and the children would stay on at the White House until after the war; their sole means of support came from Kit's family and friends, from Schuyler's monthly five-dollar check, and from the piecemeal sale of the farm and its machinery. The rest of the money from the sale went toward the purchase in 1943 of a new home for Schuyler and Laura, a small ramshackle bungalow on eight acres in Wabasso, a small town on the east coast of Florida.

Located just north of Vero Beach, Wabasso sits alongside the Indian River, a shallow, 160-mile lagoon stretching from Cape Cana-

veral south to the St. Lucie Inlet. Schuyler and Laura had first visited
the town in the fall of 1940, returning in January 1941 to rent a cabin
about a mile from the beach while Schuyler's divorce papers came
through. In addition to okra, black-eyed peas, New Zealand spinach,
and watermelon, Schuyler and Laura hoped to farm their two grapefruit groves for a living—and, of course, finish the dictionary.

IN THE THREE years following the breakup of the Jackson family, the
dictionary went through dramatic changes. In May 1941, Schuyler
and Laura decided to reorganize the word lists—not under subject
headings, as in a thesaurus, but in sections that they assumed would
follow naturally, beginning with Earth and moving outward toward
the Heavens. Initially this new approach thrilled them—Laura likened it to a Creator's plan of the universe—but it quickly proved
problematic, finally bringing on a stomach illness in Schuyler. The
impossibility of such an approach had occurred to them long before,
Laura explained to the ever patient Alfred McIntyre, but they retained it because they had felt they had committed themselves. Then
inspiration struck: putting the words in alphabetical order now
seemed the right tack.

Four months later, in September 1941, Schuyler submitted a "Plan
for Work" as part of his application for Guggenheim funding. The
new proposal included sample definitions of quagmire and quick-
sand, words that seemed to comment on the nature of their undertaking. *The Oxford English Dictionary* and *Webster's New International
Dictionary* had been retrieved and were now cited as indispensable
authorities. For the first time, too, special attention was being given
to etymologies. But in one fundamental assumption the ultimate
purpose of the dictionary remained unchanged: that a mastery of
perfect English was necessary to the moral development and spiritual
perfection of man. Their application was rejected.

In their emotional appeal to Little, Brown for a quarterly payment,
Laura conceded that the idea of synonymy might be useful; the
dictionary was now conceived as a replacement for George Crabb's
English Synonymes. Also, they had begun to look at the work of those
professional semanticists whom Laura had curtly dismissed in 1938.
In 1942 Schuyler turned his attention to his long-planned glossary

for Charles Doughty's epic poem *The Dawn in Britain* (1906) in hopes of cashing in on any interest sparked by the coming centennial of Doughty's birth. But this work seemed equally plagued; Schuyler rewrote the introduction outlining the purpose of the work over 100 times. The centenary passed, and Schuyler returned to the dictionary.

By constantly revising work already done, they kept falling behind in their goal of defining 100 words a week; one word could be defined over 200 times before they were satisfied—but even these satisfactions proved fleeting. Schuyler's recurrent bouts of illness and weakness thrust the bulk of the work on Laura, as well as the day-to-day responsibilities of housework. In 1944 Schuyler fell ill for almost six months; the end-of-the-year report alone took him three months, finally sent off in March 1945. The result was less a report of their progress than a lecture on how words must be made to have precise meanings if they did not have them already.

There was in this report, written almost five years after Schuyler began work on the dictionary, a kind of desperate plea, more from Schuyler than from Laura, as if he wanted to be challenged or have the contract canceled. Certainly, the strain of writing the report contributed to the disastrous outcome of Griselda and Maria's visit later that month. The girls were followed home by a letter from Laura explaining the in-depth critical analysis that had brought Schuyler to the decision that he could not love them anymore. Two weeks later Laura wrote Little, Brown another letter, confessional in tone. Once again she reiterated her early misconceptions about what the dictionary involved, detailing her misjudgments and former delusions at length. She ended her mea culpa with a note of how much she now owed to her husband. A year later Little, Brown canceled the contract. Laura promised that a provision would be made in their wills as a means of repaying their $3,750 advance.

Two years passed before Alfred McIntyre received another letter from Wabasso. In 1948 Schuyler and Laura wrote that the cancellation of the contract had convinced them that they had gone wrong somewhere, and as a result they had begun their work afresh. The results, they wrote, had been encouraging and would eventually justify Little, Brown's faith in them. This was the last letter in the file.

Laura and Schuyler eventually abandoned their efforts to write a dictionary. In its place they began a long philosophical narrative of the myriad difficulties that they had faced and overcome in their long struggle to provide clear and immutable definitions for words. The title for this massive work, unfinished at Schuyler's death in 1968, was *Rational Meaning: A New Foundation for the Definition of Words*. Laura Jackson completed the main body of the text in the mid-1970s. At her death it was still unpublished.

JUST WHEN DID Laura Riding renounce the gift that she had celebrated for so many years? Frank Baisden, an artist and gentleman farmer at New Hope, followed Schuyler to Florida, where he worked for him picking grapefruit before retiring to his family farm in Georgia. Laura and Schuyler had stayed at Baisden's Rising Sun farm briefly in 1941 on their way back to New Hope from Wabasso, just before they set off to be married. It was then, Baisden wrote to Tom Matthews, that he watched Laura tearfully but obediently burn armfuls of papers while Schuyler looked on "grim faced." Were these papers, as Matthews believed, her poems? It seems likely that they were. Did Schuyler, as one who had so signally failed in his own ambition to write poetry, force his wife to renounce the art in which she had invested her life and faith? Perhaps he did not need to. For Riding there would have been an undeniable "poetic" logic to the act of burning her poems, making official the transformation from Laura Riding to Laura Jackson far more credibly than a brief ceremony presided over by a Baptist minister and county clerk.

In exchange for this burnt offering, Laura's love for Schuyler was proved, and she achieved the happiness and tranquillity that had always eluded her with Graves. As long as Schuyler was alive, this love was enough for her to survive; from the correspondence with Little, Brown it appears that the dictionary mattered a good deal more to Schuyler than to her. Though some may question her decision to renounce her poetry, seeing in it the silencing of a unique female voice, it was perhaps a fair exchange at that point in her life. Even before Riding met Schuyler Jackson, her poetry had become increasingly didactic, as if she had depleted the emotional reserves required to endure the demands of her art. After she met him she was able to invest her powers in loving and protecting him from himself.

In 1948, fourteen years before the BBC reading of her work that made public her renunciation, she wrote to a young English poet interested in her poems that she regarded poetry as a relic from another time, too much at the mercy of the poet's personal needs. Her interest now was in the effort to bring truth into ordinary speech, rather than in the attempt to "perform a personal miracle of true statement," as it once had been.

Once Laura Jackson began to question her own authority, as priestess or poet, as sole arbiter of the true meaning of words, it was only a matter of time before she came to question the art that had so inspired her. With his relentless, self-destructive quest for "logic," Schuyler had perhaps been the one to hammer home the precise absurdities of those intricate circular reasonings with which Riding had always attempted to describe the poetic gift. At last she listened to this man, a voice similar to those which she had so long tried to drown out, and accepted the judgment that it held.

As for Schuyler, there is evidence that before his death he came to feel that he had forsaken his children's love for the vain and phantom promise of the utopia that the dictionary was to have ushered in. Unlike the abandonment of poetry, he could not also afford to relinquish the dream of the dictionary. To do so would have meant acknowledging a mistake that he had not the reserves to undo.

IN THE YEARS in between they made their home in the small Florida bungalow known as The Place, trying hard at first to coax a living from the sandy citrus groves. They carried picking bags and clippers, wore boots to protect themselves from snakebite, and supplied a long list of customers in the Northeast with baskets of grapefruit, tangerines, and temple oranges during the holidays. One Christmas season they shipped 3,000 orders. David Owle worked for them until he fell afoul of Schuyler; in 1948 Dorothy and Montague Simmons arrived with two small children to help pick fruit. They lived in a bungalow near the railway crossing and received no wages. This friendship with the last of the loyal Protocol endorsers ended badly. Montague, who had quit his civil service job and forsook his pension to go to Wabasso, later wrote to Robert:

As I see it, you can only renounce the world, and such gifts of yours as may be useful to the world, if by that act you are freed for giving the world a better gift. We found we had no better gift than what we were prepared to throw away. Laura and Schuyler may have such a gift; I believe they have, but they seem in their nature not able to draw out the good that may lie deep in others, but only to destroy. . . . Except at rare moments [we] felt that Schuyler was tortured and unhappy and Laura shared his tortures, and equally the rare happinesses. The atmosphere was one of critical denseness, so that real contact became impossible. What they might have won through to was something true and good . . . but they were too bogged down in their own past, from which they could not struggle free, to give out help or love or happiness to anyone else. The local people respected them, but did not like them, and none stayed working for very long.

Laura and Schuyler survived hurricanes, droughts, early freezes, mosquitos, bouts of depression, and threats of bankruptcy. Strengthened by long walks to the post office and grocery, Laura was ever less a physically fragile and indulged creature. In a letter to Griselda during one of Schuyler's long illnesses she proudly described herself as one of Wabasso's sight-seeing attractions. Without a phone or even electricity for a radio, they had few diversions. One of them in the early years was the market and Thursday matinee movie at Vero Beach where Seminole Indians could still be seen lining the market sidewalks under vividly colored capelike dresses, their necks encircled by enormous necklaces of beads and pierced coins, their flat feet bare and weathered. Schuyler was mesmerized by their aboriginal appearance; their features, he told Griselda, were at once animal and godlike. Together, Schuyler and Laura had reached some kind of frontier, even if it was not the one that they hoped and struggled for.

In 1944 Laura and Schuyler renovated the attic guest room to accommodate seventy-one-year-old Sadie Reichenthal and her wheelchair as a way of alleviating the burden that Isabel had long borne. Sadie had lost a leg some years before (perhaps to diabetes) and had written long complaining letters to her daughter about her life in a Los Angeles boarding-house. Laura hoped to make up for her years of neglect; she had even thought of writing a novel about her mother's life. But no sooner had Sadie arrived than she wanted to return to Los Angeles.

Laura tried unsuccessfully to dissuade her. It was just as well; in the four and a half months of her stay Laura had once again discovered Sadie to be a pathological liar on whom every kindness was wasted. As a condition of her return Laura made her promise that she would no longer be a drain on Isabel, who was then recovering from a serious operation. Laura and Schuyler had grown so fed up with her that Sadie was boarded at a neighbor's house before being shipped back to California. Isabel died three years later after a long and painful illness, and her husband, soon after, but Laura's letters make no mention of her mother or her mother's death after her stay in Wabasso. Her brother, Bobby, still lives as a recluse somewhere in Los Angeles, collecting vast quantities of newspaper clippings on subjects that interest him.

Schuyler and Laura clung to the grapefruit business until 1955, when they sold the last of their groves, edged out by bigger concerns in an industry that had come increasingly to rely on expensive fertilizers. After that they began taking trips cross-country in an old English Ford, camping out every night, taking in the scenery and the wildlife and the faces along the way. On one such trip they fell in love with New Mexico and bought a little house (actually an old chapel) in a small town called Watrous, about sixty miles east of Santa Fe. They also took to frequenting hot springs in Georgia and Arkansas in the never ending attempt to rid Schuyler of his aches and pains. Tests, X rays, treatments, diagnoses, remissions, and relapses of old and new problems dominated their worries; the search for the elusive cause of Schuyler's illness was as persistent and enduring as the search for the meaning of words.

In 1955, after a long silence, Griselda wrote to them about her marriage. There was a flurry of bitter letters from Schuyler in which he predicted that it would be disastrous, but their relations warmed again. They wrote to her of their vote for Eisenhower and then Nixon in 1960, judging him not only a more skillful politician than Kennedy but also a man of greater emotional maturity and depth. Barry Goldwater would later capture their imagination; they found in him a man "who says what he means." From the front lawn, Schuyler described to Griselda seeing the launch of the first space rocket from Cape Canaveral. After rising above the northern horizon, the rocket, with its tail flaming, arched out over the Atlantic. He enclosed a postcard of a chimpanzee with his mouth pursed in a kiss, a rare message of hope and humor.

Despite his many illnesses, Schuyler's death on July 4, 1968, came as a shock. He left behind numerous drafts of an unfinished will and, as Ben wrote to Tom Matthews, an "unavoidable responsibility to [Laura] through our duty and love for him which he recognized only in a few brief and fleeting moments." Ben, Maria, and Griselda created the memorial service, which included some words from Laura, the Twenty-third Psalm, a hymn, and the final intonation, "Ashes to ashes." Kit also wrote to Tom:

> . . . it was only on receiving your telegram & your letter that I could grieve—my grief was not for the loss of a beloved person—it was over my dashed hopes and recollection of my grievous faults—I not only hoped but firmly believed that those two extraordinary people would come to their senses. From what I piece together of Schuyler's final days I would not disbelieve that was exactly what happened to him and the shock of facing the enormity of his error was more than his heart could stand.

Schuyler's study remained as he left it; for many years under his pen a small scrap of paper taped to the desk announced, "This is Schuyler's pen!" The six volumes of *The Dawn in Britain* were lined up, awaiting work on the glossary of Charles Doughty's English usage to resume. Even in the dryest months, Laura, with the help of neighbors, tried to keep his grave green and in bloom.

After his death Laura began addressing envelopes as Mrs. Schuyler Jackson. Several years later another name began to appear in print, as Laura (Riding) Jackson slowly emerged from her long silence. A selected edition of her poems appeared in England and America with a manifesto announcing her renunciation of poetry as the foreword. She embarked on extensive correspondences with poets and literary scholars, obscure and well known, fascinating and exasperating them in the 1970s and 1980s as she had in the 1930s. One of them, Professor Michael Kirkham of the University of Toronto, arranged for the publication of *The Telling*, a small meditative work begun while Schuyler was still alive and expanded with passages from her letters to friends. The Guggenheim Foundation provided her grants to write her memoirs, and in 1991, soon after her ninetieth birthday, she was awarded the prestigious Bollingen Prize for poetry from Yale University. That same month she consented to the publication in England of some of her early unpublished poems, and a complete collection of them was announced for publication in the United States and England by the Carcanet Press. Sonia Raiziss, editor of *Chelsea* magazine in New York, also provided her long-standing support, publishing excerpts from various works in progress—even, in 1989, a new poem—accompanied by a long gloss by Laura (Riding) Jackson explaining this rather contradictory act.

In this later correspondence Jackson debated the endless permutations and intricacies of her thought and writing on language, as she did earlier on the question of poetry. One professor received three lengthy letters a week at the height of their correspondence; he was told to respond point by point. Laura Jackson introduced another professor in Massachusetts to a colleague in Colorado via the mails. She instructed an aspiring bibliographer of her work how to write to a scholar of it. Inevitably, each felt their understanding of her present work to be just beyond reach. Nonetheless, Laura Jackson gave every correspondent reason to presume a special intimacy and kinship, though such understandings could be imperiously revoked. At intervals a member of the coterie of "executors" would disappear from the close circle, and care was taken that the name was not raised again, except by "Mrs. Jackson"—and for excoriation only. No matter how long and loyal the correspondent, no matter how tiny the actual, presumed, or imagined misdeed, it was all over.

If Riding was deluded in her pursuit of truth, in her conviction that poetry or language or even plain persistence would bring it to her, this was a necessary delusion untempered by age, infirmity, betrayals in love and friendship, or the death of Schuyler Jackson. If she fooled herself into thinking that she alone (or with Schuyler) was to be the bearer of its glad tidings, she shared that foolishness with every great artist and visionary. Eudora Welty once wrote of Willa Cather that she made her work out of her life, "her perishable life, which is so much safer a material to build with than convictions, however immutable they seem to the one who so passionately holds them." By the same measure, Riding's poetry remains the only safe vessel to hold within it the eminently perishable lives of Laura Reichenthal, Laura Gottschalk, and Laura Riding.

In the spring of 1982, almost ten years before her death, alone in her bungalow in Wabasso, Laura Jackson wrote a short essay that was published, in part, the year she died. It is one of dozens of such works, handwritten or uncertainly typed, that languish uncataloged in the Berg Collection at the New York Public Library. Ostensibly, the subject of "The Only Possible Ending" was storytelling and the storyteller's choice of an ending. But underlying this theme it seems that Laura Jackson was also quietly considering the story of her own life, the calculations that would be made by others, the circumstances that would or would not be taken into account in the telling of this "blotched affair" of uncertain "storyending color." She offered her imagined readers a model story, one that all storytellers might do well to emulate.

Because the present story of Laura Riding's life was written without the help of its original author and in defiance of her wishes, it seems only appropriate that, in some way, Laura Jackson should have the choice of the ending. The story that she chose belonged to an old New Mexico frontier woman. Laura and Schuyler first read her story—which described an incident in her young life when she was newly arrived in the state—in the letters column of a New Mexico magazine. Like all stories, mine is a retelling, hopefully not "in the way the world speaks" but in the spirit that Laura Jackson meant it to be told.

> The bright still silence of noon settled heavily on the house, surrounded as it was by a wilderness still in danger of Indian attack. The woman within had come to the high grasslands of the northeastern quarter of the state as a young bride, following the wagon tracks of the Santa Fe Trail. She was alone now, her husband had gone away,

perhaps just to the nearest town, perhaps much further. To strengthen herself against the vast spaces and the loneliness, the woman sat down at the small player piano she had brought with her across the plains. Vigorously pumping the pedals with her small feet, she soon filled the emptiness with music; her house became a lung of song.

After a while the young woman stopped to rest and consider whether or not to continue with another scroll. In the returning silence she became aware of a presence behind her and turned to find a row of Indians standing motionless at the back of the room, arranged in neat formation. [Here, Laura interrupted herself to speculate that they were Apache Indians.]

The sight was enough to make the woman speed back to the playing of the player piano. In the face of such danger, what else was there to do? Laura Jackson asked her invisible readers intently. Without pause, roll after roll of music rang out. Finally, the woman found herself exhausted and unable to continue. Pale and trembling, she turned towards the Indians to confront her fate. After long moments one Indian in the center of the group stepped forward and in his outstretched hand he held a shiny object. She understood then, and rose quietly from her seat to accept a silver bracelet.

Laura Jackson ended her story with a moral. The truth, she felt, would always be "hidden in ominous persuasion, rapturous presentiments, day-to-day loquacious wisdoms, in ever-varying proportions and incessant change of stress and argument. The only possible ending to this is a falling quiet, a wondering what next, what *finally*. Someone will step forward, offering something shining to the other. And truth, and all present, will be safe."

As an afterthought she conceded that before long her reader will probably turn to another story. That there will be yet another story to tell was a truth that Laura (Riding) Jackson could acknowledge only with impatience.

EPILOGUE

LAURA JACKSON LONG feared that the truth she had so fervently pursued would elude final capture. She feared this not because hers was an impossible ambition but because she had lost command of time, of history, of the story of her own life.

On September 2, 1991, Laura Jackson died of heart failure at the Humana Sebastien Hospital in Sebastien, Florida. Her ashes were buried next to Schuyler's in the Wabasso graveyard. The memorial service, held in the modest house near the railroad tracks, was attended by thirty close friends and neighbors. Polly, owing to previous commitments, could not come. But it was the avatar whom Laura Jackson had so eloquently renounced who survived to provide her epitaph. Time had not run out on her.

Perhaps all along truth had been Laura Riding's pursuer rather than the imagined quarry. Snatched from her as she fled were poems—the cries, prayers, exultations, and visions of a woman perpetually *in extremis*. And so, in a moment that crossed both time and timelessness, the elegy that marked the birth of Laura Riding was read aloud on the day that marked the death of her creator. It began, "Measure me for a burial," and ended:

> Measure me by myself
> And not by time or love or space
> Or beauty. Give me this last grace:
> That I may be on my low stone
> A gage unto myself alone.
> I would not have these old faiths fall
> To prove that I was nothing at all.

NOTES

Archive Abbreviations

BERG: Henry W. and Albert A. Berg Collection, New York Public Library. Esther Antell Cohen letters and miscellaneous unpublished manuscripts; Michael Roberts letters, John Aldridge papers

BL: Beinecke Rare Book and Manuscript Library, Yale University: Gertrude Stein and Cleanth Brook letters

BPL: The Poetry / Rare Books Collection, State University of New York at Buffalo: Robert Graves papers, Alan Hodge papers

CNL: Cornell University Library. Wyndham Lewis Collection and Gussie Gaitskill papers

COL: Columbia University Library; Special Collections. Hart Crane papers, Random House papers, Isidor Schneider papers, Joseph Freeman papers

DEYA: Beryl Graves Collection in Deyá, Mallorca

FUG: The Jean and Alexander Heard Library, Special Collections, Vanderbilt University, Nashville: Fugitive papers

HRC: Harry Ransom Humanities Research Center, University of Texas at Austin

KSR: Kenneth Spencer Research Library, Department of Special Collections, University of Kansas Libraries, Lawrence

LC: Library of Congress, Manuscripts Division: Merrill Moore papers

LL: Lilly Library, University of Indiana, Bloomington: Nicholson and Karl Goldschmidt (Gay) papers

LRJ / SJ: The Laura (Riding) Jackson and Schuyler Jackson Collection at Cornell University

McK: McKeldin Library, Special Collections, University of

Maryland, College Park. Laura and Schuyler Jackson's letters to Robert Nye

NL: Newberry Library, Chicago Public Library. Malcolm Cowley papers

NWUL: Special Collections Department, Northwestern University Library, Evanston

PALMA: Karl Goldschmidt diary

PC: Private Collection

PRI: Princeton University Library, Allen Tate Papers (including papers of Caroline Gordon)

RUL: Reading University Library, Special Collections; letters to Jonathan Cape, Chatto and Windus

SU: George Arents Research Library for Special Collections, Syracuse University, Horace Gregory papers

TSM: Thomas S. Matthews papers

UC: University of Chicago, Louis R. Gottschalk papers

UCLA: University of California, Los Angeles, Department of Special Collections: Edouard Roditi papers

UCSC: University of Chicago, Special Collections. *Poetry* magazine papers and Louis R. Gottschalk papers

UD: Special Collections Department, University of Delaware: W. B. Yeats letter to Laura Riding

UT: University of Toronto, Thomas Fisher Rare Book Library: Jacob Bronowski papers

Name Abbreviations

AH: Alan Hodge
AM: Alfred McIntyre (Little, Brown editor)
AT: Allen Tate
BG: Beryl Graves
CB: Cleanth Brooks
DD: Donald Davidson
DG: David Garnett
DH: Dorothy Hutchinson
EAC: Esther Antell Cohen (Polly)

EP: Eleanor Piel (formerly Eleanor Fitzgerald)
ER: Edouard Roditi
EW: Edmund Wilson
FO'C: Frank O'Connor
GJ: Griselda Jackson
GO: Griselda Ohannessian née Jackson
GP: Geoffrey Phibbs (Taylor)
GS: Gertrude Stein

HC: Hart Crane
HK: Harry Kemp
HM: Harriet Monroe
HMB: Helen Mayers Booth
   (Isabel's sister-in-law)
HP: Herbert Palmer
HWE: Honor Wyatt Ellidge
IG: Ida Gershoy née
   Prighozy
IP: Idella Purnell
IS: Isidor Schneider
JA: John Aldridge
JC: Jonathan Cape
JCR: John Crowe Ransom
JF: Joseph Freeman
JR: James Reeves
KG: Karl Goldschmidt
KTJ: K. T. Jackson (Kit)
LB: Lucie Brown
LG: Louis Gottschalk
LR: Laura Riding
LRG: Laura Riding Gottschalk
   (1920–1926)
LRJ: Laura (Riding) Jackson
   (1941–1991)

MC: Malcolm Cowley
MK: Michael Kirkham
MM: Merrill Moore
MP: Maria Parker née
   Jackson
MS: Montague Simmons
MS-S: Martin Seymour-Smith
NC: Norman Cameron
NM: Norah McGuinness
NN: Nancy Nicholson
PH: Philip Horton, first
   biographer of Hart Crane
RG: Robert Graves
RM: Richard Mayers (LR's
   nephew)
RN: Robert Nye
RPG: Richard Perceval Graves
RPW: Robert Penn Warren
SBS: Sylvia Bernstein Seaman
SJ: Schuyler Jackson
SS: Siegfried Sassoon
TSM: T. S. Matthews
WH: Ward Hutchinson
WL: Wyndham Lewis

Introduction

In December . . . of the times: Schuyler B. Jackson, "Nine and Two," *Time*, December 26,
   1938, 41–44.
"[A]ll I know . . . prize bitch": Paul Mariani, *William Carlos Williams: A New World Naked*
   (New York: McGraw Hill, 1981), 422.
Laura Jackson had a vehement . . . invective: Cf. LRJ to Alfred Kazin, n.d., and LRJ to
   book review editor of the *St. Louis Post-Dispatch*, n.d. (ca. 1977). BERG
When the biography . . . conspiring with Robert Graves: According to MS-S (MS-S to
   GO, July 20, 1983), *The London Review of Books* would not print LRJ's letter accusing
   him of anti-Semitism and of conspiring with RG against her without first securing a
   release from him. He signed it, thus allowing her to discredit herself.

"I wish it were possible ... romance of perception": This untitled poem appears as
    epigraph to LR's *Experts Are Puzzled* (London: Jonathan Cape, 1930). Its source is
    given as "From *Automancy* by Lilith Outcome," one of LR's pseudonyms.
While still in her teens ... professor: LRJ to RN, December 16, 1964. McK.

Chapter 1: Full Epidermal Fevers

"Did I surprise you ... the terror of fulfillment": Laura Riding Gottschalk, "To a Loveless
    Lover," *Collected Poems* (London: Cassell, 1938; New York: Random House, 1938),
    38–39.
But even before ... to date: DD to Jessie B. Rittenhouse, December 15, 1923. FUG.
"His pince-nez ... massive brow": Allen Tate, *Memoirs and Opinions 1926–1974* (Chicago:
    Swallow, 1975), 24–28.
"What were we fleeing ... capable": *Memoirs and Opinions*, 24–28.
Laura (Riding) Jackson ... reductive modernism: Laura (Riding) Jackson, "About the
    Fugitives and Myself" (unpublished manuscript), Group D, Folder 1; forty heavily
    corrected pages, partly typed with many inserts, uncertain pagination. BERG.
Donald Davidson ... Ransom and Hirsch: *Memoirs and Opinions*, 26.
"It is no mere reification ... pubic": AT to HC, April 16, 1923. COL.
"We do not quote ... mind": John Crowe Ransom, *Literary Review* (July and August
    1923).
"Measure me for a burial ... nothing at all": Laura Riding Gottschalk, "Dimensions,"
    Fugitive (August–September 1923), 124.
She wrote to Joseph Freeman ... Middle West: LRG to Joseph Freeman, n.d. COL.
Her undergraduate degree ... correspondent: LRG to DD, n.d. and November 20,
    1924. FUG.
Such desolation was ... than that: LRG to Joseph Freeman, n.d. (ca. 1922). COL.
Thanking one editor ... "What every Young Poet Should Do": LRG to DD, n.d. FUG.
Tate, suffering ... Millays: This remark may not have been in this first letter, but it is one
    that LRJ has often quoted with pride, as evidence of AT's feeling about her work.
The entrance of the Fugitives ... her work: Among LR's very early poems is "On Having
    a Poem Accepted by a Magazine." Cf. Elizabeth Friedmann, Alan J. Clark, and
    Robert Nye, eds., *First Awakenings: The Early Poems of Laura Riding* (Manchester:
    Carcanet, 1992; New York: Persea, 1992), 52–53.
She confessed ... misunderstanding: LRG to AT, December 12, 1923. FUG.
She had no sense ... as well: LRG to DD, n.d. FUG.
Tate's report of the "exceedingly belle": AT to Bill Bandy, April 7, 1924. FUG.
"[Laura Gottschalk] is just about ... understatement": AT to DD, February 21, 1924.
    FUG.
"She's great! ... pericardium": AT to DD, February 27, 1924. FUG.
Her prose was as brilliant ... writing: AT to DD, March 26, 1924. FUG.
"I am more interested ... in sin": RPW to AT, n.d. (ca. March 1924). PRI.
Warren thought ... "Mrs. G.": RPW to AT, n.d. (ca. May 1924). PRI.

Perhaps it would . . . do next?: LRG to DD, November 20, 1924. FUG.

The crisis peaked . . . grew indignant.: LRG letter fragment, n.d. FUG; and "About the Fugitives and Myself," E4–6. BERG.

"Undoubtedly we were . . . an admission": Thomas Daniel Young and George Core, eds., *Selected Letters of John Crowe Ransom* (Baton Rouge: Louisiana State University, 1985), 150.

Her weekend in Nashville . . . from him: LRG to EAC, December 10, 1924. BERG.

The Fugitives sent her two dozen roses: KG interview, September 26, 1989.

Thoughts of him were . . . a stink: LRG to EAC, February 18, 1925. BERG.

Chapter 2: *The Old, Original Dust*

"Do not deny": "Incarnations," *Collected Poems*, 9.

Given his mother's maiden . . . Rydzyna: Chinen Abramsk, Maciej Jachimcczyk, and Antony Polonsky, *The Jews in Poland* (London: Basil Blackwell, 1986), 98.

Met stateside by . . . sweatshops: Melech Epstein, *Jewish Labor in the USA: An Industrial, Political and Cultural History of the Jewish Labor Union Movement* (city unknown: Ktav Publishing House, 1969), 50, 79.

By the time Nathan . . . sixteen years: *Jewish Labor in the USA*, 82; and 1900 Census, New York County, E.D. 598, Sheet 293A.

For Nathan, it was . . . in 1894: 1900 Census and LRJ to RN, n.d. McK.

"misshapen, black ideas . . . how stupid": *Everybody's Letters*, collected and arranged by Laura Riding, with an editorial postscript (London: Arthur Barker, 1933), 127–28. This book was a collection of real letters that LR found interesting. While the names and addresses have been changed, it is clear from the facts known about LR's family that this letter is from her mother and was sent to her for the book by her half sister, Isabel. The book contains several other family letters and provides the main source of information about Sadie Edersheim, LR's mother.

Her daughter Laura . . . "downtown": Cf. "To the Chairman of the Seminar on Laura Riding and Robert Graves: A Letter of Varied Commentary" (unpublished; circulated privately). December 17, 1974. LRJ's response to the proposed MLA seminar on RG and LR. LRJ/SJ.

Thus "Nathaniel" . . . "American born": "A Letter of Varied Commentary."

Nathan, by nature gay and high-spirited: RM interview, May 8, 1989.

Released from . . . rabbinical scholars: Morris Hilquit, *Loose Leaves from a Busy Life* (New York: Macmillan, 1934), 15–40.

"Jewish Socialism was . . . brotherhood": Irving Howe, *How We Lived: A Documentary History of Immigrant Jews in America 1880–1930* (New York: Richard Marek, 1979), 161.

"intense personal abuse . . . the rule": Hutchins Hapgood, *The Spirit of the Ghetto* (Boston: Belknap/Harvard University, 1967), 39–40.

"I am imbued with the idea . . . facts": *Everybody's Letters*, 112–13. This letter is dated May 1929, New York, and is signed Adolf. It refers clearly to LR's betrayal by GP, which precipitated her suicide attempt, and is written by a person who had been actively involved in the Socialist Labor party and the Socialist party as well as the garment industry. It is an affectionate and sympathetic letter written by a man who fits Nathan Reichenthal in every particular.

The editors . . . sacred duty: Moses Rischin, *The Promised City: New York's Jews 1870–1914* (Boston: Harvard University, 1962), 167.

"The difficulty with . . . Marxian socialism": Loren Baritz, ed., *The American Left: Radical Political Thought in the 20th Century* (New York: Basic, 1971), 502.

"the poetry of the oppressed miserable workingman": *The Promised City*, 167.

"fanatical internationalist . . . sensitive tinctures": *Everybody's Letters*, 112–13.

"Every poor fellow . . . not so bad": Laura Riding, "Fine Fellow Son of a Poor Fellow," *Love as Love, Death as Death* (London: Seizin, 1928), 27. The version published in the *Collected Poems* (1938) is significantly changed.

"When they die . . . personalities": *The Spirit of the Ghetto*, 39–40.

Out of their fractious . . . Dreiser: *How We Lived*, 161.

She defended her father . . . social aspiration: "A Letter of Varied Commentary." LRJ/SJ.

Among the few possessions . . . labor movement: RM to author, June 15, 1989.

As a child . . . fairy tales: LR to Jeffrey Marks, March 30, 1933. DEYA.

She reminded Nathan . . . decadents!: Laura Jackson, "Curiosities of Literary Prejudices" (unpublished). BERG.

In the old country . . . circumvention of them: Rafael Patai, *The Jewish Mind* (New York: Scribners, 1977), 499–500.

A bitter, angry argument . . . Isabel: LRJ refers to this in her memoirs and in a letter to KG on her father's death, December 24, 1938. She would most likely have moved in with Isabel, but this is speculation. LL.

Chapter 3: Back to the Mother Breast

"My mother imagined . . . suffer from it": Laura Riding, "Letter of Abdication," *Anarchism Is Not Enough* (London: Jonathan Cape, 1928; Garden City, NY: Doubleday, Doran, 1928), 209.

The Reichenthal's shared . . . Danish maid: 1900 Census, New York County, E.D. 598, Sheet 293A.

"My child . . . lie in it": *Everybody's Letters*, 127–28.

One Christmas she . . . her point: HWE interview, September 5, 1989.

She let her daughter . . . but defiance: LR to KG, December 24, 1938. LL.

"three-cornered pattern . . . successful personality": Laura (Riding) Jackson, "Introduction to a Book of Later-life Commentaries," *Sulfur* 20 (Fall 1987), 102.

Laura attended almost a dozen primary schools: Stanley J. Kunitz and Howard Haycraft, eds., *American Authors and Books, 1640–1940* (New York: H. W. Wilson, 1942), 1173.

Despite Sadie's pestering her to play outdoors: *Sulfur* 20 (Fall 1987), 101.

"An early, unpublished poem entitled "One Right, One Left": This poem originally had fifty lines. When LR's early poems were published in 1992 in a collection entitled

First Awakenings, the editors, cooperating with LRJ, decided not to include any poems in which a later published version existed, however truncated. The three lines quoted here were published in *Poems A Joking Word* (London: Jonathan Cape, 1930; pages 43–46) under the title "Fragments." In the same poem "fragments" of at least one other extant early poem can be found.

"My God, My God . . . pregnancy": *Everybody's Letters*, 127–28.

Acutely unhappy . . . precipitously worse: RM interview, May 8, 1989.

Riding told a close friend . . . attempted suicide: KG interview, September 26, 1989.

According to one . . . family lavatory: Clara Berenberg Schaap to TSM, n.d. Clara Berenberg's sister was both a friend of Isabel's and LR's piano teacher. TSM.

"My dear mother . . . loving daughter": *Everybody's Letters*, 119.

"Lida": *Poems A Joking Word*, 25–31.

With thick brown . . . Grosset and Dunlap: RM to author, June 15, 1989.

For Laura . . . golden hair: LRJ to RN, n.d. (ca. late 1964). McK.

From her accent . . . "greatly to her mortification": *Selected Letters of John Crowe Ransom*, 143.

"where the fear . . . ordinary talk": Laura (Riding) Jackson, "Twentieth Century Change in the Idea of Poetry, and of the Poet, and of the Human Being." *PN Review*, 14, (Supplement), 77–78.

Laura owed . . . the name Ellen Rogers: RM to author, June 15, 1989.

A party to . . . Laura piano lessons: Clara Berenberg Schaap to TSM, n.d. TSM.

The couple moved . . . on Ocean avenue: RM to author, June 15, 1989.

Jesse's sister . . . to school: HMB to author, June 20, 1989; Robert Weinberg to TSM, n.d. TSM.

"We could be brilliant . . . sweet dispositions": *Brooklyn Girls' High School Triennial*, 1913 ed.

She staged . . . First World War: Bertha Heller interview, December 30, 1989.

"Our hearts . . . socialism": Joseph Freeman, *An American Testament* (New York: Farrar, Rhinehart, 1936), 65.

In Jesse . . . support of her family: HMB to author, June 2, 1989.

After graduating . . . two scholarships: The Eudorus C. Kenney and a New York State Regents' scholarship. LRJ refers to three scholarships, but I could not confirm this.

During the interval . . . she became quickly bored: LRG to JF, n.d. COL; and LRG to Donald Davidson, n.d. FUG.

"Laura had completely . . . her mother": HMB to author, June 20, 1989.

"Back to the mother breast . . . there is no heart.": Laura Riding Gottschalk, "Back to the Mother Breast," *The Close Chaplet* (New York: Adelphi, 1926; London: Hogarth, 1926), 47.

In the mid-1960s . . . to resolve: LRJ to RN, January 2, 1965. McK.

The story was . . . personal matters: LRG to DD, n.d. FUG.

"Alas! . . . her position": "Fragment of an Unfinished Novel," *Anarchism Is Not Enough*, 149.

"How often have . . . unhappy": *Anarchism Is Not Enough*, 149.

There is evidence . . . self-induced: GP to RG, June 5, 1929. DEYA. See also Laura Riding, *Convalescent Conversations* (London: Constable, 1936; Deyá, Mallorca: Seizin, 1936), 14–15.

The lengths to which . . . real one: When RG's *Selected Letters* were published, LR came across references to her miserable childhood, phrased in a manner that she indignantly deemed "benevolent pity." Though she was clearly his source, in a letter to the MLA, which was sponsoring a seminar on RG and LR, LRJ minimized her childhood difficulties due to the "traits of one of [her] parents" and described her childhood as commonplace. Cf. Laura (Riding) Jackson "To the Chairman of the Seminar on 'Laura Riding and Robert Graves' MLA 1974: A Letter of Varied Commentary," n.d.; and "Postscript to A Letter of Varied Commentary," December 17, 1974. LRJ/SJ.

Her "basic . . . little being": *Sulfur* 20 (Fall 1987), 104.

Claiming the romantic . . . dirty grip: *An American Testament*, 46.

Riding, too . . . "well spoken": "Twentieth Century Change in the Idea of Poetry, the Poet, and the Human Being," 78, 88.

Chapter 4: *The Waiting Equipage*

"Chloe or her modern sister . . . end an age": "Chloe Or . . ." *Collected Poems*, 17.

Laura made a point . . . Urbana, alone: LRG to Gussie Gaitskill, n.d. (ca. December 1921 or January 1922). LRJ/SJ.

"We listened to her . . . who did": SBS interview, November 18, 1989.

"You have meant . . . injury": Morris Bishop, *A History of Cornell* (Ithaca, N.Y.: Cornell University, 1962), 149–52.

Her real name . . . hated it: EAC interview, May 17, 1989.

Her light brown hair . . . "Jewish girl": SBS interview, November 18, 1989.

All the co-eds . . . classmates. . . . "Ordinary things . . . attention": SBS interview, November 18, 1989.

Her poems . . . "buying public": Sylvia Seaman and Frances Schwartz, *Glorious to View* (unpublished novel). PC.

"It was an exciting . . . something wrong": Laura Riding, *Progress of Stories* (London: Constable, 1935; Deyá, Mallorca: Seizin, 1935), 37.

"Without the discipline . . . literary level": *Glorious to View*. PC.

"to leave me free . . . naturally": *Cornell Alumni News*, October 1983.

"passionate, scholarly good looks. . . . On an instructor's salary . . . few years": *Glorious to View*. PC.

Early in 1920 . . . "very selective": EAC interview, May 17, 1989.

"a kind of Jewish . . . brilliance": SBS interview, November 18, 1989.

Other days . . . Socialist party: Gershoy Memorial. UC.

"I may even . . . very lovely": EAC interview, May 17, 1989.

She was often . . . *Das Kapital*: LR to Jeffrey Marks, March 30, 1933. DEYÁ.

One evening in the fall of 1920 . . . Sylvia remembered: SBS interview, November 18, 1989.

"And you want everybody . . . similar glory": *Glorious to View*, PC.

a collusion of temperament and twenty: LRG to DD, n.d. FUG.

"At six little girls in love . . . I say She": "Postponement of Immortality," *Poems A Joking Word*, 87.

"direct, frequent and generally warm": LG to Warren Kuehl, January 16, 1967. UC.

"Their friendship . . . criticized him": F. G. Marcham to author, February 6, 1989.

"In defence . . . it goes": Laura Riding, *Voltaire: A Biographical Fantasy* (London: Hogarth, 1927), 3.

Laura had also . . . lakeside cottage: LRG to EAC, August 20, 1924. BERG.

"It didn't take much . . . do now": IG interview, November 16, 1989.

There she had . . . Leo and Lou: EAC interview, May 17, 1989.

Laura wrote her . . . Leo for that: LRG to EAC, August 26 and December 10, 1924. BERG.

"Ida was too much Ida": HMB to author, June 20, 1989.

"Why do you come fantastically folded . . . wantonly unviolated": Laura Riding, "Improprieties," *Fugitive* 3 (April 1924), 56–57.

Even before . . . destroyed it: LRG to DD, March 28, 1924. FUG.

"Good manners, Madame, are had these days not . . . To words": Allen Tate, "Credo: An Aesthetic," *Fugitive* 4 (June 1924), 87.

"I've observed many . . . perilous": JCR to RG, June 12, 1925. FUG.

"The requisite spot of anguish having shown . . . passion to stone": "Fragments from Alastor," *Poems A Joking Word*, 51–54.

"A very volatile . . . worthless": AT to DD, May 7, 1924. FUG.

Mindful of . . . explain later: AT to DD, August 6, 1924. FUG.

Entitled "The Mad Serenader": LRG to DD, n.d. FUG.

Any poet . . . while she dreamed: LRG to DD, n.d. (ca. August 1924). FUG.

Ransom had isolated . . . formlessness: John Crowe Ransom, "The Future of Poetry," *Fugitive* 3 (February 1924), 2–4.

"There is no common-to-all . . . gone": Allen Tate, reply to John Crowe Ransom, *Fugitive* 3 (April 1924), 34–36.

"For the poets . . . expressionists": Laura Riding Gottschalk, "A Prophecy or a Plea," *Reviewer* (April 1925), 2.

"the birth . . . insight for outsight": "A Prophecy or a Plea," 3.

In 1911 . . . below them: *Flappers, Prohibition and All That Jazz* (Louisville: Museum of History and Science, 1984), 6–24.

"Wondering how much . . . they'd like to have": Laura Riding, "Saturday Night," *Fugitive* 3 (December 1924), 144–45.

Formerly kept . . . Macauley's Theater: *Flappers, Prohibition and All That Jazz*, 22.

She had a passion . . . a reply: LRJ to GO, n.d. LRJ/SJ.

She had first hatched . . . was required: LRG to DD, July 25, 1924. FUG.

After sending . . . and tact: LRG to DD, October 13, 1924. FUG.

He wrote cheerfully . . . on Paris: LG to EAC, May 12, 1925. BERG.

"high strung . . . than most": Joyce Piell Wexler, *Laura Riding's Pursuit of Truth* (Athens: Ohio University, 1979), 7–8.

Writing to Polly . . . distinction: LG to EAC, March 26, 1925. BERG.

After her divorce . . . during the journey: LRG to IP, n.d. (ca. August 22, 1925). HRC.

"fallen into one another's arms": SBS interview, November 18, 1989.

His ex-wife . . . Greenwich Village: LRG to IP, n.d. (ca. August 22, 1925). HRC.

Chapter 5: Stranded in a Half-told Tale

"There was an insufficiency . . . in a half-told tale": "John and I," *Collected Poems*, 44–46.

From there . . . the Village: LRG to HM, n.d. UCSC.

"The more we analyzed . . . achieved": *An American Testament*, 233, 236.

"We were all . . . prominent people": Malcolm Cowley, *Exile's Return* (New York: Viking, 1959), 71, 72, 208, 222.

She dropped a few . . . Mark van Doren: LRG to HM, n.d. UCSC.

"more energy than . . . thrown in": Louise Cowan, *The Fugitive Group: A Literary History* (Baton Rouge: Louisiana State University, 1959), 217.

"Laura, incidentally . . . about everything": AT to DD, September 22, 1925. FUG.

"The little quids . . . idea of a holiday": Laura Riding, "The Quids," *Fugitive* 3 (February 1924), 10–11.

"cruellest of . . . cruel poems": Edmund Wilson, *New Republic*, March 7, 1928, 103–4.

"mad year": LR to PH, May 22, 1936. BL.

By late 1924 . . . was born: Ann Waldron, *Close Connections* (New York: G. P. Putnam's Sons, 1987), 39.

Instead of the wide . . . stomach ailment: AT to MC, March 30, 1926. NL.

"It is great . . . if strenuous!": AT to DD, September 30, 1925. FUG.

Laura (Riding) Jackson later . . . elevated: Laura (Riding) Jackson, "About the Fugitives and Myself," *Times Literary Supplement*, December 22, 1983, 61; BERG. In this letter to the editor, written after the deaths of both Caroline and AT, LRJ also suggests that it was AT who fell in love with her but refrained from acting owing to a "preceding commitment to Caroline Gordon."

"There is nothing . . . I know": *Close Connections*, 299.

"essentially without . . . moral scrutiny": *Close Connections*, 299.

"he would appear . . . ever written?": *Exile's Return*, 228–29.

"[I]f they are . . . own colors": "A Prophecy or a Plea," 2. Her early poem "Brothers" seems to contain a portrait of HC; following stanzas describing LG and AT is one of HC, the "ruthless third, exalted and devout." *First Awakenings*, 156.

"each household somewhat the worse for wear": Susan Jenkins Brown, "Hart Crane: The End of Harvest," *Southern Review* 4 (October 1968), 945–1014.

"There have been . . . well hence": John Eugene Unterecker, *Voyager: A Life of Hart Crane* (New York: Farrar, Straus and Giroux, 1969), 217.

For a time . . . their meals: LR to PH, January 1, 1937. BL.

Allen and Caroline . . . their minds: Cf. LR to PH, May 22, 1936. In this letter LR writes that she was expected to purge HC of his homosexuality by sacrificing herself to his reformation. The implication is that she never tried to do so, though this is contradicted by her comments to KG.

Polly, who described . . . what it meant: EAC interview, May 17, 1989.

Though Laura . . . directing his life: KG interview, September 26, 1989.

"There is a tendency . . . to the core": AT to HC, n.d. COL.

Crane made a point . . . in mind: Brom Weber, ed., *Complete Poems and Selected Letters and Prose of Hart Crane* (New York: Liverright, 1966), 127.

"I'll show you . . . Lorna!": LR to PH, January 1, 1937. BL.

"Astonished stood . . . the quiet": "Lucrece and Nara," *The Close Chaplet*, 16.

"But meagre was the man . . . all heaven ahead": "Druida," *Collected Poems*, 40.

"The inferiority complex . . . manifestation": AT to DD, March 3, May 14, 1926. FUG.

"good business man . . . for 'letters' ": AT to EW, December 13, 1925. BL.

"if [Laura] weren't . . . at all": AT to EW, December 13, 1925. BL.

"As soon as she . . . series!": AT to DD, January 3, 1926. FUG.

"casually affiliated . . . naiveté": AT to Horace Gregory, October 12, 1944. SU.

"after we had . . . first place": AT to Horace Gregory, October 4, 1944. SU.

"Why the special . . . me off?": "About the Fugitives and Myself." BERG.

"to save her life . . . forms": JCR to RG, September 23, 1925. FUG.

"shrewd, avant gardist . . . superficial": J. M. Bradbury, *The Fugitives* (Chapel Hill: University of North Carolina, 1958), 79.

"To these serious . . . equal basis": Louise Cowan, *The Fugitive Group: A Group Literary History* (Baton Rouge: Louisiana State University, 1959), 9, 184.

Cowan . . . subtleties of disdain: "About the Fugitives and Myself." BERG.

To become a poet . . . more for her: LRG to AT, December 12, 1923. FUG.

Their good-bye was affectionate . . . intrigue: LR to PH, January 1, 1937. BL.

"a triumph . . . conviction": Laura (Riding) Jackson, "Literary News as Literary History," *Massachusetts Review* 21 (Winter 1980), 672.

She went as . . . literary collaborators: LRG to HM, n.d. UCSC.

"I fear disaster . . . a month": AT to DD, January 3, 1926. FUG.

Chapter 6: *The Emotions of an Audience*

"You watched me act . . . of an audience": "Letter of Abdication," *Anarchism Is Not Enough*, 223.

"People don't . . . in dead earnest": Madeleine Vara (pseud.), *Convalescent Conversations*.

Laura (Riding) Jackson, counting . . . expression: "Opportunism Rampant" (unpublished) BERG. Written a year or so after MS-S's biography of RG appeared, this is a passionate denunciation of both RG and MS-S, recalling LR's early essays in intensity, colorful insult, and rage. The bitter disappointment with her love for RG, GP, and literature itself is everywhere apparent, even as LRJ describes her hope and faith that truth will appear to her and recognize the loyalty of her striving. While LRJ proposes at the outset to examine questions of documentation, in fact, she relies on the authenticity of her feelings. At one point she crosses out the phrase "I had only the comfort that I knew" and replaces it with "I had only the comfort of objectively measurable evidence."

"[Nancy]: I made [Robert] . . . stop it": Laura Riding and George Ellidge, *14A: A Novel Told in Dramatic Form* (London: Arthur Barker, 1934), 271.

Glaring at the helplessness . . . pushed off: "Opportunism Rampant." BERG.

"[Jenny]: Oh . . . falling out": *14A*, 256.

The English poet laureate . . . London and Dublin: John Betjeman and Geoffrey Taylor, eds., *English Love Poems* (London: Faber and Faber, 1957), 9–10.

The Devil! . . . him in: "Opportunism Rampant." BERG.

"[Geoffrey] is tall . . . other person": *14A*, 10.

In fact, Phibbs . . . lectures or exams: Letter and enclosures from Simon Nowell-Smith to author, now in BERG.

"With the two thirds . . . to himself": Frank O'Connor, *My Father's Son* (London: Macmillan, 1968), 21, 23, 25.

"Alas, too late . . . his theories": NM to TSM, March 6, 1978. TSM.

"I don't suppose . . . moment anyway": DG to GP, n.d. BERG.

Geoffrey's second wife . . . illustrator: Mary Taylor to author, n.d.

"Naturally the important . . . Ireland": GP to RG, October 1928. BPL.

"[Norah]: My husband is leaving . . . not real": *14A*, 11.

"Laura, as cold . . . page boys": NM to TSM, March 6, 1978. TSM.

Laura (Riding) Jackson remembered . . . work widen: "Opportunism Rampant." BERG.

"It is bad to live . . . still exists": DG to GP, September 15, 1928. BERG.

"To that phrase . . . all Ireland": FO'C to GP, n.d. BPL.

"[Geoffrey's] letters . . . was missing": *My Father's Son*, 69.

Silently calculating . . . the strain: *My Father's Son*, 69.

"He is untidy . . . bounder": *14A*, 10.

"[Geoffrey]: Couldn't . . . France": *14A*, 123.

Laura (Riding) Jackson remembered . . . he was found: "Opportunism Rampant." BERG.

"[Robert] does not allow . . . situation": *14A*, 34.

"[Laura]: We've come about . . . snake!": *14A*, 137.

"[Norah] has purposely . . . beautiful": *14A*, 8.

"[Robert]: It was just so untidy . . . to you": *14A*, 185.

"[Laura]: I know . . . in London": *14A*, 186.

"I carry her Rouen . . . futility": GP to RG, n.d. BPL.

"Where accident . . . last word": "Opportunism Rampant." BERG.

"my rug was . . . Queen": *Anarchism Is Not Enough*, 222.

"I have said . . . permitted": *Anarchism Is Not Enough*, 222.

"left the room . . . suicide": *Poems A Joking Word*, 16, 18.

Chapter 7: *The Sphinx in Egypt*

"Of old there was a spirit . . . and peace": "The Lady of the Apple," *The Close Chaplet*, 62.

"For could . . . her pleasure": from "Dedicatory Epilogue to Laura Riding," Robert Graves, *Good-bye to All That: An Autobiography* (New York: Harrison Smith, 1930), 428.

In his account . . . tone of chalk: Martin Seymour-Smith, *Robert Graves: His Life and Work* (New York: Holt, Rinehart and Winston, 1982), 122.

Later, after their relations . . . quite short: RPG interview, September 13, 1989.

More brilliant . . . speechless: LRG to EAC, March 26, 1926. BERG.

She insisted . . . for Egypt: In every instance where RPG allows LRJ a dissenting voice concerning the facts of published accounts, she invariably misremembers; contrary contemporary statements exist in her letters to EAC.

"He stayed until 7:15 . . . Oxfordshire": Anne Oliver Bell, ed., *The Diary of Virginia Woolf, 1925–1930*, vol. 3, 2nd ed. (dated April 27, 1925, entry for April 23 visit), 13.

But to Laura . . . manner: LRG to EAC, March 26, 1926. BERG.

"There is a coldness . . . insolence": *Good-bye to All That*, 13.

"I am glad . . . poets": *Good-bye to All That*, 15, 33.

"a certain Robert . . . memory": Paul O'Prey, ed., *In Broken Images*: Selected Letters of Robert Graves 1914–1916 (London: Hutchinson, 1982), 134.

"I wrote this dedication . . . hoot-fan": *Robert Graves: His Life and Work*, 135.

"Poor Robert . . . sensation": *Robert Graves: The Years with Laura 1926–1940* (New York: Viking, 1990), 133.

"not so far as I know . . . Squalling Brats": *In Broken Images*, 152.

"Despite stout assurances . . . autobiography": In a letter to RN dated April 13, 1965, LRJ comments on MS-S's "obsession with homosexuality," suggesting that he got this from RG. Curiously, she goes on to suggest that this obsession with homosexuality was something that RG picked up from her; though he might "sneer and snicker," he had never had any real distress over the subject.

"Though easily . . . shyness": Siegfried Sassoon, *Diaries* (London: Faber and Faber, 1985), 234, 271.

She found everything . . . Nancy creation: LRG to EAC, March 26, 1926. BERG.

Eleven-year old . . . were sisters: Sally Chilver to author, October 15, 1989.

"It may be . . . ever encountered": LG to EAC, February 2, 1926. BERG.

One evening in Piccadilly . . . irrevocable and fated: LRG to EAC, March 26, 1926. BERG.

Cairo . . . resisted analysis: LRG to EAC, March 26, 1926. BERG. Riding . . . called them devils: LRG to IP, May 13, 1926. HRC.

The trio did seem . . . God and Empire: LRG to EAC, March 26, 1926. BERG.

"in some distant dream of erotic bliss": Malcolm Muggeridge, *Chronicles of Wasted Time* (London: William Collins, 1975), 168.

Robert, after writing POET . . . ridiculous: *In Broken Images*, 165.

As evidence . . . Robert did: LRG to EAC, March 26, 1926. BERG.

In Egypt, too . . . revisions: LRG to EAC, March 26, 1926. BERG.

"To speak of the hallow nape . . . 'a present need.' ": Robert Graves, "The Nape of the Neck," *Poems (1914–1926)* (London: William Heinemann, 1927), 212.

It was in Egypt . . . blessed her: LRJ refers to this agreement in "Opportunism Rampant"; at the time of the breakup with RG she again refers to it.

"The Witch identifies the Devil . . . with destruction": "Samuel's Toast of Death," *The Close Chaplet*, 38–39.

"At a time of full arrival . . . vastness into dust": "The Lady of the Apple," *The Close Chaplet*, 62–65.

"As well as any other . . . rarely may be found": "As Well as Any Other," *The Close Chap-let*, 9.

One day, Laura wrote . . . ghost: LRG to IP, May 13, 1926. HRC; and evil spirits: LRG to EAC, March 26, 1926. BERG.

Chapter 8: *Nancy's Laura's Robert and Nancy's Robert's Laura*

"Cover up . . . a mask eternal": "The Mask," *Collected Poems*, 15.

Laura asked Polly . . . break the lock: LRG to EAC, undated letters from Egypt, Islip, and Vienna and October 27, 1926. BERG.

Much like the manuscript . . . Robert and Nancy: LRG to EAC, n.d. (perhaps from Vienna). BERG.

To Laura, too . . . ridiculously happy: LRG to EAC, n.d. BERG.

Undaunted, he asked . . . refused: LRJ to RN, January 2, 1965. McK.

After returning . . . no time alone: Dorothy Mayer interview, December 2, 1989: "Not once was he alone with Laura, and the whole thing was a 'bust.' "

When Polly . . . mystification: LRG to EAC, August 4, 1926. BERG.

In many respects . . . nurtured her: Joyce Piell Wexler, "Construing the Word: An Introduction to the Writings of Laura (Riding) Jackson" (diss., Northwestern University, 1974), 18.

"One no longer tries . . . by itself": Laura Riding and Robert Graves, *A Survey of Modernist Poetry* (London: William Heinemann, 1927), 124–25.

Imagism, for example . . . "never called": *A Survey of Modernist Poetry*, 117, 123, 135. However easy it was for LR to dismiss H.D. in 1926, there were confluences in their approach to their work. Hilda Doolittle, christened H.D. by her mentor and lover Ezra Pound, was an American poet whose chiseled early lyrics (D.H. Lawrence likened them to "frozen altars") gained her work wide renown in England and America before the war. In 1919 H.D. wrote a long essay entitled "Thought and Vision" that contained ideas similar to those of Riding's "A Proph-ecy and a Plea." "There is no great art period without great lovers," H.D. wrote. "We must be 'in love' before we can understand the mysteries of vision." H.D. also imagined—in a soaring language of breathless abstraction and oblique imagery— that "two or three people with healthy bodies and the right sort of receiving brains, could turn the whole tide of human thought, could direct lightning flashes of electric power to slash across the world of dead, murky thought." While Riding would disdain the Lawrentian "healthy bodies," she would second the more Nietzschean "super feelers of the super mind." H.D.'s fictional writings, though more impressionistic stylistically and less innovative structurally, devolve, like Riding's, obsessively on the story of her life and work. Showing less concern with narrative drama than with continual personal revelation, both writers plumbed and sounded their psychological depths and those of their intimates. In every-thing that they wrote they revealed an egocentric view of the world, but with "I" in constant redefinition.

Whatever enthusiasm . . . contribution: RG later came to rescind even this mild appro-
bation, following LR's lead. Cf. Julian Symons, "An Evening in Maida Vale," *London
Magazine* 3 (January 1964), 37.

Significantly, before Graves . . . discovered: Robert Graves, *Poetic Unreason and Other
Studies* (London: Cecil Palmer, 1925), 39-40.

"discover what it is we are really feeling": *A Survey of Modernist Poetry,* 89–90, 279,
282.

"Poetry must stim . . . poetic sense": Laura Riding and Robert Graves, *A Pamphlet Against
Anthologies* (London: Jonathan Cape, 1928), 122.

"I certainly remember . . . Spring of 1926": RG to "Audrey," January 29, 1934. DEYA.

In 1966 Graves modified . . . sideswipe: Cf. RG's reply to James Jensen's "The Construction of the Seven Types of Ambiguity," *Modern Language Quarterly* 27 (September
1966), 243–59.

"The book dared . . . chief virtue": Stanley Edgar Hyman, *The Armed Vision: A Study in the
Methods of Modern Literary Criticism* (New York: Knopf, 1952), 272, 294.

"I had not the book . . . pretty thick": LR to Chatto and Windus, February 9, 1931.
RUL.

In the 1947 . . . "using here": William Empson, *Seven Types of Ambiguity* (New York: New
Directions, 1947), xiv.

When Graves took credit . . . gallantry: LRJ to CB, June 25, 1977, and August 22, 1971.
BL.

"poetry on-the-way-to-becoming science": JCR to RG, June 12, 1925. FUG.

Brooks, in a 1971 . . . some time later: CB to LRJ, September 10, 1971. "I expect I was
influenced, unconsciously, if not directly and consciously, by what I learned from
the Riding and Graves text." Brooks also claims that he did not read *Seven Types of
Ambiguity* until two years after his textbook was published.

"The quids resolved . . . grammar": "The Quids," *The Close Chaplet,* 10–11.

If all felt well . . . from without: LRG to EAC, n.d. (possibly from Vienna), BERG.

In the "contemporaneous universe" . . . minor practicality: LRG to EAC, October 27,
1926. BERG.

Laura wrote . . . to get well: LRG to EAC, October 27, 1926. BERG.

An unusually pious . . . was thinking: Unpublished memoir by Amalia von Ranke Graves.
DEYA.

"Agree, it is better . . . as your own": Robert Graves, "The Taint," *Harpers* (September
1926), 502.

"What we came . . . ain't it?" *In Broken Images,* 169.

John Graves . . . "ménage à trois": John Graves to MS-S, referring to his father's diary.
BPL.

Rosaleen . . . "the Jewess": *Robert Graves: The Years with Laura,* 39, 49.

Richard Perceval Graves . . . rejects it: In a letter written two years after his biography of
RG, MS-S was insistent on the subject of LR's madness, spiritual fraudulence, and
outright capacity for evil. MS-S to GO, July 20, 1983. PC.

That APG and Amy's . . . victory: LRG to EAC, October 27, 1926. BERG.

Everything else in the trunk . . . been burned: LRG to EAC, n.d. (Vienna), BERG.

Chapter 9: Anarchism Is Not Enough

"Before that in all the periods . . . ever since": Patricia Meyerowitz, ed., *Gertrude Stein's Writings and Lectures 1911–1945* (London: Peter Owen, 1967), 31.

"In nineteen twenty-seven . . . had a greening": Laura Riding, "In Nineteen Twenty-Seven," *Love as Love, Death as Death* (London: Seizin, 1928), 59. All quotations in this chapter are from this version.

"It seems a pity . . . it up": Peter Quennell, *Weekend Telegraph*, October 20, 1990.

Deeply shocked . . . to London: *Robert Graves: The Years with Laura*, 47.

In her real life . . . mysterious affair: LRJ to RN, December 16, 1964. McK.

In the imagined . . . of her unquiet: LRJ to RN, December 16, 1964. McK.

Donald Davidson . . . for her nerves: LR to DD, n.d. FUG.

Nancy began working . . . "new pin": *Robert Graves: The Years with Laura*, 46.

In doing so . . . New York: LRG to DD, n.d. (from Vienna), FUG.

To another . . . making her unwell: LRG to EAC, n.d. BERG.

"[W]e are apt to . . . about me": *In Broken Images*, 174.

"One visitor . . . about his proceedings": Jack Lindsay, *Fanfrolico and After* (London: Bodley Head, 1963), 80–81.

"her poems of detached . . . Gertrude Stein": John Gould Fletcher's review of *The Close Chaplet*, in *Monthly Criterion: A Literary Review* 6 (August 1927), 170.

A month later . . . skirmish: LR to DD, n.d. (ca. August 1927). FUG.

Davidson addressed his reply . . . women's writing: DD to LR, October 4, 1927; LR reply on bottom. FUG.

At the Hogarth . . . 125 copies: Account books, Hogarth Press. RUL. In 1936, nine years after *Voltaire* was printed, 90 copies remained out of an edition of 250.

Drawing together . . . appeared: From the correspondence with Pinker and Sons in Lawrence, Kansas, and Northwestern University, it is clear that most of Part I of "Poetry and the Literary Universe" was written in Vienna; Part II, "T. E. Hulme, The New Barbarism, and Gertrude Stein," and Part III, "The Facts in the Case of Monsieur Poe," were written in Islip.

Begun in America . . . same issue: *Calendar of Modern Letters* 2 (October 1925).

She demonstrated how . . . Paul Valéry: Laura Riding, "The Absolute of Poetry," 12 pp. unpublished. DEYA.

Her "Worst Self" . . . *Dial*: LR to Pinker, n.d. KSR.

"In addition to . . . apartness": Arnold Bennett, *The Evening Standard Years* (London: Chatto and Windus, 1974), 132.

"put on the literary dog": Genevieve Taggard, "Cat and Mouse," *New York Herald Tribune Books* (January 6, 1929), 13.

"The rats are . . . decline of Venice": *A Survey of Modernist Poetry*, 240.

"[H]owever extreme . . . be serious": *A Survey of Modernist Poetry*, 251.

"There is a sense . . . in kind": Laura Riding, *Contemporaries and Snobs* (London: Jonathan Cape, 1928), 9.

"Even in this day . . . the Myth": *Anarchism Is Not Enough*, 10–11.

These critics . . . bourgeois society: *Contemporaries and Snobs*, 15–17.

"Never has poetry . . . dangerous to it": Roy Campbell, "A Question of Taste," *Nation and Atheneum* (March 3, 1928): 877–18.

"What, then . . . Aristotelianism?": *Contemporaries and Snobs*, 119.

"By being a mathematical . . . found correct": *Anarchism Is Not Enough*, 22–23.

"The only way . . . own devices": *Contemporaries and Snobs*, 109–10.

Poetry was deemed . . . " 'contrary fellow' ": *Anarchism Is Not Enough*, 11.

"[There is a woman] . . . divorce": *Anarchism Is Not Enough*, 134, 135.

"How came it about": *Anarchism Is Not Enough*, 133–34.

From the safety . . . stared at: LR to DH, June 8, 1936. PC.

She told Donald Davidson . . . avoid the censor: LR to DD, n.d. FUG; in this letter she refers to the book as *MSS I*, whereas in a letter to Polly it is *Miss I*.

"[I]t affected me in the same . . . no one pleasure": *Anarchism Is Not Enough*, 47, 51, 54.

Among Riding's very early poems: Laura (Riding) Jackson, "For Rebecca West (On Reading *The Judge*)," cf. *First Awakenings*, 89–90.

"Prose is the . . . poem": *Anarchism Is Not Enough*, 117.

In Emily Brontë . . . "criticism of sex": Virginia Woolf, *A Room of One's Own* (New York, Harcourt, Brace and World, 1929, 1957), 78.

"see whether you don't . . . in causes": Nigel Nicolson, ed., *A Reflection of the Other Person: The Letters of Virginia Woolf, 1929–1931*, vol. 4 (London: Chatto and Windus, 1983), 327–28. This letter to Ethel Smyth provoked a testy response. A composer and suffragist who had spent time in prison for "The Cause," Smyth was notorious for her ceaseless self-promotion and unconciliatory stand toward the male-dominated London music establishment. The editor of Woolf's letters described Smyth's "petulant" behavior as the "terror of conductors" (page xv).

"when reviewers . . . I admit": *A Reflection of the Other Person*, 329.

If Nancy had a breakdown . . . always Robert: LR to EAC, n.d. BERG.

Chapter 10: Outside the Window

"The tympanum is worn thin . . . live through love": "World's End," *Collected Poems*, 111.

After an operation . . . "half and half": LR to GS, n.d. BL.

In early April . . . only a day: RG to GS, April 9, 1929; and " 'complete retirement' " RG to WL, n.d. CNL.

"supernatural . . . contained conflict": Nancy Cunard, *Those Were the Hours: Memories of My Hours Press*, edited, with a Foreword by Hugh Ford (Carbondale and Edwardsville, Ill.: Southern Illinois University, 1969), 104.

"Analogy . . . instrument of co-ordination": *Contemporaries and Snobs*, 155.

"Discover the free will . . . not necessarily logical": Laura Riding, "The Contraband," *Calendar of Modern Letters* 2 (October 1925), 95.

This is not madness . . . in France: LR to GS, April 16, 1929. BL.

"Her beauty . . . in one breath": "Helen's Burning," *Poems A Joking Word*, 94.

In *The Savage God* . . . nihilistic expression: Alfred Alvarez, *The Savage God: A Study of Suicide* (London: Weidenfeld and Nicholson, 1971), 259, 277–78.

"one cannot talk . . . garment of Christ": *Robert Graves: The Years with Laura*, 108, 110.

As in "Helen's Burning" . . . above all else: After the death of her second husband in 1968, LRJ lived in a house without electricity for over twenty years—dependent on flashlights—rather than risk lighting the kerosene lamps that SJ had always attended to.

"The lesson . . . to a fact": Laura Riding, "The Lesson," *Though Gently* (Deyá, Mallorca: Seizin, 1930), 17.

The single most important . . . went with her: LR to GS, n.d. BL.

Laura, Helen remembered . . . her injuries: HMB to author, June 20, 1989.

"Laura went through . . . friends with her": EAC interview, May 17, 1989. Nonetheless, there are no LR letters from the 1930s in the Esther Antell collection.

Laura warned . . . than literary: LR to ER, December 13, 1928. UCLA.

Afterward she admitted . . . the magazine: LR to IS, n.d. COL.

Kay Boyle . . . company and opinion: Kay Boyle to author, n.d.

"[I]t was left . . . appreciate it": Hugh Ford, ed., *The Left Bank Revisited: Selections from the Paris Tribune 1917–1934* (University Park, Penn.: Pennsylvania State University, 1972), 265–66.

"We need new words . . . own magnificence": Eugene Jolas, ed., *transition* 3 (June 1927), 179.

"There is . . . identity to eloquence": Laura Riding, "A Note on *White Buildings* by Hart Crane," *transition* 10 (January 1928), 140.

Tate's foreword . . . was "cant": LR to DD, February 2, 1927. FUG.

"Mr. Crane is preserving . . . theme": *A Survey of Modernist Poetry*, 289.

"quietly . . . gone on . . . recognition": *A Survey of Modernist Poetry*, 188.

"A large-scale mystic . . . knew it": *Contemporaries and Snobs*, 143.

"The purer [the words] . . . expressing the age": *Contemporaries and Snobs*, 155–56.

Geoffrey was made . . . Great Goddess: LR to GS, November 29, 1929. BL. An earlier cable had referred to the connection GP made between LR and GS; LR does not ascribe these labels to GP but, with cues from LR and RG, he is the most likely source.

"Laura is so poignant . . . all my love": GS to RG, n.d. BL.

"I stand for a half hour . . . on the telephone": *The Diary of Virginia Woolf*, vol. 3, 222.

Hart Crane had second . . . when he signed: Dougald McMillan, *transition: The History of a Literary Era* (London: Calder & Boyars, 1975), 139–40.

"She told me . . . shifting of emphasis": *Poems A Joking Word*, 21.

"Pain is impossible . . . but here beyond": "Here Beyond," *Poems A Joking Word*, 166.

The difficulty . . . before the leap: LR to GS, n.d. BL.

"Its revolution . . . Symbolist unconscious": Bradford Morrow, ed., *World Outside the Window: The Selected Essays of Kenneth Rexroth* (New York: New Directions, 1987), 253.

"What to say when the spider . . . legs then none": "What to Say When the Spider," *Poems A Joking Word*, 114–18.

"But of course . . . short runs": RG to GS, January 28, 1946. BL.

Over fifty years . . . of humanity: Laura Riding Jackson, "The Word-Play of Gertrude Stein," in Michael J. Hoffman, ed., *Critical Essays on Gertrude Stein* (Boston: G.K. Hall, 1980), 242–45.

"She took the part . . . good cheer": "Interview with Laura (Riding) Jackson," conducted by Elizabeth Friedmann, *PN Review* (March/April 1991), 69.

"And how did the accounts come out": GS to LR, n.d. DEYA.

"the personal touch . . . proper state for business": RG to GS, n.d. BL.

"because of the generalization": I have seen only LR's reply to this letter and drawn from that the substance of GS's objection. Cf. LR to GS, n.d. BL.

Laura's final letter . . . about the weather: LR to GS, n.d. BL. MS-S mentions an eyewitness account of an argument between GS and LR in London as to whether one should rescue a Jew from Nazi territory; GS was for, LR against, on practical grounds; the source is unnamed. As correspondence ceased in 1930, predating the rise of Nazism, this is refutable. Referring to an earlier quarrel—again without naming the source—MS-S reports that the break was of LR's "choice." The correspondence between LR and GS refutes this as well.

In one unpublished . . . homosexuality: Unpublished essay on GS. Folder B #18 BERG.

"She was . . . everyone's edification": *Critical Essays on Gertrude Stein*, 260.

"If she kept . . . hidden it well": *Critical Essays on Gertrude Stein*, 245.

Chapter 11: Good-bye to All That

Accounts of RG's description of the leap: RG to WL, n.d. CUL; RG to HP, n.d. HRC; RG to DD, June 29, 1929. FUG.

In her letter . . . merely jumped out a window: LR to MM, n.d. LC.

"I told you . . . has risen again": NM to TSM, n.d. TSM.

"Only action . . . judging the case": *In Broken Images*, 190.

Just after . . . "sweating like a bull": Robert Graves, *But It Still Goes On* (London: Jonathan Cape, 1930), 109–14.

"I'm tired of . . . lucky bloody Nancy": NN to RG, n.d. DEYA.

"dynamic of abridged . . . social cognition": Paul Fussell, *The Great War and Modern Memory* (New York: Oxford University, 1975), 35.

Thus when he . . . "wicked nonsense": *Good-bye to All That*, 2nd ed. (Harmondsworth: Penguin, 1957), 205.

"These acres . . . loss of sense": Robert Graves, "Lost Acres," *Collected Poems 1975* (New York: Oxford University, 1975), 76–77.

"for fun . . . something to do": *Robert Graves: The Years with Laura*, 107.

She referred to the . . . "Insect": LR to GS, n.d. BL.

"I will write . . . Victorianism": Christopher Hassell, *A Biography of Edward Marsh* (New York: Harcourt Brace, 1959), 306.

Christopher MacLachlan . . . main character: Christopher MacLachlan, "Heroes and Hero-worship in Goodbye to All That," Patrick Quinn, ed., *Focus on Robert Graves and His Contemporaries*, newsletter 1 (University of Maryland, 1988), 8, 11.

One form . . . exhibitions: Laura (Riding) Jackson, *Praeterita* (unpublished). BERG.

"I feel exactly . . . frightened": *A Biography of Edward Marsh*, 345.

"It was obvious . . . circumstances": *Robert Graves: The Years with Laura*, 59–60, 341.

They were returned . . . Polly Antell: Beryl Graves, RG's second wife, with whom he had four children, comments, "This seems so out of character it is hard to believe." BG to author, January 12, 1991.

He found the *Avoca* . . . bad temper: *Voyager: A Life of Hart Crane*, 576–77.

"Laura has been thinking . . . to him": RG to HC, March 25, 1929. COL.

Upon his return . . . was consummated: "Opportunism Rampant." BERG.

"It wasn't just . . . Geoffrey-with-Laura": RG to NN (dated "Sunday night"). LL.

Laura's first, undated . . . find peace: LR to GS, n.d. BL.

The point of this . . . her beauty: "Opportunism Rampant." BERG.

"On May 6th . . . to put in": The letter to Stein describing the hospital visit is undated, but May 6 seems to have been the flashpoint. The May 12 barge conversation doubtless conflated a number of statements, some perhaps made earlier, some later in order to build a semicoherent case against GP, with NN as accessory. To have this conversation take place in the hospital, therefore, would have reflected complexities in their relationship that would not be amenable to easy litigation.

They had all . . . more wiser: LR to HC, n.d. COL.

Having heard . . . complete break: R. W. Phibbs to RG, June 24, 1929. BPL.

"If I thought. . . . Well!" RG to GS, n.d. BL.

"Do you wish me . . . not true?": NN to RG, n.d. DEYA.

"I know . . . that does it": NN to RG, May 15, 1929. DEYA.

"Act V, Scene 5": Robert Graves, *Ten Poems More* (Paris: Hours, 1930), 14.

"Geoffrey stood up . . . She's sick": *Robert Graves: His Life and Work*, 172–77.

Richard Perceval Graves . . . "appears uncertain": *Robert Graves: The Years with Laura*, 345.

Whether to influence . . . bedroom window: RG to F. J. H. Sandars, July 28, 1929. Ed Maggs Bookseller Catalogue.

By then Laura (Riding) Jackson . . . descent: Not aware that MS-S wrote his account without RG's active collaboration, LRJ nonetheless concluded that MS-S had stooped to the "lowest in vilificatory extravagances of pseudobiographical report." She described his confidence in doing so as "quite maniacal." In "Opportunism Rampant" LRJ bitterly conceded MS-S's victory in the eyes of the book press.

"The memoirs . . . of anyone": *Good-bye to All That*, 2nd ed., 8.

dubiousness . . . badly unhinged: *The Great War and Modern Memory*, 35.

"I never made . . . at the time": Jenny Nicholson to Mary Taylor, n.d. (ca. July 1956). PC.

Only William Nicholson . . . "stop Time!": *Weekend Telegraph*, October 20, 1990.

"Content in you . . . foiler of beauty": "The Age of Certainty," *Ten Poems More*, 14.

Chapter 12: A Small Circle of Meaning

"When keeping house is statecraft . . . Truth": *Laura and Francisca* (Deyá, Mallorca: Seizin, 1931).

Robert Graves . . . "derangement of wits": Robert Graves and Paul Hogarth, *Mallorca Observed* (London: Cassell, 1954), 13.

Mr. Short in Palma . . . exactly right: LR to HC, n.d. COL.

Nevertheless both . . . live untroubled: LR to GS, n.d. BL.

Len Lye . . . capable: LR to GS, n.d. BL.

Before leaving . . . inevitable: LR to EAC, n.d. BERG; and LR to HC, n.d. COL.

"Of course I am obscure . . . a host": Laura Riding, letter, *Times Literary Supplement*, March 3, 1932, 155.

Responding to Merrill Moore's . . . know herself: LR to MM, n.d. LC.

"If strange things happen . . . ever-reluctant element": Robert Graves, "On Portents," *To Whom Else* (Deyá, Mallorca: Seizin, 1931), 19.

Though Laura . . . occasions: LR to GS, January 16, 1930. BL.

"Inner is the glow . . . of contradiction": Laura Riding, "Because of Clothes," *Epilogue*, Vol. 2 (Summer 1936) 250–51.

"The unprecious jewels . . . of childhood": "Jewels and After," *Poems A Joking Word*, 169.

When he failed . . . a friend: LB memoir. TSM.

Robert asked . . . woolen jerseys: RG to JA, n.d. BERG.

With this . . . letters to her: LR to GS, n.d. BL.

Chapter 13: The Damned Thing

"Stir me not . . . once burned": "Because I Sit Here So," *Collected Poems*, 12–13.

"rather magnificent" gifts: Unpublished memoir by LB. TSM. Unsourced quotes in this chapter are from this memoir. I have preserved her misspellings. I am grateful to Margaret Bottrall for alerting me to the existence of this memoir and to the late TSM for providing me with a copy.

"a lean look of speed": T. S. Matthews, *Under the Influence: Recollections of Robert Graves, Laura Riding and Friends* (London: Cassell, 1979), 133.

Laura insisted . . . pay his passage: LR to JA, n.d. BERG.

Elfriede later . . . savage dogs: *Under the Influence*, 129.

"I like men to be men . . . case": Stanley Kunitz, ed., *Authors Today and Yesterday* (New York: H. W. Wilson, 1933), 565.

Her draft . . . as immoral: Draft of LR's statement. DEYA.

"Poets are not . . . Lawrenceland": Laura Riding, "Answers to an Enquiry" *New Verse* 11 (October 1934), 4.

"I am tidy . . . nothing go by": *Authors Today and Yesterday*, 565.

"My sexual glands . . . sexual": *Anarchism Is Not Enough*, 189.

"thoroughly unplatonic": LR to HP, January 18, 1931. HRC.

What remained important . . . "nothingness": LR to "Ken," September 21, 1933. DEYA.

She reported . . . sexual misdeeds: LR to JA, n.d. BERG; and cf. LR to Frank Lea, March 3, 1933, June 14, 1933. DEYA.

"she was a better friend . . . of women": *Everybody's Letters*, 245.

"The child . . . male child": *Anarchism Is Not Enough*, 187.

"When . . . will man . . . children?": *Anarchism Is Not Enough*, 208.

"She understood his wooing . . . than paper": Laura Riding, "Two Loves, One Madness,"
  Poet: A Lying Word (London: Arthur Barker, 1933), 96–100.

"Woman is . . . assimulate mentally": *Anarchism Is Not Enough*, 200–1.

Women's bodies . . . correspondent: LR to "Ken," September 21, 1933. DEYA.

"My head is . . . as they can": "Pride of Head": *Collected Poems*, 10.

Asked by one . . . who she was: LR to "Ken," September 21, 1933. DEYA.

He quoted . . . (taken from notes): Cf. LR to GS, n.d. BL. In this letter LR mentions how
  RG is incorporating some notes of hers into a manuscript of his own, "To Whom
  Else."

"Call me . . . " spoken words: "As It Were Poems," *To Whom Else*, 14–18.

"I agree that sex . . . rather magnificent": Rosaleen Cooper to LR, March 1, 1932. DEYA.

Writing to . . . fundamental one: LR to "Ken," January 7, 1934. DEYA.

"long-legged . . . poetry": Warren Hope and Jonathan Barker, eds., *The Collected Poems of
  Norman Cameron* (London: Anvil, 1990), 139.

With John Aldridge . . . get a job: *The Collected Poems of Norman Cameron*, 137.

Though Norman always . . . olive grove: KG to author, September 29, 1989.

"the price . . . not outrageous": NC to RG, n.d. DEYA.

"It will have . . . shoot me": LB to BG, May 11, no year. DEYA.

Chapter 14: The Dry Heart

"The world where the dead live . . . even dry": "The Life of the Dead," *Collected Poems*,
  417. All quotations are from this version.

"There is one story and one story only": The line was from a later poem of RG ("To Juan
  at the Winter Solstice") but LRJ insisted that he stole this "key axiom" from her. Cf.
  LRJ, *New York Times Book Review*, September 24, 1978: "Graves' poem 'To Juan at
  Winter Solstice' steals its punch lines from a key axiom of mine, figuring impor-
  tantly in my talk, writing, papers to which Graves had access: There is only one
  story!"

"[T]he 'shadow' . . . I would": *Under the Influence*, 335–36.

"My only claims . . . the richest": *Under the Influence*, 329.

"[I]n fact we are all . . . fewer people": *Under the Influence*, 332.

"Laura! . . . its significance": *Under the Influence*, 128.

"This is the source . . . a hole": T. S. Matthews, "The Worst Unsaid" (privately published),
  57. TSM. This poem first appeared in *Epilogue I*, heavily edited by LR. Her version
  read:

> In the forehead's calm
> A hole is wanting.

Left alone in the house . . . nice legs: Edmund Wilson, in Leon Edel, ed., *The Twenties*
  (New York: Farrar, Straus and Giroux, 1975), 448–49, 513.

"Robert summed up . . . 'wrong people!' ": *Under the Influence*, 127.

"a private exercise, between ourselves": *Under the Influence*, 149.

She had started *Fantasia* . . . he left: The masque was never finished, but *Description of Life*, a later version, was found in the Canelluñ attic in the 1970s and returned to LRJ in Wabasso. This was then published by a fine press in 1980, somewhat revised. Cf. LR to JR, November 26, 1934, in which LR refers to a film scenario called "Description of Life" and its beginnings as a collaboration and large-scale masque that she and her collaborators eventually tired of. LRJ/SJ.

"She would be looking pale . . . little purpose": *Under the Influence*, 141.

"As I read, my alarm . . . I was": *Under the Influence*, 143.

"You're still a little weak . . . stock certificates": T. S. Matthews, *The Moon's No Fool* (New York: Random House, 1936), 271–72.

I was in a rolling . . . she said: Laura Riding, "The Playground," *Progress of Stories*, 226.

"To read her . . . be understood": *Under the Influence*, 339.

The illustrations . . . self-defeating: LR to "Mr. Beedham," January 12, 1933. DEYA.

Laura had a particular fear of London traffic: LR to DH, June 8, 193ғ. PC.

Riding cautioned . . . bustle: LR to JA, December 20, 1932. DEYA.

"in the sense . . . disappearance": Laura Riding, ed., *Epilogue III: A Critical Summary* (London: Constable, 1937; Deyá, Mallorca: Seizin, 1937), 191.

"for drama I like what is happening": *Authors Today and Yesterday*, 565.

About halfway . . . state of shock: *Under the Influence*, 246.

"full spread of truth" and "metaphysical perfection": LR to JR, n.d. LRJ/SJ.

"There was a post-box . . . like it?": "The Playground," *Progress of Stories*, 226.

"He will not admit . . . is now": *Under the Influence*, 344.

Chapter 15: The Unthronged Oracle

"Your coming, asking . . . stink of hell": "The Unthronged Oracle," *Collected Poems*, 206–7.

"I attempt to comfort . . . first place": Robert Graves, *But It Still Goes On* (London: Jonathan Cape, 1930), 205.

"Somehow . . . of no kind": *But It Still Goes On*, 206.

Like Canelluñ . . . before their own: For details and specifics regarding the building of Canelluñ, the intricacies of Gelat's confidence tricks on Graves and Riding, and the perspective from the village, I am indebted to William and Elena Graves.

"Every maiden aunt . . . own books": JC to RG, October 29, 1930. RUL.

"too heavy a touch . . . have been": RG to JA, n.d. BERG; also draft of same letter. DEYA.

"This limitation . . . were final": Jacob Bronowski, "Hints on Riding," *Granta* 40 (October 10, 1930), 18–19.

"to carry the language . . . geometry": John Vice, "Jacob Bronowski and Humanism: A Philosophy for the Twentieth Century," *New Humanist* (June 1984), 8.

"It came about by chance . . . at last": Laura Riding, "Then Follows," *Twenty Poems Less* (Paris: Hours, 1930) 25–32.

"most beautiful house . . . the kitchen": Jacob Bronowski to his mother, July 8, 1932. Box 132. UT.

"I won't go . . . speak of": Jacob Bronowski to his mother, July 8, 1932. Box 132. UT.

Planned as a . . . collate: *Robert Graves: The Years with Laura*, 185–86.

"I am never . . . investigation": *Authors Today and Yesterday*, 565.

"deplorable monument . . . abused": Voltaire, *Philosophical Dictionary*, ed. and trans. by Theodore Besteman (Harmondsworth: Penguin, 1972), 8.

" 'divine' sanction of poetic life": James Reeves, "The Romantic Habit of English Poets," in *Epilogue* I (London: Constable, 1935; Deyá, Mallorca: Seizin, 1935), 200.

"In their last interview . . . 'than that' ": *Experts Are Puzzled*, 158–60.

"an occasion . . . simple targets": *Under the Influence*, 151.

"Yes, such a creature . . . peace thereof": "Then Follows," *Collected Poems*, 174. I am grateful in this instance and in other, less specific ones, to Sandra M. Gilbert and Susan Gubar's *No Man's Land: The Place of the Woman Writer in the 20th Century*, vol. 1, *The War of the Words* (New Haven, Conn.: Yale University, 1988), 264. Their discussion of recent sexual linguistic theories, their reference to Eric Neumann's 1955 text, *The Great Mother*, all contributed to my conceptual awareness of the ground on which to stand while considering this poem and other works of LR.

"She is woman . . . beyond itself": *Epilogue* I, 9.

"play with . . . extreme statement": *Critical Essays on Gertrude Stein*, 260.

"Then I must . . . Godhood": "As to Food," *Poet: A Lying Word*, 87–89.

Many years . . . their eyes: LRJ to RN, December 2, 1964. McK.

Chapter 16: *The Story Pig*

"On the mantelpiece of Hotel Moon": "The Story Pig," *Progress of Stories*, 197.

"was *jealous* . . . wretched thing": *Robert Graves: The Years with Laura*, 207–8.

"she'd have . . . ordinary meat": "Daisy and Venison," *Progress of Stories*, 72.

"What did you mean . . . stories?" *Under the Influence*, 135.

Jonathan Cape would sell . . . ever after: LR to JC, August 14, 1931. RUL.

"Her stories were . . . author": "Daisy and Venison," *Progress of Stories*, 73–74, 78.

"She could not write . . . characters": "Daisy and Venison," *Progress of Stories*, 74.

"we almost know . . . careful of accidents" and "Oh of course . . . long ago": Preface, *Progress of Stories*, 14, 15.

What would people . . . abandoning her: LR to JA, n.d. BERG.

To Robert . . . always of herself: Laura Riding, "A Crown for Hans Andersen," fragment found in Deyá.

When Riding . . . book form: LR to JC, n.d. (ca. June 1932) RUL.

"When one reads . . . crazy little sister": LRJ quotes this review in *Antaeus* (Spring/ Summer 1974), 55.

"smiling like a clergyman" and "pressing down . . . love?": "Daisy and Venison," *Progress of Stories*, 85.

"I have . . . change it": Preface, *Progress of Stories*, 8.

"His father . . . Magyar origins": "Three Times Round," *Progress of Stories*, 97.

"You can't get it . . . whatever you like": "A Fairy Tale for Older People," *Progress of Stories*, 268.

In 1934 she told . . . disentangle: LR to JR, July 15, 1934. LRJ/SJ.

"That is . . . both co-operate": "Reality as Port-Huntlady," *Progress of Stories*, 97–98.

"The effect . . . anonymity of the author": "The Anonymous Book," *Anarchism Is Not Enough*, 163.

"[A] story must . . . sorry": "Reality as Port-Huntlady," *Progress of Stories*, 124.

"If you so much . . . amuse yourselves": HWE interview, September 5, 1989.

Laura assisted . . . own surrealism: LR to LB, n.d. BERG.

"a character from . . . Nibelung": KG interview, September 26, 1989.

"[P]erhaps, indeed . . . insisted on": "Reality as Port-Huntlady," *Progress of Stories*, 152–53.

"He was more than protective . . . put it": *Under the Influence*, 129.

"What refuge here . . . than at home": Robert Graves, "The Cell," *Poems 1930–1933* (London: Arthur Barker, 1933), 6.

"She had a beautiful . . . voice of the God": Robert Graves, *I, Claudius: From the Autobiography of Tiberius Claudius Born 10 B.C. Murdered and Deified A.D. 54* (New York: Harrison Smith and Robert Haas, 1934), 17.

In Graves' "legendary mind," . . . owner desired: Robert Graves, *The Greek Myths* (Harmondsworth: Penguin, 1955), 39, 42, 120.

"I have been assaulted . . . a fifth season": "Samuel's Elegy for Amalthea of the Legends": *The Close Chaplet*, 40–43.

"To a fawning fellowship . . . speak clear": *I, Claudius*, 18.

"Augustus ruled . . . flesh": Robert Graves, *I, Claudius*, 31.

Livia consolidated . . . "for eating": *I, Claudius*, 33.

"I have never . . . too long": *I, Claudius*, 415–16, 419.

"I was thinking . . . my opportunities": *I, Claudius*, 494.

In fact, Robert actively disliked the sun: KG to author, September 8, 1990: "R.G. was no sun-worshipper: into the sea and out of up the hill—home again."

"The first time . . . loved him": *Robert Graves: The Years with Laura*, 206–7, 219.

Indeed, she conceded . . . her life: KG interview, September 26, 1989: "She did more than just kiss him, I was told."

But Deyá . . . of conclusions: LR to JA, June 11, 1934. BERG.

Robert, returning . . . pretty ring: LR to JA, n.d. BERG.

"Venison ran upstairs . . . 'go along' ": *Progress of Stories*, 64–65.

Having accepted . . . business language: LR to JC, n.d. (ca. June 1932). RUL.

Chapter 17: The Why of the Wind

"We have often considered . . . thus the next": "The Why of the Wind," *Collected Poems*, 329–30.

At one point . . . followed suit: KG interview, September 26, 1989.

When the rain . . . blue flower: KG diary, September 13, 14, October 2, 1935. This diary is an important source for this chapter in evoking the temper of the last months in Deyá and of the rhythms of work, illness, and relationships. It is presently in the possession of Kenneth Gay (formerly Karl Goldschmidt) in Palma, Mallorca. I am very grateful to him for sharing it with me and allowing me to quote from it. PALMA.

By August 1933 . . . former housemaid: KG interview, September 26, 1989.

Of this group . . . a conspiracy: LR to JR, March 14, 1935. LRJ/SJ.

"illuminating talk . . . about girls": KG diary, September 23, 1935. PALMA.

"I couldn't have . . . go right": KG's diary, October 24, 31, 1935. PALMA.

"discovering the poet": LR to JR, n.d. LRJ/SJ.

Before his return . . . admirer: Cf. Samuel Putnam, Maida Castelhun, George Reaney, Jacob Bronowski, eds., *The European Caravan* (New York: Bremer, Warren & Putnam, 1931), 439. I am grateful to Jacob Bronowski's biographer John Vice for providing me with scarce publications and research materials and for showing me his notes on the diary entries for this period.

He lectured Eirlys . . . puffy sleeves: LR to JR, July 11, 1934. LRJ/SJ.

To Robert's answer . . . even better: RG to JR, n.d. HRC.

"Quarrel with Laura": Jacob Bronowski's diary is in the possession of his widow.

To distinguish between . . . the world: LR to JR, May 2, 1934. LRJ/SJ.

In a long letter . . . his judgment: LR to JR, May 16, 1934. LRJ/SJ.

In particular . . . "on together": JR to LR, May 24, 1934. DEYA.

After Laura . . . "by reversion": LR to JR, July 11, 1934. LRJ/SJ.

In her next . . . truth as well: LR to JR, n.d. LRJ/SJ.

"literary ventriloquism": Edward Mendelsohn, *Early Auden* (New York: Viking, 1981), 124.

Similarly, the foreword . . . self-perception: Cf. LR's correspondence with Michael Roberts. BERG.

Her exercise of . . . or forgotten: "An Evening in Maida Vale," 34–41.

Though her language . . . her purposes: Cf. LR to Jeffrey Marks, March 30, 1933. DEYA.

"I want to say . . . she is": RG to JR, n.d. HRC.

Laura (Riding) Jackson . . . it herself: Laura (Riding) Jackson, "On the Final Times and After," Folder 7, Group D. BERG.

"Her undershot jaw . . . honourable men": HK to MK, n.d. PC.

"her face white with rage": LB memoir. TSM. LR later seems to have regretted this outburst, writing to the person who had given her the whip that she had disposed of it, claiming that she was not interested in "power or cruelties." LR to "Ken," September 21, 1933. DEYA.

"Of course one . . . stunting influence": Jane Aiken Hodge to author, October 9, 1990. Also, interview with KG, September 26, 1989: "Laura interfered with people's lives: She ruined Alan and Norman. She took Alan's novel to pieces. He never wrote another novel, never wrote another poem."

"the urgency . . . her delusion": Robert Fitzgerald, "Laura Riding," *Kenyon Review* 1 (Summer 1939), 342.

In a moment . . . cautious mind: LR to JR, October 25, 1933. LRJ/SJ.

"It was very awkward . . . like this": KG diary, November 5, 1935. PALMA.

But it was Karl . . . "without a blink": KG interview, September 26, 1989.

"Too reasonable . . . warty lads": W. B. Yeats to LR, May 23, 1936. UD.

When one of her . . . chastised him: LR to John Cullen, n.d. DEYA.

Still, she suggested . . . poor health: W. B. Yeats to LR, n.d. (ca. end of June 1936). HRC.

"tiny, good looking . . . imaginable": KG diary, November 4, 1935. PALMA.

"Can this be made . . . usual embraces": "Wishing More Dear," *Collected Poems*, 309.

Failing that . . . Barcelona: KG diary, November 13, 1935. PALMA.

"Why hasn't he . . . Bloody egoism": KG diary, November 24, 1935. PALMA.

"I rather wish . . . restrains her": KG diary, December 17, 1935. PALMA.

If he wanted to know . . . Deyá: LR to AH, December 20, 1935. BPL.

Chapter 18: A Trojan Ending

"The story . . . of it": Laura Riding, *A Trojan Ending* (London: Constable, 1937), 398–99.

"What was wrong . . . of Troy": *A Trojan Ending*, 134.

"No contemporary newspaper . . . viewed": *A Trojan Ending*, xxvii.

"Alas, no . . . Italy nowadays": *Focus* 14 (April/May 1935). *Focus* was the Deyá newsletter published sporadically in 1935.

When Riding came . . . under siege: RG diary, July 28 and 29, 1936. DEYA.

"the least vulnerable . . . morality": Paul Johnson, *Modern Times: The World from the Twenties to the Eighties* (New York: Harper and Row, 1983), 321–22.

Around the table . . . own neutrality: RG diary, May 21, 1936. DEYA.

Had she been . . . Spanish politics: LR to AH, May 22, 1936. BPL.

Ever sensitive . . . the elections: RG's diary, March 16, 19, 25, and April 2 and 4 shows that Gelat was very busy lining up his political allies in the wake of the Popular Front elections and edging out the doctor and "his gang." DEYA.

Gelat, canny . . . a communist: RG diary, March 31, 1936. DEYA.

"Comrades . . . capture of Troy": George Dimitroff, *The Working Classes against Fascism* as quoted in Johnson op. cit.

A few days . . . by the sea: KG diary, November 8, 1935. PALMA.

In June 1936 . . . ailing Europe: RG diary, June 2, 1936. DEYA.

"Priam mused tiredly . . . dreadful course": *A Trojan Ending*, 29.

The Mayor of Inca . . . promptly shot: *Robert Graves: The Years with Laura*, 357.

On July 22 . . . people were killed: RG diary, July 23, 1936. DEYA.

"My terror and grief . . . these isles": KG diary, October 4, 1935. PALMA.

"A pity . . . wrapping paper": Paul O'Prey, ed., *Between Moon and Moon: Selected Letters of Robert Graves 1946–1972* (London: Hutchinson, 1984), 27.

Chapter 19: Doom in Bloom

"And every prodigal greatness . . . could not be": "The Flowering Urn," *Collected Poems*, 224.

West was the daughter . . . *A Trojan Ending*: LRJ to Russell Maylone, October 1970. NWUL.

Two Irish tweed . . . with them: KG to author, October 18, 1989.

He returned . . . straight face: KG interview, September 26, 1989.

"On the set . . . Edward VIII!": "The Curse of Claudius," *Huddersfield Examiner*, October 12, 1977.

"live a peaceful, civilized existence . . . less peaceful": Laura Riding, *The World and Ourselves* (London: Chatto and Windus, 1938), flaps.

"As a poet . . . into unities": "Answers to an Enquiry," 4.

"One woman goes a long . . . capacity": "Answers to an Enquiry," 5.

"It is no use . . . hot-house": Valentine Cunningham, *British Writers of the Thirties* (New York: Oxford University, 1988), 150.

"Queen-bore among all . . . at present": Geoffrey Grigson, "First of All, Miss Laura Riding," *New Verse* (August 1938), 26. By the time he came to write his memoirs, LR was "that bluestocking whom so many have never known how to take or tackle."

"Coming at this time . . . oblivion": Geoffrey Grigson, *Recollections, Mainly of Writers and Artists* (London: Chatto and Windus, 1984), 130.

"On Auden, Graves and Norman Cameron . . . devitalized fairyland": "An Evening in Maida Vale," 40.

"The writer who grasps . . . purposeful world": Stephen Spender, *The Destructive Element: A Study of Modern Writers and Beliefs* (Folcroft, Penn.: Folcraft Library Editions, 1977), 33.

They stayed at . . . Ibizan necklace: RG's diary, October 20, 1936. DEYA.

An undergraduate approached . . . what she was: "The End of the World and After," typed notes for LR's speech. BPL.

A few months . . . that respect: LR to AH, n.d. (possibly from Lugano). BPL.

Laura reported . . . her reception: LR to WH, November 2, 1936. PC.

"A truly piteous fate . . . tells 'us' ": Harry Kemp and Laura Riding, *The Left Heresy in Literature and Life* (London: Methuen, 1939), 44.

"Many people get on well . . . humorously": *The Left Heresy*, 69.

"Too great an interest . . . good things": *The Left Heresy*, 118.

As with so many . . . "outside disorders": *The World and Ourselves*, 476.

"Georgian preferred . . . those days!": RG to Albert Mills, March 29, 1937. WR.

Gelat's imprisonment . . . his diary: RG diary, March 21, 1937. DEYA.

Thus Laura's chronic insomnia . . . with death: LR to NN, n.d. LL; and RG's diary, April 3, 1937. DEYA.

One night, suffering . . . Trojan: RG's diary. DEYA.

"When you say . . . make it oneself": *The World and Ourselves*, 73–74.

"For where . . . male or female": *The World and Ourselves*, 69.

When Alan told her . . . excellent intrigue: LR to AH, n.d. (ca. March 1937). BPL.

What real weapons . . . they deserved: LR to AH, June 6, 1937. BPL.

The real answer . . . for advice: LR to JA, June 5, 1937. BERG.

"to be *tidy* . . . guilty immodesty": *The World and Ourselves*, 413.

"moral war on evil": LR to Ronald Bottrall, April 6, 1938. HRC.

"It is written in words . . . polysyllables": Dorothy Sayers, "Ink of Poppies," *Spectator* (March 14, 1937), 897.

"All the good words . . . tainted": RG diary, April 28, 1938. DEYA.

Though Robert noted . . . session: RG diary, May 7, 1938. DEYA.

"What you really meant . . . my beer": "An Evening in Maida Vale," 36–37.

On May 4, 1938 . . . his diary: RG to JR, n.d. LRJ/SJ; also RG diary, April 28, May 4, and June 17, 1938. DEYA.

Someday, Laura wrote . . . as well: LR to JR, n.d. LRJ/SJ.

During the drafting . . . recognizing him: RG diary, April 8, 1938. DEYA.

Riding had finished hers in Surrey: The last poem, "Christmas 1937," was written in mid-December 1937 and was added to the proofs, as was another more fragile and exceedingly moving poem "Nothing So Far."

"a poet outside his poem is messianic": "The Absolute of Poetry," early unpublished version. DEYA.

"Miss Riding has few equals . . . or dead": Dudley Fitts, "The 'Right Reasons' for Writing Poetry," *Saturday Review* (March 25, 1939), 17.

"Forgive me, giver . . . perfect it": "Lines in Short Despite in Time," *Poet: A Lying Word*, 37.

"a moment" . . . "your bed": LR to JR, n.d. LRJ/SJ; and RG diary, May 30, 1938. DEYA.

Chapter 20: *Le Château de La Chevrie*

His diary followed . . . house: RG diary, July 27, 1938. DEYA.

"The kitchen ghost . . . touched it": RG diary, August 12, 1938. DEYA.

"A score of bats . . . was not hers": "A Jealous Man," *Collected Poems, 1975*, 93–94.

Among the dozens . . . coconut shell: RG's letters to Albert Mills are in private hands; the time and money he spent in Mr. Mill's shop cannot be underestimated; not only did he surround himself with these relics, he gave them away liberally to those closest to him.

"Isn't it an insult . . . Bible": NN to RG, n.d. LL; see also from this period LR to NN, n.d., and RG to NN, n.d., of the same collection.

"it would be . . . are not": RG to NN, July 10, 1938. LL.

"tolerance of . . . lexicographical richness": RG diary, April 16, 1937. DEYA.

Laura wrote . . . of her dream: LR to AH, n.d. BPL.

Regrettably . . . Downing street: LR to KG, September 20, 1938. LL.

On September 28 . . . "Germanic fury": LR to JR, September 28, 1938. LRJ/SJ.

Where Robert chopped . . . were stocked: RG diary, August 7, 1938. DEYA.

"Our guess is . . . for *Time*": *Princeton Alumni News*, January 27, 1939.

Schuyler's answer . . . American: LR to TSM, March 14 and 30, 1933. DEYA.

She found his reference . . . disrespectful: LR to SJ, March 30, 1933. DEYA.

Refusing to be baited . . . more fruitless arguments: SJ to LR, June 18, 1933. DEYA.

There had never been . . . understanding: LR to TSM, March 14, 1933. DEYA.

Five years later . . . first Protocol: A letter signed by KTJ appeared as one of the responses to LR's "Personal Letter" in *The World and Ourselves*, but KTJ insists that LR rewrote it entirely.

Along with long letters . . . "color": RG diary, December 10, 1938. DEYA.

She spoke . . . began to understand: LR to KG, n.d. (ca. early December 1938). LL.

She had planned . . . his survival: LR to KG, December 24, 1938. LL.

"[Poets] acknowledge . . . human communication": Schuyler B. Jackson, "Nine and Two," *Time,* December 26, 1938, 41–44.

Robert, writing . . . "700,000 subscriptions": RG to KG, January 13, 1939. LL.

"I think the man's in love with you": *Robert Graves: The Years with Laura,* 294–95.

To Karl, Laura . . . indispensable to her: LR to KG, March 5, 1939. LL.

"intimate omen": LR to JA, March 6, 1939. BERG.

Even the fall . . . their values: LR to KG, February 3, 1939. LL.

"stinging advertisement": LR to Ian Parsons, February 3, 1939. RUL.

She had an inkling . . . Karl: LR to KG, n.d. (ca. early February 1939). LL.

"in a perverse way": RG to KG, February 10, 1939. LL.

"Guns from the sea . . . the tears run down": "Dawn Bombardment," *Collected Poems, 1975,* 122.

"We all feel . . . no sense": RG diary, February 27, 1939. DEYA.

"as a focus for love among us": RG diary, March 1, 2, 1939. DEYA.

"joulting pig . . . one-in-the-bush": RG diary, March 18–21, 1939. DEYA.

"After so much loss . . . unwelcome": "After So Much Loss," *Collected Poems,* 325–26.

Chapter 21: New Hope

"The old ruin . . . the war": Griselda Jackson, ed., *Jackson Quarterly.* PC.

Kit said later . . . *Arabia Deserta:* KTJ interview, October 23, 1989.

Kit, two months . . . France: KTJ interview, October 23, 1989.

"There were a lot of queer ducks there": KTJ interview, October 23, 1989.

To settle them . . . to America: LRJ to RN, July 15, 1964. McK.

Later . . . getting him involved: LRJ to GO, May 14, 1956. LRJ/SJ.

"Kit was sort of gawky" . . . welcoming: EP interview, May 15, 1989.

"someone who had always . . . peacock": GJ to LRJ, n.d. (ca. November 1982). LRJ/SJ.

"He always thought he was Jesus Christ": KTJ interview, October 23, 1989.

Johnny Matthews . . . paled into insignificance: Interview with Paul and John Matthews, June 2, 1989.

Along with the special . . . puzzled them: GO to LRJ, n.d. LRJ/SJ.

"And that means . . . we all are": *In Broken Images,* 281.

"You know all . . . for all": *In Broken Images,* 282.

"Schuyler and I do": BG to author, April 8, 1991: "I don't remember [this]. [MS-S] probably had this from [AH], . . . in which case it is probably true."

She expected everyone . . . napped: BG interviews, September 1989.

According to Tom Matthews . . . sitting up with a corpse: *Under the Influence,* 205. Also EP interview, May 15, 1989.

"When I started back . . . loved her": EP, interview, May 15, 1989.

"but his lowered eyelids . . . receptive": *Under the Influence,* 203.

"Eleanor, I understand you think this is a cult": EP interview, May 15, 1989. When EP later reminded Julie Matthews what she had said about LR, Julie had no memory of it.

One evening at sunset . . . mosquitos: LB to BG, July 6, 1976. DEYA.

"It suddenly dawned . . . for months": *Under the Influence*, 206–7.

Matthews was . . . insult to the truth: LRJ to Alfred Kazin, June 22, 1977. BERG. Before writing this chapter I wrote to LRJ asking if she would like to comment on the events of the summer of 1939 and, in particular, her denunciation of KTJ as a witch. I had no reply.

If Matthews' account . . . Laura's circle: BG to author, April 10, 1991: "Tom was so frightened by the whole thing—I remember when Dorothy and I went up to Newport with the children he picked up the newspaper at breakfast, skimmed through the international news, and said 'and now for the real news' which was the weather! On the verge of a war, and after all we'd been through, I was quite shocked." To write this chapter I have offset the account set forth in TSM's book, MS-S's version (based on AH's recollection), the memories of KTJ, GO, MP, EP, and BG against letters written at the time by BG, LR, and SJ.

Sometime in late May or early June: KTJ interview, October 23, 1989. It is hard to date precisely the time of this first breakdown. KTJ believes that it was early June; by late June, early July she remembered a visit from LR's half sister, Isabel, and her son Richard and a walk they took on the boardwalks of Atlantic City. For my account of what happened I have relied on the memories of MP and GO.

"The particulars of that . . . all of us": KTJ to author, n.d. (ca. September 1989).

"Before my mother's . . . was too late:" GO interview, February 28, 1989. This contradicts TSM's version, which says that he did not see KTJ for months after the dinner at his house in which she lay her head on the table. It supports her view that TSM and Julie were, at the time, more aware of the course of events at the farm than he later cared to acknowledge, perhaps out of a sense of guilt over his powerlessness and responsibility for the situation.

"Laura would go . . . just her mind": KTJ interview, October 23, 1989.

they believed . . . earthquake in South America: GO interview, February 28, 1989.

Even the search . . . private language: One can not underestimate how much LR took her cues from RG. In *The White Goddess*, RG answers the riddle, "What is a mare's nest?" with quotations from Shakespeare and a fourteenth-century Irish lyric that purportedly provide him his answer. "The Night Mare is one of the cruellest aspects of the White Goddess. Her nests, when one comes across them in dreams, lodged in rock-clefts or the branches of enormous yellow yews, are built of carefully chosen twigs, lined with white horse hair and the plumage of prophetic birds and littered with the jawbones and entrails of poets." From *The White Goddess: A Historical Grammar of Poetic Myth* (New York: Farrar, Straus and Giroux, 1948, 1966), 26. It is extremely doubtful that LR ever made any concerted study of cabalism or gnostic thought, although MS-S seemed to believe she had and RPG refers quite confidently to LR's practice of "black magic." (*Robert Graves: The Years with Laura*, 307).

"[Although she didn't] . . . with Laura": *Under the Influence*, 208.

To Beryl . . . certified as maleficent: BG interviews, August 1990.

"Why? . . . mother was?": *Under the Influence*, 213.

In another curious . . . her father: GO interview, February 28, 1989.

As Griselda watched . . . evil, too: GO interview, February 28, 1989. GO remembers watching SJ and TSM have this argument in the White House hallway from the stairway landing.

"in borrowed severity": LR to RG, August 15, 1939. BPL.

At that time . . . to their mother: GO interview, February 28, 1989.

Among Kit's practices and black magic . . . detail: KTJ denies ever having spent much time in conversation with LR, and BG does not believe that KTJ would have confessed "sexual perversions" to LR, "though maybe Schuyler did." BG to author, April 8, 1991. It is not unlikely that KTJ's desire to make love in a field of daisies constituted her "perversion."

Only after Kit's breakdown . . . evil at work: BG to author, April 8, 1991. "The Gurdjieff connection proves nothing as [SJ] was much more involved."

As corroboration . . . "despised people": LRJ to GO, May 14, 1956. LRJ/SJ. I am grateful to Griselda Ohanessian née Jackson for letting me see this letter.

In the 1960s . . . personally attest: LRJ to RN, April 13, 1965. McK.

"I never described . . . like that": KTJ interview, October 23, 1989.

"She got in over her head": GO interview, February 28, 1989. In a letter to MS-S she also wrote, "I don't think anyone involved was evil, Laura included, though I think she generated wrong things and believed herself to be good when she was in some respects not. I do think they were a pretty sorry lot, all. Neurotic, intellectually conceited, spiritually and humanly immature, pretty second-rate and certainly not so very adult." (June 27, 1983). PC.

But, by August . . . complete surrender: LR to RG, August 12 and 15, 1939. BPL.

"What happened long ago . . . coming over": RG to NN, n.d. LL.

Ten years later . . . selfish reasons: SJ to GJ, April 3, 1949. LRJ/SJ.

one of Robert's . . . *World Has Changed*: LR to KG, n.d. (ca. July 1939). LL.

When Robert's letters . . . herself and Alan: LR to RG, August 19 and 29, 1939. DEYA.

her letters encouraging Alan . . . they would: LR to AH, August 29, 1939. BPL; cf. RG to Ronald Bottrall, September 8, 1939. HRC.

Her letter was . . . one iota: SJ to RG, January 6, 1940. DEYA.

The wickedness . . . provide her: Laura (Riding) Jackson, "Robert Graves' *The White Goddess*," 4. BERG.

"I feel now . . . premature": *Between Moon and Moon*, 206.

"Lovers in the act . . . among thieves": "The Thieves," *Collected Poems, 1975*, 123.

Chapter 22: *The Only Possible Ending*

"But something must be . . . the world speaks": "Memories of Mortalities," *Collected Poems*, 280–95.

In the weeks since . . . was Laura: SJ to GJ, April 7, 1940. LRJ/SJ.

The cockroaches . . . free of charge: SJ to GJ, April 7, 1940. LRJ/SJ.

At dawn, Still . . . of the day: SJ to GJ, April 7, 1940. LRJ/SJ.

"she has made . . . same person": *In Broken Images*, 292.

Laura, he told Karl . . . document: *In Broken Images*, 290.

Riding's earlier samples: LR, specifications for *A Dictionary of Exact Meanings*, November 7, 1938. BERG.

in contrasting . . . city setting: LR to AM, February 4, 1940. BERG.

"not a dictionary . . . included": RG to Desmond Flower, December 14, 1938. RUL.

Anyone with access to . . . ethically articulate: Laura Riding, *A Dictionary of Exact Meanings*, initial proposal submitted to Little, Brown, 1938. BERG.

Her eleven-page . . . wear off: LR to AM, July 23, 1938. BERG.

Laura, Robert . . . Beryl typing: RG diary, January 22, 1939. DEYA.

Laura wrote to . . . was discussed: LR to Ronald Bottrall, February 10, 1939. HRC.

The rebuttal to Little, Brown . . . style and grammar: This part of the letter is reminiscent of *The Reader Over Your Shoulder* that RG, with AH as coauthor, would write during the war. LRJ claimed that the idea for the book—which became a popular handbook on English prose style—had come from her.

Riding had ended . . . door-to-door salesmen: LR to AM, January 25, 1939. BERG.

In May, Schuyler . . . Harlem River: SJ to GJ, May 6, 1940, LRJ/SJ.

Laura . . . ducked into a store: EP interview, May 15, 1989.

Twice a week . . . newsreels: SJ to GJ, April 21, 1940. LRJ/SJ.

Gifts from the children . . . wordless one: SJ to GJ, April 21, 1940. LRJ/SJ.

In June 1940 . . . to Kathy: SJ to GJ, June 30, 1940. LRJ/SJ.

In one letter . . . dictionary: SJ to GJ, October 27, 1940. LRJ/SJ.

Out on a stroll . . . much faster: SJ to GJ, May 6 and 13, 1940. LRJ/SJ.

Laura's poems . . . Laura Riding: Cf. Laura Riding's "If the tree in a stormy time uttered a cry" in SJ to GJ, October 27, 1940. LRJ/SJ.

A letter from Laura . . . to complete: LR to AM, May 25, 1940. BERG.

Only after a fierce . . . progress: LR to A. P. Watt, May 25, 1940. BERG.

"Laura wants her breakfast!": GO interview, February 28, 1989.

The woman who . . . offer: LR to GJ, n.d. LRJ/SJ.

To show her industriousness . . . feedings: LR to GJ, July 22, 1940. LRJ/SJ.

Laura Riding and Schuyler Jackson were married on June 20, 1941: Application for Marriage License no. 61884, June 11, 1940, Elkton, Maryland.

Laura acknowledged . . . write with: LRJ to EAC, December 17, 1941. BERG.

She found Sadie . . . her company: LRJ to GJ, February 1, 1943. LRJ/SJ.

The rest . . . purchase in 1943 of a new home: LRJ to GJ, April 27, 1943. LRJ/SJ. The veranda was collapsing, the bedroom and the kitchen required extensive renovations and rebuilding, the stairway moved, and the foundations were replaced.

In addition to . . . dictionary: SJ to GJ, May 16, 1943. LRJ/SJ.

The impossibility of such . . . right tack: LRJ to AM, May 26, 1941. BERG.

The new proposal included . . . perfection of man: Laura Jackson and Schuyler Jackson, "Plan for Work," typescript submitted to Guggenheim and Little, Brown; September 29, 1941. BERG.

In their emotional appeal . . . in 1938: LRJ to AM, April 23, 1942. BERG.

But this work seemed . . . over 100 times: SJ to GJ, September 19, October 17, 1943. LRJ/SJ.

The girls were followed home . . . anymore: LRJ to GJ, April 4, 1945. LRJ/SJ.

Two weeks later Laura wrote . . . her husband: LRJ to AM, April 16, 1945. BERG.

In 1948 . . . faith in them: LRJ and SJ to AM, October 13, 1948. BERG.

eventually . . . definitions for words: In April 1945, AM had suggested an article for the *Atlantic Monthly* on the difficulties that they were facing; this was the germ of *Rational Meaning*. At that time LJ felt that such a work could not appear until the dictionary had been published.

Laura Jackson completed . . . mid-1970s: Cf. LRJ to Robert Gorham-Davis, September 19, 1974. COL.

Laura and Schuyler had stayed . . . married: SJ to GJ, April 27, 1941. LRJ/SJ.

Were these papers . . . her poems?: *Under the Influence*, 319.

"a personal miracle of true statement": LRJ to Gwendolyn Murphy, May 4, 1948 (copy sent to RG). DEYA.

One Christmas season . . . 3,000 orders: SJ to GJ, April 26, 1947. LRJ/SJ.

"As I see it . . . very long": MS to RG, n.d. DEYA.

In a letter . . . sight-seeing attractions: LRJ to GJ, March 22, 1944. LRJ/SJ.

One of them . . . godlike: SJ to GJ, July 12, 1943. LRJ/SJ.

Laura and Schuyler had grown . . . neighbor's house: LRJ to EAC, August 18, 1944. BERG.

They wrote to her . . . maturity and depth: LRJ to GO, February 1961. LRJ/SJ.

"unavoidable responsibility . . . fleeting moments": *Under the Influence*, 312.

"it was only on . . . could stand": *Under the Influence*, 317.

"hidden in ominous . . . be safe": Laura (Riding) Jackson, "The Only Possible Ending," *PN Review* 17 (March/April 1991), 76–77.

As an afterthought . . . another story: "The Only Possible Ending," unpublished version, April 1982. Holograph, 6 pp. BERG.

Epilogue

"Measure me . . . nothing at all": Laura Riding Gottschalk, "Dimensions," *Fugitive* 2 (August–September 1923), 124.

BIBLIOGRAPHY

Works by Laura Riding

POETRY

Laura Riding Gottschalk, *The Close Chaplet* (New York: Adelphi, 1926; London: Hogarth, 1926)

Laura Riding, *Voltaire, A Biographical Fantasy* (London: Hogarth, 1927)

——. *Love as Love, Death as Death* (London: Seizin, 1928)

——. *Poems A Joking Word* (London: Jonathan Cape, 1930)

——. *Though Gently* (Deyá, Mallorca: Seizin, 1930)

——. *Twenty Poems Less* (Paris: Hours, 1930)

——. *Laura and Francisca* (Deyá, Mallorca: Seizin, 1931)

——. *The Life of the Dead* (London: Arthur Barker, 1933)

——. *Poet: A Lying Word* (London: Arthur Barker, 1933)

——. *Americans* (Los Angeles: Primavera, 1934)

——. *Collected Poems* (London: Cassell, 1938; New York: Random House, 1938). Reprinted by Carcanet Press in Manchester and Persea Books in New York in 1980.

Laura (Riding) Jackson, *Selected Poems: In Five Sets* (London: Faber and Faber, 1970; New York: W. W. Norton, 1973; New York, Persea, 1993)

——. *First Awakenings: The Early Poems of Laura Riding*, Preface by Laura (Riding) Jackson. Elizabeth Friedmann, Alan J. Clark, Robert Nye, eds. (Manchester: Carcanet, 1992; New York: Persea, 1992)

CRITICISM AND MISCELLANEOUS

Laura Riding, *Contemporaries and Snobs* (London: Jonathan Cape, 1928; Garden City, N.Y.: Doubleday, Doran, 1928)

——. *Anarchism Is Not Enough* (London: Jonathan Cape, 1928; Garden City, N.Y.: Doubleday, Doran, 1928)

——. *Four Unposted Letters to Catherine* (Paris: Hours, 1930; New York, Persea, 1993)

——, comp. *Everybody's Letters* (London: Arthur Barker, 1933)

Laura Riding, ed., *Epilogue: A Critical Summary.* 3 vols. (London: Constable; Deyá, Mallorca: Seizin, 1935, 1936, 1937)
———. *The World and Ourselves* (London: Chatto and Windus, 1938)
Laura Riding and Robert Graves. *A Survey of Modernist Poetry* (London: William Heinemann, 1927; Garden City, N.Y.: Doubleday, Doran, 1928)
———. *A Pamphlet Against Anthologies* (London: Jonathan Cape, 1928; Garden City, N.Y.: Doubleday, Doran, 1928)
Harry Kemp and Laura Riding. *The Left Heresy in Literature and Life* (London: Methuen, 1939)
Laura (Riding) Jackson, *The Telling.* (London: Athlone, 1972; New York: Harper and Row, 1973)
———. *The Word 'Woman' and Other Related Writings.* Elizabeth Friedmann and Alan J. Clark, eds. (New York: Persea, 1993)

FICTION

Laura Riding, *Experts Are Puzzled* (London: Jonathan Cape, 1930)
Barbara Rich (pseud. of Laura Riding and Robert Graves), *No Decency Left* (London: Jonathan Cape, 1932)
Laura Riding and George Ellidge, *14A: A Novel Told in Dramatic Form* (London: Arthur Barker, 1934)
———. *Progress of Stories* (London: Constable, 1935; Deyá, Mallorca: Seizin, 1935). Reprint: (New York: Dial Press, 1982)
Madeleine Vara (pseud.), *Convalescent Conversations* (London: Constable, 1936; Deyá: Seizin, 1936)
Laura Riding, *A Trojan Ending* (London: Constable, 1937; New York: Random House, 1937). Reprint: (Manchester: Carcanet, 1984; New York: Carcanet, 1989)
———. *Lives of Wives* (London: Cassell, 1939; New York: Random House, 1939). Reprinting: (Manchester: Carcanet, 1988; New York: Carcanet, 1989)
Laura (Riding) Jackson, *Description of Life* (New York: Targ Editions, 1980)

WORKS ON LAURA RIDING

Barbara Block Adams, *The Enemy Self: Poetry and Criticism of Laura Riding* (Rochester, N.Y.: University of Rochester, 1990)
Joyce Piell Wexler, *Laura Riding's Pursuit of Truth.* (Athens, Ohio: Ohio University, 1979)
———. *Laura Riding: A Bibliography.* (New York and London: Garland, 1981)

Grateful acknowledgment is made to the Columbia University Library for permission to quote from or cite the Hart Crane, Isidor Schneider, and Joseph Freeman papers; to the law offices of Levin & Gann for permission to quote from letters by Gertrude Stein; the Lilly Library at Indiana University and Sam Graves for permission to quote from the Nicholson papers; to the Department of Rare Books, Cornell University Library, for permission to cite the letters of Laura (Riding) Jackson to James Reeves; to Helen Tate for permission to quote from the letters of Allen Tate to Donald Davidson et al.; to the Princeton University Library for permission to cite the Robert Penn Warren letters; to the Yale Collection of American Literature, Beinecke Rare Book and Manuscript Library, Yale University, for permission to cite manuscript material from its Gertrude Stein Collection; to the Harry Ransom Humanities Research Center at the University of Texas at Austin for permission to quote from the Graves, Purnell, and Bottrall papers; to Rita Bronowski and the Thomas Fisher Rare Book Library for permission to quote from a letter by Jacob Bronowski; to Sylvia S. Seaman for permission to quote from her unpublished novel *Glorious to View*; to Kenneth Gay for permission to quote from his unpublished diary; to the department of Special Collections, University of Maryland at College Park Libraries, for permission to cite letters by Laura (Riding) Jackson to Robert Nye; to Helen Ransom Forman for permission to quote from letters of John Crowe Ransom and Mary Taylor for permission to quote from letters by Geoffrey Phibbs. Letters and writings by Robert Graves are reproduced with the permissions of the Poetry/Rare Books Collection, University Library, State University of New York at Buffalo, Oxford University Press, the executors of the estate of Robert Graves, and A. P. Watt Ltd. Letters and writings by Laura Riding and Laura (Riding) Jackson are cited with the permission of the Henry W. and Albert A. Berg Collection and the New York Public Library, Astor, Lenox, and Tilden Foundations. For permission to quote from U.K.- and Commonwealth-copyrighted work of Laura (Riding) Jackson, I wish to thank the Board of Literary Management established under the terms of her will. In granting such permission for U.K. and Commonwealth editions the Board does not convey its approval of the use made of the quotations, nor its approval of the biography as a whole or in its particulars. (Under the pre-1978 U.S. copyright law, copyright has lapsed on Riding's pre-1940 poetry and prose. It remains protected in the U.K., Canada, other Commonwealth countries, and elsewhere.)

Unless otherwise noted, I have used the first published version of Laura Riding's poems with the exception of those poems that appear as epigraphs. Again, unless otherwise noted, they are from the 1938 edition of Laura Riding's *Collected Poems*. For Robert Graves' poems I have used the first published version only for those that do not appear in the 1975 edition of his *Collected Poems*.

Photographs have been provided by and are reproduced with the kind permission of:

T. S. Matthews: Laura Riding, insert p. 1; Kit Jackson and Tom Matthews, p. 7.

Sylvia Bernstein: Sylvia Seaman, p. 2.

Vanderbilt University Photographic Archives: Allen Tate, Donald Davidson, John Crowe Ransom, and Robert Penn Warren, p. 3; Laura Riding Gottschalk, p. 4.

Cornell University Library, Department of Manuscripts and University Archives: Louis G. Gottschalk, p. 4.

Richard Mayers: Isabel Mayers, p. 4.

Richard Perceval Graves: Robert Graves and Nancy Nicholson with their children, p. 5.

Simon Nowell-Smith: Geoffrey Phibbs, p. 5.

National Portrait Gallery, London: group shot of Karl Goldschmidt, Robert Graves, and Laura Riding (photographer unknown), p. 6.

Beryl Graves: Jean Marroig Gelat and Francisca, p. 6.

Griselda Ohannessian: Griselda Jackson and Schuyler Jackson, p. 7.

INDEX

Note: Laura Riding's name is abbreviated as
    LR throughout the index, except for
    in the main entry under Riding,
    Laura

"Absolute of Poetry, The," 161
Acquaintance with Description, An (Stein), 184,
    193
"Act V, Scene 5," 211
Adams, Leonie, 72
Adelphi, 160
Adelphi (publisher), 72, 83–84, 123, 128,
    373
"After Smiling," 246, 248
"After So Much Loss," 378–79
"Age of Certainty, The," 214
Albert Mills (store), 347, 354, 366–67, 370
Aldridge, John, 237, 238, 241, 249, 257,
    258, 266, 275, 325, 340, 341, 423
    collaboration with LR, 262–69, 316
    correspondence with LR, 293, 294–95,
        310–11, 316, 357, 363, 373, 375
    death of, 270
    described, 236
    literalism and, 361
    marriage to Lucie Brown, 250–51
    mother of, 275
    portrait of LR, 239
Alice in Wonderland (play), 49
Allen, Hervey, 371
"All Nothing, Nothing," 323
All That Gets Posted, see Everybody's Letters
Alvarez, Alfred, 178
"Amalthea," 304
American Money, 160
Americans (Riding), 264

Anarchism Is Not Enough (Riding), 42, 160,
    161, 164, 166–70, 171, 184, 239,
    290, 397
    reviews of, 261–62
Andersen, Hans Christian, 271, 293–94
Anderson, Sherwood, 7
"And This Hard Jealousy," 188
"Anonymous Break, An," 298
Another Future of Poetry (Graves), 139
Antell, Polly, 16, 17, 47, 55, 57, 58, 86,
    123, 126, 181, 207, 408, 412
    correspondence and confidences shared
        with LR, 59, 123, 136, 146–47,
        150, 152, 220
    correspondence with Louis Gottschalk,
        66, 67
    on Crane, 79
    as LR's roommate in New York City, 70,
        72, 76
    LR's suicide attempt and, 180
    LR's trunk left with, 81, 134–35, 136, 152
    at Sage College, 47, 49–50, 52, 54
Anthologies Against Poetry (Riding), 135
Anti-Semitism, 19, 24, 25, 85, 162–63,
    193, 194
Apple Tree Yard, 119, 121
Archer, John, 319
Aristotle, 161, 370
"Arms and the Covenant" speech,
    Churchill's, 360
Ascent of Man, The (Bronowski), 323
"As It Were Poems," 244–45, 308
"As to Food," 286–87
At Home with Anatole France (LeGoff), 72, 123
Auden, W. H., xiii, 187, 349, 350
    LR's influence on, 323, 350

Austen, Jane, 170
Authors Today and Yesterday, 238, 239, 283
"Autobiography of Baal, The," 272–74
Avoca (barge), 101, 206, 207

"Back to the Mother Breast," 41–42
Baisden, Frank, 415
Baldwin, Stanley, 348
Bara, Theda, 46
Barker, Arthur, 312, 317
Baudelaire, Charles Pierre, 50
BBC, xiii, 346, 349, 356, 416
"Because I Sit Here So," 234
"Because of Clothes," 230–31, 243
Becker, Carl Lotus, 55–56, 58
Beedham, Mr., 263
Beerbohm, Max, 119
Beezlebub's Tales to His Grandson (Gurdjieff), 255
Belknap, Mrs. William, 65
Bell, 96
Bell, Vanessa, 98
Benchley, Peter, 256
Bennett, Arnold, 161, 162
Bernstein, Sylvia, 47, 49, 50, 52, 57, 68
    Glorious to View, 50, 51, 52, 53–54
Berryman, John, 145
Betjeman, John, 96
"Beyond," 188–89
Bingham, Barry, 65
Bingham, Robert Worth, 65
Bishop, John Peale, 84
Blackmur, R. P., 144
Blake, William, 129, 186
Bloomsbury group, 120, 170, 181, 235
Blunden, Edmund, 350
Bodenheim, Maxwell, 72
Bogan, Louise, 84, 197
Bollingen Prize, 420
Bookseller, The, 359
Bottrall, Ronald, 257, 407
Boyle, Kay, 182, 183
Branson, Richard, 240
Bridge, The (Crane), 80, 86, 183
Bronowski, Jacob, 257, 278–79, 283, 287,
        316, 319–23, 324, 349, 350
    The Ascent of Man, 323
    background of, 319
    in Deyá, 280–81, 282, 319–20
    Experiment and, 319
    The Poet's Defence, 323
    quarrel with LR, 321–23, 325, 326, 327

Brontë, Emily, 170
Brooke, Rupert, 206, 287
Brooklyn Boys' High School, 39, 53
Brooklyn Girls' High School, 36–38, 39,
        45
    debating society, 38–39
Brooks, Cleanth, 144, 145
Broom, 71
Brown, Lucie, 234–38, 239, 243, 245, 249,
        250–51, 256, 258, 261, 264, 266,
        299, 326, 377
    death of, 270
Brown, Susan, 76, 79
Brown, William Slater, 76, 77–78
Buchanan, George, 370
"Burbank with a Baedeker: Bleistein with a
        Cigar," 162–63
Burtonwood, Mary, 290–91, 299–300, 306,
        309–10, 316
But It Still Goes On (Graves), 199, 274
Butler, Samuel, 129, 130, 144, 304
Byron, George Gordon, 135, 204

Calendar of Modern Letters, 160, 161
Cambridge Gownsman, 159, 319
Cambridge University, 350, 352
Cameron, Norman, 237, 248–50, 251, 257,
        266, 275, 316, 317, 326, 340, 346,
        357, 377
    LR's influence on, 350
    wives of, 251
Campbell, Roy, 164–66
Canelluñ (Riding home in Mallorca), 251,
        258, 266, 269, 274, 275, 280–81,
        288, 300, 302, 306, 311, 318
    described, 281–82, 316
    evacuation of, 338–39
    sirocco winds affecting, 313–14
    after the Spanish civil war, 339–41,
        347
C'an Pa Bo (cottage), 258, 291
Ca'n Torrent (Cameron home), 251, 314,
        316, 317, 318, 327, 340
Cantwell, Robert, 389
Cape, Jonathan (publisher):
    Graves' work and, 160, 232, 274, 276–
        78, 311–12
    LR's termination of relationship with,
        311–12
    LR's work and, 160, 221, 276–78, 290,
        291, 292, 294, 295, 296, 297, 311–
        12

Carcanet Press, 420
Carter, Elliott, 389
Cather, Willa, 421
"Celebration of Failure," 185
"Cell, The," 301–02
Chamberlain, Neville, 358, 363, 369
Champlain (ship), 379
Charles, Prince, 340
Charterhouse, 116
Château de La Chevrie, Graves and LR at,
    364–79
Chatto and Windus, 326, 375
Chelsea, 420
Chinese poetry, 138
"Chloe Or . . . ," 46, 227
Churchill, Winston, 347–48, 360
Classic, 10
Claudius, the God and His Wife Messalina
    (Graves), 305, 309
Close Chaplet, The (Riding), 83, 84, 85, 123,
    127, 128, 132–33, 136, 187, 243,
    304, 373
  reviews of, 158–59
  sales of, 159
Cobb, William, 13, 14, 135
Coleridge, Samuel Taylor, 135, 145, 204
Coles, H. G. D., 368
Collected Poems (Dickinson), 341
Collected Poems (Graves), 361, 367
Collected Poems (Riding) (1938), 34, 64, 189,
    263, 280, 361
  preface to, xii, 361
  reviews of, xii, xiii, 323, 327, 361, 372,
    373, 374
Collected Poems (Williams), xii
Colón, Don Bernardo, 274, 275, 288, 309,
    340, 341
Comintern, 335, 336
Common Asphodel, The (Graves), 139
Composition as Explanation (Stein), 182,
    184
Comstock, Anthony, 239
Condition of the Working Class in Britain, The
    (Hutt), 353
Constable (publisher), 292, 317, 347
Constructive Birth Control Society, 119
Contact, 71
Contemporaries and Snobs (Riding), 151, 160,
    161–62, 163–64, 171–72, 183,
    290
  reviews of, 161, 164–65
Contemporary Verse, 10
"Contraband, The," 176

Convalescent Conversations, 91
Cook, Thomas, 124, 132
Cook, William, 193
Cornell University, 9, 40, 48–55, 86
  Sage College, 46–47, 48–54
Cosmopolitan Club, 47
Council of the Inside People, 357, 358–59
Count Belisarius (Graves), 367
Country Sentiment (Graves), 200
"Covenant of Literal Morality," *see* First
    Protocol
Cowan, Louise, 85
Cowley, Malcolm, 70–71, 72, 73, 78, 84,
    186
Crabb, George, 413
Crane, Hart, 6, 72, 76, 80, 182–83, 186–
    87, 207, 208
  as an alcoholic, 78
  The Bridge, 80, 86, 183
  as homosexual, 79, 80, 220
  as poet, 78, 79
  LR's correspondence with, 219
  LR's friendship with, 78–79, 80–81, 86
  suicide, 81, 183, 229, 264
  White Buildings, 84, 183
"Credo: An Aesthetic," 60
Criterion, 158–59, 170, 171
Critical Vulgate, The, *see Epilogue: A Critical
    Summary*
"Crown for Hans Christian Andersen, A,"
    271, 293–94, 295
Cullen, John, 319
Cummings, E. E., 72, 142
Cunard, Nancy, 175, 214

Dadaism, 71
"Daisy and Venison," 291–92, 293, 295–
    96, 297, 311
"Damned Thing, The," 239, 240, 242–43
David Copperfield, Graves' condensed version
    of, 249, 289
Davidson, Donald, 157, 158, 161, 168,
    183, 196
  as editor, 13, 65, 66
  as Fugitive, 4, 5, 6, 7, 11–12, 13, 14, 15,
    61, 68, 85
  nom de plume, 6
  rejection of LR's poetry, 61
  review of *The Close Chaplet*, 159
  Tate's correspondence with, 12–13, 61,
    72, 76, 83, 84, 87
"Dawn Bombardment," *see* "Hostage, The"

Dawn in Britain, The (Doughty), 414, 419
Day, Dorothy, 24
"Death as Death," 227
Debs, Eugene, 10, 24, 25, 26, 40
de la Mare, Walter, 350
Denham Studios, 346, 348
Dent (publisher), 406, 412
Deyá, Mallorca:
    curate rule of, 364
    evacuation of, 328, 338–39, 345–46
    Graves' return to, 339–41
    LR and Graves in, 318–39
    LR's possessions left behind in, 339
    Spanish civil war and, 328, 334, 336,
        337, 338–39
Dial, 160, 161
Diana, Lady, 340
Dickinson, Emily, 111, 176, 341
Dictionary of Related Meanings (originally
        Dictionary of Exact Meanings), xiii,
        367–68, 389, 404, 405, 406–07,
        410–16
"Dimensions," 8–9, 11
Dimitroff, Georgi, 335
"Divestment of Beauty," 246–47
Donne, John, 135
Doolittle, Hilda, 138, 202
"Doom in Bloom," 361
Dostoevsky, Fyodor, 27
Doubleday, Doran imprint, 160, 373
Double Dealer, 6
Doughty, Charles M., 371, 383, 414, 419
Douglas, Major Clifford Hugh, 372, 407
Douglas, Michael, 340
Dreiser, Theodore, 27
"Druida," 82–83, 128
Duncan, Isadore, 61, 70

Early Poems (Riding), 187–89
Eastman, Max, 70
Eberhart, Richard, 319
Edersheim, Sadie, *see* Reichenthal, Sadie
Eisenhower, Dwight D., 418
"Elegy in a Spider Web," 189–91
Eliot, T. S., 6, 63, 138, 144, 150, 161, 162–
        63, 166, 172, 184, 278, 350
    "Burbank with a Baedeker: Bleistein with
        a Cigar," 162–63
    as editor of *Criterion*, 158–59
    Robert Graves' disagreement with, 158–
        59, 202
    private life, 186

"The Waste Land," 6, 7, 80, 146, 165,
        183
Ellidge, George, 290, 299–300, 309, 310,
        316, 377
Ellis, Havelock, 46, 97
Ellit, Doris, 206
"End of the World and After, The," 351
Ends and Means (Huxley), 359
English Club, Oxford University, 249,
        351
English Synonymes (Crabb), 413
Epilogue: A Critical Summary (previously *The
        Critical Vulgate*), 282–87, 310, 314,
        317, 318, 319, 320, 322, 323, 327,
        330, 372
    final volume of, *see World and Ourselves,
        The*
    reception of, 351
    reviews of, 323, 331
Epsom, William, 143–44, 145, 278, 279,
        319, 350
Eric Pinker and Sons, 123
"Escape from the Zeitgeist," 160
Everybody's Letters, 33, 232–33, 289
    afterword to, 241
Experiment, 319
Experts Are Puzzled (Riding), 221, 232, 276,
        283–84

Faber Book of Modern Verse, The, 329
    foreword to, 323
Fairies and Fusiliers (Graves), 117, 200
"Fairy Tale for Old People, A," 296–97
"Fallacies," 66
Faust, Elfriede, 234, 237, 238, 249–50,
        251, 257, 266, 306, 316, 317, 326
"Fine Fellow Son of Poor Fellow," 26
First Protocol, 359, 360, 361, 363, 366,
        367, 368, 369, 373, 374, 377
Fitts, Dudley, 362
Fitzgerald, Eleanor, 389, 390, 408
Fitzgerald, F. Scott, 7, 64, 255, 256
Fitzgerald, Robert, 327, 389, 390
Fitzgerald, Zelda, 7, 256
Fletcher, John Gould, 6, 158–59
Florida East Coast Railroad, xi, xii
"Flowering Urn, The," 345
"Footfalling," 323
"Forgotten Girlhood" (originally "Lida"),
        34–35, 40, 42, 57, 128
Forster, E. M., 122, 158, 169, 325
"For What Is Easy," 323

14A (Riding and Ellidge), 94, 95, 96, 100, 102, 103, 104, 106–07, 257, 299, 309, 355, 377
Four Unposted Letters to Catherine (Riding), 221
"Fragment of an Unfinished Novel," 42–43, 168
"Fragments," 87
"Fragments from Alastor," 60
Frail Barb, The (Riding), 13–14, 135
Francisca (maid), 341
Franco, General Francisco, 337, 338, 340
Frank, James, 3, 14
Frank, Rose:
    sister Goldie, 14
Frank, Ross, 3, 14, 15
Frank-Maurice, Inc., 70, 72
Freeman, Joseph, 9, 10, 37, 39, 53
    on Greenwich Village life and times, 70, 72, 79
Freud, Sigmund, 239, 349
Freudian approach to analyzing poetry, 140, 141
"Friendship on Visit," 329
Frost, Robert, 202, 371
Fugitive (magazine), 4, 7, 8, 11, 13, 15, 59, 60, 62, 85
    first issue of, 5–6
    "The Quids" in, 73
    LR's fund-raising for, 65–66
Fugitives (poetry group), 4–17, 59–60, 65–66, 68, 74, 84–85, 141, 196, 328
Fussell, Paul, 200, 212–13
"Future of Poetry, The," 62

Galicia, 19, 25, 27
Gallivant, Robin, *see* Davidson, Donald
Garnett, David, 98–99, 101, 109, 197
Gelat, Anita, 364
Gelat Marroig Más, Juan, 219, 229, 233, 267, 274–75, 287–88, 290, 300, 310, 315, 318, 336, 339, 340, 341
    arrest of, 354, 364
    building projects with Graves and LR, 274–75, 281, 287, 335, 340
    café of, 316, 337
    Robert Graves' property maintained by, 339–40, 347
    as mayor, 334–35, 337, 338
    mistress of, 224
General Disability (Landes), 39
Gershoy, Leo, 52, 55, 56, 58, 59

"Gertrude Stein and the New Barbarism," 183
Gibson, Dr. Finley, 65
Gish, Lillian, 65
Glasgow Herald, The, 159
Glorious to View (Bernstein), 50, 51, 52, 53–54
Glover, Gordon, 300, 315, 316
"Goat Alone" (previously "Samuel's Toast of Death"), 279
Goethe, Johann Wolfgang von, 27, 199
Golden Treasury of English poetry, Palgrave's, 45
Golding, Louis, 317
Goldman, Emma, 70
Goldschmidt, Karl, 314–18, 327–28, 329, 330–31, 336, 388
    from August 1936 to 1939, 347, 349, 354, 355, 357, 363, 369, 373, 374–75, 377
    background of, 314–15
    evacuation from Deyá, 338–39, 345–46
    girlfriend, Ellie, 315, 316, 317
    Robert Graves and, 315, 340, 374, 375, 388, 406
Goldwater, Barry, 418–19
Good-bye to All That (Graves), 92, 115–18, 121, 193, 208, 305
    analysis of, 204
    completion of, 210, 272
    "Dedicatory Epilogue," 113, 118, 132
    on Graves' parents, 199
    LR's suicide leap and, 197–98
    sales of, 232, 274, 276
    title of, 204
    tone of, 203
    on veracity of, 212–13
Gordon, Caroline, *see* Tate, Caroline
Goring, Hermann, 338
Gottschalk, Laura, *see* Riding, Laura
Gottschalk, Louis, 39, 52–57, 68, 72, 86, 123
    divorce from LR, 17, 66, 67
    items from LR's trunk for, 134, 135, 151
    marriage to LR, xviii, 9, 11, 16, 17, 47, 54–55, 57, 58–59, 61, 63, 64, 66–67
    politics of, 39, 53
    proposal to remarry, 136
    remarriage, 151–52
    at University of Illinois, 9, 47
    at University of Louisville, 11, 12
"Grace," 178

Grant, Duncan, 98
Granta, The, 278
Graves, Alfred Perceval (APG), 116–17,
        118, 122, 198–99, 200, 204, 272,
        274
    death of, 346
    the "Trinity" relationship and, 146, 147,
        149–51
Graves, Amy, 117, 118, 119, 121, 122, 123,
        147–48, 198–99, 200, 205, 240,
        274, 346
    memoirs, 147–48
    the "Trinity" relationship and, 146, 147,
        149–51, 158
Graves, Beryl, *see* Pritchard, Beryl
Graves, Catherine, 122, 124, 206, 209–10,
        346
Graves, David, 122, 124, 206, 209–10,
        337, 346
    World War II and, 370
Graves, Jenny, 122, 124, 206, 209–10, 213,
        346
Graves, John, 150, 179
Graves, Millicent, 122
Graves, Philip, 122
Graves, Richard, 124
Graves, Richard Perceval, 75, 114, 150,
        212, 325
Graves, Robert, 406, 416
    agent, 123
    Another Future of Poetry, 139
    appearance, 115
    autobiography of, *see* Good-bye to All That
    "The Autobiography of Baal," 272–74
    background, 15–18
    biographies of, xv, xvi, 75, 109, 113–14,
        150, 211–12, 325–26
    book on obscene language, 125
    breakup of, 203, 208, 209–10
    But It Still Goes On, 199, 274
    celibacy, 248
    character, 204
    Claudius, the God and His Wife Messalina,
        305, 309
    The Common Asphodel, 139
    Count Belisarius, 367
    Country Sentiment, 200
    David Copperfield, condensed version of,
        249, 289
    death of, 270
    diaries from 1937 to 1939, 365, 369,
        370, 373, 376, 379, 387
    disagreement with Eliot, 158–59, 202

divorce, 367
    Fairies and Fusiliers, 117, 200
    fascism and, 337
    as a father, 206–07, 209–10
    finances, 120, 121, 123, 125, 147, 151,
        154, 159–60, 204–05, 206
    Gelat and, 274, 275, 288
    after *Good-bye to All That,* 232, 274,
        275, 276
    after *I, Claudius,* 309
    in 1933, 289, 300
    in 1936, 347, 353
    the *Fugitive* and, 6
    Good-bye to All That, see Good-bye to All
        That
    grave of, 218
    Beryl Hodge (later Graves) and, 341,
        368, 369, 370, 376, 377–78, 388,
        399, 400
    I, Claudius, see I, Claudius
    Impenetrability, or, The Proper Habit of English,
        139
    infatuation with Julie Matthews, 266
    Schuyler Jackson and, 377, 401
    Laurence and the Arabs, 160, 181, 347
    loss of religious faith, 199
    The Marmosite's Miscellany, 130
    marriage to Kit, 117, 120, 121, 201, 206
        breakup of, 203, 208, 209–10
    No Decency Left, 257, 276–78, 289, 311
    On English Poetry, 139
    Phibbs and, 99, 101, 104, 108, 109, 117,
        209, 210–11
    Poetic Unreason and Other Studies, 139–40
    poetry of, 117, 126, 127–28, 130, 148,
        201, 211, 214, 229–30, 244–45,
        246, 248, 257, 301–02, 304, 350,
        367, 402
        obscure, nightmarish, 365–66
        see also individual titles
    as professor in Egypt, 86, 121, 125, 147
    pseudonym, book written under, 276–77
    return to Deyá, 339–41
    Laura Riding and, *see* Riding, Laura,
        Robert Graves and
    sexuality, 116, 121
    Gertrude Stein and, 175, 180, 185, 191–
        92, 193, 196, 209, 233
    To Return to All That, 199
    traffic accident, close escape from, 155–
        57
    trip to England in summer of 1939, 395,
        398–99, 400

Graves, Robert (*cont.*)
   wartime service and its influence on him,
     204–06
   The White Goddess, 402, 403
Graves, Rosaleen, 122–23, 136, 147, 150,
     178–79, 203, 213
   as an aunt, 206
   on sex, 247
Graves, Sally, 118–19, 122, 376
Graves, Sam, 122, 124, 147, 206–07, 209–
     10, 346
Great Gatsby, The (Fitzgerald), 64
Great Scourge and How to End It, The
     (Parkhurst), 239–40
Gregory, Horace, 84–85
Grenville (battleship), 338
Grigson, Geoffrey, 239, 349, 350, 351
Grimm Brothers, 385
Grosset and Dunlap, 36, 38
Guale Indians, xi
Guggenheim Foundation, 412, 413, 420
Gurdjieff, Georges, 255, 383–84, 396

Haines, Lett, 235, 264
Hapgood, Hutchins, 26
Hardy, Thomas, 204
Harries, Sam, 202
Haywood, "Big Bill," 70
Heap, Jane, 383
Heathen, A Mistake Somewhere, The (Wyatt and
     Glover), 317
Heinemann (publisher), 146
"Helen's Burning," 177–78, 179
Hemingway, Ernest, 7, 325
Here Beyond, see Poems A Joking Word
"Here Beyond," 186, 188–89, 279
Hirsch, Nathaniel, 14, 15
Hirsch, Dr. Sidney Mttron, 3–4
   described, 5
   as Fugitive, 4, 6, 15–16
Hitler, Adolf, 27, 315, 316, 334, 336, 337,
     338, 362–63, 365, 369
Hodge, Alan, 257, 326, 331, 338, 340, 349,
     357, 388
   collaboration on novel with LR, 348
   correspondence with LR, 351, 369, 400
   Dictionary of Related Meanings and, 368, 407
   evacuation from Deyá, 345–46
   in France, 362, 363, 368, 370, 377, 379–80
   in New Hope, 382, 391
   pre–World War II politics, 356, 357
   return to England, 395, 398–99

Hodge, Beryl, *see* Pritchard, Beryl
Hodge, Jane Aiken, 326
Hogarth Press, 57, 86, 97, 123, 128, 159,
     181
Hopkins, Gerald Manley, 145
"Hostage, The" (later "Dawn
     Bombardment"), 376
Hours Press, 214
"How Came It About?," 167–68
Howe, Irving, 23
How to Make a Revolution (Postgate), 355
Hulme, T. E., 141
Humana Sebastien Hospital, 423
Hutchinson, Dorothy, 319, 357
Hutchinson, Ward, 319, 352, 357
Hutt, Allen, 353
Huxley, Aldous, 359
Hyman, Stanley Edgar, 143

I, Claudius (film), 346, 347, 348
I, Claudius (Graves), 290–91, 299, 300–10,
     312
   analysis of, 300–09
   publisher of, 312
   reviews of, 309
   success of, 309
"Idea of God, The," 284
Imagism, 138
"Impenetrability, or the Proper Habit of
     English," 125
Impenetrability; or the Proper Habit of English
     (Graves), 139
"Improprieties," 59–60
"In a Café," 168
"Incarnations," 18
"In Nineteen Twenty-Seven," 153–54,
     155–57, 164, 172, 175, 186, 354
Institute for the Harmonious Development
     of Man, 383
Irish Songs and Ballads, 116

Jackson, Ben, 384, 391, 396, 408, 409, 419
Jackson, Griselda, 384–87, 390–400, 404–
     05, 408–09, 411, 414, 417, 418–19
Jackson, Kathy, 384, 391, 408, 409
Jackson, Kit (née Townsend), 254, 272–73,
     375, 380, 382, 386, 409, 412, 419
   accused of being evil, 394–96, 397, 398
   background of, 382
   breakdowns, 392, 395, 397–98, 405
   divorce, 413

Jackson, Kit (*cont.*)
  marriage, 382–83, 386, 409, 413
  personality of, 385
  in spring and summer of 1939, 386, 387,
    390–99
Jackson, Laura (Riding), *see* Riding, Laura
Jackson, Maria, 396, 408, 414, 419
Jackson, Philip Nye, 371
Jackson, Schuyler Brinckerhoff, II (LR's
    second husband):
  background of, 371–72
  death of, xii, xiii, 416, 419
  divorce, 413
  as a father, 384, 385, 386, 396, 399,
    404–05, 411–12, 414, 416
    letter writing, 408–09, 410, 418–19
  Robert Graves and, 377, 401
  marriage to Kit, 382–83, 386, 409
  Thomas Matthews and, 254, 255–56,
    270, 372, 373, 374, 375, 382, 383,
    385, 386, 387–88, 390, 395
  moneymaking schemes, 384, 386
  New Hope farm, 372, 381–82, 404, 405,
    406, 407, 411–12
  sale of, 412
  LR and, *see* Riding, Laura, Schuyler
    Jackson and
  as *Time* reviewer, xiii, 372, 373, 374,
    412
Jackson Monthly, 384
Jackson Quarterly, 381
Jacks or Better (Matthews), 391, 393
Jarrell, Randall, 143
"Jealous Man, A," 248, 365–66
Jean Paul Marat: A Study in Radicalism
    (Gottschalk), 57, 66
"Jewels and After," 231
Jewish Daily Forward, 24
Jewish Socialism, 23
Jews, 19, 23–25, 27, 337
  German, 22, 23–24, 315, 316, 336
  Nazi persecution of, 316, 362
  social status of, 37
  see also Anti-Semitism
Joan of Arc, 91, 105
"Jocasta," 169
"John and I," 69
John Kemp's Wager, 117
Johnson, Paul, 334
Jolas, Eugene, 173, 182–83, 186, 187
Joseph II, Emperor of Austria, 19, 29
Joyce, James, 182, 325, 350
  Ulysses, 183, 349

Judge, The (West), 169
Jung, Carl, 253

Kafka, Franz, 184
Kapital, Das (Marx), 53
Keats, John, 51, 135, 204
Kemp, Alix, 357
Kemp, Harry, 352, 357
Kennedy, John F., 418
Kerouallan, countess de, 364
King, Horatio, 36
Kipling, Rudyard, 199
Kirkham, Michael, 420
Korda, Alexander, 346–47

Labour Club, Oxford University, 368
Lady Chatterley's Lover (Lawrence), 349
"Lady of the Apple, The," 112, 130–31
Lake, Dr. (LR's surgeon), 196, 203
"Lake Isle of Innisfree," 142
Landes, Dr., 39
"Last Nuptials," 87
Laughton, Charles, 348
Laura and Francisca (Riding), 217, 220–29,
    233, 243, 263, 279, 294
  "Francisca and Scarcely More," 222,
    224–28
  "How the Poem Ends," 222, 228–29
  "The Island and Here," 222–24
  review of, 221
Lawrence, D. H., 325, 349
Lawrence, T. E., 121, 124, 125, 129, 148,
    158, 181, 204, 282
  death of, 347
Lawrence, T. E. (*cont.*)
  Graves' book about adventures of, 160,
    181, 347
  LR's suicide leap and, 197
Lawrence and the Arabs (Graves), 160, 181,
    347
Leaf, Arthur, 346
Leavis, F. R., 144, 349
Leavis, Queenie, 349
Left Book Club, 352
Left Heresy in Literature and Life, The (Riding
    and Kemp), 352, 353, 357, 362
LeGoff, Marcel, 72
Lehote, André, 102
Lenin, Vladimir Ilich, 28
"Lesson, The," 180
"Letter of Abdication," 30, 91, 109–10

Lewis, C. Day, 350, 352
Lewis, Sinclair, 7, 28, 46
Lewis, Wyndham, 196, 197, 352
Liberator, 9, 10
Libre Estampa, 354
"Lida," *see* "Forgotten Girlhood"
Liddell-Hart, Basil, 347, 405
"Life of the Dead, The," 252
Life of the Dead, The (Riding), 262–69, 270,
    279, 316
Lindsay, Jack, 158
Lindsay, Vachel, 202
"Lines in Short Despite in Time," 362
Literary internationalism, 138
Literary Review, 7
Little, Brown, 406, 407, 410, 412, 413–14,
    415
Little Review, 71, 383
Liverpool Post, 159
Lives of Wives (Riding), 348, 367, 368, 377
Lloyd, Harold, 123
London Daily Telegraph, 354
Lorber, Laura, *see* Reichenthal, Laura
"Lost Acres," 201
Love as Love, Death as Death (Riding), 181,
    187, 323
Lowell, Robert, 145
Lowry, Malcolm, 319
"Lucrece and Nara," 81–82, 128
Luna (company), 275, 287
Luxemburg, Rosa, 28, 29, 39
Lye, Jane, 316
Lye, Len, 105, 178, 208, 220, 248, 257,
    258, 316, 341, 346
Lyric West, 10

McCormacks (Deyá couple), 318–19
MacDonald, George, 385, 392
McGuinnes, Norah, 97–99, 100–02, 104,
    105–09, 194, 197, 213, 393
McIntyre, Alfred, 407, 410, 413, 414
MacLachlan, Christopher, 204
MacLeish, Archibald, 138
MacNeice, Louis, 350
"Mad Serenader, The," 61
Magdelena (maid), 317
Maine (ship), 346
Main Street (Lewis), 7
Mallarmé, Stéphane, 50, 189
Mallik, Basanta, 120, 129, 130, 202, 204, 205
Mallorca, *see* Deyá, Mallorca
Manchester Guardian, 318

Mansfield, Katherine, 255, 257, 258
"Map of Life, The," 387
Marat, Jean Paul, 56, 57, 66
"March 1937," 354, 376
Marcham, Frederick George, 55
Margarita (dressmaker), 230, 232
Maria (gardener's daughter), 317, 318
Marmosite's Miscellany, The (Graves), 130
Marsh, Edward, 121, 158, 197, 204
Marta's (restaurant), 72
Marx, Karl, 19, 23, 24, 28
    Das Kapital, 53
Marxism, 351, 352
"Mask, The," 134, 149
Mason, James, 50, 51
Masses, The, 70
Mass Observation, 359
Masters, Edgar Lee, 371
Matthews, Johnny, 387
Matthews, Julie, 254, 255–57, 259, 261,
    262, 265, 266–67, 269, 316, 351,
    373, 375, 380, 388
    death of, 270
    Graves' infatuation with, 266
    Schuyler Jackson and, 383
    mother of, 356
    reunion with Graves and LR, 346
    in spring of summer of 1939, 386, 387,
        390, 392, 393, 394, 395
Matthews, Paul, 387
Matthews, Thomas Stanley, 253–71, 284,
    291, 316, 324, 327, 339, 351, 388,
    402, 415, 419
    background of, 254–55
    death of, 271
    in Deyá, 252–53, 255, 256–62, 265,
        266–67, 269, 270, 372
    Schuyler Jackson and, *see* Jackson,
        Schuyler Brinckerhoff, II, Thomas
        Matthews and
    Jacks or Better, 391, 393
    The Moon's No Fool, 257–60, 317
    reunion with Graves and LR, 346
    LR's return to America and, 380
    in spring and summer of 1939, 389, 390,
        391, 392, 393, 395–96, 396
    as *Time's* managing editor, 270, 356, 388,
        389
Matthews, Tommy, 385, 387
Mayers, Helen, 38, 59, 68, 180, 412
Mayers, Isabel, *see* Reichenthal, Isabel
Mayers, Jesse (brother-in-law), 38, 39, 40,
    42, 418

Mayers, Richard (nephew), 40
Memoirs of a Foxhunting Man (Sassoon), 204
"Memories of Mortalities," 404
Mencken, H. L., 6, 160
  Smart Set, 55
Metaphysics (Aristotle), 161
Midsummer's Night Dream, A, 39
Mills, Albert, 347, 354, 366–67, 370
Milton, John, 135, 371
"Miss Banquett or the Populating of
  Cosmania," 294, 295, 297
Mitchison, Naomi, 355, 359
Modernism, xiii, xvii, 4, 5, 8, 162, 163,
  167, 202, 350
  Fugitive debate on, 62–63
  *A Survey of Modernist Poetry, see Survey of
  Modernist Poetry, A*
Molière, 135, 152
Monroe, Harriet, 10, 13, 63
  correspondence with LR, 70, 72, 86
Moon's No Fool, The (Matthews), 257–60, 317
Moore, Marianne, 138, 158, 160, 161, 202
Moore, Merrill, 6, 196–97, 227
Morgan, Ann, *see* Wyatt, Honor
Morrell, Lady Ottoline, 120, 200
Morris, Cedric, 235, 236
Muggeridge, Malcolm, 125
Muir, Edwin, 160
Mussolini, Benito, 334, 355, 369
"My Brother Robert," 150

"Nape of the Neck, The," 127–28
Napoleon, 19
Nashville Poetry Prize (1924), 4, 8, 10, 12,
  14, 16, 66
Nashville Tennessean, 13
Nation, 72
Nation and Athenaeum, 164
Naziism, 316, 337, 362
"Nearly," 188
"New Barbarism and Gertrude Stein, The,"
  182
New Criterion, 160, 161, 162, 164, 165, 172,
  323
New Criticism, 74–75, 143, 144, 145
New Criticism, The (Ransom), 144, 145
New Republic, 74, 160, 256
New Romanticism, 139
New Verse, 239, 349, 350
New York Call, 24, 27, 29
New York Public Library, Berg Collection,
  421

New York Times, 37
New York University, 72
Nicholson, Ben, 119
Nicholson, Nancy, 96, 99, 101, 104, 109,
  118–21, 194, 197, 204, 205, 207,
  214, 399
  appearance, 118–19
  as artist, 86, 119, 136, 157
  child-rearing ideas, 119, 121, 137
  divorce from Graves, 367
  in Egypt, 123–33
  Egyptian trip, 86, 112–13, 121–22, 123
  as feminist, 86, 119
  Graves' helplessness and, 200
  marriage, 117, 120, 121, 201, 206
    breakup of, 203, 208, 209–10, 367
  relationship with Phibbs, 207–11, 213
  reunion with Graves and LR, 346
  LR's correspondence with, 354, 367
  LR's suicide leap and, 93, 94–95, 111,
    208, 209, 212, 213
  Trinity with LR and Robert Graves, 95,
    102–03, 105, 106, 107, 110, 123–
    24, 126–28, 129, 131, 136, 147–
    58, 167–69, 172, 207, 211
Nicholson, William, 113, 114, 119, 121,
  209, 214
  the "Trinity" relationship and, 154, 158
Nihilism, 71, 177, 178, 277, 396, 397
Nimrod's Rise (Riding home), 382, 390,
  391, 411
Nixon, Richard, 418
Nobel Prize, 309
No Decency Left (Graves), 257, 276–78, 289,
  311
Nottingham Journal, 159

Oberon, Merle, 348
"Obsession," 186, 191, 221, 232
O'Connor, Frank (né Michael O'Donovan),
  97, 99, 101, 102–03
O'Donovan, Michael, *see* O'Connor, Frank
Ogden, C. K., 406–07
O'Neill, Eugene, 72
On English Poetry (Graves), 139
"One Right, One Left," 32
"Only Possible Ending, The," 421–22
"On Portents," 229–30
Open Road Press, 371, 383
"Opportunism Rampant," 109, 212
Orage, A. R., 383
"Organs of Sense," 243

Ouspensky, Pyotr, 101, 383
Owen, Wilfred, 201
Owle, David, 416
Oxford Book of Modern Verse, The, 329
Oxford English Club, 350
Oxford English Dictionary (OED), 406, 413
Oxford Magazine, 159
Oxford University, 350, 368
  English Club, 249, 351
  Labour Club, 358
Oxford University Press, 368

Palmer, Mrs., 187
Pamphlet Against Anthologies, A (Riding and
    Graves), 141–42, 151, 154, 159,
    160, 350
Pankhurst, Christabel, 239–40
Paris (ship), 86, 376, 379
Paris, France, 173, 181–82
  American writers in, 7, 71, 138, 187
Paris *Tribune*, 182
Parker, Dorothy, 256
Paul, Eliot, 182
Pavlova, Anna, 61
"Personal Letter with a Request for a Reply,
    A," 346, 353, 355, 356, 357, 359,
    372
Phibbs, Geoffrey, 95–111, 180, 185, 206,
    207, 341
  background of, 96
  death of, 213
  described, 96, 97
  Robert Graves and, 99, 101, 104, 108,
    109, 117, 209, 210–11
  marital problems, 97–99, 100, 101–02
  name change, 95–96, 109
  relationship with Nancy Nicholson,
    207–11, 213
  relationship with LR, 93, 100–09, 172,
    175–78, 207–12, 221, 232–33,
    378, 393
  LR's suicide leap and, 93, 94–95, 103,
    110–11, 178, 180, 197, 208, 209,
    212
Phillips, Mary, 327
"Philosophy of Composition," 9
Pinker, Eric, 160–61
Plath, Sylvia, 145
"Playground, The," 260–61, 269–70, 291,
    295
Poe, Edgar Allan, 6, 9
"Poem Only," 188

Poems A Joking Word (originally "Here
    Beyond"), 186, 187–91, 221, 227,
    276, 290
  reviews of, 278–79, 319
Poetics (Aristotle), 161
Poetic Unreason and Other Studies (Graves),
    139–40
Poetry (magazine), 10, 63, 67
"Poets and Poetry," 323
Poets Defence, The (Bronowski), 323
Poincaré, Raymond, 92
Pomfret (prep school), 371
Pope, Alexander, 166
Popular Front, Spain, 335–36, 337, 338
Postgate, Raymond, 355
"Postponement of Immortality" (later
    "Postponement of Self"), 54
Pound, Ezra, 138, 141, 202, 350, 372
Practical Criticism (Richards), 279
Praeterita (Riding) (memoirs), xiv–xv, 44, 420
"Precis," 211
"Pride of Head," 243–44
Prighozy, Ida, 57–59
Prim, Roger, *see* Ransom, John Crowe
Primo de Rivera, Miguel, 334
Princess and the Goblin (MacDonald), 392
Princeton Alumni News, 372
Princeton University, 254, 255, 256, 260,
    270, 371, 372
  Tuesday Evening Club, 255, 371
Pritchard, Beryl, 388, 398
  background of, 368
  as Robert Graves' wife, 341
    pregnancy, 400
    relationship before their marriage,
      368, 369, 370, 376, 377–78, 388,
      399, 400
  as Alan Hodge's wife, 362, 363, 365,
      369, 380, 382, 399, 400
  LR's nickname for, 368, 369
  as secretary to LR, 369, 370, 407
  in the summer of 1939, 388, 391, 395,
      399
Progress of Stories (Riding), 291, 292–99,
    311, 317
  preface to, 292–93, 294, 296
  review of, 295, 297
  sections of, 295
"Prophecy or a Plea, A," 62–63, 75, 78,
    139, 146, 160
Prussia, 19
Psychoanalysis, 140, 205
"Pure Death," 126

"Quids, The," 73–74, 86, 202
Quinn, John, 383

Raine, Kathleen, 319
Raizess, Sonia, 420
Random House, 347, 373
Ranpura, 112
Ransom, John Crowe, 37, 60, 138, 144–45, 158, 161, 172
  background of, 4, 6
  formal metrical structure and, 141–42, 145
  as Fugitive, 4, 5, 11, 15, 16, 62, 68, 85
  Graves' admiration for poetry of, 202
  The New Criticism, 144, 145
  nom de plume, 7
  on LR's poetry, 164
  on "The Waste Land," 7
Rational Meaning: A New Foundation for the Definition of Words (Riding and Jackson), 415
"Reality as Port Huntlady," 297–300
Reeves, David, 362, 377, 382, 388, 391, 394, 395, 405
Reeves, James, 257, 287, 317, 319, 349, 352, 358, 361, 369
  Bronowski-Riding quarrel and, 321, 322, 325, 327
  described, 329
  in Deyá, 317–18, 327–31, 340
Reeves, Laura, 358
Reichenthal, Isabel (half sister), 18, 20, 31, 66, 151, 180, 238, 364, 373, 417
  appearance of, 36
  birth of, 20
  book dedicated to, 128
  closeness with LR, 31, 36, 38, 47, 375
  death of, 418
  financial assistance for LR, 412
  literary career, 36, 38, 39
  marriage of, 29, 38, 39–40
  nom de plume, 38
  relationship with her stepmother, 21, 22, 31, 32, 33
Reichenthal, Isidor (paternal grandfather), 19
Reichenthal, Laura, *see* Riding, Laura
Reichenthal, Laura (née Lorber), 20, 22, 31
Reichenthal, Nathan (father), 34, 55, 364, 375
  death of, 27–28, 373
  jobs, 20, 24, 25–26, 28, 31, 32

  origins of, 14, 18–20, 22, 28
  politics and, 23, 24–25, 27, 29, 31, 32, 39
Reichenthal, Robert (brother), 412, 418
  birth of, 31, 33, 36, 44
  mental illness, 33, 42
Reichenthal, Sadie (née Edersheim) (mother), 20–23, 26, 27, 110
  background of, 20–21, 22
  birth of, 22
  LR and, 30–35, 41–44, 45, 232, 412, 417–18
Reichenthal, Sarah (paternal grandmother), 19
Reverdy (cubist poet), 189
"Revolution of the Word, The," 186–87
Ribbertrop-Molotov Pact, 327
Richards, I. A., 143, 144, 279, 406–07
Richards, Vyvyan, 181
Richardson, Dorothy, 170
Riding, Laura:
  accents, 37, 136, 138
  appearance, 12, 31, 37, 49, 58, 113–14, 325–26, 387
    clothing and jewelry, 230–31, 237, 240, 258, 275, 311, 326, 347, 351, 387, 390
  biographies of, xiv–xvii
  birth of, xiii, xviii, 31
  British accent, 136, 138
  childhood, 30–44
  claim to intellectual title to writing of others, 323
  collaboration, 348, 362
    with Aldridge, 262–69, 316
    on *Epilogue: A Critical Summary, see Epilogue: A Critical Summary*
    on *14A, see 14A*
    with Graves, 137–46, 151, 154, 159, 257, 276–77, 325, 367–68, 407
    with Hodge, 348
    with Schuyler Jackson, 400, 404, 405, 406–07, 410–15
    with Kemp, 352, 357
    with Matthews, 257–60
  college education, 9–10, 11, 12, 40, 46, 48–54, 57, 59, 63
  as critic, xiii, 137–46, 151, 154, 159, 160–70, 182, 183–84, 205, 350
  death of, xiv, xviii, 423
  as editor, xiii, 257–60, 317, 318, 319, 321, 324
  see also this entry under collaboration

Riding, Laura (*cont.*)
  education, 36–39, 45
    college, 9–10, 11, 12, 40, 46, 48–54,
      57, 59
  as evangelist, 351, 355
  father and, 27, 28–29, 39
  fear of insanity, 44
  feminism and, 238, 241, 349, 351, 353,
    355–56, 358
  finances, 66, 71, 86, 123, 274, 277–78,
    288, 408, 412
  the Fugitives and, 4–5, 8–17, 59–63,
    65–66, 68, 74, 84–85, 141, 328
  on God, 279–80, 283–87, 320
  Robert Graves and, xii, xv, 15, 27, 28,
    44, 57, 75, 86–87, 91–115, 117,
    118, 122–31, 172–73, 178, 181–
    82, 191, 217–71, 274–403,
    405–06
    in America, 382, 386–99
    from August 1936 to 1939, 346–79
    collaborative writing, 137–46, 151,
      154, 159, 257, 276–77, 325, 407
    contracts, linkage of, 159–60
    criticism of Graves' writing, 166, 205
    Egyptian trip, 86–87, 119–33
    end of relationship, xiii, xv, 399, 400,
      401
    end of sexual relationship, 234–35,
      237, 239, 240, 241, 246, 247, 257
    evacuation from Deyá, 328, 338–39,
      345–46
    first meeting, 112–15
    in France, 363–79
    letters disparaging Graves, xiii, xvi
    in Mallorca, xii, 217–339
    "The Quids" noticed by, 73, 86, 202
    return to America, 376, 379–80
    LR's suicide leap and, 91, 92–95, 111,
      157, 172, 179, 180, 196–98, 202–
      03, 205, 208–09, 212, 213
    Seizen Press, *see* Seizen Press
    in spring and summer of 1939, 386–
      400
    struggle for control of the historical
      records, 401–03
    Trinity with LR and Nancy
      Nicholson, 95, 102–03, 105, 106,
      107, 110, 123–24, 126–28, 129,
      131, 136, 146–58, 167–69, 172,
      207, 211
    unequal relationship, 301, 302, 309,
      310
  half sister and, *see* Riechenthal, Isabel
  on homosexuality, 349, 361
  hotel, 285, 287
  influence on 1930s British poetry, 323–
    27, 350–51
  Schuyler Jackson and, 372–75, 380,
    388–401, 404–19
    collaborative writing, 400, 404, 405,
      406–07, 410–15
    finances, 408, 412
    introduction, 372
    marriage, xiii, 92, 411
    in New York City, 404–11
    review of LR's poetry, xiii, 372, 373,
      374
    sexual relationship, 388
    in spring and summer of 1939, 386,
      388–400
    in Wabasso, Florida, xii, 412–18
  jazz, influence of, 65, 81
  as a Jew, 14, 85, 150, 158, 168, 194
  as lecturer, 351–52
  letters responding to critics and
    reviewers, xiii, xv, 11–12, 61, 159,
    221, 356
  literalism and, 360–62
  in Louisville, Kentucky, 11, 12, 16–17,
    63–65
  marriages:
    to Louis Gottschalk, xviii, 9, 11, 16,
      17, 47, 54–55, 57, 58–59, 61, 64,
      66–67
    idea of, 250
    to Schuyler Jackson, xiii, 92, 411
  memoirs, xiv–xv, 44, 420
  mother and, 30–35, 41–44, 45, 232,
    412, 417–18
  name changes, xiii, xvii–xviii, 29, 54,
    405, 419
    to Laura Riding, 152
    pseudonym, xviii
  as Nashville Poetry Prize recipient, 4, 8,
    10, 12, 14, 16, 66
  nervous breakdown, 16
  "new moral law," 357–67, 365
  in New York City, 17, 68–81, 82–83, 86,
    404–11
  as novelist, 13, 348
    The Frail Barb, 13–14, 135
    Lives of Wives, 348, 367, 368, 377
    A Trojan Ending, *see Trojan Ending, A*
  Phibbs and, *see* Phibbs, Geoffrey
  poetry of, 29, 37, 38, 44–45, 361–62, 420

Riding, Laura, poetry of (*cont.*)
  ambivalence about, xv
  attitude toward readers of, xvii, 73
  "death" in, 226–28, 262–69
  early attempts to get published, 8,
    10–11
  paradox in, 60, 81, 177, 268
  renunciation of, xiii–xiv, xv, 45, 362,
    415–16, 419
  use of words, 74, 262–63, 360
  see also individual titles
 poetry readings, 72
 politics and, 10, 28, 29, 39, 40, 53, 73,
  320
  British working class and, 352–53
  First Protocol, *see* First Protocol
  Second Protocol, *see* Second Protocol
  as World War II approached, 348–49,
    353, 354, 355–61, 365, 366, 369–
    70, 375
 portrait of, 329
 as publicist, 70, 72
 reviews of works of, *see individual titles*
 on sex, 238–40, 241–42, 243, 245, 247,
  248, 299
 sexuality, 46, 47, 58, 243
  renunciation of sex, 238–39, 241, 247
 suicidal leap of 1929, xiii, 91–111, 157,
  172–73, 176, 178, 179, 185, 205,
  208–09, 212, 213, 229, 232
  prose work about, 186
  recovery from, 174–75, 180, 185,
    196–98, 202–03, 207, 208, 209,
    249
 supernatural and, 355, 356, 393–94,
  396–98
 Tate and, *see* Tate, Allen, LR and
 as translator, 72, 123, 249
 triangle of parents and sibling, 31, 32
 university, 287
  books for a children's, 367–68
  in Urbana, Illinois, 9, 10, 34, 47
  in Vienna, 147, 151, 157
 Voltaire biography by, 56–57, 159
 works of, *see individual titles*
Rilke, Rainer Maria, 199, 319, 374
Ringrose (barge), 101, 102, 207
Rivers, W. H. R., 140, 204
Robert, Michael, 323, 329
Roberts, Eirlys, 282, 287, 316, 320, 321,
  322
Robinson, Edwin Arlington, 161
Rodakowski, Raymond, 204

Rogers, Ellen, *see* Reichenthal, Isabel
Rolland, Romain, 57
"Romantic Habit in English Poetry, The,"
  287
Romeo and Juliet, 211
"Room of One's Own, A," 170
Room of One's Own (Woolf), 241
Room with a View, A (Forster), 169
Royal Egyptian University, 12, 86, 125,
  147
Russell, Bertrand, 200

Sage College, 46–47, 48–54, 57
St. Vincent Millay, Edna, 159
Sampson, Martin Wright, 51–52
Sampson Agonistes (Milton), 371
"Samuel's Elegy for Amalthea of the
  Legends," 304
"Samuel's Toast of Death," 129–30, 279
Sand, George, 51
San Francisco Overland Express, 67
Sassoon, Siegfried, 117, 124, 129, 140,
  200, 204, 289
 friendship with Robert Graves, 120–21
 as homosexual, 120, 148
 memoirs, 204
 on Nancy Nicholson, 120–21
 the "Trinity" and, 149, 157–58
 in World War I, 120, 198, 203
"Saturday Night," 64–65
Savage God, The (Alvarez), 178
Sayers, Dorothy, 360
Schiller, Johann Friedrich von, 27
"Schoolgirls," 50–51
Schwarz, Georg, 353, 354, 364
Sebastian (gardener), 281
Second Protocol, 374, 375, 389, 390, 406
Seizen Press, xii, xiii, 181, 184, 193, 210,
  221, 232, 282, 293, 316, 317, 336,
  341
 American distributor for, 346
"Seizure of the World," 361
Seminole Indians, xi, 417
Seven Types of Ambiguity (Epsom), 143–44,
  145
Seymour-Smith, Martin, xvi, 75
 biography of Robert Graves, xvi, 109,
  113–14, 121, 211–12
 LR's reaction to, 325
Shakespeare, William, 135, 205, 320
 Sonnet 129, 142–44, 146
Shaw, George Bernard, 276

Shelley, Percy Bysshe, 51, 97, 106, 135, 204, 287
Short, Mr., 219
"Signs of Knowledge," 243
Simmons, Dorothy, 362, 368, 370, 374, 377, 405, 416–17
Simmons, Montague, 368, 377, 416–17
Sinclair, May, 170
Sinclair, Upton, 28
Sitwell, Edith, 118, 166
Smart Set (Mencken), 55
Socialism, 23–27, 29, 39, 119, 320, 368
Socialist Labor party, 25
Socialist party of America, 25, 26, 27
Society of Home Students, 368
Somerville, Maisie, 346, 356, 357, 360, 377
South Wales Argus, 159
Soviet Union, 28, 29, 327
Spanish civil war, xii, 328, 334–39, 347–48, 354, 365, 366, 375
  end of, 377
Spectator, 360
Spender, Stephen, 350, 351
Spirit of the Ghetto, The (Hapgood), 26
Squire, J. C., 350, 371
Stalin, Joseph, 336
"Stanzas in Despair, Dying," 61, 62
"Starved," 11
Stead, Christina, 355–56
Steiglitz, Alfred, 70
Stein, Gertrude, 105, 139, 153, 158, 173, 181–86, 191–95, 226, 325, 350, 397
  An Acquaintance with Transition, 184, 193
  Composition as Explanation, 182, 184
  as God, 285–86
  Graves and, *see* Graves, Robert, Gertrude Stein and
  as homosexual, 194
  Joyce and, 182
  as LR's confidant, 230, 232
  LR's criticism of writing of, 182, 183–84
  LR's decision to go to Mallorca and, 219, 220
  LR's poetry and, 189, 190
  LR's suicide attempt and, 174–75, 177, 180, 185, 191, 196, 208, 209, 219
  Seizen Press and, xiii, 181, 184, 193
Step Ladder, 10
Stevens, Wallace, 138, 202
Still, Gordon, 405
"Story Pig, The," 290

Strenge, Emmy, 353, 354, 364
"Succubus, The," 248
Sunday Times, 295
Survey of Modernist Poetry, A (Riding and Graves), 137–46, 151, 154, 160, 162, 183, 350
  reviews of, 159
Symons, Julian, 324, 350–51, 360–61

Taggard, Genevieve, 162
"Taint, The," 148
Tate, Allen, 62, 73, 75, 183, 256
  Catholicism and, 184
  Crane and, 79–80, 81
  described, 5
  description of LR, 12–13, 87
  as Fugitive, 4, 5, 6, 60–61, 62
  marriage, 76–77
  move to New York, 6–7, 15, 61
  poetry of, 6, 79–80
  LR and, 4, 13, 16, 17, 57, 59–61, 66, 68, 79, 83–86, 87, 135, 141, 172
    affair and abortion, 75–77
    encouragement of LR's poetry, 11, 72, 73
    Louisville meeting, 4, 12, 59, 75
    love for Tate, 59, 75–76, 82, 127
    in New York City, 17, 70, 72, 76–77, 82
    "Trinity" relationship and, 158
  on "The Waste Land," 7
Tate, Caroline (née Gordon), 61, 76–77, 79, 80, 82, 202, 256
  LR's correspondence with, 157
Tate, Nancy, 76, 77
Taylor, Basil, 235, 236, 237, 250
Taylor, Geoffrey, *see* Phibbs, Geoffrey
Teasdale, Sara, 159
"T. E. Hulme, the New Barbarism, and Gertude Stein," 183
Telling, The (Riding), 420
Telling Tales, 76
Tennyson, Alfred Lord, 135, 199
"Their Last Interview," 283–84
"Then Follows," 280, 284–85
"Thieves, The," 402–03
This Side of Paradise (Fitzgerald), 255
This Week, 349
Thomas, Dylan, 248
Though Gently (Riding), 221
"Tillaquils, The," 128

Time, xii, xiii, 237, 255, 270, 356, 388, 389
  Schuyler Jackson as reviewer for, xiii,
    372, 373, 374, 412
Time and Tide, 359
Times, 362
Times Literary Supplement, 221, 224, 347, 359
"To a Loveless Lover," 60
Toklas, Alice B., 186, 194, 220
Tolstoy, Leo, 27
To Return to All That (Graves), 199
To the Lighthouse (Woolf), 169
"To the Sovereign Muse," 246
To Whom Else? (Graves), 232, 244–45, 246
Townsend, Kit, *see* Jackson, Kit
Transatlantic Review, 71
transition, 173, 182–83, 184, 186, 189
Travels in Arabia Deserta (Doughty), 371, 383
Trojan Ending, A (Riding), 313–14, 332–34,
    337, 346, 347
  Graves' dramatic treatment of, 367
Tuesday Evening Club, 255, 371
Twain, Mark, 27
"Two Loves, One Madness," 242

Ulysses (Joyce), 183, 349
Understanding Poetry (Warren and Brooks),
    145
U.S. Senate, 373
University College, Hull, 326
University of Illinois, 9, 10, 47
University of Louisville, 12
University of Toronto, 420
"Unthronged Oracle, The," 272

Valéry, Paul, 161, 188, 189
Vanderbilt University, 65
Van Doren, Mark, 72
Verlaine, Paul Marie, 50
Villon, François, 50
Voltaire, 55, 56–57, 283
Voltaire: A Biographical Fantasy (Riding), 56–
    57
  sales of, 159
"Voyages," 79

Wabasso, Florida, xi–xii, xviii, 412–13, 421
Warren, Robert Penn ("Red"), 61, 76, 144
  as Fugitive, 4, 13
  meeting with LR, 4
  suicide attempts, 13
  on "The Waste Land," 7

Understanding Poetry, 145
Warshow, Robert, 72, 83–84
"Waste Land, The," 6, 7, 80, 146, 165, 183
Webster's New International Dictionary, 413
Welty, Eudora, 421
West, Kitty, 346
West, Rebecca, 30, 106, 169, 170, 295, 297
"What Is English Literature?," 153
"What to Say When the Spider," 189–91
"When Love Becomes Words," 329
"When the Skies Part," 370
White, T. H., 319
White Buildings (Crane), 84, 183
White Goddess, The, 402, 403
Whitman, Walt, 135
"Why Not Laugh," 63
"Why of the Wind," 313
Wilde, Oscar, 135, 235
Williams, William Carlos, xii, 7, 138, 202
Wilson, Edmund, 72, 84, 256, 270
Winters, Yvor, 144
"Wishing More Dear," 329
Withering of the Fig Leaf, The (Ellis), 97
Wolfe, Humbert, 350
Woolf, Leonard, 97, 123
Woolf, Virginia, 115, 169, 170–71, 172,
    186, 241, 349, 350
  on Robert Graves, 199
Wordsworth, William, 199
Word 'Woman,' The (Riding and Roberts), 321
World and Ourselves, The (Riding), 356, 357,
    358, 359, 375
World Has Changed, The (Jackson and
    Riding), 400
World's End (cottage), 122, 133, 135, 152,
    154
"World's End," 174, 176
World War I, 39, 48, 71, 116, 120, 198–
    203, 323–24, 331
World War II, 334, 338, 405
  march of events toward, 348, 358, 363,
    369–70, 373, 376, 390
  outbreak of, 250, 400
Wyatt, Honor, 300, 316, 317, 318, 327,
    356, 360, 377
  collaboration on novel with LR, 348
  nom de plume, 318

Yale University, 420
Yeats, William Butler, 95, 100, 142, 161,
    197, 328–29
  Schuyler Jackson and, 371